THE ENGLISH
POETIC EPITAPH

THE ENGLISH POETIC EPITAPH

*Commemoration and
Conflict from
Jonson to
Wordsworth*

JOSHUA SCODEL

CORNELL UNIVERSITY PRESS

ITHACA AND LONDON

Contents

Acknowledgments

Thomas M. Greene and Ronald Paulson oversaw the earliest version of this work, and I am indebted to their scholarly examples more deeply than I can say. John Hollander and Gordon Williams helped me conceive the project, and Geoffrey Hartman, George deF. Lord, and Lowry Nelson, Jr., provided encouraging criticism.

Many friends and colleagues at the University of Chicago were of assistance in my rethinking and revising. I am extremely grateful to the members of the English department who listened to, read, and commented upon portions of this book: David Bevington, James Chandler, J. Paul Hunter, Gwin Kolb, W. J. T. Mitchell, Janel Mueller, Michael Murrin, Bruce Redford, Tom Stillinger, Richard Strier, and John Wallace. Jay Schleusener provided moral—or at least psychological—support, and Robert von Hallberg and Joseph Williams answered inquiries. Mark Kishlansky of the History department and A. W. H. Adkins and the late George Walsh of the Classics department kindly allowed me to attend relevant graduate seminars. Three work-study students, Heidi Beck, Lee Garver, and the ever-resourceful Priscilla Barlow, gave essential aid.

A Whiting Foundation fellowship at Yale partly supported me as I began the book, and a fellowship at the University of Wisconsin at Madison's Institute for Research in the Humanities provided an ideal atmosphere in which to transform it. At Madison, David Bordwell, Phillip Harth, Ullrich Langer, and Howard Weinbrot were wonderful colleagues and critics. I am very grateful to my two readers at Cornell

University Press, Ann Baynes Coiro and Steven N. Zwicker, for their helpful suggestions. For help of various kinds, I also thank Anne Badger, Michael Balfour, Hugh Brogham, Phil Mottram, David Riggs, and Frederic B. Tromly. Let me also acknowledge the long-standing support of David Quint, Ed Schiffer, and David Mikics; of Ruth Scodel, who helped more than any younger sibling had a right to expect; and of my wife, Mayumi Fukui, who, among other things, forced me to conclude.

Many vicars, rectors, and churchwardens graciously allowed me to photograph monuments and transcribe inscriptions in their parish churches in the summer of 1987. The staffs of the Regenstein Library of the University of Chicago, the Sterling and Beinecke libraries at Yale, the Butler Library at Columbia University, the Newberry Library, and the British Library, enabled me to make the best of their resources. I thank the editors of *SP* and *ELH* for permission to use two articles that are revised and incorporated as chapters 3 and 8: "Genre and Occasion in Jonson's 'On My First Sonne,'" *Studies in Philology* 86 (1989):235–259, and "'Your Distance Keep': Pope's Epitaphs upon Himself," *ELH* 55 (1988):615–642.

JOSHUA SCODEL

Chicago, Illinois

THE ENGLISH
POETIC EPITAPH

Introduction

The poetic epitaph, a poem inscribed or purporting to be inscribed upon a tomb, participates in the social, and therefore historical, construction of the dead. Though death is a biological reality that human beings share with all other living things, the beliefs, emotions, rituals, and works of art that determine and express its human meaning are culturally constructed.[1] Anthropologists have emphasized that a society's conception of its dead is central to its self-understanding. Since the existence of a social order presupposes its survival despite the death of its individual members, a society must treat the dead in such a way that they undergird rather than undermine the reproduction of social life and its fundamental values and practices. Changes in the treatment of the dead are thus closely and dialectically linked to changes in social relations among the living.[2]

[1] Not even contemporary scientific definitions of death and the dead escape cultural presuppositions. For a philosophical examination of some of the premises underlying biological definitions of death, see Hans Jonas, "Against the Stream: Comments on the Definition and Redefinition of Death," in his *Philosophical Essays: From Ancient Creed to Technological Man* (Chicago: University of Chicago Press, 1974), 132–140; for a radical critique of the cultural assumptions underlying scientific conceptions of death, see Jean Baudrillard, *L'échange symbolique et la mort* (Paris: Gallimard, 1976), 191–282.

[2] For anthropological discussions of the relationship between social orders and their treatment of the dead, I have found especially useful Maurice Bloch and Jonathan Parry, "Introduction: Death and the Regeneration of Life," in *Death and the Regeneration of Life*, ed. Bloch and Parry (Cambridge: Cambridge University Press, 1982), 1–45; Richard Huntington and Peter Metcalf, *Celebrations of Death: The Anthropology of Mortuary Ritual* (Cambridge: Cambridge University Press, 1979); and Jean-Pierre Vernant's introduction to *La*

Societies often respond to death by asserting the new and enduring status of some of their dead, who do not just decompose and disappear but take on a new role in the social order. They may exist simply as part of the collective memory or may become members of another world connected in some way to the living. While publicly marking the undeniable manifestation of physical death, the spot where a corpse is buried, tombs and their inscriptions also assert the continuing "social being" of the deceased.[3] The funerary monument and its epitaph differentiate the dead by commemorating this person rather than that person for certain attributes rather than others. Such memorials thus contribute to the continuous reconstruction of the social order by acknowledging the reality of death while proclaiming the posthumous existence of certain persons and the social values they represent.

A literary genre is, as Fredric Jameson writes, a "socio-symbolic message... [that is] immanently and intrinsically an ideology in its own right."[4] As a literary genre the poetic epitaph exploits both the distinctive features of verse and its own specific conventions in order to define the dead in ways that not only reinforce but also extend, challenge, and reshape prevailing cultural assumptions. The development of the poetic epitaph is thus a continuous process of assimilation and modification of cultural norms.

The reciprocal dynamic between the poetic epitaph and contemporaneous culture may be traced back to the earliest Western tradition of the genre. In the seventh century B.C., Greeks began inscribing tombs with prose epitaphs that briefly identified the deceased for posterity. They also inscribed verse epitaphs that used the expressive resources of poetic tradition to enhance the inscription's cultural function of asserting the enduring social importance of the dead. Because of space limitations and the time and expense involved in inscribing a monument, epitaphs tended to be brief. Poets treated this functional constraint as an ex-

---

mort, les morts dans les sociétés anciennes, ed. Gherardo Gnoli and Vernant (Cambridge: Cambridge University Press, 1982), 5–16.

[3] In his pioneering study of funerary practices, Robert Hertz argued that the "social being grafted upon the physical individual" determines how a person is treated in death; see "A Contribution to the Study of the Collective Representation of Death," in his *Death and the Right Hand*, trans. Rodney and Claudia Needham (Glencoe, Ill.: Free Press, 1960), 76–78. Bloch and Parry refine Hertz's argument in one crucial respect: they argue that the treatment of the dead is a constitutive part, rather than a mere reflection, of the "social being" of the dead, just as society is not simply reaffirmed in its treatment of the dead but always being reconstituted by such treatment (pp. 3–7).

[4] See Fredric Jameson, *The Political Unconscious: Narrative as a Socially Symbolic Act* (Ithaca: Cornell University Press, 1981), 141. On the ideological functions of genre, see also Gian Biagio Conte, *The Rhetoric of Imitation: Genre and Poetic Memory in Virgil and Other Latin Poets*, ed. and trans. Charles Segal et al. (Ithaca: Cornell University Press, 1986), 100–208; and Maria Corti, *An Introduction to Literary Semiotics*, trans. Margherita Bogat and Allen Mandelbaum (Bloomington: Indiana University Press, 1978), 115–143.

pressive challenge, using brevity to ensure the memorability of the message. Early verse epitaphs exploited the mnemonic power of meter and gnomic utterances to convey with epigrammatic forcefulness the significance of the dead.[5] Linking their own verbal artistry to the powerful visual effects of funerary sculpture, some poets consciously related their compositions to the tombs upon which they were inscribed in order to elaborate the meaning of the memorial as a whole.[6] Through resemblances between their epitaphs and other kinds of poetry, moreover, poets located their epitaphs within the system of literary genres, exploiting other genres' functions and values. Epitaphs often resorted, for example, to epic formulae in an effort to link the dead to Homeric heroes and their "undying fame."[7] Epitaphic use of diverse meters further suggested the connection of this genre to others: dactylic hexameter reinforced the association with the heroic values of epic, while elegiac couplets signaled a departure from epic norms and might have implied, by contrast, a link to ritual expressions of grief, since contemporary funerary laments used this meter.[8]

Greek poets also adapted the conventions of the funerary inscription for new varieties of poetic epitaphs that diverged from dominant conceptions of the dead. They wrote pseudo-inscriptional epitaphs, poems commemorating the dead in the style of actual tomb inscriptions. They also produced wholly imaginary epitaphs, including compositions that expressed comic and satiric attitudes toward the dead that would never have been inscribed upon actual tombs. By increasing the distance between the poetic epitaph and actual funerary practices, Greek practitioners increased the flexibility of both the genre's and the culture's treatment of the dead.

English poetic epitaphs similarly revealed and reshaped their society's

[5] On gnomic utterances in epitaphs, see Jules Labarbe, "Aspects gnomiques de l'épigramme grecque," in Fondation Hardt pour l'étude de l'antiquité classique, L'épigramme grecque (Geneva: Vandoeuvres, 1968), 349–369. On the conversion of a genre's functional constraints into expressive features, see Alastair Fowler, Kinds of Literature: An Introduction to the Theory of Genres and Modes (Cambridge: Harvard University Press, 1982), 152–153.

[6] See the discussion of the variety of relationships between verse inscriptions and their tombs in Christoph W. Clairmont, Gravestone and Epigram: Greek Memorials from the Archaic and Classical Periods (Mainz: Verlag Philipp Von Zabern, 1970).

[7] On epic formulae in Greek epitaphs, see Paul Friedländer and Herbert B. Hoffleit, Epigrammata: Greek Inscriptions in Verse from the Beginnings to the Persian Wars (Berkeley: University of California Press, 1948), 7–64 and passim; and Werner Peek's introduction to his Griechische Grabgedichte (Berlin: Akademie-Verlag, 1960), 8–11.

[8] On the epitaph's connections to the epic tradition and contemporaneous elegiac laments, see Friedländer and Hoffleit, 65–66; and Peek, 12–15. The alleged link between inscriptions in elegiac meter and contemporaneous laments in the same meter depends on a now controversial inference that elegiac meter was originally used primarily for such laments. For arguments against this inference, see Bruno Gentili, "Epigramma ed elegia," in Fondation Hardt, 37–68; and Martin L. West, Studies in Greek Elegy and Iambus (Berlin: Walter de Gruyter, 1974), 1–21.

attitudes toward the dead. This book traces the English poetic epitaph from the early seventeenth to the early nineteenth century, the period of its greatest importance to English literature and culture. Over this span English society endured extremely high rates of mortality.[9] In the face of omnipresent death, epitaphs sought to assert the enduring social roles of the deceased. They did so in various and often opposing ways, however, for writers enlisted the dead in competing social, religious, and political visions. Epitaphs differentiated and evaluated the dead according to such diverse and often contested criteria as social rank, gender, age, religion, and personal achievements.[10] They posited widely differing links—spiritual, ethical, and emotional—between the dead and the living. Thus the epitaph engaged in the central conflicts of English collective life.[11]

English writers composed both prose and verse, inscriptional and pseudo-inscriptional epitaphs. Like their Greek counterparts, English epitaphic poets used the mnemonic properties of meter, verbal concision,

[9] See the table of life expectancy at birth in E. A. Wrigley and R. S. Schofield, *The Population History of England, 1541–1871: A Reconstruction* (Cambridge: Harvard University Press, 1981), 231. The period of my study witnessed considerable variations in mortality rates, but life expectancy never surpassed forty-one (Wrigley and Schofield, 235–236) and there is no correlation between such variations and the social treatment of the dead. Lawrence Stone has argued that a decline in infant mortality beginning in the mid eighteenth century "enabled" parents to feel profound grief at the death of their children; see *The Family, Sex and Marriage in England, 1500–1800* (New York: Harper, 1977), 81–82. Other historians, however, have convincingly denied Stone's correlation between demography and affect by refuting his claim that parents did not mourn intensely for their children before the mid eighteenth century; see, for example, Alan Macfarlane, "Death and the Demographic Transition: A Note on English Evidence on Death 1500–1750," in *Mortality and Immortality: The Anthropology and Archaeology of Death*, ed. S. C. Humphreys and Helen King (London: Academic Press, 1981), 249–259.

[10] For a cross-cultural discussion of the various factors that enter into what he calls the "social personality" of the dead and their differential funerary treatment, see Lewis R. Binford, "Mortuary Practices: Their Study and Their Potential," in his *An Archaeological Perspective* (New York: Seminar Press, 1972), 208–251.

[11] Joachim Whalley's salutary warning that studies of the history of death must attend to the relevant particulars of social organization, religion, politics, and family formation has encouraged my attempt to embed the epitaph in something other than the "history of death" conceived of as an autonomous field of historical inquiry; see the introduction to his anthology, *Mirrors of Mortality: Studies in the Social History of Death* (New York: St. Martin's, 1981), 9. Though I owe a great debt to two broad histories of death in Western culture, Philippe Ariès's *The Hour of Our Death*, trans. Helen Weaver (New York: Random, 1982) and Michel Vovelle's *La mort et l'Occident de 1300 à nos jours* (Paris: Gallimard, 1983), I have tried to situate the development of the English poetic epitaph within the specificities of English social, religious, political, and artistic history. As models for detailed contextualization of the history of death, I have learned from studies of different cultures and periods, especially Jacques Chiffoleau, *La comptabilité de l'au-delà: Les hommes, la mort, et la religion dans la région d'Avignon à la fin du moyen âge (vers 1320–vers 1480)* (Rome: École Française de Rome, 1980); James J. Farrell, *Inventing the American Way of Death, 1830–1920* (Philadelphia: Temple University Press, 1980); and David E. Stannard, *The Puritan Way of Death: A Study in Religion, Culture and Social Change* (New York: Oxford University Press, 1977).

and other literary devices to support their commemoration of the dead. They also parlayed epitaphic brevity into a device of great expressive and ideological range by exploring its implications for literary and social hierarchies based upon contrasts between "small" and "great." Funerary monuments and their church or churchyard settings played a central role in the social and religious conflicts of early modern English society. Poets posited a variety of relationships between epitaphs and their (real or imaginary) tombs that revealed a profound awareness of such relationships' social and religious, as well as aesthetic, implications. In addition, they combined or contrasted the epitaph with other genres. They were especially interested in the relationship between the brief epitaph and the longer elegy: their decisions to write in one or the other of these genres, or to combine them, involved crucial judgments about the relationship between the living and the dead.

The history of the English poetic epitaph exhibits continuous interactions between the compositions of those who stood as poets in their own and others' regard, on the one hand, and, on the other, the compositions of bereaved survivors from various social ranks and of the parsons and stonecutters who on occasion produced such works.[12] As a brief, occasional genre with numerous practitioners, the epitaph was often considered minor or "low," so that most epitaphic poets felt compelled to stake out a position, implicit or explicit, concerning the status of the genre and thereby either to support or to challenge traditional hierarchical notions of literary kinds. By cultivating analogies between the literary status of the epitaph and the social status of the deceased, poets often contrived to suggest the connection between literary hierarchies and the social hierarchies they upheld. Certain poets and critics, among them Ben Jonson, Robert Herrick, Alexander Pope, Samuel Johnson, and William Wordsworth, indeed considered the epitaph a crucial literary genre precisely because it called into question prevailing conceptions of who and what was high and low, major and minor, central and marginal, in life, death, and poetry.

As a rule, generic conventions survive longer than the cultural beliefs and practices out of which they arise.[13] English epitaphic poets often

---

[12] I have read as many English poetic epitaphs as possible from the seventeenth through the nineteenth centuries in order to make confident assertions concerning the tradition. This study draws its materials from a variety of sources in addition to the major authors and the major anthologies of English poetry, including the numerous anthologies of epitaphs from the Renaissance to the present; sixteenth- through eighteenth-century epigram collections; eighteenth- through twentieth-century magazines and journals; seventeenth- to twentieth-century antiquarian and topographical works; collections of monuments and brasses; parish register collections; local histories; biographies; and, finally, actual monuments and tombstones.

[13] See Corti, 118; and the discussion of the "sedimentation" of generic conventions in Jameson, 140–141.

exploited conventions that presupposed discarded beliefs and practices in order to imagine relationships between the living and the dead that differed from the conceptions of their contemporaries. Thus, for example, poets often worked variations upon a traditional classical formula, "Sit tibi terra levis," "May the earth rest lightly upon you." Although in Christian belief, the grave housed only the insentient body of the deceased, the formula nevertheless allowed a Christian poet to express, with classical authority and sententious brevity, a solicitude for the body of the deceased that had different emotional and intellectual resonances depending upon the precise historical context. The very diversity of the epitaphic traditions upon which English poets could draw—classical, medieval, Renaissance, and Reformation—afforded broad perspectives and an imaginative freedom that would have been unavailable if poets had simply accepted as absolute constraints the dominant beliefs and practices of their age.[14]

This book narrates the rise and fall of the English poetic epitaph as a vital literary genre. It consists of three major sections, the first two concerning the seventeenth-century epitaph, and the third concerning the eighteenth- and early nineteenth-century epitaph. The epitaph flourished in the seventeenth century when writers struggled over the cultural function of the dead in poetically fruitful ways. During the early eighteenth century the most interesting epitaphs reveal a crisis stemming from extreme dissatisfaction with contemporary conceptions of the social role of the deceased. From the mid eighteenth to the early nineteenth century, the most important poetic epitaphs seek new ways of validating the importance of the dead. In so doing they simultaneously fight against and expose the increasing anachronism of a literary genre that sought to assert the vital public role of the dead.

Throughout the book I have sought to strike a balance between the analysis of individual poets and the tracing of general historical trends. My first section focuses on Jonson as the first major English poet to forge an original and influential epitaphic poetics by exploiting and transforming the classical, medieval, Renaissance, and Reformation epitaphic traditions. Chapters 1 to 3 discuss Jonson's epitaphs in terms of three central, recurring issues for the book: the relation of the epitaph to its (real or imaginary) funerary monument and setting; the aesthetic and ideological use of epitaphic brevity; and the relation of the epitaph to other genres, including, most importantly, the elegy. Jonson's distinction between the "matter" of an epitaph and the mere "materiall" of an

---

[14] Fowler claims that genres that embody "values of very long standing" may "offset the bias or oppression of a particular society" (p. 36). This book attempts to substantiate Fowler's claim.

opulent funerary monument exploits humanist and Protestant iconoclastic motifs in order to declare the superiority of the virtuous man's
"goodness" as commemorated in plain poetic statement to the aristocrat's
social grandeur as expressed in funerary show. Announcing their own
"much in little" power, his epitaphs use brevity to divide merit from
social rank by quickly consigning the corrupt courtier to oblivion and
by raising and immortalizing the more socially humble but virtuous. His
greatest short poem, "On My First Sonne," transforms a classical generic
combination, the elegy with final epitaph. Jonson uses the composite
form in order to bear witness to his grief as a father and then to move
beyond his personal feelings by proclaiming the enduring public value
of both the deceased and the impersonal "maker" who commemorates
him.

The second section of the book locates the epitaphs of Jonson's contemporaries and seventeenth-century successors in relation to the social,
religious, and political conflicts of the period. Chapter 4 discusses two
poets who commemorated John Donne, Donne himself and the Jonsonian Thomas Carew. Unlike Jonson, Donne did not write many poetic
epitaphs, but he did compose one major poem in the genre, a highly
unusual epitaph upon himself. Donne's epitaph imagines a spiritual exchange between the living and the dead that diverges sharply from
mainstream Protestant views and implicitly criticizes contemporaneous
social relationships among the living. Donne's poetic, theological, and
social daring suggests why his epitaph was not imitated. Taking a different tack, in his elegy with final epitaph upon Donne, Carew absorbs
his older contemporary into his own Jonsonian poetics and his partisan
view of the church and state of England. Carew's poem thus exemplifies
the increasing polemical use of the dead in the struggles of seventeenth-
century England.

The next three chapters examine the epitaph in a period of intense
historical crisis, before, during, and after the Civil Wars. Chapter 5
analyzes early and mid-seventeenth-century epitaphs treating a controversial ideal of humanists and of Puritans, the "honest" man. Frequently
placed in opposition to the "great" man, the "honest" man of unpretentious virtue or humble godliness is a central figure in the ideological
conflicts of the period. Epitaphs that celebrate or denigrate the "honest"
man add an intensely topical dimension to the genre's treatment of
monuments as signs of rank and to its use of brevity to exalt or disparage
the lowly. The two major epitaphic poets who commemorate "honest"
men, James Shirley and Richard Crashaw, are both indebted to Jonson.
Shirley intensifies Jonson's humanist contrast between mere rank and
virtue, while Crashaw adapts a Jonsonian style to address new religious
and political tensions. Struggling against the religious polarization within

the established church during the late 1620s and 1630s between traditional Calvinists and Puritans, on the one hand, and the Arminians
patronized by Charles I, on the other, Crashaw commemorates an "honest" man who combined features of both factions and thus embodied all
the poet's (futile) hopes for a *via media* of religious and political peace.

Moving from broad trends to the generic contributions of an individual poet, chapter 6 discusses Herrick's idiosyncratic treatment of the
grave as a place of beneficent retreat from social disorder. During the
Civil Wars the social elite on both sides sought to defend their private
property and their concomitant rights as free men. Herrick boldly imagines the grave as the necessary and sufficient property of the contented
dead, who can dwell there free from worldly strife. Though Herrrick is
a devoted disciple of Jonson, he avoids Jonsonian proclamations of the
epitaph's "much in little" power. Instead he treats epitaphic brevity as
the decorous textual analogue to the small but secure homes of the dead,
and he embeds epitaphs within longer poems that dramatize a retreat
from the world.

While Herrick uses the dead to imagine an escape from the living, the
most interesting late seventeenth-century epitaphs, which are examined
in chapter 7, enlist the idealized dead to attack the living. Though the
social elite's eagerness to avoid renewed civil war restrained conflict during
this period, political, religious, and social tensions continued because of
the unhealed religious divisions and persistent distrust between successive kings and their Parliaments. Discontented in various ways with the
intensely factionalized late seventeenth-century order, poets as diverse
as Abraham Cowley, Andrew Marvell, and John Dryden develop a polemical rhetoric of nostalgia that makes the dead, often by willful biographical distortion, into representatives of the virtues that have
purportedly been destroyed by the iniquities of the times. Poets transform martyrs and supposed martyrs of war into symbols of lost honor
and virgins or supposed virgins into symbols of lost purity. Many features
of the early and mid-seventeenth-century epitaph decline in popularity
as a reaction to recent history. Thus, for example, poets anxious that
the iconoclasm and social upheaval of the Civil Wars not be repeated
write epitaphs that defend rather than attack the tombs upon which they
are inscribed and avoid the epigrammatic motifs that Johnson and other
early seventeenth-century poets used to challenge distinctions between
high and low. The epitaph becomes plainer in style at the same time as
it becomes more polemically duplicitous.

The intensely partisan exploitation of the dead in turn undermines
the credibility of epitaphic praise. The third and final section of the book
addresses the eighteenth- and early nineteenth-century attempts to resolve the controversies concerning the proper objects and manner of

epitaphic commemoration. Pope's influential attempts to "correct" the genre are the focus of chapters 8 and 9. Pope's obsession with death and the art of definitive statement drew him inexorably to the epitaph. Considering the contemporary epitaph both as a symptom of and a contribution to the evils of the age of Walpole, Pope tries to purify the genre. In his epitaphs upon himself, he attempts to define himself for posterity and thus exempt himself from the misrepresentations of flatterers and slanderers. Erecting his own modest memorial tablet in his parish church and announcing that he does not wish to be buried or commemorated in Westminster Abbey among the "great," Pope portrays himself as a "poor poet" who will not make his peace, even in death, with a social order that he despises. By commemorating vulnerable women and fellow poets who have been harshly judged or shamefully forgotten, he presents himself as the defender of society's outcasts. Anxious to distinguish his epitaphs upon the "great" from mere flattery, Pope blends elements of epitaph and elegy in a new way. Rather than dramatizing the movement from personal grief to public praise, Pope seeks to validate his epitaphic praise by expressing his "sincere" elegiac grief for "friends" rather than patrons. Though he tries to use his own fame and status as a moral arbiter to link his personal feelings to public values, Pope decisively shifts attention away from the "social being" of the dead to the feelings of the individual mourner.

Ubiquitous echoes of Pope's elegiac epitaphs reveal their extensive influence from the mid eighteenth through the early nineteenth century. In the absence of uncontested social criteria for differentiating the dead, grief-filled epitaphs from Pope's time onward often suggest that the individual mourner's sense of loss provides the most compelling, and perhaps the only authentic, demonstration of the dead person's significance. The values of personal elegy, articulated as an individual's overriding sense of loss for another unique and irreplaceable mortal, rise to dominance and thereby spell the ultimate decline of the epitaph as a literary genre dedicated to the brief definition of the public significance of the dead.

The problem is signaled in chapter 10, which analyzes the way English epitaphic poets in the wake of Pope attempt to shift the genre's source of validation from the mourning poet to the readers of the epitaph. Poets such as Thomas Gray and Johnson voice a desperate need for highly sensitive readers who alone can truly appreciate and mourn the deceased in all of his or her vulnerable uniqueness and thereby reintegrate him or her into the community of the living. Such calls for ideal readers come at the same time as the growth and social diversification of the reading public made the responses of readers all the more unpredictable. In the face of a larger, more heterogeneous readership, epitaphs beg the feeling few to reverence the deceased. This anxious focus upon the reactions of the reader, which has parallels in contemporaneous funerary art's treatment of the spectator, reveals great uncertainty concerning the enduring social role of the dead. Indeed a growing number of "anti-epitaphs" reject all attempts to reconnect the dead to society at large.

During the same period, however, many epitaphic writers attempt to recapture common values by broadening the social range of the genre, a development analyzed in chapter 11. The upper and middle classes began to admire the churchyard inscriptions of the lowly and to compose their own benevolent epitaphs upon the humble. Commemorating the simple, generic virtues of such lowly creatures as contented laborers and devoted servants, paternalist epitaphs redeploy the language of impersonal panegyric increasingly avoided in the subjectivized, individualized epitaphs upon the elite. Though they celebrate a realm of supposedly uncontested social values, such epitaphs are in fact nostalgic responses to, and participants in, vast and unsettling social change. In the face of the mounting tension between classes that accompanied the onset of capitalist relations, epitaphs upon exemplary members of the lower orders, or upon animals such as faithful dogs that could represent the lower orders, attempt to demonstrate in a radically new way the enduring mutual affection of high and low. Such epitaphs quickly become formulaic, however, a development that further erodes the commitment of poets to the epitaph's task of briefly defining, in credible fashion, the social role of the dead.

The expressive and representational shifts detailed in chapters 10 and 11 bring on the ultimate decline of the epitaph as a culturally significant literary genre. Chapter 12 treats Wordsworth's epitaphic theory and practice as the culmination of the focus on humble creatures and on the reader's response. Wordsworth suggests that because of their weak sense of community and their contempt for the past, the educated, urbanized classes of an increasingly industrial England have forgotten their bonds to the deceased. He turns nostalgically to pious rural churchyard inscriptions upon the lowly as affirmations of a traditional intimacy between the living and the dead. Defending the commonplaces of such epitaphs as fitting expressions of our "common nature," he stresses that the educated reader must humble himself or herself in order to respond properly to such compositions. Not part of a traditional community himself, however, Wordsworth normally responds to, rather than composes, lowly epitaphs. His treatment of short, humble inscriptions primarily as the stimuli for his longer, personal, elegiac meditations rather than as literary compositions in their own right is symptomatic of the epitaph's new subliterary status.

epitaph → *elegy*.

Deprived of many of its conventions but retaining its crucial function of lament, the elegy sustains vitality into the twentieth century as the preeminent lyric genre for expressions of personal feeling and insight concerning the dead. By contrast, poets after Wordsworth generally consider the poetic epitaph anachronistic. In poetry the epitaphic project of defining the public significance of the dead is itself dead, and many of the poetic epitaph's conventions now sound hollow and inappropriate as responses to human mortality. Contemporary poets concerned with death tend to focus not on the enduring social significance of the deceased but on their personal responses to the dead, and scholars who study the history of literary treatments of the deceased reflect contemporary interests and concerns by focusing on the elegiac strain of funerary literature and its psychological roots. G. W. Pigman's and Peter M. Sacks's recent studies of the elegy, for example, have skillfully analyzed its conventions and development in terms of psychoanalytic accounts of the individual's mourning process.[15] This book, by contrast, explores a genre whose fundamental emphases differ radically from our own "natural" feelings toward the dead. I have tried to describe with both sympathy and rigor the once crucial cultural functions of the poetic epitaph. I hope that this study of past attempts to capture the enduring spirit of the dead has itself captured something that endures.

Editorial Note: I have modernized i, j, u, v, and y and most scribal and inscriptional contractions when citing English and Latin texts. I have changed extended passages in italics to roman type and reduced the use of italics and capitals in brief quotations. Otherwise I have not avoided the inconsistencies of spelling, punctuation, typography inevitable in a book based on a variety of sources. When citing an epitaph that appears in several printed sources, I have selected my source according to the particular point I wish to make: some sources provide more reliable texts, some fuller historical information, while some provide crucial evidence for dating the composition. Unless otherwise indicated, all quotations and translations of standard classical works are from the editions in the *Loeb Classical Library*. When no reference for an epitaph or its translation is given, the transcription or translation is mine.

[15] See G. W. Pigman III, *Grief and English Renaissance Elegy* (Cambridge: Cambridge University Press, 1985) and Peter M. Sacks, *The English Elegy: Studies in the Genre from Spenser to Yeats* (Baltimore: Johns Hopkins University Press, 1985). Though my focus and method differ from both these works, I have profited from Pigman's extraordinary learning and Sacks's sensitive readings.

PART 1

BEN JONSON AND THE
EPITAPHIC TRADITION

Chapter *1*

Monumental Poetics:
The Epitaph and the Tomb

Ben Jonson is the first major English poet to compose a substantial number of epitaphs and to leave a decisive legacy to his successors. He therefore provides an excellent starting point for a discussion of the English epitaphic tradition. Because his compositions reveal an intense awareness of the genre's history and possibilities, they must be read against the classical, medieval, Renaissance, and Reformation traditions that Jonson both draws on and transforms in his struggle to make the genre embody his view of poetry's role as a bridge between the dead and the living. I will examine Jonson's epitaphs from three standpoints—the epitaph's relationship to the tomb, the expressive function of epigrammatic brevity, and the epitaphic response to elegiac mourning—in order to elucidate both the major conventions of the genre and his particular use of those conventions to forge his poetics of death.

A poetic epitaph evokes a real or imagined tomb containing the physical remains of the deceased. By asserting the enduring significance of the deceased, the epitaph perforce addresses the relationship between the tomb as the resting place of a corpse and the vital spirit, however defined, of the dead. Jonson's epitaphs on Sir Charles Cavendish and Margaret Ratcliffe reveal two different but complementary approaches to this relationship. In the Cavendish epitaph, Jonson exploits humanist and Protestant attacks on the aristocratic tomb in order to distinguish the mere container of a body from the epitaphic message that conveys the lasting meaning of a man's life. In the Ratcliffe epitaph, a poem that only pretends to be inscribed upon marble, Jonson creates a purely poetic monument that can convey the immortal achievement of the deceased better than any material tomb.

One cannot understand Jonson's treatment of the tomb without considering the central and controversial role of funerary monuments during the late sixteenth and early seventeenth centuries. Tombs were above all indicators of social distinctions. At the beginning of the seventeenth century, Jonson's mentor and friend William Camden noted, "Monuments answerable to mens worth, states, and places, have alwaies been allowed, yet stately sepulchers for base fellows have alwaies lyen open to bitter jests."[1] Writing in 1631, John Weever echoed Camden's remark and contended that "sepulchres should bee made according to the qualitie and degree of the person deceased, that by the Tombe every one might be discerned of what ranke he was living."[2] During the late sixteenth to mid seventeenth century, the erection of magnificent tombs for the ostentatious display of lineage and rank became a veritable craze among the English nobility and gentry, who not only raised monuments to their next of kin but also built or rebuilt tombs for their illustrious (though sometimes imaginary) ancestors. By 1600 it was considered almost obligatory for a landed family to have a series of grand monuments in the local church.[3] People left provisions in their wills for suitably opulent monuments to themselves or erected such monuments during their lifetimes, lest an heir should fail to provide them with memorials befitting their station.[4] Because of the low quality of most funerary sculpture, tombs could normally not be sharply differentiated by the talents of their craftsmen. Sheer size, costly materials, and rich decoration therefore served to distinguish monuments.[5] Contemporary comments on funerary art closely associate beauty and expense: when in 1592, for example, Francis Bacon adduced England's many "beautiful and costly tombs and monuments" as proof of the nation's flourishing state, his two adjectives, though not quite a hendiadys, indicate the mingling of aesthetic and economic criteria.[6]

[1] William Camden, *Remaines of a Greater Worke, Concerning Britaine* . . . (London, 1605), 29–30. Camden's discussion of monuments and epitaphs appears in a separately paginated section at the end of the work.

[2] John Weever, *Ancient Funerall Monuments* (London, 1631), 10.

[3] See Clare Gittings, *Death, Burial and the Individual in Early Modern England* (London: Croom Helm, 1984), 183–186; Richard L. Greaves, *Society and Religion in Elizabethan England* (Minneapolis: University of Minnesota Press, 1981), 729–736; Eric Mercer, *English Art, 1553–1625* (Oxford: Oxford University Press, 1962), 217–220; and Lawrence Stone, *The Crisis of the Aristocracy: 1558–1641* (Oxford: Oxford University Press, 1965), 579–581.

[4] Gittings, 184; and Graves, 731–732.

[5] Mercer, 217–218.

[6] Francis Bacon, "Observations on a Libel" (1592), in *The Letters and the Life of Francis Bacon*, ed. James Spedding, 7 vols. (London, 1861–1874), 1:158; cited for a different point in Gittings, 144.

The placement of tombs reinforced their social significance. The monuments of the most distinguished members of the community normally either dominated the chancel, where they could be seen by all worshipers during services, or were housed in family chapels attached to the church that provided an exclusive, semiprivate place of commemoration while displaying the family's special status to the community at large.[7] The lowest members of the social hierarchy, by contrast, were buried in unmarked graves in the churchyard. Between these extremes, commemoration of various degrees of prestige was possible: lesser gentry and prominent yeomen, for example, might have more modest monuments such as brasses within the church or—though this was rare before the late seventeenth century—churchyard monuments.[8] From the nobility commemorated in opulent church tombs to the majority of the population buried in anonymous churchyard graves, the dead were thus made to support the hierarchy of the living. All men must die, but the social order based on distinctions of rank endured. Monuments kept death the leveler at bay with visible "proof" that social distinctions prevailed over death.[9]

Some complained, however, that tombs did not in fact sufficiently uphold the traditional hierarchy because they often reflected wealth rather than noble lineage. Weever lamented that a "rich quondam Tradesman" all too often received a "huge great" tomb, while Thomas Fuller complained in 1642 that often "some rich man of mean worth [was] loaden under a tombe big enough for a Prince to bear."[10] The late sixteenth and early seventeenth century was a time of considerable social mobility when rich tradesmen and professionals could enter the gentry or attain almost equal status.[11] Those who identified "worth" with lineage disliked

---

[7] On the rise of the family chapel in the sixteenth and seventeenth centuries as a "specially designated space" for wealthy families, see Philippe Ariès, *The Hour of Our Death*, trans. Helen Weaver (New York: Random, 1982), 288–292.

[8] See Gittings, 141–146. On brasses as monuments for those of limited wealth, see Malcolm Norris, *Monumental Brasses: The Craft* (London: Faber, 1978), 52–57. Burial in the church was more expensive than churchyard burial, and sometimes rent was exacted for church monuments: see Gittings, 142; Greaves, 715; and Christopher Hill, *Economic Problems of the Church from Archbishop Whitgift to the Long Parliament* (Oxford: Clarendon, 1956), 168–169.

[9] For a cross-cultural argument that tombs in various cultures represent the "continuity of the property-holding kinship group" and thus the "permanent social order" based on such groups, see Maurice Bloch and Jonathan Parry, "Introduction: Death and the Regeneration of Life," in their anthology *Death and the Regeneration of Life* (Cambridge: Cambridge University Press, 1982), 32–38.

[10] Weever, 11; and Thomas Fuller, *The Holy State and the Profane State* (1642), ed. Maximilian Graff Walten, 2 vols. (New York: Columbia University Press, 1938), 1:188.

[11] On the upward mobility of merchants and professionals, see Lawrence Stone, "Social Mobility in England," *Past and Present* 33 (1966):16–55. Keith Wrightson discusses the complicated interplay between lineage and wealth as relative determinants of social status

the fact that upwardly mobile men could assert their high status by building grand monuments that should have been reserved for those of higher birth. Wealthy merchants and tradesmen, the social elite of London and the major towns, indeed often had very impressive monuments.[12] The nobility and gentry, on the other hand, sometimes avoided the expense of large tombs out of financial necessity or prudence. Economic exigencies affected the very summit of the hierarchy: though he erected grand monuments in Westminster Abbey for his predecessor, Elizabeth I, and his mother, Mary Queen of Scots, as well as smaller monuments to his infant daughters Sophia and Mary, King James I never had monuments built for Prince Henry or Queen Anne, apparently because money was diverted to more pressing projects.[13]

Those who rejected the identification of lineage with worth launched more fundamental attacks on the hierarchy of funerary monuments. Widely inculcated in grammar schools and universities and espoused with varying degrees of fervor by many in the upper ranks of society, Christian humanism, with the support of classical precedents, identified "true nobility" with virtue.[14] Humanists often blunted the meritocratic implications of the concept of "true nobility" by arguing that gentlemen were in fact normally the most virtuous or by asserting that lineage and virtue together constituted the highest nobility.[15] Some proponents of humanist views, however, were upwardly mobile men eager to denigrate mere lineage. Humanism fueled attacks on those considered "great" but not "good," and writers treated the grand tomb covering a corpse as a vivid example of the central aristocratic vice, conspicuous outward show without inner moral substance. In his *Microcosmographie* (1628), for example, John Earle develops the analogy between a worthless aristocrat,

---

in early modern England in *English Society: 1580–1680* (New Brunswick, N.J.: Rutgers University Press, 1982), 17–38.

[12] On the monuments of wealthy London citizens, see Jeremy Boulton, *Neighbourhood and Society: A London Suburb in the Seventeenth Century* (Cambridge: Cambridge University Press, 1987), 149–150; and Mercer, 236.

[13] On James I's checkered career in monument construction, see Graham Parry, *The Golden Age Restor'd: The Culture of the Stuart Court, 1603–1642* (New York: St. Martin's, 1981), 254–259.

[14] For ancient *loci classici* asserting that virtue is "true nobility," see Seneca's *Epistulae morales* 44. 5 and Juvenal's *Satire* 8. Quentin Skinner discusses the development of the idea of *vera nobilitas* first among the Italian and then among the Northern, primarily English, humanists in *The Foundations of Modern Political Thought*, 2 vols. (Cambridge: Cambridge University Press, 1978), 1:81–82, 236–241. Mervyn James discusses the English development of humanist ideology in *English Politics and the Concept of Honour, 1485–1642* (Kendal, Cumbria: Past and Present Society, 1978); see especially pp. 58–65. On the diffusion of humanist principles in late sixteenth- and early seventeenth-century English education, see Mervyn James, *Family, Lineage, and Civil Society: A Study of Society, Politics, and Mentality in the Durham Region, 1500–1640* (Oxford: Clarendon, 1974), 100–102.

[15] See Skinner, 1:236–241. James I was an eminent proponent of the view that "vertue followeth oftest Noble bloud"; see his *Basilikon Doron* (Edinburgh, 1603), 47.

a "mere great man," and the aristocratic monuments in which he delights: "His virtue is, that he was his father's son.... One of just as much use as his images [family monuments], only he differs in this, that he can speak himself, and save the fellow of Westminster [the guide to the monuments in the Abbey] a labour.... Thus he lives till his tomb be made ready, and is then a grave statue to posterity."[16] The "grave statue" reveals the "great" man's essence in both life and death to be an empty show.

Humanists often contrasted the aristocratic monument either with the monument of fame a virtuous man built for himself, or with the salvation he received from God, or with both fame and salvation as separate but correlative forms of posthumous survival.[17] In *Virgidemiarum* (1597), Joseph Hall attacks an aristocrat for building himself a "ritch monument" rather than making a monument of his "living deeds," which is the only "tombe...that true vertue needs."[18] In *Abuses Stripped and Whipped* (1603), George Wither similarly criticizes those who think it does not matter how they live so long as they receive a "carved Marble": "Doost thou suppose, by a few carved stones, / ... / To be *immortall*? If thou long to live / After thy death; let noble *Vertue* give / And adde that living glory to thy name."[19] Jonson's friend Richard Corbett composed an elegy upon Thomas Ravis, the bishop of London who died in 1609, which contrasts the deceased, who was buried without a monument, and those who trust in "perjur'd stone." The good bishop needs no monument because he both lives in the "Tongues of living men" and is "assured" of salvation at the Day of Judgment.[20] Comparing tombs to the legendary triumphs of Greek illusionistic art, Corbett suggests that they are only for those who try in vain to fool God with artful surfaces:

> Let those that feare their Rising, purchase vaults,
> And reare them statues to excuse their faults,

[16] Henry Morley, ed., *Character Writings of the Seventeenth Century* (London, 1891), 234–235.

[17] Ariès notes the frequent association between earthly fame and heavenly salvation in the sixteenth and seventeenth centuries; see pp. 214–215 and 228. Erwin Panofsky discusses the biblical and patristic associations of salvation with fame and their influence upon Italian Renaissance and Baroque funerary monuments in "Mors Vitae Testimonium. The Positive Aspect of Death in Renaissance and Baroque Iconography," in *Studien zur Toskanischen Kunst*, ed. Wolfgang Lotz and Lise Lotte Möller (Munich: Prestel-Verlag, 1964), 221–236.

[18] Joseph Hall, "Satire III. ii," in *The Collected Poems of Joseph Hall*, ed. Arnold Davenport (Liverpool: Liverpool University Press, 1949), 36.

[19] George Wither, "Satyr II. 1 (Vanitie)," in his *Juvenalia* (1622; rpt., Menston, England: Scolar Press, 1970), 187.

[20] Richard Corbett, "An ELEGIE *written upon the death* Of Dr. RAVIS Bishop of LONDON," ll. 23, 26, and 33 in *The Poems of Richard Corbett*, ed. J. A. W. Bennet and H. R. Trevor-Roper (Oxford: Clarendon, 1955), 3–4.

As if, like Birds that peck at painted Grapes,
The Judge knew not their *persons*, from their *shapes*.[21]

With satiric verse Corbett portrays the contemporary craze for tombs as
a monumental but fruitless coverup.

Such attacks center on those who vainly erect monuments to themselves instead of leading good lives. Though some critics attacked
all ostentatious tombs, it was widely felt that the living owed their
dead relatives commemoration befitting their social station. Epitaphs
announce that heirs have erected monuments out of piety to those
who have given them so much. Thus the inscription upon one early
seventeenth-century tomb announces that the son "being liberally bred
in ye university of Oxon / Thought himself bound to erect" his parents'
monument.[22] As one early seventeenth-century epitaph upon a gentleman explains, piety demands that a monument be erected even for a
virtuous man who, on humanist principles, does not need one: "Not that
hee needeth Monements of Ston / For his well gotten Fame to rest upon,
/ But this was rear'd to testifie that hee, / Lives in their Loves that yet
surviving bee."[23] Another epitaph of the same period attacks the "mau-
solean monument[s]" and "painted sepulchre[s]" of the unworthy but
defends the tomb upon which it is itself inscribed as the legitimate sign
of "due respect" to a gentleman who had built himself a lasting, im-
material "monument" by virtuous "action."[24] Humanism itself encouraged such protestations of pious respect for the dead: medieval epitaphs
do not normally mention the commemorators of the deceased, and the
emphasis on the survivors who piously erected the monument and wrote
or commissioned the epitaph was a humanist practice deriving from the
imitation of classical inscriptions.[25] Thus the living contrived to have it
both ways: they simultaneously affirmed that virtue was the truest mon-

---

[21] Corbett, "An ELEGIE," ll. 29–32 in *Poems*, 4.

[22] The epitaph of Ralph Quelche, d. 1629, and his wife is in D. J. Enright, ed., *The
Oxford Book of Death* (Oxford: Oxford University Press, 1983), 325.

[23] Epitaph upon Nathaniel Still, Esquire, d. 1626, in John Le Neve, ed., *Monumenta
Anglicana: Being Inscriptions on the Monuments of several Eminent Persons . . . 1600–1715*, 5
vols. (London, 1718–1719), 4:104. Compare the nearly identical epitaph upon John
Heigham, Esquire, d. 1632, in Elias Ashmole, *The Antiquities of Berkshire*, 3 vols. (London,
1733), 1:178–179.

[24] Epitaph upon Edward Sherland, Esquire, d. 1609, in Thomas F. Ravenshaw, ed.,
Antiente Epitaphes (from A.D. 1250 to A.D. 1800) (London, 1878), 50.

[25] On the rediscovery of the classical epitaph identifying both the deceased and the
commemorator(s), see Ariès, 230–231; and Iiro Kajanto, "Origin and Characteristics of
the Humanistic Epitaph," *Epigraphica: Rivista Italiana di Epigrafia* 40 (1978):20–21. Though
Kajanto provides fifteenth-century examples from Rome, Ariès's assertion that the form
reappears in Europe in the sixteenth century is true of England. By the seventeenth century
the two-part epitaph is standard in England; for numerous examples see the fourth volume
of Le Neve's collection, containing inscriptions from 1600 to 1649.

ument and defended the tombs that revealed the social status of both the deceased and themselves.

By radically altering the relationship between the living and the dead, Protestantism further contributed to both the popularity of tombs and the conflicts surrounding them. Protestantism severed the various links across the barrier of death posited by Catholicism. The denial of purgatory meant that the living could not help the dead by prayer, while the abolition of the cult of saints meant that the living could not pray to the dead for help. Most Catholic theologians, including the major Scholastic, Aquinas, and the most influential humanist, Erasmus, believed that the dead knew and cared about the actions of the living.[26] Calvin and most English Protestant theologians, by contrast, thought that the dead were unconcerned with earthly events.[27] The disappearance of the "sacred economy" that regulated exchanges between the living and the dead increased the popularity of monuments: assertions of familial continuity served as partial and secular compensation for the breaking of the sacred connection between the generations envisaged by Catholic theology.[28] The Protestant denial of purgatory and prayers for the dead eliminated the donation of vast sums to chantries. Chantries had allowed the elite not only to secure relief for their souls but also to perpetuate their memory. Church monuments provided permissible substitutes for such commemoration.[29] Some of the money once spent on adorning the church with religious images now deemed idolatrous by Protestants was transferred to monuments, and the removal of such images and saints' shrines from church walls provided the space needed for the proliferation of tombs.[30]

Much in Protestantism was nevertheless hostile to the erection of grand

[26] On the Catholic view, see Edward Surtz, S. J., *The Praise of Wisdom* (Chicago: Loyola University Press, 1957), 86–87.

[27] See Calvin, *Institutes of the Christian Religion*, trans. Ford Lewis Battles, ed. John T. McNeill, 2 vols. (Philadelphia: Westminster Press, 1960), 2:882–883 (3.20.24). On the mainstream English Protestant view, see Lucien Carrive, "La doctrine de la mort et la vie future en Angletere à l'époque de la Réforme," in Centre de Recherches sur l'Angleterre des Tudors à la Régence, Université de Lille, *La mort, le fantastique, et le surnaturel du XVième à l'époque romantique* (Lille: Presses Universitaires de Lille, 1979), 23, 29. Richard Strier analyzes the way in which George Herbert espouses the Protestant view by casting doubt upon, and suggesting the irrelevance of, the dead's awareness of the living in "'To all Angels and Saints': Herbert's Puritan Poem," *MP* 77 (1979):132–145; see especially pp. 141–142.

[28] See Keith Thomas, *Religion and the Decline of Magic* (New York: Scribner's, 1971), 604; and Michel Vovelle's *La mort et l'occident de 1300 à nos jours* (Paris: Gallimard, 1983), 327, 357.

[29] See Lorraine C. Attreed, "Preparation for Death in Sixteenth Century Northern England," *The Sixteenth Century Journal* 13, no. 3 (1982):64.

[30] On the new space for memorials, see J. G. Mann, "English Church Monuments, 1536–1625," *The Walpole Society* 21 (1933):19.

monuments. Most English humanist critics of the aristocratic tomb were also, of course, Protestants, and Protestant impulses both reinforced and challenged the humanist treatment of the dead. Protestantism encouraged the denigration of tombs that honored men "great" but not "good." While humanism often celebrated the virtuous person's "monument" of earthly fame, however, the specifically Protestant emphasis fell upon the godly person's humility in the face of his or her savior. Early Protestant reformers had attacked lavish tombs as manifestations of pride. Arguing that monuments were proper as signs of pious "hope of the future resurrection," rather than as expressions of "glory" for "posterity," Calvin criticized great expenditure on tombs.[31] In the 1560s or 1570s, Myles Coverdale, like Calvin, attacked "gorgeous graves and sepulchres" as manifestations of "pride."[32] Calvin himself chose to be buried in an unmarked churchyard grave, and a late sixteenth-century English translation of an epigram by Théodore de Bèze claimed that the lowly grave of "godlie" Calvin "doest surpasse" the "Marble toumbs" and "sepulchers" of kings.[33]

During the late sixteenth and early seventeenth centuries, the social elite of the Puritan faction within the English church generally spent as much on monuments as other men of rank.[34] Some of the "godly" nobility and gentry did, however, express misgivings concerning the vainglory of monuments. After having built an opulent monument upon the death of his father, the early seventeenth-century Puritan Sir Edward Lewkenor, for example, decided that such expense was "of all others worst bestowed."[35] The early seventeenth-century poet and deeply Calvinist humanist Fulke Greville planned a gigantic monument for Sir Philip Sidney and himself that was to have included an epitaph condemning it as a "Vaine affected immortalitie" and a foolish attempt "By stones to seeke aeternitie againe."[36] The large tomb he actually built for himself in Warwick Cathedral proclaims his social importance. The somber black

[31] John Calvin, *Commentary on Genesis*, trans. John King, 2 vols. (Edinburgh: Calvin Translation Society, 1847–1850), 2:245.

[32] Myles Coverdale, "Treatise on Death," in *Remains of Myles Coverdale*, ed. Rev. George Pearson (Cambridge: Cambridge University Press, 1846), 109.

[33] Timothe Kendall, "An Epitaphe upon...John Calvin, poorely and plainly enterred at Geneva," in *Flowers of Epigrammes* (1577), Spenser Society no. 15 (1874; rpt., New York: Burt Franklin, 1967), 165.

[34] See J. T. Cliffe, *The Puritan Gentry: The Great Puritan Families of Early Stuart England* (London: Routledge, 1984), 131–133; and Greaves, 732–733.

[35] See the discussion of the Lewkenors in Patrick Collinson, "Magistracy and Ministry: A Suffolk Miniature," in his *Godly People: Essays on English Protestantism and Puritanism* (London: Hambledon Press, 1983), 453–466. I quote from p. 462.

[36] Fragments of the inscription are preserved in a letter that Sir John Coke sent to Greville in 1615, which is printed in Norman K. Farmer, Jr., "Fulke Greville and John Coke: An Exchange of Letters on a History Lecture and Certain Latin Verses on Sir Philip Sidney," *Huntington Library Quarterly* 33 (1970):220–223. I quote from p. 222.

sarcophagus has an inscription, however, that concludes "A monument of sin" ("Trophaeum peccati").[37] Like survivors who displayed their social status by erecting tombs to the dead while at the same time declaring in humanist fashion the superfluity of such monuments, Greville has it both ways by building himself a grand sepulcher while declaring it proof of his own sinful pride.

Protestant suspicions concerning tombs were revealed most dramatically in the destruction of funerary memorials. During early and mid-sixteenth-century outbreaks of iconoclasm, English Protestants demolished or mutilated many funerary monuments.[38] Many pre-Reformation monuments were destroyed because they had "idolatrous" pictures of the Virgin and saints as well as "superstitious" inscriptions requesting prayers for the dead.[39] Some iconoclasts believed, moreover, that all church monuments featuring images of the dead, not only those with specifically Catholic elements, encouraged idolatrous worship of the deceased.[40]

The destruction of tombs challenged the social hierarchy, and a 1550 statute ordering that religious images in churches be removed or destroyed specifically excluded funerary monuments of any "dead person which hath not been commonly reputed and taken for a saint."[41] Destruction of tombs continued, however, despite government prohibitions. An Elizabethan proclamation of 1560 against further destruction made explicit its concern for the lineage-based social hierarchy: it deplored the "extinguishing of the honorable and good memory of sundry virtuous and noble persons deceased" and the loss of "the true understanding of divers families" caused by the destruction of tombs.[42]

A telling contradiction in the government's attitude toward church monuments reveals the tension between aristocratic concern for honoring one's ancestors and Protestant fears of idolatrous worship of the dead. The Elizabethan proclamation distinguishes between the "monuments of idolatry and false feigned images" that were to be destroyed

[37] See Ronald A. Rebholz, *The Life of Fulke Greville, First Lord Brooke* (Oxford: Clarendon, 1971), 316–318.

[38] For accounts of sixteenth-century iconoclastic destruction of monuments, see Margaret Aston, *England's Iconoclasts*, vol. 1, *Laws against Images* (Oxford: Clarendon, 1988), 269–271, 314–315, and passim; and John Phillips, *The Reformation of Images: Destruction of Art in England, 1535–1660* (Berkeley: University of California Press, 1973), 117–118, passim.

[39] On destruction of Catholic imagery and inscriptions upon tombs, see Malcolm Norris, *Monumental Brasses: The Memorials*, 2 vols. (London: Phillips and Page, 1977), 1:258–263.

[40] Phillips, 117.

[41] The decree is cited and discussed in Aston, 269–271.

[42] "Prohibiting Destruction of Church Monuments" [Windsor, 19 September 1560, 2 Elizabeth 1], in Paul L. Hughes and James F. Larkin, eds., *Tudor Royal Proclamations*, 3 vols. (New Haven: Yale University Press, 1964–1969), 2:146. The statute is cited and discussed in Aston, 314–316; and Phillips, 117–119.

and monuments of the dead "set up for . . . [their] memory . . . in common churches and not for any religious honor."[43] The proclamation relies on a traditional distinction between legitimate images that merely aid the memory (in this case, of the dead) and idols that are worshipped.[44] Issued in 1563 and read in every church during the late sixteenth and early seventeenth centuries, the *Second Tome of Homilies* contains a homily on idolatry that makes a similar distinction between legitimate images and idols but points out the danger of even the former in churches: "Images used for no religion, or superstition rather, we meane Images of none worshipped, nor in danger to be worshipped of any, may be suffered. But Images placed publikely in Temples, cannot possibly bee without danger of worshipping and idolatrie."[45] The homilist warns that even images intended simply as memorials could nevertheless become objects of worship when placed in the house of God. Citing an oft-quoted passage from the Wisdom of Solomon (14:14), the homilist notes that idolatry, the worship of "dead Images" instead of the "living God,"[46] first arose with the forming of an image to the dead: "For . . . the origine of Images, and worshipping of them, as it is recorded in the eight Chapter of the booke of Wisedome, began of a blinde love of a fond father, framing for his comfort an Image of his sonne, being dead, and so at the last men fell to the worshipping of the Image of him whom they did know to bee dead."[47] The homilist further describes the Catholic cult of saints as an idolatrous worshiping of tombs and the dead, attacking "worshippers of tombes and pictures . . . [who] doe burie themselves upon the buried."[48] It is therefore not surprising that church monuments

---

[43] Hughes and Larkin, 2:146–147.

[44] Phillips, 117–118. Protestants often exploited this distinction to define and defend an often shifting realm of legitimate, non-idolatrous images. For its use in defense of images in texts, see John N. King, *English Reformation Literature: The Tudor Origins of the Protestant Tradition* (Princeton: Princeton University Press, 1982), 144–160; and Huston Diehl, "Graven Images: Protestant Emblem Books in England," *Renaissance Quarterly* 39 (1986):49–66.

[45] "The second part of the Homilie against *perill of Idolatry*," in *Certaine Sermons or Homilies*, intro. Mary Ellen Rickey and Thomas B. Stroup, 2 vols. (1623; rpt., Gainesville, Fla.: Scholars' Facsimiles & Reprints, 1968), 2:44.

[46] *Certaine Sermons or Homilies*, 2:19.

[47] *Certaine Sermons or Homilies*, 2:61. For other late sixteenth- and early seventeenth-century citations of the Book of Wisdom's account of the origins of idolatry, see, for example, John Jewel, "The Reply to Harding's Answer," in *The Works of John Jewel*, ed. Rev. John Ayre, 4 vols. (Cambridge, 1845–1850), 2:645–646; the work ascribed to Nicholas Ridley, "A Treatise on the Worship of Images," in *The Works of Nicholas Ridley*, ed. Henry Christmas (Cambridge, 1841), 85; and John Donne, *Devotions upon Emergent Occasions*, ed. Anthony Raspa (1975; rpt., New York: Oxford University Press, 1987), 94. The first two works use the passage to argue against images in churches; Donne's *Devotions* uses the passage as part of a careful distinction between idolatry of the dead and proper "*offices of piety*" toward them.

[48] *Certaine Sermons or Homilies*, 2:25.

could be feared, even by those who erected them, as dangerous invitations to idolatry. In a 1615 letter to Fulke Greville, Sir John Coke claimed that the custom of constructing memorials to the dead in churches arose from the Catholic worship of saints: "That superstition which taught to worshipp the reliques of the dead brought their tombs into churches."[49] Though Coke simply demanded "moderation" in the erection of church monuments, other members of the established church criticized aristocratic monuments as potentially idolatrous. Thus when a Low Church Oxford divine, Daniel Featley, complained in 1613 that money was "ambitiously, if not superstitiously, consumed in erecting Statues, Obelisques, Tombes, or Monuments for the dead" instead of in "erecting Temples to the living God," he hinted that aristocratic tombs were not only vainglorious but also objects of superstitious reverence that turned people from the living God to "dead" images of dead men.[50]

Jonson's epitaph upon Sir Charles Cavendish participates in the controversies surrounding the cult of the grand tomb. The epitaph exploits humanist and Protestant suspicions of aristocratic monuments in order to denigrate the very tomb on which it is inscribed. Sir Charles Cavendish, who died in 1617, was the wealthy second son of the immensely rich Bess of Hardwick, the countess of Shrewsbury, and the son-in-law of Baron Ogle. His tomb is a fine example of the sepulchral monuments of the early seventeenth-century aristocracy: its alabaster covers the entire south wall of the Cavendish Chapel at Bolsover, Derbyshire, and is sumptuous in design and ornamentation (Figure 1).[51] It is a memorial not only to Sir Charles himself but also to his entire family: the family arms are emblazoned near the top of the tomb, with the life-size recumbent effigy of Sir Charles under a richly coffered arch beneath, followed below by the similar recumbent effigy of his wife and then, at the base, the much smaller kneeling figures of his three sons, each identified by name. Such compositions are common on large monuments of the late sixteenth and early seventeenth centuries: the parents restfully gaze toward heaven with their hands in prayer while the smaller, kneeling children display both religious devotion and familial piety toward their parents, placed genealogically and hierarchically above.[52] In the tym-

[49] The quotation is from Sir John Coke's letter to Greville in Farmer, 221.

[50] Daniel Featley, "The Arke under the Curtaines...," in his *Clavis Mystica* (London, 1636), 575.

[51] See also the description in Nikolaus Pevsner, *Derbyshire*, revised by Elizabeth Williamson, The Buildings of England (Harmondsworth: Penguin, 1978), 92.

[52] For examples of similar late sixteenth- and early seventeenth-century compositions, see Brian Kemp, *English Church Monuments* (London: B. T. Batsford, 1980), 81–82; Mercer, 222; and Margaret Whinney, *Sculpture in Britain: 1530 to 1830* (Baltimore: Penguin, 1964), p. 14 and plates 8a-b. Lawrence Stone notes that early modern English children of the

Figure 1. Monument of Sir Charles Cavendish, d. 1617, in Bolsover Church. By permission of the Royal Commission on the Historical Monuments of England.

panum behind Cavendish a cartouche of complexly patterned strapwork, a common decorative item of the period, adds to the lavish display, while at the top of the black marble pillars small obelisks, traditional symbols of immortality, here garnished with the snake of the Cavendish crest, complete the proclamation of family pride.[53] Two other branches of the Cavendish family erected similarly grandiose monuments in family chapels in the early seventeenth century.[54] The Cavendishes had been minor gentry until Bess of Hardwick, through marriage and the shrewd promotion of her sons, dramatically raised the family fortunes. Like the other Cavendish tombs, the Bolsover monument loudly testifies to the family's (recently acquired) prominence.

The Cavendish chapel at Bolsover simultaneously announced the family's status within the community and allowed living kin to visit the dead and thus reaffirm familial continuity in a semiprivate setting. The inscriptions on the tomb accordingly have a double focus, outward on the public and inward on the family. Just above the coat of arms the title of Jonson's poem, "SIR CHARLES CAVENDISH TO HIS POSTERITIE," is blazoned in large gold letters; just below the arms stands the poem itself, with a prose eulogy of Sir Charles further below, followed by a final prose inscription below his recumbent effigy. While the eulogy describing Cavendish as one whom *"Wisdome, Honour, Content* made *Happie"* is addressed to "strangers," the final prose inscription between his effigy and his wife's concentrates on the feelings of the surviving family that erected the monument in his (and their own) honor:

From which happines, he was translated to the better, on ye 4th of Aprill. 1617. yet not without the sad, & weeping remembrance of the sorrowfull Lady Katherine ... who, of her pietie, with her two surviving sonnes, have dedicated this humble monument to his memorie, & doe all desire, in their tyme, to be gathered to his dust, expecting the happy howre of resurrection. . . . [55]

The two prose inscriptions together combine in typical fashion a panegyric of the deceased and a description of the survivors whose piety

---

upper classes kneeled before their parents daily as a show of respect; see *The Family, Sex and Marriage in England, 1500–1800* (New York: Harper, 1977), 171.

[53] On the popularity of decorative strapwork and of obelisks as symbols of immortality, see Kemp, 62–63, 71, 177.

[54] During her lifetime Bess of Hardwick erected her large monument in what became the Cavendish Chapel of Derby Cathedral, where she was buried in 1607; for a description of the monument, see Pevsner, *Derbyshire*, 170. Later in the chapter I will discuss the monument in the Cavendish Chapel of Edensor Parish Church that commemorates Sir Charles's two older brothers, Henry and William, who died in 1616 and 1626, respectively.

[55] *Ben Jonson*, ed. C. H. Herford and Percy and Evelyn Simpson, 11 vols. (Oxford: Clarendon, 1925–1952), 8:387–388 (date corrected). All quotations of Jonson are from this edition. References indicating the volume and page number will be incorporated into the text of this and the following two chapters.

moved them to construct the tomb. The final prose inscription reveals that the monument is not only a representation of the piety connecting the family's living and dead members—a piety to be affirmed by visits to the tomb—but also a proleptic representation of the physical closeness to which the family will return when they are all "gathered" in the same "dust." This emphasis upon family continuity is what justifies the monument's inclusion of effigies of both the living and the dead and its lack of precise discrimination between these different states: Lady Katherine lies below her husband in the recumbent posture of the dead in anticipation of her future reunion with him, while Sir Charles's already dead first son kneels alongside his living brothers at the base of the tomb in perpetual devotion.

Inscribed in large gold letters on three black tablets just under the crowning arms, Jonson's poetic epitaph denies meaning, however, to the monument:

> Sonnes, seeke not me amonge these polish'd stones:
> these only hide part of my flesh, and bones:
> which, did they neere so neate, or proudly dwell,
> will all turne dust, & may not make me swell.
>
> Let such as justly have out-liv'd all prayse,
> trust in the tombes, their care-full freinds do rayse;
> I made my lyfe my monument, & yours:
> to which there's no materiall that endures;
>
> nor yet inscription like it. Write but that;
> And teach your nephewes it to aemulate:
> it will be matter lowd inoughe to tell
> not when I die'd, but how I livd. Farewell.
>
> (8:387)

The poem's central contrast between the "polish'd stones" of the tomb and the true monument of the deceased, his virtuous life, expresses, as we have seen, humanist ideology. In the early years of James I's reign Jonson, who had risen from humble status as a menial bricklayer and lowly actor to the more exalted role of a poet-dramatist patronized by the king and the aristocracy, conveniently discovered the gentle blood of his own Scottish ancestors and thus legitimized and furthered his social ascent. His poetry nevertheless often proclaims the humanist doctrine of "true nobility" so appealing to a self-made man.[56] In his epigrams

---

[56] On Jonson's insistence upon his own gentle ancestry, which coexisted uneasily with his contempt for "mere" lineage, see "Ben Jonson's Conversations with William Drummond of Hawthornden" (*Ben Jonson*, 1:139); and David Riggs, *Ben Jonson: A Life* (Cambridge: Harvard University Press, 1989), which notes that Jonson's assertion of his gentle ancestry in the early years of James I's reign constituted an act of "retrospective self-fashioning" (pp. 4–5 and 115–116).

he declares that "to live great, was better, then great borne" ("To Sir William Jephson," l. 12; 8:75) and praises a man whose "deedes, unto thy name, will prove new wombes, / Whil'st others toyle for titles to their tombes" ("To Sir Henry Nevil," ll. 17–18; 8:70). The eighth part of his funerary poem *Eupheme* echoes Juvenal (*Satire* 8.20) to claim, "'Tis Vertue alone, is true Nobilitie" (8:282). In the epitaph, Jonson has Cavendish proclaim from the grave the superiority of his virtuous life and consequent immortality to the mere "materiall" greatness represented by his opulent tomb.

Jonson borrowed the dismissal of tombs as the vain monuments that "freinds do rayse" (l. 6) for those whose lives have "out-liv'd all prayse" (l. 5) from the final couplet of an earlier, more conventional proclamation of the humanist credo, an epigram by Thomas Bastard, one of Jonson's older contemporaries:

> *De Francisco Walsingham & Philippo Sidneo Equit.*
> Sir *Francis* and sir *Philip*, have no Toombe,
> Worthy of all the honour that may be.
> And yet they lye not so for want of roome,
> Or want of love in their posteritie.
> Who would from living hearts untombe such ones,
> To bury under a fewe marble stones?
> *Vertue dyes not, her tombe we neede not raise,*
> *Let them trust tombs which have outliv'd their praise.*[57]

Both the ideal courtier-poet-soldier Sir Philip Sidney and his father-in-law, Francis Walsingham, Elizabeth's principal secretary, lay buried in old Saint Paul's Cathedral without memorials.[58] Their lack of monuments provided the perfect occasion for a humanist declaration. After claiming that the posthumous survival of Sidney and Walsingham in "living hearts" is far greater than a nugatory "fewe marble stones," Bastard concludes with a generalizing couplet that proclaims the standard contrast between those whose virtue makes them immortal and the worthless "great" who rely upon merely material monuments.[59]

[57] Thomas Bastard, "*Liber Quartus*: Epigr. 31," in *Chrestoleros: Seven Books of Epigrames* (1598), Spenser Society no. 47 (1888; rpt., New York: Burt Franklin, 1967), 103. (My emphasis on lines seven and eight.)

[58] Sidney and Walsingham lacked monuments because the latter went heavily into debt after giving the former a lavish funeral; see the note in Katherine Duncan-Jones and Jan Van Dorsten, eds., *The Miscellaneous Prose of Sir Philip Sidney* (Oxford: Clarendon, 1973), 145–146.

[59] In the epigram following that upon Sidney and Walsingham, Bastard describes the Westminster Abbey monuments of the once-great dead as only "a play-game of a painted stone" ("*Liber Quartus*: Epigr. 32," l. 9, in *Chrestoleros*, 104). Bastard's contention that Sidney and Walsingham do not lack a "tombe" because of "want of roome" probably replies to the poem that the antiquarian John Stow claims was scrawled in old Saint Paul's under

Though Jonson echoes Bastard's final couplet, the central paradox of the Cavendish epitaph radically distinguishes the poem from Bastard's more conventional composition: the voice of the dead Cavendish emanates from his grand tomb in order to deny that he is to be found there. Classical epitaphs often represent the dead speaking from their tombs, sometimes only to deny that anything but dust remains of them. Thus in one Latin inscription the deceased proclaims from the grave, "I was a knight, now I am but dust made from a knight," while in another the deceased informs the reader, "If you ask who I am, behold I am dust and dried-up ash."[60] Contact between the dead and the living is thus both affirmed and denied: the dead deliver to the living the somber message that they no longer exist except as dust. Medieval epitaphs adapt the classical motif of a grim warning to the living. Often describing themselves in shockingly visual terms as corpses at various levels of decomposition, the dead proclaim some version of the memento mori formula, "Such as you are, such was I, / Such as I am, such shall you be."[61] These epitaphs make the tomb not only a memorial to the dead but also a charitable exhortation to the living to remember their own end and repent. With the rise of humanist and Protestant epitaphic motifs, the memento mori message from the deceased was heard with diminishing frequency. The voice of the corpse still resounds, however, in some late sixteenth- and early seventeenth-century epitaphs, as the following two examples illustrate:

> Come nere my friends, behould and see
> Suche as I am suche shall you bee:
> As is my state within this tombe
> So must yours be before the doome.

> Even Dust as I am now
>   And thou in time shall be

---

the grandiose monument of Sir Christopher Hatton, the lord chancellor who died in 1591: "Philip [Sidney] and Francis [Walsingham] have no Tombe, / For great Christopher takes all the roome" (A Survey of London [1603], ed. Charles Lethbridge Kingsford, 2 vols. [Oxford: Clarendon, 1908], 1:338). Since Hatton was widely perceived to have been unqualified for the high office bestowed upon him, his opulent monument exemplified the ostentation of the worthless "great" man. Rather than focus upon one aristocrat's vainglorious tomb, however, Bastard voices the general humanist critique of material monuments.

[60] "Miles eram, sum deinde cinis de milite factus"; "Si quaeris quae sim, cinis en et tosta favilla" (Franciscus Buecheler, ed., Anthologia Latina, Pars Posterior: Carmina Latina Epigraphica [Leipzig: Teubner, 1895–1897], 1:189 and 2:442 [nos. 409 and 960]).

[61] For examples and discussion of the medieval memento mori epitaph, see Ariès, 218–219; and Rosemary Woolf, The English Religious Lyric in the Middle Ages (Oxford: Clarendon, 1968), 312–324, 401–404.

Such one was I as thou
Behold thy self by me.[62]

With his denigration of his monument as mere "polish'd stones" that "hide" his "flesh, and bones" (ll. 1–2) destined to "dust" (l. 4), Cavendish recalls the demystifying tradition of the memento mori. Cavendish does not identify himself, however, with his buried body: the self-assured "I" of his opening command treats his own body as an *other* and thus distances himself from the speaking corpse of tradition.

Cavendish's denigration of the tomb as the container of a *foreign* body has a Stoic resonance. Seneca tells a bereaved mother, Marcia, that she need not "hurry to the tomb" of her son because "what lies there is his basest part . . . bones and ashes are no more parts of him than were his clothes."[63] Yet while Seneca goes on to console Marcia by celebrating the purified soul of her son "dwelling in the highest heaven," Cavendish does not identify himself with a spirit above. He thus ignores both the Stoic conception of a celestial afterlife and the traditional Christian alternative to the speaking corpse, the voice of the soul speaking from heaven.[64] While the decomposed corpse speaks from the grave in order to frighten the sinner into remembering his end, the voice of the soul speaks from above the grave in order to comfort the bereaved and testify to the joys of heaven. An early seventeenth-century epitaph ends, for example, with this comforting couplet: "Then cease deare Infant, Husband, Parents, Friends / To wayle my woes, in Heaven I have amends."[65] Though Protestants generally believed that the dead were not aware of earthly events, such epitaphs provided consolatory fictions that reconnected the blessed dead to the living.

Cavendish, by contrast, locates his vital remains solely in his self-immortalizing way of life. Though his central claim—"I mayde my lyfe my monument" (l. 7)—is yet another version of the humanist topos Bastard expresses in "Virtue dyes not," the power of the first-person,

---

[62] Epitaphs upon John Trustlowe, d.1593, in Ravenshaw, 38–39; and Robert Gippes, d. 1624, in Le Neve, 4:95. The speaking corpse's warning survives into the early nineteenth century, but over the course of the seventeenth century it virtually disappears from the church monuments of the elite and is relegated to modest churchyard inscriptions. For examples from the Middle Ages to the late eighteenth century, see Thomas Joseph Pettigrew, *Chronicles of the Tombs* (London, 1857), 62–67.

[63] "Proinde non est quod ad sepulcrum fili tui curras; pessima eius . . . istic iacent, ossa cineresque, non magis illius partes quam vestes aliaque tegimenta corporum" (Seneca, *De consolatione ad Marciam* 25.1). Compare Seneca's argument that the wise man does not care what happens to his mortal body after death in *Epistulae morales* 92.34–35 and *De tranquillitate animi* 14.3.

[64] See Seneca, *De consolatione ad Marciam* 25.1–3. On the Stoic heaven, see also Seneca's *De consolatione ad Polybium* 9.3; *Epistulae morales* 93.9–10 and 102.22–30; and compare Cicero, *Tusculan Disputations* 1.19.43–1.32.81; and *De senectute* 21.77–23.84.

[65] Epitaph of Anne Wylde, d. 1624, in Le Neve, 4:89–90.

plain-style voice belittling the "polish'd stones" of the very tomb from which it speaks revivifies the humanist commonplace and suggests that Cavendish's life-as-monument is embodied in his enduring words. His imperious tone, his proud rejection of a foolish pride in his monument reveal his presence as a voice even as he disparages the monument covering his corpse. His words may be glossed by Jonson's declaration of poetic faith in *Discoveries*: "Language most shewes a man: speake that I may see thee" (8:625).

Jonson emphasizes the importance of Cavendish's message by dramatically reversing an epitaphic topos. When Cavendish tells his children that his life is not only his own monument but also theirs (l. 7), he reverses the common assertion that a person's children are his or her monument. Some poems send the reader from a material monument of the deceased to the truer monument, the progeny of the deceased, as in the following composition, once attributed to George Herbert:

> Sir John Danvers' earthly part
> Here is copied out by art;
> But his heavenly and divine,
> In his progenie doth shine.
> Had he only brought them forth,
> Know that much had been his worth.
> There's no monument to a sonne,
> Read him there, and I have done.[66]

Cavendish, by contrast, emphatically—even stridently—asserts that his life is a monument for his sons rather than their lives being a monument for him. This reversal emphasizes the sons' continued need to heed their father's ways as expressed in his message. Some epitaphs of this period assert that the "best part" of a father remains in his children: "But if in hopefull issue parents live, / I'm not halfe dead, my beste part doth survive."[67] Cavendish tells his sons that only "part" of his body rests in the tomb, because the other part lies in the sons themselves. Nevertheless his "best part"—the meaning of his life—is to be found in the message itself.

The final stanza completes the identification of Cavendish's lasting spirit with the message he delivers. The enjambed phrase, "nor yet in-

---

[66] "On John Danvers," in *The Works of George Herbert*, corrected ed., ed. Frederick E. Hutchinson (Oxford: Oxford University Press, 1945), 208. This poem is in fact the inscription for a memorial portrait rather than for a tomb, but the two kinds of memorial were closely related. See Roy Strong, *The Cult of Elizabeth: Elizabethan Portraiture and Pageantry* (London: Thames and Hudson, 1977), 84–110, which discusses the popularity of such memorial portraits in the Elizabethan and Jacobean periods and describes them as "a curious hinterland between the living portrait and the funeral or tomb effigy" (p. 84).

[67] Epitaph upon Nicolas Luttrell, d. 1607, in Ravenshaw, 47.

scription like it" (l. 9), at first suggests that the poetic inscription, like the physical tomb, cannot adequately represent his life. Such denigration of the poetic medium in comparison to the virtues of the subject is a familiar rhetorical strategy: one praises by asserting the inexpressible qualities of the subject.[68] Jonson's epitaph, however, does not rest content with positing a virtue beyond language. Though "nor yet" initially means "and also not," the following clause, "Write but that" (l. 9), activates another meaning for "nor yet" that redeems the poem as Cavendish's vital message: "nor till now." Up to now there has been no inscription worthy of him, the deceased proclaims, but he begins to make up for this deficiency by dictating his appropriate epitaph with the proud command "Write but that." Presumably he refers to the pith of his message— "I mayde my lyfe my monument, & yours"—and his command suggests that his true epitaph is not the actual inscription on the tomb but an inscription that the sons must rewrite for themselves. Cavendish's command to rewrite his epitaph is, of course, a poetic fiction emanating from the already inscribed epitaph. Nevertheless, the command suggests a vital bridge between the dead and the living: the sons can "write" the essential message of their father, in their hearts if not on a material monument, and thus make that message truly their own.[69] They will then be able to teach their descendants ("nephewes," l. 10, from Latin *nepotes*, "descendants") "it to aemulate" (l. 10). The antecedent of "it" is "that" of "Write but that," so that the message and the life it encapsulates merge as the object that Cavendish's descendents must be taught. In declaring how "loud" the "matter " (l. 11) of his message is, Cavendish implicitly contrasts its "matter" with both the "materiall" of a monument and the mere *verba* of an ordinary inscription: the enduring message has *res*, substance, as opposed to mere materiality, and meaning, as opposed to mere sound.

The transmission of Cavendish's message requires not simply its appropriation by Cavendish's sons but also their departure—announced by the final, definitive "Farewell"—so that they may go and spread it to future generations. The final emphasis on transmitting the didactic message transforms a classical epitaphic topos. In ancient times the dead were buried along the major highways, and many Greek poetic epitaphs request that the passing wayfarer carry the message concerning the de-

---

[68] See the classic discussion of "inexpressibility topoi" in Ernst Robert Curtius, *European Literature and the Latin Middle Ages*, trans. Willard R. Trask (Princeton: Princeton University Press, 1953), 159–162; and William N. Fisher, "*Occupatio* in Sixteenth- and Seventeenth-Century Verse," *Texas Studies in Language and Literature* 14 (1972):203–222.

[69] For a discussion of Jonson's general emphasis upon "receptivity," including the giving and receiving of poetic lessons, see Thomas M. Greene, *The Light in Troy: Imitation and Discovery in Renaissance Poetry* (New Haven: Yale University Press, 1982), 282–283.

ceased to a third party, normally the surviving relatives.[70] Such poems stress both the pathos of a death far from relatives and friends and the epitaph's role as a verbal link between the dead and the living far away. Several compositions in the Planudean Anthology, which was widely accessible in Henri Estienne's 1566 edition of the Greek text as well as in various translations, exploit the topos. The following Hellenistic example is to be imagined as the inscription upon a cenotaph for a man drowned at sea: "Ye sailors on the sea, Aristo of Cyrene prays you all by Zeus the Protector of strangers to tell his father Meno that he lost his life in the Aegean main, and lies by the rocks of Icaria."[71] Though the message itself concerns the place of death, the command to transmit the message seeks to transcend this place through renewed communication with the living. Other Greek epitaphs make transmission of the message a matter of deep ethical import. In Simonides' famous epitaph on the dead of Thermopylae, for example, the message concerns the when and where of death, but by transmitting that message the "stranger" would learn a patriotic lesson transcending time and place: "Tell, stranger, the Spartans that you have seen us lying here. / We fell obeying the sacred law of our fatherland."[72] Pointedly denying the importance first of the place of burial and then of the time of death ("not when I die'd," l. 12), Cavendish stresses further the message's space- and time-defying power and gives ethical import to the act of transmission itself. The sons are to be vitally linked to their father and transformed by the message that they have (re)written and will transmit to their descendants.[73]

---

[70] For an analysis of this motif in Hellenistic epitaphs, see Sonya Lida Tarán, *The Art of Variation in the Hellenistic Epigram* (Leiden: Brill, 1979), 132–149. For a complex, enigmatic use of the motif in Latin poetry, see Propertius, *Elegy* 1.21.

[71] "Nautiloi ô plôontes, ho Kurênaios Aristôn / pantas huper Xeniou lissetai umme Dios, / eipein patri Menôni, par' Ikariais hoti petrais / keitai, en Aigaiôi thumon apheis pelagei" (*Greek Anthology*, 7.499). The epitaph was translated into Latin in the sixteenth century; see James Hutton, *The Greek Anthology in Italy* (Ithaca: Cornell University Press, 1935), 502. Other epigrams from the Planudean Anthology that exploit the message motif, such as *Greek Anthology* 7.500, 7.521, and 7. 540, were also translated into Latin during the Renaissance; see Hutton, *Greek Anthology in Italy*, 502, 504; and James Hutton, *The Greek Anthology in France and in the Latin Writers of the Netherlands to the Year 1800* (Ithaca: Cornell University Press, 1946), 644, 653–654.

[72] This distich epitaph was well known in Cicero's version: "Dic, hospes, Spartae nos te hic vidisse iacentes. / Dum sanctis patriae legibus obsequimur" (*Tusculan Disputations* 1.42.101).

[73] Lady Katherine Cavendish, Sir Charles's wife, died in 1629 and was buried, as she had vowed in the prose epitaph upon her husband's tomb, alongside her spouse. Jonson composed an epitaph upon her that was probably intended for a memorial tablet to be placed beside the Cavendish monument in the family chapel. Calling his epitaph a "coppie" (l. 40) of the "Record in heaven" (l. 40), Jonson emphasizes once more the spreading of the epitaphic message: "You, that were / Her Children, and Grand-children, reed it heere! / Transmitt it to your Nephewes, ffreinds, Allies, / Tenants, and Servants" (ll. 1–3, 8:399).

Cavendish's assertion, "I made my lyfe my monument . . . / to which there's no materiall that endures" (ll. 7–8), recalls Horace's claim concerning his poetic achievement, "I have completed a monument more lasting than bronze" ("Exegi monumentum aere perennius," *Ode* 3.30.1). Cavendish's identification of his life-as-monument with his enduring verbal message gives special meaning to the echo. Jonson, who presented himself as the English Horace and defined the poet as "a Maker" (8:635),[74] makes Cavendish the Horatian "poet" or "maker" of his immortal life and message. In his quarrel with Inigo Jones, Jonson draws on the traditional hierarchy of the liberal and mechanical arts to contrast poetry's concern with the "soul" and inner "meaning" of things and architecture's inferior concern with the "body" and surface "sense."[75] Cavendish's dismissal of "polish'd stones" in favor of his enduring verbal message allows Jonson to enunciate his own deeply held belief in the superiority of poetic to material monuments.

Since there is no evidence that Jonson knew the deceased, it is not surprising that the epitaph reflects Jonson's values rather than Cavendish's own. There is nevertheless considerable irony in Cavendish's dismissal of material monuments, since like his mother, Bess of Hardwick, he was in fact known for his passion for architecture and status-enhancing structures.[76] His mock-castle at Bolsover, which he rebuilt after buying its ruins from his more illustrious stepbrother, Gilbert Talbot, the seventh earl of Shrewsbury, was probably meant to suggest that Sir Charles came of more ancient, distinguished lineage than was the case.[77] His mother's epitaph provides an interesting contrast to Jonson's composition, for as the culmination of its panegyric it notes that Bess "built the houses of Chatsworth, Hardwick, and Oldcotes, highly distinguished by their mag-

[74] On Jonson's identification with Horace (and the difficulties such an identification entailed), see Richard Helgerson, *Self-Crowned Laureates: Spenser, Jonson, Milton, and the Literary System* (Berkeley: University of California Press, 1983), 103, 113–116.

[75] See D. J. Gordon, "Poet and Architect: The Intellectual Setting of the Quarrel between Ben Jonson and Inigo Jones," in *The Renaissance Imagination: Essays and Lectures by D. J. Gordon*, ed. Stephen Orgel (Berkeley: University of California Press, 1975), 77–101.

[76] On Sir Charles Cavendish as an enthusiastic builder, see Mark Girouard, *Robert Smythson and the Elizabethan Country House* (New Haven: Yale University Press, 1983), 205–245.

[77] Though he confuses Sir Charles with his older brother William, who bought himself into the peerage, Conrad Russell's claim that Cavendish "was pretending to a more ancient lineage than he possessed . . . by building himself a sham castle at Bolsover" rightly underscores the social function of the building; see *The Crisis of Parliaments: English History 1509–1660* (London: Oxford University Press, 1971), 164. In "To Penshurst" Jonson himself praises a material monument of the aristocracy, a country house, but he distinguishes the ideal represented by Penshurst from the mass of ostentatious houses "built to envious show" (l. 1, 8:93). In his concluding contrast between Penshurst and bad houses—"Now, PENSHURST, they that will proportion thee / With other edifices . . ." (ll. 99–100, 8:96)—the "Now," furthermore, can only refer to the temporality *within* Jonson's own poem, thus implying that Jonson's poem has itself helped *remake* Penshurst so that it can "now" stand fully as an ideal.

nificence." These were her monuments, the magnificent testaments to her and her family's importance.[78] The son's epitaph, by contrast, presents him as an ideal by making him speak like the proud poet Jonson.

The epitaph's presentation of Cavendish must have satisfied the surviving family: it not only was inscribed upon the tomb but also was the first of many works that the poet composed for the Cavendishes. William, the duke of Newcastle, the eldest son, became one of Jonson's best patrons.[79] Nevertheless, in a poem of patronage, Jonson does not make the concessions he might have in his treatment of the aristocratic monument. The prose inscription presents the tomb as an expression of the surviving family's piety toward the deceased. Unlike other humanist poetic epitaphs, however, Jonson's poem refuses to weaken its denigration of the monument by conceding the tomb's piety. Instead it proclaims that such "materiall" piety is irrelevant. Satisfaction with building and visiting a grand tomb containing "dust" would be like the misplaced aristocratic pride that Jonson criticizes in his ode of 1611 to Sir William Sidney, when he bids the young man not to "rest" on his ancestry: "For they, that swell / With dust of ancestors, in graves but dwell" ("Ode. To Sir William Sydney, on his Birth–day," ll. 39–40, 8:121). The monument might join the dead and the living in stone, but Jonson wants to bind them in spirit. The Cavendish sons have to leave the grand monument that hides their father's dust in order to spread the epitaphic message that represents his vital legacy. Jonson's patrons have it both ways: the grand tomb and prose inscription proclaim the family's social status, Jonson's verse the virtuous achievement of the paterfamilias. Nevertheless, Jonson maintains his integrity by expressing his own humanist beliefs, thereby making the poem his own lesson, heeded or not, to the family.

The final command that Cavendish's sons teach the emulation of his life has a Christian subtext that further supports the transition from a monumental place to verbal transmission: the biblical episode of the women's visit to Christ's empty tomb (Mark 16:1–8, Matthew 28:1–8, Luke 24:1–11). The opening "Sonnes, seeke not me amonge these polish'd stones" harks back to the angel's question at Christ's tomb: "Why do you seek the living among the dead?" (Luke 24:5). Jonson probably borrows from an intermediate source between the biblical text and his poem, yet another epigram in Thomas Bastard's collection, a sonnet-

---

[78] I cite the English translation in Thomas Noble, *The History and Gazeteer of the County of Derby*, 2 vols. (Derby, 1833), 2:245, which also gives the Latin inscription. Although this inscription was placed upon the monument in the later seventeenth century, it accurately reflects Bess's own values. On her passion for building, see Girouard, *Smythson*, 143–162.

[79] On William Cavendish as Jonson's patron, see Riggs, 301–302, 325–329, 334–337.

epigram only two pages away from the earlier one cited as a source for the Cavendish epitaph:

In cultum reliquiarum
To seeke thee in thy Tombe sweete Jesu when,
The women with their oyntment hastened:
Two Angels did appeare, forbidding them
To seeke thee living there among the dead.
Did *Rome* by diving in the tombes of saintes,
But seeke the living whence they now are fled,
Yet might they heare the Angels making plaint.
Seeke not the living *Rome* among the dead.
But to tye holy worshipp to dead bones.
To bowe religion to the wicked trust
Of crosses, reliques, ashes, sticks, and stones.
To throwe downe living men to honour dust:
  Is not to seeke, but like *Mezentius* rather,
  To joyne the living and the dead together.[80]

Bastard changes the angel's question of Luke 24:5 into an indirect command (ll. 3–4) and then adapts the command to an attack on the Catholic cult of saints ("Seeke not the living *Rome* among the dead," l. 8). Jonson's opening command is closer to Bastard's poem than to the Bible, but the Cavendish epitaph also clearly exploits the biblical text itself. Jonson constructs an implicit analogy between the Cavendish of his poem and Christ and the angel(s) of the New Testament. Both the poem and the biblical passages move from a futile concern for a dead body to the teaching of a vital message: just as the angels send the women away from the empty tomb of Christ to tell the disciples of Christ's teaching concerning his Resurrection (Mark 16:7), so Cavendish sends his sons away from the tomb of his decomposing body that they might teach his message concerning self-immortalization. By echoing the biblical contrast between a message of life and a tomb of death, Jonson provides a deeply resonant analogue to his humanist contrast between the living message of a virtuous man and the aristocratic monument of a corpse.

Both Bastard and Jonson echo the biblical message to attack the veneration of tombs and dead bones rather than of a living spirit. Bastard's iconoclastic assault upon saints' shrines parallels his critique of grand monuments in the epigram on Sidney and Walsingham, and the Cavendish epitaph exploits Protestant fears that the aristocratic tomb, like the Catholic shrine, encourages idolatrous worship of the dead. One may contrast the Cavendish poem with other early seventeenth-century epitaphs that describe the tomb as the "shrine" of the deceased and

---

[80] Bastard, *"Liber Quartus:* Epigram 27," in *Chrestoleros*, 100.

intimate that the body buried within deserves some of the devotion once given to the wonder-working relics of saints:

> Reader, stand back: dull not this Marble Shrine,
> With irreligious Breath: the Stone's divine,
> And does enclose a Wonder—Beauty, Wit,
> Devotion, and Virginity with it.
>
> This [epitaph] only points the reader where thy dust
> Is, till the worlds last audit, left in trust;
> That those, whose zeale can gladly spend an age
> In a long, tedious, barefoot Pilgrimage
> And merit by't, may each neglect the shrine
> Of his once honour'd Saint & visit thine.
>
> This Toomb's sublimed to a shrine, and doth containe
> An holier Saint than could all legends faine.[81]

All three poems use the language of Catholic cult rhetorically, not literally, and the final two clearly mock the "idolatrous" cult of saints. They all nevertheless adapt that cult in order to heighten respect for the physical remains of the dead and for the glorious "shrine" that contains them. Jonson, by contrast, invokes Scripture to attack such reverence for mere "stones" that cover dead "flesh, and bones."

While exploiting Protestant iconoclastic impulses, however, Jonson does not turn in Protestant fashion from a dead idol to the living God. Instead he pushes the humanist celebration of man's virtue to a proud extreme. His biblical echo secularizes the scriptural message concerning life and death and thereby reveals his desire to assert the radical autonomy of human achievement: Cavendish transmits a living message that substitutes for, rather than depends upon, the living Word of Christ and the Resurrection.[82] Christian humanists often correlated earthly fame

[81] Epitaphs upon Anne Burton, d. 1642, in T. Webb, ed., *A New Select Collection of Epitaphs*, 2 vols. (London, 1775), 1:30; Katherine Dent, d. 1637, in Le Neve, 4:176; and Shilston Calmady, Knight, d. 1645, in Ravenshaw, 95. William Browne's altar-shaped epitaph for Sir Thomas Manwood, d. 1613, asks for an "offering" of "tears and sighs" at the "Shrine"; see *Poems of William Browne*, ed. Gordon Goodwin, 2 vols. (London, 1894), 2:142. See also the "shrine" image in the epitaphs upon Catherine Mountague, d. 1612, and Lady Mary Salter, d. 1613, in Ravenshaw, 52, 56.

[82] Ernest B. Gilman compares Jonson's iconoclasm to that of Protestant religious writers in *Iconoclasm and Poetry in the English Reformation: Down with Dagon* (Chicago: University of Chicago Press, 1986), 50–54, 89–90. While highly suggestive, Gilman's comparison obscures the crucial difference between attacking idols in the name of man's words and in the name of God's Word. Louis Marin's semiological (and therefore inherently secularizing) reading of the biblical narrative of the visit to the tomb as an allegory of the movement from a language about objects (the tomb and the body) to a language about itself (the command to transmit the message of the *Logos*), instructively parallels Jonson's transformation of the biblical episode; see Marin, "Les femmes au tombeau: Essai d'analyse structurale d'un texte évangélique," in his *Études sémiologiques* (Paris: Klincksieck, 1971), 221–231.

and salvation, and Jonson's epitaph does not necessarily preclude, simply because it ignores, the celestial bliss of the deceased. While not wholly incompatible with beatitude as the reward for a virtuous life, however, Jonson's transformation of the biblical message renders problematic a conception of salvation as the gift of grace brought by Christ's sacrifice for sinful humanity.

Jonson's epigram "Of Life, and Death" takes the proclamation of human independence to its limit by claiming that the virtuous can, wholly unaided by God, earn a blessed afterlife:

> The ports of death are sinnes; of life, good deeds:
> Through which, our merits leads us to our meeds.
> How wilfull blind is he then, that would stray,
> And hath it, in his powers, to make his way!
> This world deaths region is, the other lifes:
> And here, it should be one of our first strifes,
> So to front death, as men might judge us past it.
> For good men but see death, the wicked tast it.
>
> (8:53-54)

Though its opening expounds the traditional Christian view of death as the wages of sin, the theology of this epigram is highly unusual. Probably written during Jonson's Catholic period of 1598–1610, the poem explicitly contradicts the central tenet of mainstream Protestantism, that one cannot "merit" salvation.[83] Indeed, by extending the elevation of human powers beyond even Catholic—including Catholic humanist— views of the joint role of human merit and God's grace in salvation, the poem propounds what from a Catholic as well as a Protestant perspective is a heretical Pelagian belief in the ability to gain a blessed afterlife solely by means of one's own will and virtuous acts.[84]

Heterodoxy goes hand in hand with classicism. The "good men" of Jonson's poem embody the Stoic ideal of the autonomous wise man, and the epigram describes an afterlife that recalls the starry realm of freedom and knowledge earned by the wise Stoic more than the Christian heaven

---

[83] On Jonson's conversion to Catholicism in 1598 and return to the English church in 1610, see Riggs, 50–52, 176–177.

[84] One may contrast Jonson's Pelagianism with the views of the Catholic humanist whose great learning and religious moderation he most respected, Erasmus. In his dispute with Luther, Erasmus argued that God's grace and human free will together lead to salvation and explicitly eschewed the Scylla of the "Pelagians" as well as the Charybdis of the Lutherans; see *Luther and Erasmus: Free Will and Salvation*, ed. and trans. E. Gordon Rupp et al. (Philadelphia: Westminster Press, 1969), 95–96 and passim. On Jonson's admiration for Erasmus, see Graham Bradshaw, "Three Poems Ben Jonson Did Not Write: A Note on Jonson's Christian Humanism," *ELH* 47 (1980):484–499.

attained through grace.[85] Jonson is elsewhere more orthodox: in some of his religious lyrics he begs for God's mercy and in some of his funerary poems he celebrates the dead's attaining salvation through Christ.[86] Precisely because of its heterodoxy, however, the epigram "Of Life, and Death" reveals the intensity of Jonson's desire to assert humanity's independence. Though the Cavendish epitaph avoids any celestial realm, pagan or Christian, it is clear that Cavendish's enduring spirit, like the afterlife of the epigram, depends no more upon a transcendent power than it does upon a material tomb.

While the Cavendish epitaph attacks the tomb upon which it is inscribed as the mere covering of a corpse, its progression from such an attack to the assertion of the enduring monument of the deceased paradoxically resembles the movement elicited by some grand sepulchral monuments themselves. Such tombs acknowledge the dead body buried beneath them in order further to demonstrate fame's victory over death. Such monuments are thus both memento moris, teaching that all must die, and proud assertions of the vital difference between those doomed to oblivion and those deserving remembrance. Emblems provide the most common way of showing the "rise" from death to fame. The tomb of the wealthy merchant Thomas Sutton in the London Charterhouse chapel, for example, erected by Nicholas Stone in 1615, has emblems of death in the lower portion of the tomb—an hourglass and skull flanked on one side by a child blowing bubbles, the ubiquitous symbol of earthly vanitas, and on the other by Father Time with his scythe, a common symbol of earthly transience—but has at the top of the monument two amorini who, while leaning upon skulls, blow trumpets of fame.[87] Epitaphs often allude to monumental height as a symbol of achieved or

---

[85] Seneca imagines the wise man's claiming that he has "indeed earned admission to their [the gods'] presence" upon death ("Merui quidem admitti . . . inter illos . . . ," Epistulae morales 93.10). Compare Jonson's assertion that Sir Henry Morison "leap'd the present age" to see "that bright eternall Day" in heaven ("To the immortall memorie, and friendship of . . . Sir Lucius Cary, and Sir H. Morison," ll. 79–96, 8:245–246). Katharine Eisaman Maus analyzes Jonson's adoption of the Stoic ideal of the autonomous wise man in Ben Jonson and the Roman Frame of Mind (Princeton: Princeton University Press, 1984), 14–18 and passim; Richard S. Peterson notes the Senecan basis of the Cary-Morison ode's portrait of self-propelled human ascent to the afterlife in Imitation and Praise in the Poetry of Ben Jonson (New Haven: Yale University Press, 1981), 216–217. Neither Maus nor Peterson directly treats the conflict between Jonson's Stoicism and Christian conceptions of grace.

[86] For Jonson's more traditional treatments of grace, see, for example, "To Heaven" (8:122), "The Sinners Sacrifice" (8:126–130), and "Eupheme: 9. Elegie on my Muse," ll. 131–152 (8:286).

[87] See the description and picture of the monument in Walter Lewis Spiers, "The Note-Book and Account Book of Nicholas Stone," The Walpole Society 7 (1919):40–41 and plate 3.

desired fame, and the movement up Sutton's monument, which reaches to the chapel ceiling, enacts fame's defeat of death.[88]

The double tomb, which arises in the fifteenth century, provides another visual analogue to the Cavendish epitaph: on its bottom layer lies a representation of the body buried below the ground, either as a skeleton or corpse, and on top a representation of the deceased more or less as he appeared in life.[89] Sixteenth-century examples figured the ascent that the dead would undergo at the Resurrection: Dean Colet's tomb in old Saint Paul's, which is no longer extant, contrasted the corpse below and the bust of the restored body above, enclosed in a scallop shell of beatitude.[90] Seventeenth-century double tombs depict the secular contrast between death and earthly fame either in addition to or instead of the Christian contrast. The monument erected in the 1620s in memory of Henry and William Cavendish, Sir Charles's older brothers, is a slight variation on the double tomb: a recumbent skeleton and shrouded corpse lie below a marble table; on the left hangs the suit of armor of Henry, who had fought in the Low Countries; on the right hang the official robe, coronet and sword of William, the earl of Devonshire; and on both sides stand imposing martial figures (Figure 2). The monument thus contrasts the horizontality and nakedness of death with the verticality and sartorial splendor of earthly honors and achievement. An angel blowing a trumpet holds two inscriptional tablets above the middle of the table.[91] The tablets' panegyric epitaphs upon the two brothers verbally "answer" the skeleton and corpse that they surmount by proclaiming both the future Resurrection and present fame of the deceased. While Henry's epitaph claims that his skeleton awaits "the trumpet-call of the Resurrection" ("Classicam Resurrectionis"), the title "Fame's Archives" ("Famae Archiva") caps the two epitaphs.

The double tomb of Robert Cecil, Lord Salisbury is even closer to the Cavendish epitaph in its assertion of fame's conquest over death. Commissioned during Cecil's lifetime but completed a few years after his death in 1612, the tomb features a portrait of Cecil, clad in his official

---

[88] The epitaph of Sir Thomas Stanley, d. 1600, describes "sky aspiring pyramides" as attempts to preserve one's name (Ravenshaw, 43). On verticality as a cross-cultural symbol of high status and enduring achievement, see Rudolf Arnheim, *The Dynamics of Architectural Form* (Berkeley: University of California Press, 1977), 33–34.

[89] For accounts of the origins and general features of the double-tomb, see Kathleen Cohen, *Metamorphosis of a Death Symbol: The Transi Tomb in the Late Middle Ages and the Renaissance* (Berkeley: University of California Press, 1973), 1–119; and Erwin Panofsky, *Tomb Sculpture*, ed. H. W. Janson (London: Thames and Hudson, 1964), 63–66.

[90] The tomb's aphoristic inscription celebrated the true life after death: "The glory of the body returns to this. / Die to the world that you might live for God. / Love and lyve" ("Istuc recidit gloria carnis / Morere mundo ut vivas deo / Love and lyve"). See Cohen, 125–128.

[91] See the description of the tomb in Pevsner, *Derbyshire*, 205–206.

Figure 2. Monument of Henry Cavendish, d. 1616, and William Cavendish, First Earl of Devonshire, d. 1626, in Edensor Church. By permission of the Royal Commission on the Historical Monuments of England.

robes and holding the staff of the lord treasurer, lying on a table-slab supported on the shoulders of four kneeling life-size female figures representing the cardinal virtues. Below the table a skeleton lies on a straw mat.[92] The tomb, while providing a shocking memento mori below, asserts that the cardinal virtues have raised Cecil above the indistinction of death the leveler and assured him of his individualizing fame.[93] Since there are no visual representations of Salisbury's beatitude, the message is, as in the Cavendish epitaph, secular: Cecil made his life his earthly monument.

A final example reveals rhetorical strategies, both visual and verbal, resembling the Cavendish epitaph. The enormous alabaster and black marble double tomb of Sir Lawrence Tanfield, who died in 1625, dominates a chapel in Burford Parish Church. A skeleton lies underneath a slab, above which lie the praying recumbent effigies of Tanfield and his wife, he in his judge's robes and she in a black mourning mantle. Six large marble pillars, surmounted by obelisks of immortality, support a canopy over the recumbent figures, at the corners of which allegorical figures of various virtues suggest that Tanfield's achievement raises him up from the death represented by his skeleton below.[94] One of the several inscriptions upon the monument simultaneously justifies the visual ascent—from the skeleton through the effigies to the crowning figures of immortality—and denigrates the tomb:

> Not this small heape of stones & straightned Roome
> The Bench, the Court, Tribunall are his tombe
> This but his dust, but these his name interre
> And these indeed now but a sepulcher
>
> Whose meritts only raised him; and made good
> His standing there, where few so long have stood.... [95]

Tanfield rose from minor country gentry to become judge of the King's Bench and chief baron of the Exchequer, and the inscription claims that

[92] On the Salisbury monument, see Erna Auerbach and C. Kingsley Adams, *Paintings and Sculpture at Hatfield House: A Catalogue* (London: Constable & Co., 1971), 111–113, 159–160.

[93] On the use of the four cardinal virtues for the glorification of the individual in fourteenth-century Italian tombs and sixteenth-century French tombs see, respectively, Panofsky, *Tomb Sculpture*, 74–76; and Cohen, 142–145. Whinney notes the probable influence of French depictions of the virtues upon the Salisbury monument (p. 20). For another double tomb that celebrates the earthly fame of the deceased, see the monument of Edward Fitton, d. 1608, in Gawsworth, Cheshire, described in Nikolaus Pevsner and Edward Hubbard, *Cheshire*, The Buildings of England (Harmondsworth: Penguin, 1971), 222.

[94] See the description of the monument in Jennifer Sherwood and Nikolaus Pevsner, *Oxfordshire*, The Buildings of England (Harmondsworth: Penguin, 1974), 506–507.

[95] Cited in Kurt Weber, *Lucius Cary, Second Viscount Falkland* (New York: Columbia University Press, 1940), 10 (text modified slightly).

his "meritts only raised him" to high government office just as the monument dramatizes his ascent from death to immortality through virtue.[96] Yet the inscription also adopts a humanist topos, the claim that the true monument of a great man is much larger than a small, confining material tomb, in order to denigrate the supposedly "small heape of stones" that merely covers a corpse. One may compare an epitaph upon Sir Philip Sidney, which claims that England, the Netherlands, heaven, the arts, the military, and the "world" are the true monuments of the deceased, whom "a small heape of stones" cannot "enclose."[97] Like Sir Charles Cavendish's surviving family, Lady Tanfield, the erector of the monument, contrives to have it both ways. While the enormous memorial ostentatiously proclaims Tanfield's rise to status and wealth, the epitaph dismisses the material tomb in favor of the even larger, authentic monument of Tanfield's enduring achievement, the institutions that he adorned and in which his immortal fame now dwells.

In these monuments, spatial configurations—above versus below, horizontality versus verticality—act as powerful visual metaphors. The practice initiated by Greek poets of composing verse epitaphs that only purport to be inscribed upon monuments became widespread during the sixteenth and seventeenth centuries.[98] Both classical and early modern pseudo-inscriptional epitaphs had a wider tonal range than actual inscriptions, for they included satiric, comic, and fantastic poems as well as traditional panegyrics. Pseudo-inscriptional epitaphs also had a wider formal range than actual inscriptions: the popularity of figured poems, printed poems in the shape of material objects, led to pseudo-inscriptional epitaphs in various monumental shapes, including pyramids, pillars, and altar-tombs.[99] Such poems could simultaneously imitate a monumental form and explicitly or implicitly assert that wholly verbal memorials were as good as, or better than, monuments of marble, brass, or stone.[100] Not unlike double tombs, some figured poems force the

[96] On Tanfield, see R. H. Gretton, *The Burford Records: A Study in Minor Town Government* (Oxford: Clarendon, 1920), 268–274; and Weber, 8–10.

[97] Cited in Camden, *Remaines*, 54. Compare the epitaphs upon William Camden, d. 1623, in Oxford University, *Camdeni Insignia* (Oxford, 1624), B1v–B2r; and James I, d. 1625, in Cambridge University, *Cantabrigiensium Dolor & Solamen: Seu Decessio Beatissimi Regis Jacobi...* (Cambridge, 1625), 7–8.

[98] Ariès, 227–228.

[99] For some examples of these various forms, see the epitaphs on Sir Philip Sidney in Oxford University, *Exequiae Illustrissimi... Sidnaei* (Oxford, 1587), C2v, E4r–v, F4v; and Oxford University, *Peplus. Illustrissimi... Sidnaei* (Oxford, 1587), A3r. These and other funerary collections in honor of Sidney are reprinted in *Elegies for Sir Philip Sidney*, ed. A. J. Colaianne and W. L. Godshalk (Delmar, N.Y.: Scholars' Facsimiles & Reprints, 1980).

[100] On figured poetry, see Elizabeth Cook, *Seeing through Words: The Scope of Late Renaissance Poetry* (New Haven: Yale University Press, 1986), 21–47; and John Hollander,

reader to read upward as a visual metaphor for an ascent to glory.[101] Such a maneuver violates, however, normal ways of reading a text, and in his acrostic epitaph on Margaret Ratcliffe, Jonson instead foregrounds the descending vertical axis of the text:

M Arble, weepe, for thou dost cover
A dead beautie under-neath thee,
R ich, as nature could bequeath thee:
G rant then, no rude hand remove her.
A ll the gazers on the skies
R ead not in faire heavens storie,
E xpresser truth, or truer glorie,
T hen they might in her bright eyes.
R are, as wonder, was her wit;
A nd like *Nectar* every flowing:
T ill time, strong by her bestowing,
C onquer'd hath both life and it.
L ife, whose griefe was out of fashion,
I n these times. Few so have ru'de
F ate, in a brother. To conclude,
F or wit, feature, and true passion,
E arth, thou has not such another.

(8:39)

Margaret Ratcliffe, one of Queen Elizabeth's favorite maids of honor, died in 1598, after starving herself, so it was rumored, in grief at the recent deaths of several brothers. The queen paid for a funeral more elaborate than Ratcliffe's rank required.[102] Jonson's epitaph, written early in his career as a playwright-poet rising from a lowly past, is a bid for recognition from court circles. The epitaph praises Ratcliffe for both her rare familial sorrow, whose effects he tactfully does not specify, and her beauty and wit, two qualities expected of, and normally ascribed to, Elizabeth's maids of honor.[103] Though he may have written the poem for Ratcliffe's tomb, Jonson probably intended the poem as a pseudo-inscription that would demonstrate that a poem can itself be an impressive monument for the dead.[104] The verticality of the acrostic creates

---

"The Poem in the Eye," in his *Vision and Resonance: Two Senses of Poetic Form* (New York: Oxford University Press, 1975), 252–268.

[101] See, for example, the columnar poem in praise of Elizabeth's "immortalitie" cited and discussed in Hollander, 261.

[102] See Herford's and Simpson's note in *Ben Jonson*, 11:7–8.

[103] See Violet A. Wilson, *Queen Elizabeth's Maids of Honour* (London: John Lane, 1922), 5–6.

[104] A far less interesting epitaph was in any case inscribed upon the tomb in Saint Margaret's, Westminster; see the text in John Stow, *A Survey of the Cities of London and Westminster . . . corrected, improved, and very much enlarged by John Strype (1720) . . . brought down to the present time*, 2 vols. (London, 1754–1755), 2:622.

a "stately Pyle,"[105] and the poem begins and ends with apostrophes to "Marble" (l. 1) and "Earth" (l. 17), thus emphasizing the movement down the monument from its visible top to its invisible ground.

The descent from marble to earth is, paradoxically, an "ascent" into glory that repeats and intensifies another descent described within the poem itself:

> A ll the gazers on the skies
> R ead not in faire heavens storie,
> E xpresser truth, or truer glorie,
> T hen they might in her bright eyes.
> (ll. 5–8)

The living Ratcliffe allowed men to "read" a "glorie" upon earth that they would normally have sought by looking up at heaven. Now men must read down the acrostic poem itself to find the glory of the buried Ratcliffe. The poem ends with a lesson concerning the buried Ratcliffe's enduring uniqueness: "Earth, thou hast not such another" (l. 17). The concluding line means both that there is nobody else like Ratcliffe left *upon* earth and nobody like her buried *in* earth.[106] In the second sense the concluding line pointedly contradicts the speaking corpse's assertion of the ultimate indifferentiation of mortal men, the "such as I am, such shall you be" formula. The movement down into Ratcliffe's grave issues in a humanist assertion of individual glory instead of a memento mori.[107]

While Cavendish rejects the monumental locus in favor of the verbal message and its movement in time and space, the Ratcliffe epitaph commemorates the deceased with both a spatial monument and a temporal sequence. The poem's opening command, "Marble, weepe," treats the "sweating" of the marble as if it were an emotional response to be elicited by the poet. This command also initiates the poem's combination of solidity and flow. While the verticality of the name emphasizes the spatial form of the text, the initial command and the obtrusive announcement of cessation ("To conclude," l. 15) emphasize temporal process. The

---

[105] I borrow the phrase from the epitaph on Katharine Dent, d. 1637, in Le Neve, 4:176.

[106] One may compare the double sense of this line with the two assertions of the concluding couplet of an epitaph upon Sidney: "The world does not have another like him, / nor will the dust offer anyone similar" ("Orbis non habet alterum, / Nec pulvis similem dabit"; "Epitaphium," in *Exequiae . . . Sidnaei*, L4v). The sententious compression of Jonson's line provides a strong close to the poem.

[107] For another example of Jonson's transformation of the speaking corpse's assertion, see the concluding couplet of his epitaph on Philip Gray: "For, if such men as he could die, / What suretie of life have thou, and I?" ("*An Epitaph on Master* PHILIP GRAY," ll. 6–7, 8:168). Although this final rhetorical question suggests the traditional message that all men must die, Jonson the humanist insists that death does *not* erase the distinction between outstanding men "such" as Gray and common men like the rest of us.

poem's mixture provides an appropriate memorial for Ratcliffe as she is represented in the poem: the "marble" monument is a compensatory substitute for the "feature" (l. 16) of the beautiful woman, while the temporal movement of Jonson's verse echoes, wittily, her departed "wit" (l. 9), compared to "*Nectar* ever flowing" (l. 10).[108]

Both the Cavendish and Ratcliffe epitaph capture Jonsonian poetic ideals. Some three years after the Ratcliffe epitaph, Jonson had Caesar claim in *Poetaster* (1601) that poetry could preserve Rome's perishable "monuments" within the "liquid marble" of her lines (V.i.21–24, 4:290). While the Cavendish epitaph's verbal denigration of the tomb affirms the superiority of verbal to material monuments, the Ratcliffe epitaph's textual weeping marble embodies the poet's claim to be able to construct "liquid marble" as enduring as a tomb. The different kinds of poetic monuments Jonson creates in the Cavendish and Ratcliffe epitaphs reveal, however, his differential treatment of gender. While Jonson identifies with Cavendish as a male, independent subject, he depicts Ratcliffe as a womanly, "rich" (l. 3) object. Jonson, who elsewhere suggests that men must overcome emotional weakness by restraining grief, praises a woman's extreme "true sorrow" for a man.[109] Jonson gives Cavendish a Stoic contempt for all externals, including his tomb and the body it covers. The poet adopts, by contrast, the neo-Platonic correlation between outward beauty and inward virtue that was often used for the courtly idealization of women in order to praise the "Expresser truth" of Ratcliffe's beauty.[110] The shift from a Stoic to neo-Platonic register is clearly gender-based, for while Jonson often praises women and occasionally children (who are not fully gender-differentiated) for outward grace, he invariably praises adult men for inner virtue alone. Thus the plain-style iconoclasm of the Cavendish epitaph and the elegant surface of the Ratcliffe poem reveal Jonson's desire to compose in what he considers decorously gender-specific modes.

By making the acrostic a vertical monument, Jonson's epitaph on

---

[108] The poem thus foregrounds for expressive purposes the space-time combination that W. J. T. Mitchell argues structures our decoding of all literary texts; see his "Spatial Form in Literature: Toward a General Theory," in *The Language of Images*, ed. W. J. T. Mitchell (Chicago: University of Chicago Press, 1974), 271–300.

[109] On Jonson's implicit reliance in this and other funerary poems upon the tradition that grief befits a woman but not a man, see G. W. Pigman III, *Grief and English Renaissance Elegy* (Cambridge: Cambridge University Press, 1985), 86–88. Jonson's epitaph on Sir Charles Cavendish's sister-in-law, Lady Jane, the countess of Shrewsbury, praises a widow who wedded no second husband besides "Sorrow," "Deaths Harbinger" ("To ye memorye of . . . Ladie *Jane* . . . Countesse of Shrewsbury," ll. 17, 21, 8:394). Jonson never praises a man, by contrast, for such extreme sorrow.

[110] For a popular Renaissance exposition of this neo-Platonic doctrine, see Baldesar Castiglione, *The Book of the Courtier*, trans. Charles S. Singleton (Garden City, N.Y.: Doubleday, 1959), 342–345.

Ratcliffe gives new meaning to a traditional epitaphic form. Acrostic epitaphs are popular from the Roman inscriptions collected by Renaissance humanists to the compositions, both inscriptional and pseudoinscriptional, of Jonson's own times.[111] The essential core of an epitaph is normally the name of the deceased, and the acrostic epitaph tries to make the name both memorable, thus ensuring the fame of the dead, and meaningful, thus bridging the gap between the mere name that survives and the essence of the deceased. Jonson would later scorn the acrostic, but it was an appropriate choice for a poem upon a member of the Elizabethan court, which loved such rhetorical "fancies."[112] He himself deemed his acrostic epitaph worthy of inclusion in his *Epigrammes* (1616), and it certainly belongs in a book that focuses on the significance of names.[113] Epitaphs are an integral part of the epigram collection, which seeks to preserve "good, and great names ... to their remembrance with posteritie," as Jonson says in the preface (8: 25–26). In panegyric epigrams throughout the collection, Jonson declares the names of the good expressive of their virtues. Sometimes the poet claims that the name in itself has a poetic plenitude of meaning (e.g., "So PHOEBUS makes me worthy of his bayes, / As but to speake thee, OVERBURY, is praise," "To Sir Thomas Overbury," 8:73), while other times he asserts that the good man's merits give him his resonant name (e.g., "Thy deedes, unto thy name, will prove new wombes," "To Sir Henry Nevil," l. 17; 8:70). The acrostic on Margaret Ratcliffe's name literalizes such panegyric declarations: it is both the kernel that generates the poem's epigrammatic praise (so that the poem enacts the conceit of the Overbury epigram that a name is itself praise) and the product of the praise that the deceased receives from Jonson for her good qualities (so that the poem

[111] On the acrostic in Roman inscriptions, see Judson Allen Tolman, Jr., *A Study of the Sepulchral Inscriptions in Buecheler's "Carmina Epigraphica Latina"* (Chicago: University of Chicago Press, 1910), 17. On Renaissance interest in, and collection of, Latin inscriptions, see Ida Calabi Limentani, *Epigrafia Latina* (Milan: Istituto Editoriale Cisalpino, 1968), 40–51. For a few late sixteenth- and early seventeenth-century English acrostic epitaphs, see the epitaphs upon Thomas Eyer, d. 1581, Richard Swift, d. 1620, and Charles and Grace Cutliffe, d. 1637, in Ravenshaw, 31, 65, 87; on Sir Philip Sidney in Cambridge University, *Academiae Cantabrigiensis Lacrymae ... Sidneii* (Cambridge, 1587), 48–49; and *Exequiae Illustrissimi ... Sidnaei*, F4v; and on Richard Cosin, d. 1598, in William Barlow, *Vita et Obitus ... Richardi Cosin* (London, 1598), 63.

[112] For a courtly acrostic see, for example, Sir John Davies's panegyrics upon Elizabeth, the *Hymnes of Astraea in Acrosticke Verse* (1599), in *The Poems of Sir John Davies*, ed. Robert Krueger (Oxford: Clarendon, 1975), 71–86. In *"An Execration upon* Vulcan," which Jonson wrote after his library was destroyed by fire in 1623, Jonson makes fun of shaped poems and "Acrostichs " (ll. 32–39, 8:204).

[113] On Jonson's poetics of naming, see Anne Barton, *Ben Jonson, Dramatist* (Cambridge: Cambridge University Press, 1984), 170–193; Eric Partridge, "Jonson's EPIGRAMMES: The Named and the Nameless," *Studies in the Literary Imagination* 6 (1973):153–198; and David Wykes, "Ben Jonson's 'Chast Booke'—The *Epigrammes*," *Renaissance and Modern Studies* 13 (1969):76–87.

enacts the process of "getting" a name through virtue). Camden, whose intense interest in names influenced his pupil's onomastic poetics, relates names and personal distinctions in his *Remaines*: "Names ... were first imposed for the distinction of persons. ... After for difference of families ... and have been especially respected as whereon the glorie and credite of man is grounded."[114] Jonson's verbal monument makes a similar point in its final line, which simultaneously completes the acrostic of Ratcliffe's name and asserts her enduring distinctiveness.

[114] Camden, *Remaines*, 28. Both Barton (pp. 170–172) and Wykes (p. 86) explore Camden's influence on Jonson's poetics of naming.

Chapter 2

Much in Little:
The Poetics of Brevity

One cannot discuss the poetic epitaph without considering its relationship to the more inclusive genre of the epigram. The epigram was originally a short poem written for inscription, and the sepulchral inscription has been the major subcategory of the inscription since the latter's emergence in post-Homeric Greek literature.[1] The labor and expense of engraving and the limitations of space on stones necessitated that sepulchral inscriptions be brief, but poets from the Greeks onward have turned this originally functional constraint to expressive advantage in both inscriptional and pseudo-inscriptional epitaphs that are epigrammatic in the modern sense.[2] In his commonplace book, *Discoveries*, Jonson, echoing the humanist Juan Luis Vives, commends the "briefe style" as one that "expresseth much in little" (1972–1973, 8:623). His epitaphs, many of them included in his *Epigrammes*, exemplify such a style. Jonson not only writes brief epitaphs but also asserts within them the power of brevity. In the Cavendish epitaph, a relatively short poem, for example, the deceased commands his sons to write an even shorter inscription, one that will be very brief but full "enoughe" because it says all that need be said concerning his virtuous life.

Interest in the poetics of epitaphic brevity increased in the late six-

---

[1] On the early Greek verse inscription, see Werner Peek's introduction to his *Griechische Grabgedichte* (Berlin: Akademie-Verlag, 1960), 1–42.

[2] See Barbara Herrnstein Smith, *Poetic Closure: A Study of How Poems End* (Chicago: University of Chicago Press, 1968), 196–197.

teenth and early seventeenth centuries, partly as a response to the growing popularity of long panegyric inscriptions. Over the course of the sixteenth century, funerary inscriptions moved from the edges of tomb-chests, their normal position on medieval tombs, onto square or rectangular panels set prominently in the sides, backplates, or canopies of monuments, positions that made possible much longer compositions. In addition, the inscriptional tablet without effigies, a monumental form encouraging verbosity, arose in the late sixteenth century and slowly grew in popularity decade by decade.[3] These changes in the relationship between inscription and monument had a multiplicity of causes: the spread of literacy made desirable a greater role for the inscription in the tomb's overall message; the humanist emphasis on virtue encouraged long edifying accounts of the lives of the deceased in both prose and verse; and the relative inexpensiveness of inscriptional tablets made them attractive to the increasing minority of the population that desired memorials.[4] The suspicion of visual display we have seen in humanist attacks on grand monuments and Protestant attacks on idolatrous images further contributed to the greater emphasis on the verbal message. Medieval inscriptions, made up of one or more of three possible elements—the brief biography or praise of the deceased, the memento mori warning, and the request for prayers—often used brevity effectively, but rarely self-consciously. By contrast, from the sixteenth century onward the increasingly common long panegyric contributed to a counteremphasis on brevity as a deliberate, "literary" feature of the carefully crafted epitaph.

Many considered expressive brevity the major criterion for evaluating epitaphs. In *The Arte of English Poesie* (1589), George Puttenham defined an epitaph as "a Kind of Epigram . . . in few verses, pithie, quicke, and sententious." An early seventeenth-century antiquarian argued that the only essential for epitaphs is "that which is required in an epigram, viz. witt and brevity." Camden's historical collection of epitaphs singled out from the medieval past those that exemplified the pithy ideal, such as the epitaphs upon Queen Maud, whose two lines "contained her princely parentage, match, & issue," and upon John Kempe, whose "one verse comprehended all his dignities, which were great." Sir John Coke re-

---

[3] See Brian Kemp, *English Church Monuments* (London: B. T. Batsford, 1980), 83.

[4] On the influence of rising literacy and humanism upon the new form of monument, see Ralph A. Houlbrooke, *The English Family, 1450–1700* (London: Longman, 1984), 205–206. Philippe Ariès notes the rise of long edifying biographies of the dead in sixteenth-century Europe in *The Hour of Our Death*, trans. Helen Weaver (New York: Random, 1982), 222–230; Thomas Pettigrew provides several examples of lengthy sixteenth-century English epitaphs in *Chronicles of the Tombs: A Select Collection of Epitaphs* (London, 1864), 74–82.

marked as if it were a truism that an "epitaphe should couch much matter in few woords."[5]

Both the composition and appreciation of brief forms were marks of humanist cultivation. The preference for brief epitaphs reflected the taste for various related short forms: "strong lines," sententiae, proverbs, emblems, mottoes, and devices. All such forms purported to say a great deal in a small compass and often challenged the cultivated reader to see how they did so.[6] Brevity in poetic epitaphs was encouraged by the popularity of the classically influenced humanist epigram in the sixteenth and seventeenth centuries. Throughout the sixteenth century, neo-Latin epigram collections printed in England contained epitaphs, while later in the century and early in the next epigram collections in English, like those of John Weever, Thomas Bastard, Sir John Davies, Sir John Harington, and Jonson himself, all included epitaphs. Epigrammatic epitaphs by wits such as John Hoskyns and John Donne circulated, meanwhile, in manuscript, to be appreciated by the cognoscenti.[7]

The cult of sententious brevity had a range of aesthetic and ideological implications. Brevity was often used in sixteenth- and seventeenth-century epitaphs for the incisive panegyric of individual achievement: epitaphs praised men and women briefly because those who had truly earned their fame needed extensive praise no more than a grand tomb. When Queen Elizabeth ended her first speech to Parliament in 1559

[5] I cite George Puttenham, *The Arte of English Poesie*, ed. Gladys Doidge Willcock and Alice Walker (Cambridge: Cambridge University Press, 1936), 56; Thomas Hearne, ed., *A Collection of Curious Discourses written by Eminent Antiquaries...*, 2 vols. (London, 1771), 1:239; William Camden, *Remaines of a Greater Worke, Concerning Britaine...* (London, 1605), 35, 45; and Norman K. Farmer, Jr., "Fulke Greville and John Coke: An Exchange of Letters on a History Lecture and Certain Latin Verses on Sir Philip Sidney," *Huntington Library Quarterly* 33 (1970):221. With a laconic brevity mirroring the object of his praise, Camden also commends an epitaph as "short and sufficient" (*Remaines*, 55). Sir William Segar contrasts the decorous brevity of classical epitaphs and the unfortunate prolixity of modern ones in his *Honor, Military and Civil* (1602), reprinted in *The Book of Honor and Armes* (1590) *and Honor, Military and Civil* (1602), intro. Diane Bornstein (Delmar, N.Y.: Scholars' Facsimiles and Reprints, 1975), 256.

[6] On the pursuit of expressive brevity in Renaissance literature, see Rosalie Colie, *The Resources of Kind: Genre-Theory in the Renaissance*, ed. Barbara K. Lewalski (Berkeley: University of California Press, 1973), 32–75; and Kitty W. Scoular, *Natural Magic: Studies in the Presentation of Nature in English Poetry from Spenser to Marvell* (Oxford: Clarendon, 1965), 38–119.

[7] On the epigram during this period, see Mary Thomas Crane, "*Intret Cato*: Authority and the Epigram in Sixteenth-Century England," in *Renaissance Genres: Essays on Theory, History, and Interpretation*, Harvard English Studies no. 14, ed. Barbara Kiefer Lewalski (Cambridge: Harvard University Press, 1986), 158–186; Hoyt Hopewell Hudson, *The Epigram in the English Renaissance* (Princeton: Princeton University Press, 1947); and T. K. Whipple, *Martial and the English Epigram from Sir Thomas Wyatt to Ben Jonson*, University of California Publications in Modern Philology no. 10 (Berkeley: University of California Press, 1925).

with a discussion of the epitaph she supposedly wanted engraved on her simple marble stone—"And in the end, this shall be for me sufficient, that a marble stone shall declare that a Queen, having reigned such a time, lived and died a virgin"—she used epitaphic brevity to inaugurate her self-definition as the Virgin Queen.[8] She singled out those two aspects of herself she would manipulate throughout her reign to assert her power—her regal authority and her sexual purity and inaccessibility— and defined herself by distinguishing, as Jonson's Cavendish would later do, between the brief but sufficient praise that she chose for herself and the superfluous praise that others might have thought to give. Brevity thus defined a self by what it excluded.

Such self-definition is central to humanist epitaphs that insist that the name of the deceased is epitaph enough. Dr. John Caius, a wealthy medical humanist who was private physician to Edward VI and Mary I and cofounder of Gonville and Caius College, Cambridge, died in 1573 after designing his tomb and composing his inscription. He erected to himself a sarcophagus with a richly decorated canopy and the following inscription in large gold letters: "Virtue lives on after death. I was Caius. He died July 29, 1573 at the age of sixty-three" ("Vivit post funera virtus. Fui Caius. Aetatis suae LXIII obiit XXIX Iuli Anno Do[mini] 1573").[9] The Society of Antiquaries, which included Jonson's mentor Camden and his friend Sir Robert Cotton, held a series of talks on epitaphs in 1599–1600. Three of the society's members, including Camden, singled out this epitaph for praise.[10] Ignoring the age and date of death and the conventionally phrased humanist assertion that virtue endures, the antiquarians treated "I was Caius" ("Fui Caius") as the whole epitaph— "of much signification," said one, though "but a word."[11] "Fui Caius" on one level appears as yet another memento mori, the message from the corpse hidden in the sarcophagus stating who it "was" but is no longer. This loss of identity bypasses medieval formulae, however, and returns to classical cadences. The epitaph echoes, as one of the antiquarians pointed out, the lament of Panthus in the *Aeneid* who, witnessing the fall of his city to the Greeks, laments to Aeneas, "We Trojans are not, Illium is not, and the great glory of the Teucrians" ("fuimus Troes, fuit Illium

[8] Cited in J. E. Neale, *Elizabeth 1 and Her Parliaments*, 2 vols. (London: Jonathan Cape, 1953–1957), 1:49.
[9] See the description of the monument in Nikolaus Pevsner, *Cambridgeshire*, 2d ed., The Buildings of England (Harmondsworth: Penguin, 1954), 79.
[10] See Hearne, 1:243, 342; 2:377. On the activities of the Society, see Kevin Sharpe, *Sir Robert Cotton, 1586–1631: History and Politics in Early Modern England* (Oxford: Oxford University Press, 1979), 17–47. Sharpe plausibly suggests that Camden introduced the topic of epitaphs to the Society (p. 20).
[11] Hearne, 1:243. Eric Mercer notes that the humanist aphorism "Vivit post funera virtus" is common upon funerary monuments; see *English Art, 1553–1625* (Oxford: Oxford University Press, 1962), 246.

et ingens / gloria Teucrorum," *Aeneid* 2.325–326).[12] Panthus is both correct and incorrect: the Trojans are dead but their glory is preserved by
Aeneas and Virgil's epic. By means of this allusion Caius's epitaph, even
without the preceding "Vivit post funera virtus," reverses the traditional
memento mori message and proclaims the continuing glory of Caius's
name at the same time as it announces that he himself no longer exists.

Indeed the audacity of this brief epitaph lies in its implication that
Caius's name alone is praise enough, that nothing more specific need be
said about him since the passerby will know upon reading "Fui Caius"
just how much greatness was lost and how much glory remains upon
the death of this very successful academic. The epitaph implicitly invokes
an idea made explicit in two-line Italian quattrocento epitaphs like Ercole
Strozzi's on the philosopher Pico della Mirandola and Michele Marullo's
on the military commander Braccio Perusino: "Giovanni della Mirandola
lies here; the rest concerning him / both the Tagus and Ganges, perhaps
even the Antipodes, know"; "Braccio lies here: you ask what were his
family and deeds; / if you do not grasp both when his name is said, may
you grasp nothing."[13] Such distichs instantiate Jacob Burckhardt's claim
that Italian humanists, in their glorification of the individual, treated
the epigram as "the concentrated essence of fame."[14] With his brief,
assertive epitaph, Caius does the same.

Caius's late sixteenth-century epitaph is one of the earliest English
examples of the proud name-as-praise motif that arose in Renaissance
Italy. Such epitaphs became very popular in early seventeenth-century
England for high-ranking ecclesiastics and academics, professionals
whose careers so often embodied the humanist ethos of personal achievement. The epitaphic distich upon William Goodwin, the dean of Christ
Church Cathedral, Oxford, who died in 1620, is typical: "It is enough
for the name to remain upon the tomb for him who seeks to know. /
GOODWIN lies here: Fame will speak the rest."[15] In Phineas Fletcher's

---

[12] The allusion is noted by an anonymous antiquarian in Hearne, 2:377.

[13] "Joannes iacet hic Mirandola, caetera norunt / Et Tagus et Ganges, forsan et Antipodes"; this epitaph is included in an oft-reprinted Renaissance collection of brief
biographies with epitaphs, Paulus Jovius [Paulo Giovio], *Elogia... Virorum Literis Illus-
trium...* (Basel, 1577), 51. "Braccius hic situs est: quaeris genus actaque: utrunque /
Ni teneas dicto nomine, nil teneas" ("Epitaphium Bracci Perusini," *Michaelis Marulli Carmina*,
ed. Alessandro Perosa [Zurich: Artemis-Verlag, 1951], 92). Compare Angelo Poliziano's
epitaph upon Ficino in Jovius, 57.

[14] Jacob Burckhardt, *The Civilization of the Renaissance in Italy*, trans. S. G. C. Middlemore
(Oxford: Phaidon Press, 1944), 160–161. Ariès notes the use of "the name alone" in
epitaphs but incorrectly dates its rise to the seventeenth century (p. 229).

[15] "Est Satis in Tumulo nomen constare petenti, / GOODWINUS iacet hic, caetera fama
dabit" (Le Neve, 4:76). For other early to mid-seventeenth-century examples of the motif,
see John Prideaux's epitaph upon the founder of the Bodleian library, Thomas Bodley,
d. 1612, in Oxford University, *Iusta Funebria...Thomae Bodleii...* (Oxford, 1613), 8; and

six-line epigram commemorating Doctor Thomas Playfere, Margaret Professor of Divinity at Cambridge and chaplain to James I, who died in 1609, the deceased briefly proclaims his enduring fame and concludes with a command reminiscent of Cavendish's "Write but that" but using the name-as-praise motif: "My soul in heaven breathes, in schools my fame: / Then on my tombe write nothing but my name."[16] Praised by Jonson as a translator and historian (*Epigrammes* XCV, 8:61–62) and as a "grave, and truly letter'd" man (*Discoveries* 921–922, 8:591), Sir Henry Savile, the provost of Eton, was one of the most learned and successful humanists of his day. Savile reputedly asked only for the two words "Savillius erat" ("He was Savile") upon his tomb, and when he died in 1622 he received this epigram glossing the two-word epitaph: "To have placed the name of Savile upon his tomb is praise enough, / And that one word, 'He was,' is grief enough."[17] Caius's epitaph is more memorable than such later compositions precisely because it implies rather than states the great significance of the name.[18]

With its pithy and novel combination of memento mori, classical allusion, and humanist pride, the Caius epitaph was addressed to a learned audience that alone could appreciate its generic sophistication. Other humanist epitaphs are more explicit concerning their intended readers. In his epitaph upon Perusino, Marullo heaps scorn upon those who do not know the achievements of the deceased and therefore cannot grasp the great significance of his name. An English example of the name-as-praise motif from the same period as the Caius epitaph, John Weever's distich upon Bishop John Jewel, who died in 1571, similarly castigates the ignorant: "Here lyeth *Juell*, who knoweth not the rest, / Is worthie to be ignorant at least."[19] Marullo's and Weever's distichs reveal most clearly a feature of all humanist name-as-praise epitaphs: they not only praise the dead who have won personal fame but also implicitly or ex-

---

the epitaph upon Donne, d. 1631, in John Donne, *The Epithalamions, Anniversaries and Epicedes*, ed. W. Milgate (Oxford: Clarendon, 1978), 99.

[16] Phineas Fletcher, "On Doctor Playfer," ll. 5–6 in Giles and Phineas Fletcher, *Poetical Works*, ed. Frederick S. Boas, 2 vols. (1909; rpt. Grosse Pointe, Mich.: Scholarly Press, 1968), 2:257. On Playfere, see the entry in the *DNB*.

[17] "Sufficit ad laudes nomen posuisse Savilli, / Et verbum ad luctum sufficit illud, Erat" (Oxford University, *Ultima Linea Savilii, sive in obitum Henrici Savilii* . . . [Oxford, 1622], C1v).

[18] The humanist name-as-praise motif, which glorified personal achievement rather than lineage, was naturally less commonly applied to nonprofessional gentlemen. When it is so used, it is transformed. The epitaph of Sir Robert Stanley, d.1632, in Chelsea Parish Church, for example, begins "To say a STANLEY lyes here that alone / Were Epitaph enough. . . ." Significantly this epitaph differs from the others in stating that the fame of the deceased depends upon his bearing the *family* name ("a STANLEY") rather than proclaiming the name as the sign of the deceased's *individual* achievement.

[19] John Weever, "In tumulum Iuelli," in his *Epigrammes in the Oldest Cut and Newest Fashion* (1599), ed. R. B. McKerrow (London: Sidgwick and Jackson, 1911), 94.

plicitly divide the living into the learned elite who understand the brief message and the ignorant masses who do not. Such epitaphs thus attempt to unite the dead and living members of an aristocracy of "merit."

It is instructive to contrast humanist name-as-praise epitaphs with that of Robert Grosseteste, the renowned medieval scholar and bishop who died in 1253. His epitaph partakes of an older tradition of self-abasement in death. Camden emphasizes (and approves of) the brevity of the Grosseteste epitaph when he notes in the *Remaines* that the bishop "commanded this only to be engraven over his Tomb": "Do you wish to know who I am? putrid flesh, nothing but worms; / Whoever you are, may this be enough for you to know of me."[20] Unlike most medieval epitaphs, the composition uses brevity self-consciously. The refusal to reveal the name of the deceased, a name identified with his past life as opposed to his present state, and the assertion that the unadorned, anonymous memento mori message should be lesson enough adds a new and pointed pithiness to the traditional reminder of death. This medieval epitaph exploits brevity, but to enunciate an old moral concerning how paltry, rather than how great, is the deceased.

Pithy expressions of the loss of personal identity in death continue to appear in sixteenth- and seventeenth-century epitaphs. William Lenthal, the Caroline Speaker of the House of Commons and Civil War parliamentarian, for example, declared in his will that "so great a sinner" as himself should receive no monument or, at most, a "plain stone" with only the two-word epitaph "Vermis sum."[21] In the sixteenth and seventeenth centuries, however, brief epitaphs in which the deceased declares the extinction of his identity are often deliberately ambiguous. Sometimes epitaphs express the conflict between modesty in the face of death and an enduring concern for social status and posthumous fame. Camden and another antiquarian singled out for praise a stone in old Saint Paul's Cathedral with the bare inscription "Oblivio" and the arms of the deceased. Camden commends it for being "conceyted," since the deceased "would not willingly have been forgotten, when he adjoyned his armes to continew his memorye"; the other antiquarian admires its brevity and irony, since "the writer said one thing and intended another . . . [for] he undoubtedly meant that the word *oblivio* should be his monument."[22] This seemingly trivial paradox is a witty analogue to Greville's grand monument with its inscription concluding "Trophaeum peccati." Such an epitaph fulfills the common desire to have it both ways in the face of death, to juxtapose, since one could not truly reconcile,

---

[20] "Quis sim nosse cupis? caro putrida, nil nisi vermis; / Quisquis es, hoc de me sit tibi scire satis" (Camden, *Remaines*, 43).

[21] I quote from the extract of his will in the *DNB*.

[22] Hearne, 1:232, 243.

Christian modesty and worldly pride. It also bespeaks its author's sense that wit, rather than the mere announcement of his lineage, was necessary to capture a sophisticated audience's attention and thus to attain whatever fame could be won from oblivion.

Epitaphic brevity could also express the conflict between Christian modesty and humanist pride in specifically personal achievement. According to Anthony à Wood, John Marston was buried in 1634 under a stone inscribed "Sacred to oblivion" ("Oblivioni Sacrum").[23] The inscription, probably written by Marston himself, pointedly transforms a formulaic epitaphic opening, "Sacred to the memory" ("Memoriae Sacrum") followed by the name of the deceased.[24] The Marston epitaph is thus both self-abasing and witty in its novel inversion of tradition. It befits both the older Marston, the parish minister, and the satiric poet-dramatist of earlier days. Indeed the words echo the title of the final poem in Marston's *The Scourge of Villany* (1598), "To everlasting *Oblivion*." This poem ironically reverses such a proud conclusion to a poetic volume as Horace's *Ode* 3.30 by proclaiming *not* the immortality of the book and its author but rather the disappearance of the poems into oblivion and the consequent peaceful "death" of the poet, undisturbed by critical voices:

> Farre worthier lines in silence of thy [oblivion's] state,
> Do sleepe securely free from love or hate....
> . . . . . .
> Peace hatefull tongues, I now in silence pace,
> Unlesse some hound doe wake me from my place,
>   I with this sharpe, yet well meant poesie,
>   Will sleepe secure, right free from injurie
>   Of cancred hate, or rankest villanie.[25]

This malcontent pose is knowingly self-contradictory: Marston publishes a work proclaiming his radical privacy. The echo of this early poem fills the anonymous, two-word epitaph with further ambiguity: for those in the know, "Oblivioni Sacrum" paradoxically identifies the unnamed deceased and recalls his early poetic fame. By echoing his pseudo-rejection of the public in his early satires, the epitaph also perhaps suggests that the older clergyman, confronting death, has indeed sought what he only pretended to seek as an angry young man. The brief epitaph thus combines wit and Christian humility in a way not susceptible to precise dis-

---

[23] See the editor's note in Arnold Davenport, ed., *The Poems of John Marston* (Liverpool: Liverpool University Press, 1961), 6.

[24] John Le Neve's epitaph anthology provides thirty-one examples from 1612 to 1647 of "Memoriae Sacrum," or, as it was often abbreviated, "M. S.," followed by the name of the deceased: see *Monumenta Anglicana: Being Inscriptions on the Monuments of several Eminent Persons . . . 1600–1715*, 5 vols. (London, 1718–1719), 4:35–230.

[25] Marston, 175.

criminations. It thereby evokes the individual commemorated more elusively but effectively than could the name that is so pointedly omitted. Like so many contemporaneous compositions, Marston's epitaph tries to have it both ways. It is more successful than most.

Jonson's fascination with names reveals his humanist allegiances. In the Ratcliffe epitaph he displays his sense of a name's power, and in both his panegyric epigrams and epitaphs he uses the name-as-praise motif. When he applies the motif to an aristocratic title like *Pembroke* he assimilates that title—not without strain—to the humanist ethos of virtuous achievement. He supports his assertion that the title *Pembroke* is itself "an *Epigramme*, on all man-kind; / Against the bad, but of, and to the good" ("To William Earle of Pembroke," ll. 1–3, 8:66) by praising Pembroke's virtue, not his lineage. The Pembroke epigram suggests that for Jonson, as for his humanist predecessors, the name divides the world into two groups, the "good," who appreciate its significance, and the "bad," who do not. One may compare the way Jonson implicitly divides his readers at the opening of his *Epigrammes*, between those who "take care . . . / to understand," as he advises, and those who do not ("To the Reader," 8:27).

In his elegant and enigmatic pseudo-inscriptional "Epitaph on Elizabeth, L. H.," Jonson simultaneously names and refuses to name the deceased and in so doing challenges his cultivated reader "to understand" a lesson greater than a name. The epitaph commemorates a woman of whom we know only that she died before 1616, when the epitaph was published:

> Would'st thou heare, what man can say
>   In a little? Reader, stay.
> Under-neath this stone doth lye
>   As much beautie, as could dye:
> Which in life did harbour give
>   To more vertue, than doth live.
> If, at all, shee had a fault,
>   Leave it buryed in this vault.
> One name was ELIZABETH,
>   Th'other let it sleepe with death:
> Fitter, where it dyed, to tell,
>   Than that it liv'd at all. Farewell.
>
> (8:79)

The opening question implies an analogy between the poem and the deceased, asking the reader to see not only how much the poet can "say / In a little" (ll. 1–2) but also how much the deceased was able to "say" in the "little" statement that was her life.[26] Jonson thus suggests that expressive brevity is the formal analogue to the great achievements of the deceased as an individual. Jonson's initial question pointedly replaces a common opening. Like the Grosseteste epitaph, many sixteenth- and seventeenth-century epitaphs begin by asking whether the reader wants to know the identity of the deceased. Thus an epitaph upon Thomas Bodley, who died in 1612, begins, "Do you ask, o wayfarer, whose tomb this is?"[27] By encouraging the reader's curiosity concerning what one "can say / In a little," rather than in the name of the deceased, Jonson hints that the question of the dead woman's true identity will be answered in a novel manner. He also hints that the reader will have to *work* to understand the poem and that its puzzles will be both a challenge to, and a judgment upon, the reader.

The next two pithy couplets assert the woman's "much in little" accomplishment. They also attempt to demonstrate the poet's "much in little" power. Working by implication rather than direct statement, line four suggests the neo-Platonic notion of an eternal, noncorporeal beauty that survives after the mortal beauty of the body has gone,[28] while the graceful parallelism of "much beautie" and "more vertue" in lines four and six suggests the neo-Platonic connection between outward beauty and inward virtue that Jonson often uses, as in the Ratcliffe epitaph, for the praise of women. The progression from "little," to "much," and finally to "more" in the second lines of the first three couplets emphasizes the poem's attempt to find "much in little."

While lines three to six straightforwardly praise the harmonious outward and inward excellence of the deceased, lines seven to ten are more puzzling. The poet gives the reader the Christian name of the deceased, "ELIZABETH" (l. 9), but asks that her other name "sleepe with death" (l. 10). This request for silence parallels the poet's request that the reader "leave" any "fault" of Elizabeth "buryed" in the tomb (ll. 7–8). Elizabeth's second name and her possible flaws are as closely related as her beauty

[26] See Jack D. Winner, "The Public and Private Dimensions of Jonson's Epitaphs," in *Classic and Cavalier: Essays on Jonson and the Sons of Ben*, ed. Claude J. Summers and Ted-Larry Pebworth (Pittsburgh: Pittsburgh University Press, 1982), 111.

[27] "Quaeris viator cuius est iste tumulus?" (Oxford University, *Iusta Funebra...Bodleii*, 12). For other sixteenth- and seventeenth-century epitaphs that begin with the traditional question, see Ludovico Ariosto, "Lirica Latina XLVI," in his *Opere Minori*, ed. Cesare Segre (Milan: Riciardi, 1954), 74; and the epitaph upon Prince Henry, d. 1612, in Oxford University, *Iusta Oxoniensium* (Oxford, 1612), K1r. Epitaphs also often begin by simply postulating the reader's question concerning the identity of the deceased. The epitaph upon Thomas Nuce, d. 1617, for example, begins "Here who lyes if you now Enquere..." (Le Neve, 4:63). For other examples, see the epitaphs upon Rachel Eliot, d. 1608; and Richard Ferris, d. 1649, in Le Neve, 4:18, 233.

[28] See O. B. Hardison, Jr., *The Enduring Monument* (Chapel Hill: University of North Carolina Press, 1962), 125.

and virtue in the preceding pair of couplets, for each is a mysterious "it" denied the reader in parallel commands to silence. In the most convincing discussion of these lines, Nathaniel Strout cites Camden's etymological definition of the name "Elizabeth" as "Peace of the Lord" or "Quiet rest of the Lord" in order to argue that Jonson implies a contrast between the Christian name, whose meaning suggests the present blessed state of the deceased, and her family name and possible faults, both part of Elizabeth's earthly life but now to be firmly buried with the perishable body.[29] The learned reader is no doubt expected to grasp the great meaning of the single word "Elizabeth" and realize, as in the Caius epitaph, that he has been told enough.

Jonson superimposes upon the implicit contrast between spiritual perfection and earthly flaws, moreover, the humanist contrast between fame based on individual achievement and mere social rank. "L. H." presumably stands for "Lady H———." While the full title of the deceased would emphasize the social identity of the deceased as the wife of a knight or peer, the solitary name "Elizabeth" emphasizes her enduring personal achievement.[30] Despite his attempt to fit a title like "Pembroke" into the humanist framework, Jonson distinguishes the poet from the herald precisely because the former concerns himself with individual virtue while the latter treats "strict degrees of ranke, or title" ("To all, to Whom I Write," 8:29). In this epitaph Jonson suppresses the title in favor of a virtuous name. There might well have been, as some have speculated, a scandal in the mysterious Elizabeth's family. Whatever the historical circumstances, Jonson takes the opportunity to promote his humanist views.

Jonson's poem transforms the riddle epitaph, a form practiced by the ancients and cultivated by humanists.[31] Riddles often have as their solution a name whose full meaning is suggested by the riddle itself, and thus they have a generic affinity to epitaphs, so concerned with names and their significance.[32] Riddles, which so often play a role in initiatory

---

[29] Nathaniel Strout, "Jonson's Use of a Name in 'Epitaph on Elizabeth, L. H.,' " *English Language Notes* 17 (1979):30–33; see Camden, *Remaines*, 79. For other attempts to interpret the puzzles of this poem, see Howard S. Babb, "The 'Epitaph on Elizabeth, L. H.' and Ben Jonson's Style," *JEGP* 62 (1963):738–744; Ossi Ihalainen, "The Problem of Unity in Ben Jonson's *Epitaph on Elizabeth, L. H.*," *Neuphilologische Mitteilungen* 80 (1979):238–244; and John M. Major, "A Reading of Jonson's 'Epitaph on Elizabeth, L. H.,' " *SP* 73 (1976):62–86.

[30] Compare Ihalainen, 243.

[31] On the tradition of the riddle epitaph, see Archer Taylor, *The Literary Riddle before 1600* (Berkeley: University of California Press, 1948), 75–79. For a Renaissance selection of riddle epitaphs, see Nicholas Reusner's *Aenigmatographia sive Sylloge Aenigmatum et Griphorum Convivalium*, 2 vols. (Frankfurt, 1599), 2:187–190. This popular work went through several editions.

[32] On riddles as lessons concerning the meanings of names and their role in (mainly

rites, create an exclusive community, uniting the riddler and those who can solve the riddle but excluding those who cannot.[33] Thus, like the name-as-praise epitaph, the riddle epitaph, which normally posits the name of the deceased as the solution, separates those who understand the name from those who do not. Though some riddle epitaphs remain unsolved to this day, generally such epitaphs are playful, highly literary, pseudo-riddles. The name of the deceased is usually given in the title, and the "riddle" simply encourages the reader actively to appreciate its wit, grasp the name's full meaning, and thereby join those who "understand." Jonson adapts a kind of riddle epitaph particularly popular in the Renaissance and the seventeenth century, the logograph, in which the letters of a name are embedded within a larger phrase that simultaneously hides the name (or at least pretends to do so) and reveals its "true" significance. A frigid logograph in a French epitaph from the 1622 Oxford collection commemorating Jonson's friend Savile begins by imagining the reader asking the perennial question of identity—"Tell me; who lies here in this mournful coffin?"—and ends with the name "hidden" in a phrase that simultaneously reveals the supposed nature of the deceased: "It is he who has enriched his community [*Ha ENRIchi SA VILLE*]."[34] In a lovely late sixteenth-century riddle epitaph upon a little girl, Giovanni Battista Guarini reveals some of the expressive possibilities of the form: "If you would like to know who I am, / you who admire my small urn; weep. / There will spring from my ashes, if you water them / With a little tear, / a sweet-smelling and gently swaying little violet [*violetta*], / and thus from your gift / you will know who I am."[35] Making the usual assumption that the reader wishes to know the name of the deceased, the epitaph informs the curious reader that he or she can (at least partially) discover that name, Pargoletta Violante, from the *violetta* a tear will produce (Pargo-*letta Vio*-lante). Guarini's riddle playfully but tenderly links the living and the dead. In order to learn the name of the deceased as well as her true nature—the violetlike

---

modern) poetics, see Andrew Welsh, *Roots of Lyric: Primitive Poetry and Modern Poetics* (Princeton: Princeton University Press, 1978), 25–46.

[33] For a discussion of the community that riddles imply and create, see André Jolles, *Formes simples*, trans. Antoine Marie Buguet (Paris: Le Seuil, 1972), 103–119. For a suggestive exploration of the riddling nature of literature as such in terms of the linguistic community it seeks to create, see Geoffrey Hartman, *Saving the Text: Literature / Derrida / Philosophy* (Baltimore: Johns Hopkins University Press, 1981), 134–136 and passim.

[34] " 'Dis-moy; Qui gist icy dans ce triste cercueil?'. . . . 'C'est luy qui plus de tous Ha ENRIchi SA VILLE' " (Oxford, *Ultima Linea Savilii*, B1v ["Epitaphe Enigmatique"]).

[35] "Se vuoi saper chi sono / O tu, che miri la brev' urna; piagni. / Spunterà dal mio cenere, se 'l bagni / D'una tua lagrimetta, / Un'odorata, e vaga violetta, / E così dal tuo dono / Intenderai chi sono"; the poem is cited as the source of one of William Drummond's *Madrigals* (1616) in L. E. Kastner, ed., *The Poetical Works of William Drummond*, 2 vols. (Manchester: Manchester University Press, 1913), 1:227.

beauty and fragility embodied in her name—the good reader must sorrowfully respond to the epitaph with a tear.

Jonson transforms such riddling in his treatment of the title of the deceased "L. H." He does not provide clues as to what the initials really stand for, but he does embed the abbreviation in words that reveal, instead of the family title itself, what its significance *should be*. The first name "E*l*izabet*h* " contains the abbreviation "L. H." in itself and thereby signals the absorption of the mortal and social into the spiritual and individual. The command that the family title should be allowed to fall into oblivion, which comes where the family name would normally be, also contains "L. H." embedded in itself ("th'other, *l*et it sleep with deat*h*"), thus substituting for the revelation of the title the assertion that this title is irrelevant. Like the author of the Savile epitaph and Guarini, Jonson appeals to a curious reader, but unlike them he tries to forge a specifically ethical link between the deceased and the reader by making the riddle a humanist lesson concerning the superiority of virtue to lineage.

The final couplet of Jonson's epitaph has troubled readers, and it indeed seems deliberately to challenge its reader, unto the end, to understand. Its general sense seems to be that it is "fitter" to "tell" the place of the family name's "death" than to emphasize its ever having existed at all. The name "dyed" at the epitaphic site itself, the place at which it was buried in oblivion to make way for plain "Elizabeth" as the dead woman's name of glory. The association of a name with death's superiority to life recalls a well-known passage in Ecclesiastes: "A good name is better than a good ointment; and the day of death, than the day that one is born" (Ecclesiastes 7:1). Saint Jerome glosses the passage by noting that death simultaneously frees us from the world and awards us our earthly fame by revealing conclusively "what kind of men we are."[36] Jonson similarly suggests that the death by which the deceased has simultaneously gained the "Peace of the Lord" and her enduring reputation, both adumbrated in her "good" name of "Elizabeth," is better than the earthly birth by which she became the imperfect mortal "Elizabeth ———."

A significant shift occurs in the last three couplets: the poem no longer simply relates Elizabeth's virtues but instead asks the reader to cooperate in the telling by passing over her faults in silence and letting her family name rest in oblivion. The last couplet's "Fitter where it dyed to tell" thus refers to both what it is fitter for the poet to tell the reader and

---

[36] Erwin Panofsky cites Saint Jerome's commentary on Ecclesiastes in "Mors Vitae Testimonium. The Positive Aspect of Death in Renaissance and Baroque Iconography," in *Studien zur Toskanischen Kunst*, ed. Wolfgang Lotz and Lise Lotte Möller (Munich: Prestel-Verlag, 1964), 230–231.

what it is fitter for the reader, once he or she has left the poetic monument, to tell others. The reader who understands the meaning of Jonson's riddle will comprehend Elizabeth's achievement and will spread the good news. The poem's opening invites the reader to "heare," but by the close of the poem the reader has learned what to "tell." The short poem seeks to convert a curious reader into an instructed, participating newsbearer, and at the end of the poem the "man" that can say "much in little" refers not only to the poet and Elizabeth but also to the proper reader. Like the Cavendish epitaph, the poem ends with "Farewell," sending the reader from the (fictive) stone with a message, a message concerning man's ability to express much, both in the little that he says and in all that he does not.

In the final couplet Jonson invokes one of the central concepts of classical and Renaissance aesthetics and ethics: the fitting or decorous. Decorum depends on knowing not only what to do or say in a given situation but also what not to do or say: Cicero, arguing that to express too much is generally worse than to express too little, cites the famous example of the painter who rightly veiled the face of Agamemnon sacrificing Iphigeneia because he could not portray the proper expression on the face (*Orator* 21); Horace suggests keeping violent acts offstage and being brief when seeking to instruct (*Ars Poetica* 179–189, 336–337). As in the Cavendish and Ratcliffe epitaphs, Jonson normally follows conventional notions of decorum, which demand that panegyric epitaphs admit no fault in the deceased. He thereby confronts the problem of flattery, with which he often struggles in his poems: he sometimes flatters in the very act of denying he is doing so; sometimes admits to having flattered in the past but denies doing so in the present; and sometimes advances the argument common in classical antiquity that flattery is legitimate because it creates a positive ideal for men to live up to or be judged against.[37] Jonson's panegyric epitaphs could not, of course, change a Cavendish or Ratcliffe, but whatever the dead were actually like in life, Jonson as a didactic poet can legitimately present them in death as ideals for others' imitation and admiration. In the Elizabeth, L. H. epitaph, however, Jonson directly involves the reader in the process of decorous idealization and thereby puts forward a solution to the problem of flattery unique in his work. Whatever earthly flaws she may have had, Elizabeth has gained the "peace of the Lord." The poet and

[37] For excellent discussions of Jonson's struggles with flattery and his assertions of its didactic value, see Richard Helgerson, *Self-Crowned Laureates: Spenser, Jonson, Milton and the Literary System* (Berkeley: University of California Press, 1983), 176–179; and Katharine Eisaman Maus, *Ben Jonson and the Roman Frame of Mind* (Princeton: Princeton University Press, 1984), 65–67. Hardison provides Roman examples of the defense of flattery as didactic (pp. 31–32).

the reader who remember her virtues but suppress her flaws decorously and charitably grant her the earthly correlative of salvation, a good name. They thereby improve themselves by making her an exemplary pattern for their own edification. Both the epitaph's admissions and the active, forgiving reader it demands are unique in the period.[38] Jonson had good reason to feel that he had said much in a small compass.

The brief epitaph that claims to contain a great message fights against a persistent principle in the formation of canons and generic hierarchies: length has always been one major determinant of generic status, so that short works such as epigrams have often been considered naturally lower than long works such as epics.[39] Brevity is indeed often used in six-teenth- and seventeenth-century epitaphs not only for ambivalent self-abasement in death but also for dismissive epitaphs upon the "low." Though in the chapter specifically devoted to epitaphs Puttenham em-phasizes the genre's powerful sententiousness, elsewhere he holds up as models for his contemporaries the "slight" poems with which ancient poets commended "the maner of life or death of anie meane person . . . by some litle dittie or Epigram or Epitaph in fewe verses & meane style comfortable to his subject."[40] Here brevity is not supposed to express much with little but is rather meant decorously to reflect its "slight" subject matter. Classical epitaphs indeed sometimes use brevity for the fitting commemoration of the lowly. Simonides' distich on a laborer, "Man, you do see not the grave of Croesus, / but a hired hand's small tomb, yet sufficient for me," is *about* such decorum: the small tomb, and implicitly the small distich poem purporting to be inscribed upon it, is "sufficient for" or "befitting" ("hikanos") the laborer, who is equally "small" in social terms.[41] One rarely finds such a serious epitaph upon the lower ranks in the sixteenth or seventeenth centuries, brief or otherwise, but short comic epitaphs upon holders of various lower-class occupations are an unpleasant staple. The early seventeenth-century distich "On Bell the Tinker"—"*Bell* though thou dy'dst decrepit, lame[,] forlorn, / Thou was't a man of mettle, I'll be sworn"—is typical in its use of brevity to reinforce the poem's condescension toward its lowly subject by assuming that there

[38] Contrast Hal's speech over Hotspur: "Thy ignominy sleep with thee in the grave, / But not remember'd in thy epitaph!" (William Shakespeare, *The First Part of Henry IV*, ed. A. R. Humphreys, The Arden Shakespeare [London: Methuen, 1960], 159 [V.iv.99–100]). The self-conscious idealization of the dead normally occurs before the writing of the commemorative epitaph rather than becoming a constituent part of the epitaph itself.

[39] See Alastair Fowler, *Kinds of Literature: An Introduction to the Theory of Genres and Modes* (Cambridge: Harvard University Press, 1982), 216–217.

[40] Puttenham, 44.

[41] "Anthrôp', ou Kroisou leusseis taphon, alla gar andros / khernêteô mikros tumbos, emoi d' hikanos" (*Greek Anthology*, 7. 507a). I have modified the Loeb translation.

is no more to be said or made of such a "meane person" beyond the quick flash, or thud, of supposed wit.[42]

Humanists also use such dismissive brevity, however, to treat the morally, rather than socially, "low." The cult of individuating fame expresses itself not only in sententious panegyrics on the virtuous but also in brief epitaphs that consign to oblivion those who did not perform good deeds. Thus John Hoskyns, a friend of Jonson and a master of the comic epitaph, writes an epitaphic distich upon "a man ... doyinge nothinge": "Here lyes the man was borne and cryed / tould three score yeares, fell sick and dyed."[43] The epitaph's brevity conveys the quick passage of an anonymous nonentity from birth to death, without significant action in between. Hoskyns's "Of ye losse of time" ends by imagining the curt pronouncement of passers-by, the traditional epitaphic *viatores*, upon an idle man: "not here he lives: but here he dyes."[44] By treating the idle man as if he were in need of an epitaph, Hoskyns evokes the Stoic equation of the idle and the dead. Seneca claims that upon passing the country house of the lazy, rich hedonist Vatia he always says to himself, in epitaphic style, "Here lies Vatia!"[45] For both Seneca and Hoskyns, the pursuit of pleasure and idleness, as opposed to virtuous cultivation of the self, are a kind of self-burial, and both use brevity to suggest that all that need be said of the lazy hedonist is that he is dying or dead.

In his satiric epigrams and epitaphs, Jonson uses dismissive brevity in a similar way. He denies the satirized object the proper, individualizing name proclaimed in the panegyric poems, substituting instead a generic name that curses unto eternity the vice of the person. In "To my Lord Ignorant," the "naming" of the enemy quickly dispatches a foolish lord: "Thou call'st me *Poet*, as a terme of shame: / But I have my revenge made, in thy name" (8:29). In "On some-thing, that walkes some-where," Jonson confronts a courtier resembling Seneca's and Hoskyns' idlers:

> At court I met it, in clothes brave enough,
>   To be a courtier; and lookes grave enough,
> To seeme a statesman: as I neere it came,
>   It made me a great face, I ask'd the name.
> A lord, it cryed, buried in flesh, and blood,
>   And such from whom let no man hope least good,

[42] Included in *Facetiae: Musarum Deliciae and Wit Restor'd and Wits Recreations*, 2 vols. (London, 1817), 2:230; other examples may be found in *Facetiae*, 2:219–221.

[43] Included in Louise Brown Osborn, *The Life, Letters, and Writings of John Hoskyns, 1566–1638* (New Haven: Yale University Press, 1937), 171.

[44] Osborn, 170.

[45] "Vatia hic situs est" (*Epistulae morales* 55. 4). The passage was well known: Camden, for example, quotes it in his introductory discussion of epitaphs in *Remaines*, 30. Seneca elsewhere imagines the houses of idle hedonists as their tombs, upon which epitaphs could be inscribed registering the occupants' death-in-life (*Epistulae morales* 60.4).

> For I will doe none: and as little ill,
>   For I will dare none. Good Lord, walke dead still.
>   (8:30)

Though Jonson asks "the name," the courtier foregoes his chance of immortality in the poet's book by identifying himself as a worthless "lord," a titled, nameless, and above all dead "thing." Jonson's Stoic view of the body as foreign to the true, virtuous self, expressed so strongly in the Cavendish epitaph, clearly emerges in this epigram upon a courtier who loses himself in his body. The courtier's claim to have "buried" his spirit in his "flesh, and blood" makes the man's very body, like an aristocratic tomb, a mere showy covering of the dead. The epigram inverts the panegyric epitaph's presentation of an enduring spirit that transcends the tomb: the lord speaks from the body in which he is buried as Cavendish speaks from his tomb, but instead of a brief yet resonant message, all that the lord reveals is his inconsequential death-in-life, a humanist version of the epitaphic speaking corpse.[46] Jonson's response— "Good Lord, walke dead still"—is, like Seneca's "Here lies Vatia!" and Hoskyns's "here he dyes," the curt but decorously definitive response to such a man.

Jonson's "To Fine Lady Would-Bee," which treats a court lady similarly immersed in her body, attacks its subject for taking drugs to prevent pregnancy lest she lose time for "sport." It ends with a half-line epitaph: "Write, then on thy wombe, / Of the not borne, yet buried, here's the tombe" (ll. 11–12, 8:46). The poem viciously strips the woman of her pretensions and inscribes the definitive epitaph upon the empty, bodily tomb. The lady is forever mere "would-be," her child will forever not be: neither has acquired ontological substance or name, and the very brief inscription pithily describes the woman's body as the tomb both of her nameless child and of unfulfilled human potential. No more need be said because nothing more has come to be.

While Hoskyns's brief satiric jabs attacked the idle as such, Jonson's targets were idle courtiers. His attacks upon unnamed, generic courtiers betray his strong desire to reveal the lowliness of those "great" but not good. Like the epitaph upon Elizabeth, L. H., such poems present a personal "solution" for Jonson to the problem of flattery. The aesthetic efficacy of Jonson's refusal to name the bad should not obscure its prag-

---

[46] Though the comparison of the body to a tomb in which the spirit lies buried is ubiquitous in classical philosophy and Christian theology, Jonson is here closest to the Senecan use of the analogy to attack the idle hedonist. Compare Jonson's own self-castigation at the opening of "An Ode. To himselfe": "Where do'st thou careless lie, / Buried in ease and sloth?" (8:174). For a thorough survey of the many philosophical and theological uses of the body-tomb comparison in classical and Christian antiquity, see Pierre Courcelle, "Le corps-tombeau," *Revue des Études Anciennes* 68 (1966):101–122.

matic origins: Jonson, who suffered several times for veiled criticisms of powerful people in his plays, could not in fact publish a poem naming the "worthlesse lord" whose "great image" he admitted to having praised with "most fierce idolatrie" ("To My Muse," ll. 2–4, 8:48).[47] He could, with less danger, consign a nameless lord to spiritual death. Quick deflating epitaphic "murders" of generic courtiers were undoubtedly a necessary expressive outlet for a poet whose idealizing magnification of particular ones inevitably involved compromises with truth.[48]

Brevity could also be used, however, not to dismiss the base but rather to assert the high value of someone normally considered low. In such cases brevity directly challenges rather than confirms conventional hierarchies of style and subject. The overturning of the hierarchy of great and small, broached in such a poem as the Elizabeth, L. H. epitaph, is crucial to sepulchral writings seeking to raise traditionally humble subjects. A Greek epitaph upon a slave (Greek Anthology 7.538), which was faithfully translated into Latin by Thomas More, suggests that death obliterates any distinction between high and low: "While he lived, this man was a slave. But now, in death, he / Wields no less power than you, mighty Darius."[49] While this Greek epitaph raises the humble by lowering the mighty, Martial's Roman compositions elevate the low more directly. His epigrams on small creatures frozen in amber, for example, which were often imitated in the Renaissance, describe a viper receiving a "nobler tomb" than Cleopatra's and an ant made "precious by its death."[50] The poet's art, as much as the amber, converts small, low creatures into something noble and precious. Though these are whimsical poems, their magnification of the small resembles the strategy of some of Martial's most serious epitaphs. His epitaph on a virtuous Roman matron contrasts her modest monument with enormous tombs: "A marble, o traveler, you read small in truth, but one that shall not give place to the stones of Mausolus and the Pyramids."[51] The small marble will

[47] On Jonson's troubles for attacks upon James I's Scottish courtiers in Eastward Ho!, a drama he wrote in collaboration with George Chapman and Marston in 1605, and upon Arabella Stuart, first cousin of the king, in Epicoene, composed in 1609, see David Riggs, Ben Jonson: A Life (Cambridge: Harvard University Press, 1989), 122–126, 156–157.

[48] Praising named individuals and attacking unnamed or pseudonymous vicious men is traditional epigrammatic practice (cf. Martial, Epigram 10.33), but traditional practice had a pragmatic function for both his predecessors and Jonson himself.

[49] "Hic servus dum vixit, erat, nunc mortuus idem / Non quam tu Dari magne minor potest" (Thomas More, "On a Dead Slave. From the Greek" ["In Servum Mortuum. E Graeco"] in The Complete Works of St. Thomas More, vol. 3, part 2, Latin Poems, ed. Clarence H. Miller et al. [New Haven: Yale University Press, 1984], 126–127).

[50] Martial, Epigrams 4.59 and 6.15; see also 4.32; on these epigrams' numerous Renaissance imitations, see Scoular, 100.

[51] "Marmora parva quidem sed non cessura, viator, / Mausoli saxis pyramidumque legis" (Martial, Epigrams 10.63. 1–2).

not yield to greater tombs because its brief inscription commemorates a virtuous lady. The monument, the poem, and its subject are all in one sense small but in another sense great. A similar reversal of value is implicit in Martial's several brief, tender epitaphs upon slave children.[52]

In the sixteenth and seventeenth centuries, the epitaph's association with other brief forms encouraged its undermining of traditional hierarchical distinctions. With varying degrees of reflection on their own brevity, the various forms of sententious wisdom admired in this period often celebrated littleness. Like the other Old Testament and apocryphal wisdom books, the Book of Proverbs was an important model for Renaissance epigrams. It pithily recommends pious contentment with little and praises the wisdom of little creatures: "There be four things which are little upon the earth, but they are exceeding wise" (30:24); "Better is little with the fear of the Lord, than great treasure and trouble therewith" (15:15).[53] The oft-translated *Disticha Catonis*, a collection of Latin hexameter couplets proffering ethical advice, probably from the third century, was a popular school text and another major model for Renaissance epigrams.[54] The *Disticha* briefly recommends a moral economy of littleness: "Fly what is excessive; remember to be content with little; / The ship is safer, which is borne on a small stream."[55]

Christian overturnings of both social and stylistic hierarchies further legitimated the reversals of high and low enacted in the epigram and epigrammatic epitaph. Jesus declared to his disciples that "he that is least among you all, the same shall be great" (Luke 9:48). His message concerned things hidden from "the wise and prudent" but "revealed... unto babes [Vulgate, "parvulis," or "little ones"]" (Matthew 11:25 and Luke 10:21). While according to Cicero, the low style was fit only for "small things" ("parva," *Orator* 29.101), Augustine dignified the low style as a crucial feature of the Bible, a low style accessible to humble "little ones" but containing the greatest truths concerning a God whose Incarnation broke down such absolute distinctions as low and high, little and great.[56] The Christian transvaluation of the low and high provided

---

[52] See Martial, *Epigrams* 1.88, 6.28, 6.29.

[53] On these biblical models for short religious poems, see Barbara K. Lewalski, *Protestant Poetics and the Seventeenth-Century Religious Lyric* (Princeton: Princeton University Press, 1979), 55–57.

[54] On the importance of the *Disticha* as models for sixteenth-century epigrammatists, see Crane, 165–169.

[55] "Quod nimium est fugito; parvo gaudere memento: / Tuta mage est puppis, modico quae flumine fertur" (*Catonis disticha: Facsimiles, notes, liste des editions du xve siècle*, ed. Joseph Neve [Liège: H. Vaillant-Carmanne, 1926], 27 [2.6]).

[56] Augustine, *On Christian Doctrine*, trans. D. W. Robertson (Indianapolis: Bobbs-Merrill, 1958), 142–144 (3.17–18). For classic discussions of the Christian *sermo humilis*, see Erich Auerbach, "Sermo Humilis" in his *Literary Language and Its Public in Late Latin Antiquity and in the Middle Ages*, trans. Ralph Manheim (London: Routledge, 1965), 25–82; and Erich

an implicit authority for brief epitaphs affirming the greatness of the little.

Sir Henry Wotton's 1628 epitaph on the wife of his nephew, Sir Albert Morton, for example, subverts traditional hierarchies: "He first deceased, she for a little tried / To live without him, liked it not, and died."[57] Though Jonson approves only of women's extreme sorrow, both widows' and widowers' sorrow-unto-death was an early modern ideal. Several late sixteenth- to mid-seventeenth-century epitaphs tenderly commemorate married couples whose love was so great that husband and wife died simultaneously or shortly after one another and were buried together.[58] Because it was a remarkably pithy, understated depiction of this conjugal ideal, the Wotton epitaph was often adapted for seventeenth-century epitaphs upon widows and widowers.[59] Though the epitaph's implicit commendation of extreme love for a creature would have troubled Augustine and the writers of Christian consolatory treatises, the poem nevertheless exploits the reversals of the Christian *sermo humilis*. While resembling Hoskyns's epitaph upon the lazy man in its use of brevity to represent a "little" life quickly over, the couplet's understated brevity praises a "little" action that yet embodies great, even

Auerbach, *Mimesis: The Representation of Reality in Western Literature*, trans. Willard R. Trask (Princeton: Princeton University Press, 1953), 72–73, 151–155.

[57] The poem first appears in a letter Sir Henry Wotton sent to John Dynely on November 13, 1628; see Logan Pearsall Smith, *The Life and Letters of Sir Henry Wotton*, 2 vols. (Oxford: Clarendon, 1907), 2:311. It subsequently appeared in numerous anthologies and miscellanies.

[58] See, for example, the epitaphs upon John and Florence Windham, d. 1596, in Thomas F. Ravenshaw, ed., *Antiente Epitaphes (from A.D. 1250 to A.D. 1800)* (London, 1878), 40; Gyles and Katherine Reed, d. 1611, in Thomas Habington, *A Survey of Worcestershire*, ed. John Amphlett, 2 vols. (Oxford, 1895–1899), 1:113–114; William Cotton and his wife in Richard Bruch, *Epigrammatum Hecatontades Duae* (London, 1627), D2r–v (Epigram 2.84); Robert and Mary Leman, d. 1637, in Le Neve, 4:172; Richard Crashaw's much-anthologized "An Epitaph Upon Husband and Wife, which died, and were buried together," published in 1646, in *The Complete Poetry of Richard Crashaw*, ed. George Walton Williams (New York: Norton, 1970), 478; John Hall's "On a Gentleman and his Wife, who died both within a very few days," in his *Poems* (1646–1647), reprinted in *Minor Poets of the Caroline Period*, ed. George Saintsbury, 3 vols. (Oxford: Clarendon, 1905–1921), 2:206; and the epitaph on Thomas and Martha Russell, d. 1656, in John Thorpe, *Registrum Roffense: or, A Collection of Antient Records ... of the Diocese and Cathedral Church of Rochester* (London, 1769), 842.

[59] For echoes of Wotton's distich, sometimes alone and sometimes as part of slightly longer compositions, see the epitaphs upon William Cotton, d. 1656, in A. C. Bizley, ed., *The Slate Figures of Cornwall* (Marazion and Penzance: Worden Printers, 1965), 109; the "sympathizing wife" of Thomas Barington in Thomas Fuller, *The History of the Worthies of England* (1662), reprinted in Fuller, *The Poems and Translations in Verse*, ed. Alexander B. Grosart (Edinburgh, 1868), 190; John Whiting, d. 1681, in E. A. Webb, *The Records of St. Bartholomew's Priory and of the Church and Parish of St. Bartholomew the Great, West Smithfield*, 2 vols. (London: Oxford University Press, 1921), 2:467; and Bartholomew Doidge, d. 1681, in Horatio Edward Norfolk, ed., *Gleanings in Graveyards: A Collection of Curious Epitaphs* (London, 1866), 28.

heroic, love. Both its form and content thereby undermine conventional notions of small and great.[60]

Children epitomize littleness, and epitaphs on children naturally treat the value of the small. Jonson's epitaphs upon children, the "little ones" beloved of Christ, challenge conventional evaluative judgments concerning little and great, sometimes in a more purely classical and sometimes in a more Christian register. In the English poetic tradition, Jonson is a pioneer in composing epitaphs and elegies upon children that treat them as little-but-great, from his epitaph on his own daughter Mary, written sometime around 1600, to that on Elizabeth Chute, who died in 1627.

Anthropologists have noted that in many societies children constitute a special category of the dead. Children are often not considered full members of the social order, and thus in many societies they do not receive the full funerary rituals and memorials accorded adults.[61] In England up through the fourteenth century, children were not commemorated with monuments or epitaphs. In fifteenth- and early sixteenth-century England, monuments and inscriptions commemorating children were very rare. Though still uncommon, they became more frequent by the end of the sixteenth century, and became widespread only over the course of the seventeenth century.[62] A similar development occurred in pseudo-inscriptional epitaphs on children.[63]

Epitaphs on children through the late sixteenth century reflect primarily the familial pride of the nobility and gentry. They normally emphasize

[60] Some epitaphs of the period attempt to reconcile the conjugal ideal, with its extreme love for a fellow creature, and Christian love of God. The epitaph upon Cecely Bridges, d. 1625, for example, praises her desire to join her husband in the grave but notes that by dying she has gained two "bridegrooms," Christ as well as her husband (Le Neve, 4:99–100). The monument of Frances Poulton, who died in 1642, depicts the deceased and his widow crossing hands over a skull (see Nikolaus Pevsner, *Middlesex*, The Buildings of England [Harmondsworth: Penguin, 1951], 159). The inscription glosses the visual assertion of conjugal love's transcending death by explaining that the widow "Liveth but desireth with him [her husband] to bee dissolved and to bee with Christ...." The echo of Saint Paul's "desire to depart, and to be with Christ" (Philippians 1:23) links the widow's loving desire to rejoin her husband to a pious Christian yearning for union with God.

[61] See Lewis R. Binford, "Mortuary Practices: Their Study and Potential," in his *An Archaeological Perspective* (New York: Seminar Press, 1972), 233–234; and Robert Hertz, "A Contribution to the Study of the Collective Representation of Death," in *Death and the Right Hand*, trans. Rodney and Claudia Needham (Glencoe, Ill.: Free Press, 1960), 76.

[62] See the accounts of the rise of brasses commemorating children in Malcolm Norris, *Monumental Brasses: The Memorials*, 2 vols. (London: Phillips and Page, 1977), 1:90–91, 147–148, 170–171, 232, 246–247; and John Page-Phillips, *Children on Brasses* (London: Allen, 1970). More elaborate monuments for children are very rare indeed until the later sixteenth century and still not common in the early seventeenth century.

[63] See Leah Sinanoglou Marcus, *Childhood and Cultural Despair: A Theme and Variations in Seventeenth-Century Literature* (Pittsburgh: University of Pittsburgh Press, 1978), 39, 256, note 96.

the unfulfilled potential of the child, who was to have continued the familial line.[64] Thus John Parkhurst's epitaph upon Mary, the infant daughter of Thomas Seymour and Catherine Parr who died in 1548, has the deceased praise herself for the virtues that she too would have attained from her regal mother if she had only lived: "If Death had allowed me to live, / the virtue of the best mother . . . / Would have lived again in me. . . ."[65] When the three-year old son of Robert Dudley died in 1584, he was given a miniature but still ostentatious tomb in the family chapel of Warwick Cathedral and an inscription emphasizing all that the boy, Dudley's only legitimate son, might have become: "A childe of great parentage, but of farre greater hope and towardnes. . . . " By emphasizing the child's unfulfilled potential, such epitaphs confirm that the deceased did not attain his or her hoped-for place in society; by singling out for commemoration a mere child, such epitaphs also implicitly assert the high status of the surviving family, even whose children deserve commemoration.

Such unfulfilled potential could be conveyed with great pathos through decorously expressive littleness. Consider the lovely quatrain of trimeters and dimeters on Dorothy Drury, who died in 1597 at the age of four:

> She, little, promis'd much,
> Too soone untyed:
> She only dreamt she liv'd,
> And then she dyde.[66]

"Little" would have become "much," but sadly did not, and the poem's brevity underlines how little the deceased was allowed to live.

Jonson's funerary poems upon his own first daughter and son, poetic monuments as compelling as any tomb, are on one level claims for his own "true nobility" and proud commemorations of his own family line. In all his epitaphs upon children, however, Jonson treats the young not as figures of unfulfilled potential but rather as examples of completed, "much in little" perfection. The child is a necessary "other" for Jonson. The passive product of nature's or God's craftsmanship, the child has a corporeal innocence that is the idealized opposite of Jonson's own stren-

---

[64] Marcus notes that Elizabethan laments emphasize that the child "died too early to make a mark on the world" but cites no examples (p. 24).

[65] "Si Mors dedisset vivere, / Illa illa[e] matris optimae / Virtus . . . / . . . / In me revixisset. . . . " (John Parkhurst, "Inclytae puellae Mariae eiusdem Reginae filliae, Epitaphion," in his *Ludicra sive Epigrammata Iuvenilia* [London, 1573], 154.)

[66] The epitaph is cited in R. C. Bald, *Donne and the Drurys* (Cambridge: Cambridge University Press, 1959), 29.

uous self-making and struggle against the lures of the body.[67] The Elizabeth, L. H. epitaph reveals Jonson's sense of death as a beneficent end, and he normally imagines children's deaths as removals—unhappy only for the living mourners—from the pains of the adult world.[68] Most of his funerary poems upon children were written during his Catholic period, and his stress upon the perfect innocence of the child is in line with post-Reformation Catholic dogma. In sharp contrast to the Protestant belief in the child's inherited sinfulness, the Council of Trent pronounced the baptized child innocent and incapable of mortal sin.[69] Jonson's last epitaph upon a child, in memory of Elizabeth Chute, reveals, however, that even after his return to the English church the poet retained his conception of child as the innocent opposite of the fallen adult. This belief coexists with Jonson's conviction, when reflecting upon his own moral condition, that he was "Conceiv'd in sinne, and unto labour borne" ("To Heaven," l. 18, 8:122). The perfect little child is not only, though, an idealized, innocent counter to Jonson's own fallen condition. As a creature made rather than self-made, the child also becomes analogous to the small poem Jonson "makes" in honor of the child. Jonson has both the child and the brief epitaph implicitly demonstrate that the little can yet be great. His brief, tender epitaphs on children thus also assert the power of his epigrammatic art.

The declared slightness of the "Epitaph on S[alomon] P[avy] a child of Q. El[izabeths] Chappel," which commemorates a child actor who died in 1601, allows Jonson to praise the deceased without seeming to violate traditional social and literary decorum:

> Weepe with me all you that read
> This little storie:

[67] Jonson's glorification of the child is striking given his attraction to Stoicism. The Stoic normally treated the child as mere potential, one who has not yet reached the stage where one can fashion oneself to be wise and virtuous. Though Seneca argues that it is virtue, and not mere longevity, that matters in life (*Epistulae morales* 93)—an argument that Jonson adopts in the Cary-Morison ode's funerary praise of a young man who died at twenty-one (ll. 21–74, 8:243–245)—the Roman Stoic treats children as *tabula rasa* not yet capable of the virtuous life. Seneca argues that a small boy who died lost nothing, for although the child, in growing up, might "have been moulded to a better standard" ("in melior formari"), more likely he would have "become just like the [inferior] many" ("fieri pluribus similis"); see *Epistulae morales* 99.12–13. Jonson finds something much more positive in the child.

[68] The Cary-Morison ode's praise of the "Brave Infant of *Saguntum*" for avoiding the miseries of life by refusing ever to leave the womb (ll. 1–10, 8:242–243) is the extreme version of Jonson's sense of the child's death as a beneficent escape; see Achsah Guibbory, *The Map of Time: Seventeenth-Century English Literature and Ideas of Pattern in History* (Urbana: University of Illinois Press, 1986), 122–123; and William Kerrigan, "Ben Jonson Full of Shame and Scorn," *Studies in the Literary Imagination* 6 (1973):214–216.

[69] On the Catholic view, see Houlbrooke, 137; and John McManners, *Death and the Enlightenment: Changing Attitudes to Death in Eighteenth-Century France* (New York: Oxford University Press, 1985), 66–67.

And know, for whom a teare you shed,
   Death's selfe is sorry.
'Twas a child, that so did thrive
   In grace, and feature,
As *Heaven* and *Nature* seem'd to strive
   Which own'd the creature.
Yeeres he numbred scarse thirteene
   When *Fates* turn'd cruell,
Yet three fill'd *Zodiackes* had he beene
   The stages jewell;
And did act (what now we mone)
   Old men so duely,
As, sooth, the *Parcae* thought him one,
   He plai'd so truely.
So, by error, to his fate
   They all consented;
But viewing him since (alas, too late)
   They have repented.
And have sought (to give new birth)
   In bathes to steepe him;
But, being so much too good for earth,
   Heaven vowes to keepe him.
                    (8:77)

The epitaph is a small poem about a small figure who is made even more so by the abbreviation that hides his name.[70] Like Martial's creatures in amber, however, art raises lowly Pavy: the poet describes him as a small but precious "jewell" (l. 12), the object of all attention, and the "error" (l. 17) of the Fates that destroys him aestheticizes but dignifies his death Jonson's conceit of the mistake concerning the child's age is based on Martial's epitaph upon a young charioteer who won so many races that Lachesis makes the same error (*Epigram* 10.53). The imitation of a Roman epitaph gives classical authority to Jonson's poem on apparently so slight a subject.

Jonson here links the littleness of childhood to the littleness of humble social station. The Pavy epitaph tells a "little storie" (l. 2) not only because the deceased was a mere child but also because he was a lowly actor. Until their rise in status in the eighteenth century, actors normally received only comic, condescending epitaphs that humorously identified them with the peculiarities of their menial occupation, as in "—Exit Burbage."[71] Jonson's epitaph, by contrast, is witty but not humorously

---

[70] Herford and Simpson notes that the identity of the epitaph's subject was in fact only discovered in 1942 (*Ben Jonson*, 11:27).

[71] The Burbage epitaph may be found in *Facetiae*, 2:216. Besides Jonson's epitaph, I have found no other even semi-serious seventeenth-century epitaph on an actor. There are, by contrast, numerous eighteenth- and nineteenth-century panegyric epitaphs on

condescending and brief but not truly modest. Jonson himself had risen from journeyman actor to playwright only four years before Pavy's death, and his praise of "S. P." honors an occupation all too often despised. Indeed his imitation of Martial's epitaph upon a charioteer challenges his contemporaries' parochial snobbery by reminding them that public performers of all kinds received more respect in the ancient world than in early modern England.[72]

Jonson celebrates the greatness of littleness more explicitly in the sepulchral inscription for the six-year old Elizabeth Chute, which appeared in *The Under-wood* as follows:

> What Beautie would have lovely stilde,
> What manners prettie, Nature milde,
> What wonder perfect, all were fil'd,
> Upon record, in this blest child.
> And, till the comming of the Soule
> To fetch the flesh, we keep the Rowle.
>
> (8:188)

The poem praises the child for having all different forms of perfection. Its progression of praise from "lovely / prettie / mild" to the culminating "perfect" is self-consciously extravagant. Jonson adopts the panegyric motif that one person contains all the different virtues. This was a ubiquitous theme in the Renaissance because of the widespread belief, stated most succinctly and memorably by Aristotle, that the highest excellence combined the individual kinds of excellence: "But the superiority of good men over the mass of men individually... really consists in this, that a number of scattered good points have been collected together into one example" (*Politics* 3.6.5).[73] Excerpts from three early seventeenth-century epitaphs, the third also upon a child, show the typical use of such praise:

> She that lyes heere within this gloomy grave
> Enjoyd all virtues that a minde coulde have.

---

actors; see Silvester Tissington, ed., *A Collection of Epitaphs and Monumental Inscriptions*... (London, 1857), 196–207.

[72] See also Martial's panegyric epitaphs upon the actors Latinus and Paris (*Epigrams* 9.28, 11.13). Jonson's only other epigram in praise of an actor begins with an explicit appeal to Roman appreciation of actors: "If *Rome* so great, and in her wisest age, / Fear'd not to boast the glories of her stage, / ... / How can so great example dye in mee, / That, ALLEN, I should pause to publish thee?" ("To Edward Allen," ll. 1–2, 7–8, 8:56–57).

[73] On this and other classical formulations of the "many in one" as both an ethical and aesthetic ideal, see Erwin Panofsky, *Idea: A Concept in Art Theory*, trans. Joseph J. S. Peake (New York: Harper, 1968), 14–15. On Renaissance applications of the notion to the hero, see James Nohrnberg, *The Analogy of the Faerie Queene* (Princeton: Princeton University Press, 1976), 32–34.

> Love Justice Honoure Here,
> All at once in one appeare.
>
> Birth, breeding, beauty, grace & carriage sweet
> In thee Deare Saint did all together meet.[74]

Jonson enriches the motif by making the expressive brevity of his poem a formal analogue to the single, small child who yet embodies all excellence. The poem describes the child herself as a kind of text, thus blurring the distinction between her and the poem describing her. The living Elizabeth was a public office in which the documents of her virtue were "fil'd / Upon record" (see *OED* "file" v 3), and the "roll" that concludes the poem is both the "flesh" that remains as the "record" of her virtue and the poem itself as textual memorial.

Powerfully attracted to the idea of escaping historical contingency and worldly struggle into the perfection of death, Jonson provides himself and his reader a brief glimpse of such perfection. The original text was inscribed upon a small brass along with a prose inscription giving the names of the mourning parents, a knight and his wife; the name of the child; and the date and age at which she died. The poem was published in *The Under-wood*, however, without the name of the child and with the generic title "An Epitaph." It is uncertain how much the text of *The Under-wood*, published posthumously by Sir Kenelm Digby in 1640, reflects Jonson's own editorial decisions.[75] Yet whether or not it was planned by Jonson, the exclusion of the historical facts concerning the deceased is in keeping with the poem's generalizing thrust. All specificity, including the poem's origin in a patronage relationship, is effaced, and the child is idealized all the more by being removed from concrete particulars.

Jonson's masterpiece of expressive brevity among his epitaphs is "On My First Daughter." Unlike the poems we have thus far discussed, the epitaph does not directly proclaim or clearly thematize its own brevity, for Jonson the father restrains the proud maker's claims. Its twelve lines are nevertheless a triumph of compact implication. The epitaph is, as Jonson surely knew it to be, the first major poetic epitaph in English

[74] Epitaphs upon Magdalen Curson, d. 1610, in Ravenshaw, 50; Francis Fitzherbert, d. 1619, in Tissington Parish Church; and Cecilia Puckering, d. 1636, in Warwick Cathedral. See also the epitaph upon Jonson's poetic disciple, Thomas Randolph, d. 1635, and William Whately, d. 1647, in Ravenshaw, 82, 98. The "all-in-one" motif is even clearer in the inscriptional version of Jonson's epitaph, where "blest" read "one" (8:188).

[75] See Herford and Simpson's notes in *Ben Jonson*, 11:47–48; and Ian Donaldson, ed., *Ben Jonson*, The Oxford Authors (Oxford: Oxford University Press, 1985), 680–681. See also Annabel Patterson, *Censorship and Interpretation: The Conditions of Writing and Reading in Early Modern England* (Madison: University of Wisconsin Press, 1984), 126–143, which argues that Jonson himself carefully arranged *The Under-wood* in order to encode veiled political messages.

upon a child. While the Ratcliffe epitaph, written in the same period, is a conspicuously artful composition seeking the attention of court circles, "On My First Daughter" is a poetic monument that plainly but forcefully rivals the most ostentatious tomb:

> Here lyes to each her parents ruth,
> MARY, the daughter of their youth:
> Yet, all heavens gifts, being heavens due,
> It makes the father, lesse, to rue.
> At sixe moneths end, shee parted hence
> With safetie of her innocence;
> Whose soul heavens Queene, (whose name shee beares)
> In comfort of her mothers teares,
> Hath plac'd amongst her virgin-traine:
> Where, while that sever'd doth remaine,
> This grave partakes the fleshly birth.
> Which cover lightly, gentle earth.
>
> (8:33-34)

After iambic pentameter couplets, used by Jonson in the Cavendish epitaph, the iambic tetrameter couplets found in "On My First Daughter" are the most common English epitaphic meter.[76] Both types can function similarly to classical elegiac couplets, which have a high degree of syntactic and rhetorical independence within the poems of which they are a part. Jonson's first three couplets all have independent clauses and are, like classical elegiac couplets, rhetorically self-contained units. Jonson uses both the sense of the couplets as discrete units and the space between them to express the intellectual and emotional turns of the poem.

The opening couplet could in syntactic and formal terms be a complete epitaph: "Here lyes to each her parents ruth / MARY, the daughter of their youth." A comparison of this couplet to classical and Renaissance neoclassical distichs reveals how Jonson's opening captures the compressed pathos of the ancient epigram and its Renaissance imitations. Consider the fifteenth-century neo-Latin poet Marullo's epitaph on the infant Alcino: "I, Alcino, lie here, where my sorrowful parents laid me. / This is the price of life and of childbearing."[77] Both Jonson's couplet and Marullo's epitaph pack within their two lines the double emphasis typical of ancient and humanist epitaphs, giving the name of the deceased and expressing the great sorrow of the survivors. Both are pagan

---

[76] For another Jonsonian example, see the epitaph upon Henry West, Lord La Warr, d. 1628 (8:233–234). For a few other early seventeenth-century examples, see Le Neve, 4:63, 83, 86, 97, 103, 104.

[77] "Alcinus hic iaceo, moesti posuere parentes. / Hoc pretium vitae est atque puerperii" ("Epitaphium Alcini Infantis," in *Michaelis Marulli*, 49).

in spirit, for they suggest that all of the child is buried in the grave. Marullo's Alcino delivers from the grave a stark, gnomic generalization that places the parents' particular grief in a universal perspective. Jonson more subtly expresses the great grief of the parents by placing the name of the deceased, which in English epitaphs normally follows the "Here lies..." formula directly,[78] between rhyming phrases concerning the parents that implicitly identify the death of their child with the loss of the most joyful period of their shared lives ("to each her parents ruth," "the daughter of their youth"). Jonson's opening two lines thus evoke the burial place not only of Mary's remains but also of a family's youthful joy.

Jonson's opening couplet has the restrained, third-person point of view found in many Greek two-line epitaphs. A sixth-century Athenian distich reads: "Diocles set up for all to see this monument to his son / Stesias, whom tearful death holds fast."[79] The father expresses his grief in the single word "tearful," and he distances his sorrow by recording in the third person, for posterity, his child's name and his own. Such an epitaph envisages no consolation to the living beyond the memorialization of names and the impersonality that distances, even as it records, grief. A Hellenistic epitaph by Callimachus is very similar: "His twelve-year old son the father Philipus laid / here, his great hope, Nikoteles."[80] Writing for the surviving father Philippus, Callimachus uses the same impersonal form, with the brief phrase "his great hope" rendering all the father's loss.[81] Jonson emphasizes the power of an inscription to mute a personal voice of grief by the shift from the first-person point of view of the title, "On My First Daughter," to the impersonal statement of the opening couplet.[82] While the Cavendish and Elizabeth, L. H. epitaphs convey messages to be "heard" by their readers and transmitted

[78] On the normal use of the "Here lies... (X)" formula, see Fowler, 101.

[79] "Sêma phi[l]ou paidos tode idein Di[oklês kat]ethêken / Stêsiou, hon thanato[s dakru]oeis kath[e]khei" (Paul Friedländer and Herbert B. Hoffleit, *Epigrammata: Greek Inscriptions in Verse from the Beginnings to the Persian Wars* [Berkeley: University of California Press, 1948], 74). This is one of several examples of the restrained Greek epitaphic distich in Friedländer and Hoffleit, 70–94. For other examples, see also Peek, 60–75, 88–93.

[80] "Dôdeketê ton paida patêr apethêke Philippos / enthade, tên pollên elpida, Nikotelên" (*Greek Anthology*, 7. 453, my translation).

[81] Discussing this impersonal form, Francis Cairns claims that the classical epitaph most frequently uses an "unidentified human" as "speaker"; see his *Generic Composition in Greek and Latin Poetry* (Edinburgh: Edinburgh University Press, 1972), 216. The lapidary impersonality of such epitaphs suggests, however, not the personal voice of a speaker so much as an inscription's suppression of such a voice.

[82] On the distinction between literary genres that "represent" or imitate spoken discourse and those that "represent" or imitate inscribed discourse, see Barbara Herrnstein Smith, *On the Margins of Discourse* (Chicago: University of Chicago Press, 1978), 30. Jonson's pseudo-inscriptional epitaph here imitates an inscription, but at its end the poem shifts, we shall see, to an imitation of spoken discourse.

to others, here a message is externalized by being inscribed. By echoing the traditional impersonal epitaph, the opening couplet not only distances personal sorrow but also suggests, as a small consolation, that Mary's parents are suffering the grief that so many parents before them have suffered and recorded.

Callimachus delays till the end of his brief epitaph the central piece of epitaphic information, the name of the deceased, "Nikoteles." Coming immediately after the poignant "his great hope," the name suggests an irony: "Nikoteles," which means "he who fulfills a victory," expresses the father's "great hope," but the name is now all that is left of a hope brutally unfulfilled. Jonson, too, plays with names, though the significance is not immediately clear. The juxtaposition of "ruth / Mary" across the couplet hints at a pun on the two words. The lines suggest two possible readings. One may find in them an irony like Callimachus's: the parents who in hope named their child "Mary / merry" (i.e., "happy," OED 3b) ironically find her, instead, to be "ruth / Ruth." The sequence "ruth / Mary" may also suggest, however, that the child who now seems to her parents "ruth / Ruth" is in fact, as they had named her, "Mary / merry." By raising such questions about its own meaning, the couplet weakens its otherwise strong sense of closure and thereby propels the poem forward.

The corrective "yet" (l. 3) introduces a Christian vision that modifies the classical opening: the daughter, one of "heavens gifts" (l. 3), has returned to heaven. According to Catholic theology, Jonson's daughter, as a baptized infant, is innocent, and her soul assured of heavenly bliss.[83] Jonson does not yet enunciate, however, a dualism of body and soul but instead gives two different perspectives on his daughter and her new home. In the opening couplet, Mary the earthly daughter is "here," while in the next four lines she has gone "hence" (l. 5). These successive views suggest an unwillingness to relinquish his sense of the unified being he knew as his daughter, but the poem finally mediates between these extremes by distinguishing but carefully linking body and soul in lines five through eight. By announcing that the Virgin Mother has placed Mary's soul amongst the "virgin-traine" (l. 9), the poem indeed emphasizes that virginity is both a corporeal state of the buried body and a spiritual state of the soul above.

These lines connect the soul's ascent not only to the buried body but also to the daughter's name, whose true significance is revealed. The name "Mary" appears in heaven only in periphrasis and pun, as if it had become an unspeakable, holy name. The daughter and the Virgin Mary

[83] Riggs notes that no Church of England baptismal record for Mary Jonson has survived and plausibly speculates that her parents had a Catholic priest secretly perform the rite (p. 86).

are linked by their name in the most semantically complex phrase of the poem: "Whose soul heavens Queene, (whose name shee beares)" (l. 7). Though one can distinguish between the first "whose" as referring to the daughter and the second "whose" as referring to the Virgin, the shifting referent of "whose" reinforces the two Mary's fusing of spiritual identities in their shared name.[84] Furthermore, the ascent of Mary's soul hints at the name's etymological meaning of "exalted," so that the daughter in effect fulfills, like Elizabeth, L. H., the spiritual meaning of her name.[85] The daughter's association with the Virgin Mary suggests, retrospectively, that Jonson's description of Mary's life as "heavens due" not only uses the ancient commonplace of life as a loan requiring repayment by death but also transforms the daughter to correspond to another meaning of "Mary": she becomes *ros coeli*, "heaven's dew," a liturgical appellation of the Virgin Mary.[86] Thus the name "Mary" turns out indeed to express in little not a pregnant irony about man's vain hopes, like Callimachus's "Nikoteles," but a Christian message of heavenly bliss. Whatever her parents' ruth, "Mary" is herself now "happy" or "merry."

Jonson's attempt to suggest the continuing relationship between the body, soul, and name of his beloved daughter radically transforms a procedure common in sixteenth-century epitaphs, which often divide the deceased into his or her body, soul, and fame (or name). Thus George Buchanan's Latin epitaph upon Sir Nicholas Bacon, who died in 1579, asserts that Bacon "lives a second life among the souls of heaven. His fame fills the world, which is a third life to him. His body, once the home of his soul, is placed in this coffin." The Latin epitaph of John Borough, who died in 1595, reads, "This shrine is the Mausoleum of his body, the world that of Borough's name, the heavens that of his soul."[87] Sometimes the combination of fame or name on earth and bliss in heaven leads to the minimizing or total neglect of the actual body in the grave, as in these two examples:

[84] Patrick J. Mahony notes this fusion in "Ben Jonson's 'best piece of *poetrie*,'" *American Imago* 37 (1980):74.

[85] Camden defines "Mary" as "exalted" and notes the name's appropriateness to the Virgin in *Remaines*, 83.

[86] On the topos of repayment, see Richmond Lattimore, *Themes in Greek and Latin Epitaphs* (Urbana: University of Illinois Press, 1962), 170–171; on the pun, see Mahony, 72.

[87] " . . . agit / Vitam secundam caelites inter animos. / Fama implet orbem, vita quae illi tertia est. / Hac positum in arca est corpus, olim animi domus" (Camden, *Remaines*, 53); "Corporis hoc fanum, Burghenis nominis orbis / Est Mausoleum, spiritus ipse Polus" (William Camden, *Reges, Reginae, Nobiles . . . in ecclesia . . . Westmonasterii sepulti . . .* [London, 1600], H4r). For other examples of this triple division, see the epitaphs upon the French humanist William Budé translated in Timothe Kendall, *Flowers of Epigrammes* (1577), Spenser Society no. 15 (1874; rpt., New York: Burt Franklin, 1967), 156; Sir John Leigh, d. 1564, in John Stow, *A Survey of London* (1603), ed. Charles Lethbridge Kingsford, 2 vols. (Oxford: Clarendon, 1908), 1:283; and William Barker, d. 1575, in Norris, 1:239.

>Now lives thy soule, through from thy corps dissevered,
>There high is blisse, here cleare in fame the while. . . .
>
>His soule in heaven dooth live in endles joye
>his woorthy woorks, such fame in earth have sowne,
>As sack nor wrack, his name can there destroy.[88]

Such poems sacrifice the survivor's remembrance of the whole person for the consolatory affirmation that the person has been divided in such a way that each part of him or her has reached its proper place. The extreme clarity and formulaic nature of the division attempts to free the living from regretting the whole person who was by making them acknowledge the parts that endure. Jonson cannot, however, accept such a division. Though he can imagine the adult Cavendish rejecting his mere body in the tomb, his daughter is for him an ideal of total bodily and spiritual innocence. Through puns, juxtaposition, and implication, Jonson therefore blurs the conventional epitaphic divisions, seeking consolation in a vision of the deceased closer to the whole child he knew.

Jonson's attempt to retain a sense of his whole child depends heavily upon the most Catholic element in the poem, the depiction of the Virgin Mary's special tenderness toward her virginal infant namesake. The picture of the soul of Jonson's daughter beatified in heaven is not, by itself, either Catholic or Protestant. In an otherwise useful discussion of views on the soul after death, Helen Gardner incorrectly treats the belief in the soul's immediate translation to heaven (or hell) upon death as a Catholic view rarely found among English Protestants.[89] English Protestants in fact held two different views of the fate of the soul after death, one of which resembled that of their Catholic contemporaries. Since the twelfth century the Roman church had held that there was an immediate judgment at death and that the soul immediately began to experience heaven, hell, or purgatory. Asserting the primacy of the Resurrection, Calvin, by contrast, maintained that the soul of the deceased entered into a period of waiting for the Last Judgment, a period in which it felt joy or sorrow but in a temporary and provisional way. He refused to identify the "paradise" or "Abraham's bosom" that the souls of the elect entered upon death with heaven.[90] Though English Protestants were

[88] Sir John Harington, "*An Epitaph in Commendation of* George Turbervill, *a learned Gentleman*," in *The Letters and Epigrammes of Sir John Harington*, ed. Norman Egburt McClure (Philadelphia: University of Pennsylvania Press, 1930), 30; and "*An Epitaph*, written by G. W. of the Death, of M. G. Gaskoygne," ll. 6–8 in *The Works of the English Poets from Chaucer to Cowper*, ed. Alexander Chalmers, 21 vols. (London, 1810), 2:466.

[89] See Helen Gardner, ed., *John Donne: The Divine Poems* (Oxford: Clarendon, 1978), 114–117. Gardner analyzes views on death in relation to Donne's belief in immediate beatification or damnation, which she claims is highly unusual among Protestants.

[90] See Calvin, *Institutes of the Christian Religion*, trans. Ford Lewis Battles, ed. John T. McNeill (Philadelphia: Westminster Press, 1960), 1:996–998 (3.25.6).

divided between the older, Catholic view (minus purgatory) and the Calvinist,[91] funeral sermons and epitaphs suggest that the pre-Reformation view was far more widespread. Some otherwise firm English Calvinist ministers explicitly rejected Calvin's view of the soul's fate.[92] Like the epitaphs we have seen which divide the deceased into his or her buried body, immortal fame, and heavenly soul or imagine the soul of the deceased speaking from heaven, the majority of late sixteenth- and seventeenth-century English epitaphs that explicitly treat the after-life of the soul situate it in heaven.[93] The continuing strength of the pre-Reformation view in England, even among otherwise strong Calvinists, probably stems from its greater consolatory power. It allowed the be-reaved to know that their departing loved ones were enjoying full heav-enly bliss, in comparison to which Calvin's mysterious place of waiting was emotionally unsatisfying.[94] But Jonson's Catholic Mariolatry enables him to go further than his Protestant contemporaries in picturing such heavenly bliss: it licenses his imagining the Virgin Mary's personal, ma-ternal concern for his child.

Only after presenting such a consoling picture does Jonson enunciate a clear separation of body and soul: "Where, while that sever'd doth remaine / This grave partakes the fleshly birth" (ll. 10–11). "While," how-

---

[91] While countenancing both the (modified) Catholic and Calvinist positions, the Church of England condemned as heretical the third major Christian position, the belief that the souls of the dead slept or lay dead until the Resurrection. Though Luther was an early proponent of "soul sleep," the doctrine quickly became associated with radical Anabaptists; in England, "soul sleep" or "mortalism" was espoused only by a small minority of religious radicals who became vocal during the Civil Wars and Interregnum, when censorship was relaxed and heterodoxy flourished. See Paul Althaus, *The Theology of Martin Luther*, trans. Robert C. Schultz (Philadelphia: Fortress Press, 1966), 404–425; and Norman T. Burns, *Christian Mortalism from Tyndale to Milton* (Cambridge: Harvard University Press, 1972).

[92] The prominent Puritan divine Thomas Gataker, for example, attacks the "unsound assertion . . . of those that denie unto the soules of the Saints deceased entrance into heav'n, and accesse unto the presence of Christ, until the last day." He argues that "Paradise" is none other than "the third Heaven, the present place of Christ's residence and abode"; see *Two Funeral Sermons: Paul's Desire of Dissolution . . .* (London, 1620), 28. Other Puritan funeral sermons assume the instant translation of the soul to heaven: see, for example, Robert Harris, *Samuels Funerall . . .* (London, 1630), 22; and William Harrison, *The Christian Life and Death of Mistress Katherin Brettergh* (London, 1634), C3v.

[93] Twenty-four of the inscriptions upon persons who died between 1600 and 1640 in Le Neve's anthology, for example, claim that the soul of the deceased is in heaven. A few inscriptions claim that the deceased has given back his or her soul to God (or Christ) or that the soul is now with God (or Christ); such epitaphs could be implying the Calvinist position by deliberately omitting mention of heaven or, as seems more likely, they may simply be using variant expressions for heavenly bliss. See the epitaphs upon Jane Con-ingsbie, d. 1608; Margeria Fortescu, d. 1613; William Becke, d. 1614; John Rudston, d. 1616; Mary Cleere, d. 1618; and Frances Layer, d. 1629, in Le Neve 4: 18–19, 42–44, 53, 69, 116.

[94] English Calvinists were at any rate not alone in rejecting Calvin's own position: many seventeenth-century French Calvinists did the same (McManners, 145; 501, n. 126).

ever, means not only "although," thus introducing a separation of body and soul similar to "Now lives thy soul, though from thy corps dissevered," but also—and more importantly—"as long as," thus pointing forward to the final resurrection when body and soul will "partake" of one another once more.

The final line of the poem, moreover, returns once more to the classical viewpoint of the opening couplet: "Which cover lightly, gentle earth." The wish that the earth not weigh heavily upon the dead body is ubiquitous in Greek and Latin epitaphs.[95] Noting that this formulaic wish appears even in epitaphs that treat death as total annihilation or that place the soul of the deceased in some place other than the grave, Richmond Lattimore concludes that the wish should be read as an expression not of actual belief in the sentience of the corpse but rather of emotional "discomfort at the thought of its [i.e., the body's] being cramped or suffocated under a heavy weight."[96] The formulaic wish allows the living, whatever their conscious beliefs, to project unto the corpse their own bodily sensations. Such projection is a common, cross-cultural phenomenon, for human beings often find it difficult fully to accept the distinction between an unfeeling corpse and the live, sentient body of those they knew and loved.[97] The movement in Jonson's poem from the dualism of lines ten and eleven to the concluding wish dramatically enacts a movement from Christian faith back to a feeling that is both classical and, so the father-poet no doubt felt, natural. The final line does not cancel, but rather supplements, the consolations of theological dogma. Simply ignoring the theological distinctions of the body "here" and the soul "there," the father expresses the continuing protective concern he feels for the whole child he knew.

The period at the end of the penultimate line makes the concluding, grammatically fragmentary line sound almost like an afterthought. Jonson may be following the habit of Latin inscriptions, in which the formula "Sit tibi terra levis" or its abbreviated form, "S. T. T. L.," is often tacked on to the end of the epitaph.[98] If he is self-consciously joining his predecessors in grief, however, he makes what was formulaic ineptitude a

[95] Lattimore, 65–74.

[96] Lattimore, 74.

[97] See Erwin Panofsky's discussion of the cross-cultural "law of inconsistency" governing funerary rituals, which often seem to imply the sentience of the corpse despite the beliefs of the living to the contrary, in *Tomb Sculpture*, ed. H. W. Janson (New York: Harry Abrams, 1964), 12.

[98] Judson Allen Tolman notes that Latin inscriptions often have the phrase "tacked on as though it were an afterthought" in *A Study of the Sepulchral Inscriptions in Buecheler's "Carmina Epigraphica Latina"* (Chicago: University of Chicago Press, 1910), 27. Camden notes the use of the formulaic abbreviation "S. T. T. L." in ancient inscriptions (*Remaines*, 31).

highly meaningful break. The paternal "I" must be the implied speaker of this final address to the earth, and thus Jonson's own voice, in all of its urgency, finally makes itself heard in a hitherto impersonal poem. This voice seems to enter the poem not as a part of the poetic monument and its impersonal inscription, but as a detached personal *response* to the inscription of the preceding lines. The poem's new sense of voice, separate from the impersonal commemoration of the preceding nine lines, reminds one of Latin epitaphs which, instead of simply adding the wish to the end of the poem, ask the passerby to express the wish himself as he leaves the monument.[99] Here are a popular Latin inscription and a Ovidian passage that illustrate this variation: "Wish, o traveler, / of your piety that earth be light upon him"; "Grudge not, o lover, as thou passeth by, / A prayer: 'Soft may the bones of Naso lie.'"[100] Such epitaphs convert the break between the impersonal epitaphic statement and the final wish into the distance between the tomb and its inscription and the departing, but potentially responding, reader. In a similar but more oblique fashion, Jonson himself seems to become the reader of the poetic monument he has created but now confronts, bidding sorrowful farewell to its occupant.

The final line is not, however, without Christian precedents. In medieval epitaphs prayers for the souls of the dead are occasionally coupled with prayers that the body, too, be at peace. Excerpts from two medieval English epitaphs reveal this combination: "I beseech you [o readers] pray, that the gifts of blessed / life among the saints be given him; and that here he may rest without strife"; "For such merits may You [o Christ] grant her the blessed realms, / Nor let her earthly tomb press heavily [upon her,] but let the court of God make her blessed."[101] Such examples fully express the continuing emotional significance of the body in the grave even for Christians who believe that the soul has departed. Jonson the Catholic adapts the double prayer of these medieval Catholic epitaphs. While his final request replaces the request that the body be at peace, the tears of the mother, answered by the Virgin Mary's personal

---

[99] Tolman, 27.

[100] "Tu opta, viator, / cum pietate tua ipso terra leve" (Lattimore, 71); "AT.TIBI. QUI.TRANSIS.NE.SIT.GRAVE.QUISQUIS.AMASTI. / DICERE.NASONIS.MOLLITE.OSSA.CUBENT" (Ovid, *Tristia* 3.3.75–76).

[101] "Vos [lectores] precor orate, quod sint sibi dona beatae / Cum sanctis vitae; requiescat et hic sine lite" (epitaph upon Robert Waldby, d. 1398, in Camden, *Reges*, G1r); "Pro tantis meritis sibi dones [Criste] regna beata / Nec premat urna rogi sed beet aula dei" (epitaph upon Joan Clopton, d. 1430, in Cecil T. Davis, *The Monumental Brasses of Gloucestershire* [1899; rpt., Bath: Kingsmead Reprints, 1969], 31). I cite the Waldby inscription from Camden's collection of the epitaphs in the Abbey, published in 1600. As a friend of Camden, a student at Westminster School, and a perennial Londoner, Jonson might have seen the epitaph either in Camden's collection or in the Abbey himself.

intercession, play the role of the traditional Catholic prayer for the soul of the deceased, which are often addressed to the Virgin.[102]

Jonson deepens the significance of such double prayers by linking it to the gender distinction between father and mother. Beginning with the opening line's use of "each" rather than "both" to refer to the parents' grief, Jonson carefully distinguishes between the responses of father and mother to the child's death. He consoles himself with the thought that his daughter is "heavens due," but the mother weeps and requires the comforting intervention of the Virgin Mary. Just as Jonson praises Margaret Ratcliffe, as a woman, for an intensity of grief that he considers improper in men, so this poem suggests that the father is more rational in response to his daughter's death, the mother more emotional.[103] While such a contrast implies a patriarchal hierarchy of superior male reason and inferior female passion, the Catholic elements of the poem afford greater respect to the feminine response. The mother's tears link her to the heavenly realm of her daughter's soul and of the Virgin Mary, while the father's final solicitude for the body in the grave reveals his own earthly focus. Thus the mother is treated not only as more emotional but also as closer to (a feminized) heaven than the father.[104] The two grieve differently, but that difference does not resolve itself into a simple, unequivocal hierarchy.

Jonson's pride as a father and poet shapes and transforms the Catholic elements of the poem. Normally, Catholic epitaphs pray to the Virgin for souls in purgatory, not for the blessed souls of infants, and they never assert that the Virgin has answered their prayers. It is in fact Jonson, a punning mythmaker as well as a Catholic, who invents the personal intercession of the heavenly Mary and thus consoles the

[102] On the Virgin Mary as Our Lady of Mercy in the iconography of Catholic funerary monuments, see Ariès, 256–258. Prayers to the Virgin Mary may be found in numerous medieval epitaphs. For famous instances, see John of Garland's and Petrarch's respective epitaphs upon themselves in *The Parisiana Poetria of John of Garland*, ed. and trans. Traugott Lawler (New Haven: Yale University Press, 1974), 102–103; and Jovius, 8. For an English example, see the epitaph of William Read, d. 1447 in Ravenshaw, 11. Prayer scrolls issuing from the mouths of the figures on English medieval monumental brasses often petition the Virgin; see Herbert W. Macklin, *Monumental Brasses* (London: Allen, 1913), 125.

[103] See G. W. Pigman III, *Grief and English Renaissance Elegy* (Cambridge: Cambridge University Press, 1985), 87.

[104] Jonson is not the only Catholic to imply a connection between women's supposed emotionalism and their spiritual intimacy with the souls of the dead. Giovanni Boccaccio, for examples, writes of how plague destroyed women's normal "feminine concern for the salvation [*la donnesca pietà per salute*] of the souls of the dead"; see the *Decameron*, trans. G. H. McWilliam (Harmondsworth: Penguin, 1972), 55; and *Decameron*, ed. Vittore Branca (Florence: Presso L'Accademia Della Crusca, 1976), 14. The Virgin Mary herself combined intense emotion and spiritual concern, and treatments of Mary presumably both arose from, and reenforced, this view of femininity; on the Virgin Mary's relationship to ideals of femininity, see Marina Warner, *Alone of All Her Sex: The Myth and the Cult of the Virgin Mary* (New York: Knopf, 1976).

mother—and himself—with a divine response to the mother's tears. Instead of simply stating, as epitaphs usually do, that the deceased is in heaven, Jonson makes his child an honored member of heaven's royal entourage. Thus during the same period in which he commemorated a maid of honor at Elizabeth's court, Jonson gave his daughter, by force of his poetic assertions, an equivalent status at the greater court of "heavens Queen."

His poetic exaltation of his daughter in heaven is paralleled by the dignifying of his daughter below. The one unusual word in the last line's request, the address to the earth as "gentle," is richly evocative. Though "gentle" is a common polite form of address in this period ("gentle," *OED* 3b), here Jonson gives the word great meaning: he calls the earth "gentle" both because he wishes it to be physically gentle towards his daughter's remains and because he wants to endow it with a gentle dignity befitting his daughter's worth. Jonson did not erect a material monument to his daughter, but he seeks by poetic assertion to raise her otherwise "common" earth to "gentle" status, thereby making his daughter an earthen grave of great rank. Compare this epitaphic distich composed by Jonson's Scottish host of 1619, William Drummond: "This deare (though not respected) Earthe doth hold. / One for his Worth, whose Tombe should bee of Gold."[105] The earth is "gentle" to Jonson, as it is "deare" to Drummond, because of the poet's respect for the deceased it holds. Both poets thus assert that the low is truly high.

[105] William Drummond, "Epitaph," in his *Poetical Works*, 2:119.

Chapter 3

Mourning and Praise: The Elegy and Epitaph

Throughout the Western literary tradition longer works have included brief poetic epitaphs. One finds them in biographies and romances, philosophical treatises and love laments.[1] Epitaphs are especially common at the end of literary texts because they provide strong closure. The subject of an epitaph, the ultimate state of the dead, thematically evokes finality, and its epigrammatic brevity makes it seem, in formal terms, all "end."[2] This chapter will first examine the most important classical and Renaissance generic combination involving a final epitaph, the long funerary poem that ends with an epitaph. I will then discuss Jonson's transformation of this composite form in his most compelling funerary poem, "On My First Sonne."

A number of features normally distinguish the epitaph from the longer funerary poem, the form we now commonly call the elegy, which in the Renaissance went by that name and a host of others.[3] Puttenham's

[1] For general discussions of longer genres' incorporations of smaller ones, see Francis Cairns, *Generic Composition in Greek and Roman Poetry* (Edinburgh: Edinburgh University Press, 1972), 158–176; and Alastair Fowler, *Kinds of Literature: An Introduction to the Theory of Genres and Modes* (Cambridge: Harvard University Press, 1982), 179–181.

[2] On the use of "closural allusions" and epigrammatic style for strong closure, see Barbara Herrnstein Smith, *Poetic Closure: A Study of How Poems End* (Chicago: University of Chicago Press, 1968), 172–182, 196–210.

[3] On the various names for funerary laments, see O. B. Hardison, Jr., *The Enduring Monument* (Chapel Hill: University of North Carolina Press, 1962), 113. "Elegy" in both classical and Renaissance poetry referred to a poem in elegiac meter, but both classical and Renaissance poets and critics believed that this meter was originally used for laments and remained especially appropriate for such poems. See Georg Luck, *The Latin Love Elegy*,

definition of the epitaph usefully distinguishes between the epitaph and the longer funerary poem:

An Epitaph is but a kind of Epigram only applied to the report of the dead persons estate and degree, or of his other good or bad partes...and is an inscription such as a man may commodiously write or engrave upon a tombe in few verses...for the passer by to peruse and judge upon without any long tariaunce: So as if it exceede the measure of an Epigram, it is then...rather an Elegie than an Epitaph which errour many of these bastard rimers commit, because they be not learned.[4]

Relating the epitaph's brevity to its inscriptional character, Puttenham complains that long epitaphs are in fact indecorous "elegie[s]." His earlier discussion of "Poeticall lamentations" suggests that there is more to the epitaph-elegy distinction, however, than difference in length:

The lamenting of deathes was chiefly at the very burialls of the dead, also at monethes mindes and longer times...which was done...by wofull countenaunces and voyces, and besides by Poeticall mournings in verse. Such funerall songs were called *Epicedea* if they were song [sic] by many, and *Monodia* if they were uttered by one alone.[5]

Using the imprecise terminology of his times, Puttenham here speaks of "epicedea" and "monodia," rather than the term he later uses, "elegie."[6] Nevertheless, one can derive several central distinctions between the epitaph and the elegy from his discussions. Puttenham considers the epitaph a brief, inscribed "report" in praise or blame of the dead addressed to all passersby, the "poeticall lamentation" a longer composition sung by mourners at a funerary ritual, either at the burial itself or at a commemorative ceremony. Besides their differing lengths, the two genres thus differ in subject matter, since the epitaph is a "report" concerning the deceased, the elegy an expression of mourners' sorrow, and

---

2d ed. (London: Methuen, 1969), 25–26; and for classical and Renaissance associations of the meter with lament, see Ovid, *Amores* 3.9.3; and Joannes Secundus, *Elegy* 3.7 in Clifford Endres, *Joannes Secundus: The Latin Love Elegy in the Renaissance* (Hamden, Conn.: Archon Books, 1981), 189–195.

[4] George Puttenham, *The Arte of English Poesie*, ed. Gladys Doidge Willcock and Alice Walker (Cambridge: Cambridge University Press, 1936), 56.

[5] Puttenham, 48–49.

[6] Puttenham discusses "elegie" as a "long lamentation" in this section, but uses the term to refer to love rather than funerary lament (p. 49). Renaissance critics often used "elegy" for both kinds of lamentation, sometimes distinguishing between "mourning elegies" and "love elegies" (Fowler, 136).

in setting or occasion, since the epitaph is part of a spatial monument, the elegy of a temporal ritual.[7]

Defining genres in terms of their (real or supposed) original occasions, Puttenham does not directly confront the issue of fictional settings. He therefore ignores the elegy that is not actually part of a death ritual and the epitaph that only purports to be inscribed upon a tomb. His distinctions nevertheless shed light upon the composite form consisting of an elegy that imagines a funeral or commemorative ritual and concludes with a pseudo-inscriptional epitaph. This generic combination dramatizes the relationship between elegy and epitaph and uses the movement from one to the other in order to enact successive responses to the dead. Virgil, Ovid, and pseudo-Tibullus provide ancient examples of the composite form.[8] Mopsus's lament for Daphnis in Virgil's *Eclogue* 5 (ll. 20–44), the earliest and most influential example of the form, begins by describing the funeral ceremony for Daphnis (ll. 20–26) but shifts to recording the funeral lament (ll. 27–42). The lament concludes with the command that the mourners erect a monument for Daphnis and inscribe his epitaph upon it: "And build a tomb and on the tomb place, too, this verse: / 'I am Daphnis of the woodlands, known from here even to the stars. / The guardian of a fair flock, fairer myself.'"[9] While the twenty-three-line elegiac section is concerned with the mourners' feelings and actions in time, the final two-line epitaph renders Daphnis's praise of his own time-transcending achievement. By heightening the reader's awareness of the temporality of reading, the relative lengthiness of the first section underscores the temporal process of mourning. The extreme brevity of the final distich, by contrast, minimizes the reader's sense of time and encourages his or her perception of the inscription as a spatial form. The spatial verbal monument provides a decorous formal analogue to Daphnis's proud description of his fame in spatial terms as extending "from here even to the stars."[10]

---

[7] On the differing subject matters of the two forms, compare Fowler: "Epitaphs are normally about the deeds and qualities of a particular deceased person and their claim on our attention; funeral elegies are about the thoughts and feelings of those who mourn" (p. 65).

[8] See Virgil, *Eclogue* 5.20–44; Ovid, *Amores* 2.6; and pseudo-Tibullus, *Elegy* 3.2. The pseudo-Tibullan composition provides the poet's directives for his own funeral and epitaph but otherwise follows the same patterns as the Virgilian and Ovidian poems. Fowler cites the major example of the composite form, Virgil's *Eclogue* 5, as an example of the "inclusion" of one genre within another, but because he conflates the elegy with final epitaph and a different generic phenomenon, the pseudo-inscriptional epitaph with a final inscriptional formula, he does not elucidate the ceremonial and aesthetic logic of the Virgilian example or of the composite form as a whole (p. 179).

[9] "Et tumulum facite et tumulo superaddite carmen: / 'Daphnis ego in silvis, hinc usque ad sidera notus, / formosi pecoris custos, formosior ipse'" (Virgil, *Eclogue* 5.42–44). I have substantially altered the Loeb translation.

[10] By foregrounding in turn temporal and spatial aspects of the text in shifting from

Death rituals generally seek to bring about or affirm the new status of the deceased. The person who has been violently torn from the living must be incorporated into the world of the dead, however conceived, so that he or she can be related in a new way to the community of the living.[11] A monument and epitaph appropriately close such a ritual by declaring the survivors' tempering of their sense of loss and final acceptance of the new "place" of the deceased. In Virgil's use of the composite genre, the elegiac section presents the mourners' lamenting of Daphnis's absence, whom the Fates "carried off" ("tulerunt," l. 34), while the final epitaph affirms that he has not simply vanished but has rather become one of the famous dead. The strong aesthetic closure of the epitaph helps answer the brute fact of death, that most abrupt and uncontrollable of endings, with a new end regulated and made meaningful by human action and art.

While the generic combination's elegiac portion often records the mourners sorrowfully addressing the deceased as an absent "you," the epitaph is normally either a first-person declaration by the deceased himself, as in Daphnis's distich, or third-person, impersonal praise. In either case, the mourners' grief is left behind when a point of view beyond theirs affirms, with unequivocal finality, the new state of the dead. Angelo Poliziano's late fifteenth-century neo-Latin poem upon Albiera Albitia, one of the most important Renaissance instances of the composite form, underscores the contrast between the elegiac and epitaphic sections by making the former a weighty 286 lines, the latter a mere 4.[12] The very length of the elegiac portion dramatizes the survivors'

the mourners' lament to the panegyric upon the deceased, the elegy with final epitaph exploits the space-time combination inherent, according to W. J. T. Mitchell, in our experience of literary texts ("Spatial Form in Literature: Toward a General Theory," in *The Language of Images*, ed. W. J. T. Mitchell [Chicago: University of Chicago Press, 1974], 271–300) to dramatize different treatments of the dead.

[11] For an anthropological discussion of the way funerary rituals seek the separation of the dead from the world of the living and their integration into the community of the dead, see Arnold van Gennep, *The Rites of Passage*, trans. Monika B. Vizedom and Gabrielle L. Caffee (Chicago: University of Chicago Press, 1960), 146–165; and the extension and refinement of Van Gennep's formulations in Richard Huntington and Peter Metcalf, *Celebrations of Death: The Anthropology of Mortuary Ritual* (Cambridge: Cambridge University Press, 1979), 8–13, 61–120.

[12] For a rhetorical analysis of this poem, which does not, however, discuss its place in the tradition of elegies with final epitaphs, see Hardison, 131–137. George Chapman imitates Politian's poem, including its move from elegiac mourning to epitaphic praise, in his "AN EPICED, or Funerall Song: On . . . HENRY Prince of WALES, &c." (1613); see the text and note in *The Poems of George Chapman*, ed. Phyllis Brooks Bartlett (New York: Modern Language Association; London: Oxford University Press, 1941), 254–268, 453. Another well-known fifteenth-century Italian example of the composite form, Lycidas's song in Jacopo Sannazaro's *Piscatorial Eclogue* 1.44–105, is closely modeled on Mopsus's song in Virgil's *Eclogue* 5; for the Latin text and an English translation, see Sannazaro, *Arcadia and the Piscatorial Eclogues*, trans. Ralph Nash (Detroit: Wayne State University Press, 1966), 158–163.

difficult and slow overcoming of their feelings of loss, and toward its
close the section makes vivid the mourners' grief by describing the burial
service as if it were occurring in the present:

> The crowded procession now leads the way, the priest sings sorrowful words
> now, and the bronze bells ring from the churchtowers. . . . Oh how much gloom
> do their uncombed hair, their eyes and their cheeks express! How much grief
> clouds their faces!

The poem moves from the temporal sorrow of the mourners, whose
immersion in time is emphasized by the repeated "now," to the impersonal epitaph's brief and definitive proclamation of Albiera's permanent
state of death and glory, located spatially in an earthly monument and
the heavenly stars:

> And finally the tomb of elaborately worked marble shuts in the icy limbs, and
> has on it a short verse: "The beautiful body of Albiera lies beneath this marble.
> Surely no marble has such fame. Her body adorns the tomb, but her spirit the
> stars: oh how much glory and fame are added to the heavens!"[13]

The rhetorical similarity of the two exclamations, "How much grief
clouds their faces!" and "oh how much glory and praise are added to
the heavens!" further highlights the contrast between the sorrows of the
living and the glorious new state of the deceased.

One of Pierre de Ronsard's poems upon the death of King Charles
IX in 1574 reveals how much a sophisticated poet can omit and still have
his readers grasp the generic signals of the composite form. The poem,
which consists of a French sonnet as its elegiac portion and a concluding
Latin quatrain as its epitaph, moves from a sorrowful valediction to
epigrammatic, third-person praise of the deceased:

> Seeing you in your coffin, alas! three times alas!
>
> .   .   .   .   .
>
> Farewell, Charles, farewell, o newest star of heaven,

---

[13] "Praecedit iam pompa frequens, iam moesta sacerdos / Verba canit, sacris turribus
aera sonant, /. . . . / O quantum implexi crines, oculique, genaeque / Noctis habent! Quantus
nubilat ora dolor! / . . . . / Et tandem gelidos operosi marmoris artus / Includit tumulus, &
breve carmen habet. / Hoc iacet Albierae pulchrum sub marmore corpus / Nulla quidem
tantum marmora laudis habent / Exornat tumulum corpus, sed spiritus astra. / O quanta
accessit gloria, lausque Polo!" (Politian, "Elegia, sive Epicidion. In Albierae Albitiae im-
maturum exitum . . . ," ll. 267–268, 273–274, 281–286 in *An Anthology of Neo-Latin Poetry*,
ed. and trans. Fred J. Nichols [New Haven: Yale University Press, 1979], 267–269). I have
in places modified the punctuation of Nichol's text and translation, following Angelo
Ambrogini Poliziano, *Prose volgari inedite e poesie latine e greche edite e inedite*, ed. Isidoro del
Lungo (Florence, 1867), 247–248.

While I prepare a grander monument for you,
Accept these sighs and tears from your servant.

Charles on earth lived as the greatest glory of the world,
With his great love of justice and of piety;
Now likewise dwelling in heaven he is the glory of the skies,
To which he bore himself upwards on wings of justice and piety.

(*Te voyant au cercueil, helas! trois fois helas!*
. . . . .

Adieu, Charles, adieu, du Ciel Astre nouveau:
    Tandis que je t'appreste un plus riche Tombeau:
    Pren de ton serviteur ces souspirs & ces larmes.

Carolus in terris terrarum gloria vixit
Maxima, Justititae magno & Pietatis amore:
Nunc idem coelo vivens est, gloria coeli,
Quò se Justitiae & Pietatis sustulit alis.)[14]

Ronsard shifts from expressions of sorrow at a burial ceremony, evoked by the speaker's sight of the dead king in his coffin, to praise of a monarch whose death is described as a spatial ascent from glory on earth to glory in heaven. Though the elegiac section of the poem is itself relatively brief, Ronsard makes the epitaph three times shorter and thus preserves the sense of emphatic closure. Ronsard's composition differs from other major examples of the composite form, however, in several respects. While the elegiac section normally includes mourners' laments within the description of a collective funerary ritual, the elegiac section here consists entirely of the poet's personal lament for his king. The epitaph is normally presented as an inscription upon a tomb, but Ronsard's is a purely verbal monument. While the shift from elegy to epitaph is normally clarified by references to the erection of a monument, Ronsard signals this shift only by changes in language and meter and—though this may be the printer's decision rather than Ronsard's—the blank space between the sections. The poem moves from a first-person French sonnet, a vernacular genre of love lament here adapted for a personal funeral lament, to impersonal Latin, the enduring language of solemn, public inscriptions, and dactylic hexameter, the meter of the highest panegyric genre, the epic. Ronsard's transformations of the form suggest the epitaphic poet's ability both to transcend his own personal sorrow and to provide, without any supporting material monument, a fitting public memorial for the dead.

[14] Pierre de Ronsard, "Sonnet de luy-mesme [Charles IX]," ll. 6, 12–18 in *Les oeuvres de Pierre de Ronsard: Texte de 1587*, ed. Isidore Silvor, 8 vols. (Chicago: University of Chicago Press; Paris: Librairie Marcel Didier, 1966–1970), 8:16.

George Pigman has noted that Jonson was deeply suspicious of mourning, often treating it as a dangerous outbreak of emotion revealing a sinful distrust of God and of the blessed state of the dead.[15] Jonson did not, however, wholly reject mourning. In "On My First Sonne," he adapted the elegy with concluding epitaph precisely because the composite form allowed him to mourn the loss of a beloved son while finally acknowledging, as he both wished and felt compelled to do, his child's new state and enduring achievement. Since the epitaph in honor of his son also explicitly testifies to the power of Jonson's public, commemorative art, the poem dramatizes Jonson's "making" of a verbal monument in order to free himself from the personal grief of a father through public praise not only of the deceased but also of himself as poet.

The circumstances surrounding his first son's death help explain Jonson's use of the composite form. While residing in Huntingdonshire with his mentor William Camden and friend Sir Robert Cotton during the plague that struck London in May, 1603, Jonson learned in a letter from his wife that his son had died.[16] Jonson had been estranged from his wife and therefore away from his children since sometime before February 1603.[17] By contemporary standards, he had neglected his patriarchal obligations: it was considered the particular responsibility of the male head of a household to look after his family in time of plague. The official prayer of 1603 for times of plague stated that "the chief remedy to be expected from man is that everyone would be a magistrate to himself and his whole family."[18] Jonson could not have attended the burial of his son, which would have taken place quickly after the boy's death. He thus failed to fulfill his final duty toward his child.[19] He could

---

[15] See G. W. Pigman III, *Grief and English Renaissance Elegy* (Cambridge: Cambridge University Press, 1985), 85–95.

[16] The circumstances are given in the "Conversations with Drummond" in *Ben Jonson*, 1:139–140.

[17] On Jonson's separation from his wife from sometime before February 12, 1603 to about 1605, see David Riggs, *Ben Jonson: A Life* (Cambridge: Harvard University Press, 1989), 92–93, 145.

[18] The prayer is cited in Paul Slack, *The Impact of Plague in Stuart and Tudor England* (London: Routledge, 1985), which notes that the plague "isolated the individual family and left it to its own resources" (p. 290). Peter M. Sacks suggests that Jonson may have felt guilt, "however irrationally," concerning his absence from London in *The English Elegy: Studies in the Genre from Spenser to Yeats* (Baltimore: Johns Hopkins University Press, 1985), 122. The historical context makes this possibility a high probability and suggests the (culturally relative) rationality of Jonson's guilt. Riggs argues that *Sejanus*, written during the same period as "On My First Sonne," "displaced" Jonson's "potentially intolerable burden of anxiety" concerning his abandonment of his children during plague-time (pp. 98–102); he does not seem, however, to find such anxiety in the poem itself (pp. 96–97). I argue that "On My First Sonne" is a more direct, though still not fully explicit, attempt to deal with the feelings Riggs finds encoded in *Sejanus*.

[19] Jonson's guilt feelings could only have been increased by having Camden for a companion during the 1603 plague. In the chapter on epitaphs in his *Remaines*, Camden

not have been satisfied with the burial his son received: during plague, funeral ceremonies were sharply curtailed, and most of the dead, instead of being buried in the consecrated ground of churches or churchyards with burial services, were quickly covered with a winding-sheet and flung without last rites into pest-pits.[20] Having been raised a Catholic, Jonson's child would have had even less chance of being properly buried during such troubled times.[21] In "On My First Sonne" Jonson therefore provides a compensatory burial ritual and an individualizing, immortalizing tomb-stone inscription for the boy who was in all likelihood unceremoniously buried in an unmarked grave. Like Ronsard's poem on Charles IX, but in a far more personal, emotional context, Jonson's poem implicitly asserts the power of poetry's verbal rituals and constructs: poetry can provide a proper burial for the dead without a body or a priest and a worthy public monument to the dead without a material tomb.

Several English humanists before Jonson had exploited the elegy-epitaph combination.[22] Like Ronsard, Jonson relies upon his reader's intimate knowledge of the composite form when he transforms it in "On My First Sonne." The poem's first ten lines provide an innovative but

---

describes the "care of burial" among all but "savage nations" and attacks those who neglect "the last duty" toward those "nearest unto them" by failing to bury them properly; see *Remaines of a Greater Worke, Concerning Britaine*...(London, 1605), 27–28. Though he did not publish the *Remaines* until 1605, Camden had clearly already formed his opinions concerning the importance of burials and memorials, since he played a major part in the Society of Antiquaries' discussions concerning funerals and epitaphs in 1599–1600 and published his guide to the epitaphs of Westminster Abbey in 1600.

[20] F. P. Wilson, *The Plague in Shakespeare's London* (Oxford: Oxford University Press, 1927), 42–44.

[21] Catholics considered the churches and churchyards of the established church consecrated burial grounds because they normally predated the Reformation, and there were numerous seventeenth-century cases of struggles between Catholics wishing to inter their children in consecrated ground with the Catholic burial rites, on the one hand, and unwilling parsons, on the other. Catholics frequently had to resort to secret night burials and other subterfuges. See John Bossy, *The English Catholic Community, 1570–1850* (New York: Oxford University Press, 1976), 140–142; and John Miller, *Popery and Politics in England, 1660–1688* (Cambridge: Cambridge University Press, 1973), 52. During plagues, by many viewed as God's punishment on mankind for such sins as the toleration of Catholics, it would be even harder for a Catholic to receive a proper burial; on scapegoating of Catholics during plagues and other calamities, see Keith Thomas, *Religion and the Decline of Magic* (New York: Scribner's, 1971), 86, 542–543.

[22] See George Turberville's late sixteenth-century "Another Epitaph upon the death of Henry Sydhnam, and Gyles Bampfield, gent.," in his *Epitaphes, Epigrams, Songs and Sonets (1567) and Epitaphes and Sonnettes (1576)*, facsimile reprint with introduction by Richard J. Panofsky (Delmar, N.Y.: Scholars' Facsimiles & Reprints, 1977), 409–412; "A Commemoration of the generall mone...for and of...Sir Phillip Sidney," appended to George Whetstone's *Sir Phillip Sidney, his honorable life, his valiant death, and true virtues* (1587), C3r–C4r, reprinted in *Elegies for Sir Philip Sidney*, ed. A. J. Colaianne and W. L. Godshalk (Delmar, N.Y.: Scholars' Facsimiles & Reprints, 1980); and William Browne's "An Elegy on Mr. William Hopton," who probably died in 1591, in *The Poems of William Browne of Tavistock*, ed. Gordon Goodwin, 2 vols. (London, 1894), 2:246–248.

still recognizable example of the elegy with final epitaph, while its final couplet breaks with the generic model more radically and thus foregrounds the crucial differences between Jonson's poem and earlier works:

> Farewell, thou child of my right hand, and joy;
>   My sinne was too much hope of thee, lov'd boy,
> Seven yeeres tho'wert lent to me, and I thee pay,
>   Exacted by thy fate, on the just day.
> O, could I loose all father, now. For why
>   Will man lament the state he should envie?
> To have so soone scap'd worlds, and fleshes rage,
>   And, if no other miserie, yet age?
> Rest in soft peace, and, ask'd, say here doth lye
>   BEN. JONSON his best piece of *poetrie*.
> For whose sake, hence-forth all his vowes be such,
>   As what he loves may never like too much.
>
> (8:41)

The first eight and a half lines suggest the funeral of the poet's son. The occasion of the poem, the father's relinquishing of his son, is emphasized by the temporal markers "just day" (l. 4) and "now" (l. 5). Jonson represses the moment of the son's actual death, of which he was informed after it had already occurred. In its place he creates a moment of positive psychological and ritual action in which he can actively "pay" back his son to "fate" (ll. 3–4) by giving him a poetic substitute for burial. "Rest in soft peace" (l. 9) adapts the prayer normally said by the priest at a Catholic burial service, first before the body was brought into the cemetery for burial and then when the burial service was completed: "May his soul and the souls of all the departed faithful by God's mercy rest in peace. Amen" ("Anima eius & animae omnium fidelium defunctorum per Dei misericordiam requiescant in pace. Amen").[23] Jonson thus sug-

---

[23] See the English Catholic prayer book, *Sacra Institutio Baptizandi* . . . (Salisbury, 1604), 99, 144. Since Protestants rejected prayers to the dead, no such prayer is to be found in *The Book of Common Prayer*. Some might object that Jonson's "Rest in soft peace" recalls not the Catholic burial service but the well-known epitaphic formula *Requiescat in pace*. This formula, however, which itself derives from the burial service, becomes common in English epitaphs only much later than Jonson's poem and normally appears at the end of epitaphs. *Cuius anima requiescat in pace* was common at the end of Italian and French medieval epitaphs; see Philippe Ariès, *The Hour of Our Death*, trans. Helen Weaver (New York: Random, 1982), 218; and Iiro Kajanto, "Origin and Characteristics of the Humanistic Epitaph," *Epigraphica: Rivista Italiana di Epigrafia* 40 (1978):17. I have found no examples of this or the shorter version *Requiescat in pace*, however, in English medieval epitaphs. *Requiescat in pace* does not appear regularly on post-Reformation English tombstones until the eighteenth and nineteenth centuries, when its increasing appearance reflects the greater tolerance, de facto and eventually de jure, of Catholicism, with which the formula was associated. For discussion and examples of the use of the formula or the abbreviation R.

gests the completion of a last rite befitting his son. The "here doth lye" of the second half of the same line uses the ubiquitous *hic iacet* of sepulchral inscriptions and thus reveals that the poem has shifted from the elegy appropriate at a funeral to the brief panegyric inscription.[24] Though Jonson, like Ronsard, has compressed the elegiac section and omitted the erection and inscribing of the tomb, the first ten lines of his poem maintain the basic formal characteristics of the elegy with final epitaph.[25]

These lines nevertheless differ importantly in intent from the generic model. While other elegies with concluding epitaph end by acknowledging the new "place" of the deceased separate from though related to the world of the living, in "On My First Sonne" Jonson seeks above all to bring back the son that he lost and to "place" him in a monument that reasserts the intimate connection between the dead son and his father. In the elegy of lines one through nine, he simultaneously calls back and offers to relinquish his son, while in the epitaph of lines nine and ten he constructs a monument firmly bonding the son to himself. His central strategy is to substitute for the already lost flesh-and-blood

---

I. P.—the sure sign that the phrase has become commonplace—on English Catholic tombstones, see John Hobson Matthews, "Catholic Memorial Inscriptions," *Publications of the Catholic Record Society* 12 (London: Strowger and Son, 1913), 232–272, whose earliest example is the epitaph upon Mary Vaughan, d. 1713 (p. 266); and the numerous Catholic inscriptions from Old Saint Pancras Church and churchyard in Frederick Teague Cansick, ed., *A Collection of Curious and Interesting Epitaphs . . . of Saint Pancras, Middlesex*, 2 vols. (London, 1869), 1:1–169, whose earliest example is the epitaph upon Catherin Brent, d. 1709 (p. 81). I will discuss the significance of Jonson's modification of the prayer later in the text.

[24] Turberville adapts the form for men who died at sea and were consequently deprived of burial and monuments: in the first twelve stanzas the poet "waile[s] their sodain deaths" (l. 70); in the penultimate two stanzas he bids "water Nimphes" (l. 73) provide the dead with a grave and inscribe a monument with the three-line panegyric epitaph with which his poem concludes (ll. 82–84); see Turberville, 410–412. Jonson's use of the composite form for one who was not buried and commemorated properly is thus not unprecedented.

[25] Several critics have assumed the whole poem is an epitaph, including W. David Kay, "The Christian Wisdom of Ben Jonson's 'On My First Sonne,'" *SEL* 11 (1971):125–136; Wesley Trimpi, *Ben Jonson's Poems: A Study of the Plain Style* (Palo Alto, Calif.: Stanford University Press, 1962), 182–183; and Jack D. Winner, "The Public and Private Dimensions of Jonson's Epitaphs," in *Classic and Cavalier: Essays on Jonson and the Sons of Ben*, ed. Claude J. Summers and Ted-Larry Pebworth (Pittsburgh: Pittsburgh University Press, 1982), 113–118. Kay writes of the unusual attention given to the "mourning poet" in what is "essentially an epitaph" (p. 125). Others have noticed the switch to an epitaphic formula at line nine but either ignore its generic sources and implications or argue that one discovers at this point that the whole poem is an epitaph; for the first approach, see Francis Fike, "Ben Jonson's 'On My First Sonne,'" *Gordon Review* 11 (1969):205–220; Katharine Eisaman Maus, *Ben Jonson and the Roman Frame of Mind* (Princeton: Princeton University Press, 1984), 119–123; for the second, see Pigman, 88; and Arnold Stein, *The House of Death: Messages from the English Renaissance* (Baltimore: Johns Hopkins University Press, 1986), 152.

child associated with the mother and mortality a name that connects father and son and can be recalled and immortalized by art.

In the first four lines Jonson espouses the commonplace of life as a loan and purports to pay back the child that was but "lent" (l. 4). Yet his very first word, "Farewell," suggests the poet's unwillingness to accept his son's new state. Elegies often close with an explicit expression of farewell: Catullus concludes the elegy on his brother with his famous valediction, "ave atque vale" (101, l. 10), Ronsard's elegiac sonnet has a final "Adieu, Charles, adieu"; while an English elegy with final epitaph upon Sir Philip Sidney records the "farewells" of the mourners near the end of the elegiac section.[26] By beginning with such a "farewell," Jonson makes the rest of the poem seem an attempt to qualify this valediction's finality.

While in his other funerary poems upon children Jonson imagines the child as "other," Jonson cannot here accept this conception of his first son. He addresses the child with an etymological version of their shared first name, Benjamin: "thou child of my right hand, & joy" (l. 1). The Hebrew name "Benjamin," which Jacob gave his youngest son (Genesis 35:18), literally means "son of the right hand," the "filius dexterae" of the Vulgate. Saint Jerome and the *Glossa Ordinaria* interpret "filius dexterae" to mean "filius virtutis," that is, "son of manliness."[27] Thus the name conveys all the patriarchal pride of a father in his male offspring. Jonson strengthens the bond of "virtus" between father and son by modifying the translation: whereas most commentators and both the Coverdale and King James versions translate the name as "son of *the* right hand," Jonson calls his son "child of *my* right hand."[28]

By his marked silence concerning the boy's mother, Jonson further asserts the absolute dependence of the son's identity upon the father. In the biblical narrative, Jacob's son was first named "Ben-oni" ("son of my sorrow") by his dying, despairing mother, Rachel, and then renamed "Ben-jamin" by his proud father Jacob (Genesis 35:18). By opening with the biblical meaning of the name "Benjamin," Jonson recalls the Old Testament episode and thereby associates the name with the absence of the mother and the unmediated patriarchal bond between father and son.[29] While he treated his daughter Mary as the joint offspring of two parents, he imagines his male child as his alone. A neglectful father who

[26] "Farewell the worthiest Knight, that liv'd, the multitude did crie: / Farewell that hon'rd arte, by lawrell and the Launce, / Farewell the frend (beloved) of all, that hadst no foe but chaunce" ("A Commemoration," in Whetstone, *Sidney*, C3v).

[27] See Fike, 206–208.

[28] See J. Z. Kronenfeld,"The Father Found: Consolation Achieved through Love in Ben Jonson's 'On My First Son,'" *SP* 75 (1978):72.

[29] Several critics note the absence of the mother but do not link it to the biblical allusion: see Maus, 120; Pigman, 88; and Winner, 116.

had left his child with the boy's mother, Jonson fiercely reclaims his son even as he agrees to pay back what was only lent and has already been taken from him. It was the wife and mother who witnessed the son's death and actual but inadequate burial; it was she through whom Jonson heard the news of his loss. Jonson the father therefore has to reassert his patriarchal possession in order to be able to "recall" the son enough to reenact the son's burial in poetry.

Jonson's desire to assert the sole possession of his child has particular pathos and significance because of the son's age. In early modern England seven was a crucial age of transition, the usual age that children became subject to gender-specific behavior and boys left the feminine, nurturing world of their mothers, nurses, and school dames in order to enter the masculine, disciplined world of fathers and schoolmasters.[30] A sixteenth-century family manual's recommendation that siblings of the opposite sex no longer sleep together when they reach seven presupposes gender-differentiation at that age.[31] In *The Book of the Governor* (1531), Sir Thomas Elyot advises that boys be taken "from the company of woman" at age seven and given to male tutors; in a work of the 1560s or 1570s, Myles Coverdale assumes the practice amongst his readers: "After seven years the child [i.e. the boy] has his [male] tutors and schoolmasters to rule him."[32] Jonson himself entered Westminster School and discovered his spiritual father, Camden, sometime after he turned seven.[33] Thus Jonson neglected and then lost his Benjamin before he could truly experience the child as the bearer of his own masculine *virtus*. Even as he purports to relinquish his son, Jonson invokes his son's name,

[30] See Ralph A. Houlbrooke, *The English Family, 1450–1700* (London: Longman, 1984), 150; and Lawrence Stone, *The Family, Sex and Marriage in England, 1500–1800* (New York: Harper, 1977), 409–410. The importance of age seven derives from the long-standing division of the ages of man (i.e., of males) into seven-year periods; see the classical and medieval citations in J. A. Burrow, *The Ages of Man: A Study in Medieval Writing and Thought* (Oxford: Clarendon, 1986), 38–39, 191, 200–201.

[31] William Harrington's recommendation regarding siblings in *The Commendacions of Matrymony* (London, 1528), E2v, is cited in Alan Macfarlane, *The Family Life of Ralph Josselin: A Seventeenth-Century Clergyman* (Cambridge: Cambridge University Press, 1970), 91.

[32] Sir Thomas Elyot, *The Book of the Governor* (1531), ed. S. E. Lehmberg (London: Dent, 1962), 19; *Remains of Myles Coverdale*, ed. George Pearson (Cambridge: Cambridge University Press, 1846), 57. The notion that boys should leave home for school at seven is ancient: see, for example, Aristotle, *Politics* 7.15.7 and 7.15.11. Erasmus's counterargument that boys should begin their education before the traditional age of seven reveals the close link between the beginning of education and the assertion of male, patriarchal values. Erasmus opens his treatise *De Pueris Instituendis* by dismissing "silly little women" ("mulierculas") who worry lest boys receive instruction too early and later attacks mothers who "keep their infant in their laps almost to the age of seven" ("infantes suos usque ad annum pene septimum in sinu detinent"); see *Declamatio de Pueris Statim ac Liberaliter Instituendis*, ed. and trans. Jean-Claude Margolin (Geneva: Librairie Droz, 1966), 380–381, 396–397, 414–417.

[33] Rosalind Miles notes that seven was the youngest age for admission to Westminster School in *Ben Jonson: His Life and Work* (London: Routledge, 1986), 13.

with all its patriarchal resonances, in an attempt to enter the son into the masculine world denied him by death. Jonson thereby asserts both his son's status as a proper male heir and his own role as a proper father.

The first couplet's confession of the sin of "too much hope" (l. 2) seems to imply that the son's death is punishment for Jonson's excessive hopes for the boy. Blaming the deaths of those dear on one's own faults was for Jonson's contemporaries not only, as it is today, a common psychological reaction to death, but also a respectably rational explanation based on the assumption that God sometimes punished people's sins with the death of loved ones.[34] Fathers of the early modern era commonly spoke of their sons, particularly their oldest or only sons, as their "hope," for sons embodied the glorious future of the patriarchal line and name.[35] To have excessive hope in one's heir was to forget, however, one's mortality and thereby to court punishment for ignorance and pride.

Yet Jonson fights against his own admission of responsibility for his son's death. The second couplet's description of the son as a gift lent for seven years and then repaid to fate ascribes the boy's death to the workings of inevitable destiny. This new formulation suggests that Jonson's punishment for his sin is his own intense sorrow and disappointment, rather than the death of the child.[36] Whatever the nature of the punishment, however, Jonson's confession of sin is difficult to interpret, because it is not clear how much truth or mystification the confession contains. While excessive hope may in some sense have caused Jonson to neglect his paternal duties by preventing him from believing that his son could fail as his heir, Jonson's admission may also be a way of denying that what he had truly evinced was not too much but too little concern for the boy. In any case the poem seeks in fact not to suppress but rather to declare and finally fulfill Jonson's hope.

Jonson's etymologizing of "Benjamin" suggests that the father's sin is embodied in the very "hopeful" name that he gave to his son.[37] Since

---

[34] Thomas notes that Ralph Josselin blamed the 1648 death of his infant son on his own vanity and frivolity in *Religion and Decline of Magic*, 83. Sara Heller Mendelson notes that Stuart women diarists often blamed the deaths of their children upon their own sins in "Stuart Women's Diaries and Occasional Memoirs," in *Women in English Society, 1500–1800*, ed. Mary Prior (London: Methuen, 1985), 197.

[35] In *The Spanish Tragedy* Hieronimo, speaking over the corpse of his only son Horatio, laments: "Here lay my hope, and here my hope hath end"; see Thomas Kyd, *The Spanish Tragedy*, ed. Philip Edwards, The Revels Plays (London: Methuen, 1959), 115 (IV. iv. 90). For a plausible argument that Jonson was responsible, about three years before his son's death, for making additions to Kyd's play that focus upon Hieronimo's loss of his child, see Anne Barton, *Ben Jonson, Dramatist* (Cambridge: Cambridge University Press, 1984), 13–28. Compare also Ralph Josselin's brief, poignant note in his diary upon the death of his oldest son in 1673: "he was my hope" (discussed in Macfarlane, 166).

[36] See Maus, 120.

[37] Camden's long discussion of names in the *Remaines* specifically links them, including

Jonson considers one of the poet's primary tasks to be the proclamation and immortalization of virtuous men's supposedly appropriate names, his own son's name has a special complexity. In the opening of the poem, the name appears both as an unwitting paternal curse, harmful to the father himself and possibly fatal for the child, and as a compensatory poetic blessing, an affirmation of what can be preserved by the father-poet despite the child's physical death. In the first two lines, Jonson lovingly recalls his son by name not once but twice. Since "Benjamin" was also glossed as "loved and cherished,"[38] "lov'd boy" (l. 2), which means both "once loved" and "still loved," is yet another version of the name that preserves against death the father-son bond.

The epitaphic phrase "BEN. JONSON his best piece of *poetrie*" (l. 10) simultaneously memorializes the name shared by father and son and reveals its ultimate significance. Jonson puns on the original meaning of *poetry* as "that which is made or created" and thereby identifies his fatherhood with his poetic craft as a "maker."[39] In being "made" into a poem, the son is also made true to his name, etymologized as the "child of my right hand," for the son-as-poem is indeed the product of his poet-father's writing hand.[40] The epitaph thus completes the movement of the son from the temporal sphere of physical generation, the mother, and mortality to the realm of poetic, paternal immortalization.[41] Jonson's evident pride in the poem-child as the product of his hand, and his alone, may be compared to his later proud declaration that *Volpone* came "from his owne hand, without a co-adjutor, / Novice, journeyman, or tutor" ("Prologue," ll. 17–18, 5:24).[42] His hope in his son has, in a sense,

---

Hebrew names like "Benjamin," to parental "hope": "The first imposition of Names was grounded upon...many occasions...but the most common in most antient times among all nations, as well as the *Hebrewes*, was upon future good hope conceived by parents of their children, in which you might see their first and principall wishes toward them" (p. 29).

[38] Fike cites Robert Estienne's *Biblia* (Geneva, 1577); and Henry Ainsworth's *Annotations upon...Genesis* (Amsterdam, 1616) for such definitions of the name (p. 208).

[39] Trimpi, *Ben Jonson's Poems*, 182–183.

[40] See Pigman, 88.

[41] Jonson's contrast between his masculine immortalizing of a name and the feminine conception of a mortal child draws upon the widespread contrast between man's "superior" cultural creativity and woman's "mere" natural reproduction of life; for a cross-cultural study of this contrast, see Sherry B. Ortner, "Is Female to Male as Nature Is to Culture?" in *Woman, Culture, and Society*, ed. Michelle Zimbalist Rosaldo and Louise Lamphere (Palo Alto, Calif.: Stanford University Press, 1974), 67–88. Compare Erasmus's similar association of the male with the spiritual/cultural and the female with the physical/natural in the argument of *De Pueris Instituendis* that male tutors must nourish the minds of infants just as nurses nourish their bodies (see Erasmus, 378–381 and Margolin's note, 477–478).

[42] Jonson elsewhere expresses his conception of poetry as a realm of self-sufficient and specifically masculine power: in *The Forrest* 10 he rejects all sources of inspiration outside himself and contrasts the superfluous "ladies of the *Thespian lake*" with the source of his inspiration, "My owne true fire" (ll. 25–29, 8:108).

been fulfilled: the father who tragically wished for a flesh-and-blood child to continue his line grants himself his wish, with full awareness of its deep costs, in the epitaphic perpetuation of the name.

"On My First Sonne" uses a device found elsewhere in Jonson's poetry: the display of a name that purportedly has great significance at or near the end of a poem. Jonson's epitaph upon Cecilia Bulstrode ends with her name and the claim that it is the ultimate term of praise: "She was 'Sell Boulstred. In wch name, I call / Up so much truth...." (8:372). "My Answer. The Poet to the Painter" concludes, "Yet when of friendship I would draw the face, / A letter'd mind, and a large heart would place / To all posteritie; I will write Burlase" (8:227). In "On My First Sonne," the elegiac portion twice calls upon the meaning of the boy's name, while the final epitaph resoundingly gives the name and its full meaning in one compact phrase. Jonson's triple use of the name has an obvious psychological power as a repetitive assertion of the enduring link between father and son. It adapts, moreover, the classical burial ritual of *vocatio*, the calling three times upon the name of a dead person whose body is not available for burial. Aeneas thrice calls the name of Deiphobus in order to bury his fellow Trojan (*Aeneid* 6.505–506), while Ausonius claims in the prologue to the *Parentalia* that "even he who lacks the urn of mournful burial will be well-nigh as though interred, if his name be uttered thrice."[43] Without sharing any literal belief in the magical power of the ceremony, as a poet Jonson can take comfort in a verbal ritual sanctioned by poetic tradition that purports to bury the absent dead. He can use it as a substitute for the burial service denied his son. In the traditional *vocatio*, the mourners build a cenotaph for the deceased and call upon him to enter the monument by crying out his name. Jonson builds a verbal cenotaph with his right hand—the epitaph itself—and by calling upon the meanings of the name "Benjamin" rather than the name itself, he further assimilates the ritual to his own poetics. He implicitly asserts that one best buries the dead by acknowledging their immortal essence, by invoking their name insofar as it embodies their lasting significance.[44]

The epitaph does not simply lay to rest and commemorate the son. It

[43] "Ille etiam, maesti cui defuit urna sepulcri, / nomine ter dicto paene sepultus est" (Ausonius, "Item praefatio versibus adnotata," ll. 13–14, Loeb translation modified). On the *vocatio*, see also J. M. C. Toynbee, *Death and Burial in the Roman World* (Ithaca: Cornell University Press, 1971), 54.

[44] In his discussion of Jonson's poetics of naming, Eric Partridge argues that Jonson's manipulations of names draw upon "magical" beliefs that name and essence are so inextricable that, for example, to honor or injure a name is to honor or injure its bearer. Partridge does not fully clarify whether Jonson uses such beliefs as potent fictions or in some sense actually subscribes to them; see "Jonson's EPIGRAMMES: The Named and the Nameless," *Studies in the Literary Imagination* 6 (1973):195–197. I hold the former view.

also allows Jonson to escape from his own suffering as a father. Jonson uses the traditional shift from temporal mourning to spatial praise in order to move from his unbearable sense of the absence of his son "now" to a "here" in which father and son can join as poet and poem. In the middle lines of the poem, Jonson's outcry of paternal suffering "now"— "O, could I loose all father, now" (l. 5)—belies his acceptance of the piously generalized "just day" and expresses intense desire to escape an intolerable predicament. Jonson's despairing question further reveals his intense need for release: "For why / Will man lament the state he should envie?" (ll. 5–6). Jonson here draws a highly unorthodox distinction between lamentation for and envy of the dead, wishing he could feel the latter rather than the former. A topos of consolatory literature, both classical and Christian, is that lamentation for the dead shamefully betrays the mourner's selfish envy of the blessed state of the deceased. Seneca concisely expresses the idea: "To weep for one who is happy is envy."[45] In his elegy on Lady Jane Paulet, the Marchioness of Winchester, composed some twenty-eight years after "On My First Sonne," Jonson follows tradition in identifying lament as a disguised form of envy and advises the bereaved to be happy at their daughter's bliss: "Goe now, her happy Parents, and be sad, /. . . . / If you can envie your owne Daughters blisse, /And wish her state lesse happie then it is!" (ll. 77, 83–84, 8:271).[46] Such a feeling of happiness requires concentration on the blissful state of the other rather than on one's own feelings of loss. This is an attitude that Jonson cannot even approach in "On My First Sonne," because he cannot accept his son's having an identity apart from himself.

Trapped in his own grief, Jonson can only postulate the equally sterile alternatives of lamenting the loss of his son or envying the son's imperviousness to such loss. He imagines the posthumous existence of his son not as a positive state of beatitude but simply as an escape from the "now" of anguish in which he is himself entrapped. The son has "scap'd worlds, and fleshes rage" (l. 7). In traditional theological taxonomies, the

[45] "Beatum deflere invidia est . . . " (Seneca, *De consolatione ad Polybium* 9. 3, cited in Pigman, 156). For a Christian example, compare the Elizabethan humanist Roger Ascham's chiding of his wife for mourning their dead son: "And now, Margaret . . . do your love your sweet babe so little, *do you envy his happy state so much*, yea, once to wish that nature should have rather followed your pleasure in keeping your child in this miserable world, than grace should have purchased such profit for your child in bringing him to such felicity in heaven?" (*The Whole Works of Roger Ascham*, ed. Rev. Dr. Giles, 2 vols. [1864; rpt. New York: AMS Press, 1965], 2:172 [emphasis mine]).

[46] Lady Paulet died in 1631. In "Eupheme," his funerary tribute to Lady Venetia Digby, who died in 1633, Jonson similarly claims that he "blaspheme[s]" by lamenting Digby's death and thereby envying her bliss: "I murmure against *God*, for having ta'en / Her blessed Soule, hence, forth this valley vane / Of teares, and dungeon of calamitie! / I envie it the Angels amitie! / The joy of Saints! the *Crowne* for which it lives, / The glorie, and gaine of rest, which the place gives" ("Eupheme: 9. Elegie on my Muse," ll. 33–38, 8:283).

world is associated with avarice and the flesh with lust.[47] These are the sins that Jonson confesses to having committed and continues to commit in lines one to four by not wishing to pay his debt and by having excessive hope in the child of his own flesh. The son has also escaped "age" (l. 8), the temporal "miserie" (l. 8) Jonson himself keenly feels upon the loss of his first son.[48]

Jonson begins to escape from his unbearable condition with "Rest in soft peace" (l. 9). By changing the *requiescant in pace* formula of the Catholic burial service from third to second person and from optative subjunctive to imperative, Jonson transforms a prayer to God into his own command to his son.[49] Just as at the opening of the poem he ignored the mother's role in bearing his son, so here he ignores God's role as the answerer of prayers in order to assume sole responsibility for his son's "peace." While in his epitaph upon his first daughter Jonson acknowledges the role of the Virgin Mary in the child's blessed fate, in this poem so concerned with sole possession of his child, he suppresses all others, human and divine, who would come between his son and himself.

Jonson closely associates his son's "peace" in death with his own peace of mind. In the command "rest in soft peace," Jonson addresses not only his child but also himself, bidding that the "rage" he has just noted and exhibited in his outburst of passion should cease. The elliptical brevity of the following words, "ask'd, say" (l. 9), allows one to read them similarly as the father's command both to his deceased child, who is told what to say when asked concerning his identity, and to himself. These two readings are, in fact, the same: Jonson's instructions to his dead son reveal that the filial response must be a fiction invented by his father. In making a reply for his child, Jonson underscores that his son has indeed been made into a poem, a poem that brings Jonson emotional peace with the consolatory fiction of his son's response. Jonson thereby "looses," as he wished, the role of elegiac, mourning "father," and be-

---

[47] See Patrick Cullen, *Infernal Triad: The Flesh, the World, and the Devil in Spenser and Milton* (Princeton: Princeton University Press, 1974), xxv–xxxvi.

[48] Jonson's substitution of "age" for the traditional third sin of the devil, pride, is important: the very unconventionality of "age" in this series suggests its powerful significance for Jonson. William Kerrigan argues that "worlds, and fleshes rage" is "deliberately close to pulpit cliché" and that the lines suggest that for Jonson "the conventional rages of world and flesh may not be, after all, so miserable, [but] 'age' certainly is"; see "Ben Jonson Full of Shame and Scorn," *Studies in the Literary Imagination* 6 (1973):216. Although I disagree that the "rage" of the world and flesh is conventional within this specific poetic context, Kerrigan correctly points out that "age" is a deeply felt misery both here and elsewhere in Jonson's works.

[49] "Rest in soft peace" might be read as a contracted optative subjunctive, "[May you] rest in soft peace," rather than as an imperative. The imperative reading better fits, however, the poem as a whole.

comes the epitaphic poet, "a Maker, or a fainer.... that fayneth and formeth a fable," to quote the definition of a poet in *Discoveries* (2347–2353, 8:635).[50]

One may contrast the epitaphic message Jonson "makes" with that sought by the sixteenth-century Italian neo-Latin poet Giovanni Pontano in his elegy on his daughter Lucia. Punning on his daughter's name just as Jonson puns on the name of his son, Pontano claims that he sees his Lucia reborn as a light (*lux*) in heaven. The poem ends with the father begging his daughter to speak of her happiness at having escaped life's miseries: "I behold you my daughter in heaven; do you, o my daughter, your parent / behold? Or does your father feign [*fingit*] for himself these delusions? / ... / But if any part of you nevertheless survives, o my daughter, confess / you are happy that earliest youth snatched you away."[51] All too aware that he may have feigned the responsive glance of his child, Pontano begs his daughter to speak to him without any certainty of her answer. Jonson, by contrast, eliminates the possibility of failure by "fayning" the response he needs rather than awaiting an answer. The epitaph's status as the poet's self-consoling fiction perhaps explains why it is not in formal terms a self-contained whole: while a concluding epitaph is normally metrically independent from the elegy, the epitaph of "On My First Sonne" begins in mid-line, and its *hic iacet* clause identifying the deceased is not a self-sufficient couplet but only a portion of two lines connected by rhyme to the fifth and sixth lines of the preceding elegiac lament.

Based on the common epitaphic assumption that the passerby will wish to know the name of the deceased, "ask'd, say" signals the transition from the elegiac to the epitaphic portion of the poem by introducing a new element, the future readers who will inquire concerning the identity of Jonson's child. As in Ronsard, the movement from elegy to epitaph thus also entails a shift from personal lament to public proclamation.[52] One may compare Jonson's "ask'd, say" to the opening of a humorous epitaph by his friend John Hoskyns. Hoskyns addresses the inscription

---

[50] Compare Winner, 116.

[51] "Coelo te natam aspicio: num, nata, parentem / aspicis? An fingit haec sibi vana pater? /.../ siqua tamen de te superat pars, nata, fatere / felicem, quod te prima iuventa rapit" ("Tumulus Luciae Pontanae Filiae," ll. 5–6 and 9–10 in Joannus Pontanus [Giovanni Pontano], *Carmina*, ed. Johannes Oeschger [Bari: Gus, Laterz e Figli, 1948], 221).

[52] Both Turberville and Browne similarly move from personal lament to public proclamation in their composite elegy-epitaphs. Turberville moves from an elegiac section heavily marked by the first-person singular pronoun (ll. 4, 5, 9, 15, 17, 26) to a final impersonal inscription for "passers by" to "read" (l. 80); see Turberville, 409–412. After fifty-six lines in which the solitary poet mournfully addresses the deceased, Browne turns to the dead man's tombstone and pronounces the seven-line, impersonal panegyric upon the deceased (ll. 60–66) that the stone will "instruct some after-age to say" (l. 59); see Browne, *Poems*, 2:248.

itself, telling it what to say to the questioning reader: "If Any aske, who here doth lie, / Say, 'tis the Devills Christmas Pye."[53] Though Jonson bids not the inscription but the dead son—that is, himself—speak, the epitaph uses the *hic iacet* form that evokes not the voice of either son or father but rather the impersonality of an inscription. In many epitaphs the dead reply in the first person to the reader's imagined inquiry concerning their identity.[54] Jonson avoids such a first-person response, however, because it would once more separate him too greatly from his son. The third-person point of view, which is so clearly a product of Jonson's writerly hand rather than of any voice, creates a verbal "space" in which father and son can join together and be publicly remembered in "soft peace." The epitaph contains a highly meaningful pun: both father and son have indeed achieved the "best piece / peace" of poetry, the "peace" that only Jonson's poetic artifact can provide.[55]

The epitaphic response is thus really the product of a poetic inscription. Indeed the phrase "ask'd, say" echoes another tradition concerning the power not of voice but of writing, the poet's address to his poem or book as it goes off to face the public. Compare Spenser's "To his book" at the opening of *The Shepheardes Calender* (1579):

> Goe little booke: thy selfe present,
> As child whose parent is unkent:
>
> . . . . .
>
> And asked, who thee forth did bring,
> A shepheards swain saye did thee sing,
>
> . . . . .
>
> But if that any aske thy name
> Say thou wert base begot with blame.[56]

---

[53] Included in Louise Brown Osborn, *The Life, Letters, and Writings of John Hoskyns, 1566–1638* (New Haven: Yale University Press, 1937), 214.

[54] For Greek examples, see the dialogues between the curious passerby and the deceased in *Greek Anthology*, 7.163–165; for Renaissance translations of these epitaphs, see James Hutton, *The Greek Anthology in France and in the Latin Writers of the Netherlands to the Year 1800* (Ithaca: Cornell University Press, 1946), 645. The epitaph upon "a good old Erle of Devonshire" cited in E. K.'s commentary upon Spenser's *The Shepheardes Calender* (1579) provides an English example; see *The Yale Edition of the Shorter Poems of Edmund Spenser*, ed. William A. Oram et al. (New Haven: Yale University Press, 1989), 101.

[55] Winner views the "peace" / "piece" pun as troubling rather than consolatory (117). The pun testifies, however, to Jonson's power over words, the only power that he wields in the poem and one in which he puts his hopes for overcoming grief.

[56] Edmund Spenser, "To His Booke," ll. 1–2, 8–9, 13–14, *The Shepheardes Calender* in *Yale Edition of Spenser*, 12. For other poets' addresses to their poems that use similar constructions, see the Elizabethan poet Sir Edward Dyer's "My song, if anie aske whose greivous Case is such, / *Dy er* thou let his name be knowne..." ("A Fancy," ll. 77–78, included in Ralph M. Sargent, *At the Court of Queen Elizabeth: The Life and Lyrics of Sir Edward Dyer* [London: Oxford University Press, 1935], 187); Thomas Bastard's "If any aske thee what I doe professe, / Say that, of which thou art the idlenesse" ("Ad librum

Spenser uses "asked . . . / saye" in advising his book/child what to tell the curious reader concerning the book and its parent, the poet. In "making" his child his best poem, Jonson reverses the poetry-as-child topos. Jonson's use of the "ask'd, say" formula emphasizes, however, that his seeming address to his son is really a figure for his confrontation with his own written words, the medium by which he can publicly assert his son's immortal identity as poem and his own as poet. Spenser's notion of the book as the child of the masculine poet clearly presupposes the same effacement of the female as Jonson's notion of the child as poem. Thus the evocation of this tradition of public writing reinforces Jonson's cultural "recreation" of his son.[57]

Jonson opposes the productions of his "right hand" not only to the physical procreation of man and woman but also to the material productions of the tomb-maker. Critics have plausibly suggested that Jonson's praise of his son as his best poem is indebted to Montaigne's discussion of artists' relative love for their children and their artistic creations.[58] Here are relevant excerpts from the 1603 translation of Montaigne by Jonson's friend John Florio:

For what we engender by the minde . . . are brought forth by a far more noble part, than the corporall, and are more our owne. We are both father and mother together in this generation.

There are few men given unto Poesie, that would not esteeme it for a greater honour, to be the father of *Virgils Aeneidos*, than of the goodliest boy in *Rome*, and that would not rather endure the losse of the one than the perishing of the other. . . . Nay, I make a great question, whether *Phidias* or any other excellent Statuary, would as highly esteeme, and dearely love the preservation, and suc-

---

suum," ll. 9–10 in *Chrestoleros: Seven Books of Epigrames* (1598), Spenser Society no. 47 [1888; rpt., New York: Burt Franklin, 1967], 83); and Anne Bradstreet's "If for thy Father askt, say, thou hadst none: / And for thy Mother, she alas is poor" ("The Author to her Book," ll. 22–23 in *The Works of Anne Bradstreet*, ed. John Harvard Ellis [1867; rpt., Gloucester, Mass.: Peter Smith, 1962], 390).

[57] Bradstreet's address to her book, quoted in the preceding note, registers the usual effacement of the female by reversing its terms: *her* book has no father. Like Spenser, Samuel Daniel in *Delia* describes his poetry as the motherless child of the masculine poet, but with a twist appropriate to a collection of love sonnets, the poet sends off his child with the request that it speak not of his creativity but of the beloved's disdain: "Goe wailing Verse, the Infants of my love, / *Minerva*-like, brought foorth without a mother /. . . . / Say her disdaine hath dryed vp my blood" ("Sonnet II," ll. 1–2, 9 in *The Complete Works of Samuel Daniel*, ed. Alexander B. Grosart, 5 vols. [1885; rpt., New York: Russell, 1963], 1:38).

[58] See Wesley Trimpi, "BEN. JONSON his best piece of *poetrie*," *Classical Antiquity* 2 (1983):147–150; and Winner, 116. Herford and Simpson note that Jonson owned both a 1580 French edition of Montaigne (1:268) and Florio's 1603 English translation (1:264).

cessefull continuance of his naturall children, as he would an exquisite and
match-lesse-wrought Image, that with long study, and diligent care he had perfected according unto art.[59]

Jonson rejects Montaigne's crucial distinctions and categories. Montaigne
follows Plato's *Symposium* in his division between corporeal children, the
products of physical union between mother and father, and intellectual
or artistic progeny, of which the parent is "both father and mother."
Jonson blurs this distinction by making the identity of his child-poem
dependent upon himself alone.[60] While Montaigne distinguishes between physical children, on the one hand, and the spiritual children
produced by various kinds of "makers," including the poet and sculptor,
on the other, Jonson sharply distinguishes the work of the poet as
"maker" from what he considers the inferior physical labor of the tomb
maker. An epigram from the Planudean Anthology, here translated
from the literal Latin version contained in the Eilhard Lubin edition of
the Anthology that Jonson owned, concerns the sculptor Architeles and
his erection of a tomb for his son Agathanoris: "The sculptor Architeles
for his dead son Agathanoris / made this tomb with mournful hands. /
Alas, alas, this grave-stone, iron did not cut, / but it wore away, flooded
by many tears. / Ah, headstone, rest lightly upon the dead, so that he
may say, / 'Truly a father's hand placed the stone upon me.' "[61] In
addition to the general resemblance between this poem of a father
mourning his son and "On My First Sonne," there is a strikingly similar
emphasis upon the fathers' creative hands and upon their desires that
their sons in some sense acknowledge, beyond the grave, their fathers'
vocations. Architeles the sculptor asks his son to tell of his building the
tomb ("Truly a father's hand placed the stone upon me"), while Jonson
asks his son to tell of his father's *poesis*. The final line of the Greek poem,
like "Here doth lie / BEN. JONSON his best piece of *poetrie*," may be read
as the epitaph for the son dictated by the father: "Truly a father's hand
placed the stone upon me" recalls early Greek one-line epitaphs that
record a father's erection of the monument to his son as proof of paternal

---

[59] Michel de Montaigne, *The Essayes*, trans. John Florio, 3 vols. (London: Dent, 1910),
2:85, 88.

[60] Compare Winner, 116.

[61] "Scalptor Architeles Agathanori filio mortuo / Manibus misseris concinnavit tumulum. / Hei, hei, petram illam, quam non incidit ferrum, / Sed contabuit crebris lacrumis ir-
rigata. / Hei, columna, mortuo levis mane, ille ut dicat, / Vere paterna manus me imposuit
lapidem" (Eilhard[us] Lubin[us], *Anthologia diaphorôn epigrammatôn palaiôn. Florilegium,
hoc est veterum graecorum poetarum epigrammata comprehensa libris septem* [Heidelberg,
1604], 595). Jonson owned a 1603 edition of Lubin's work; see David McPherson, "Ben
Jonson's Library and Marginalia: An Annotated Catalogue," *SP* 71, no. 5 (1974):46–47.

love.[62] Thus the poems have a similar movement from a command that the son be at peace ("Ah, headstone, rest lightly upon the dead"; "Rest in soft peace") to the dictating of the son's epitaph. But although Architeles and Jonson both desire acknowledgement, the Greek father longs for recognition of the "paternal hand" that carves a material monument, the English one for recognition of a "right hand" that "makes" a purely verbal monument. Indeed by avoiding, like Ronsard, the description of the tomb usual in an elegy with concluding epitaph, Jonson elides the one funerary act upon which the Greek poem centers, the building of the tomb. In so doing he implicitly asserts that his brief poem alone provides a sufficient monument for his son.

The Greek poem may have had a personal resonance for Jonson in his desire to define his paternal relationship to his child. Although based on widespread cultural prejudices, Jonson's contempt for manual labor was undoubtedly increased by his own lowly beginnings; both his stepfather and he himself, briefly, were bricklayers.[63] In Jonson's time tomb making was the province not of artists but of masons, manual laborers comparable in social status to bricklayers.[64] Jonson might well have associated the making of tombs with his own humble past as a lowly builder. Mildmay Fane's elegy on Jonson reveals the possible association between the bricklayer and tomb maker by combining, in a way that would have been highly repugnant to its subject, Jonson's roles as poet and as a supposed maker of tombs:

> He who began from brick and lime
> The Muses' hill to climb
> And whilom busied in laying stone,
> Thirsted to drink of Helicon
>
> . . . . .
>
> Now since that he is turned to clay, and gone,
> Let those remain of th'occupation
> He honored once, square him a tomb may say
> His craft exceeded far a dabbler's way.[65]

---

[62] Compare this early Greek inscription: "This tomb to Spinther his father placed over his body" ("Sama tode Spinthêri patêr epethêke thanonti"). Paul Friedländer and Herbert B. Hoffleit provide this and other examples of the one-line form in *Epigrammata: Greek Inscriptions in Verse from the Beginnings to the Persian Wars* (Berkeley: University of California Press, 1948), 11–13.

[63] See Riggs, 9–10, 17, 53; and Walter George Bell, *A Short History of the Worshipful Company of Tylers and Bricklayers of the City of London* (London: H. G. Montgomery, 1938), 21–22.

[64] On masons and tomb-making, see Katharine A. Esdaile, *English Church Monuments, 1510 to 1840* (New York: Oxford University Press, 1946), 44–45.

[65] Mildmay Fane, "[On Ben Jonson]," ll. 1–4 and 7–10 in *Ben Jonson and the Cavalier Poets*, ed. Hugh Maclean (New York: Norton, 1974), 205. Such an association was plausible because of fluidity among the various building trades; see Stella Kramer, *The English Craft*

In "On My First Sonne," a poem so concerned with what it means to be a proper father and a "best" son, Jonson might well have considered his own patrimony and early years as a stepson. His pointed omission of the fiction of a material tomb may here imply not only the general superiority of poetry to physical monuments but also his more personal sense that what he as a poet-father has given, and made of, his son far surpasses what his stepfather gave to, and would have made of, him.

Jonson does not end his poem, however, with the epitaphic proclamation of his "best piece of *poetrie*." Like the final line of "On My First Daughter," in which the poet seems to confront the verbal monument he has made, the conclusion of "On My First Sonne" registers the poet's partial separation from the tomb of paper that he has just constructed. The final couplet—"For whose sake, hence-forth all his vowes be such, / As what he loves may never like too much" (ll. 11–12)—subverts the distinctions between epitaph and elegy by mixing epitaphic impersonality and elegiac temporality. While in the first two lines of the epitaph Jonson uses the mediation of the text to escape time as the "maker" of a mortal child who has become an immortal poem, in the last two lines of the poem he uses the externalized text to reflect back upon himself as a man who must finally return to lived time: the "here" of the poet's epitaphic pride yields to the "hence-forth" of the father's elegiac resolution. The continuing description of the father-poet in the third person emphasizes that the poet has only begun the difficult task of detaching himself from the proud impersonality of the epitaph and opening himself to the future.

The last line echoes the concluding line of an epigram in which Martial consoles a friend for the loss of a beloved slave: "may you wish that what you love has not pleased you excessively."[66] The final line is the nearest the poem comes to a simple quotation of another text, and Jonson's use of so close an echo at the end of so original a poem further suggests the difficulty of his truly making these words, and the resolve that they express, his own. The Martial allusion clarifies the poet's wish that the things he loves, including the things he has himself created, not please him excessively. Jonson's use of "like" in the sense of "please," however, underscores how difficult it will be for him to attain his wish. The reader's trouble comprehending the distinction between the normally synonymous words "loves" and "like" is the interpretive analogue to the father-poet's difficulty in actually living, outside the poem, this distinction. The poem thus ends not with the space of "peace" created by a verbal monument but with a problematic future.

Guilds: Studies in their Progress and Decline (New York: Columbia University Press, 1927), 12–14, 79–83, and passim.

[66] "Quidquid ames, cupias non placuisse nimis" (Martial, *Epigrams* 6.29.8).

The elegy with final epitaph traditionally provides strong aesthetic closure as a compensatory substitute for the brute ending of death. Jonson counters the loss of his son and his own failure as a father by giving his son a poetic burial and a verbal monument that answers death with a brief but enduring "piece / peace" of poetry. Yet just as he refuses to give the epitaph its traditional formal independence from the preceding elegy in order to emphasize that the poetic monument arises as a fictive defense against unbearable elegiac feelings of sorrow, so he refuses to end with the aesthetic closure of the public monument. He concludes, instead, with a couplet of uncertain generic status that suggests he cannot permanently rest in his poetic fictions but must confront, anew, time and loss. Thus the consolatory aesthetic closure of the traditional form gives way to a more complex sense of the relationship between poetic conclusions and continuing life. Jonson's second son, Joseph, probably died of plague shortly after the first. We do not know how Jonson responded to the death of this child or to that of his third and last legitimate son, his final chance for an heir, who was born some four years and died some eight years after Jonson's first son. We only know that the poet-father, filled no doubt both with memories and renewed hope, followed a traditional practice in naming this son, too, Benjamin.[67]

[67] On Jonson's second and third sons, see Riggs, 97, 145, 180.

PART 2

CONFLICT AND COMMEMORATION
IN THE SEVENTEENTH-
CENTURY EPITAPH

Chapter 4

Reconceiving the Dead:
Donne and Carew on Donne

John Donne's preoccupation with death—death in general, the deaths of others, and his own death—expressed itself in sonnets, hymns, elegies, the generically unique *Anniversaries*, devotions, funeral sermons, and, occasionally, epitaphs.[1] The epitaph was not an especially favored genre: compared to Jonson and many of the Sons of Ben, Donne composed few epitaphs, and most reveal little of his genius. Donne's verse "Epitaph on Himselfe" is, however, a major though neglected poem with important ramifications for Donne's treatment of death throughout his writings.[2]

[1] For my understanding of Donne's treatment of death and the dead in various phases of his career, I owe general debts to John Carey, *John Donne: Life, Mind and Art* (New York: Oxford University Press, 1981), 198–230 and passim; Barbara K. Lewalski, *Donne's Anniversaries and the Poetry of Praise: The Creation of a Symbolic Mode* (Princeton: Princeton University Press, 1973); and Arnold Stein, *The House of Death: Messages from the English Renaissance* (Baltimore: Johns Hopkins University Press, 1986), 49–66, 94–110, and passim. I cite Donne's poems from the following editions: *The Divine Poems*, ed. Helen Gardner, 2d ed. (Oxford: Clarendon, 1978); *The Elegies and The Songs and Sonnets*, ed. Helen Gardner (Oxford: Clarendon, 1965); *The Epithalamions, Anniversaries, and Epicedes*, ed. W. Milgate (Oxford: Clarendon, 1978); and *The Satires, Epigrams, and Verse Letters*, ed. W. Milgate (Oxford: Clarendon, 1967).

[2] In addition to the epitaph with which I will be concerned, Donne composed some early verse epitaphs on mythological figures and prose inscriptions for the monuments of his wife Ann, Sir Robert Drury, Elizabeth Drury, and finally for his own. One of the early verse epitaphs, "Hero and Leander," is a minor masterpiece of expressive brevity (Donne, *Satires*, 50); see Barbara Herrnstein Smith, *Poetic Closure: A Study of How Poems End* (Chicago: University of Chicago Press, 1968), 204–206. The prose inscriptions are interesting compositions that shed light upon Donne's other works, his personal relationships, and his sense of his own career. Neither the early verse epitaphs nor the prose inscriptions are,

Though he adapts Catholic prayers for the dead in his epitaphs on his son and daughter, Jonson's most influential epitaphs forge an ethical relationship between the dead and the living, preserving examples of virtue and vice for imitation, admiration, avoidance, or execration. Such epitaphs were acceptable to Protestants, who envisaged no other relationship possible between the living and the dead, and most seventeenth-century English poets continued Jonson's ethical focus. In his epitaph upon himself, Donne, by contrast, depicts an intense spiritual reciprocity between the living and the dead well outside the mainstream of both English poetic tradition and Protestant theology. By its very lack of influence, Donne's epitaph sheds light on the imaginative bounds of the English epitaphic tradition: the poem attracted no imitators because it was too daring an expression of a highly personal poetic and theological vision.[3]

Probably written sometime between 1608 and 1612, Donne's "Epitaph on Himselfe. *To the Countesse of Bedford*," has resemblances of theme and tone to both his secular poems and his sacred writings. My reading of the poem will therefore branch out to include many other Donne compositions, both secular and sacred.[4] The poem consists of two parts, an introductory address to the countess of Bedford and the epitaph proper, addressed to all ("Omnibus"). Here is the actual epitaph:

Omnibus
My Fortune and my choice this custome break,
When we are speechlesse grown, to make stones speak,
Though no stone tell thee what I was, yet thou
In my graves inside see what thou art now:
Yet thou'art not yet so good, till us death lay
To ripe and mellow here, we'are stubborne Clay.
Parents make us earth, and soules dignifie
Us to be glasse; here to grow gold we lie.
Whilst in our soules sinne bred and pamper'd is,
Our soules become wormeaten carkases;
So we our selves miraculously destroy.
Here bodies with lesse miracle enjoy
Such priviledges, enabled here to scale
Heaven, when the Trumpets ayre shall them exhale.

---

however, representative of his major achievements. Furthermore, unlike the *Anniversaries*, whose panegyric hyperboles greatly influence late seventeenth-century epitaphs, these works have little impact upon the epitaph tradition.

[3] I strongly agree with Lewalski's claim that in his funerary poetry Donne "was engaged in working out a personal, often original, theological synthesis" (Lewalski, 132).

[4] Despite the great variety of Donne's writings—their vast differences in occasion, purpose, and tone—and the important distinctions between the poet and preacher, I assume that there are profound connections in thought and feeling among his works. For a persuasive argument for the unity of Donne's oeuvre, see Carey, 10 and passim.

Heare this, and mend thy selfe, and thou mendst me,
By making me being dead, doe good to thee,
And thinke me well compos'd, that I could now
A last-sick houre to syllables allow.[5]

The epitaph makes two central, interwoven claims and two final requests. The "I" of the poem, the speaking corpse of the poet imagined within his grave, claims that his state is in fact that of the living reader, "what thou art now" (l. 4), because the sinful souls of the living are themselves becoming "wormeaten carkases" (l. 10). He qualifies this claim with another, however, for he argues that the reader as a living "corpse" is in fact "not yet so good" (l. 5) as the buried one, since only in death do corpses begin the process of transformation that will culminate in the resurrection of the body at the Last Judgment. He finally asks the reader to reform in order to "mend" (l. 15) the deceased by allowing him to do good to the reader, and, in a coda, asks the reader to think well of the dying man who has "now" (l. 17), it is revealed, just composed the poem. The initial claim expounds, possibly for the first but certainly not for the last time in the English epitaphic tradition, a central theme of contemporaneous English Protestant thought about death. The second claim in idiosyncratic fashion treats death as a dynamic process rather than a state. The final request that the reader mend himself or herself in order to mend the deceased is wholly unique among English epitaphs and reveals Donne's interest in adapting Catholic modes of thought in order to radically reconceive the bonds between the living and the dead. The coda, finally, underlines the fictionality of the speaking corpse in order to emphasize the reader's necessary participation in thus reimagining the relationship of the living and the dead.

The opening couplet announces the iconoclastic novelty of Donne's stance. Out of supposed penury and, more importantly, personal inclination, the speaker pointedly rejects a tombstone and its inscription, which he treats as fraudulent attempts to cover up the scandal of death by making "stones speak" when dead men are themselves "speechlesse" (l. 2). The topos of the speaking stone is ancient: classical epitaphs often have the tombstone relate in the first person who is buried under it, suggesting a compensatory movement whereby memorializing ob-

---

[5] I here extract the epitaph from the composite text of the address to Bedford and epitaph presented by Milgate in Donne, *Satires*, 103. Manuscripts give various titles to both the poem as a whole and to the sections; they also separate the introductory epistle and epitaph. The 1635 edition of Donne's work, in which the poem was first printed, has two versions, one containing the epistle and the first ten lines of the epitaph, the other the epitaph as a whole; see Milgate's note in Donne, *Satires*, 271–272. Though I will explore the significance of the opening epistle at the end, since I am mainly interested in the epitaph itself, the possibility that the epitaph proper was at some stage a separate poem does not affect the major thrust of my analysis.

jects proclaim for posterity the identities of the silent dead.[6] Early seventeenth-century English epitaphs adapt the motif for hyperbolic praise. They treat the tombstone's ability to speak as a miracle proving the greatness of the wonder-working deceased, as in the following examples: "One greater than Orpheus lies beneath me. / He does more than makes stones move, he makes them speak"; "Do you marvel how stones have learned to speak, o traveler? / A heavenly trust is buried in this tomb."[7] In his epitaph Donne baldly rejects the artificiality of such "miracles" as foolish attempts to mystify death. In so doing he underlines the artificiality of his own voice from the dead, which can no more speak from a piece of paper than can a stone. The major effect of this opening couplet is thus to unsettle the reader, alerting him that his conventional expectations will not be fulfilled.[8]

Indeed they are not. Donne rejects the panegyric speaking stone in order to present himself as a speaking corpse. He rejects the central purpose of commemorative epitaphs—he does not identify himself by name or by any of the traits he had in life—but instead proclaims what he is in death, a corpse awaiting the Resurrection. The brusque substitute of present condition for past identity is reminiscent of the medieval

---

[6] For Greek examples that were translated into Latin or the continental vernacular languages by the seventeenth century, see The Greek Anthology 7. 272, 521, 591; and for discussion and examples of "speaking objects" in Greek inscriptions, see Mario Burzachechi, "Oggetti parlanti nelle epigrafi greche," Epigraphica: Rivista Italiana Di Epigrafia 24 (1962):3–54; and A. E. Raubitschek's paper, "Das Denkmal-Epigramm," and the ensuing remarks in Fondation Hardt pour l'étude de l'antiquité classique, L'épigramme grecque (Geneva: Vandoeuvres, 1968), 1–36.

[7] "Sub me iacet orphea vincens. / Iste facit plusquam, saxa movere, loqui" (epitaph upon Dean Eedes, d. 1604, in Thomas F. Ravenshaw, ed., Antiente Epitaphes (from A.D. 1250 to A.D. 1800) [London, 1878], 46); "Miraris qui saxa loqui didicere, Viator? / Coeli depositum conditur hoc tumulo" (Henry, Prince of Wales, d. 1612, in Cambridge University, Epicedium Cantabrigiense In obitum...Henrici...Principis Walliae [Cambridge, 1612], 13). For other examples of this panegyric topos, see the epitaphs upon Sir John Newdigate, d. 1610, in Harefield Parish Church; Edward Fitton, d. 1617, in Gawsworth Parish Church; and Dorothy Pooley, d. 1625, in John Le Neve, ed., Monumenta Anglicana: Being Inscriptions on the Monuments of several Eminent Persons... 1600–1715, 5 vols. (London, 1718–1719), 4:102.

[8] In later works Donne uses the topos of the speaking stone with a restraint far closer to Greek treatments than to seventeenth-century English panegyrics. Avoiding the miracle motif, he emphasizes that it is really the mourning survivors who make stones speak, to console themselves. In his epitaph upon his wife, who died in 1617, Donne bids the stone express what his overwhelming sorrow cannot: "at which he himself, speechless when confronted with the sorrow, commanded this stone tablet to speak" ("Quod hoc saxum fari iussit / Ipse, prae dolore Infans"; Epithalamions, 78, 215). In the "Third Meditation" of his Devotions, he imagines communicating as a dead man through the stones but notes that his "friends" will actually make the stone speak: "In the Grave I may speak thorough the stones, in the voice of my friends, and in the accents of those wordes, which their love may afford my memory"; see Donne, Devotions upon Emergent Occasions, ed. Anthony Raspa (1975; rpt., New York: Oxford University Press, 1987), 15. Like Jonson in his epitaph on his son, Donne thus emphasizes that the dead "speak" only through the graces of the living. His "Epitaph on Himselfe" reveals this truth, I shall argue, in another way.

memento mori warning from the grave.[9] Donne dramatically changes, however, a usual feature of the warning: he declares that his grave shows not what the living reader *will* be but rather what the reader is *now*.

While Jonson rejects the memento mori of medieval tradition in order to assert the individual's earthly immortality, Donne provides a novel but still religious variation of the memento mori in order to bring back some of the shock value to a formula that was losing its force. Donne's new formulation is more than a rhetorical innovation, however, for the assertion of the present identity of the living and the dead expresses a central religious concern of the period, the spiritual death of the living. While sermons and meditations on physical death continue throughout the sixteenth and seventeenth century, there is also increasing emphasis among English Protestant preachers upon the living's present state of sin as a death from which they can be reborn only through God's grace.[10] In Richard Sibbes's sermon "The Dead-Man, or, the State of Every Man by Nature," for example, the sinful are compared to "open sepulchres."[11] The epitaph's claim that life itself is a kind of suicide in which "we ourselves miraculously destroy" (l. 11) resembles views Donne expounds throughout his career, as poet and as preacher, in jest and seriousness. As a young wit Donne defends the paradox "that all things kill themselves," while in a famous passage from his final sermon as the dean of Saint Paul's Cathedral he compares the world to "an universall church-yard," our lives to "a week of deaths."[12] In his *Devotions upon Emergent Occasions* (1624), Donne asserts that another's death reminds him not only that he must die but also that he is, already, dead. In the eighteenth meditation he cries out: "I *am dead*, I was *borne dead*, and from the first laying of these *mud-walls* in my *conception*, they have *moldred* away, and the whole course of *life* is but an *active death*."[13]

It is instructive to compare Donne's equation of the living and the dead in his epitaph upon himself to the argument of Francis Quarles's poetic meditation, "On a Monument" (1632):

[9] Donne's refusal to tell "what" he was, rather than "who" he was, suggests that the speaker has indeed taken a position beyond that of mortal man and comprehends even his own past nature from a transcendent point of view. See Hannah Arendt's discussion of the crucial difference for Augustine between the questions "Who am I?" (asked by man of himself) and "What am I?" (asked by man of God) in *The Human Condition* (Chicago: University of Chicago Press, 1958), 10–11.

[10] See Barbara K. Lewalski's discussion of the Protestant metaphor of sin as death in *Protestant Poetics and the Seventeenth-Century Religious Lyric* (Princeton: Princeton University Press, 1979), 88–89.

[11] Cited in Lewalski, *Protestant Poetics*, 88.

[12] John Donne, *Paradoxes and Problems*, ed. Helen Peters (Oxford: Clarendon, 1980), 1–2; *The Sermons of John Donne*, 10 vols., ed. Evelyn M. Simpson and George R. Potter (Berkeley: University of California Press, 1953–1962), 10: 234. All citations of Donne's sermons will be from this edition.

[13] Donne, *Devotions*, 96.

Seest thou that *Monument?* Do'st see how Art
Does polish Nature to adorne each part
Of that rare Worke, whose glorious Fabricke may
Commend her beauty to an after-day?
Isn't not a dainty Peece? And apt to raise
A rare advantage to the Maker's praise?
But knowest thou what this dainty Peece encloses?
Beneath this glorious *Marble* there reposes
A noysome putrid *Carkas*, halfe devour'd
By crawling *Caniballs*; disguiz'd, deflour'd
With loath'd Corruption, whose consuming sent
Would poyson Thoughts, although it have no vent:
Ev'n such a *Peece* art thou, who ere thou be
That readst these Lines: This *Monument* is *Thee*:
Thy Body is a Fabricke, wherein Nature
And Art conspire to heighthen up a Creature
To summe Perfection, being a living Story
And rare *Abridgement* of his Maker's Glory;
But full of lothsome *filth*, and nasty *mire*
Of lust, uncurb'd Affections, base desire;
Curious without, but most corrupt within;
A glorious *Monument* of inglorious *Sin*.[14]

Like the opening of Donne's epitaph, Quarles's "Ev'n such a *Peece* art thou.../ This *Monument* is *Thee*" (ll. 13–14) transforms the medieval memento mori formula into a seventeenth-century Protestant message by asserting the present identity of the living reader, filled with sin, to a rotting corpse. All "dead" sinners are like the hypocritical Pharisees of the Gospels, "whited sepulchres, which indeed appear beautiful outward, but are within full of dead men's bones, and of all uncleaness" (Matthew 23:27). There is, however, a revealing difference between Donne's and Quarles's identification of the living with the dead. The surprise of the Quarles poem depends upon erecting and then destroying a presumed distinction between the self and an object "out there": "that Monument" (l. 1) becomes "this Monument" and, finally, "Thee" (l. 14). The surprise is diminished, however, by the poem's highly methodical, standard procedure, which has numerous parallels in contemporary sermons, meditations, and religious poetry: twelve lines propose an object for study, while ten make the "application" to the believer.[15]

[14] Francis Quarles, "III. 40. *On a Monument*," in *Divine Fancies: Digested into Epigrammes, Meditations, and Observations* (1632), reprinted in his *Complete Works in Prose and Verse*, ed. Alexander B. Grosart, 3 vols. (London, 1880–1881), 3:246.

[15] On the importance of the personal "application" in Protestant sermons and meditations, see Lewalksi, *Donne*, 85–86; on its typological basis, see Lewalski, *Protestant Poetics*, 131–140. The poem's division into balanced sections increases this sense of control: six lines conjure up the visual image of the grand tomb that the reader is asked to "see," six

Donne's composition, by contrast, is truly surprising. In the very first four lines Donne asserts the identification that Quarles treats as his didactic goal. Beginning rather than ending with an identification of the living and the dead, Donne asserts the unsettling proposition of identity only to unsettle that proposition as well.

According to Donne, the living are in fact "not yet so good" as the corpse in the grave: though without the worldly fortune to buy a useless tombstone, the speaking corpse reveals that it is itself further along the process that turns "wormeaten carkases" into a spiritual fortune, "gold" (l. 8). Even as the speaker details the processes "we" mortals all experience, the oft-repeated "here" of a grave belonging to the "I" alone emphasizes the gap between the dead and the living. This simultaneous identification of, and distinction between, the living and dead is an idiosyncratic but characteristic feature of Donne's poetics of death. Written during the same period as the epitaph upon himself, Donne's epitaph upon Elizabeth Drury, who died in 1610, begins with a similar double message: "Thou knowest not, wayfarer, whither thou goest. Thou hast come to the Cadiz of all men, even to thine own. Thou liest here thyself [*ipse*], if thou art virtuous [*si probus es*]; for indeed here lies Virtue herself [*ipsa . . . Probitas*], Elizabeth."[16] Donne here recalls epitaphs that inform the passerby that wherever he or she is going now, his or her final destination is the grave. A Roman inscription begins, "Oh, tired wayfarer, you who pass by me, / although you wander for a long time, nevertheless you must come to this."[17] Crashaw begins an epitaph for a fellow Cambridge student, William Herrys: "Stop for a while, wayfarer, where you will have to remain for a long time; of course you know that hither you are hastening wherever you hasten."[18] As in his epitaph upon himself, Donne radicalizes a traditional epitaphic warning by asserting the present rather than future death of the reader: Donne's virtuous traveler already lies in the grave, since Elizabeth Drury, "Virtue herself,"

lines invoke the inner reality that the reader is made to "know," and after two lines proposing the application to the self, four describe the outer man, four the inner.

[16] "Quo pergas, viator, non habes. / Ad Gades omnium venisti, etiam et ad tuas: / hic iaces, si probus es, ipse; / ipsa etenim hic iacet probitas, / Elizabetha . . ." (Donne, *Epithalamions*, 76, 212). Milgate presents convincing arguments for Donne's authorship of this epitaph in Donne, *Epithalamions*, 211–212.

[17] "Heus tu, viator lasse, qu[i] me praetereis, / cum diu ambulareis, tamen hoc veniundum est tibi"; this is one of several such inscriptions cited in Richmond Lattimore, *Themes in Greek and Latin Epitaphs* (Urbana: University of Illinois Press, 1962), 257.

[18] "Siste te paulum (viator) ubi Longum Sisti / Necesse erit, huc nempe properare te scias / quocunque properas" (Richard Crashaw, "*Epitaphium in Dominum* Herrisium," in *The Complete Poetry of Richard Crashaw*, ed. and trans. George Walton Williams [1970; rpt., New York: Norton, 1974], 572–573). Herrys died in 1631 (Crashaw, 466). Compare the opening of Thomas Bancroft's "*An Epitaph on Mistresse* Anne Roberts of Naylston"—"Stay, Passenger, and see thy journies end"—in his *Two bookes of Epigrammes and Epitaphes* (London, 1639), B4v.

lies dead. Yet though the buried Drury is an ideal in which the wayfarer participates (in the Platonic sense) insofar as he is virtuous, he and she are by no means the same. In the very act of asserting the reader's death, Donne suggests the difference between the reader and the actual deceased: the "probus" wayfarer is masculine, Elizabeth, or "Probitas," is feminine, and the juxtaposition of "ipse / ipsa" emphasizes the gap between the living and the dead. The virtuous male wayfarer is in fact challenged to discover just how the death of the sixteen-year old virgin whom the inscription goes on to describe relates to his own. Donne's epitaph upon himself similarly challenges its reader.

Donne gives different answers at different times to how another's death both is and is not one's own. (The *Anniversaries* broaden the problem to that of how one girl's death both is and is not the world's). In the epitaph upon himself, Donne's sense of the inseparably joined living and dead issues in a sense of their mutual responsibilities: "Heare this, and mend thy selfe, and thou mendst me, / By making me being dead, doe good to thee" (ll. 15–16). The chiastic interplay of "thee," "thy selfe," and "me" conveys the intertwining of the fates of the living and the dead. Charitably revealing to the living reader what that reader now is and soon must be, the deceased requests that the reader mend himself and thereby mend the deceased. But how can the behavior of the living affect the dead? Donne's alchemical description of the corpse "grow[ing] gold" in the grave and his subsequent claim that the corpse in the grave is "enabled . . . to scale / Heaven" (ll. 13–14) transforms the state of death into a process of spiritual purification. Donne the preacher would later describe death in more traditional theological terms as the moment at which the soul goes to heaven and the body begins the humiliating disintegration it suffers until the Resurrection.[19] In poems close in date to the epitaph, however, Donne adapts alchemical images like those in the epitaph in order to present an unusual vision of the corpse's undergoing a process of purification as it awaits the Last Judgment.[20] Donne's epitaph upon himself is more daring than any of his other poems from the period, for the epitaph uses this notion of a spiritual process between individual death and the Last Judgment in order to suggest that the living can help the dead progress spiritually. The reader who reforms

---

[19] See, for example, Donne, *Sermons*, 10:238–239.

[20] See the sonnet "Resurrection," ll. 9–11, written circa 1609, and "Elegie on the Lady Marckham," ll. 20–28, which commemorates a woman who died in 1609 (*Divine Poems*, 4; *Epithalamions*, 57–58); and for discussion of these and related Donne passages, see Edgar Hill Duncan, "Donne's Alchemical Figures," *ELH* 9 (1942):277–280. Kathleen Cohen's discussion of medieval alchemical treatments of the corpse's putrefaction as part of the process of spiritual regeneration provides useful background; see *Metamorphosis of a Death Symbol: The Transi Tomb in the Late Middle Ages and the Renaissance* (Berkeley: University of California Press, 1973), 96–112.

upon reading Donne's poem both begins the process of improvement for him- or herself and, by allowing the deceased a virtuous act of edification, quickens that process for the deceased. The reader thereby, in effect, hastens on the general Resurrection, when the bodies of all the virtuous shall be made "gold."

The epitaph expresses a belief rejected by mainstream Protestantism but held by Donne throughout his life, that the behavior of the living could affect the dead for good and ill. In *Biathanatos*, written circa 1608 and thus during the same period as the epitaph, Donne claimed that those who were scandalized by suicide committed the sin of uncharitableness, and by so sinning they caused greater posthumous punishment to be inflicted upon the suicide who had led them to sin. Donne generalized: "For certaynly God often punisheth a Sinner, much more severely because others have taken occasion of sinning by his fact. If therefore we did correct in our selfs this easinesse of being scandaliz'd, how much easier, and lighter might we make the punishment of many transgressors? For God, in his judgement hath allmost made us his assistants, and councellors, how farre he shall punish; and our interpretation of anothers Sinne doth often give the measure to Gods Justice or Mercy."[21] As a minister of the established church, Donne continued to expound such unorthodox belief. In a funerary sermon probably of 1624, Donne justified the provisions of the deceased for an annual commemorative sermon in his honor with a description of the blessings or torments that the living could bestow upon the dead through virtuous or vicious action:

His intention was not so much to be yearly remembred himself, as that his posterity, and his neighbours might be yearly remembred to doe as he had done. For, this is truly to glorifie God in his Saints, to sanctifie our selves in their examples; To celebrate them, is to imitate them. For, as it is probably conceived, and agreeably to Gods Justice, that they that write wanton books, or make wanton pictures, have additions of torment, as often as other men are corrupted with their books, or their pictures: so may they, who have left permanent examples of good works, well be beleeved, to receive additions of glory and joy, when others are led by that to do the like: And so...they who dwelt about him, may assist their own happiness, and enlarge his, by following his good example in good proportions.[22]

Just as in the epitaph Donne imagines himself being "mended" by the good behavior of the living whom he has edified, so in *Biathanatos* and

---

[21] John Donne, *Biathanatos*, ed. Ernest W. Sullivan II (Newark: University of Delaware Press, 1984), 32–33.

[22] Donne, *Sermons*, 10:190–191.

the funerary sermon he imagines the dead being rewarded or punished for the actions of the living whom they have corrupted or inspired.[23]

While expressing a unique personal vision, Donne's epitaph is reminiscent of medieval Catholic epitaphs, not in specific doctrinal content but in its sense that the living and the dead are bound to mutual spiritual improvement. In some medieval memento mori epitaphs, the charitable edification of the living is to be reciprocated by the charitable prayers of the living for the dead, as these two examples reveal:

> Ho that wil sadly beholde me with hys ie,
> May see hys owyn merowr and learne for to die.
> . . . . .
> Wherfor ye pepil inweye of charitie
> With yor good prayeris I prey yu help me.
> For lych as I am right so shall ye all be....
>
> Remembyr your-selfe well duryng tyme & space:
> I was as ye are nowe; and as I, ye shalbe.
> Wherfor I beseche you of your benygnite,
> ffor the love of Jhesu & hys Mothyr Mare,
> ffor my sowle to say A pater noster & An Ave.[24]

While in such medieval epitaphs the prayer is the living reader's charitable response to the edification he has received from the dead, in Donne's poem the edification is itself the charitable response. In the medieval inscriptions the dead wish to gain release from purgatory; in Donne's epitaph the deceased wishes to attain the Resurrection. Despite these crucial theological differences, however, Donne is here closer in spirit to these medieval epitaphs than to anything written by his English contemporaries or successors.[25]

---

[23] In the generation after Donne, Jeremy Taylor similarly deviates from mainstream Protestantism in suggesting that the virtuous actions of the living may help the dead. Discussing the duties that the living owe the dead in *Holy Dying* (1651), Taylor argues that for the living to "do all those parts of personall duty which our dead left unperformed, and to which the lawes do not oblige us, is an act of great charity, and perfect kindnesse: *and it may redound to the advantage of our friends also, that their debts be paid even beyond the Inventory of their moveables*"; see *Holy Living and Dying*, ed. P. G. Stanwood, 2 vols. (Oxford: Clarendon, 1989), 2:233 (emphasis mine). Taylor is, however, less assured and specific than Donne concerning the living's effects upon the dead.

[24] Epitaph on John Baret, d. 1467, cited in Pamela M. King, "Eight English *Memento Mori* Verses from Cadaver Tombs," *Notes and Queries* 226, n.s. 28 (1981): 495 (orthography modernized in places); "A Tombstone Inscription" in Rossell Hope Robbins, ed., *Secular Lyrics of the XIVth and XVth Centuries* (Oxford: Clarendon, 1952), 119. King provides several other examples of a memento mori followed by requests for prayer (495–496).

[25] Donne the minister preached against both purgatory and prayers for the dead; in a sermon of 1626 he advanced the typically Protestant argument that the living should pray not for the dead but for their own souls, "dead in their sins" (*Sermons*, 7:188). In the period immediately preceding his ordination in 1615, however, Donne's belief that the living

It is fitting that Donne, the voracious reader of theology, the ex-Catholic convert to the Church of England who strove for a vision of the "true church," should write an epitaph that simultaneously announces a theme central to contemporary English Protestantism and hearkens back to Catholic ways of thought. Although critics have interpreted Donne's relationship to his Catholic origins in radically different ways, it is undeniable that he retained some aspects of his Catholic past throughout his life.[26] One may instructively contrast the epitaph with the treatment of Catholic doctrine concerning the dead in the *Songs and Sonnets*. In such poems as "The Canonization," "The Funerall," and "The Relique," Donne at once mocks and exploits the cult of saints in his fantasy concerning his and his beloved's power over future generations, who will idolize them with "mis-devotion" ("The Relique," l. 13).[27] The epitaph incorporates Catholic sentiments in a more subdued and less ambivalent fashion by imagining a relationship between the dead and the living that does not depend upon Catholic "idolatry" but nevertheless sustains a link between the living and dead not envisaged in mainstream Protestantism.

The poem's picture of edifying reciprocity indeed moralizes Donne's long-standing desire to assert his continuing influence over the living.

---

could help the dead led to his advocating prayers for the deceased that focused, like the epitaph, on the Resurrection. In *Essays in Divinity*, probably completed in 1614, he claims that "discreet" prayers to "hasten" the Last Judgment may "benefit" the dead suffering the "solitude of the grave"; see John Donne, *Essays in Divinity*, ed. Evelyn M. Simpson (Oxford: Clarendon, 1952), 76. Donne is probably recalling the prayer in the Church of England's burial service that God "haste" his "kingdom"; see *The Book of Common Prayer, 1559: The Elizabethan Prayer Book*, ed. John E. Booty (Charlottesville: Folger Shakespeare Library and University Press of Virginia, 1976), 313. The Puritan *Admonition to the Parliament* of 1572 had attacked this section of the English burial rite as a "popish" prayer for the dead, while defenders of the established liturgy such as John Whitgift had vehemently asserted that the prayer was for the living rather than for the deceased; see *The Works of John Whitgift*, ed. John Ayre, 3 vols. (Cambridge: Cambridge University Press, 1851–1853), 3:364–365. While not espousing the doctrine of purgatory, Donne embraces a "popish" belief in the efficacy of prayers for the dead condemned by Protestant attackers and defenders of the English church alike. *Essays in Divinity* is thus even closer to Catholic attitudes toward the dead than the poetic epitaph.

[26] Carey argues that a sense of apostasy is the crucial element in Donne's anxiety-ridden psychological and poetic makeup (15–59 and passim). Dennis Flynn analyzes Donne's Catholic sympathies in his middle years and his feelings of being a "survivor" of the persecution of Catholics in "Donne's Catholicism I," *Recusant History* 13 (1975):1–17; "Donne's Catholicism II," *Recusant History* 13 (1976):178–195; and "Donne the Survivor," in *The Eagle and the Dove: Reassessing John Donne*, ed. Claude J. Summers and Ted-Larry Pebworth (Columbia: University of Missouri Press, 1986), 15–24. Richard Strier argues that Donne's early Catholicism made him unable fully to feel and express the Protestant conception of salvation by grace alone in his *Holy Sonnets*; see "John Donne Awry and Squint: The 'Holy Sonnets,' 1608–1610," *MP* 86 (1989):357–384. I differ from these critics in exploring Donne's emotionally positive, psychologically liberating use of his Catholic inheritance.

[27] Donne, *Elegies*, 89.

John Carey argues that in his secular lyrics Donne, dreading the thought that after his death life will go on as before and he will be forgotten, constantly imagines death precisely so that he can imagine overcoming it. Carey notes that the "dead" Donne of the love lyrics is unusually "active and influential."[28] In the epitaph, however, Donne morally redeems such fear and his compensatory assertions of posthumous influence: the epitaphic poet seeks to overcome, as Donne the preacher would later try to do, the fear that death will cause the loss of his specifically *edifying* influence. Mixing his own voice with that of David the psalmist, Donne in one sermon presents death as the loss of the preacher's ability to help his flock: "Howsoever I shall enjoy God my selfe [when I am dead], yet I shall be no longer a meanes, an instrument of the propagation of Gods truth amongst others; And, till we come to that joy, which the heart cannot conceive, it is, I thinke, the greatest joy that the soule of man is capable of in this life, (especially where a man hath been any occasion of sinne to others) to assist the salvation of others."[29] This sermon weighs the seemingly incompatible joys of union with God in death and helping his fellow men in life. The epitaphic poet tries, however, to avoid choosing between these two joys by imagining his purification as an opportunity for the edification of others.

While the first sixteen lines of Donne's epitaph seem to be the message of a speaking corpse, the concluding couplet provides the final twist of this very sinuous poem by returning us to the dying man who, in the final fiction of the poem, has actually just composed the epitaph. The "now" of the speaking corpse abruptly gives way to the "now" of a dying writer. Though one might treat the final couplet as a regrettable retreat from the daring of the preceding lines, I think it enriches the poem as a whole. While the epitaph thus far has reminded the reader that he or she is in a sense dead like the corpse in the grave, the coda reminds the reader that the epitaph was itself actually and necessarily written by a still living man. In the *Devotions* Donne claims that "a sicke bed, is a grave; and all that the patient saies there, is but a varying of his owne *Epitaph*."[30] The epitaph, as its final couplet reveals, has literalized such a claim. The final couplet not only looks forward to a future death, however, but also records a "now" that has already past. Indeed, insofar as the epitaph marked "Omnibus" is addressed to posterity, the final "now" of the dying man is no more and no less imaginary than the "now" of the speaking corpse. Donne thus underscores the evanescence of all "nows" recorded in poetry. He thereby suggests the reader's necessary imaginative role in "hearing" the dying man preparing his final speech

---

[28] Carey, 201; the argument is set forth on pp. 198–204.
[29] Donne, *Sermons*, 5:384.
[30] Donne, *Devotions*, 15.

for an otherwise speechless corpse. Only if the reader will truly "heare this" (l. 15) can the living-but-dead reader mend him- or herself and, in turn, mend the dead-but-living Donne.

The opening epistle, to which I now turn, further complicates the relationship between the author and his audience by focusing upon one specific reader, Donne's patroness:

> Madame,
> That I might make your Cabinet my tombe,
> And for my fame, which I love next my soule,
> Next to my soule provide the happiest roome,
>   Admit to that place this last funerall Scrowle.
>   Others by Testaments give Legacies, but I
>   Dying, of you doe beg a Legacie.[31]

The poem's precise occasion is not known. Milgate suggests two possibilities: either Donne has "died" because he did something that earned the displeasure of his patroness, the countess of Bedford, or his poem is a valediction to the countess upon his departure for France with the Drury family in 1611, and the poet has thus "died," because parting from his "beloved" patroness is, by amatory convention, "death."[32] Whatever the precise occasion, the poem seems at its opening to be merely verse of social compliment to an important patroness. The poet asks that his poem be placed in her cabinet, because it is there that his soul, in the language of compliment, is also buried. Donne moves from the initial compliment, however, to a meditation on his own death independent of its supposed occasion. Much of the poem's wit indeed lies in its adopting a complimentary premise and then using it for a self-exploration that transcends that initial premise.

In this poem Donne uses the poetry of patronage for his own ends, converting flattery into didacticism, the dependent poet-client into the authoritative teacher. While some of his other verse letters reveal a violent oscillation between self-abasement and self-assertion in his relationship to his addressee, this poem's principle of charitable reciprocity seeks

---

[31] Donne, *Satires*, 103.

[32] Milgate's note in Donne, *Satires*, 272. The latter explanation is supported by Donne's "To the Countesse of Bedford; *Begun in France but never Perfected*," which begins "Though I be *dead*, and buried, yet I have / (Living in you,) Court enough in my grave" (Donne, *Satires*, 104). The poem mixes the conceit common in love poetry of absence from the beloved as death with the conceit common among Renaissance courtiers of absence from the court as death. The double conceit reveals the realities of patronage: Donne's "beloved" Lady Bedford was one of his possible avenues toward courtly advancement. Donne's verse epitaph is determined, I will argue, to transcend these social parameters. (For another example of absence from the court as death, see Donne's "Epithalamion at the Marriage of the Earl of Somerset," in which the poet presents himself as "dead, and buried" because far from court [l. 101; *Epithalamions*, 14].)

to transcend the social reality of the patron-client relationship. Donne begins the sinuous logic of the whole poem by purporting to "beg a Legacie" of Lady Bedford instead of giving one. Donne in fact here initiates a dizzying number of reversals. The dead normally leave legacies, but poet-clients normally beg them of patronesses, so that the "dead" man is in fact behaving decorously as a poet of patronage. The true irony is, however, that the legacy Donne begs is actually a charitable gift to Bedford—and to all his readers—so that the "dead" man has become a spiritual patron. Nevertheless, since Bedford, like all readers, receives a lesson in edification which in turn will aid Donne, she in fact will give him the legacy he begs for insofar as she responds properly to his poem. The serious playfulness of the poem's ideal of spiritual exchange thus breaks down the distinctions between giving and receiving upon which the patron-client relationship, conventionally defined, depends.[33]

Donne breaks down not only the distinction between giving and receiving but also the traditional distinctions among body, soul, and fame. He announces that the epitaph concerns his fame, an odd claim for a poem that refuses to identify the dead. This claim is in fact deliberately misleading, forcing the reader to rethink the status of fame. One may compare this claim to the final lines of the *First Anniversarie* (ll. 473–474), which similarly associate Donne's poetry with fame: "Verse hath a middle nature: heaven keepes soules, / The grave keeps bodies, verse the fame enroules."[34] Donne adapts the division common in sixteenth-century epitaphs of the deceased into the body in the grave, the soul in heaven, and fame on earth, associating poetry with the middle region of earthly fame. His association of poetry with a "middle nature" is, however, a strikingly inappropriate final summary of a poem obsessed

---

[33] On Donne's poetry of patronage, see Patricia Thomson's "Donne and the Poetry of Patronage: The Verse Letters," in *John Donne: Essays in Celebration*, ed. A. J. Smith (London: Methuen, 1972), 308–323, which emphasizes Donne's treatment of larger, religious topics in the midst of flattery; and Arthur F. Marotti's *John Donne, Coterie Poet* (Madison: University of Wisconsin Press, 1986), 202–231, which stresses Donne's uncomfortable role as subordinate and his consequent subversion of panegyric so that he is "competing with, rather than self-effacingly paying tribute to, his addressee" (p. 207). Though Marotti's account of Donne's relationship to his patroness Lady Bedford is often convincing and always provocative, his treatment of Donne's epitaph upon himself reveals the reductiveness of his approach. He argues that Donne's "poetic lecture . . . on the soul and the body . . . might really have been intended to disguise the fact that, in journeying with Drury, Donne was giving up hope that the Countess could be an avenue to courtly advancement and was looking elsewhere for patronage" (p. 229). The telltale "really" underscores that Marotti treats theological meditation, like all other "intellectual complexity" (p. 207), merely as a stratagem in the poet's struggles with patronage. In the epitaph Donne consciously moves from secular social relationships to a theological relationship in which he seeks to establish mutual charity as the connection between human beings. From a secular point of view this may be mystified, but it is not mere subterfuge.

[34] Donne, *Epithalamions*, 35.

with extremes, the departure of a now heavenly soul and the anatomy of an corpse. In the *First Anniversarie*, Donne emphasizes that Drury's fame cannot in fact be separated from her soul above and her body—and the body of the world!—below. In the epitaph, Donne's fame similarly resides not, as one would expect, in his earthly name but rather in his universal significance as a buried corpse aspiring and seeking help to be at one with its heavenly soul. Jonson blurs the distinctions among body, soul, and fame in his epitaph on his daughter, trying to hold on to the whole infant he loved and loves. Donne wholly subverts these distinctions in order to suggest that the goal of life and death is the wholeness to be attained at the Resurrection. His epitaph seeks the moment, in other words, when earthly fame will disappear. The ultimate irony of his poem is that its very idiosyncrasy makes the work a more accurate and memorable monument to his unique personality and intellect than could any mere proclamation of his name.

Poets generally exercised more imaginative freedom in pseudo-inscriptional epitaphs than in actual inscriptions, and Donne certainly did not intend this highly unorthodox poem as the inscription for his tomb. In the prose inscription he wrote for his monument some ten years later, a more conventional but also perhaps more honest composition, Donne subordinates rather than transforms his concern for personal fame. The epitaph inscribed on his monument in Saint Paul's Cathedral begins with his own name, but ends with another's: "he beholdeth Him Whose name is the Rising [or "the East"; *Oriens*]."[35] "Oriens," a striking and unusual appellation of Christ based on Zechariah 6:12,[36] embodies Donne's hope in the Resurrection through and in Christ. It also tempers his personal pride: while epitaphs normally play on the great meaning of the name of the deceased, here Donne, who elsewhere puns so well on "Donne," avoids such self-regard and instead consecrates the composition's only wordplay to God.

Helen Gardner has rightly questioned Isaac Walton's famous account of the dying, shrouded Donne standing on an urn posing for his funerary monument. She has plausibly argued that the dying Donne arranged that his shrouded face be painted, either in his last days or as he lay in state, and that this painting was subsequently used as a model, probably at his behest, for the frontispiece to his posthumously published final sermon, *Death's Duell*, and for Nicholas Stone's monument of Donne erected in Old Saint Paul's Cathedral in 1631 (Figure 3).[37] Donne's desire

[35] "Aspicit eum cuius Nomen est Oriens" (text and translation in Donne, *Epithalamions*, 80, 219).

[36] Milgate cites other passages in which Donne quotes Zechariah 6:12 and applies it to Christ (Donne, *Epithalamions*, 219).

[37] Helen Gardner, "Dean Donne's Monument in St. Paul's," in *Evidence in Literary Schol-*

Figure 3. Monument of John Donne, d. 1631, in Saint Paul's Cathedral. By permission of the Royal Commission on the Historical Monuments of England.

for a likeness of his face, either dying or dead, reveals once more a concern for personal fame: the face is the corporeal equivalent of the name, the wholly individual aspect of the self. Yet Donne also reveals his wish to maintain after death his edifying influence over the living: as an accurate record of Donne's features, the portrait expresses a desire for personal continuance, but as a shrouded, emaciated face it serves as a memento mori. Personal commemoration is ethically redeemed by its edifying purpose. The early seventeenth century witnessed the growing popularity of actual portraits as opposed to stock figures upon monuments.[38] Like the name-as-praise motif in epitaphs, the trend in funerary art reflects the humanist cult of personal achievement. While Donne's desire for a final portrait reveals his humanist concern for personal renown, the shroud, like the final name "Oriens" on his epitaph, tempers his desire for fame on earth with an acknowledgment of final things.

Both as poet and preacher Donne continually reimagined his legacy to posterity, but when he died his poetic contemporaries had to determine, for themselves, the precise nature of that bequest. In the greatest funerary tribute to Donne, "An Elegie upon the death of the Deane of Pauls, Dr. John Donne," Thomas Carew, a Jonsonian who yet like many other Sons of Ben felt the power of Donne's highly original verse, seeks not only to define Donne's achievement but also to relate it to his own. Indeed the poem implicitly asserts the author's necessary remaking of his great predecessor in order to make him serve Carew's own literary, cultural, and political needs and values.[39]

An elegy with concluding epitaph, Carew's poem reveals both Donne's and Jonson's influence: while the paradoxes, images, and metrics of the elegiac portion of the poem recall Donne's daring and original poetic mode, the poem's imitative poetics and traditional generic combination, as well as the style of the concluding epitaph, recall the humanist neo-classicism of Jonson. Adopting the long-standing composite form of elegy with final epitaph, Carew moves from a lengthy "I-thou" lament for the absent poet fictively set on the funeral day to a brief, impersonal, panegyric epitaph that places Donne in the tomb and describes his lasting

---

arship: Essays in Memory of James Marshall Osborn, ed. René Wellek and Alvaro Ribeiro (Oxford: Clarendon, 1979), 29–44.

[38] On the growing demand for portraits on monuments in the early seventeenth century, see Eric Mercer, English Art, 1553–1625 (Oxford: Oxford University Press, 1962), 238–241; and Lawrence Stone, The Family, Sex and Marriage in England, 1500–1800 (New York: Harper, 1977), 225–226.

[39] Though he does not discuss Carew's elegy, Lawrence Lipking's exploration of how elegists put poetic predecessors "to use" in a series of seventeenth- to nineteenth-century elegies on poets is relevant to my concerns here; see The Life of the Poet: Beginning and Ending Poetic Careers (Chicago: University of Chicago Press, 1981), 138–179.

achievement.[40] Carew uses the reversals inherent in the generic combination to enact a reversal in his relationship to Donne.[41] In the elegy itself, he simultaneously mourns and praises the deceased by denying that he can deliver an elegy measuring up to Donne's greatness:

> Can we not force from widdowed Poetry,
> Now thou art dead (Great DONNE) one Elegie
> To crowne thy Hearse?...
>
> (ll. 1–3)

> Oh, pardon mee, that break with untun'd verse
> The reverend silence that attends thy herse,
> Whose awfull solemne murmures were to thee
> More than these faint lines, A loud Elegie,
> That did proclaime in a dumbe eloquence
> The death of all the Arts....
>
> (ll. 71–76)

> I will not draw the envy to engrosse
> All thy perfections, or weepe all our losse;
> Those are too numerous for an Elegie,
> And this too great, to be express'd by mee.
>
> (ll. 87–90)

Like Carew's elegy, many other funerary tributes to Donne use the inexpressibility topos to praise the deceased.[42] In much of the elegy Carew's rugged meter, violent conceits, and paradoxes also clearly imitate, however, what Carew calls Donne's "masculine expression" (l. 35). Carew thus demonstrates his ability to praise Donne in a Donnean style even as he protests that he cannot adequately praise the deceased.[43] Yet because Carew stresses Donne's rejection of imitation in favor of "fresh

[40] I use the text in *The Poems of Thomas Carew*, ed. Rhodes Dunlap (Oxford: Clarendon, 1949), 71–74.

[41] Ada Long and Hugh Maclean argue that the poem is deliberately "indecorous (in the context of genre)" because it does not have the *consolatio* and exhortation that elegies should have according to Joseph Scaliger, as expounded by O. B. Hardison, Jr., and further contend that the poem ends with a "witty transmutation of elegy to epitaph"; see " 'Deare Ben,' 'Great DONNE,' and 'my *Celia*': The Wit of Carew's Poetry," *SEL* 18 (1978):84–87. The first claim is false, the second misleading, and both are based on the methodological error of describing a genre wholly in terms of a critic's rules instead of investigating poetic practice. Though Carew's poem *is* unusual and witty, this is because Carew uses a traditional generic pattern for his own particular ends.

[42] The elegies of Henry King, Edward Hyde, Richard Corbett, Izaac Walton, Jasper Mayne, Endymion Porter, and Sidney Godolphin all argue that only Donne could adequately praise Donne. All of these elegies appeared with Carew's composition in the "Elegies upon the Author" appended to Donne's posthumous *Poems* (1633) and are reprinted in Donne, *Epithalamions*, 81–84, 86–88, 93–95, 100, 104–105.

[43] Carew's imitation of Donne has been noted and interpreted in differing ways: see Michael Murrin, "Poetry as Literary Criticism," *MP* 65 (1968):204–205; and Lynn Sadler, *Thomas Carew*, Twayne's English Author Series (Boston: Twayne, 1979), 88–90.

invention" (l. 28), his imitation of Donne paradoxically underscores his mournful distance from the absent Donne, the great original. Indeed Carew's simultaneous imitation and praise reveals his quite un-Donnean, Jonsonian neoclassicism, since the model for his strategy is Horace's panegyric imitation of the great original poet Pindar, whom Horace imitates in the course of claiming inimitable (*Ode* 4.2.1–27). Carew's Horatian stance toward Donne is highly ironic: Carew praises Donne for not having a "Mimique fury" (l. 31) that would merely borrow "Anacreons Extasie, / Or Pindars" (ll. 32–33), but Carew himself self-consciously does "worse" than imitate such Greek originals, since he himself imitates neither Anacreon nor Pindar but the Latin imitator of both Greek poets, Horace.[44] In the elegy Carew is twice removed from the original invention he seeks to capture. The elegy thus wittily reveals that imitation of Donne can only lead to a highly successful enactment of poetic defeat.

While the Donnean style of the elegy cleverly demonstrates the sad truth that Donne's death entailed the loss of original poetic force, the epitaph is in Carew's normal, untroubled neoclassic style:

> Here lies a King, that rul'd as hee thought fit
> The universall Monarchy of wit;
> Here lie two Flamens, and both those, the best,
> Apollo's first, at last, the true Gods Priest.
>   (ll. 95–98)

The epitaph's rhyme on "fit" and "wit" underscores Carew's change of style by echoing the rhyme in one of the elegy's most Donnean passages:

> Since to the awe of thy imperious wit
> Our stubborne language bends, made only fit
> With her tough-thick-rib'd hoopes to gird about
> Thy Giant phansie, which had prov'd too stout
> For their soft melting Phrases.
>   (ll. 49–53)

In this elegiac passage Carew imitates and abases himself before Donne's "Giant phansie," using harsh cadences and violent enjambments that imitate the process by which Donne's "imperious wit" made "stubborn

---

[44] Carew's contemporaries would have readily associated Horace as an imitative poet with Anacreon and Pindar as two of his major Greek models. In Jonson's 1629 "Ode to Himself," to which Carew wrote a critical reply, Jonson bids himself take up "Or thine own *Horace*, or *Anacreons* Lyre; / Warme thee, by *Pindares* fire" (ll. 43–44); see *Ben Jonson*, ed. C. H. Herford and Percy and Evelyn Simpson, 11 vols. (Oxford: Clarendon, 1925–1952), 6:493. Jonson plans either to imitate Horace or the Greek poets that Horace himself imitated; Carew imitates only the Latin imitator.

language...fit"; in the epitaph, by contrast, Carew resumes his own habitual style, writing graceful couplets of lapidary clarity that owe more to Jonson than to Donne.

In the elegy Carew praises Donne's rejection of the "Pedantique weeds" (l. 25) of classical learning and the "gods and goddesses, which in thy [Donne's] just raigne, / Were banish'd" (ll. 64–65). Carew prophesies, however, that soon Donne's "strict lawes will be / Too hard for Libertines in Poetrie" (ll. 61–62). The classical allusions in the epitaph's panegyric description of the deceased as "two Flamens" and "Apollo's ...Priest" already rebel against Donne's "strict lawes." Carew's designation of Donne the poet as "Apollo's...Priest" recalls the depictions of the poet-as-priest in Carew's classical and neoclassical imitative masters, Horace, who describes himself as "the Muses' priest," and Jonson, who calls himself the "priest" of the "Muses," a "priest" seeking "*Delphick* fire," and writes of "we *Priests,* and *Poets.*"[45] Carew presents himself in the concluding epitaph as the first of the post-Donnean "libertine" poets, breaking the laws of Donne's "monarchy" but not those of neoclassical decorum. Donne's kingdom allowed but one form of verse, his own: it was truly "uni-vers[e]-all." Thus to re-present Donne's enduring achievement in the epitaph Carew must self-consciously remake him in Carew's own style and from his own perspective.[46]

The epitaph's neoclassicism does more, however, than signal Carew's stylistic allegiances. In the elegy Carew moved from the rhetorical power of Donne the preacher to that of Donne the secular poet without noting any break in the life of the deceased (ll. 14–60). The epitaph's neoclassicism enables Carew not only to assert the fundamental continuity of Donne's career but also aggressively to "sanctify" both the secular poet and the Christian minister as "flamens" and "priest[s]." The "true God" is superior to Apollo, but just as the two are balanced in the neat chiasmus of the final line, so each has its place in the totality of Donne's priestly

---

[45] "Musarum sacerdos" (Horace, *Ode* 3.1.3); Ben Jonson, "*Epistle.* To KATHERINE, LADY AUBIGNY," ll. 100–101; "*An Ode to* JAMES *Earle of Desmond, writ in Queene* ELIZABETHS *time, since lost, and recovered,*" ll. 11–12; "*To the immortall memorie...of...Sir Lucius Cary, and Sir* H. MORISON," l. 82 (8:119, 177, 243). Carew would undoubtedly have known the first of these Jonson poems, which was published in Jonson's *Works* of 1616, and the last, which was composed some two years before Carew's elegy.

[46] Two other elegists end their compositions with epitaphs, but both epitaphs emphasize that only Donne could truly praise Donne. A great historian but a mediocre poet, Edward Hyde, in "On the death of Dr Donne," notes that only Donne's "owne" language could adequately praise him (l. 4) and ends "Hee then must write, that would define thy parts: *Here lyes the best Divinitie, All the Arts*" (ll. 19–20); though not intentional, the very flatness of the one-line epitaph suggests that "all the Arts," including the arts of praise, are indeed dead. Mr. R. B.'s "In Memory of Doctor Donne," which argues that Donne's death has quenched all "Poetique fire" (l. 92), ends with an epitaph that uses the name-as-praise motif in order to allow Donne, in effect, to praise himself: "*Heere lies Deane Donne*; Enough..." (l. 103). See Donne, *Epithalamions,* 83, 99–100.

career. Since flamens were priests specially appointed to carry out the rituals of particular deities in polytheistic Rome, Carew's use of the Latin term indeed daringly and wittily suggests that the distinction between the Christian God and Apollo is almost on the same level as the distinction between the various gods honored by the different Roman flamens.[47] In his own sepulchral inscription upon himself, Donne briefly, perhaps evasively, describes his life before his ministry as a time of successful "studies": he subordinates the secular to the sacred without either dwelling upon or abjuring his past. Confronted by the contrast between his secular and religious writings, several elegists upon Donne go farther and stress the discontinuities of Donne's life and the reformation that transformed Jack Donne into Dean Donne of Saint Paul's.[48] Himself a secular poet, Carew by contrast uses the final epitaph to legitimize his own secular values by hallowing the whole of Donne's accomplishment, profane as well as sacred.

A comparison of Carew's composition to Lord Herbert of Cherbury's elegy on Donne further elucidates the significance of Carew's final epitaphic definition of Donne's achievement. Lord Herbert's elegy shares with Carew's elegiac section the paradoxical strategy of imitating Donne while declaring him inimitable.[49] Unlike Carew, however, Lord Herbert maintains to the end the inexpressibility topos and the self-effacing imitation of Donne's style. Lord Herbert ends his elegy with a negative definition of Donne, implying that this is the best—and faithfully Donnelike—description that can be given of the deceased.[50] In his paradoxical elegy he also declares his inability to emulate Carew: "With my witty *Carew* I should strive / To celebrate thee [i.e., Donne] dead, did I not need / A language by it self, which should exceed / All those which are

---

[47] On flamens as the priests of particular deities, see Cicero, *De legibus* 2.8.20; and Varro, *De lingua latina* 5.84. Thomas Godwin's popular textbook on Roman antiquities, which was first published in 1614 and went through many editions over the course of the seventeenth century, claims that "every God" had his particular flamen; see his *Romanae Historiae Anthologia Recognita et Aucta* . . . (Oxford, 1631), 55.

[48] In "To the deceased Author, Upon the Promiscuous printing of his Poems, the Looser sort, with the Religious," a certain Tho[mas] Browne contrasts Donne's "loose" (l. 1) secular love poetry, his "confession," with his sacred writings, his "glory" (l. 14); John Chudleigh's "On Dr John Donne, late Deane of S. Paules, London" praises Donne's transferral of wit to "pietie, which it doth best become" (l. 16); Sir Lucius Cary concludes "An Elegie on Dr. Donne" with a combination of "first" and "last" that echoes Carew's final epitaph but sharply distinguishes the secular and sacred Donne: "Then let his last excuse his first extremes" (l. 89); see Donne, *Epithalamions* 82–83, 105, 91–93. For a general discussion of the differing ways in which the elegists treated the "two Donnes," see also Sidney Gottlieb, "Elegies upon the Author: Defining; Defending; and Surviving Donne," *John Donne Journal* 2 (1983):23–38.

[49] Murrin, 205.

[50] Lord Herbert of Cherbury, *"Elegy for Doctor* Dunn," in *The Poems, English and Latin, of Edward, Lord Herbert of Cherbury*, ed. G. C. Moore Smith (Oxford: Clarendon, 1923), 59.

in use.... "[51] Lord Herbert's ostensible inability to "strive" with Carew in praise may be read as a friendly rival's rejection of the bold, independent manner with which Carew offers a positive definition of Donne's achievement in the epitaph.[52]

Carew's pride in the final epitaph is clear from the lines with which he introduces it. Only the uncultured could accept at face value the poet's self-denigration in the final couplet of the elegy: "Let others carve the rest, it shall suffice / I on thy Tombe this Epitaph incise" (ll. 93–94). Carew's couplet exploits in subdued fashion the rhetoric of dismissal used so often in classical and classically influenced poems for contrasting the inferior activities of others—evoked in Latin with a subjunctive clause, in English with a "let" clause—and one's own superior activity.[53] Jonson and his disciples in particular make this rhetoric their own. Thus in "To Sir Robert Wroth" Jonson conjures up the activities of the bad with a succession of "let" clauses—"Let others," "Let this man," "Let him," "Let that," "Let thousands more"—in order to return at the end, resoundingly, to the uniquely virtuous activities of Wroth: "But thou, my WROTH" (ll. 67–91).[54] In a poem from the same period as the Donne elegy, Carew decorously uses the form to criticize Jonson's own "immodest rage" at the vulgar public's response to Jonson's *The New Inne*: "Let the Rowte say"; "Let them the deare expence of oyle upbraid"; and, finally, "Let others glut on the extorted praise / Of vulgar breath, trust thou to after dayes."[55] In the elegy upon Donne, Carew is polite toward others who would "carve the rest," but he leaves no doubt in the minds of the reader familiar with his Jonsonian rhetoric that he is sure he will in fact say all that needs to be said concerning Donne's enduring achievement.

Carew indeed leaves nothing for others to inscribe except superfluities like Donne's lineage or dates of birth and death. Far from being a beginning, the epitaph is very much an end that overturns the proclamations of expressive failure in the elegy and testifies not only to Donne's but also to Carew's poetic power. While in the "panting numbers" (l. 77) of his elegy Carew declares that Donne's "perfections" and "our losse"

[51] Lord Herbert, "*Elegy*," ll. 50–53 in *Poems*, 58.

[52] For an interesting argument that in his elegy on Donne, Henry King, Donne's executor, angrily attacks Carew's independent stance as presumptuous, see Michael P. Parker, "Diamond's Dust: Carew, King, and the Legacy of Donne," in Summers and Pebworth, 191–200.

[53] For Roman examples, see *Aeneid* 6.847–853, Horace, *Ode* 1.31.9–20, Tibullus, *Elegy* 1.1.1–6, and Ovid, *Amores* 2.10.31–38.

[54] Jonson, 8:98–99. For other Jonsonian uses of such rhetoric, see also "*An Epistle answering to one that asked to be Sealed of the Tribe of* BEN" (ll. 9–30) and the Cavendish epitaph (ll. 5–7) in Jonson, 8:218–219, 387.

[55] Carew, "To Ben Johnson. *Upon occasion of his Ode of defiance annext to his Play of the new Inne*," ll. 29, 33, 43–44 in Carew, 65.

are "too numerous for an Elegie" (ll. 88–89), the brief but forceful verse of the epitaph literally numbers Donne's entire achievement from "first" to "last" as a "uni-vers[e]-all" king and "two Flamens."

In asserting that both a king and two flamens lie in one grave, the epitaph recalls a common type of riddle epitaph, that involving numbers.[56] Compare this labored epitaph on Michelangelo: "Halt: I will show you wonderful things, traveler, a small urn contains Apelles, Dinocrates, and Phidias. Are three therefore buried in one tomb? You are mistaken: here one man is buried, but he fulfills the role of three."[57] The small urn wondrously contains a trio of classical masters in painting, sculpture, and architecture because the deceased it holds is one but of threefold stature. With more inventive wit, Carew does not explain the riddle by noting that Donne is really one: he simply asserts that "here lies a King" and "here lie two Flamens," allowing the sophisticated reader to grasp for himself Donne's wondrous combination of roles.

Carew's praise of Donne as three-in-one supports his "sanctification" of Donne's entire career. Three-in-one epitaphs were especially popular in the Renaissance because of the privileged status of triads in both neo-Platonic and Christian thought. A riddling epitaph on the much-bewailed Prince Henry of Wales, who died in 1611, is based on the anagram of the name "Henrice Stuarte": "Ter-uni charus est" ("To Thrice-one he is dear"). The epitaph descants on all the sacred triads to whom Henry was dear: "Who is this one? or rather who is this thrice-one, / To whom he is thrice dear? / A sacred three-in-one triad."[58] An epitaph upon Queen Anne, who died in 1619, identifies her with the sacred triad of Juno, Minerva, and Venus, the goddesses of Virtue, Wisdom, and Beauty: "Now in heaven you are made Juno, Minerva, Venus. / Farewell Anna, most perfect in number, happy / now may you rest in the bosom of the divine triad."[59] With witty daring, Carew hints that there is also

---

[56] See Wilhelm Franke, *Gattungskonstanten des englischen Vers-Epitaphs von Ben Jonson zu Alexander Pope* (Nuremberg: Carl, 1964), 104.

[57] "Siste gradum: pandam tibi mira viator, Apellem, / Dinocratem, Phydiam continet urna brevis. / Tres igitur tumulo clauduntur? falleris: unus / Hic tantum situs est, instar at ille trium" (included in *The Divine Michelangelo: The Florentine Academy's Homage on his Death in 1564*, tr. with intro. Rudolf and Margot Wittkower [London: Phaidon, 1964], 79–80 [translation modified]). See also the very similar riddle-epitaphs concerning Michelangelo as four-in-one on pp. 76 and 80.

[58] "Iste quis est unus? vel (si placet) iste ter-unus, / Cui ter charus hic est? Sancta triuna trias" (Cambridge, *Epicedium . . . Henrici*, 53).

[59] "Caelica nunc facta es Iuno, Minerva, Venus. / Anna Vale, numeris o perfectissima, foelix / Divinae in Triadis nunc requiesce sinu" (Cambridge University, *Lacrymae Cantabrigienses: In obitum Serenissimae Reginae Annae* [Cambridge, 1619], 87). See also the similar epitaphs upon Anne in Cambridge, *Lacrymae . . . Annae*, 64; and Oxford University, *Academiae Oxoniensis Funebria Sacra. Aeternae Memoriae Serenissimae Reginae Annae . . . Dicata* (Oxford, 1615), H3r; and upon Elizabeth in Oxford University, *Oxoniensis Academiae Funebre Officium in Memoriam . . . Elisabethae . . . Reginae* (Oxford, 1603), 133.

a holy mystery to be found in his riddling three-in-one epitaph, for his epitaph suggests Donne's *imitatio Christi*. Since Apollo is the god of prophecy as well as poetry, Donne was a king, a prophet ("Apollo's ... Priest"), and a priest ("the true Gods Priest"); the totality of his career, secular and sacred, fulfilled the three mediatorial offices of Christ.[60]

Carew not only describes Donne in conformance with Carew's own imitative, neoclassical point of view and his high valuation of secular poetry. He also uses Donne to promote Carew the courtier poet's own sense of the relationship between poetry and society. Carew's description of Donne as ruler of "th'universall Monarchy of wit" adapts a Donnean motif. The deceased poet and preacher was fascinated by the idea of royal power, and in his lyric poetry he portrayed himself as a king far superior to mere political rulers:

> All Kings, and all their favorites,
> All glory'of honors, beauties, wits,
>
> . . . . .
>
> All other things, to their destruction draw,
> Only our love hath no decay;
>
> . . . . .
>
> Here upon earth, we'are Kings, and none but wee
> Can be such Kings, nor of such subjects bee....[61]

The devaluation of all kingdoms outside the realm of the lover-king is a powerful fantasy in Donne's love poetry: "She'is all States, and all Princes, I, / Nothing else is" he proclaims at his most outrageous.[62] While Carew's "universall Monarchy" captures Donne's hyperbolic self-aggrandizement, "of wit" transforms the relationship between the poet's kingdom and the political realm. Like Jonson's description of John Selden as "Monarch *in letters!*"[63] Carew's description of Donne treats the kingdom of the deceased as a literary heterocosm analogous to, rather than in subversive tension with, the political realm.

Writing during a time of tension between Charles I and the country, Carew the courtier poet indeed pays tribute not only to a great poet but

---

[60] On Christ's three mediatorial offices, see Barbara Kiefer Lewalski, *Milton's Brief Epic: The Genre, Meaning, and Art of Paradise Regained* (Providence: Brown University Press, 1966), 182–187.

[61] Donne, "The Anniversarie," ll. 1–2, 6–7, 23–24 in *Elegies*, 71–72.

[62] Donne, "The Sunne Rising," ll. 21–22 in *Elegies*, 73. On Donne's fascination with royal power, see Carey, 116–117; and Jonathan Goldberg, *James I and the Politics of Literature* (Baltimore: Johns Hopkins University Press, 1983), 107–112. Goldberg argues that in the love lyrics Donne "appropriated royal absolutism for his own private sphere" (p. 107) and thus both upheld, and subverted, the logic of royal absolutism.

[63] Jonson, "*An Epistle to Master* JOHN SELDEN," 1.65 in Jonson, 8:160 (emphasis mine).

also to a real king. In praising Donne as "a King, that rul'd as he thought fit" (l. 94), Carew makes Donne a hyperbolic analogue to Charles I himself, ruling his heterocosm of wit as Charles ruled England. When Carew composed the poem, Charles I was indeed ruling as he thought fit. Carew composed the elegy sometime between 1631 and 1632, and thus between the third and fourth years of Charles's eleven-year rule without Parliament.[64] A few years later Carew celebrated Charles's rule for its "peace and plenty, which the blessed hand / Of our good King gives this obdurate Land."[65] A major cause of the tensions between the king and Parliament that had led to Charles's decision to do without the latter in 1629 had been the issue of whether the king was bound by the "fundamental laws" of the kingdom.[66] Carew's implicit analogy between Donne and Charles I cleverly articulates a procourt position on this issue. Complaints against the king, his advisors, and his court were often based on their alleged belief that the king could rule as he pleased. In 1629 Christopher Sherland complained to the House of Commons that the kings' councillors "tell him [the king] that he may command what he listeth and do what he pleaseth."[67] In the original version of Phillip Massinger's *The King and the Subject*, Don Pedro, the king of Spain, proclaims, "Wee'le rayse supplies what ways we please." Since the playwright undoubtedly expected viewers to apply these lines to England's own king, Charles I ordered that the insolent lines be changed.[68] Defenders of the king argued, by contrast, that the king's "absolute rule" did not allow him to rule as he pleased, since he still had to rule as was fitting, under God.[69] Thus Sir Robert Heath argued in 1628 that the king had absolute power in some matters but would not act "unfitly, for the Hurt of his People: ... The King will not break the Trust committed unto him by God. But, my Lords, do I by this say, or maintain, that a King hath Liberty to do what He list? No, God forbid: He is set over His People for their Good; and, if He do transgress, and do unjustly, there is a greater power than He."[70] Carew's formulation "rul'd as hee thought fit" proclaims Donne's absolute power (he ruled just as he

[64] See Dunlap's note in Carew, 207.

[65] Carew, "*In answer of an Elegiacall Letter . . .*," ll. 47–48 in Carew, 75.

[66] On the debate over the king's relation to the "fundamental laws," see Margaret Atwood Judson, *The Crisis of the Constitution: An Essay in Constitutional and Political Thought in England, 1603–1645* (1949; rpt., New York: Octagon Books, 1964); Conrad Russell, *Parliaments and English Politics, 1621–1629* (Oxford: Clarendon, 1979), 323–389; and J. P. Sommerville, *Politics and Ideology in England, 1603–1640* (London: Longman, 1986), 9–111.

[67] Wallace Notestein and Frances Helen Relf, eds., *Commons Debates for 1629* (Minneapolis: University of Minnesota Press, 1921), 16.

[68] Cited in Judson, 151.

[69] On the king's accountability to God in absolutist theory, see Sommerville, 34–35.

[70] Cited in Judson, 145.

"*thought* fit") but denies that he ruled willfully as he "pleased" (he ruled only as he "thought *fit*"). Thus Carew enlists Donne in defense of the court's conception of monarchy, describing Donne as a king whose absolute but not arbitrary exercise of power in the "Monarchy of wit" corresponds to Carew's flattering vision of Charles I in the political realm.[71]

Carew's description of Donne the poet and the preacher as "priest[s]" or "flamens" also has a polemical, procourt resonance. With its emphasis upon the ritual aspects of religious life, the Arminian faction backed by Charles I and dominating the Church hierarchy in the 1630s promoted the term "priest" at the expense of "minister" in order to heighten the distinction between the clergy, the administers of the holy sacraments, and mere laymen. The Puritan faction within the Church, as well as many traditional Protestants, despised the term as a betrayal of the Protestant emphasis upon the godly layman.[72] The term "flamens" provocatively reinforces the procourt, ritualistic resonance of the term "priest." The Roman flamens were officers of state ritual, reputedly created by the legendary king Numa Pompilius when he decided that the Roman kings could not themselves perform all Rome's sacred rites in honor of the gods.[73] Carew's polemical use of the term "priest" is faithful to the Dean of Saint Paul's, who as a preacher with court connections and subject to court pressures explicitly argued in his sermons for the interchangeability of "priest" and "minister."[74] By making not only Donne the cleric but also Donne the poet into a "priest" or "flamen," however, Carew suggests that not only clergymen (like the dean of Saint Paul's) but also secular poets (like Jack Donne) are important servants of the Caroline state. Carew thereby also indirectly suggests his own significant role as a poetic supporter of royal power, a role he fulfilled as much in his elegy

[71] A later Royalist panegyric upon a writer recalls Carew's praise of Donne as monarch and his implicit analogy to Charles I. Among the commendatory verses appended to Beaumont and Fletcher's *Comedies and Tragedies* (London, 1647), which form a veritable anthology of Royalist poets (including Robert Herrick, Richard Lovelace, and James Shirley), John Harris, a minor Cavalier, claims that Fletcher was "sole Monarch, and did raign / In Wits great Empire, abs'lute Soveraign" (F4v). Harris's 1647 elegy for an all-powerful monarch of letters clearly expresses sorrow that another, actual monarch had lost power.

[72] A member of the 1629 Parliament claimed with outrage that the Arminian John Cosin had had *The Book of Common Prayer* newly printed with "the word *minister* [changed] into the word *priest*"; see Notestein and Relf, 60. On the politics of the word "priest" in the late 1620s and 1630s, see the introduction to Conrad Russell, ed. with intro., *The Origins of the English Civil War* (London: Macmillan, 1973), 21.

[73] Livy, 1. 20; and Godwin, 54. A 1641 Puritan tract attacked the bishops for resembling flamens (*The Petitition for the Prelates briefly examined* [London, 1641], 10).

[74] See Donne, *Sermons*, 2:221–222, 9:122. Some of the elegies on Donne are explicitly anti-Puritan: see Cary's elegy, ll. 47–49 and Mayne's elegy, ll. 65–72 (Donne, *Epithalamions*, 92, 95). Carew, by contrast, does not stoop to explicit argument: he simply and gracefully asserts.

and epitaph upon the monarch of wit as in his explicit panegyrics of Charles I and his court. His epitaph upon Donne thus exemplifies the polemicization of the dead that is, as we shall see, a central feature of the mid- and late seventeenth-century epitaph.

Chapter 5

Praising Honest Men: Social and Religious Tensions in the Early and Mid-Seventeenth-Century Epitaph

By commemorating the dead for certain attributes, epitaphs suggest what qualities society should value and accordingly preserve in its collective memory. A number of early and mid-seventeenth-century epitaphs celebrating or mocking a controversial social and religious ideal, the "honest" man, articulate conflicting conceptions of the virtues that society should uphold. The "honest" man emerges first and foremost as a challenge to the "great" man. While continuing the traditional humanist emphasis upon virtue as opposed to mere lineage, epitaphic praise of the "honest" man heightens the antiaristocratic tendency of humanist thought by associating virtue positively with the humble rather than simply arguing that virtue matters more than exalted lineage for determining true nobility. Zealous Protestants, moreover, adopt the term "honest" to evoke their own humble godliness, and epitaphs upon the "honest" man as a synonym for the godly, rather than noble or gentle, man play a role in the intense religious and social conflicts of the period before, during, and after the Civil Wars. Short panegyric epitaphs upon "honest" men provide additional impetus to attacks upon grand tombs as representations of mere rank and wealth and give new social and religious significance to the epitaph's poetics of brevity by insisting that the most expressive epitaph is, quite simply, "Here lies an honest man."

The uses of the word "honest" are intimately linked to the social divisions of early modern England. From its older sense of "honorable," the word gradually became associated in the sixteenth and seventeenth centuries with the necessarily plain, unostentatious virtue of the lower ranks.[1] During this period "a plain honest man" or a similar phrase using "honest" was the most common term of approbation among yeomen for others of their rank.[2] When used of a gentleman, "honest" could imply a contrast to his more ostentatious social superior, a peer: refusing to marry his daughter to an earl, Sir William Holles said in the late sixteenth century that he wished "to see hir married to an honest gentleman with whome [he] may have friendship and conversation."[3] Used by social superiors, the term could have a touch of condescension, implying that "honesty," rather than some more distinguished virtue, was all that one could praise an inferior for.[4] It was also used, however, in assertions that the humble were morally superior to the great. In his book of characters, *The Good and the Bad* (1616), Nicholas Breton, for example, glorified the lowly but virtuous "honest man" who strives for "plainness" and whose "content is his kingdom." "An honest poor man," he further noted, may be "more rich in grace than the greatest of the world."[5]

The word's very ambiguities could be used to forge a definition of worth independent of traditional social distinctions. "Honest" in the more general sense of "honorable" did not wholly disappear among the educated. Roman philosophers had argued that *honestum* ("that which is morally honorable") was the *summum bonum*. Rendering *honestum* as "honest" despite the English word's newer, humbler connotations, Thomas Lodge's 1614 edition of Seneca states that being "honest" is "the chiefest good."[6] Jonson used "honest" in both its old and new senses and sometimes combined aspects of both to stake out his own ethical ideal. In *Catiline*, when the Stoic Cato asks "What honest act is that, / The *Roman*

---

[1] I owe a general debt to the important treatment of the history of the word "honest" in William Empson, *The Structure of Complex Words* (London: Chatto & Windus, 1977), 185–250. I will be mainly concerned, however, with aspects of the word's history not covered by Empson.

[2] See Mildred Campbell, *The English Yeoman under Elizabeth and the Early Stuarts* (New Haven: Yale University Press, 1942), 377–378. Campbell cites the above phrase and such variants as "a plain honest good man," "a plain honest man," "a very honest good man," or "plain honest countryman" as the most frequent positive designations of a yeoman. In Thomas Dekker's, John Ford's, and William Rowley's *The Witch of Edmonton*, published in 1658 but probably written in 1621, the yeoman John Carter denies he is a gentleman and proclaims his "honest" yeoman stock: "No Gentleman, I . . . [My father and grandfather were] Honest *Hertfordshire* Yeomen; such an one am I"; see *The Dramatic Works of Thomas Dekker*, ed. Fredson Bowers, 4 vols. (Cambridge: Cambridge University Press, 1955–1961), 3:498 (I.ii.3–7).

[3] Cited in Lawrence Stone, *The Crisis of the Aristocracy: 1558–1641* (Oxford: Oxford University Press, 1965), 746.

[4] See Empson, 187–188.

[5] Henry Morley, ed., *Character Writings of the Seventeenth Century* (London, 1891), 270, 277.

[6] *The Workes of Lucius Annaeus Seneca*, trans. Thomas Lodge (London, 1614), 290 (*Epistulae morales* 71.4). For other Roman discussions of *honestum*, see Seneca, *Epistulae morales* 120.1–3 and Cicero, *De finibus* 2.45.

Senate should not dare, and doe?" (IV.526–527),[7] the word has all its Roman *dignitas*. In the *Discoveries*, on the other hand, Jonson compares the Muses' bad treatment of poets, who are rarely granted a decent living, to the treatment that "the times *Grandes*" mete out to "an old Client, or honest servant, bound by his place to write, or starve."[8] The poet is like an "honest servant," full of humble integrity but little rewarded.[9] In the second introductory poem to his *Epigrammes*, Jonson explains why he does not write libellous or obscene poems: "He that departs with his owne honesty / For vulgar praise, doth it too dearely buy."[10] Honesty makes one stand above the *vulgus*, yet it is clearly a plain rather than aristocratic virtue. Jonson combines the Roman connotations of *honestum* with some of the earthy resonance of the English word in order to assert his own humanist sense of the ideal man, neither one of the vulgar nor an ostentatious courtier. It is this rich sense of "honest" that Jonson invoked when he told Drummond in 1619 that "of all stiles he loved most to be named honest."[11]

Jonson's proclamation of his own "honesty" was itself open to deflation by those who seized upon the word's humbler connotations. The poet enjoyed a doggerel epitaph that a friend had written upon him enough to recite it to Drummond: "here lyes honest Ben / that had not a beard on his chen."[12] In an epitaph affectionately implying, like comic epitaphs on members of lowly occupations, that all that need be said of the "dead" is a trivial witticism, the use of "honest Ben" pricks the dignified bubble of Jonson's Roman *persona*. The epitaph underlines that the poet of avowed honesty was in social terms far from exalted and even somewhat ridiculous.

James Shirley, a member of the tribe of Ben, wrote several elegant panegyric epitaphs upon nobles and gentlemen. In his most interesting epitaph, however, Shirley intensifies the humanist position of his master Jonson by contrasting the humble memorial and brief but pregnant epitaph upon a lowly, "honest" parson with the grand monuments and empty, flattering epitaphs of an immoral social elite. The anonymous

---

[7] *Ben Jonson*, ed. C. H. Herford and Percy and Evelyn Simpson, 11 vols. (Oxford: Clarendon, 1925–1952), 5:514.

[8] Jonson, *Discoveries* 622–633, 8:583.

[9] Jonson elsewhere identifies honesty with the lowly but virtuous. In a letter to the secretary of Lord Ellesmere, the lord chancellor, he requested help for "a most honest man, & worthie of a much better fortune" (1:201). Jonson's epigram to Ellesmere interceding for an unidentified "poore Man" (*The Under-wood*, XXXI, 8:185) probably refers to the "most honest man" of the letter. In Jonson's masque, "Love Restored," first performed in 1612, the representative of simple rural pleasures, Robin Goodfellow, introduces himself as an "honest plaine countrey spirit" (7:378).

[10] Jonson, 8:27.

[11] Jonson, 1:150.

[12] Jonson, 1:149.

subject of the epitaph and the precise date of composition are unknown, but the poem certainly dates from Shirley's years in London, the mid-1620s or 1630s, when he composed most of his epitaphs:

> For them that leave no monument
> Behind them good, much gold is spent
> To build a tomb: the gentle son
> Will turn his father into stone,
> And on a cushion carved fair
> Cut him into form of prayer,
> And in jet beneath command
> To be writ in golden hand
> (If no other good beside,)
> His worship's name, and when he died.
> But when did charity find room
> To raise an honest parson's tomb,
> Or bestow upon his hearse
> Figure, or a marble verse?
> Then let her, whom he did trust
> With life and love, enclose his dust
> At the cost of double mite,
> (The widow's all,) and underwrite
> This epitaph, which she'd have read
> To shew her duty to the dead.
>
> *Epitaph inscribed on a small piece of marble.*
>
> No more marble let him have;
> He hath treasure in his grave,
> And his piety will survive,
> To keep his memory alive:
> A glorious nothing it would be,
> To say, his tomb were rich, not he.[13]

Ten lines attacking the flattering monuments of rich but morally worthless gentry, those who have "gold" but are not "good" (l. 2), are balanced by ten lines defending the rights of a humble parson to a tomb. The satiric description of a "gentle" (l. 3) son's transformation of his dead father into a stone praying figure refers to a very popular monumental form in the early seventeenth century, the kneeling figure, or "kneeler." The kneeling figure, which originally appeared on monuments for such ancillary figures as the surviving children (as in the Cavendish monument), quickly replaced the recumbent effigy as the most popular early seventeenth-century pose not only for the surviving family but also for the dead. Unlike the recumbent effigy's commemoration of the deceased

---

[13] James Shirley, *Dramatic Works and Poems*, ed. William Gifford and Alexander Dyce, 6 vols. (London, 1833), 6:501–502.

peacefully recumbent in death, the kneeler purports to depict and me-morialize the pious life that the deceased had led. The kneeler thus obscures the brute fact of death in order to connect the dead more closely to the living.[14] Shirley singles out the kneeler both because it was popular and because its portrait *au vif* could be used as a direct and unequivocal cover-up of a life ill spent.

The contrast between the worthless gentleman who customarily re-ceives a grand tomb and the "honest parson" (l. 12) who normally lacks one brings out clearly the opposition between "gentle" and "honest" lives. The humble, uncommemorated parson was very much a reality of the times. Due to the great differences in benefices, the wealth and status of the lower clergy varied enormously in the early seventeenth century: while some lower clergy were financially and socially on a par with the lesser gentry, others lived in poverty and were treated by the nobility and gentry with contempt.[15] If patrons or local parishes were not forth-coming and the surviving family was without resources, a vicar or curate might well be uncommemorated when he died.[16] The penurious but

---

[14] On the rise of the kneeler and the parallel decline of the recumbent effigy in sev-enteenth-century England, see Brian Kemp, *English Church Monuments* (London: B. T. Batsford, 1980), 80; J. G. Mann, "English Church Monuments, 1536–1625," *The Walpole Society* 21 (1933):16–17; and Michel Vovelle, *La mort et l'occident de 1300 à nos jours* (Paris: Gallimard, 1983), 353–354. There were practical reasons for the kneeler's growing pop-ularity. Kneelers made possible compact grouping of figures and took up less horizontal space than recumbent figures in the increasingly crowded churches. While tradition re-quired that recumbent figures be life-size, kneelers, having originally been used for the smaller figures of children, could appear in all sizes without noticeable incongruity. Like inscriptional tablets without effigies, small monuments with kneelers clearly appealed to those with less money or inexpensive tastes. The many large monuments with kneelers, on which "much gold" was indeed spent, nevertheless suggest that the major cause of the shift from recumbent to kneeling figures was not economic; the kneeling figures are rather the expression of a new desire to portray and eternalize the dead as they were when they lived rather than to commemorate them as dead (Vovelle, 353–354). The continuity of the family, portrayed in the Cavendish monument and similar compositions consisting of recumbent parents and kneeling children, is emphasized even more strongly in the nu-merous monuments that consist entirely of kneelers, the husband and sons on one side and the wife and daughters on the other, with no visual acknowledgement of the death that divided family members. (For a very different interpretation of the kneeler as a representation of the soul in Paradise rather than "a man on this earth," see Philippe Ariès, *The Hour of Our Death*, trans. Helen Weaver [New York: Random, 1982], 254–259. The literary evidence does not, however, support this interpretation, as Ariès himself concedes.)

[15] See Rosemary O'Day, *The English Clergy: The Emergence and Consolidation of a Profession, 1558–1642* (Leicester: Leicester University Press, 1969), 172–189; and Christopher Hill, *Economic Problems of the Church from Archbishop Whitgift to the Long Parliament* (Oxford: Clarendon, 1956), 199–223.

[16] There are many modest but respectable seventeenth-century monuments of parish clergymen; see Katharine A. Esdaile, *English Church Monuments, 1510 to 1840* (New York: Oxford University Press, 1946), 103. Such commemoration wholly depended, however, upon local circumstances. In Preston, Dorset, the patron of the living erected a very modest wall monument consisting of a small kneeler and this brief epitaph: "The Vicar here

worthy parson was therefore a perfect representative of an "honest" man, low in social status though high in the eyes of God.

"The double mite, / (The widow's all)" (ll. 17–18) that alone provides the parson with his small memorial alludes to Jesus's contrast between the donations that the rich gave to the temple's treasury and the offerings of a poor widow who "threw in two mites": "Verily I say unto you, That this poor widow hath cast more in, than all they which have cast into the treasury: For all they did cast in of their abundance; but she of her want did cast in all that she had, even all her living" (Mark 12:41–44; cf. Luke 21:1–5). Biblical authority thus asserts the moral superiority of the humble widow who spends her all for her dear husband to the gentleman who spends great amounts on his worthless father. By hinting at the deceased minister's role as a Christian anti-type of the Temple treasury, the Biblical allusion also neatly prepares for the epitaph's panegyric of a man materially poor but spiritually rich.

According to the fiction of the poem, the widow herself composed the final, six-line epitaph, which uses brevity to express the modesty of the deceased and his widow while continuing to attack the values of the great. The opening announces that the exiguous marble is the product of moral choice as well as fortune, since the small monument befits a man whose spiritual "treasure in his grave" (l. 22) makes a grand tomb unnecessary. The opening "No more" (l. 21) suggests the inscribed poem's own quick rush toward closure, and the epitaph pits its form of brevity against that of the bad gentleman: the brief praise of the deceased, unidentified by irrelevant, vainglorious names or dates, stands in pointed contrast to the epitaph upon the hypothetical worthless gentleman bearing only "his name and when he died" (l. 10). The final couplet provides effective and witty closure: "A glorious nothing it would be, / To say, his tomb were rich, not he" (ll. 25–26). Though it here lacks the richly ambiguous tone it has in its source, Donne's "Aire and Angels," the semi-oxymoronic phrase "glorious nothing" pithily deflates the cult of monumental show and allows the parson's widow a final, verbal revenge against the proud and uncaring of the world.[17]

The poem adumbrates two ideological positions, one explicit and the

---

entombed lies; / Whose patron him doth eternize / That his fair works of charity: / May not with him still buried be / But live in lasting memory / He died in 1614 aged 32" (photo and text in Sir Owen Morshead, *Dorset Churches* [Norwich: Dorset Historic Churches Trust and Jarrold and Sons, 1975], 41). The patron proclaims his voluntary act of commemorating the vicar for the edification of parishioners, and the monument thus announces his own, as well as the deceased vicar's, "charity." Other clergymen did not have such generous patrons.

[17] John Donne, "Aire and Angels," l. 6 ("Some lovely glorious nothing I did see"). On the complexity of Donne's phrase in its original context, see the editor's note in Donne, *The Complete English Poems*, ed. A. J. Smith (Harmondsworth: Penguin, 1971), 353–354.

other submerged. The poem criticizes the "great" who fail to live up to the responsibilities their rank imposes upon them. It calls on them to fulfill their obligations to their inferiors, which include such charitable acts as providing suitable commemoration for poor ministers. The biblical allusion evokes, by contrast, Jesus's assertion of the humble's moral superiority to the rich. Thus while the poem explicitly attacks social abuses, Shirley hints at a more radical critique of the social hierarchy. Though as he rose in the world he adopted two (equally false) coats of arms, Shirley was himself of common background and had been a humble parson and schoolmaster circa 1618–1624, before he came to London and embarked on his career as a professional and court dramatist.[18] Shirley seems to idealize the "honest" minister as an image of an earlier, humbler self, morally superior to the world in which Shirley dwells.

One may compare Shirley's praise of a humble cleric with his exaltation of a "new man" in *The Bird in a Cage* (1632–1633). Having disguised himself as the lowly malcontent Rolliardo in order better to pursue his beloved, the protagonist of the play proudly announces his humble birth and noble daring:

> Fortune, and courtesie of opinion
> Gives many men Nobility of Birth,
> That never durst doe nobly, nor attempt
> Any designe....
>
> . . . . .
>
> ...[It] is my chiefe glory, that perhaps being sprung
> From humble Parentage, dare yet attempt
> A deed so farre above me....
>
> . . . . .
>
> Let Scorners know...
> My memory after death, receives more honour
> Than all your marble Pinnacles can raise you,
> Or alabaster figures....[19]

Like the epitaph, Rolliardo's speech exposes the emptiness of the grand tomb as a sign of mere rank and wealth. Denigrating mere lineage, Rolliardo proclaims his greatness as an individual. In this speech one can hear Shirley encoding—and idealizing—his position as a low-born but ambitious dramatist at a court dominated by "great" men.[20] While

---

[18] See George Bas, "James Shirley, dramaturge caroléen (1596–1666)," diss., University of Paris IV (Lille: Université de Lille, 1973), 21–23, 27–30.

[19] James Shirley, *The Bird in a Cage: A Critical Edition*, ed. Frances Frazier Senescu (New York: Garland, 1980), 31 (II.i.7–10, 15–17, 20–23).

[20] Marvin Morillo argues that this speech, which is not strictly relevant to the dramatic situation, expresses Shirley's own feelings in "Shirley's 'Preferment' and the Court of Charles I," *SEL* 1 (1961):106–107.

the parson could represent to Shirley an earlier self whose humility makes him superior to the "gentle," the malcontent could represent an actual self whose glorious daring renders him superior to the idle nobility. Like the epitaph's biblical allusion, the malcontent's speech allows Shirley to vent some of his own frustration against the high-born and rich. Since, however, the lowly malcontent is in reality Lord Philenzo, the aristocratic hero, the play provides "proof" that noble actions (at least sometimes) reflect noble blood. Thus the play as a whole, like the poem as a whole, calls for men of rank to justify their place in the social hierarchy through virtuous action. Though Shirley attaches different values to the lowly in the poem and the play—"honest" humility versus "noble" ambition—both works use the lowly to attack the social hierarchy while containing that attack within a more moderate plea that the social elite reveal their moral worth.

Shirley, who was undoubtedly Catholic when he wrote the funerary poem, emphasizes the social position and moral value of the parson, not his religious allegiances. "Honest" increasingly took on a specifically Protestant resonance, however, over the course of the late sixteenth and early seventeenth centuries. Honesty became the central virtue of the zealous Protestant, so that "honest" and "godly" became near synonyms. The epitaph of Anne Horswell, who died in 1599, praises her "honneste godlye lyfe," while that of John Green, who died in 1615, eulogizes his "true devotion" and "tryde honesty."[21] When the epitaph of Richard Manning, who died in 1604, describes the deceased as "Zealous of God's truth, hateing sin, to honest men right kinde," it is clear that "honest" men are deeply religious men.[22]

The Puritans aggressively promoted the new conception of honesty. Retaining the virtue's plainness while closely linking it to godliness, the Puritans contrasted true honesty not only with aristocratic ostentation but also with the mere good behavior thought to be valued by "unreformed" members of the lower orders. Both the similarities and the differences between the honesty of the godly Puritan and that of the plain yeoman emerge in Arthur Dent's oft-reprinted work, *The Plaine Mans Path-way to Heaven* (1601), a dialogue between a godly minister and his respectful companion, on the one hand, and two ignorant villagers, on the other. The villagers believe that honesty in the sense of good neighborliness and outward shows of devotion assures salvation. When

[21] I cite Thomas F. Ravenshaw, ed., *Antiente Epitaphes (from A.D. 1250 to A.D. 1800)* (London, 1878), 42; and John Le Neve, ed., *Monumenta Anglicana: Being Inscriptions on the Monuments of several Eminent Persons... 1600–1715*, 5 vols. (London, 1718–1719), 4:48–49.
[22] John Thorpe, *Registrum Roffense: or, A Collection of Antient Records... of the Diocese and Cathedral Church of Rochester* (London, 1769), 1018.

one of them finally learns that his kind of honesty is not sufficient—"For though outwardly I have lived honestly to the worldward, yet inwardly I have not lived religiously to Godward"—the other is appalled at the idea that "an honest man . . . a good neighbour" could be damned.[23] Dent makes clear that the ignorant do not understand the real meaning of honesty by introducing the minister's humble and faithful companion, Philagathes ("Lover of the Good"), as himself an "honest man": the true honest man is not the ignorant yeoman who trusts in good deeds but the Protestant believer who has—to use another common expression— an "honest heart."[24] In his posthumously published biography of the godly layman John Bruen, William Hinde, a prominent Puritan divine in Chester until his death in 1629, described how Bruen established a veritable "Church in his house" by hiring "honest and faithfull, godly and gracious servants."[25] The social and religious resonances of "honesty" merge in this portrait of humble servants who were honest and faithful toward both their master and their God.[26]

A poem at the end of the Puritan Thomas Oldmayne's funeral sermon on Sir Edward Lewkenor (1619) reveals the Puritan cult of the honest man. The poet imagines readers' perusing the inscriptions on Lewkenor's tomb:

> There they shall read, how worshipfull his Berth,
> (To which ambitiously all sorts aspire,
> How e're in other worth they suffer dearth)
> There they his wealth, (which worldlings so desire)
> There (that which only gentle mindes admire

[23] Arthur Dent, *The Plaine Mans Path-way to Heaven* (London, 1601), 372–373.

[24] Early in the seventeenth century, John Barlow advises sinners to "get faith in *Christ*; [and] labour for an honest heart" in *The Joy of the Upright Man* (London, 1619), 36.

[25] William Hinde, *A Faithfull Remonstrance* (London, 1641), 55.

[26] George Herbert suggests a continuity between the good behavior of plain, humble countryfolk and godly faith. He writes in *The Country Parson* that "country people (as indeed all honest men) do much esteem their word" and in "Jordan: 1" asserts that "shepherds are honest people" (l. 11), a claim presumably true of literal as well as metaphorical shepherds. In "Constancie," he praises the "honest man" (l. 1) as the ideal Christian in his relation both to God and man: "To God, his neighbour, and himself most true" (l. 3). See *The Works of George Herbert*, corrected ed., F. E. Hutchinson (Oxford: Clarendon, 1945), 228, 57, 72–73. Richard Strier points out that the conception of godliness in "Constancie" allows greater room for the self's exertions toward God than is normal in Herbert, who usually stresses fallen man's lack of a stable self that could seek God and man's total dependence upon God's grace; see *Love Known: Theology and Experience in George Herbert's Poetry* (Chicago: University of Chicago Press, 1983), 11; and "Ironic Humanism in *The Temple*," in *"Too Rich to Clothe the Sunne": Essays on George Herbert*, ed. Claude J. Summers and Ted-Larry Pebworth (Pittsburgh: University of Pittsburgh Press, 1980), 32–52. Such inconsistency is frequent in Protestant appropriations of the ethical concept of honesty as an ideal. Despite their belief in humanity's absolute dependence upon God's grace, even Puritans who praise the "honest" man often stress his virtuous attitude toward God rather than his total dependence upon Him.

And doth embellish wealth and parentage)
His Learning and Religion entire:
I, for my part, (how e're in this nice age
  It sound but ill, and homely seeme) will span
  His spatious praises thus, Hee was an honest man.[27]

In recounting the inscriptional message of the grand tomb, the poet has it both ways. He informs us of Lewkenor's rank and fortune while contrasting such things, regarded so highly by the worldly, with the learning and godliness of the deceased, which only the truly "gentle," that is, the virtuous, admire. The poet concludes, moreover, by contrasting the monument's more lengthy praise of lineage, wealth, and virtue with the "homely" but "spatious" praise that the poet will himself give in what should be, for the proper reader, epitaph enough: "Hee was an honest man." One may compare the poet's use of "Hee was an honest man" as the brief but sufficient description of a plain, Protestant ideal with the short and simple epitaph upon godly Robert Kerwin, who died in 1615, which implicitly treats honesty as the humble but sufficient Christian virtue: "ROBERT KERWIN now here doth lie, / A man of proved honestie: / Whose sowle to heaven hense did flie, / To enjoy Christ his felicitie, / The seventh of Februarie. 1615."[28]

Because of the religious tensions of the early seventeenth century, the association of honesty with religious zeal was highly controversial. One epigram writer of the period, Sir Thomas Wroth, depicts a supposed honest man as a religious hypocrite: "Honest Sir John doth to his neighbours cry, / Forsake the world, and learne the way to dye; / If this be wholesome counsell he doth give, / Why then makes he himselfe such shift to live."[29] Anti-Puritans denied Puritans' claims of true honesty. An early seventeenth-century epigrammatist, Thomas Freeman, for example, concludes a poem describing his encounter with an austere religious man by quipping, "'tis a Puritan, / Trust me, I tooke him for an honest man."[30]

Richard Crashaw's pseudo-inscriptional "*An Epitaph upon Mr. Ashton a conformable Citizen,*" probably composed before Crashaw left London to enter Pembroke College, Cambridge, in 1631, commemorates a man

<hr/>

[27] Timothy Oldmayne, *Gods Rebuke in Taking from us . . . Sir Edward Lewkenor* (London, 1619), 99–100.
[28] Ravenshaw, 58.
[29] Sir Thomas Wroth, *The Abortive of an Idle Houre: or A Centurie of Epigrams* (London, 1620), 15.
[30] Thomas Freeman, "In Puritanum," in his *Rubbe, and A Great Cast* (London, 1614), I2v–I3r (Epigram 2.62). In the next epigram Freeman underscores that for him the true "honest man" is not the grave Puritan but the bluff, plain-speaking man: he praises a "free spirit" who "Speakes honest English, without complements" ("Morum amorum amicorum . . . ," Freeman, I3r [Epigram 2.63]).

who is made to embody all of the young poet's hopes for peace within the increasingly tension-filled English church. The opening of the epitaph seeks to link the Protestant ideal of the honest man promoted especially by the Puritan faction to the ideal of the citizen who is "comformable" both in the general sense of "tractable, submissive... of compliant disposition or practice" (*OED*, 3b) and in its more specific, topical sense of "conforming to the usages of the Church of England" (*OED*, 3c):

> The modest front of this small floore
> Beleeve mee, Reader can say more
> Then many a braver Marble can;
> *Here lyes a truly honest man.*
> One whose Conscience was a thing
> That troubled neither Church nor King.
> One of those few that in this Towne,
> Honour all Preachers; heare their owne,
> Sermons he heard, yet not so many,
> As left no time to practise any.
> Hee heard them reverendly, and then
> His practice preach'd them o're agen.
> For every day his deedes put on
> His Sundayes repetition.
> His *Parlour-Sermons* rather were
> Those to the Eye, then to the Eare.
> His prayers tooke their price and strength
> Not from the lowdnesse, nor the length.
> Hee was a Protestant at home,
> Not onely in despight of *Rome*.
> Hee lov'd his *Father*, yet his zeale
> Tore not off his Mothers veile.
> To th'Church hee did allow her Dresse,
> True *Beauty*, to true *Holinesse*.
> Peace, which hee lov'd in Life....
>
> (ll. 1–25)[31]

"Here lyes a truly honest man" (l. 4) has the plain, Protestant resonances of the Lewkenor poem. Crashaw differs from many of his English Protestant countrymen, however, in depicting the "truly honest man" as one fully content with the established order. Crashaw's stress on "peace" was a major theme of defenders of the church in the 1620s and 1630s: Bishop Joseph Hall's vain attempts to quell tension in the Church have such

---

[31] I cite the text in *The Complete Poetry of Richard Crashaw*, ed. George Walton Williams (New York: Norton, 1970), 464–465. Williams notes that a manuscript version of the poem describes Ashton, who remains unidentified, as a "Citizen of London."

titles as *Via Media: The Way of Peace* (1622), *The Peacemaker* (1626), and *De Pacis Ecclesiasticae Rationibus* (1634). In the early seventeenth century, there was much discontent in Parliament and among the Puritan ministry and citizens of London with a Church that had turned its back on further Calvinistic reform. The late 1620s brought especially strong opposition to the Church's rising Arminian faction and a king in sympathy with that faction. With its emphasis on church ritual and its anti-Calvinist contention that men were not predestined to salvation or damnation but could accept or reject divine grace, Arminianism was widely perceived as an attempt to restore "popish" doctrine and idolatrous practice.[32] William Laud, bishop of London from 1628 until he was raised to the governing see of Canterbury in 1633, used his authority to stifle Calvinist views and promote Arminian ones in London sermons and religious publications.[33] Crashaw, who became a fervent Arminian at Cambridge, promotes a delicate compromise position in this early poem by commemorating a rare exemplum of religious moderation, a comfortable London citizen faithful to the major religious ideals of traditional Protestantism but fully contented with the increasingly Arminian Church.[34]

Crashaw's opening claim that "honest" Ashton's "conscience.../... troubled neither Church nor King" (l. 5–6) has particular topical import. As I noted in my discussion of Carew's elegy on Donne, one of the chief sources of tension between Charles I and Parliament was disagreement over the extent of royal power, and many felt that the king's Arminian supporters were encouraging royal absolutism and, consequently, the suppression of the subject's conscience. In 1627 Roger Manwaring preached before the king two sermons, published shortly thereafter,

[32] On Puritanism in London in the mid-1620s and 1630s, see Valerie Pearl, *London and the Outbreak of the Puritan Revolution: City Government and National Politics, 1625–1643* (Oxford: Oxford University Press, 1961); see especially pp. 160–176. On the rise of Arminianism and the opposition it provoked, see Godfrey Davies, "Arminianism versus Puritanism in England, ca. 1620–1640," *Huntington Library Bulletin* 5 (1934):157–179; Nicholas Tyacke, *Anti-Calvinists: The Rise of English Arminianism, c. 1590–1640* (Oxford: Clarendon, 1987); and Tyacke's earlier essay, "Puritanism, Arminianism and Counter-Revolution," in *The Origins of the English Civil War*, ed. with intro. Conrad Russell (London: Macmillan, 1973), 119–143.

[33] Tyacke, *Anti-Calvinism*, 181–185; Tyacke, "Puritanism," 137. In 1629 members of Parliament of 1629 expressed outrage against Laud's "restraint of books written against Popery and Arminianism"; see Wallace Notestein and Frances Helen Relf, eds., *Commons Debates for 1629* (Minneapolis: University of Minnesota Press, 1921), 58–59.

[34] Paul M. Parrish suggests that the Ashton epitaph tacitly supports Laudian High Anglicanism in "Carew's Funeral Elegies," in *Essays on Richard Crashaw*, ed. Robert M. Cooper (Salzburg: Universität Salzburg Press, 1979), 58–60. Parrish fails to distinguish between the self-conscious (and for Crashaw, not ultimately sustainable) *via media* of this early epitaph and Crashaw's later vehement Arminianism. On the Arminianism of Crashaw's mature poetry, see Austin Warren, *Richard Crashaw: A Study in Baroque Sensibility* (Ann Arbor: University of Michigan Press, 1939), 3–63 and passim; and Thomas F. Healy, *Richard Crashaw* (Leiden: Brill, 1986), 66–93 and passim.

claiming that to resist the "Soveraigne will" was a "breach of Conscience."[35] In 1628 the parliamentary leader John Pym reported to an alarmed Parliament that Manwaring had asserted that the king had absolute power and that subjects had to submit to illegal commands against their conscience.[36] Parliament ordered that Manwaring's sermons be burned and Manwaring himself imprisoned, fined, and barred from all offices. Under parliamentary pressure, the king issued a proclamation suppressing the sermons but pardoned and granted ecclesiastical preferment to Manwaring.[37] Though Manwaring was not in fact an Arminian in theology, parliamentarians quickly branded him an Arminian because of his support for, and by, the court.[38] In 1628 the Puritan minister Henry Burton accused the Arminians of arguing that "kings are partakers of God's owne omnipotency."[39] In 1629 members of Parliament continued to complain that the Arminians were preaching that the king "may command what he listeth."[40] Crashaw thus makes Ashton a laudable example of conscientious "conformity" at a time when many wished to safeguard conscience's rights against the encroachment of ecclesiastical and royal authority.

Ashton lived up to Protestant ideals promoted by the Puritans without falling into the subversive vices their enemies attributed to them. As one that "honour[ed] all Preachers" but heard his own (l. 8), Ashton displayed pious Protestant devotion to hearing the Word while rejecting the Puritan practice of "gadding to sermons."[41] Since Puritan worship centered around sermons as calls to saving faith, many of the godly would leave their parish church for another if the parish minister did not preach often enough for their needs or if his sermons were insufficiently Calvinist. In the early 1620s John Lambe, chancellor of the Canterbury Diocese, complained of the "manifest contempt" parishioners too often displayed "of their owne Minister" and contended that "Puritans goe by troupes from their owne parishe Church (though there be a Sermon)

[35] Margaret Atwood Judson quotes Manwaring's support of royal absolutism and analyzes its limits in *The Crisis of the Constitution: An Essay in Constitutional and Political Thought in England, 1603–1645* (1949; rpt., New York: Octagon Books, 1964), 214–217 (quotation from p. 215).
[36] Pym's claims are summarized in James F. Larkin and Paul L. Hughes, eds., *Stuart Royal Proclamations*, 2 vols. (Oxford: Clarendon, 1973–1983), 2:198, n. 2.
[37] For the proclamation and its context, see Larkin and Hughes, *Stuart Proclamations*, 2:197–199.
[38] Tyacke, *Anti-Calvinists*, 159.
[39] Henry Burton, *Israel's Fast* (London, 1628), cited in Tyacke, *Anti-Calvinists*, 158.
[40] I cite once more the remark of Edward Sherland in Notestein and Relf, 16.
[41] On "gadding to sermons" as a Puritan phenomenon, see Patrick Collinson, *The Elizabethan Puritan Movement* (Berkeley: University of California Press, 1967), 373–374; and Christopher Hill, *Society and Puritanism in Pre-Revolutionary England*, 2d ed. (New York: Schocken, 1967), 66–67.

to heare another whom their humour better affecteth."[42] In his *Micro-cosmographie* (1628), John Earle portrayed a hypocritical Puritan woman who "will go in pilgrimage five mile to a silenced minister, when there is a better sermon in her own parish."[43] To the church hierarchy, such "gadding" undermined the parish as the unit of a compulsory, national church organization and encouraged a semicongregationalism of like-minded Protestants. Especially worried were Laud and his Arminian allies, who feared a Puritan "fifth-column" within the Church. London's many parish churches and numerous city-wide Puritan lectureships (endowed preaching positions) made "gadding" especially easy and common. Crashaw therefore praises Ashton as one of the "few...in this Towne" (l. 7) who piously heard the Word but avoided such divisive practices.

By claiming that Ashton heard sermons but "not so many" that he neglected to "practise" them (ll. 9–10), that is, to perform good works, Crashaw further suggests that the deceased was a pious Protestant who avoided the extremism with which opponents charged Puritans. The balancing of sermons and good works was associated with religious moderation and irenicism during this period, as these two epitaphs upon ministers, from the mid 1620s and the early 1630s respectively, reveal:

> Meeke, loveing, lovd, onely with sinne at strife,
> Who heard him sawe life in his doctrine shine,
> Who sawe him heard sounde doctrine in his life....
>
> He was a man of peace; only some strife
> There was between his doctrine & his life,
> Which should be more instructive, for indeed
> His Actions were all Sermons....[44]

Though Puritans themselves continually emphasized the necessary harmony of preaching and practice,[45] their opponents frequently charged that the Puritans' emphasis upon sermons and salvation by faith alone

[42] Cited in J. T. Cliffe, *The Puritan Gentry: The Great Puritan Families of Early Stuart England* (London: Routledge, 1984), 178–179.

[43] Morley, 194.

[44] Epitaphs upon John Broadley, d. 1625, in E. W. Crossley, ed., *The Monumental and Other Inscriptions in Halifax Parish Church* (Leeds: John Whitehead, 1909), 3–4; and George Birkhead, d. 1631, in Le Neve, 4:132–133.

[45] In a funeral sermon of 1627 Thomas Gataker was conventional in praising a fellow minister whose "doctrine and...practice concurred." William Haller cites Gataker's *Abrahams Decease. A meditation...delivered at the Funerall of...Mr. Richard Stock* (London, 1627) along with several other panegyrics upon Puritan ministers for their unity of doctrine and practice in *The Rise of Puritanism* (1938; rpt., New York: Harper, 1957), 115–116.

led to contempt for good works.[46] A 1626 sermon by the Arminian John Cosin attacked ministers who tell their flocks that "all is well if they can but say their catechism and hear sermons" and who "make them believe that there is nothing to be done more but to believe and so be saved." Earle described his hypocritical Puritan woman as one "so taken up with faith she has no room for charity, and understands no good works." In *The Muses' Looking Glass* (1630), Thomas Randolph had a Puritan exclaim, "I say no works are good; / Good works are merely popish, and apocryphal."[47]

Crashaw's claim that Ashton's "prayers tooke their price and strength / Not from the lowdnesse, nor the length" (ll. 16–17) similarly praises the deceased for having practiced private devotions, a central feature of traditional Protestant piety, without the excesses ascribed to Puritan prayer style. Satirists often mocked what they considered the ostentatiously lengthy and noisy prayers of Puritans: John Marston's 1598 *Certaine Satyres*, for example, ridicules a "Precisian" who "says . . . a solemne grace / Of halfe an hour"; John Webster's *The Duchess of Malfi*, first performed in 1612, jokes about "puritans that have sore throats with over-straining."[48]

The description of Ashton as a "Protestant at home, / Not onely in despight of *Rome*" (ll. 19–20) reveals just how far Crashaw's godly man concurred with the Arminian directions of the Church. In the 1620s and 1630s the Arminians attempted to modify the English church's long-held and virulent anti-"popery." Richard Montagu, for example, argued that the Roman church was a true though unsound church and rejected as unproven the long-standing Protestant identification of the pope with the Antichrist. Though Montagu and his fellow Arminians insisted that they were adamantly opposed to Catholic "superstitions," their outraged opponents attacked their milder attitude towards Rome as proof of the their crypto-Romanism.[49] In 1626, Charles I issued a proclamation, writ-

---

[46] In 1628 the moderate Puritan member of Parliament Sir Simonds D'Ewes, discussing his own "lively faith" and "godly life," inveighed against the "the devilish sophisms and errors" of those who contended "that assurance [of grace] brings forth presumption and a careless wicked life"; see *The Autobiography and Correspondence of Sir Simonds d'Ewes*, ed. James Orchard Halliwell, 2 vols. (London, 1845), 1:369. D'Ewes was attacking a widespread charge.

[47] Cosin cited in Tyacke, *Anti-Calvinists*, 124; Earle in Morley, 194; Randolph in William P. Holden, *Anti-Puritan Satire, 1572–1642* (New Haven: Yale University Press, 1954), 110.

[48] John Marston, "Satyre 2," ll. 56, 61–62 in *Poems*, ed. Arnold Davenport (Liverpool: Liverpool University Press, 1961), 73; and John Webster, *The Duchess of Malfi*, ed. John Russell Brown, The Revels Plays (Cambridge: Harvard University Press, 1964), 121 (IV.ii.84–85). Holden cites the Marston passage (p. 55). On the long prayers of Puritans and the quarrels among English Protestants over prayer length throughout the sixteenth and seventeenth centuries, see also Horton O. Davies, *The Worship of the English Puritans* (Glasgow: University Press of Glasgow, 1948), 67–69, 109–110, 135, 151, 280.

[49] On the conflict between the traditional English Protestant identification of the pope

ten with Laud's aid, that banned further controversy concerning Montagu's opinions "for the establishing of the Peace and Quiet of the Church
of England."[50] In 1629 London clergyman launched a petition complaining that Charles's proclamation was being used to promote Arminian at the expense of Calvinist doctrine.[51] In the 1629 Parliament Francis
Rous compared ascendant Arminianism to a "Trojan horse" containing
men "ready to open the gates to Romish tyranny."[52] By implicitly dismissing those whose consciences (unlike Ashton's) were worried by in-
novations within the established church as "Protestant[s] . . . / . . . *onely* in
despight of Rome" (emphasis mine), Crashaw combats the traditional
anti-papist sentiment that fueled intense fears concerning the new directions of the Church.

Ashton's visible "sermons" addressed to the "eye" (l. 16) are implicitly
linked to his respect for the English church's visible beauty, its "veile"
and "dresse" (ll. 22, 23). Those who feared and criticized the Church's
visible beauty, Crashaw would have his reader believe, are the same as
those who do not practice, and thus make visible, what they preach. The
Puritan emphasis upon preaching had led, according to their opponents,
to a mere "religion in the ear," and in the early seventeenth century the
Arminians strongly reasserted the centrality of the visual aspects of
church worship.[53] In 1635 the Arminian Robert Shelford, for example,
argued that "the beauty of preaching (which is a beauty too) hath preacht
away the beauty of holinesse."[54] Crashaw presents Ashton, the embodiment of a middle way, as having constantly sought to balance the beauties
of eye and ear.

The memorial for Ashton reveals a similar balance. Crashaw's plain-
style epitaph in iambic tetrameters owes a general stylistic debt to Jonson,
and the opening assertion that the "modest front of this small floore" is
able to "say more" than a showier tomb recalls Jonson's announcements
of his poems' expressive brevity.[55] Jonson, however, either exalts the
verbal message at the expense of the (real or imaginary) monument or
celebrates the power of poetry to create its own visual monument, while
Crashaw imagines a harmony between his inscription and the (imaginary)
floor slab upon which it is inscribed. Both the epitaph and the slab dec-

---

with the Antichrist and the more moderate Arminian attitude toward the Roman church,
see Christopher Hill, *Antichrist in Seventeenth-Century England* (London: Oxford University
Press, 1971), 1–41; and Tyacke, *Anti-Calvinism*, 55, 149, 247, and passim.

[50] The proclamation is in Larkin and Hughes, *Stuart Proclamations*, 2:90–93.

[51] See Tyacke, *Anti-Calvinism*, 181–182.

[52] See Notestein and Relf, 13.

[53] See Hill, *Society*, 63–64. Hill cites the dismissive description of Puritanism as "religion
in the ear" from a supposed retort of King James to the Puritans at the Hampton Court
Conference.

[54] Cited in Tyacke, *Anti-Calvinists*, 55.

[55] On Crashaw's debt to Jonson in his early funerary poetry, see Warren, 96.

orously reflect the values of the deceased. The inscription's short lines and calm statement reflect Ashton's modest adjuring of the "lowdness and length" associated by many with Puritan devotions. Though the thirty-eight line epitaph is not truly brief, especially when compared to con-temporaneous epigrammatic epitaphs, Crashaw makes the fourth line of the poem—"Here lyes a truly honest man"—both the sententious epitome of the entire message and a self-contained epitaph statement that can stand, like the praise of Lewkenor as an honest man, for the esential epitaph to which the rest of the poem acts as a mere gloss. The floor monument expresses Ashton's virtue in complementary visual terms. A Christian innovation, the floor slab, whether of marble, brass, or stone, was the humblest of church monuments. It was walked upon rather than looked up to and thus evoked the body laid low. Such a monument could therefore represent, as in this poem, a pointed choice of humility in an age of grand funerary display.[56] The smallness of Ashton's slab further conveys humility. Carefully distinguishing the properly humble visual image from the controversial and ostentatious display of the aristocratic monument, Crashaw suggests that the beauty of the Church has nothing whatever to do with vainglorious or courtly show. Ashton and his visual monument are as plain as any Protestant "honest man" could wish.

The poem suggests that moderate conformity has its own religious power. Ashton's peaceful life earns him a similarly quiet death:

> Peace, which hee lov'd in Life, did lend
> Her hand to bring him to his end;
> When Age and Death call'd for the score,
> No surfets were to reckon for.
> Death tore not (therefore) but sans strife
> Gently untwin'd his thread of Life.
>
> (ll. 25–30)

The life strings of the good citizen who "tore not" the Church's "veil" are gently untied so that Ashton experiences the calm death that was an ideal of the period.[57] The poem ends by turning to the reader and asserting the potentially transformative force of such gentleness:

[56] See Ariès's sensitive discussion of the significance of the horizontal tomb (pp. 237–240). William Browne's pseudo-inscriptional epitaph upon himself, which begins "Loaden with earth, as earth by such as I.../ Tread on me he that list," evokes a floor slab and makes explicit its moral significance; see "My Own Epitaph," in *The Poems of William Browne of Tavistock*, ed. Gordon Goodwin, 2 vols. (London, 1894), 2:293.

[57] On the calm, quiet death as an ideal in the sixteenth and seventeenth centuries, see Ariès, 310–312. Though in his final sermon Donne stresses that "an easie, a quiet death" (or its opposite) is not proof of salvation (or damnation), he beautifully depicts the ideal of the quiet death in his funerary sermon on Lady Danvers and in the opening of "A Valediction: forbidding Mourning." For sensitive observations on Donne's presentation of

What remains then, but that Thou
Write these lines, Reader, in thy Brow,
And by his faire Examples light,
Burne in thy Imitation bright.
So while these Lines can but Bequeath
A Life perhaps unto his Death,
His better Epitaph shall bee,
His Life still kept alive in Thee.

(ll. 31–38)

In marked contrast to Jonson's use of the motif, the spreading of the
message is here both a verbal and visual act. The primary meaning of
"front" is "forehead" (*OED* I.1), and the "modest front" announced in
the opening line yields at the end of the poem to the good reader's
"brow." The poem asks that the inscription appear where it belongs, as
a mark upon the modest brow of the good reader. The reader who
inscribes this verbal message and "burne[s]" with Ashton's "light" becomes a Christian messenger like John the Baptist, "a burning and a
shining light" who "bare witness" of Christ (John 5:33, 35). The reader
also thereby obeys Christ's injunction to his disciples concerning the
visual proclamation of good works: "Let your light so shine before men,
that they may see your good works, and glorify your Father which is in
heaven" (Matthew 5:16).

Like the praise of Ashton as a man of peace whose actions were sermons, the comparison of the deceased to a light recalls seventeenth-
century epitaphs upon ministers. Such epitaphs describe the dead as,
for example, "a burninge and a shininge light" like John the Baptist; a
"lamp divine / Which here with zeal did burn, with knowledge shine";
and "A shining saint / A burning taper."[58] By applying panegyric motifs
normally used of ministers to Ashton, Crashaw emphasizes that Ashton
embodied the traditional Protestant ideal of the godly or "honest" layman. The Arminians sought to exalt the church hierarchy above the
layman—the bishops who held office *iure divino*, the "priesthood" (rather
than the traditional Protestant "ministry") who administered the sacraments—but Crashaw provides supposed assurance that the godly laymen

---

the "good death" in these and other passages, see Arnold Stein, *The House of Death: Messages
from the English Renaissance* (Baltimore: Johns Hopkins University Press, 1986), 49–66,
211–212, and passim.

[58] Epitaphs on John Day, d. 1622, in Ravenshaw, 67; John Down, d. 1631, in W. H.
Beable, ed., *Epitaphs: Graveyard Humour and Eulogy* (1925; rpt., Detroit: Singing Tree Press,
1971), 240; and Richard Russell, d. 1654, in Ravenshaw, 109. For similar images used of
ministers, see also the epitaphs upon Edward Marshall, d. 1625, in Le Neve, 4:97–98; and
James Robins, d. 1652, in F. N. Davis, ed., "Anthony à Wood's and Richard Rawlinson's
Parochial Collections (Third Part)," *Oxfordshire Record Society* 11 (1929):238. I have not
found a similar image in any seventeenth-century epitaph upon a laymen other than
Crashaw's poem.

is still an ideal fully compatible with support for the Church and the king.[59]

Crashaw could not himself sustain the balance between "honesty," with its increasingly Puritan resonances, and "conformity," with its increasingly Arminian consequences. In the poems written at Cambridge he wholeheartedly espoused Arminian positions. In 1635 he composed an introductory poem to Shelford's Arminian *Five Pious and Learned Discourses* that espoused three positions of the earlier epitaph: reverence for the beauties of religion addressed to the eye (ll. 1–48); the necessary unity of belief and action, rather than reliance upon "faith, a *mountaine word*, made up of aire" (ll. 49–58); and, finally, the rejection of anti-popery as the defining characteristic of the true Protestant ("... no longer shall our people hope, / To be a true Protestant, 's but to hate the Pope," ll. 67–68).[60] Gone is the epitaph's attempt, however, to forge a moderate position by absorbing the values and rhetoric of "honesty." By 1635 the king had ruled without Parliament for six years, Laud had been archbishop of Canterbury for two, and Arminianism had conquered the established church. Now fully committed to Arminian doctrine and ritual, Crashaw no doubt viewed his praise of a conforming "honest man," in retrospect, as a naive attempt to square the circle by mingling incompatible religious trends.

The Ashton epitaph did not, of course, stem the tide of "honest" dissatisfaction with the Church and the king any more than it provided Crashaw himself with a permanent credo. While the poet himself moved from Laudianism to exile and Catholicism in the 1640s, honesty as a religious and social ideal continued to play an important role in the turmoil of the years immediately before, during, and after the Civil Wars. The Arminians' rise to complete control of the church hierarchy when Laud became archbishop of Canterbury in 1633 radicalized the Puritan movement of the 1630s and early 1640s. The 1640 London Root and Branch petition for the elimination of the episcopacy, an early radical salvo in the attack upon the Caroline-Laudian Church, was mastermined by the wealthy Puritan merchant elite of London but subscribed to by many men of the middle ranks. In his defense of the petition to Parliament, Alderman Pennington affirmed the worth of humble but zealous "honest" men by arguing that "if ther weere anie meane mens hands to it, yet if they weere honest men, ther was noe reason but ther

---

[59] On the Arminian exaltation of the episcopacy, see William M. Lamont, *Godly Rule: Politics and Religion, 1603–1660* (London: Macmillan, 1969), 56–77; on the attempted elevation of the ministry not as preachers but as "priests" administering the sacrament, see Tyacke, "Puritanism," 140.
[60] Crashaw "*Upon the ensuing Treatises [of* Mr. Shelford]," in Crashaw, 69–70.

hands should bee received."[61] During the Civil Wars and Interregnum, the "honest" party came to mean the junior officers and common soldiers who fought for Parliament and supported the radical actions of 1648 and 1649, including the execution of the king.[62] When Richard Baxter spoke of "a plain hearted, honest, godly man, entirely beloved and trusted by the soldiers for his honesty," he was describing a potent ideal.[63] In 1643 Cromwell defended his acceptance of a nongentleman as a captain of cavalry by noting the fighting spirit of "honest" men: "If you choose godly honest men to be captains of horse, honest men will follow them.... A few honest men are better than numbers."[64] In a 1646 report to the Parliament on the army's progress and needs, the Puritan Independent Hugh Peter, a great believer in the "honest" soldiers for whom he was a chaplain, stressed that men of "faithfulnesse, and honestie" should be valued over men of "honour, friends, and estate."[65] Tempering the ideal of godliness with conservative respect for the social hierarchy, many Puritan gentry, by contrast, took alarm at such developments.[66] By 1649, when the army grandees and the gentry who controlled the Rump Parliament prevented the more extreme religious and social reforms sought by the Army radicals and their allies among the Levellers and radical religious sects, the "honest" party had lost whatever unity it had. Struggles raged for the hearts and minds of the "honest": a 1649 tract coauthored by a group of Independent ministers, for example, attacked the Levellers for "corrupting and dividing ... the honest and true-hearted party" and "abusing simple-hearted honest men."[67]

---

[61] Quoted in *The Journal of Sir Simonds D'Ewes from the Beginning of the Long Parliament to the Opening of the Trial of the Earl of Strafford*, ed. Wallace Notestein (New Haven: Yale University Press, 1923), 339.

[62] See David Underdown, "'Honest' Radicals in the Counties, 1642–1649," in *Puritans and Revolutionaries: Essays in Seventeenth-Century History presented to Christopher Hill*, ed. Donald Pennington and Keith Thomas (Oxford: Clarendon, 1978), 186–205, which cites numerous examples of such uses of "honest" during the period.

[63] Cited in Underdown, "'Honest' Radicals," 188.

[64] Cited in Christopher Hill, *God's Englishman: Oliver Cromwell and the English Revolution* (London: Weidenfeld & Nicolson, 1970), 67. Hill discusses Cromwell's promotion of officers from among the lower ranks and the social implications of low-born officers in the Parliamentary army (pp. 65–68, 100–102).

[65] Cited in Raymond Phineas Stearns, *The Strenuous Puritan: Hugh Peter, 1598–1660* (Urbana: University of Illinois Press, 1954), 264.

[66] On the conflict between "radical Puritanism" and "gentry conservatism" during the Civil Wars and post–Civil Wars period, a conflict not simply between groups but also within individual minds like Cromwell's, see David Underdown, *Pride's Purge: Politics in the Puritan Revolution* (1971; rpt., London: Allen, 1985), 336–360 and passim.

[67] *Walwins Wiles* (London, 1649) in William Haller and Godfrey Davies, ed., *The Leveller Tracts, 1647–1653* (New York: Columbia University Press, 1944), 285–317 (quotations from pp. 288 and 306). Allusions to "honest" men appear throughout the tract. The principal author was a minister associated with John Godwin's Independent Calvinist congregation (Haller and Davies, 285). James E. Farnell notes that Godwin's gathered church, while dissociating itself from the Levellers, proclaimed its "own doctrine of democratic politics

The same tract accused the Levellers of deliberately pushing for inopportune and wild measures, such as replacing professional judges with a rotation system whereby common workers would be relieved of work in order to judge civil and criminal cases. Thus "a Cobler from his Seat, or a Butcher from his Shop, or any other Tradesman that is an honest and just man" would sit in judgment.[68] Throughout the period Royalists satirized cobblers as the grubby proponents of radical social and religious policies, and even the Independent ministers who attacked the Levellers expected their readers to be shocked by the notion of an "honest" cobbler and his ilk's meting out the law of the land.[69] Such shock provides the context for understanding the following two epitaphs, printed consecutively in the 1650 version of the anthology *Wit's Recreations*:

An honest Epitaph

Here lyes an honest man, reader, if thou seek more,
Thou art not so thy selfe; for honesty is store
Of commendations; and it is more praise,
To dye an honest man, than full of dayes.

On a Cobler

Here lyes an honest cobler, whom curst fate,
Perceiving nere worn out, would needs translate;
'Twas a good thrifty soul, and time hath bin,
He would well liquor'd wade through thick and thin:
But now he's gone, 'tis all that can be said,
Honest John Cobler is here under-laid.[70]

First issued in 1640 and revised several times up to its last, 1663 edition, *Wit's Recreations* is an anthology of epigrams and epitaphs adhering throughout its "career" to a conservative sense of stylistic decorum: it includes many panegyric and a few satiric epitaphs upon kings, the aristocracy, gentry and clergy, but only comic epitaphs—and many of them—upon the lower orders.[71] While the epitaph on the cobbler is

---

by honest men" in "The Usurpation of Honest London Householders: Barebone's Parliament," *English Historical Review* 82 (1967):28–29.

[68] Haller and Davies, 303.

[69] For Royalist attacks upon radical Protestant cobblers in the 1640s, see the satires cited in Holden, 61, 63, 66. A Royalist song upon the Restoration looked to the happy future when "the *Cobler* shall edify us no more"; see "A SONG. *For General* Monk's *Entertainment at Cloth-workers-Hall,*" in *A Collection of Loyal Songs Written against the Rump Parliament between the Years 1639 and 1661*, 2 vols. (London, 1731), 1:263.

[70] I cite the text reprinted in *Facetiae: Musarum Deliciae and Wit Restor'd and Wits Recreations*, 2 vols. (London, 1817), 2:251.

[71] The collection includes numerous poems on Hobson the carrier, the Cambridge postman commemorated by a number of condescending university wits including, most notably, John Milton, though his two efforts did not make it into the collection; see *Facetiae*, 2:227–228, 249–250.

present from the first edition, the epitaph on an honest man appears for the first time in 1650.[72] The juxtaposition of the two epitaphs reveals both the contradictions and the conservatism of such an anthology. The first poem, the doggerel but serious descendant of the Lewkenor poem, is a concession to the times, using supposedly sententious brevity to assert that "honest man" is the highest and most expressive praise. The second, by contrast, uses reductive brevity to assert that an "honest cobler" is an object of comic condescension about whom little could or should be said. The second, older epitaph limits the significance of the first epitaph by suggesting that the latter's lack of social specification is not truly an egalitarian, leveling proclamation. The second epitaph suggests that only a man of substance could truly be a virtuous "honest man," since other men are definable only in terms of their limiting and inherently comic occupations. *Wit's Recreations* thus reveals both the ultimate thrust, and the thwarting, of the "honest" ideal. Both the godly yearnings that helped initiate the Civil War and the social conservatism that prevented a more radical revolution from occurring in the late 1640s and 1650s are here inscribed in a few doggerel lines, full of meaning in a way not wholly envisaged by their authors.

Outspoken Royalist poets during the Interregnum meanwhile treated all Puritans as social upstarts and ridiculed the "honest" ideal on both the religious and social fronts. A Royalist anthology of 1658, *Wit Restor'd*, included both a version of the cobbler epitaph from *Wit's Recreations* and a similar comical, condescending epitaph upon an "honest" tailor.[73] It offered no version, by contrast, of the panegyric epitaph upon an honest man. Instead it explicitly attacked the godly ideal. During Elizabeth's reign Sir John Harington composed an epigram attacking a Puritan minister who sang "Geneva Psalmes" but would not give a poor man alms.[74] Reprinting Harington's epigram, the editors of *Wit Restor'd* replaced his misleading designation of the minister as a "priest" with the more appropriate and topical appellation, an "honest vicar."[75] The "honest vicar" satirized in the poem is both a socially humble clergyman like Shirley's "honest parson" and a Puritan fanatic whose obsession with

---

[72] I have consulted the 1640, 1641, 1650, and 1663 editions; in the 1650 edition the two epitaphs are numbered 150 and 151.

[73] "On the Death of Cut. Cobler" and *"An Epitaph upon* Hurry *the Taylor"* in *Musarum Deliciae* (1655) *and Wit Restor'd* (1658), facsimile reprod. with intro. Tim Raylor (Delmar, N.Y.: Scholars' Facsimiles & Reprints, 1985), 78–79, 129.

[74] See "Of Blessing without a crosse," in *The Letters and Epigrammes of Sir John Harington*, ed. Norman Egburt McClure (Philadelphia: University of Pennsylvania Press, 1930), 164. The epigram was published several times in the first half of the seventeenth century.

[75] "A Vicar," in *Musarum & Wit*, 130.

faith excludes charity. In 1658 *Wit Restor'd* attacked the humble and zealous "honest" man with the resentful wit of the defeated. In 1660 the defeated re-emerged triumphant, however, when more than wit was restored.

Chapter 6

Herrick and the
Epitaph of Retreat

This chapter examines one poet's adaptation of the epitaph in response to the turmoil of the mid seventeenth century. Robert Herrick's epitaphs are unique treatments of the relationship between the grave and the social world during times of civil disorder, but they are also an extreme version of the seventeenth-century celebration of contented retirement, a literary trend that was partly a reaction to the religious and social conflicts England experienced in the years preceding, during, and after the Civil Wars.[1] Herrick imagines the grave as a small but secure place of retreat where the self is safely buried. During the Civil Wars men on both sides fought to defend their private property and their concomitant rights as free men. With strange originality, Herrick seeks contentment during such troubled times by figuring the grave as the necessary and sufficient property, the ultimate home, of the truly free man.

Herrick similarly seeks contentment in the brief epitaph as a small but sufficient message concerning the dead. Though he was a devoted pupil of Jonson, his epitaphs for the most part avoid the Jonsonian emphasis on transmitting the exemplary virtues of the deceased. They try, instead, to preserve the deceased from the disorder experienced by the living. The epitaph is normally a highly public genre, addressing or purporting to address all passersby and proclaiming the enduring social value of

[1] For discussions of this retirement tradition, see Earl Miner, *The Cavalier Mode from Jonson to Cotton* (Princeton: Princeton University Press, 1971), passim; and Maren-Sofie Røstvig, *The Happy Man: Studies in the Metamorphoses of a Classical Ideal*, rev. ed. (Oslo: Norwegian University Press, 1962), vol. 1, especially pp. 69–225.

the dead. By contrast, even as they assert the continuing connection between the dead and the living, Herrick's self-avowedly modest epitaphs try to maintain a beneficent distance between the small, private domain of the dead and the large, threatening world of the living.

Though some of the epitaphs contained in Herrick's *Hesperides* have been closely analyzed and justly praised, critics have not adequately discussed the relationship of Herrick's compositions to the epitaphic tradition.[2] One can begin to elucidate the connections by considering Herrick's epitaph upon Jonson, which implicitly treats the relationship of Herrick's epitaphic poetry to that of his master:

> Here lyes *Johnson* with the rest
> Of the Poets; but the Best.
> Reader, wo'dst thou more have known?
> Aske his Story, not this Stone.
> That will speake what this can't tell
> Of his glory. *So farewell.*
>
> (H-910)[3]

Purporting to be the inscription upon Jonson's tomb, the poem praises Jonson as the best of poets and then sends the reader away from the monument to Jonson's "story," that is, to Jonson's own "account of the events of his life" (*OED*, 4d) in his self-portraying poems. Though the poem's brevity and plain-style simplicity reveal its general debt to Jonson's epigrams and epitaphs, its avowed modesty differs greatly from Jonson's pride in his "much in little" poems. The final "tell" / "farewell"

---

[2] Kathryn Anderson McEuen has a brief and not always convincing discussion of the influence of the *Greek Anthology* and Martial on Herrick's epitaphs in *Classical Influence upon the Tribe of Ben* (1939; rpt., New York: Octagon Books, 1968), 31–32, 235–239. For my discussion of Herrick's epitaphs, I have found useful Gordon Braden, *The Classics and English Renaissance Poetry: Three Case Studies* (New Haven: Yale University Press, 1978), 154–254; Ann Baynes Coiro, *Robert Herrick's "Hesperides" and the Epigram Book Tradition* (Baltimore: Johns Hopkins University Press, 1988), especially pp. 207–216; Robert H. Deming, *Ceremony and Art: Robert Herrick's Poetry* (The Hague: Mouton, 1974), 99–126; A. Leigh DeNeef, *"This Poetick Liturgie": Robert Herrick's Ceremonial Mode* (Durham: Duke University Press, 1974), 142–163; Achsah Guibbory, *The Map of Time: Seventeenth-Century English Literature and Ideas of Pattern in History* (Urbana: University of Illinois Press, 1986), 137–167; U. Milo Kaufman, *Paradise in the Age of Milton* (Victoria, B.C.: University of Victoria, 1978), 51–57; and Leah Sinanoglou Marcus, *Childhood and Cultural Despair: A Theme and Variations in Seventeenth-Century Literature* (Pittsburgh: University of Pittsburgh Press, 1978), 120–139. Though I am principally concerned with Herrick's book of secular poetry, *Hesperides*, which contains almost all of his epitaphs, my notes sometimes refer to relevant compositions in *Noble Numbers*, the book of sacred poems. Though different in focus and sometimes contradictory in attitude, the two books nevertheless reveal the same poetic voice.

[3] All citations and the numbering of the poems are from *The Complete Poetry of Robert Herrick*, ed. J. Max Patrick (Garden City, N.Y.: Doubleday, 1963). I have profited from the notes on Herrick's sources in this edition and in L. C. Martin, ed., *The Poetical Works of Robert Herrick* (Oxford: Clarendon, 1956).

rhyme echoes the final rhyme of Jonson's epitaphs upon Elizabeth, L. H. and Sir Charles Cavendish.[4] In both of Jonson's poems a final clipped "farewell" announces that the speaker has said all that need be said and dismisses the reader with magisterial authority. Herrick's valediction, which follows a confession of supposed inability to say what needs to be said, creates a very different effect by the simple addition of the adverbial particle "so." Herrick presents to his readers the logical consequences of his poem's ostensible inadequacy ("so" in the sense of "that being the case"): the reader is gently persuaded to seek Jonson's story elsewhere rather than commanded to depart.

The epitaph thus seems to belong not at all to the proud Jonsonian tradition but rather to the countertradition of the explicitly slight epigrammatic epitaph. It recalls such a modest epitaph as Ausonius's distich on Ulysses: "Ulysses son of Laertes is buried in this tomb; / read the *Odyssey* if you wish to know all."[5] A late Latin author with a self-consciously minor and belated relation to poetic tradition, Ausonius appropriately writes an epitaph that makes little claim for itself. Part of a series of "tiny" ("parvula") epitaphs upon Greek epic heroes, Ausonius's epitaph decorously upholds the traditional hierarchy of genres by sending the reader from the epigrammatic confines of the epitaph to the greater epic poem that alone can portray the glory of the deceased. Herrick's epitaph seems even more pointedly modest, since it suggests the inability of the poet's epigrammatic art to tell of the great things concerning a poet who proclaimed the expressive power of the epigram as a genre.

Herrick's poetic modesty is not, however, as straightforward as it appears. "Here lyes *Johnson* with the rest / Of the Poets; but the Best" echoes one of Jonson's assertions in *Discoveries* (2578–2579): "To judge of Poets is only the facultie of Poets; and not of all Poets, but the best."[6] Herrick's echo implies that he is one of those poets able to judge Jonson the best precisely because he himself is one of the best. Since Herrick

---

[4] It is not certain that Herrick knew the Cavendish epitaph, composed circa 1619, since the poem was never published. Herrick's association with Jonson and the "tribe of Ben" in London during the 1620s, however, makes it likely that he knew the composition; see Marchette Chute, *Two Gentle Men: The Lives of George Herbert and Robert Herrick* (New York: Dutton, 1959), 184–191.

[5] "Conditur hoc tumulo Laerta natus Ulixes: / perlege Odyssean omnia nosse volens" (Ausonius, *Epitaphia heroum . . .* , 5).

[6] *Ben Jonson*, ed. C. H. Herford and Percy and Evelyn Simpson, 11 vols. (Oxford: Clarendon, 1925–1952), 8:642. *Discoveries* was published posthumously in the 1640 *Works* (8:557). Though Jonson's burial in 1637 is the terminus a quo for Herrick's poem, it is likely that Herrick wrote the poem after the publication of (and perhaps in response to) the publication of Jonson's *Works*. This would explain, at any rate, why Herrick's composition was not included in the 1638 commemorative anthology upon Jonson, *Jonsonus Virbius*.

has presumably learned his poetic skill and consequent ability to judge poetry from Jonson, his humble praise of his master in fact expresses the pride of filiation. To be a worthy poetic son of "Father *Johnson*" (H-575), the best of poets, is a large poetic claim. Herrick, with humble pride, claims no more.

The poetic self-assertion of this seemingly modest poem is reflected in a highly artful simplicity quite unlike Ausonius's unadorned elegiac distich. The alliteration of the contrasting words "story" and "stone" is carefully matched by the internal rhyme of the conceptually linked words "story" and "glory," placed in identical metrical positions in their respective lines. Herrick clearly expect the reader to pause, consider the relationship between these three crucial words, and appreciate the poem as an elegant artifact—one that in fact says all that it wishes to say— before moving on.

Herrick's unique mixture of modesty and assertion reveals itself most clearly in the numerous epitaphs upon himself that are scattered through the *Hesperides*. Like Donne in his "Epitaph on Himselfe," Herrick in his many pseudo-inscriptional epitaphs upon himself constructs a highly original relationship between himself and the world of the living. In an epitaph of disyllabic triplets, Herrick finds a modest authority in death:

> Thus I,
> Passe by,
> And die:
> As One,
> Unknown,
> And gon:
> I'm made
> A shade
> And laid
> I'th grave,
> There have
> My Cave.
> Where tell
> I dwell,
> *Farewell.*
> ("Upon his departure hence," H-475)

The poem is indebted to medieval epitaphs in which the deceased says farewell to the living as if he or she were in the process of leaving the world. The valedictory speaker normally delivers a simple message: the inevitability of death.[7] Herrick's poem explores the double movement inherent in such poems, however, whereby the speaker simultaneously departs from, and gains authority over, the living.

Herrick's unusual meter gives a highly self-effacing tone to this description of his own death and burial. There is little pathos, for the poet does not make enough of a textual appearance for his disappearance to be strongly felt. The short lines make the reader experience instead the speed with which the poet departs. The opening, "Thus I / Passe by" (ll. 1–2) describes the poet disappearing into death as quickly as the reader himself "passes by" the dimeter lines. The parallel between the swift disappearance of the "I" and the brief reading experience is reinforced because the reader of an epitaph is traditionally the passerby or, as Herrick calls him in another poem, the "passenger" ("To the Passenger," H-821).[8]

Normally an epitaph tells the passerby to stop: "Stay, view this stone," begins Jonson's epitaph upon Cecilia Bulstrode.[9] Some classical inscriptions emphasize, desperately, how short a stop is needed for the busy passerby to read the message of the epitaph and thus rescue the deceased, even if but for a moment, from oblivion.[10] Sixteenth- and seventeenth-century epitaphs sometimes do the same: Ludovico Ariosto's neo-Latin epitaph upon Raphael, for example, entices the passerby to pause and read with the assurance that "the stop is not long" ("non longa mora est"), while the early seventeenth-century English poet Huntington Plumptre bids the traveller "stay a brief moment" ("Paulum siste").[11] Demanding even less from the reader, Herrick does not ask the reader to stop at all: both the writer and the reader, the dead and the living, quickly pass each other by after the briefest of encounters.

The poet who "passes by" also finds a place, however, from which he can finally deliver a message, in the last triplet, that establishes a more

---

[7] An inscription from a late fifteenth-century English tombstone is typical: "Farewel my frendes, the tyde abideth no man / I am departed hense and soe shall ye" (included in Thomas F. Ravenshaw, ed., *Antiente Epitaphes [from A.D. 1250 to A.D. 1800]* [London, 1878], 14). Herrick could have seen such epitaphs both on tombs and in antiquarian works. Some fifteenth-century versions are to this day legible on brasses, and early seventeenth-century works by John Stow and John Weever recorded variants; see D. Gray, "A Middle English Epitaph," *Notes and Queries* 206, n. s., 8 (1961):132–135.

[8] One of Jonson's epitaphs treats the terms "passenger" and "passerby" as equivalent: see "*An Epitaph, on* HENRY L. La-Ware. *To the Passer-by*," which opens "If, Passenger . . ." (8:233).

[9] Jonson, 8:371.

[10] See Richmond Lattimore, *Themes in Greek and Latin Epitaphs* (Urbana: University of Illinois Press, 1962), 232–234.

[11] Ludovico Ariosto, "Raphael of Urbino," in *Renaissance Latin Verse: An Anthology*, ed. Alessandro Perosa and John Sparrow (Chapel Hill: University of North Carolina Press, 1979), 182; and Huntington Plumptre, "Epitaphium Henrici 6," in his *Epigrammatôn Opusculum Duobus Libellis Distinctum* (London, 1629), 64.

permanent connection with the world. The final rhyme "dwell" / "Farewell" (ll. 14–15) once more recalls Jonson's epitaphs upon Cavendish and Elizabeth, L. H., and his concluding command that the reader "tell" (l. 13) where he now "dwell[s]" recalls the commands of the same two Jonson epitaphs. Like the Cavendish and Elizabeth, L. H. epitaphs, Herrick's poem adapts the classical epitaphic topos of bidding the passerby to deliver a message concerning the deceased to a third party. Unlike Cavendish's proclamation of personal identity and glory, Herrick's final message is not proud: it does not tell who the departed is or why he should be remembered, but simply where he now lies buried. The deceased and his qualities will thus remain "unknown" (l. 5) even though news will be spread of where he lies. Nor does the final message seem, like the final couplet of the Elizabeth, L. H. epitaph, a deeply resonant ethical pronouncement. Herrick's emphasis is closest to the epitaphs from the *Greek Anthology* that ask the reader to tell relatives and friends where the deceased lies buried far from home. Herrick strips the emphasis upon the place of burial of its pathetic specificities, however, by giving the reader no location other than "my Cave" (l. 12), no identifying name, and no specific third party to address. The puzzling thinness of the message forces the reader, so ready to pass by, to pause at the conclusion and consider the poem's oddities. The final message is on one level a memento mori, telling us and asking us to tell others that one more man no longer dwells among the living. The speaker sounds oddly contented, however, for he has not simply left the world but has also taken possession of a place in which he can "dwell" and from which he can deliver commands, however small, to the world he has left behind.[12]

The sepulchral "cave" of "Upon his departure hence" is Herrick's most bizarre but characteristic version of his central ideal, "home." Home takes different forms in *Hesperides*, but it is above all a little haven of retreat in which one can find contentment, safety, and freedom from the cares of the larger, threatening world. In a celebration of his modest "cell" indebted to Horatian retirement poetry, Herrick praises the place where he "securely" dwells ("*An Ode to Sir* Clipsebie Crew," ll. 1, 25, H-544). In a panegyric on country life that echoes Jonson's claim that Sir Robert Wroth can stay "at home, in ... securer rest,"[13] Herrick praises his own brother's life "at home, blest with securest ease" ("*A Country life: To his Brother, Master* Thomas Herrick," l. 69, H-106). Like Jonson, Herrick proclaims that such security is based upon being "content" with what

[12] I owe a general debt to Braden's discussion of Herrick's "strategy of effacement" (see especially pp. 158–161 and 193–194). I am particularly concerned, however, with Herrick's *double* movement of retreat and assertion.

[13] Jonson, "To Sir Robert Wroth," l. 13, 8:97.

one has at "home" ("Country Life," 1. 22, "To Sir Robert Wroth," l. 65). Throughout *Hesperides* Herrick imagines the grave, too, as a small, safe, and carefree home. Contemplating the fall of daffodils, he learns that he shall die and be "safely buried" (H-107). In "His Winding-sheet," he describes the grave as a "securer place" free from worldly desires (H-515). In one epitaph upon himself he describes the grave as a "Chamber fit" (H-306), in another he compares it to the "long'd for lodging" of pilgrims (H-617). While in one poem he professes contentment with the "poore Tenement" in which he lives (H-552), in another he asks the grave digger for "one Tenement" in which to lie when dead (H-853).[14]

In "Upon his departure hence," Herrick's imagining and accepting of the "cave" as his ultimate home is a lesson in contentment with the most minimal of possessions. The slight epitaphic message is the verbal correlative of the small grave, and in the same epitaph Herrick's acceptance of the brief message as his ultimate legacy to the world verbally enacts his contentment with little. Unlike Jonson, who proudly and openly announces that he is making much out of little, Herrick professes contentment with little as an oblique means of claiming or gaining much. He makes his strategy most explicit in brief epigrams advising contentment: "Who with a little cannot be content, / Endures an everlasting punishment" ("Again," H-606); "Let's live with that smal pittance that we have; / *Who covets more, is evermore a slave*" ("The Covetous still Captives," H-607). The first distich suggests the discontented suffer perpetually both in this life and, presumably, in the world to come; the second echoes Horace (*Epistle* 1.10.41) to argue that the discontented suffer lives of perpetual bondage. Both distichs recall the similar distich from the *Disticha Catonis*: "Be sure to flee excess; enjoy what is little. / The ship is safe, which sails upon a moderate stream."[15] While Cato's little poem simply recommends littleness, however, both of Herrick's distichs imply the transvaluations of the Christian *sermo humilis* by suggesting that contentment with little is "great," for it has consequences "everlasting" or "evermore."[16] These small poems concern contentment in

---

[14] Coiro discusses Herrick's embracing of death but does not link it to his general desire for a small but safe "home" (pp. 207–216). Kaufman discusses Herrick's desire for death in terms of the poet's search for a "secure space" (pp. 51–57). Ignoring the poet's sense of external threats, Kaufman contends that Herrick tries to escape from his own "troubled conscience." I argue, by contrast, that Herrick tries to escape from the troubles of the outside world and from desires that would subject him to the world.

[15] "Quod nimium est, fugire; parvo gaudere memento. / Tuta est puppes, modice quo flumina fertur" (*Catonis disticha: Facsimiles, notes, liste des editions du xve siècle*, ed. Joseph Neve [Liège: H. Vaillant-Carmanne, 1926], 27 [2.6]).

[16] In *Noble Numbers*, Herrick makes Cato's praise of contentment more explicitly religious in order to expound the message of the Christian *sermo humilis* that the little is great. Cato recommends contentment with "whatever time offers": "If material things and one's perception [of things] are not what they once were, / Live content with whatever times offers"

life, but contentment with the small grave and the slight epitaphic message is perhaps for Herrick the greatest achievement, for it frees one from the most human and tenacious form of slavish desire for more, being "greedie of ... life" ("To his Booke," l. 17, H-405).

As "Upon his departure hence" reveals, however, Herrick imagines the grave not only as a small refuge from worldly desires and troubles but also as a place from which the deceased can communicate with the living whom he has left behind. Such communications derive their modest authority precisely from the speaker's unworldly position. "The cruell Maid" (H-159) treats the vital link between the poet's retreat to the grave and his small but authoritative message. The poem begins with the poet's withdrawal and ends with his epitaph:

> And Cruell Maid, because I see
> You scornfull of my love, and me:
> Ile trouble you no more; but goe
> My way, where you shall never know
> What is become of me: there I
> Will find me out a path to die;
> Or learne some way how to forget
> You, and your name, for ever: yet
> Ere I go hence; Know this from me
> What will, in time, your Fortune be:
>   . . . . .
> ... yet this thing doe,
> That my last Vow commends to you:
> When you shall see that I am dead,
> For pitty let a teare be shed;
> And (with your Mantle o're me cast)
> Give my cold lips a kisse at last:
> If twice you kisse, you need not feare,
> That I shall stir, or live more here.
> Next, hollow out a Tombe to cover
> Me; me, the most despised Lover:
> And write thereon, *This, Reader, know,*
> *Love kill'd this man.* No more but so.
>   (ll. 1–10, 20–31)

("Rebus et in sensu, si non quod fuit ante, / Fac vivas contentus eo, quod tempora praebent"; *Catonis disticha,* 29 [3.11]). Herrick recommends contentment with "whatever comes" on the grounds that nothing which comes from God is in fact small: "Whatever comes, let's be content withall: / Among Gods Blessings, there is no one small" ("Welcome what comes," N-55). Herrick's transformation of this Latin distich into a Christian reversal of small and great has English antecedents. An early seventeenth-century translator renders the epigram thus: "Content is great; though little bee the meate; / The Great in Little, makes the Little, Great" (Sir Richard Baker, *Cato Variegatus or Catoes Morall Distichs* [London, 1636], 65). See also the discussion of Herrick's "love of littleness," which notes the Christian but not the classical sources of the motif, in Marcus, *Childhood,* 120–129.

The opening section of the poem treats the relationship between withdrawal and communication in conventional Petrarchan terms. Like the rest of Herrick's mistresses, the "cruell Maid" has no substance independent of her role: she is simply the cold woman who impels the poet to seek "a path to die" (l. 6) and to tell her what must be told.[17] I have omitted much of what Herrick actually tells the cruel fair, because it is for the most part a conventional warning that her beauty will decay and that she might then be smitten with love. At the end the poet's message returns, however, to his true interest, his own posthumous fate. Herrick imagines his reappearance as a dead man with a characteristic mixture of meekness and assertion. Just as the departing poet claims he will trouble his beloved "no more" (l. 3), so he reappears dead and thus unable to "stir, or live more here" (l. 27). Yet just as his voyage to death gives him the authority traditionally vouchsafed dying men to make his beloved "know" (l. 9) her fate,[18] so the poet's death will allow him (if his beloved does as she is told) an epitaph that will authoritatively teach its reader: "This, Reader, know" (l. 30). There is thus a clear analogy between the cruel maid, who learns from her would-be lover as he departs, and the reader, who will learn from the epitaph of the departed poet.

The whole poem is about what it means to do and say something and "no more." In the epitaph Herrick takes brevity as far as it can go: the two hemistiches of the enjambed epitaph together make up a single iambic tetrameter line. The epitaph has a combination of elements typical of Herrick: an authoritative command that the reader learn the epitaphic lesson ("This, Reader, know") followed by a paucity of actual information ("Love killed this man," l. 31). Herrick underlines his contentment with this small message by ending the poem not with the epitaph but with his self-effacing gloss, "No more but so."

He further underscores his contentment through imitation. "The cruell Maid" and its epitaph are based upon Theocritus's *Idyll* 23, in which a lover bewails his unrequited love and dictates the epitaph that he wants inscribed upon his tomb: "*Love killed this man.* Traveler, do not pass by, / *But pause and read this.* He had a cruel beloved."[19] Adapting only one clause from each of Theocritus's two hexameters, Herrick re-

---

[17] See Braden's excellent remarks on the "absolute imperviousness" and unreality of Herrick's imaginary mistresses (pp. 218–222).

[18] For classical instances of the commonplace that dying men's last words are authoritative and prophetic, see Homer, *Iliad* 16.851ff. and 22.358ff.; Plato, *Apology* 39c; and Robert Garland, *The Greek Way of Death* (Ithaca: Cornell University Press, 1985), 20, 136. For Renaissance examples, see the opening of John of Gaunt's dying speech in *Richard II* and the parallels adduced in William Shakespeare, *Richard II*, ed. Peter Ure, The Arden Shakespeare, 5th ed. (London: Methuen, 1961), 47 (II.ii.5–11 and notes).

[19] "Touton erôs ekteinen. Hodoipore, mê parodeusêis, / alla stas tade lexon. Apênea eikhen hetairon" (Theocritus, *Idyll* 23. 47–48, translation and italics mine). Modern scholars reject Theocritus's authorship of this poem.

duces the two hexameters of the Greek to a four-foot epitaph that the reader can presumably take in without stopping. Herrick demands "no more."

Such a miniaturizing imitation of Theocritus's idyll is highly untraditional. The Greek poem spawned a long tradition of lovers' complaints, but poets after Theocritus typically expanded and made more assertive, rather than reduced and rendered more self-effacing, the epitaphic message. Beginning with pseudo-Tibullus's *Elegy* 3.2, in which the poet-lover adapts the composite form of elegy with concluding epitaph in order to provide directions for his own funeral and sepulchral inscription, post-Theocritean complaints normally end with an epitaph whose strong closural message embodies the lover's ultimate act of self-assertion. The lover dictates an epitaph that names to the world both himself and the beloved who caused his death, thus consoling himself with both posthumous fame and revenge. The conclusions of the pseudo-Tibullan composition and of a well-known English pastoral complaint, the shepherd Harpalus's lament concerning his cruel Phillida, are typical:

But the sad cause of my death let a legend show, and on the stone's face which all may see let it set out these lines: Lygdamus lies here. Sadness and anxiety because of his wife Neaera's being stolen from him [by another man] caused him to die.[20]

> Write you my friends upon my grave,
>   this chaunce that is befall.
> Heere lyeth unhappy *Harpalus*,
>   by cruell Love now slaine:
> Whom *Phillida* unjustly thus,
>   hath murdred with disdaine.[21]

Like Theocritus's lover but unlike these Latin and English lovers, Herrick does not ask that his inscription record either his own or his beloved's name; he asks only to be remembered as a man killed by love. This anonymity is clearly another gesture of modesty by which the deceased does not obtrude himself too much upon either his beloved or the reader.

---

[20] "Sed tristem mortis demonstret littera causam / atque haec in celebri carmina fronte notet: / LYGDAMUS HIC SITUS EST. DOLOR HUIC ET CURA NEAERAE / CONIUGIS EREPTAE CAUSA PERIRE FUIT" (Pseudo-Tibullus [Lygdamus], *Elegy* 3.2.27–30). I have modified the Loeb translation.

[21] The English poem appeared in two major Renaissance anthologies, *Tottel's Miscellany* (1557–1558) and *England's Helicon* (1600; 1614); see *Tottel's Miscellany* (1557), ed. Hyder Edward Rollins, 2 vols., rev. ed. (1925; Cambridge: Harvard University Press, 1965), 1:133–135; and *England's Helicon: 1600, 1614*, ed. Hyder Edward Rollins, 2 vols. (Cambridge: Harvard University Press, 1935), 1:40–43 (from which I quote). For other examples, see Ovid's *Heroides* 2.145–148 and 7.193–196; and Jacopo Sannazaro's "If I should die..." in Sparrow and Perosa, 148–149.

At the beginning of the poem Herrick hopes to forget his beloved and her name: "Or learne some way how to forget / You, and your name, for ever" (ll. 7–8). In his final, self-effacing epitaph he manages to forget both her name and his own. Not seeking fame or revenge as an unrequited lover, Herrick is content to dictate a brief exemplary lesson on the dangers any man faces who falls in love. Recording this humble experience—"so" and not otherwise—is, he insists, message enough.[22]

In "The Argument of his Book" (H-1) Herrick alternates between claims to "sing" and to "write"; the book as a whole combines lyrics that imitate song or speech and epigrams that announce their status as writing.[23] Individual poems also combine lyric and epigrammatic elements. "The cruell Maid" simultaneously moves from life to death and from the representation of speech to the representation of writing. The poet's speech to his beloved gives way to the inscriptional record Herrick bequeaths to his reader. The poet's evident need to confront the world at a safe distance leads him not only to write but also to treat writing as a theme. In the two-line epigram "Writing," he echoes Ovid's Phaedra in *Heroides* 4.10 on the difference between speaking and writing: "When words we want, Love teacheth to endite; / And what we blush to speake, she bids us write" (H-846). In "The cruell Maid" Herrick seems to treat a lover's speech as a model for poetic communication as such, and we may apply the distich's description of writing as a substitute for speech to Herrick's treatment of writing in general. He retreats from direct self-presentation, but converts such retreat into re-presentation through inscriptions that substitute for the presence he does not wish to show. Writing thus becomes a means of publicizing, while preserving the privacy of, the self. In "The cruell Maid," the impersonality that an in-

[22] Besides Herrick's epitaph, the only epitaph in this tradition I know that preserves Theocritean anonymity is the epitaph Propertius tells his beloved Cynthia to put on his tomb: "HE THAT NOW LIES NAUGHT BUT UNLOVELY DUST, / ONCE SERVED ONE LOVE AND ONE LOVE ONLY" (*Elegy* 2.13.35–36; "QUI NUNC IACET HORRIDA PULVIS, / UNIUS HIC QUONDAM SERVUS AMORIS ERAT"). Propertius, however, imagines his death not because he is unhappy in love but because he wants to imagine his immortality, and his couplet presents in brief his supposed central claim to eternal fame: the fact that he loved and was true to one woman (*Elegy* 2.1.47–48). Indeed his brief epitaph in *Elegy* 2.13 is part of a series of diminishments that play implicitly with the idea of the power of brevity: he asks Cynthia to bury his *three* little books with him (l. 25) and to inscribe his epitaph with *two* lines of poetry (l. 35) which describe his *one* love. The movement from three to two to one is an act of powerful concentration, a distilling of Propertius's glory in his single beloved. This epitaph's proud brevity is thus the very opposite of Herrick's self-consciously modest brevity.

[23] On epigram and lyric in *Hesperides*, see Coiro, 30–42 and passim; and Alastair Fowler, *Kinds of Literature: An Introduction to the Theory of Genres and Modes* (Cambridge: Harvard University Press, 1982), 197–198. Fowler associates the "I sing" of the "The Argument" with both epic and ode and the "I write" with epigram (p. 198), but the dominant contrast is surely between lyric (including ode) and epigram.

scription allows further separates the writer from the world: Herrick retreats to become a universal lesson for his fellow man. While earlier poets use the impersonality of an inscription for public praise of the dead, Herrick uses such impersonality further to support his strategy of simultaneous assertion and retreat.

In another poem of departure unto death, Herrick adapts to the needs of his own poetics the "much in little" topos used by Jonson:

> Go I must; when I am gone,
> Write but this upon my Stone;
> Chaste I liv'd, without a wife,
> That's the Story of my life.
> Strewings need none, every flower
> Is in this word, Batchelour.
> ("To his Tomb-maker," H-546)

"To his Tomb-maker" could have been a simple epitaph entitled "Upon himself," but by adding the introductory couplet, Herrick dramatizes the movement from direct speech to writing. He thus emphasizes the mediation inherent in an inscription that both links him to and separates him from the world of the living. "Write but this upon my Stone" prepares for the expressive brevity of the ensuing epitaph. It recalls such proud moments of epitaphic self-assertion as Sir Charles Cavendish's "I made my life my monument, & yours. / Write but that" or Thomas Playfere's "on my tombe write nothing but my name." It thus prepares us for a vigorous self-definition that would counter the opening constraint of "Go I must" with an assertion of the dead's enduring value. Herrick does not wholly subvert the convention. His glory, he declares, is that he lived a celibate life. Herrick indeed has reason to be proud as a Christian, a parson in the Laudian Church, and a prudent seeker of domestic tranquility. Chastity is a major Christian virtue. With their attempt to reemphasize the distinction between the "priesthood" and the laity, moreover, influential members of the Laudian Church, including the celibate Archbishop Laud himself, downgraded the mainstream Protestant celebration of wedded love and promoted celibacy among its "priesthood."[24] Seventeenth-century misogynistic epitaphs praised bachelorhood as a shrewd escape from marital strife. An epitaph of 1629, for example, commemorates a man who "free from wedlocke, care, or stryfe, / . . . wedded was to single life."[25] In similar misogynistic fashion,

---

[24] On Laud's and other High Church ecclesiastics' promotion of clerical celibacy, a policy supported by Charles I, see Charles Carlton, *Archbishop William Laud* (London: Routledge, 1987), 83; and Austin Warren, *Richard Crashaw: A Study in Baroque Sensibility* (Ann Arbor: University of Michigan Press, 1939), 8–9; 208, n. 12.

[25] Epitaph on Richard Best, d. 1629, in Ravenshaw, 76.

Herrick elsewhere finds his "only comfort" in his bachelorhood and consequent escape from marital woe ("His Comfort," H-1052).[26]

Herrick's assertions in "To his Tomb-maker" nevertheless have a self-conscious, almost smug modesty quite different from the norms of proud self-praise. Herrick's culminating claim to fame does not actually identify the highly idiosyncratic poet. "Batchelour" has great rhetorical force as the last and longest word of the poem and as a substitute for the word normally asserted to mean so much in an epitaph, the name of the deceased. Instead of the usual pun on the personal name, Herrick's conclusion—"every flower / Is in this word, Batchelour"—puns on "batchelour" and "bachelor's-button," the name given to various flowers of round or buttonlike form (*OED*). By substituting the name of a *class* of people or flowers for a personal name of glory, Herrick tempers the humanist cult of fame. His achievement is, furthermore, essentially privative, based upon what he did not do ("without a Wife") and does not need ("Strewings needs none"). The padding of the message in so short a poem— "batchelour" following "Chaste . . . without a Wife," the wholly pleonastic "That's the Story of my life"—reveals how little Herrick in fact purports to claim for himself. He celebrates not his glory, but rather, once more, his contentment with little in life and death: contentment with a solitary life, with being honored as an anonymous bachelor, and with having no floral embellishments.

While all Herrick's communications from the grave seek to establish both his distance from and his enduring connection to the world he has left behind, they oscillate between the modest assertions discussed thus far and even more humble requests that his mortuary home be protected from the outside world. The assertiveness of "To his Tomb-maker," for example, is balanced by the beseeching tone of a poem that comes shortly after. *Hesperides* is filled with short sequences of consecutive poems that qualify and enrich the meaning of one another.[27] The three poems that follow "To his Tomb-maker" complement the epitaph:

> Our mortall parts may wrapt in Seare-cloths lye:
> *Great Spirits never with their bodies dye.*
>   ("Great Spirits supervive," H-547)

[26] An epitaph attributed to Herrick treats a man who died from marital "strife"; see "Epitaph on a man who had a Scold to his Wife" (S-10).

[27] For the most extensive argument concerning the organization of Herrick's *Hesperides*, see Coiro, passim, which argues that Herrick carefully arranged not only sequences of contiguous poems but also thematically related poems dispersed throughout the volume. Regarding Herrick's epitaphs I accept the former but not the latter argument. I have not found that the arrangement of the epitaphs dispersed throughout *Hesperides* significantly illuminates the individual compositions except in special cases, such as the final epitaph of the book, which explicitly draws attention to its position.

Out of the world he must, who once comes in:
No man exempted is from Death, or sinne.
("None free from fault," H-54)

Let me sleep this night away,
Till the Dawning of the day:
Then at th'opening of mine eyes,
I, and all the world shall rise.
("Upon himselfe being buried," H-549)

The two distichs qualify the epitaph in opposing ways. The first poem asserts the immortality of "Great Spirits." Though Herrick presumably includes himself among these and thus suggests more pagan pride than in his declaration of Christian chastity, he modestly states the general case for man's immortality through greatness. The second distich states that all men must die just as all men are sinners; implicit is the Pauline message that "the wages of sin is death" (Romans 6:23). Herrick again states the general case, but the truism that all men as sinners "must" go "out of the world" reveals the sinner in the chaste bachelor who begins "To his Tomb-maker" by acknowledging, "Go I must." The two epigrams thus encompass in brief man's potential greatness and his sinfulness, death, and immortality, and hint that Herrick, whatever his claims to uniqueness, is also an Everyman, spanning the human spectrum.

The final poem, "Upon himselfe being buried," explicitly returns to the poet, but here he lacks even the generic virtue of bachelorhood. His sole claim to individuality in this poem is that "this night" of death is his and not those he addresses, that he sleeps alone until he rejoins all other men at the Last Judgment, when "all the world shall rise." By identifying himself with his buried remains as they await the Resurrection, Herrick qualifies both the first distich's one-sided emphasis on secular immortality (even the "mortal parts" of man shall at last be awakened and made new) and the second distich's one-sided emphasis upon death as leaving the world (which the deceased will rejoin when "all the world" rises and is transformed).

"Upon himselfe being buried" also adds a new sense of vulnerability to the picture of the poet's death. Unlike in "To his Tomb-maker," the speaker in this poem needs something more from his reader than respectful attention to his self-defining message. The poem may be read as the dead man's prayer to God as he is buried, begging that He allow the speaker to sleep peacefully till the Resurrection. Since God is not explicitly addressed, however, one may also read the poem as a humble request to the living, who are implored not to disturb the sleep of the deceased.

Herrick's imagining himself asleep in his grave until the Resurrection recalls scriptural descriptions of death. Jesus "awake[s]" the dead Lazarus from "sleep" (John 11:11–14); Saint Paul describes the dead as "asleep" and "sleep[ing] in Jesus" (1 Thessalonians 4:13–14) and as having "fallen asleep in Christ" (1 Corinthians 15:18). According to the sermon against the fear of death in the *Book of Homilies*, in order to give "comfort" to mortals "holy Scripture calleth . . . bodily death a sleepe, wherein man['s] senses be (as it were) taken from him for a season, and yet when hee awaketh [at the Resurrection], he is more fresh then he was when he went to bed."[28] The image is comforting because it suggests the body's peacefulness between death and Resurrection.[29] Herrick, however, emphasizes not the peacefulness but the vulnerability of the sleeping body in its interim state. Epitaphs usually request that the "sleeping" dead not be awakened as a comic motif. Both classical and seventeenth-century English epitaphs playfully warn readers not to disturb irritable people whose awakening would be unpleasant.[30] A seventeenth-century comic epitaph asks the reader to let a lowly rustic "clown" sleep who got no rest from his labor during life.[31] Herrick's request that he not be awakened from his sleep in the grave dramatizes, by contrast, a genuine and anxious desire to be free from disturbance by the world.

In another epitaph upon himself, Herrick more directly wishes that the living not disturb his rest:

> Here I have found a Chamber fit,
> (God and good friends be thankt for it)
> Where if I can a lodger be
> A little while from Tramplers free;

[28] "An exhortation against the feare of death" in *Certaine Sermons or Homilies*, intro. Mary Ellen Rickey and Thomas B. Stroup, 2 vols. (1623; rpt., Gainesville, Fla.: Scholars' Facsimiles & Reprints, 1968), 1:61.

[29] The scriptural descriptions of death as peaceful sleep provided the basis for the doctrines of "soul sleep" and "mortalism" deemed heretical by the English church. The homilist, however, treats only the bodies of the dead as asleep. He also claims that death provides for the souls of the deceased "a tasting of heavenly pleasures" (*Certaine Sermons*, 1:60).

[30] Herrick himself uses the motif in a comic epitaph upon a quarreling couple: "Quiet yet; but if ye make / Any noise, they both will wake, / And such spirits raise, 'twill then / Trouble Death to lay agen" ("Upon a Wife that dyed mad with Jealousie," ll. 3–6, H-145). Compare the two Greek epitaphs upon the biting satirist Hipponax (*Greek Anthology* 7.405, 7.408), both of which were translated into Latin and the European vernaculars during the Renaissance (see James Hutton, *The Greek Anthology in Italy* [Ithaca: Cornell University Press, 1935], 499; and James Hutton, *The Greek Anthology in France and in the Latin Writers of the Netherlands to the Year 1800* [Ithaca: Cornell University Press, 1946], 650); and Huntington Plumptre's "Epitaphium Mariae cuiusdam foeminae asperrimae" (*Epigrammatôn*, 68–69).

[31] "On a Clown" in *Facetiae: Musarum Deliciae and Wit Restor'd and Wits Recreations*, 2 vols. (London, 1817), 2:231.

> At my up-rising next, I shall,
> If not requite, yet thank ye all.
>   ("On himselfe," ll. 7-12, H-306)

Just as in "Upon himselfe being buried" Herrick hopes that he will be allowed to sleep a mere "night away," so in "On himselfe" he hopes that "tramplers" will not disturb his home for the brief period before the Last Judgment. By seeking only "a little while" of peace, Herrick underscores his Christian faith in the biblical promise that the Resurrection is to come in "a little while" (John 16:17–25; Hebrews 10: 37). As in "Upon himselfe being buried," however, his hope that he not be disturbed expresses his sense of the grave as a private realm that must be kept safe from the living, for however brief a time.

Though Herrick's epitaphs upon himself reveal an idiosyncratic poetic temperament, his treatment of the grave as the ultimate retreat from the world is not wholly unique. Cavalier retirement poems sometimes praise a retreat so extreme that the distinction between life and death is minimized. In "The Garden," for example, James Shirley imagines escaping from erotic entanglement to "a little plot of ground" in which he will

> I'th' Center of my ground compose
> Of Bayes and Ewe my Summer room,
> Which may so oft as I repose,
> Present my Arbour, and my Tombe.

The poet is "dead" to the world, so the garden is metaphorically his tomb as well as his place of retirement.[32] William Habington, one of the most indefatigable proponents of country retirement in the late 1630s and 1640s, praises the actual grave as a retreat:

> Welcome thou safe retreate!
> Where th'injured man may fortifie
> 'Gainst the invasions of the great:
> Where the leane slave, who th'Oare doth plye,
> Soft as his Admirall may lye.[33]

---

[32] James Shirley, "The Garden," ll. 25–28 in *Poems (1646) together with Poems from the Rawlinson Manuscript*, A Scolar Press Facsimile (Menston, England: Scolar Press, 1970), 69–70.

[33] William Habington, "*Solum mihi superest sepulchrum.* Job," ll. 1–5 in *The Poems of William Habington*, ed. with intro. Kenneth Allott (London: Hodder and Stoughton; Liverpool University Press, 1948), 124. On Habington, see Røstvig, 1:88–99.

Though Habington's heavy-handed moralizing, loosely based on Job's bitter praise of the grave (Job 2:13–19), is very different from Herrick's light touch, he shares Herrick's celebration of the grave as haven.

Some retirement-unto-death poems suggest a desire to escape from the sociopolitical realities of the mid seventeenth century, and Herrick's epitaphs clearly respond to his particular social and political predicament. As a "citizen" of London (H-713) who was "exiled" to the modest country parsonage of Dean Prior in "dull *Devon-shire*" (H-51) and as a Royalist minister confronting the Civil Wars and finally suffering ejection by the Parliamentarians in 1647, Herrick had compelling reasons to preach contented retirement from the world. Although it is difficult to date his poems, at least some of his epitaphs, like many Cavalier retirement poems, seek a private place secure from the public disorder of the Civil Wars. "Upon the troublesome times" suggests why the epitaph was an irresistible genre for this poet:

> O! Times most bad,
> Without the scope
>   Of hope
> Of better to be had!
>
> Where shall I goe,
> Or wither run
>   To shun
> This publique overthrow?
>
> No places are
> (This I am sure)
>   Secure
> In this our wasting Warre.
>
> Some storms w'ave past;
> Yet we must all
>   Down fall,
> And perish at the last.
>   (H-596)

Herrick here searches, as he often does, for a place "secure" (l. 11), and the poem suggests that much of his love of private places represents an attempt to evade "publique overthrow" (l. 8). Yet the final stanza moves from a topical lament to a more general fear of death surprising in this poet who so often embraces death. Given his frequent treatment of the grave as a safe place of retreat, it initially seems odd that in the final stanza he should identify the horror of the Civil Wars with the inevitability of death. The poem moves, however, from an "I" (l. 5) seeking to escape the general ruin in a "secure" place to a "we" (ll. 13, 14) who will surely die, and what Herrick seems to fear most is not death as such but the indistinction of death. The Civil Wars cause general death, but his epitaphs allow the poet to die in his own personal way. In one despairing poem upon his own death, Herrick asks that the living "weepe for the dead, for they have lost this light: / And weep for me, lost in an endlesse night" ("On Himselfe," ll. 1–2, H-952). Lost in "endlesse night" rather than "safely buried," the speaker here imagines himself as simply one among the numerous dead. The epitaphs, on the other hand, try to claim a place safe from worldly disorder, sparing the poet indistinction by creating and defending a place, however small, of his own.

The Civil Wars might well have led Herrick to conclude that the only place one could ultimately possess, and therefore the home that one could most safely desire, was the grave. In the distich "Buriall," he finds solace in the fact that "man may want Land to live in; but for all, / Nature finds out some place for buriall" (H-807). In an odd but revealing epigram, "Large Bounds doe but bury us," he develops the association of the grave with land as property:

> All things o'r-rul'd are here by Chance;
> The greatest mans Inheritance,
> Where ere the luckie Lot doth fall,
> Serves but for place of Buriall.
>
> (H-542)

Herrick preaches, once more, contentment. The poem suggests that since chance determines how much property one inherits and such property, however large, ultimately only serves as one's grave, one should be content with the little property that one receives. In "The Country life ..." (H-662), Herrick praises Endimion Porter for traversing "thine own dear bounds / Not envying others larger grounds: / For well thou know'st, *'tis not th'extent / Of Land makes life, but sweet content*" (ll. 15–18). "Large Bounds doe but bury us" suggests the futility of discontent with one's "bounds" in the face of both chance and ultimate death. The epigram is similar to the argument of Horace's *Ode* 2.18, in which the ancient poet contrasts his contentment upon his small Sabine farm with those who seek ever larger estates. Such greed is foolishness, argues Horace, for all men in death receive sufficient land: "Why strive for more and more? For all alike doth Earth unlock her bosom—for the poor man and for princes' sons."[34]

Herrick grounds his advice in biblical as well as classical tradition. Herrick's declaration that chance determines all things "here" on earth,

---

[34] "Quid ultra tendis? aequa tellus / pauperi recluditur / regumque pueris ... " (Horace, *Ode* 2.18.32–34).

including the amount of land one inherits, may sound wholly pagan, but chance is in this context the sublunary agent of Judaeo-Christian Providence. The claim that a man's "inheritance" results from "where ere the luckie lot doth fall" echoes God's commands to Moses and Joshua concerning the land of the Jews: "And ye shall divide the land by lot for an inheritance among your families . . . *every man's inheritance shall be in the place where his lot falleth*" (Numbers 33:54; cf. Joshua 13:6). Herrick's allusion implies that all men, like the Jews, must accept the rule of chance that is in fact God's law.

Oddly, however, Herrick's point depends on the false premise that men of his own time were buried on their actual property. Herrick had both classical and biblical precedents for his conceit that a man's private property would eventually serve him only as a burial site. Greeks and Romans owned their burial plots and rich Roman landowners sometimes had themselves and their dependents buried on their estates.[35] An epigram by Martial concerns a daughter buried in her parents' garden (*Epigrams* 1.114), while his epitaph on the same girl asserts that the parents will join her in the grave and that the site will remain in their everlasting possession (*Epigrams* 1.116). The Jews sometimes used their property as their own place of burial: Joshua was buried "in the border of his inheritance" (Joshua 24:30, Judges 2:9). Herrick's contemporaries, however, were not interred on their private property but in the public grounds of the church or churchyard; though they often payed dearly for the honor of a certain burial site, they did not legally own their place of burial.[36] Herrick's anachronistic association of the grave with a landed inheritance is thus especially revealing. His epigram not only advises contentment with the small property one has. Ignoring legal niceties, the poem also suggests that the grave is the ultimate essence of property, the necessary and sufficient form of property for the truly wise and contented man.

Herrick's epitaphic defenses of the grave as a "home" of retreat is in fact an extreme, idiosyncratic extension of the defense of property that so preoccupied his contemporaries. Parliamentarians reluctantly fought against a king whose actions seemed to them arbitrary attacks on "the right of property, [and] the liberty of the subjects." Many who opposed Parliament's actions, however, did so precisely because they feared civil war would in fact further harm their property rights. Sir John Cole-

---

[35] On Roman burial upon estates, see J. M. C. Toynbee, *Death and Burial in the Roman World* (Ithaca: Cornell University Press, 1971), 49.

[36] In *De Sepultura* (1641), Sir Henry Spelman attacked burial fees precisely on the grounds that canon law designated churches and churchyards "loci sacrati" that were "severed from humane Property" and therefore allowed "no buying or selling"; see Spelman, *English Works* (London, 1727), 180 and passim.

pepper warned that the Parliament's appeals to the people against the king would eventually "destroy all rights and proprieties...in a dark, equal chaos of confusion." The moderate Parliamentarian Sir Simonds d'Ewes lamented in June 1642 that "all right and property, all *meum* and *tuum*, must cease in a civil war." In the mid-1640s local gentry protested that the Parliamentary government had indeed—like Charles I in his years of personal rule—abrogated the "Liberties and Properties of the Subject" and used "arbitrary power...upon persons and estates."[37] As these various complaints reveal, men closely associated their property—their lands, their homes, their chattels—and their personal liberty. Property rights were indeed the model of all rights: the free man owned all of his rights just as he owned his property (which included his "property" in himself, i.e., his body). An attack upon a man's property was ipso facto an attack upon the individual's status as a free man.[38] Herrick's epitaphs establish the connection between an irreducible piece of personal property and a self free not only from the disturbance of unruly desires but also from the intrusions of others. Herrick was deprived of his property by Parliament when he was ejected in 1647 from his Dean Prior living, but his epitaphs seek to claim and defend his ultimate estate, the grave, as the last bastion of the free self.

Herrick's imagined contentment in death thus has a crucial ideological limit. One can see more clearly the conceptual "bounds" of his attempt to preserve the individual grave as the minimal unit of personal integrity by contrasting it to a contemporaneous writer's rejection of such an attempt. Gerrard Winstanley the Digger was perhaps the most important of the radical Interregnum theorists who denied the sanctity of prop-

[37] I cite the following: Parliament's "Act declaring the illegality of Ship-Money" (1641) in Samuel Rawson Gardiner, ed., *The Constitutional Documents of the Puritan Revolution: 1625–1660* (Oxford: Clarendon, 1889), 117; Sir John Colepepper's reply to the "Nineteen Propositions" (1642), quoted in J. S. Morrill, *The Revolt of the Provinces: Conservatives and Radicals in the English Civil War, 1630–1650* (London: Allen, 1976), 34; Sir Simonds D'Ewes's diary note of June 8, 1642, quoted in Christopher Hill, "The Many-Headed Monster," in his *Change and Continuity in Seventeenth-Century England* (Cambridge: Harvard University Press, 1975), 198; and the "Wiltshire Clubmen's Petition to the King," July 1645, and the Sussex Clubman petitions, September 26, 1645, cited in Morrill, *Revolt*, 197, 198.

[38] On the close relationship between property and rights in seventeenth-century English political theory, see C. B. Macpherson, *The Political Theory of Possessive Individualism: Hobbes to Locke* (Oxford: Oxford University Press, 1962); J. G. A. Pocock, *The Machiavellian Moment: Florentine Political Thought and the Atlantic Republic* (Princeton: Princeton University Press, 1975), especially pp. 375–377 and 385–391; and Richard Tuck, *Natural Rights Theories: Their Origin and Development* (Cambridge: Cambridge University Press, 1979). These works' important disagreements do not affect my general point concerning seventeenth-century views. I am also indebted to Janel M. Mueller, "On Genesis in Genre: Milton's Politicizing of the Sonnet in 'Captain or Colonel,'" in *Renaissance Genres: Essays on Theory, History, and Interpretation*, ed. Barbara Kiefer Lewalski, Harvard English Studies no. 14 (Cambridge: Harvard University Press, 1986), 213–240, which brings seventeenth-century theory to bear upon Milton's defense of property in his prose and the sonnet "Captain or Colonel."

erty.[39] In *The Law of Freedom* (1652), he offered his last and most systematic argument for communal use of the land. Winstanley contends that man's earthly nature demands that all men should have "free enjoyment" of the earth: "As Man is compounded of the four Materials of the Creation, *Fire, Water, Earth,* and *Ayr*; so is he preserved by the compounded bodies of these four, which are the fruits of the Earth; and he cannot live without them.... therefore this restraining of the Earth from brethren by brethren, is oppression and bondage; but the free enjoyment thereof is true Freedom."[40] Such communal use, Winstanley claims, would restore "Peace in the Earth" and unite "all people in a Land into one heart and mind."[41] Winstanley despaired of convincing his countrymen to transform England, however, and he ends the work with a poem that bitterly asks how one can "change the heart of Man" and concludes by welcoming death:

> O death where art thou? wilt thou not tidings send?
> I fear thee not, thou art my loving friend.
> Come take this body, and scatter it in the Four,
> That I may dwell in One, and rest in peace once more.[42]

The frustrated pursuit of commonality in life issues in longing for commonality in death. Winstanley envisions his dead body not at rest in its individual grave but instead scattered to the four elements that make up and support humankind. Such decomposition into the cosmos leads not to loss of self but to ultimate peace and unity with a pantheistically conceived One.[43] It thus provides what the truly communal life would achieve upon earth—harmonious union. Such a scattering is precisely, however, what Herrick fears most. While Winstanley's egalitarian communism ends in posthumous dispersal and blending, Herrick's Royalist last stands end in a place very much his and his alone.

Herrick's "To the Passenger" (H-821) affects a nonchalance concerning burial that in fact proves just how important the issue is for him:

> If I lye unburied Sir,
> These my Reliques, (pray) interre:

---

[39] For a discussion of Winstanley's theory and practice, see Christopher Hill, *The World Turned Upside Down: Radical Ideas during the English Revolution* (New York: Viking, 1972), 86–147, 313–319, and passim.

[40] Gerrard Winstanley, *The Law of Freedom* (1652), in *The Works of Gerrard Winstanley*, ed. George H. Sabine (Ithaca: Cornell University Press, 1941), 519–520.

[41] Winstanley, 515–516.

[42] Winstanley, 600.

[43] On Winstanley's pantheism, see Hill, *World*, 111–112.

> 'Tis religio[n]s part to see
> Stones, or turfes to cover me.
> One word more I had to say;
> But it skills not; go your way;
> He that wants a buriall roome
> *For a Stone, ha's Heaven his Tombe.*

This poem recognizes what the distich "Buriall" does not: one is no more absolutely assured of a grave than of any other property. Herrick imagines being unburied, however, precisely so that he can assure himself, and assert to the world, that he would still be "safely buryed" in a more important sense. The poem is based on classical epigrams spoken by unburied corpses. Such poems are fictional extensions of the epitaphic tradition in which the dead are made to speak from their tombs.[44] In Horace's *Ode* 1.28, the ancient poem closest to Herrick's epigram, a drowned corpse asks a passing sailor for burial. While Horace's ode ends with the dead man's request, however, the deceased in Herrick's poem changes his mind halfway through, moving abruptly from a humble request that the passerby bury him to an imperious command that the passerby go away. Herrick's poem in a sense becomes a true epitaph when the speaker realizes that he in fact already speaks from his tomb, which is beneficent heaven itself. The poem becomes another lesson in contentment, for the deceased discovers that he has all he needs, since lack is really possession: "He that wants a buriall roome / *For a Stone ha's Heaven his Tombe*" (ll. 7–8). He is content not only with his new-found grave but also with speaking a brief message and no more: "One word more I had to say: / But it skills not" (ll. 5–6).

In a characteristic move from first to third person, the speaker achieves contentment by moving from a vulnerable "I" (ll. 1, 5) to an impersonal, generic "he" (l. 7). The final couplet could indeed stand independently like one of Herrick's many impersonal, distich epigrams. Its separability from the original situation of the poem signals the withdrawal of the poet from a direct encounter with the living passerby and his transformation of the self into an impersonal lesson for both himself and the world. The poem's strategy recalls that of "The cruell Maid," but impersonality is here used not only to support but also to create the necessary and sufficient grave of retreat.

Herrick's poem participates in contemporary conflicts over the burial of the dead and responds to the harsh realities of civil war. The speaking corpse's final realization that he does not actually need burial does not

---

[44] For a discussion of Greek epigrams of this type and variations upon the motif in Propertius and Horace, see Gordon Williams, *Tradition and Originality in Roman Poetry* (Oxford: Clarendon, 1968), 172–185.

invalidate his assertion that it is "religions part," whether heeded or not, for the living to bury the dead. By asserting religion's role in burial, Herrick attacks the contemporaneous Puritan attempt to desacralize it.[45] Puritans felt that burial should be a civil rather than religious ceremony lest it encourage superstitious beliefs that the living could in any way help the dead. The 1644 *Directory for the Public Worship of God*, which the Westminster Assembly devised as a replacement for the banned *Book of Common Prayer*, prescribed that the dead be "immediately interred, without any Ceremony" since "praying, reading, and singing, both in going to, and at the Grave, have been grossly abused, are no way beneficial to the dead, and have proved many wayes hurtfull to the living." The *Directory* was quick to add that "civill respects or differences...suitable to the ranke and condition of the party deceased" should be maintained; the Puritans were combatting "popery," not the social hierarchy that depended upon respect for the dead and the continuity of lineage.[46] The Puritan elimination of religious funerary rites nevertheless seemed to many to express and encourage a shocking contempt for the dead. One observer claimed in 1649 that the dead were often simply "thrown into the ground like dogs."[47] Herrick imagines as the ultimate outcome of Puritan disrespect for the dead the ultimate indignity, not being buried at all.

The brute reality of civil war undoubtedly increased Herrick's apprehension that he would not receive proper burial. Herrick seems to imagine himself as one of the dead strewn upon the battlefields of the English Civil Wars, whose burial was at the mercy of the local country folk who would be less respectful of the dead, so he might fear, as a consequence

---

[45] Deming and Marcus have explored Herrick's defense, against Puritan charges of "popery" and superstition, of both the Caroline church's ceremonies and traditional country festivals; see Deming, 141–142, 156–157, and passim; Marcus, *Childhood*, 129–139; and Leah Sinanoglou Marcus, *The Politics of Mirth: Jonson, Herrick, Milton, Marvell, and the Defense of the Old Holiday Pastimes* (Chicago: University of Chicago Press, 1986), 140–168. Neither Deming nor Marcus focuses upon Herrick's defense against the Puritan desacralization of burial.

[46] *An Ordinance of the Lords and Commons...The Directory for Publique Worship* (London, 1645), 73–74.

[47] N. Strange is cited in Keith Thomas, *Religion and the Decline of Magic* (New York: Scribner's, 1971), 605. Parliament was in fact noticeably unsuccessful in replacing the *Book of Common Prayer* with the *Directory*, and the traditional rites of burial seem to have been the norm throughout the 1640s and 1650s; see John Morrill, "The Church in England, 1642–9," in *Reactions to the English Civil War*, ed. John Morrill (New York: St. Martin's, 1983), 89–114; and Clare Gittings, *Death, Burial and the Individual in Early Modern England* (London: Croom Helm, 1984), 53–55. Morrill cites the 1648 case of an alderman of Ripon who was indicted and convicted of assault for trying to prevent the burial of a child according to the old burial service (p. 108). Herrick himself probably officiated at traditional burials before his ejection from Dean Prior in 1647. The directives concerning burial suggest one major reason why the *Directory* failed: it eliminated "superstitious" ceremonies without providing emotionally resonant alternatives.

of Puritan belief and practice.[48] The final couplet of the poem recalls
Lucan's well-known phrase, "He who lacks an urn has the sky to cover
him."[49] Christians adopted the adage to assert that God looked after the
Christian's bodily remains: Augustine quoted Lucan when arguing that
Christians, with their faith in the resurrection of the body, need not
worry about lack of burial (*The City of God* 1.12); the cenotaph of an
early seventeenth-century Londoner who died while on a pilgrimage to
the Holy Land ends with Lucan's words.[50] The original context of the
phrase is, however, especially relevant to Herrick's epigram. In his epic
upon Roman civil war, Lucan uses the phrase to condemn Caesar's inhuman rage in forbidding the cremation and burial of his enemies after
the battle of Pharsalia; such cruelty is useless, Lucan claims, because
heaven covers those whom a burial mound does not. The allusion to
Lucan's epic inevitably evokes the parallel reality of English civil war,
and Lucan's phrase allows the poet to achieve at least a verbal victory
over the ultimate uncertainty of the times, one's burial.

Herrick's continual rewriting of his epitaph reveals an obsessive need
to reimagine his ultimate place of retreat and his ultimate connection to
the world. The basic dilemma is unresolvable: all the graves that Herrick
claims and all the epitaphs upon himself that he writes are, necessarily,
fictions. (In fact his precise grave site at Dean Prior, where he was buried
in 1674, is unknown.) At times he indeed rebels against the fictionality
of these epitaphs, showing us his construction and then rejection of a
fictional retreat. Consider this sequence of three poems near the opening
of *Hesperides*:

> Laid out for dead, let thy last kindnesse be
> With leaves and mosse-work for to cover me:
> And while the Wood-nimphs my cold corps inter,
> Sing thou my Dirge, sweet-warbling Chorister!
> For Epitaph, in Foliage, next write this,
> *Here, here the Tomb of Robin Herrick is.*
> ("To Robin Red-brest," H-50)

> More discontents I never had
> Since I was born, then here;

[48] See the description of the postbattle scene in Brigadier Peter Young and Wilfrid
Emberton, *The Cavalier Army: Its Organization and Everyday Life* (London: Allen, 1974), 135–
136. Young and Emberton note that local bystanders often buried the dead for hygienic
reasons, but they give one example of local men who stripped all belongings from a soldier
they thought was dead and then left him on the battlefield unburied.

[49] "Caelo tegitur, qui non habet urnam" (Lucan, *De Bello Civili* 7.819).

[50] See the inscription upon the cenotaph of Sir Robert Chamberlayne, d. 1615, in
E. A. Webb, *The Records of St. Bartholomew's Priory and of the Church and Parish of St.
Bartholomew the Great, West Smithfield*, 2 vols. (London: Oxford University Press, 1921),
2:458.

Where I have been, and still am sad,
    In this dull *Devon-shire*:
Yet justly too I must confesse;
    I ne'r invented such
Ennobled numbers for the Presse,
    Then where I loath'd so much.
                    ("Discontents in Devon," H-51)

O Earth! Earth! Earth heare thou my voice, and be
Loving, and gentle for to cover me:
Banish'd from thee I live; ne'r to return,
Unlesse thou giv'st my small Remains an Urne.
                    ("To his Paternall Countrey," H-52)

"To Robin Red-brest" is one of Herrick's many innovative extensions of the traditional last injunction of a dying man or a man anticipating his death. In such poems Herrick addresses not only men and women, as is traditional, but also plants and animals: laurels (H-89), the yew and cypress (H-280), flowers (H-343), and, as in "To Robin Red-brest," birds. Such poems go farther than "The cruell Maid" and "To his Tomb-maker" in distancing the poet from his readers: the poet addresses nature instead of his fellow men. "To Robin Red-brest" adopts the folk belief that the robin redbreast covers an unburied corpse with moss, a belief alluded to in a famous passage from John Webster's *The White Devil*: "Call for the robin-red-breast and the wren, / Since o'er shady groves they hover, / And with leaves and flow'rs do cover / The friendless bodies of unburied men."[51] The robin is needed only when man has failed: presumably a friendless, solitary man, Herrick turns not to another human being for his final home and epitaphic message but to the attendant of last resort.[52] The robin is imagined, however, as a true friend. According to classical and Renaissance friendship theory, a friend should be "another self." The robin is precisely such another self: the bird sings, writes, and shares the name "Robin" with Herrick.[53] Herrick's fantasy

[51] John Webster, *The White Devil*, ed. John Russell Brown, The Revels Plays (London: Methuen, 1960), 165 (V.iv.95–98).

[52] Compare Abraham Cowley's retirement poem, "Ode II: That a pleasant Poverty is to be preferred before discontented Riches" (1637), which also associates burial by the robin with the solitary life: "Thus I would waste, thus end my carelese dayes, / And *Robin-red-brests* whom men praise / For pious birds, should when I dye, / Make both my *Monument* and *Elegie*" (Cowley, *Essays, Plays, and Sundry Verses*, ed. A. R. Waller [Cambridge: Cambridge University Press, 1906], 61).

[53] Herrick implicitly identifies himself with the robin in "*Upon Mistresse* Elizabeth Wheeler ..." (H-130) and uses the nickname "Robin" for himself in "*To Master* Kellam," l. 3 (H-918). Though possibly unintentional, ambiguities in "To the Robin Red-brest," reinforce the sense that the robin is "another self." Mourner and mourned are syntactically confused: the dangling modifier that opens the poem means that "laid out for dead" seems at first to refer to the bird addressed rather than to the speaker, since the true reference ("me," l. 2) is delayed till the end of the couplet. Similarly, "thy last Kindnesse" is ambiguous,

of an avian alter ego allows the poet once more to receive proleptically a tomb and epitaph from which he can be re-presented to men: "Here, here the Tomb of Robin Herrick is." Once more Herrick modestly seeks for little and no more: he asks only for an epitaph written in foliage, which, like words written in water, will quickly disappear.

The second poem provides another, less fanciful, description of the poet's lonely plight and his strategies of self-assertion. Herrick's discontented life in "dull *Devon-shire*," exiled from London, resembles the loneliness-unto-death in a pastoral landscape of the preceding poem. Like the pastoral epitaph in foliage (though far more lasting!), however, the "Ennobled numbers for the Presse" provide the poet with a compensatory text by which he can re-present himself to the world.

Lest the reader fail to make the connection between the first two poems, the third combines the earlier two poems' themes of death and exile. In "To his Paternall Countrey," Herrick rejects both the whimsical compensation for death offered in the first poem, the pastoral epitaph, and the more substantial compensation for exile offered in the second, wonderful poems for publication. "My country" in the seventeenth century often meant "my [local] county,"[54] and the titular "his Paternall Countrey" refers in one sense to Herrick's birthplace, London.[55] In "His returne to London" (H-713) Herrick suggests that he would rather be buried in London, his "native countrey" (l. 16), than be forced to return to Devonshire; in "On himselfe" (H-860) he expresses a desire to join "his Paternall grave" (l. 4) and London "Ancestrie" (l. 8) in death, so that he can finally rest "at home" (l. 6). By requesting burial in London in "To his Paternall Countrey," Herrick reveals the inadequacy of the epitaphic fiction of "To Robin Red-brest"; in begging the earth that his "voice" be heard ("O earth! Earth! Earth heare thou my voice"), he reveals his desire to overcome the distance of writing accepted in "Discontents in Devon." The movement from the first poem's epitaphic "Here, here" to "heare thou my voice" signals the rejection of writing that merely creates its own self-enclosed fictive place "here" in favor of a voice that attempts to call forth what is not "here." "Heare" is what Christopher Ricks calls an anti-pun, meaning "hear (not, alas, here!)."[56]

---

for it suggests both the last act the bird will perform for the poet and the bird's last good act as such.

[54] See Lawrence Stone, *The Causes of the English Revolution, 1529–1642* (1972; rpt., New York: Harper, 1972), 106.

[55] Both John L. Kimmey ("Robert Herrick's Persona," *SP* 67 [1970]:231) and Coiro (p. 209) interpret the "paternall country" as London.

[56] See Christopher Ricks, *The Force of Poetry* (Oxford: Clarendon, 1984), 142–144, 265–267. Herrick elsewhere uses the "hear / here" homophone to make a traditional, and triumphant, pun. At the end of "His Creed" (N-78) Herrick states: "I do believe, the One in Three, / And Three in perfect Unitie: / Lastly, that JESUS is a Deed / Of Gift from God: *And heres my Creed*" (ll. 13–16). To present one's creed to Christ *is* to be heard by

Herrick's ordinary movement of retreat, from lyric speech to epigrammatic writing, is thus reversed. No fictional epitaph, no amount of writing, can substitute for London's hearing his plea and granting him burial.

Herrick's "paternall country" refers not only to London, however. The phrase is also a Latinate equivalent for "fatherland," a word used in its present sense by 1623 (*OED* 1). The poem's opening line echoes Jeremiah 22.29: "O earth, earth, earth, hear thou the word of God." As the Lord's mouthpiece, Jeremiah castigates the Jews whose sins brought about their exile from Israel and prophesies that they will not be able to return to their promised land even in death (22: 12, 26). Commentators interpreted the triple cry of "earth" as a rhetorical reproof of the deaf Jews.[57] Herrick, by contrast, hopes that his voice, rather than the Lord's, will be heard, and his modification of Jeremiah suggests that though Herrick has been exiled from his promised land he hopes that he, unlike the Jews, may at least receive burial on native ground. He thus literalizes the call to the earth, hoping for a response from the material ground of his country that he presumably no longer can expect from his fellow countrymen. The Civil Wars have caused his "exile" from the England of the "golden Age" when Charles I reigned ("The bad season makes the Poet sad," ll. 7–8, H-612), and the only return to harmony he can now imagine is death and burial.[58] His calling upon the earth thus resembles his calling upon the robin: both signal a loss of faith in human society. "To his Paternall Country" suggests, however, that the charming pastoral fiction of "To Robin Red-brest" is not enough. One must implore for a true burial with the full knowledge that in troubled times the only grave one might indeed receive is heaven.

Despite their variety, Herrick's epitaphs upon himself provide only a partial picture of the poet's representations of the self's relation to death.

---

him. Communication with the ubiquitous Christ solves the problems of absence and distance inherent in poetry addressed to the nondivine.

[57] Calvin argues that "in this repetition we see that there is an implied reproof, as though he had said [of the Jews] that they were indeed deaf" (*Commentaries on the Book of the Prophet Jeremiah*, trans. and ed. John Owen, 3 vols. [Grand Rapids, Mich: Baker Book House, 1984], 3: 124–125). Milton assumes that the address to the earth rather than to the Jews themselves shows that the prophet must "tell the very soil it self, what her perverse inhabitants are deaf to" (*The Readie and Easie Way to Establish a Free Commonwealth*, 2d ed. [1660], in *The Complete Prose Works of John Milton*, vol. 7, rev. ed. Robert W. Ayers [New Haven: Yale University Press, 1980], 462–463).

[58] Claude J. Summers argues that in various poems, including "To his Paternall Countrey," Herrick creates a "counterplot" by which he laments his expulsion from Devonshire at the same time he longs for or celebrates his homecoming to London; see "Herrick's Political Counterplots," *SEL* 25 (1985):167–173. By suggesting that in several poems Herrick is lamenting not only his expulsion from Dean Prior but also the Royalist defeat that caused it, Summers is close to my own argument that his exile is from a land much larger than either London or Devonshire.

His epitaphic search for a "Chamber fit" is both complemented and countered by his proud assertions that he will live forever within his book, the *Hesperides*.[59] Claims that the poet has immortalized himself and others abound in *Hesperides*, beginning with the book's epigraph, "Effugient avidos Carmina nostra Rogos," and concluding with the final page's "The pillar of Fame." Many such claims are mere tags lifted from the classical poets: the epigraph itself is a pastiche of Ovidian lines. The most original of his assertions of immortality, by contrast, reveal the same impulse as the epitaphs, the desire to retreat to a place of safety. Consider this boasting poem:

> Live by thy Muse thou shalt; when others die
> Leaving no Fame to long Posterity:
> When Monarchies trans-shifted are, and gone;
> Here shall endure thy vast Dominion.
> ("On himselfe," H-592)

Herrick severs the link made between the immortality of the poet and the endurance of the state asserted in such classical models as Horace's *Ode* 3.30 and the end of Ovid's *Metamorphoses*, both of which connect the poet's fame to the continuing rule of Rome. Writing during a period of political "trans-shifting," Herrick asserts the autonomy of his poetic dominion. He treats the book itself, like the grave of the epitaphs, as a place of escape. Though the poet proudly proclaims his "vast Dominion" rather than noting his contentment with a "Chamber fit," "Here shall endure thy vast Dominion" undercuts itself by parading its own excess: the book may indeed endure and be temporally vast, but it is spatially vast only in a highly figurative sense.

One may contrast this epigram, which depends upon treating the book as a self-enclosed, private realm, with one in which Herrick imagines the book's fate in the world:

> If hap it must, that I must see thee lye
> *Absyrtus*-like all torne confusedly:
> With solemne tears, and with much grief of heart,
> Ile recollect thee (weeping) part by part;
> And having washt thee, close thee in a chest
> With spice; that done, Ile leave thee to thy rest.
> ("To his Booke," H-960)

Foreseeing the possibility of the book's being torn apart by its readers, Herrick promises to perform a funeral rite and bury it. The supposed

[59] On Herrick's claims for the immortalizing power of *Hesperides*, see also Coiro, 133–154; and Guibbory, 153–159.

ruler of a "vast Dominion" registers once more his fear of the outside world and his attraction to protected, delimited spaces. He grants his book the grave-as-home that he so often seeks for himself.

The last sixteen lines of *Hesperides* shift from the poet's pride in his book as a self-enclosed artifact to a more modest epitaphic assertion of self in the face of the public realm:

The pillar of Fame.
Fames pillar here, at last, we set,
Out-during *Marble, Brasse,* or *Jet,*
Charm'd and enchanted so,
As to withstand the blow
Of o v e r t h r o w :
Nor shall the seas
O r   O U T R A G E S
Of storms orebear
What we up-rear,
Tho Kingdoms fal,
This pillar never shall
Decline or waste at all;
But stand for ever by his owne
Firme and well fixt foundation.

To his Book's end this last line he'd have plac't,
Jocond his Muse was; but his Life was chast.
(H-1129–H-1130)

The formal and thematic relationship between the first fourteen lines and the final, detached couplet is unclear. One may consider the conclusion of the book one poem of sixteen lines (with the final couplet as an inscription at the base of the pillar) or two separate poems (with the final couplet a separate coda). This deliberate ambiguity raises the question of the thematic relationship between the fourteen lines' proclamation concerning "Fames pillar" and the final couplet's statement concerning the poet. The first fourteen lines present the book as an enduring monument. The number of lines recalls a sonnet, so often used by poets to proclaim their immortalizing power, and the visual pun of this poem's construction emphasizes the materiality of the text as monument. Herrick once more separates the endurance of his textual monument from the survival of "kingdoms," the dearest of which Herrick has seen fall. He also, more strikingly, separates the monument's endurance from his own immortality. Unlike Horace's claim at the end of his *Odes* to have completed a monument more lasting than bronze, Ovid's similar boast at the end of the *Metamorphoses,* or Herrick's own proud vaunt in "His Poetrie his Pillar" (H-211), the poet does not represent himself as having built the monument so that *he* can be immortal. In the fiction of the poem, Herrick may or may not have built the monument. In "On Himselfe" (H-1128), the poem immediately preceding "The pillar of Fame," the poet asks to be be crowned by "young men, and maidens" (l. 1) and be mourned for by the "Muses . . . when I am dead" (l. 6); either of these, with or without Herrick's participation, may be the "we" who are imagined erecting the pillar.[60] The poem-as-pillar does not claim to grant Herrick immortality but only to immortalize itself: it asserts, verbally and visually, its power to stand "By his owne / Firme and well fixed foundation." The pillar's endurance as an autonomous written artifact seems to be dependent upon the suppression of Herrick as either the maker or subject of the monument. He does not simply retreat into death, a poetic "home," and impersonality: he disappears.

The final, untitled couplet reintroduces the poet as subject and thus highlights his curious absence from the preceding lines. Unlike the previous fourteen lines, the couplet is extremely modest. It may be read as Herrick's final epitaph upon himself, with the book substituting for the grave as the site of a self-defining inscription. With the exception of the epitaph in "The cruell Maid," this final line is Herrick's shortest, most deprecating self-portrait. The line recalls his praise of bachelorhood in "To his Tomb-maker," but Herrick does not here, as in the earlier poem, link his chastity to self-sufficiency. His implicit relationship to the world is suggested by the final line's echo of Ovid's and Martial's contrasts between their playful poetry and their supposedly innocent lives: "my life is moral, my muse is gay"; "wanton is my page; my life is good" ("vita verecunda est, Musa iocosa mea," *Tristia* 2.354; "lasciva est nobis pagina, vita proba," *Epigrams* 1.4.8).[61] The exiled Ovid addresses Augustus, Martial addresses Domitian. Both the ancient poets are not providing epitaphic self-definitions but humbly, even obsequiously, excusing their poetry—Ovid too late, Martial in advance—to the greatest of authorities. Both not only protest the innocence of their lives but also denigrate their poems as harmless trifles: Ovid speaks of his "light task" ("leve opus," l. 339), Martial of his "harmless trifling" ("innocuous . . . lusus," l. 7). Herrick in effect ends his book with a self-denigrating cliché, deliberately reducing his proud monument to one more "jocond" collection of epigrammatic trifles and asserting once more his chaste life of bachelorhood as if that were his only claim to the reader's favor. Such a palinode may be praiseworthy for Herrick the Christian but is extremely deflating for Herrick the poet.[62]

[60] See Kimmey, 223; and Coiro, 215.

[61] Braden notes these and other sources (pp. 226–227).

[62] The palinode is also, of course, excellent preparation for *Noble Numbers* insofar as that collection humbles the proud, secular strains in *Hesperides*.

Unlike Ovid and Martial, who write their apologies in the first person and directly address their judging reader, Herrick has an unidentified speaker address the printer in the first line (Herrick himself describing his wishes in the third person? the "we" of the preceding lines?) and uses the impersonal form throughout. By avoiding "I" and "my" in his final distich, the poet emphasizes unto the end his retreat from direct encounters with his readers and the mediated nature of his final communication. He thus acknowledges, with hope and fear, that he must win his readers' approval of his pillar of fame, a synecdoche for the *Hesperides* itself, the textual "home" that establishes the poet's distance from the disturbing world outside its confines.

Herrick writes epitaphs on a wide range of mortals, both imaginary and real. His comic and satiric epitaphs upon characters with generic follies and vices resemble those of many of his contemporaries, and his panegyric epitaphs upon matrons with equally generic virtues seem little more than literary exercises. His epitaphs upon unnamed infants and virgins, by contrast, are not only highly original but also deeply felt poems. The poet identifies himself with figures of innocence whose emergence into the world is minimal. Their anonymity does not make them simply generic types: it also emphasizes how small a role they played in the world. They thus exemplify the littleness so central to Herrick's own self-representation.

Herrick's epitaphs upon children differ sharply from those of his master Jonson: while the child is very much an "other" to Jonson, an innocent foil to the adult man of experience, the child embodies in prettified, sentimental form Herrick's own retreat into the littleness of death.[63] Just as his epitaphs upon himself try to find a small but secure "home" for the poet, so his epitaphs upon infants try to protect their graves:

> Here she lies, a pretty bud,
> Lately made of flesh and blood:
> Who, as soone, fell fast asleep,
> As her little eyes did peep.
> Give her strewings; but not stir
> The earth, that lightly covers her.
> ("Upon a child that dyed," H-310)

[63] Marcus discusses Herrick's self-identification with the child in *Noble Numbers* (*Childhood*, 120–139). Her concern is with the child's religious significance for Herrick as the simple, obedient member of the established church; my concern is with the child as embodiment of his poetics of retreat in *Hesperides*. Both uses of the child respond to the "troublesome times."

The poem describes the earth that "lightly covers" the dead child as a consolatory protector, and the sound patterns of the poem reinforce the movement from loss to compensation: the poem moves from "lies" and "lately," both associated with loss, to a word that combines them but reveals the kindness of earth, "lightly." The child sleeping in the hospitable earth has the peacefulness Herrick associates with being-at-home, but also the vulnerability to intrusion with which Herrick is concerned in some of his epitaphs upon himself. The sleeper must not be awakened, and the reader is asked to perform a ritual of mourning but warned not to disturb the child.

A similar epitaph emphasizes even more strongly that the living should not disturb the sleep of a dead child:

> Here a pretty Baby lies
> Sung asleep with Lullabies:
> Pray be silent, and not stirre
> Th'easie earth that covers her.
> ("Upon a child," H-640)

The movement from "lullabies" to "Pray be silent" underscores that the reader has arrived too late either to hear or to speak. Only the final line's mention of "th'easie earth" unequivocally tells the reader that the child is actually dead, and this retrospective realization further emphasizes the belatedness of the reader, who can never know the child except as the sleeping creature she has become.[64] All the reader can and must do is to remain silent and not disturb the infant's gentle rest. A vision of peaceful death is thus proffered to, but protected from, the reader.[65]

While in his epitaphs upon himself Herrick attempts to discover contentment by accepting his own death and small grave, in his epitaphs upon virgins he attempts to discover contentment by accepting the small remains of another who is yet very much like the self. One brief epitaph upon a maid reveals just how little is left to the living:

[64] See DeNeef's discussion of the fourth line (pp. 158–159).
[65] These requests that the living not disturb a sleeping child remind one of Herrick's childlike folk charms for protecting sleeping children: "Bring the holy crust of Bread, / Lay it underneath the head; / 'Tis a certain Charm to keep / Hags away, while Children sleep" ("Charmes," H-888); "Let the superstitious wife / Neer the childs heart lay a knife: . . . / This 'mongst other mystick charms / Keeps the sleeping child from harms" ("Another," ll. 1–2, 5–6, H-889). Folk charms appealed to Herrick that, like his epitaphs, seek to protect a vulnerable self or the vulnerable "space" of the self from intruders: "The old Wives Prayer" tries to "Drive all hurtfull Feinds us fro" (l. 7, H-473); "The Spell" is supposed to "affright / Far from hence the evil Sp'rite" (ll. 8–9, H-769); the sprinkling of water "farre keepes the evil Spright" ("Another," l. 6, H-1064).

> Hence a blessed soule is fled,
> Leaving here the body dead:
> Which (since here they can't combine)
> For the Saint, we'l keep the Shrine.
> ("Upon a Maide," H-593)

"Blessed soule" and "Saint" suggest beatification, but Herrick provides no image of the heavenly state. Instead the poem emphasizes that the soul of the deceased has "fled" from the living, leaving them only the "body dead," and the metrical and rhetorical stress upon the final word "dead" is harshly blunt. The speakers, however, have a consolatory response to the grim reality: ". . . (since here they can't combine) / For the Saint, we'l keep the Shrine." "For" here means both "in honor of" and "in place of." "For" in the first sense makes the last line a vow to reverence the shrine and suggests, as do many contemporaneous epitaphs, a new version of the cult of the saints. This "saint" has, however, only left a corpse, not wonder-working relics,[66] and "for" in the second sense underscores that the shrine is small compensation for the loss of the deceased.

In another epitaph upon a maid, Herrick imagines even more minimal consolation for the living:

> Gone she is a long, long way,
> But she has decreed a day
> Back to come, (and make no stay.)
> So we keepe till her returne
> Here, her ashes, or her Urne.
> ("Upon a Maid," H-848)

The epitaph's speakers—the "we" of the poem—do not fully understand the central Christian doctrines of the afterlife and the Resurrection: they know only that the deceased has gone far away but has "decreed" to return. Herrick seems to imagine such ignorant personae in order to demonstrate the possibility of consolation even given severe limitations. In the final couplet the speakers make do with the little they have been left, "her ashes, or her Urne." By evoking the pagan practice of cremation, "ashes" and "urne" emphasize the limits of the speakers' spiritual understanding of the dead, but the odd and striking use of "or" suggests that these speakers know what matters most, how to content themselves

---

[66] One may contrast Herrick's epitaph in this regard with such a hyperbolic composition as the epitaph upon Anne Burton, d. 1642, cited in chapter 1 of this work: "Reader, stand back; dull not this Marble Shrine, / With irreligious Breath: the Stone's divine, / And does enclose a Wonder—Beauty, Wit, / Devotion, and Virginity with it" (included in T. Webb, ed., *A New Select Collection of Epitaphs*, 2 vols. [London, 1775], 1:30). Herrick's tomb has no such "wonder" left.

with whatever remains, however small. These speakers are thus examples, the poem suggests, to us all.

The final couplet recalls the conclusion of Jonson's epitaph upon Elizabeth Chute: "And, till the comming of the Soule / To fetch the flesh, we keepe the Rowle" (ll. 5–6).[67] In its published version this epitaph upon a child is Jonson's only serious, panegyric epitaph upon an unnamed subject and therefore the closest to Herrick's epitaphs upon anonymous children and virgins. There is a crucial difference, however, between Jonson's and Herrick's epitaph. While Jonson fills his "rowle" with praise of the little girl's excellence and blurs the distinction between the poem as "rowle" and the deceased as "record," Herrick emphasizes how little his poem can capture of the deceased. Herrick's echo of his poetic master suggests another, intertextual example of making do with little: just as the epitaph's speakers rest content with the small remains of the deceased, so Herrick the epitaphic poet implicitly rests content with the small remains of the Jonsonian poetic tradition, all, supposedly, that the humble disciple can assimilate.

In the seventeenth century the term "maid," though normally applied to women, could also be used of chaste men (OED, 2c), and Herrick once calls himself a "maid" ("Upon himselfe," l. 2, H-235).[68] One of the epitaphs above is not explicitly gendered, while the other concerns a female, but gender as such does not seem as significant a difference for Herrick as for most other poets of his time. Thus in a sense Herrick is commemorating himself in these epitaphs upon anonymous, unworldly "maids." Imagining his own death from the standpoint of the living, he expresses in displaced form his hope that they will cherish the little of him that will endure.

Herrick's epitaphs upon patrons and relatives are for the most part his most conventional compositions in the genre. In one composition, however, he makes the epitaph upon patrons also an epitaph upon himself. The inscription upon the tomb of Sir Edward Giles, the patron of the Dean Prior living, and his wife, was attributed to Herrick by the Devonshire antiquarian John Prince in 1701:

> No trust to Metals nor to Marbles, when
> These have their Fate, and wear away as Men;
> Times, Titles, Trophies, may be lost and Spent;
> But Vertue rears the eternal Monument.
> What more than these can Tombes or Tomb-stones Say

[67] Jonson, 8:188.
[68] In *Noble Numbers*, Herrick offers a "Virgin-Flower" to Christ, his "Maiden-Saviour" ("His Offering, with the rest, at the Sepulcher," ll. 5–6, N-270).

But here's the Sun-set of a Tedious day:
These Two asleep are: I'll but be Undrest
And so to Bed: Pray wish us all Good Rest.
                              (H-354B, italics removed)

Prince claimed that Herrick wrote this poem when he was "very Aged."[69] It would have been appropriate for Herrick, as a vicar with great poetic talent, to write the epitaph upon his patron, and the epitaph is, I shall argue, characteristic of Herrick's distinctive epitaphic style. He could not, however, have composed the epitaph in extreme old age. Sir Edward died in 1637, his wife in 1642. The monument shows husband and wife kneeling in prayer facing one another. A smaller kneeling figure slightly below and to the left of Sir Edward has the position and relative size normal for a son, but since Sir Edward was childless and had adopted his great nephew Edward Yarde as his heir, it is presumably he who is represented (Figure 4).[70] Since this was an old-fashioned monumental composition by the 1640s, it is highly improbable that the monument was erected long after Lady Giles's death. At the time of her death, Herrick, who was born in 1591, was in his early fifties.[71] Probably Prince, relying on local tradition that Herrick was the author of the epitaph, guessed that Herrick composed the poem in his late sixties after his return to Dean Prior at the Restoration because of the final lines in which the speaker vows shortly to die. Readers of Herrick's epitaphs upon himself will not, however, fall into that particular biographical fallacy!

The first four lines propound the humanist doctrine that virtue is the truest, most enduring monument. Herrick's claim that material memorials "have their Fate" is traditional: one may compare Juvenal's *Satire* 10, which ridicules the human desire for an inscription ("titul[us]") upon one's tombstone with the sardonic reflection that "even tombs have their fates assigned to them."[72] In the effective alliterative sequence dismissing perishables—"Times, Titles, Trophies"—the last two items, "Titles" or inscriptions (cf. "title," *OED* 1) and "Trophies" or monuments (cf. "tro-

---

[69] See John Prince, *Danmonii Orientales Illustres, or The Worthies of Devon* (1701; rpt., London, 1810), 423.

[70] On Sir Edward Giles's adoption of Edward Yarde, see Chute, 211–212. Yarde was Sir Edward's grand-nephew; see the genealogies of the Giles and Yarde families in Sir Henry Saint-George, *The Visitation of the County of Devon in the Year 1620*, ed. Frederic Thomas Colby, Publications of the Harleian Society no. 6 (London, 1872), 129, 320–321.

[71] Nikolaus Pevsner describes the monument as "old-fashioned" for 1642 in *South Devon*, The Buildings of England (Harmondsworth: Penguin, 1952), 118. Brian Kemp notes that depictions of kneelers in prayer grew less common after 1630 and virtually disappeared by 1650 in *English Church Monuments* (London: B. T. Batsford, 1980), 97.

[72] "...data sunt ipsis quoque fata sepulcris" (Juvenal, *Satire* 10.146). I have modified the Loeb translation.

Figure 4. Monument of Sir Edward and Lady Giles, d. 1637 and 1642, in Dean Prior
Church. By permission of the Royal Commission on the Historical Monuments of England.

phy," *OED* 2b), are conventional. The first word is, by contrast, surprising and topical, for it evokes the crisis of the 1640s, when times were indeed in flux. Though he died before the outbreak of the Civil Wars, Sir Edward Giles experienced the growing tensions between court and country: he was one of the Devonshire county commissioners who opposed Ship Money in 1634, and it was only on account of his age that he was excused from a summons to Whitehall for reprimand.[73] By 1642, when his wife died, the troublesome times had indeed come.

Like "To the Passenger," the poem breaks into a surprising new direction in the second half. The turn begins with Herrick's characteristic stress upon how little and no "more" the monument can say. The poem moves from the limited expressive power of the epitaph, which can say "but" that life is mercifully over for the deceased, to an "I" that briefly appears "but" to die. As is his wont, Herrick thereby links the littleness of the epitaphic message and the minimal assertion and retreat of an "I."

The identity of the "I" in the final couplet is, however, ambiguous. The viewer of the monument would most likely imagine the living heir depicted on the monument as the primary speaker of the final lines, asserting his pious plan to join the two dead relatives also represented upon the monument. Although publishing poets generally avoided such outpourings in epitaphs as more appropriate for elegiac laments, seventeenth-century tomb inscriptions sometimes express the fervent desire of a widow or widower, who is depicted upon the monument, to quickly join his or her spouse in the grave. The tomb of Sir Lawrence Tanfield, who died in 1625, depicts husband and widow lying side by side in death. An inscription declares the widow's desire to die and be "with him I loved."[74] The tomb of Sarah Latch, who died in 1644, presents her husband half-reclining and gazing in sorrow on her body bundled up in a shroud. In the inscription the widower declares his preparation for imminent death: "Lyveing and dead thou seest how heere wee lie. / I doate on Death preparing how to die. / Ah fleeting life she'es gone. Age somons me / Unto the grave...."[75]

---

[73] See Eugene A. Andriette, *Devon and Exeter in the Civil War* (Newton Abbot, Devon: David and Charles, 1971), 33–34; 192, note 55.

[74] This inscription is in Ravenshaw, 72.

[75] The epitaph and description of the monument may be found in Nikolaus Pevsner, *North Somerset and Bristol*, The Buildings of England (London: Penguin, 1958), 164–165. For similar emotional declarations of widows and widowers, see the tomb inscriptions upon Sarah Heiton, d. 1600, in John Thorpe, *Registrum Roffense: or, A Collection of Antient Records ... of the Diocese and Cathedral Church of Rochester* (London, 1769), 955; Lucy Bromfield, d. 1618, in Ravenshaw, 62; Sir William Dyer, d. 1641, in Horatio Edward Norfolk, ed., *Gleanings in Graveyards: A Collection of Curious Epitaphs* [London, 1866], 1; and Mary Penelope, d. 1641, in John Le Neve, ed., *Monumenta Anglicana: Being Inscriptions on the*

Yet unlike widows and widowers, whose epitaphic declarations express their legitimate marital devotion unto death, heirs were expected to live and preserve the family line. The prose inscription on Sir Charles Cavendish's monument declares that the widow and surviving sons "do all desire, *in their tyme*, to be gathered to his dust, expecting the happy howre of resurrection"; such a pious but controlled declaration is appropriate for the declaration not only of the widow but also of the sons who must carry on their father's legacy. Herrick's own obsession with retreat-unto-death has thus unmistakably influenced the assertion of longing for death in the final couplet.

Indeed, since the "I" is not explicitly identified nor his precise relation to "these two" specified, the final lines also allow the poet to voice his own resolve to die and follow the Giles couple. With such a gesture, Herrick the faithful parish vicar can vow to die in sorrow for his patron and patroness, and Herrick the poet can, as is his wont, assert his presence in a moment of retreat. By entering and disappearing in the inscription with an "I" that some readers will recognize, some not, he ensures that one epitaph upon himself, appropriately discreet, is in fact inscribed upon actual stone. Herrick's own fascination with a retreat into death indeed helps explain the lack of fit between the monument, whose kneeling figures *au vif* represent the death-transcending continuity of lineage, and the final couplet of the inscription, which envisages the reestablishment *in death* of the continuity between the dead and the living but soon to die.

Having adopted the death-as-sleep image found so often in his poetry,[76] the poet ends with a characteristic request of the living reader that is backed up by the sanctity of the dead: "Pray wish us all Good Rest." Herrick's epitaph upon his niece Elizabeth Herrick concludes by seeking to preserve her deathly sleep: "Sleep, while we hide thee from the light, / Drawing thy curtains round: *Good night*" (H-376). In the Giles epitaph, Herrick requests that the same solicitude be shown to Herrick's patrons, their heir, and himself. Indeed the word "all," by its generality, suggests that his request concerns the whole local community of the dead. Writing in the early years of the Civil Wars, when the disruptions of the times were all too apparent, Herrick seeks to bridge the gap between the living and the dead not by denying it but by requesting that the living respect and preserve the peace of the dead and their do-

---

Monuments of several Eminent Persons . . . 1600–1715, 5 vols. (London, 1718–1719), 4:194–195.

[76] Both the poem's related image of the grave as a bed and its image of death as a sunset are also found elsewhere in Herrick's poetry. For the former, see "His Own Epitaph," ll. 5–6 (H-617), and "Upon a Maide," l. 1 (H-838); for the latter, see "On himselfe," l. 6 (H-306).

main. This is a request he would make throughout the "troublesome times," over and over again in *Hesperides*, in the epitaphs upon infants, upon virgins and, most importantly and characteristically, upon himself.

Chapter 7

The Politics of Nostalgia in the
Late Seventeenth-Century Epitaph

The Civil Wars decisively impressed upon late seventeenth-century English poets an awareness of disruptive historical change. Few could look upon the period from 1642 to 1659 happily. Though it was a time of hope for some, the majority suffered. Most viewed the execution of the king as an unprecedented national tragedy, and others felt a deep disappointment at Parliament's failure to devise a permanent settlement. The Restoration settlement did not resolve the conflicts of the past. Though there was an inherent restraint upon political conflict, stemming from the ruling elite's eagerness to avoid renewed civil war, tensions continued because of the unabated mutual distrust between the king and Parliament and the deep religious divisions, with members of the reestablished Church, Protestant dissenters, and Catholics all deeply suspicious of one another's past and present roles in the nation. Widely circulated satiric epitaphs upon controversial public figures, often composed while their subjects were still very much alive, provide direct and often crude testimony to the continuing political and religious tensions.[1]

---

[1] For a few examples of such satiric epitaphs upon public figures, see the epitaphs upon Edward Coleman and Captain William Bedloe, a victim and perpetrator respectively of the Popish Plot hysteria, in Elias F. Mengel, Jr., ed., *Poems on Affairs of State: Augustan Satirical Verse, 1660–1714*, vol. 2, *1678–1681* (New Haven: Yale University Press, 1965), 360; upon Anthony Ashley Cooper, the earl of Shaftesbury, composed during the Exclusion Crisis, in Howard H. Schless, ed., *Poems on Affairs of State: Augustan Satirical Verse, 1660–1714*, vol. 3, *1682–1685* (New Haven: Yale University Press, 1968), 401–402; and upon Laurence Hyde, earl of Rochester, composed when the latter "died" by being dismissed from office in 1687, in Galbraith M. Crump, ed., *Poems on Affairs of State: Augustan*

Panegyric epitaphs expressing nostalgia for an idealized past constitute, however, the most significant development. From the Civil Wars to the end of the century, with each public crisis epitaphic poets compose works in which the gulf between the living and the dead is made to stand for the break between the way things are and the supposedly far better way they were. Like Herrick these poets of nostalgia distance the dead from the living rather than link the two, but while Herrick defended the dead, the late seventeenth-century poets more aggressively and polemically use the dead to condemn the living. While other genres explore the positive achievements of late seventeenth-century England, the most interesting panegyric epitaphs attack a degraded present and mourn a vanished ideal.

The historical crises of the mid and late seventeenth century inspired long discursive and narrative forms treating public life and historical process.[2] Although such longer compositions often contained couplets that resemble epigrammatic distichs, the epigram as an independent form and the aesthetic of "much in little" decreased in popularity.[3] In epitaphs, epigrammatic praise of individuals alternated more and more with lengthy panegyrics detailing the role of the dead in momentous historical events. The rise in popularity of the plain inscriptional tablet, to be discussed below, further contributed to the lengthening of the epitaph. In the absence of visual ornamentation, the inscription became the sole memorial assertion of the enduring value of the deceased. Late seventeenth-century epitaphic poets tended toward seemingly straightforward assertions concerning the dead, rather than the riddles and rhetorical play with the names of the deceased that were so popular in early seventeenth-century epigrammatic epitaphs. This tendency partly reflected general intellectual shifts: there was a movement in thought about language during the late seventeenth century away from lexical considerations concerning the links between specific words and particular things, *verba* and *res*, and toward syntactical considerations con-

---

Satirical Verse, *1660–1714*, vol. 4, *1685–1688* (New Haven: Yale University Press, 1968), 97–99.

[2] On the rise of public poetry and of narrative forms in the late seventeenth century, see Earl Miner, *The Restoration Mode from Milton to Dryden* (Princeton: Princeton University Press, 1974).

[3] Discussing the influence of the epigram on longer forms in the late seventeenth and early eighteenth centuries, Alastair Fowler notes that major works of the period sometimes seem to consist of "catenas of epigrams"; see his *Kinds of Literature: An Introduction to the Theory of Genres and Modes* (Cambridge: Harvard University Press, 1982), 200. For a general discussion of the inclusion of minor genres within major ones in neoclassical aesthetics, see Ralph Cohen, "On the Interrelations of Eighteenth-Century Literary Forms," in *New Approaches to Eighteenth-Century Literature*, ed. Phillip Harth (New York: Columbia University Press, 1974), 33–78.

cerning the makeup of acts of judgment.[4] Stylistic changes were also a response to the needs and desires of a new readership. For a variety of reasons, including increased popular participation in politics, the post–Civil Wars period witnessed a significant rise in literacy.[5] The new, plainer style addressed this growing reading public, which was interested less in aesthetic niceties than in the more direct rhetoric of the tracts, broadsides, pamphlets, and newspapers of sectarian religion and partisan politics.[6] While epitaphs of the late seventeenth century sometimes attacked, as we shall see, the "rabble," they did so in language that many of the middle ranks and at least some of the lower ranks could understand.

A plainer style often supported willful, highly polemical distortions of the biographies of the dead. History was simply too intractable, peoples' loyalties too divisive, for epitaphs to be fully truthful. Political opponents in the Restoration advocated their conflicting positions by appealing to ostensibly uncontested values such as liberty, property, and the necessary balance between the king and Parliament, all of which were vague enough to support the drastically different positions of various political and religious factions. Members of a highly polarized ruling elite could thus advance their polemics from a common ground to which they all claimed adherence.[7] In a similar fashion, epitaphic poets advanced as incontestable historical truths about the lives of the dead what were in fact highly partisan formulations from whose perspective the present order could be criticized. Thus late seventeenth-century epitaphs simultaneously addressed historical events to an unprecedented degree and idealized the dead in order to obscure, or indeed escape from, history's more troublesome particularities.

Charles Cotton's two epitaphs upon his neighbor and distant relative Robert Port are early examples of the common Restoration epitaphic practice of rewriting the most difficult aspects of the recent past. Charles II's Act of Indemnity and Oblivion of 1660 sought national reconciliation by absolving all those who had served the Parliamentary cause (except

[4] See Murray Cohen, *Sensible Words: Linguistic Practice in England, 1640–1785* (Baltimore: Johns Hopkins University Press, 1977); see especially pp. 25–30.

[5] On the rise in literacy and its causes, see David Cressy, *Literacy and the Social Order: Reading and Writing in Tudor and Stuart England* (Cambridge: Cambridge University Press, 1980), 177.

[6] See Paul J. Korshin, *From Concord to Dissent: Major Themes in English Poetic Theory, 1640–1700* (Menston, England: Scolar Press, 1973), 5–8.

[7] See the discussion of Restoration political rhetoric in Steven N. Zwicker, *Politics and Language in Dryden's Poetry: The Arts of Disguise* (Princeton: Princeton University Press, 1984), 3–34.

the actual regicides and a few major Parliamentarians) from all future punishment and consigning their deeds to "utter oblivion."[8] Epitaphs similarly forgot the past: many nobles and gentlemen repressed the Parliamentarian careers of parents or other relatives when erecting their Restoration monuments, and those few who did wish to commemorate Parliamentary allegiances were sometimes prevented from doing so.[9] Robert Port, who died in May 1648, was too old to have fought in the Civil Wars, but he seems to have been in sympathy with the Parliamentary cause. His eldest son, John Port, was a captain in the Parliamentary army until his death in 1651, and Port himself was trusted enough by the Parliamentary County Committee for Staffordshire to be asked to help with local tax assessments in 1643.[10] As Parliamentary control over the country disintegrated in early 1660, Cotton wrote two epitaphs upon Port, presumably to oblige Port's son Ralph, who erected a monument to his father sometime during the early years of the Restoration in the local church of Ilam, Staffordshire.[11] Probably at the son's request, the epitaphs suppressed Port's Parliamentarian connections. In a poem that treats at length the difference between an idealized past and a degraded present, Cotton falsifies Port's true position so that the deceased can stand for the virtues destroyed by the Civil Wars:

[8] See the discussion and selection from the act in J. P. Kenyon, ed., *The Stuart Constitution, 1603–1688: Documents and Commentary*, 2d ed. (Cambridge: Cambridge University Press, 1986), 336, 339–344.
[9] G. E. Aylmer and J. S. Morrill note two examples in York alone of monuments suppressing the Parliamentary allegiances of the dead in *The Civil War and Interregnum: Sources for Local Historians* (London: Bedford Square Press, 1979), 35. The struggle over the epitaph of Colonel John Birch, a prominent member of Parliament who had fought for Parliament before welcoming Charles II's return and who later supported the Glorious Revolution of William of Orange, is a good example of the repression of Parliamentary sentiment in late seventeenth-century epitaphs. Before his death in 1691 he built a huge monument to himself in the local church with an inscription proclaiming his vindication of "ye laws and liberties of his country in war." In 1693, the vicar and churchwardens complained to the diocesan bishop that his epitaph seemed to "reflect upon the justice of King Charles ye first of ever blessed memory and to justify ye late impious and unparalleled Rebellion against him." The bishop accordingly ordered the inscription defaced. See E. Heath-Agnew, *Roundhead to Royalist: A Biography of Colonel John Birch, 1615–1691* (Foley Trading Estate, Hereford: Express Logic, 1977), 215–221.
[10] See D. H. Pennington and I. A. Roots, ed., *The Committee at Stafford, 1643–1645: The Order Book of the Staffordshire County Committee* (Manchester: Manchester University Press, 1957), p. 193 on Robert Port and pp. 48 and 129 on John Port.
[11] The epitaph inscribed upon Port's monument is dated January 1659 (Old Style) in a manuscript of Cotton's poems transcribed by various of his friends and now in Derby Borough Library; the other epitaph was presumably written in the same period; see the editor's note in John Buxton, ed., *Poems of Charles Cotton* (London: Routledge, 1958), 273. There is unfortunately no complete modern edition of Cotton's works. In addition to Buxton's selection, I have used *Poems of Charles Cotton: 1630–1687*, ed. John Beresford (London: Richard Cobden Sanderson, 1923); and Charles Cotton, *Selected Poems*, ed. Ken Robinson (Manchester: Carcanet New Press, 1983).

Virtue in those good times that bred good men
No testimony crav'd of tongue; or pen;
No marble columns; nor engraven brass,
To tell the World that such a person was;
For then each pious act, to fair descent,
Stood for the worthy owner's Monument:
But in this change of Manners, and of States,
Good names, though writ in marble, have their fates.
Such is the barb'rous and irrev'rent rage
That arms the rabble of this impious Age.

Yet may this happy stone that bears a name
(Such as no bold survivor dares to claim)
To Ages yet unborn unblemish't stand,
Safe from the stroke of an inhuman hand.

Here, Reader, here a Port's sad relics lie
To teach the careless World mortality;
Who while he mortal was unrivall'd stood
The crown, and glory of his ancient blood:
Fit for his Prince's, and his Country's trust,
Pious to God, and to his neighbour just.
A loyal Husband to his latest end,
A gracious father, and a faithful Friend.
Belov'd he liv'd, and died o'er charg'd with years,
Fuller of Honour than of silver hairs.
And, to sum up all his Virtues, this was he
Who was what all we should, but cannot be.[12]

Cotton praised his friend Alexander Brome's poetry for its "pure...
unaffected strain, / As shows wit's ornament, is to be plain."[13] The epitaph
exemplifies Cotton's stylistic ideals. Straightforward in style, it uses a
rhetoric of clear statement in order to distort the past: "Fit for his
Prince's, and his Country's trust" (l. 19) falsely implies, without actually
stating, Port's Royalist allegiances.

There is a revealing oscillation in the poem's presentation of the causes
of the Civil Wars, the tragic "change of Manners, and of States" (l. 7).
The opening nostalgic contrast between the "good times" that "bred
good men" (l. 1) and the sinful present separates all of the living from
the virtuous dead. The final couplet of the poem similarly emphasizes
the difference between Port, the vanished ideal, and all men of the
present age: "And, to sum up his Virtues, this was he / Who was what
all we should, but cannot be" (ll. 25–26). Cotton clearly includes himself
and the men of his own class among those who cannot be what they

---

[12] Cotton, "An Epitaph on Robert Port...," in *Poems*, ed. Beresford, 281.
[13] Cotton, "The Answer (To Alexander Brome)," ll. 19–20 in *Selected Poems*, ed. Robinson, 84.

should. At the end of the first verse paragraph, however, Cotton singles out for especial attack the "rage" of the "rabble of this impious Age" (ll. 9–10). By blaming the lower ranks for the disorder of the times, he adopts the ubiquitous Royalist practice of falsely identifying the Parliamentarians with the *vulgus* or "rabble."[14] Along with his idealization of the Parliamentarian Port, Cotton's attack upon the lower ranks as the major source of disorder reveals his desire to avoid the unpleasant fact that during the Civil Wars the social elite had in fact fought against itself. The poem acknowledges in vague, general terms that the social elite had in fact debased itself in internecine strife but deflects and obscures this acknowledgment by idealizing Port and using the "rabble" as the scapegoat for Cotton's sorrow and anger at the bitter course of history.

The falsity of Cotton's portrait of Port and the vagueness of his attack upon his own social class does not diminish his genuine sorrow over the loss of what he considered the noble virtues of an earlier time. Cotton's earliest compositions lament the executions of various aristocratic Royalist soldiers. In one such he vows to die in solidarity with the deceased: "But I'll go to him, though he lie / Wrapped in the cold, cold arms of death."[15] He nevertheless continued to live on, tainted in his own mind as a survivor.[16]

In the Port epitaph Cotton contrasts the present, when "Good names" (l. 8) are no longer respected, with the past, when "each pious act, to fair descent, / Stood for the worthy owner's Monument" (ll. 5–6). He combines two early seventeenth-century panegyric topoi—that virtue and children are the dead's enduring monuments—and claims that these are no longer valid. Cotton's claim helps explain why these topoi become less common in the late seventeenth century: they depend on the strong sense of the dead still being vitally connected to, and respected by, the living.[17] Historical "change" (l. 7), so Cotton suggests, has destroyed such unproblematic links between the living and the dead.

[14] On the Royalists' caricature of the Parliamentarians as the "rabble," see Joyce Lee Malcolm, *Caesar's Due: Loyalty and King Charles, 1642–1646* (London: Royal Historical Society, 1983), 146–149, 157–159.

[15] Cotton, "Song. Montross," ll. 13–14 in *Selected Poems*, ed. Robinson, 22.

[16] The final line of Cotton's epitaph is suggestively similar to the end of Alexander Brome's elegy on Charles I, published in the 1661 collection praised by Cotton: "...in this impious time / Virtue's a vice, and piety's a crime. / *The sume of all whose faults being understood, / Is this, We were too bad, and you too good*"; see "On the Death of King Charles," ll. 65–68 in Brome, *Poems*, ed. Roman R. Dubinski, 2 vols. (Toronto: University of Toronto Press, 1982), 1:296. Both poets sadly identify themselves with the shameful present age, and in both poems the concluding "sum" of praise reveals the moral distance between the deceased ideal and those still living in "impious times." Though Cotton might be echoing Brome, the verbal similarity is probably due to the shared predicament and attitude of the two young survivors of the Royalist cause.

[17] For late examples of the virtue-as-monument and children-as-monument topoi respectively, see the epitaphs upon Frances Tipping, d. 1698, in F. N. Davis, ed., "Anthony

By decrying the "irrev'rent rage / That arms the rabble" against names inscribed in "marble" (ll. 8–10), Cotton treats the supposedly low-class Parliamentarians' attacks upon monuments during the Civil Wars as a synecdoche for the destruction of historical continuity and of a virtuous social order based upon such continuity.[18] He can only hope that Port's monument will escape the attacks of an "inhuman hand" so that it can preserve his name unto "Ages yet unborn" (ll. 13–14). The poem thus views the violent, degraded present in terms not only of an idealized past but also of an uncertain future. The sole potential connection between past and future is the vulnerable monument itself.

Cotton is typical in treating the destruction of funerary monuments as both a manifestation and potent symbol of the breakdown of the social order during the Civil Wars and Interregnum. As had the iconoclasm act of 1550, the 1643 Parliamentary act explicitly excluded funerary monuments from the mandated destruction of superstitious monuments.[19] Though eager to destroy the remnants of Laudian "popery" and superstition, most of the Parliamentary elite wished to preserve grand funerary monuments and the continuity of lineage they represented.[20] Despite their views, however, many funerary monuments and inscriptions were destroyed or damaged during the Civil Wars and Interregnum.[21] Not only tombs and brasses with "papist" images and inscriptions were attacked. Radical separatists expressed their revulsion for monuments as such, viewing them all as idols: as early as 1641 there

---

à Wood's and Richard Rawlinson's Parochial Collections (Third Part)," *Oxfordshire Record Society* 11 (1929):337; and upon Lady Vincent Elinor, d. 1645, in Thomas F. Ravenshaw, ed., *Antiente Epitaphes (from A.D. 1250 to A.D. 1800)* (London, 1878), 96–97.

[18] Compare the attack on "sacrilegious hands[s]" that desecrate the dead in Cotton, "Death," in *Poems*, ed. Beresford, 222.

[19] Parliament's 1644 ordinance repeated the 1550 exclusion of funerary monuments verbatim; see *Two Ordinances... for the speedy Demolishing of... all manner of Superstitious Monuments* (London, 1644), 4.

[20] The troubled times probably did intensify some moderate Puritans' suspicions of grand monuments with images. The religious tone of the Interregnum helps explain, for example, the request made in 1653 by the Puritan rector of Kedington, Simon Fairclough the younger, to his patroness, the widow of Sir Nathaniel Bernardiston. Although the Bernardistons, a family of solid Puritan gentry, had a series of grand tombs with effigies in the local church, Fairclough asked that Lady Bernardiston not follow custom and erect to her husband's memory a "pictur'd stone" lest the rector be encouraged to pray to "the Image of this Saint"; see J. T. Cliffe, *The Puritan Gentry: The Great Puritan Families of Early Stuart England* (London: Routledge, 1984), 133. While flattering the deceased husband of his patroness as a saint whose image could plausibly induce worship, the rector expresses fears of idolatry strong enough to warrant discontinuing a venerable tradition.

[21] On the iconoclasm of the Civil Wars, see Margaret Aston, *England's Iconoclasts*, vol. 1, *Laws Against Images* (Oxford: Clarendon, 1988), 62–95; and John Phillips, *The Reformation of Images: Destruction of Art in England, 1535–1660* (Berkeley: University of California Press, 1973), 183–200. On the destruction of "superstitious" commemorative brasses during this period, see Malcolm Norris, *Monumental Brasses: The Memorials*, 2 vols. (London: Phillips and Page, 1977), 1:260–263.

were reports of separatists defacing monuments in various London churches.[22] According to the Puritan gentleman Sir Simonds D'Ewes, the lower orders took advantage of the civil disorder to destroy monuments of the nobility and gentry even though Parliament had declared that "noe tombs should be meddled withall."[23] Soldiers on both sides destroyed the monuments of enemy leaders; common soldiers perhaps enjoyed venting their resentment of aristocratic generals.[24] Some people stripped brasses and monuments and sold the materials.[25] Royalist propaganda exaggerated the number and extent of such incidents on the Parliamentary side and portrayed the Parliamentary leaders themselves as upstart destroyers of monuments and the social order that monuments upheld.

Royalists unfairly branded Oliver Cromwell himself as a destroyer of monuments. Like several other Parliamentary leaders, Cromwell was buried with great pomp in Westminster Abbey. His funeral effigy, which portrayed him for the first and only time in the full regalia of a monarch, lay in state for many weeks. Considered by some an idolatrous manifestation of religious and social corruption, it might well have provided a model for a grand tomb to join those of bygone monarchs had the Stuart monarchy not been restored and the effigy (along with Cromwell's corpse) been hanged in public as posthumous punishment for the regicide.[26] Nevertheless a Royalist song attacked Cromwell as one who "did ... Monuments defie" and sardonically gave him his just deserts: "And on his Grave since there may be no Stone / Shall stand this Epitaph; *That he has none.*"[27]

Other epitaphic poets responding to the iconoclasm of the Civil Wars

[22] Anthony Fletcher, *The Outbreak of the English Civil War* (New York: New York University Press, 1981), 119.

[23] D'Ewes is cited in Cliffe, 131–132.

[24] See Christopher Hill, *Milton and the English Revolution* (New York: Viking, 1977), 171–181; see especially p. 175.

[25] See Aston, *England's Iconoclasts*, 83.

[26] On Cromwell's effigy and its probable fate, see David Piper, "The Contemporary Portraits of Oliver Cromwell," *Walpole Society* 34 (1958):36–37. After criticizing Cromwell's fall from Protestant purity into idolatrous pursuit of "flattering titles" and "false worships," the Quaker Edward Burroughs exclaimed concerning Cromwell's funeral effigy: "Is this the end and final farewell of once noble Oliver? What, only the sight of an image carried and set up?" (cited in Christopher Hill, *God's Englishman: Oliver Cromwell and the English Revolution* [London: Weidenfeld & Nicolson, 1970], 192–193). From an avowedly Royalist, anti-Puritan perspective, Abraham Cowley exploited the rhetoric of iconoclasm in order to attack Cromwell's funeral and effigy: "The Herse was magnificent, *the Idol Crowned....* a great show, and yet after all this, but an ill sight"; see Cowley, "A Discourse By way of Vision, Concerning the Government of Oliver Cromwell" (1661) in his *Essays, Plays, and Sundry Verses,* ed. A. R. Waller (Cambridge: Cambridge University Press, 1906), 342 (italics mine).

[27] "Cromwell's Panegyrick," in *Rump: Or an Exact Collection of the Choycest Poems and Songs relating to the Late Times* (London, 1662), 225.

share Cotton's fervent wish that the material monument be allowed to stand as the sole remaining sign of the dead. Contemplating time's eventual destruction of monuments, earlier epitaphic poets could easily, even glibly, assert that the fame or progeny of the deceased would outlast the material tomb. The iconoclasm of the Civil Wars made funerary monuments seem, by contrast, vulnerable but crucial bulwarks against man's inhumane disrespect for the dead. The inscription upon the monument of Edward Hunter, a child who died in 1646, has the stone itself beg for preservation:

> To the courteous souldier
> Noe crucifix you see, noe Frightful Brand
> Of Superstition's here. Pray let me stand.
> *Grassante bello civili.*
> [While Civil War rages.][28]

A child is dead, war continues. The speaking monument, taking on the burden of humane values, proclaims its freedom from idolatrous "superstition" and begs at least to be allowed to endure as all that remains of the poor child.

Closer in date and tone to the Cotton epitaph is Edmund Waller's pseudo-inscriptional epitaph upon Lady Elizabeth Sedley, a poem written sometime after 1660. After praising Sedley's virtues during the "calmer days" of peace, Waller concludes by praising her conduct during the Civil Wars and wishing that her monument be preserved:

> ...(her person and her state,
> Exempted from the common fate)
> In all our civil fury she
> Stood, like a sacred temple, free.
> May here her monument stand so,
> To credit this rude age! and show
> To future times, that even we
> Some monuments did of virtue see;
> And one sublime example had
> Of good, among so many bad.[29]

Sir Anthony Weldon, the most powerful and eventually most hated Parliamentarian in Kent, was an old friend of the Sedley family, and he helped Lady Sedley avoid the fines normally levied on "delinquents"

---

[28] Cited in Katharine A. Esdaile, *English Church Monuments, 1510 to 1840* (New York: Oxford University Press, 1946), 134.

[29] Edmund Waller, "Epitaph on the Lady Sedley," ll. 25–34 in *Poems of Edmund Waller*, ed. G. Thorn Drury (1893; rpt., New York: Greenwood Press, 1968), 243. The poem was printed posthumously in 1693 and cannot be dated precisely.

who refused to take oaths of loyalty to the Commonwealth.[30] Like Cotton, Waller idealizes the deceased by obscuring unglamorous historical realities. Describing Sedley's good fortune in heroic style as an exemption from the "common fate," Waller treats it not as the product of political compromises but as an unequivocal moral victory. The poem does not explicitly attack iconoclasm, but its treatment of Sedley and her monument rejects the strains of Protestant thought that fuelled iconoclasm. While many Protestants stressed that the "lively stones" of the faithful were far superior to any potentially idolatrous material temple,[31] Waller compares Lady Sedley to a material "sacred temple" and proceeds to blur the distinction between Sedley herself and her material tomb, both of which are "monuments...of virtue." Like the Port monument, Sedley's tomb should be preserved, so the poet asserts, as the sole link in "this rude age" between the virtuous deceased and "future times."

The "happy stone" (l. 11) that the Port epitaph wishes preserved is a small unembellished wall tablet. In the second half of the seventeenth century the wall tablet without effigy or bust, which had arisen in the late sixteenth and early seventeenth centuries, became extremely popular among the social elite.[32] During the Civil Wars and Interregnum there had been, not surprisingly, a marked decline in the erection of grand tombs with images of the dead.[33] Lacking the time and funds for the erection of large monuments, many of the elite no doubt considered monuments that could arouse iconoclastic fury a poor investment in any case. Royalists, moreover, did not wish to erect expensive monuments when they lacked the freedom to proclaim their loyalties upon their tombs. Though grand monuments reemerged with the Restoration, the hiatus in their erection contributed to the increased acceptance and popularity of more modest, imageless monuments in the late seventeenth century.

Nevertheless the funerary monument did not lose its importance as a sign of family status. The Port monument's placement in the chancel

[30] On Weldon and Sedley, see Vivian de Sola Pinto, *Sir Charles Sedley, 1639–1701: A Study in the Life and Literature of the Restoration* (London: Constable, 1927), 27–38; on Weldon's control of Kent, see Alan Everitt, *The Community of Kent and the Great Rebellion, 1640–1660* (Leicester: Leicester University Press, 1966), 126–185 and passim.

[31] On the Pauline and Puritan conception of Christians as the "lively stones" of the "living temple," see John S. Coolidge, *The Pauline Renaissance in England: Puritanism and the Bible* (Oxford: Clarendon, 1970), 23–54; see especially pp. 46–47.

[32] See Brian Kemp, *English Church Monuments* (London: B. T. Batsford, 1980), 115–120.

[33] On the decline of aristocratic monuments during the Interregnum, see Margaret Whinney, *Sculpture in Britain: 1530 to 1830* (Baltimore: Penguin, 1964), 39. Anthony Fletcher notes the dramatic decline of visual representations of the dead in Sussex during the 1640s and 1650s in *A County Community in Peace and War: Sussex 1600–1660* (London: Longman, 1975), 74–75.

of Ilam Church testifies to the family's leading position in the parish. This makes it all the more striking that Cotton does not praise Ralph Port, the erector of the monument, by seeking to connect the son to his virtuous father. Cotton asserts that no "bold survivor" (l. 12) can live up to Robert Port's name and places all of his hope in the survival of the material monument. This is no personal idiosyncrasy. In his epitaph upon Lady Sedley, Waller does the same: instead of insisting that Lady Sedley's living offspring are her enduring monument, Waller proffers the monument itself as the only potentially enduring proof of Sedley's virtue.

This implied denigration of the surviving family must have been acceptable to the relatives who commissioned the poems. Such treatment of the living may be partially explained in psychological terms as one stage in the process of mourning: mourners control the ambivalence and anger they feel by splitting their emotional reactions into positive and negative parts, idealizing the dead and directing their anger against themselves.[34] The absence in these poems of any of the customary epitaphic attempts to bridge the gap between the dead and the living nevertheless demands a historically specific explanation. Cotton and Waller are mourning and idealizing not simply the deceased but a nobler, simpler time that vanished when gentlemen became engaged in internecine strife. Both argue that only the monument can preserve the (whitewashed) past, in real or imaginary marble, from the contamination of the present.

The plain inscriptional tablet may have encouraged Cotton, like many other poets of the late seventeenth and eighteenth centuries, to write a relatively lengthy epitaph. Not only could a long composition describe the momentous historical changes Cotton felt had taken place, but the epitaph's verbal weight—so it was hoped—could make up for the monument's material and visual modesty. Cotton could still be loyal, however, to the epigrammatic ideal, and he composed a second, equally idealizing but highly pithy epitaph upon Port. Four tetrameter lines describe Port's death as the destruction of a virtuous way of life:

> Here lies he, whom the Tyrant's rage
> Snatch't in a venerable age;
> And here, with him, entomb'd do lie
> Honour, and Hospitality.[35]

---

[34] For a discussion of epitaphic idealization in terms of the psychology of mourning, see G. W. Pigman III, *Grief and English Renaissance Elegy* (Cambridge: Cambridge University Press, 1985), 5, 8.

[35] Cotton, "Epitaph On Mr. Robert Port," in *Poems*, ed. Beresford, 282.

Unlike earlier poets who stress their "much in little" message, Cotton uses brevity without fanfare for seemingly straightforward assertion. His plainness is nevertheless highly polemical. Asserting that the civilized virtues of honor and hospitality vanished with the deceased, Cotton suggests no way of reviving them. The "Tyrant's rage" refers on the most general level to death, which is often called or compared to a tyrant in funerary poetry from the Middle Ages to Cotton's own time.[36] The reference to death is normally, however, made explicit, and Cotton's use of "tyrant" rather than "Death the tyrant" or some such variant licenses a second, more topical reading. Throughout the 1640s and 1650s committed Royalists, conservative Presbyterians, and localists who distrusted the central government referred to the successive Interregnum governments and their officials as "tyrannies" and "tyrants."[37] Cotton's own elegy upon the Royalist Lord Derby, beheaded in 1651, attacks the "Blood-thirsty Tyrants of usurped state! / In facts of death prompt, and insatiate!"[38] Sir John Denham's elegy upon the Royalist Francis Villiers, who was killed in a 1648 uprising, exclaims that Villiers' death "compleats the Ages [sic] Tyrannies."[39] Cotton's "Tyrant's rage" thus can refer to both the perennial ravages of death and the "rage" of tyranny experienced by Royalists in the 1640s and 1650s. The ambiguity is indeed strategic, allowing Cotton to falsify Port's life and death without unequivocally lying. For the few who knew that Port was no Royalist and had died of old age, Cotton repeats the sad commonplace of Death the tyrant. For others, the poet vaguely but falsely suggests that Parliamentary "rage" caused Port's death and the accompanying destruction of virtues.

In blaming Port's death on the political sins of the age, Cotton adopts a common idealizing motif of the period. In laments upon royalty, early

[36] For a medieval example of death as "tyrant," see "On the Untimely Death of a Fair Lady," l. 15 in Carleton Brown, ed., *Religious Lyrics of the XVth Century* (Oxford: Clarendon, 1939), 242. For a few seventeenth-century examples, see "To Death," in *Facetiae: Musarum Deliciae and Wit Restor'd and Wits Recreations*, 2 vols. (London, 1817), 2:273–274; and the epitaphs upon Ann Harley, d. 1603, in John Thorpe, *Registrum Roffense: or, A Collection of Antient Records . . . of the Diocese and Cathedral Church of Rochester* (London, 1769), 769–770; Mary Draper, d. 1652, in Thorpe, 999; and Richard Richards, d. 1656, in Ravenshaw, 112.

[37] See the numerous examples of attacks upon Parliamentary "tyranny" in Robert Ashton, "From Cavalier to Roundhead Tyranny, 1642–1649," in *Reactions to the English Civil War, 1642–1649*, ed. John Morrill (London: Macmillan, 1982), 185–207; and J. S. Morrill, *The Revolt of the Provinces: Conservatives and Radicals in the English Civil War, 1630–1650* (London: Allen, 1976); see especially pp. 201–207. The Royalist Alice Thornton recalled the "groaneing [sic] under . . . tyranny" and "the raige, rapine, and destruction" of the Interregnum; see *The Autobiography of Mrs. Alice Thornton* (Edinburgh, 1875), 99.

[38] Cotton, "On the Lord Derby," ll. 41–42 in *Poems*, ed. Buxton, 130.

[39] Sir John Denham, "An Elegie upon the Death of the Lord Hastings," l. 16 in *The Poetical Works of Sir John Denham*, ed. Theodore Howard Banks, 2d ed. (1928; rpt., Hamden, Conn.: Archon Books, 1969), 145.

seventeenth-century poets commonly use the argument that the sins of the living killed the deceased. They rarely applied this argument, however, to nonroyalty.[40] The Civil Wars and their aftermath broaden the use of the motif: no matter how he actually died, any man worth commemorating—that is, any member of the aristocracy and gentry—could be praised as having died because of the times. James Rivers died in 1641 but his monument was erected during the Civil Wars by his prominent Parliamentary family. His epitaph describes his death as a Stoic response to royal and ecclesiastical tyranny: "Who when ambition tyranny and pride / Conquer'd the age, conquer'd himself and dy'd." Sir William Davenant's epitaph on Mr. John Sturmy portrays a neutralist "in a sad and furious Age" who "Consum'd with grief, to see the publick crimes, / ... dy'd as thou should'st wisely do, betimes." William Hammond portrays a Royalist who died of the age's sins: "... his vitals fail'd; / To show, this feeling member's health / Was wrapt up in the commonwealth." An epitaph upon the Royalist Edward Wood, who died in 1655, claims that he "chose to dye, rather than view the crimes."[41] Men on all sides longed too much for peace to allow the celebration of military valor to be the dominant form of panegyric during the Civil Wars. Though there was certainly praise for victorious military men on both sides, martyrs were most often celebrated. Cotton transforms Port's death into a martyrdom. Like the other poets cited, he thereby suggests that the survival of the living reveals their lack of heroic virtue-unto-death.

In his "Epitaphium vivi Auctoris," the poem that concludes his posthumously published *Several Discourses by Way of Essays, in Verse and Prose* (1668), Abraham Cowley, like other late seventeenth-century poets, idealizes the dead and attacks the living. Cowley distinguishes himself from his contemporaries, however, by praising himself as the ideal deceased. Describing his retirement as a "death-in-life," Cowley stakes out a small home of contentment far from the public realm. In his retirement stance Cowley resembles Herrick, but unlike the latter, he not only re-

---

[40] See Barbara K. Lewalski, *Donne's Anniversaries and the Poetry of Praise: The Creation of a Symbolic Mode* (Princeton: Princeton University Press, 1973), 23, 29–30; and Pigman, 144, n. 5. Both Lewalski and Pigman note the motif's frequent use in poems upon the death of Prince Henry.

[41] The epitaph on James Rivers is in E. A. Webb, *The Records of St. Bartholomew's Priory and of the Church and Parish of St. Bartholomew the Great, West Smithfield*, 2 vols. (London: Oxford University Press, 1921), 2:461–462. On the Rivers family, see Everitt, 117–118. The other epitaphs cited are: Sir William Davenant, "Epitaph. On Mr. John Sturmy" (no date), in Davenant, *The Shorter Poems, and Songs from the Plays and Masques*, ed. A. M. Gibbs (Oxford: Clarendon, 1972), 151; William Hammond, "Epitaph on Sir R. D." (1655) in *Minor Poets of the Caroline Period*, ed. George Saintsbury, 3 vols. (Oxford: Clarendon, 1905–1921), 2:518; and the epitaph on Edward Wood, d. 1655, in *The Life and Times of Anthony Wood*, ed. Andrew Clark, 5 vols. (Oxford: Clarendon, 1891–1900), 1:198.

treats from the world but also aggressively insists upon his superiority to it.

Intermittently throughout his literary career Abraham Cowley espoused a retirement that he closely linked to death. In poems published in the late 1630s he imagined a country life in which he could have "sleepe, as undisturb'd as death" and a life of deathlike solitude culminating in a death commemorated only by "Robin-red-brests."[42] During the Interregnum he once more declared his longing for a deathlike retreat. Like Herrick, his fellow retirement poet, Cowley suffered as a Royalist during the Interregnum, but he was far more active in the Royalist cause and far more harshly punished than the obscure parish minister Herrick. Cowley served as a Royalist spy in the 1650s and was imprisoned in 1655.[43] In 1656, while in prison, he wrote a preface to a collection of his poems in which he officially renounced Royalism as a defeated cause and announced his submission to the "unaccountable Will of God" that had given Cromwell victory. In the same preface he also declared his intention to retire to a kind of death: he announced that his reader could look upon him as "a Dead, or at least a Dying Person," for he was resolved to retire to America, write no more, and thus "bury" himself "in some obscure retreat."[44] The declaration was on one level a playful, witty ploy supporting his plea that readers treat his works with the "favor" normally only given to "Deceased Poets."[45] At the same time it expressed in extreme form the poet's desire to escape from England's—and his own—harsh plight.

During the early years of the Restoration, Cowley quickly published celebrations of the restored monarchy and attacks upon the Puritan rebels. Influential courtiers, including Edward Hyde, the earl of Clarendon, nevertheless considered him a renegade because of his abjuring of Royalism in the late 1650s, and much to the poet's disappointment, he received no court position. Primarily through the largesse of his two major patrons at court, George Villiers, the duke of Buckingham, and Henry Jermyn, earl of Saint Albans, Cowley was nevertheless able to retire in the mid-1660s with a good-sized income to a succession of

[42] See Cowley, "A Vote" and "Ode II: That a pleasant Poverty is to be preferred before discontented Riches," from *Sylva* (1637) in his *Essays*, 48–50, 60–61.

[43] See Arthur H. Nethercot, *Abraham Cowley: The Muse's Hannibal* (New York: Russell, 1931), 142–157; and Jean Loiseau, *Abraham Cowley: Sa vie, son oeuvre* (Paris: 1931), 112–122.

[44] Abraham Cowley, *Poems: Miscellanies, The Mistress, Pindarique Odes, Davideis, Verses Written on Several Occasions*, ed. A. R. Waller (Cambridge: Cambridge University Press, 1905), 8.

[45] Cowley, *Poems*, 8. It was an ancient commonplace (as well as often true) that readers were kinder to dead poets than to living ones: Cowley himself cites Martial's *Epigrams* 8.99; compare Horace, *Epistle* 2.1.1–92.

comfortable country estates.[46] In his posthumously published work, *Essays, in Verse and Prose*, Cowley uses translations and imitations of Roman poems and original compositions in both verse and prose to portray himself as the exemplary man of retirement. He proclaims his contentment with a life of "Liberty, Tranquility, Security and Innocence."[47] In the last, most personal essay of the collection, "Of Myself," Cowley contends that he had indeed wished for retirement since his earliest days, and the *Essays* as a whole seek to prove that temperament and choice, not mere failure at court or sour grapes, led him to his final retreat from the world and its strife.[48] Cowley's idealized portrayal of his own checkered career was in one sense hugely successful: during the late seventeenth and early eighteenth centuries, the *Essays* were the most influential English work in praise of the retired man.[49]

The *Essays* once more associate retirement with death. Cowley purports to desire a retirement so private as to exclude even an epitaph upon his grave. In the essay "Of Obscurity," Cowley cites with approval Horace's praise of those who "live and dye so obscurely, that the world takes no notice of them." At the conclusion of the same essay he includes in his free translation of a famous chorus praising retirement from Seneca's *Thyestes* the wish, not in the original Latin, that his "homely Death [not] embroidered be / With Scutcheon or with Elegie."[50] At the end of the book Cowley includes an epitaph upon himself, however, that attempts to sum up for the public and for posterity the meaning of his retirement:

> *Hic, O Viator, sub Lare parvulo,*
> Couleius *Hic est Conditus, Hic Iacet;*
>   *Defunctus humani Laboris*
>   *Sorte, supervacuaque vita.*
>
> *Non* Indecora pauperie *Nitens,*
> *Et Non* inerti *nobilis* otio,

---

[46] See Nethercot, 194–254; and Loiseau, 139–148. In "The Complaint" Cowley explicitly expressed his disappointment but hinted at continuing hopes for royal patronage: "Kings have long hands, they say, and though I be / So distant, they may reach at length to me"; the poem is cited and discussed in Nethercot, 213–215.

[47] Cowley, "Of Greatness," in *Essays*, 432. On the singleness of theme in the *Essays*, which justifies my reading the final epitaph in the light of the work as a whole, see Arthur H. Nethercot, "Abraham Cowley's *Essays*," *JEGP* 29 (1930):114–130. See also Nicholas Jose's thoughtful treatment of Cowley's relation to the court in the *Essays*, slightly marred by an inattention to the literary traditions behind the work and a tendency to take Cowley's statements at face value, in his *Ideas of the Restoration in English Literature, 1660–1671* (Cambridge: Harvard University Press, 1984), 90–96.

[48] See Cowley, *Essays*, 456.

[49] See Maren-Sofie Røstvig's discussion of Cowley's historical significance as the English *summa* of the retirement tradition in *The Happy Man: Studies in the Metamorphoses of a Classical Ideal*, rev. ed., 2 vols. (Oslo: Norwegian University Press, 1962), 1: 15–41, 212–221.

[50] Cowley, *Essays*, 397, 400.

Vanóque dilectis popello
   Divitiis animosus hostis.

Possis ut illum dicere mortuum;
En Terra iam nunc Quantula *sufficit?*
   Exempta sit Curis, viator,
      Terra sit illa Levis, precare.

Hic sparge Flores, *sparge breves* Rosas,
Nam vita gaudet Mortua Floribus
   Herbisque Odoratis Corona
      Vatis adhuc Cinerem Calentem.[51]

(Here, o traveler, under a small roof, here Cowley is buried, here he lies, finished with the human lot of labor and a superfluous life; splendid in his not unfitting poverty, and noble in his not inactive ease, a fearless enemy to riches loved by the foolish mob. Behold, does not so little land already now suffice him, that you can say that he is dead? Wish, o traveler, that his grave be free from cares and that the earth lie light upon him. Here strew flowers, short-lived roses, for death-in-life enjoys flowers, and crown the still warm ashes of the bard with sweet-smelling herbs).

Early editions of the *Essays* noted that the epitaph was originally "written on his [Cowley's] House" while "yet alive, but withdrawn from the busie World to a Country-Life."[52] A Latin ode in the Alcaic meter, Horace's favorite meter in his *Odes*, Cowley's Horatian ode-as-epitaph in praise of retirement-as-death is filled with echoes of Horatian and Virgilian retirement poetry. The language, genre, and classical allusions of the poem all suggest Cowley's determination to distance himself from his actual historical predicament. The poem is unlike any poem that the ancient poets themselves would have composed, however, for Cowley's retirement poem echoes but pointedly radicalizes the Augustan poets' rejections of the public realm. Ignoring his own dependence upon aristocratic patrons for his *otium cum dignitate,* Cowley contrasts his own rejection of the great with Horace's and Virgil's continuing deference to their great patrons Augustus and Maecenas. He thus idealizes himself as the truest, because most independent, representative of the ancient retirement ideal and therefore as the most appropriate judge of the public realm's iniquities.

   While the Roman retirement poems echoed by Cowley humbly link the Augustan poets to their great worldly patrons, Cowley's ode pointedly rejects such humility and presents the poet as a solitary "fearless enemy" ("animosus hostis," l. 8) of the world. The first stanza's posi-

[51] Cowley, "Epitaphium Vivi Auctoris," in his *Essays,* 461–462.
[52] Cited from the seventh edition of Cowley's works in Røstvig, 1:212.

tioning of Cowley "under a small roof" ("sub Lare parvulo," l. 1) echoes
the description of Horace's modest life at home "under a small roof"
("parvo sub lare") from one of his best-known Alcaic odes (3.29.14). In
this ode Horace invites his rich and powerful patron Maecenas to leave
Rome and visit his humble country home, arguing that "often a change
is pleasant to the rich" (l. 13). In the second stanza Cowley thus implicitly
contrasts his own supposed stance as "a fearless enemy to wealth" ("Divitiis animosus hostis," l. 8) with the modest stance of Horace toward his
rich patron. Cowley's self-proclaimed bravery itself echoes Horace's *Ode*
3.4, where Horace, using "animosus" in exactly the same position in the
Alcaic stanza as Cowley does, portrays himself in a serio-comic tone as
a poet "fearless" since childhood because of the Muses' companionship—
"with the gods' help a fearless child" ("non sine dis animosus infans," l.
20). Horace thereby modestly links himself to his truly brave patron,
Augustus, who also has the Muses as his companion during his respite
from warfare (ll. 37–42). Rejecting Horace's deference, Cowley proudly
portrays his own supposedly independent bravery. With similar point-
edness Cowley's praise of himself as "noble in his not inactive ease" ("Et
Non inerti nobilis Otio," l. 6) echoes Virgil's self-denigrating contrast
between the "ignoble ease" ("ignobilis oti") of the retired poet and the
glorious military action of Augustus (*Georgics* 4.559–566).[53] Cowley
changes "ignoble" to "noble" in order to proclaim his own dignity as a
retired poet who refuses to abase himself before any Augustus-like figure.[54] Cowley's rejection of the "popello" (l. 7), a word first used by
Horace to describe the lower classes (*Epistles* 1.7.65), thus takes on a new
meaning: Cowley the "noble" poet purports to reject the "mob" of all
those, high and low, whose attachment to wealth makes them part of
the "world." Cowley's famous version of the opening of Horace's *Ode*
3.1, "I hate the uninitiate mob and keep them far away" ("Odi profanum

[53] I excerpt from the passage: "... while great Caesar thundered in war by deep Eu-
phrates and gave a victor's laws unto willing nations, and essayed the path to Heaven. In
those days I, Virgil, was nursed of sweet Parthenope, and rejoiced in the arts of ignoble
ease" ("...Caesar dum magnus ad altum / fulminat Euphraten bello victorque volentis /
per populos dat iura viamque adfectat Olympo. / illo Vergilium me tempore dulcis alebat
/ Parthenope, studiis florentem ignobilis oti," Virgil, *Georgics* 4. 560–564).

[54] Elsewhere in the *Essays*, Cowley separates the retirement stance of Horace and Virgil
from its association with Augustus. In "Of Solitude," Cowley says that the "Innocent
Deceiver of the world, as *Horace* calls him ... I take to have been more happy ... then the
greatest Actors ... even then *Augustus* himself" (Cowley, *Essays*, 399); in "The Garden"
Cowley writes of his "no unactive Ease, and no unglorious Poverty," quotes Virgil's self-
description in the *Georgics* but corrects the modesty of "ignobilis otii" by asserting that
Virgil "had rather said '*Nobilis otii*'" (Cowley, *Essays*, 420–421). Cowley wishes that Virgil
had centered praise on himself rather than on Augustus, just as Cowley centers praise on
himself. See also Cowley's denigration of Augustus's conquering Rome "With so much
Falshood, so much guilt" in "Of Greatness" (Cowley, *Essays*, 431).

vulgus et arceo," Loeb translation modified) fully reveals the retired
poet's impartial attack on both the high and low "mob" of worldly men:
"Hence, ye Profane; I hate ye all; / Both the Great, Vulgar, and the
small."[55] Cowley expands Horace's "vulgus" to include the great as well
as the small. In the epitaph, similarly, Cowley presents himself as the
solitary "noble" who has escaped the snares of the worldly, high and low
alike.[56]

Cowley's last two stanzas focus on the "death-in-life" of the poet-hero.
Lines nine and ten make explicit the conceptual basis of Cowley's central
conceit. While Herrick expresses contentment with the grave as a small
but sufficient piece of property, Cowley suggests that his small but sufficient property, his country estate, is a kind of grave. He can be called
dead because, like a dead man, he finds his tiny plot of earth sufficient:
"Behold, does not so little land already now suffice him?" ("En Terra
iam nunc Quantula sufficit?" l. 10). Declaring his present satisfaction
with a state others supposedly accept only in death, Cowley alludes to
the commonplace that a small grave suffices even the great man—once
he is dead. Thus Juvenal contrasts Alexander the Great in life and in
death: "One globe is all too little for [non sufficit] the youth of Pella [i.e.,
Alexander]; he chafes uneasily within the narrow limits of the world...
[but when he dies] a sarcophagus will suffice him [sarcophago contentus
erit]! Death alone proclaims how small [quantula] are our poor human
bodies!"[57] "A small home [now] suffices [sufficit] the great lord" states
the epitaph upon William the Conqueror preserved in Camden's Remaines.[58] "I love Littleness almost in all things," Cowley claims in the
essay "Of Greatness," and this love allows him to accept in the present
the contracted state to which all men must eventually come.[59] By adopting in life the contraction of death Cowley avoids the fate of the great
man to whom, as Cowley writes in an imitation of Seneca, death will

[55] Cowley, Essays, 434.
[56] An anonymous eighteenth-century translation of Cowley's epitaph recognizes the
enlarged force of popello by having the poet condemn "Riches...as trifling Things, / The
Vulgar's Wish, and Pride of Kings"; see Nathaniel Frobisher (publisher), Frobisher's New
Select Collection of Epitaphs: Humorous, Whimsical, Moral & Satyrical (London, 1790s), 68.
[57] "Unus Pellaeo iuveni non sufficit orbis; / aestuat infelix angusto limite mundi /.../
sarcophago contentus erit. mors sola fatetur / quantula sint hominum corpuscula" (Juvenal,
Satire 10.168–173).
[58] "Sufficit & magno parva domus domino" (William Camden, Remaines of a Greater
Worke, Concerning Britaine...[London, 1605], 34). Compare the similar epitaph upon
Henry II (Camden, Remaines, 37); and Antony's apostrophe upon the smallness of great
Caesar's corpse in Julius Caesar: "O mighty Caesar! dost thou lie so low? / Are all thy
conquests, glories, triumphs, spoils, / Shrunk to this little measure?" (William Shakespeare,
Julius Caesar, ed. T. S. Dorsch, The Arden Shakespeare [London: Methuen, 1955], 71
[III.i.148–150]).
[59] Cowley, "Of Greatness," in his Essays, 429.

appear terrible because he "does not himself, when he is Dying know /
Nor what he is, nor Whither hee's to go."[60]

Cowley's addressee, the "viator," is told both to strew "short-lived
roses" ("breves Rosas," l. 13) upon Cowley, thus humbling the poet with
a reminder of his own transience, and to crown the "warm ashes of the
bard" ("Vatis...Cinerem Calentem," ll. 15–16). "Warm ashes of the
bard" echoes Horace's *Ode* 2. 6, in which Horace contrasts his humble
life of retirement with the active life of his friend Septimius, who is going
off to defend the Roman *imperium*. While Horace humbly bids Septimius
shed a single tear over the "warm ashes" of a "friendly bard" ("calentem
/...favillam / vatis amici," ll. 22–24, Loeb translation modified) when
the poet dies, Cowley proudly asks the modern representative of the
active life, the passerby, to show his respect for the poet-hero of retirement by crowning him. Contentment with little, Cowley suggests, is both
a figurative death to the world and an immortal victory over actual death.

Cowley's praise of his retired contentment and attack on the "mob,"
both great and small, implies both his rejection of the royal court and
his retrospective repudiation of the defeated rebels, the two major powers in England's recent history. In *Epistle* 1.10, Horace advises the addressee to "flee grandeur: though humble be your roof, / yet in life's race
you may outstrip kings and the friends of kings."[61] Cowley's version in
the *Essays* strengthens the assertion of superiority and dwells on the
emptiness of courtly life: "An humble Roof, plain bed, and homely
board, / More clear, untainted pleasures do afford, / Then all the Tumult
of vain greatness brings / To Kings, or to the favorites of Kings."[62]
Elsewhere in the *Essays* he balances such attacks on the court with condemnation of ambitious would-be acquirers of greatness like Cromwell:
"A famous person of their Off-spring [i.e., the rebellious Titans], the
late Gyant of our Nation, when from the condition of a very inconsid-
erable Captain, he had made himself Lieutenant General of an Army
of little Titans...is believed to have dyed with grief and discontent,
because he could not attain to the honest name of a King, and the old
formality of a Crown."[63] In his Pindaric ode *Brutus* (1657) Cowley had
praised, however ambiguously, Cromwell in the guise of Brutus the
tyrannicide.[64] In the *Essays*, by contrast, Cowley proclaims his contempt

---

[60] Cowley, "Seneca, ex Thyeste, Act. 2. Chor," in his *Essays*, 400.

[61] "Fuge magna: licet sub paupere tecto / reges et regum vita praecurrere amicos"
(Horace, *Epistle* 1.10.32–33). I have modified the Loeb translation.

[62] Cowley, "A Paraphrase upon the 10th Epistle of the First Book of Horace: Horace
to Fuscus Aristius," in his *Essays*, 417.

[63] Cowley, "Of Greatness," in his *Essays*, 433.

[64] On the ambiguities of the *Brutus* ode, see Jose, 81–83; and Annabel Patterson, *Censorship and Interpretation: The Conditions of Writing and Reading in Early Modern England*
(Madison: University of Wisconsin Press, 1984), 144–158. Such ambiguities do not alter

for Cromwell as a discontented would-be king and for the rebels as would-be grandees. The ambition that led Cromwell and his "little Titans" to rebel against the established order are the very opposite of Cowley's supposed contentment-as-"death." Cowley thus insists that he rejects the court out of contented self-sufficiency rather than out of the ungovernable ambition that nurtures a rebel.

Classical epitaphs upon those with pretensions to intellectual and cultural grandeur also use the motif of the great man being at last reduced to a small grave.[65] Cowley's contentment with his small "grave" thus suggests his repudiation of his poetic as well as social ambitions. The very form of the epitaph underscores Cowley's repudiation of his specifically literary ambition to be an influential public poet. In 1657 he claimed that the Pindaric ode was "the noblest and highest kind of writing in Verse."[66] Though not conducive to his success at the Restoration court, his English *Pindarique Odes* (1657) were widely imitated and the foundation of his fame. These long, grand style public poems consisting of stanzas of irregular length and meter, surprising transitions, and extended passages of daring images, sought to astonish readers by their sublime treatment of major political, metaphysical, or scientific issues. During the Restoration Cowley wrote two Pindaric funerary odes, magnifying his subjects and placing their lives and deaths within the context of major developments in political or literary history.[67] Indebted to Cowley, Pindaric funerary odes celebrating persons of supposed national or universal significance became a staple of late seventeenth-century (and subsequent) funerary poetry. They appealed to the taste for extended panegyric and historical "placement" of the dead.[68] In the *Essays* Cowley writes Pindaric odes in praise of simple retirement. He no longer em-

---

the fact that powerful people were scandalized by the poem's treatment of tyrannicide/regicide, nor that in his Restoration works Cowley, in atonement, more straightforwardly attacked Cromwell.

[65] Horace's *Ode* 1.28 is an epitaph upon the philosopher Archytas, who measured the whole universe while he lived but now lies buried in a small grave (ll. 1–6). Thomas Bancroft furnishes an early seventeenth-century imitation in "An Epitaph on *William Holorenshaw*, the Mathematician": "Loe, in small closure of this earthly bed / Rests he, that Heav'ns vast motions measured" (*Two bookes of Epigrammes and Epitaphes* [London, 1639], C1r).

[66] Cowley, "Preface," *Pindarique Odes*, in *Poems*, 156.

[67] See Cowley's "Upon the Death of the Earl of Balcarres" and "On the Death of Mrs. Katherine Philips" in *Poems*, 413–416, 441–443.

[68] The university funerary anthologies reveal the great popularity of the Pindaric ode in the late seventeenth century: the Cambridge collection commemorating General Monck has eight would-be grand Pindarics on the military hero of the Restoration (*Musarum Cantabrigiensium Threnodia in Obitum . . . Georgii Ducis Albemarlae* [1670], S2v–T1r, T2r–T3r, U1v–X1r, X2v–Y3v); the anthology commemorating Charles II has seven (*Moestissimae ac Laetissimae Academiae Cantabrigiensis Affectus, Decedente Carolo II . . .* [1684/1685], Aa2v–Bb3r, Cc4v–Dd2v, Dd4v–Ee2v, Ff1v–Gg3v); and the anthology commemorating Queen Mary, five (*Lacrymae Cantabrigienses in obitum . . . Mariae* [1694/1695], X4r–Y1r, Y4r–Aa4r, Cc2v–Cc3v).

phasizes the form's grand, public style but instead treats its metrical freedom as an analogue to the liberty of retirement: "The more He-roique strain let others take, / Mine the Pindarique way I'le make. / The Matter shall be grave, the Numbers loose and free."[69] For his final ep-itaph upon himself, however, he rejects even this more modest Pindaric style in favor of the shorter, humbler Horatian ode. In his famous ode in praise of Pindar, Horace contrasts himself as a small, laborious beelike craftsman to the grand, high-flying swan Pindar (*Ode* 4.2.25–32). In his imitation of this ode in his *Pindarique Odes*, Cowley increases the humility of the Horatian self-portrait; "my *tim'erous Muse* / *Unambitious* tracks pursues; . . . / Like the laborious *Bee*, / For little drops of *Honey* [does] flee, / And there with *Humble Sweets* contents her *Industrie*."[70] "Tim'erous," "unambitious," "little drops," "humble" and "contents" are all Cowley's intensifying gloss upon Horace's description of himself as "small" ("par-vus"). By adopting the Alcaic ode form used by Horace for his brief epitaph upon himself, Cowley suggests that he is a truly contented poet who no longer needs to impress the public with large, ambitious gestures.

In order to support its governing metaphor of retirement as death, the epitaph presents Cowley's love of littleness as more extreme than was in fact the case. Elsewhere in the *Essays* Cowley glorifies not a humble life of poverty but the comfortable life of an independent retired country gentleman with an income of five hundred pounds.[71] He praises "mod-erate plenty" and "the Golden Mean, / . . . not with the Poor, nor with the Great."[72] He celebrates what he no doubt felt that he had attained, "an Estate neither too great nor small."[73] What Cowley does not ever embrace, however, either in the body of the *Essays* or in his final epitaph, are the court grandees who actually helped ensure his life of supposedly radical independence. Cowley's sharp contrast between himself as the true man of retirement and the deferential Augustan poets Horace and Virgil is in fact highly misleading, for Cowley was as indebted to his great court patrons as Virgil and Horace were to theirs.

Though use of Latin for epitaphs was by no means uncommon throughout the seventeenth century, Cowley's decision to sum up his relation to the world in Latin rather than his native tongue further signals his desire to retreat from the realities of his historical situation. Trans-lations of the classics were very popular in the late seventeenth century: for the cultural elite such works as Dryden's *Virgil* attested to the neo-classical grandeur of "Augustan" English, which could assimilate the

[69] Cowley, "Ode. Upon Liberty," in his *Essays*, 391.
[70] Cowley, "The Praise of Pindar," in his *Poems*, 179.
[71] See Cowley, "Of Greatness," in his *Essays*, 431.
[72] I cite Cowley's "Of Liberty" and "Ode. Upon Liberty," in his *Essays*, 386, 388.
[73] Cowley, "Martial L. 10. Ep. 47," in his *Essays*, 460.

riches of the classical past, and for those with small Latin and less Greek such works made accessible the storehouse of classical wisdom. With their numerous translations and imitations of classical poems, Cowley's *Essays* are clearly part of this trend.[74] The *Essays* simultaneously give an English stamp to the Roman retirement tradition and make that tradition accessible to readers ignorant of the classics. In writing his final epitaph in Latin with highly meaningful Horatian and Virgilian allusions, however, Cowley not only affirms his allegiance to retirement but also firmly bids adieu to the unlearned English "mob."[75] More fundamentally, however, he describes himself, and demands to be judged as, an immortal *vates* rather than as an English poet of the late seventeenth century involved in the major social and intellectual tumults of the age. He retires not only from "life" into "death" but also from the flux of a living, changing English and the society in which that language is spoken into a Latinity whose antiquity makes it the best linguistic embodiment of timelessness. Through his idealized Latin self-portrait, Cowley escapes from his times in word if not in deed.

Marvell sympathized with, though he did not wholeheartedly embrace, the rhetoric of nostalgia. His "Nymph Complaining for the Death of Her Fawn," a poem written sometime during the Civil Wars, ends with a monument both similar to, and significantly different from, the monuments of bygone virtue defended by Cotton in his inscription upon Port and by Waller in the Sedley epitaph. The nymph's loss of her fawn, shot by "troopers" (l. 1), a term used of armies during the Civil Wars, recalls her loss of Sylvio, the lover who abandoned her (ll. 49–50).[76] In both cases "cruel men" (l. 54) destroy innocence. By depicting the historical reality of male military violence as the reenactment of a traditional

[74] On the popularity of translations, see Korshin, 6. Waller's epitaph for John Howard, son of Viscount Andover, d. 1663, reveals that pride in English and perhaps solicitude for those without Latin sometimes played a role in Restoration epitaphs. The poem begins: "'Tis fit the English reader should be told, / In our own language, what this tomb does hold" ("Epitaph to be written under the Latin Inscription upon the Tomb of the only Son of the Lord Andover," in Waller, 191).

[75] John Dunton's *The Art of Living Incognito* (London, 1700) provides a striking example of Cowley's popular influence. Though an extremely odd and original production, this praise of retirement-unto-death by a dissenter, hack writer, and publisher-projector has no trace of classical influence but takes its title, epigraph, and general inspiration from Cowley's *Essays*; see especially Dunton, 1–11, and compare Dunton's title to Cowley's remark that "the pleasantest condition of Life, is in *Incognito*" (Cowley, "Of Obscurity," *Essays*, 398). Like Cowley, Dunton provides a final epitaph upon himself, but he naturally writes his epitaph in rough English pentameters (p. 215).

[76] Andrew Marvell, "The Nymph complaining for the death of her *Faun*," in *The Poems and Letters of Andrew Marvell*, ed. H. M. Margoliouth, rev. Pierre Legouis and E. E. Duncan-Jones, 2 vols. (Oxford: Clarendon, 1971), 1:23–24. The term "troopers" first became current circa 1640 with reference to the Scottish Covenanting Army (see note in Marvell, *Poems*, 1:251).

tale of male betrayal, Marvell suggests the tragic inevitability of the destruction of innocence. Marvell's gendered treatment also allows him to suggest his own distance from the nymph's perspective: he can sympathize but not fully identify with a female victim of "cruel men." The nymph's response to such destruction is to imagine the tomb that will preserve against time the memory of her innocent fawn and herself:

> ...I
> Will but bespeak thy Grave, and dye.
>   First my unhappy Statue shall
> Be cut in Marble; and withal,
> Let it be weeping too: but there
> Th'Engraver sure his Art may spare;
> For I so truly thee bemoane,
> That I shall weep though I be Stone:
> Until my Tears, still dropping, wear
> My breast, themselves engraving there.
> There at my feet shalt thou be laid,
> Of purest Alabaster made:
>   For I would have thine Image be
> White as I can, though not as Thee.
>   (ll. 109–122)

The final turn of the poem is indebted to a pair of Ovidian love complaints, *Heroides* 2 and 7. The poems' respective heroines Phyllis and Dido, abandoned by their lovers, end with the epitaphs they have composed upon themselves in order to record their lovers' perfidy and their own consequent suicides. Yet by also borrowing from the Niobe myth the motif of a woman turning into a monument that sheds tears, Marvell has his nymph imagine for her fawn and herself a material rather than a verbal memorial, one which can preserve innocence and sorrow in stone but, unlike Phyllis's and Dido's epitaphs, cannot identify culprits.[77] Marvell hints at his own, fuller perspective upon the events of the poem by basing his plot on Ascanius's killing of the stag of Sylvia (*Aeneid* 7.475–510), the tragic event initiating the civil war between Trojans and Latins that issued, finally, in the founding of Rome. Though the nymph cannot know it, the fawn's death is thus part of a larger and ultimately beneficial historical process.[78] The poem appropriately ends with a monument that will not attack history's violence but will instead stand in commemoration for what has sadly been destroyed.

---

[77] On the transformation of Niobe into a weeping stone, see Ovid, *Metamorphoses* 6.301–312. Niobe was a popular subject for epitaphs: see, for example, *Greek Anthology* 7.549; and Ausonius, *Epitaphia heroum...*, 27.

[78] On the Virgilian allusion and its significance, see Earl Miner, "The Death of Innocence in Marvell's 'Nymph Complaining for the Death of her Fawn,'" *MP* 65 (1967):9–16.

In the "Horatian Ode" Marvell similarly memorialized the king's dignified acceptance of his death while affirming his own commitment,
however fraught with reservations, to the new order. Recognizing the
necessity of the momentous changes that had occurred in England, Marvell served the Cromwellian regime. After the collapse of the Protectorate and the return of the Stuarts, both as a member of Parliament
and a writer in verse and prose, he fought against absolutist monarchy
and for the rights of Parliament and Protestant dissenters. Often despairing of the political order, he treated the major political crises of the
times as symptoms of the age's moral depravity. Marvell's epitaph upon
Frances Jones, who died in 1672, is his only verse epitaph, and the poem
both critiques and exploits the rhetoric of nostalgia. Marvell simultaneously attacks those who idealize the dead out of partisan self-interest
and, while purporting not to, idealizes the deceased for his own polemical
purposes as a virginal, virtuous Protestant whose exceptional virtues
reveal all that is wrong with the Restoration settlement. Unlike early
seventeenth-century poets, he does not suggest that his poetic *exemplum*
can influence society. By echoing but significantly modifying motifs from
early seventeenth-century poetry, Marvell instead contrasts his own pessimistic sense of poetry's impotence with the more optimistic poetics of
the past. Thus his epitaph, inscribed upon a tablet in Saint Martin's-in-
the-Fields, mourns both the passing of virtues all too exceptional in an
age of moral decay and the poet's inability to change the way things are:

> Here lyes buried the body of
> Mistress Frances JONES daughter of ARTHUR
> Lord vicecount of Ranelagh, by his wife the
> Lady KATHERINE BOYLE, who was daughter
> to RICHARD BOYLE Earl of Corke, and Lord
> high Treasurer of Ireland.
> She dyed in the prime of her Age, have-
> ing never been marryed, the XXVIII of
> March in the year MDCLXXII.

> Enough; and leave the rest to Fame;
> 'Tis to Commend her but to name.
> Courtship, which Liveing she declin'd,
> When dead to offer; were unkind.
> Where never any could speake ill,
> Who would officious Praises spill?
> Nor can the truest Wit or Friend
> Without Detracting her Commend.
> To say she liv'd a Virgin Chast,
> In this Age loose and all unlac'd;
> Nor was, where vice is so allow'd,
> Of Virtue or Asham'd or Proud;

That her Soule was on heav'n so bent,
No minute but it Came and Went;
That, ready her last debt to pay,
She summ'd her life up every day;
Modest, as Morne, as Midday, Bright;
Gentle, as Evening, Coole, as Night;
'Tis true, but all so weakly said,
'Twere more Significant: She's Dead.[79]

Marvell probably met Francis Jones's mother, Lady Ranelagh, at Milton's home in Westminster. Lady Ranelagh had entrusted the education of her son to Milton, and according to Edward Phillips both Marvell and Lady Ranelagh frequently visited the poet in the 1650s.[80] In agreeing to write the epitaph for Frances Jones, Marvell's problem was to praise the humble, retired scion of an illustrious, historically active family. The prose inscription proudly presents her aristocratic parents and maternal grandfather. Viscount Ranelagh was in fact an unsavory alcoholic. Unhappily wedded to him, Katherine Boyle, Lady Ranelagh, was, however, a truly impressive figure, the intellectual companion of her brother, the scientist Robert Boyle. She had been prominent in learned circles in the 1650s, when she patronized various Puritan intellectuals who had millenarian hopes for widespread political, religious, and scientific reform.[81] Her father Richard Boyle, the first earl of Corke and lord high treasurer of Ireland, was an important political figure of the early seventeenth century, best known for his incriminating testimony in the trial and execution of the lord deputy of Ireland, Thomas Wentworth, the earl of Strafford. The 1642 execution of Strafford, whom Parliament considered the great instrument of Charles I's years of absolute and arbitrary rule, was a major Parliamentary victory. Though his animus against Wentworth was not predominantly ideological, the earl had thus played a major role in the defense of Parliament.[82] Yet unlike her mother or grandfather, Frances Jones had played no important role in history, and instead of seeking to drape her in the luster of her family lineage, the

---

[79] The inscription is cited and discussed in Hugh Brogan, "Marvell's 'Epitaph on ———,'" RQ 32 (1979):197–199.

[80] See Brogan, 198–199; and Edward Phillips, The Life of Mr. John Milton (London, 1694), reprinted in John Milton, Complete Poems and Major Prose, ed. Merritt Y. Hughes (New York: Odyssey Press, 1957), 1035.

[81] On Lady Ranelagh and her circle, see J. R. Jacob, Robert Boyle and the English Revolution: A Study in Social and Intellectual Change (New York: Burt Franklin, 1977), 16, 25, 121–126 and passim; and Charles Webster, The Great Instauration: Science, Medicine and Reform, 1626–1660 (New York: Holmes and Meier, 1975), 40, 62–63, and passim.

[82] On Strafford and Boyle, see C. V. Wedgwood, Thomas Wentworth: First Earl of Strafford, 1593–1641 (London: Jonathan Cape, 1961), 180–187, 390–392, and passim; and Nicholas Canny, The Upstart Earl: A Study of the Social and Mental World of Richard Boyle, First Earl of Cork (Cambridge: Cambridge University Press, 1982), 9–26 and passim.

verse epitaph makes her lack of historical importance the source of her true significance. Marvell presents the deceased as the embodiment of ideals that have no currency but against which the age can and must be judged.

The opening couplet of the poem introduces the rhetorical strategy that continues through the next seventeen lines: "Enough; and leave the rest to Fame; / 'Tis to Commend her but to name." Using the rhetorical device of *occupatio*, the poem begins its praise by arguing that further praise is unnecessary. The prose inscription has supposedly said all that need be said, for by the simple act of naming the deceased it has already praised her and assured her fame. The next seventeen lines of praise purport to explain why the meaning of the name of the deceased is enough and all further praise simultaneously excessive and deficient. Marvell begins to explain by arguing that to praise the deceased further would be not only superfluous but also a selfish and self-serving violation of her integrity: "Courtship, which Liveing she declin'd, / When dead to offer; were unkind" (ll. 3–4). The poet identifies all further praise with a "courtship" inimical to Jones's supposed way of life. The word "courtship" exemplifies Marvell's expressive compression, for Jones's rejection of "courtship" embodies her entire attitude toward the world as expounded in the rest of the poem. She rejected the "paying of court or courteous attention" (*OED*, 5) because she was "Modest, as Morne" (l. 17), and she spurned "courting or wooing" (*OED*, 6) because she lived "a Virgin Chast" (l. 9). She also, more broadly, rejected anything resembling the "arts of the court" (*OED*, 4), for she was not of the world but rather one whose "Soule was on heav'n...bent" (l. 13). By the early years of the Restoration the sexual immorality of Charles II and many of his courtiers had become a major source of anticourt sentiment.[83] In a private letter to his nephew and confidant William Popple written circa January 1671, Marvell complained that "the Court is at the highest Pitch of Want and Luxury."[84] In the public epitaph Marvell more prudently criticizes the decadent court by presenting the chaste, humble, pious deceased as its opposite. In order to praise the deceased without violating her integrity with his own brand of indecorous courtship, however, the poet can praise her only by arguing the irrelevance and presumptuousness of praise. Indeed he underscores the supposed irrelevance of his own remarks by asserting at length the superfluity of stating anything beyond a name that does not itself appear in his poem.

Normally the epitaphic poet or the mourner "sums up" the virtues of

---

[83] See Ronald Hutton, *The Restoration: A Political and Religious History of England and Wales, 1658–1667* (Oxford: Clarendon, 1985), 185–190.

[84] Marvell, *Poems*, 2:322.

the deceased, as Cotton does at the end of his inscription upon Port.[85] Marvell, on the other hand, sums up Jones's life while insisting that he need not do so since she in fact did it herself. Indeed, in a witty reversal, he claims that the deceased not only "summ'd her life up ev'ry day" (l. 16) but also summed up the best qualities of "ev'ry day" in the way she led her life—"Modest, as Morne, as Midday, Bright; / Gentle, as Evening, Coole, as Night" (ll. 17–18).[86] It is thus all the more superfluous and "weakly said" (l. 19) to attempt to supplement her more than adequate self-definition.

The purported repudiation of flattering courtship reflects a deep concern of Marvell, who had long linked failures of literary decorum to the political—and therefore ultimately moral—failings of the times.[87] His commendatory poem upon Lovelace's *Lucasta*, composed sometime between 1647 and 1649, lamented that poets had lost the art of "speaking well" of others during the "degenerate" times of civil strife: "Our wits have drawn th'infection of our times."[88] The infection was as strong in the year of Jones's death. In the poem upon Lovelace, Marvell concentrates on the dangers of detraction, but in the Jones epitaph he equates unnecessary praise and detraction: "Nor can the truest Wit or Friend / Without Detracting her Commend" (ll. 7–8). His attack upon Samuel Parker's arguments for royal absolutism in religion and enforced religious conformity, *The Rehearsal Transpros'd* (1672–1673), is from the same period as the epitaph and sheds particular light upon the polemical purposes of its panegyric rhetoric. Marvell suggests in *The Rehearsal* that both excessive praise and blame stem from men's self-interested use of

[85] In addition to the Port inscription and Brome's elegy on Charles I, see Cotton's "whole summe of prais [*sic*]" at the end of "An Epitaph on my Dear Aunt, Mrs. Ann Stanhope" (*Poems*, ed. Buxton, 136); and Dryden's presentation of the widower "sadly summing what he had, and lost" in "An Epitaph on the Lady Whitmore" [d. 1690], l. 4 in *The Poems of John Dryden*, ed. James Kinsley, 4 vols. (Oxford: Clarendon, 1958), 2:845.

[86] The comparison of Jones to the four phases of the day probably derives from a visual tradition. Michelangelo's sculptures of Aurora, Giorno, Crepusculo, and Notte on the Medici tombs in Florence sparked numerous seventeenth-century visual treatments of the times of day, including many widely circulated prints. Michelangelo's sculptures represent the temporal decline toward old age and, implicitly, death, and other treatments link the times of day to the Ovidian four ages of man, so that the times of day represent both man's and the world's inevitable decline; see Sean Shesgreen, *Hogarth and the Times-of-the-Day Tradition* (Ithaca: Cornell University Press, 1983), 25–88. Marvell's penultimate couplet avoids the pessimistic and funereal connotations of a topos that originated upon a funerary monument—Night is "coole" (l. 18) rather than a symbol of decline, Jones combines the qualities of the four times in a triumphant simultaneity—only so that the final couplet, as we shall see, can reassert, with more shock, the inescapable triumph of death.

[87] I am indebted to the analysis of the Jones epitaph in the context of Marvell's evolving epideictic theory in Annabel M. Patterson, *Marvell and the Civic Crown* (Princeton: Princeton University Press, 1978), 50–59.

[88] Marvell, "To his Noble Friend Mr. Richard Lovelace, upon his Poems," ll. 1–6 in Marvell, *Poems*, 1:2 (on the poem's date of composition, see note in Marvell, *Poems*, 1: 239).

epideictic rhetoric to further themselves and their partisan causes. At the opening of the work, he castigates his opponent for his indecorous, self-serving idealization of the early seventeenth-century bishop of Derry, John Bramhall, whose works Parker had reissued with a laudatory preface: "These improbable Elogies too are of the greatest disservice to their own design, and do in effect diminish alwayes the Person whom they pretend to magnifie.... our Author speaks the language of a Lover, and so may claim some pardon, if the habit and excess of his Courtship do as yet give a tincture to his discourse upon more ordinary Subjects. ...if the Bishop were alive, he would be out of love with himself [as presented by Parker]."[89] Marvell's criticism here introduces the larger argument that Parker is incapable of the moderation that underlies decorum: Parker's excessive panegyric upon the dead bishop is the other side of his excessive railing against contemporary nonconformists.[90] In his epitaph upon Jones, Marvell purports to avoid precisely the faults that he ascribes to Parker's panegyric upon Bramhall: praising and "courting" the dead in a self-serving way that actually diminishes them. Marvell praises Jones while purporting not to do so. Thus he can simultaneously use the deceased as an ideal against which to judge the age and claim, in sharp contrast to a Parker, to preserve the vulnerable deceased from partisan appropriations by the living.

Marvell's contrast between the pious virgin Jones and "this Age loose and all unlac'd" (l. 10) suggests a further connection between the epitaph and the topical prose work. In the *Rehearsal* Marvell sharply disagrees with Parker's argument that "debauchery" is a less dangerous threat to the social order than nonconformist religious practices. Marvell points out the danger of Parker's tolerance toward moral laxity "at such a time, when there is so general a depravation of Manners, that even those who contribute towards it do yet complain of it; and though they cannot reform their practice, yet feel the effects, and tremble under the apprehension of the Consequences."[91] Marvell sharply attacks Parker's arguments for royal absolutism in religion and enforced religious conformity, on the other hand, with the venerable Protestant principle that true Christianity "is the most short and plain Religion" and should not be bound by conformity in "indifferent" matters of ritual and ceremony. He treats Parker as the representative of an arrogant church hierarchy that would, like the popish and Laudian priests of times past,

[89] Andrew Marvell, *The Rehearsal Transpros'd and The Rehearsal Transpros'd, Second Part*, ed. D. I. B. Smith (Oxford: Clarendon, 1971), 12–13.

[90] On Marvell's critique of Parker's indecorum, see Patterson, *Marvell and Civic Crown*, 58, 189–210; and John M. Wallace, *Destiny His Choice: The Loyalism of Andrew Marvell* (Cambridge: Cambridge University Press, 1968), 194–195.

[91] Marvell, *Rehearsal*, 55.

fetter religion with "an innumerable rabble of Rites and Ceremonies."[92] Though himself a conformist, Marvell nevertheless agrees with the non-conformists that conscientious Protestant devotion, rather than enforced conformity to the specific rites of the Church of England, is essential to "Christian Liberty."[93] Good "manners" would follow inevitably, he suggests, from such true Protestant piety. Lady Ranelagh, and presumably her daughter, agreed on the all-importance of Christian liberty. In the 1650s Lady Ranelagh hailed the profusion of Protestant sects in millenarian terms as the "breaking forth . . . of that light of truth, which shews liberty of conscience to be one of the most unquestionable rights belonging to men as men."[94] In the epitaph Marvell does not defend Christian liberty in strident, polemical terms, for that would undermine his claim to disinterested respect for the dead. The epitaph's idealization of Jones as a humble laywoman who sought her salvation not through communal ritual but through an individual chastity and piety inimical to the values of the "loose" age and the immoral court nevertheless makes her the embodiment of the Protestant ideal threatened by polemicists like Parker.

Marvell suggests that Jones's way of life can have no influence on the degraded age but can only be contaminated by contact with it. The final line of the poem makes a new claim about the deceased beyond the simple assertion that nothing need be said beyond her name. The epitaph ends, as it begins, with a gesture of finality that rejects what has preceded as superfluous: "'Twere more Significant: She's Dead" (l. 20). The two final heavy syllables coming at the end of the long *occupatio* assert that the most significant statement about the deceased is that she is gone. Thus the poem moves from a name that supposedly means so much but is absent from the poem to a phrase that means so much because it signifies absence. The whole poem glosses its opening and closing feet: "Enough; She's Dead." Instead of trying strongly to evoke the deceased and to transmit her virtues to the living, as do so many earlier epitaphs, the poem purports simply to leave the deceased in peace by stressing the absence inherent in epitaphic representation and bidding the reader feel the loss of one whose perfection he or she can only know from a distance, through a distorting representation, once it is gone.

Marvell emphasizes his loss of faith in the power of the dead to affect the living by echoing but pointedly modifying earlier poetry. He underscores the contrast between the uncommunicable virtues of this virgin and the supposedly exemplary virtues of an earlier period's panegyric

[92] Marvell, *Rehearsal*, 238.
[93] Marvell, *Rehearsal*, 246.
[94] Cited in Jacob, 125, who discusses Lady Ranelagh's support of toleration (pp. 121–126).

subjects by basing the major portion of the epitaph upon a Jonsonian poem concerning a supposedly influential public figure. Lines nine through nineteen echo the structure of Jonson's panegyric epigram to the composer Alfonso Ferrabosco:

> To urge, my lov'd ALPHONSO, that bold fame
>   Of building townes, and making wilde beasts tame,
> Which *Musick* had; or speake her knowne effects
>   That shee removeth cares, sadnesse ejects,
>   .   .   .   .   .
> T[o]'alledge, that greatest men were not asham'd,
>   Of old, even by her practise, to be fam'd;
> To say, indeed, shee were the soule of heaven,
>   That the eight spheare, no lesse, then planets seaven,
> Mov'd by her order...
>   .   .   .   .   .
> I, yet, had utter'd nothing on thy part,
>   When these were but the praises of the Art.
> But when I have said, The proofes of all these bee
>   Shed in thy Songs; 'tis true: but short of thee.[95]

Marvell's "To say" (l. 9), "'Tis true" (l. 19), and final declaration of expressive failure, "but all so weakly said" (l. 19), echo Jonson's infinitives ("To urge, "T[o]'alledge," and "To say"), "'tis true," and final proclamation of inexpressibility ("but short of thee"). The echo only underscores, however, the differences between the two poems. Jonson honors a figure with an Amphion-like power over his audience, and since the praise of music derives from Horace's praise of poetry (*Ars Poetica* 391–396), Ferrabosco's supposed musical power parallels and is implicitly linked to Jonson's most exalted, mythopoetic conceptions of the poet's own public power. Marvell, on the other hand, praises a private figure whose exceptionality can have no more influence on the times than can— so one suspects him to be implying—his own partial revival of a panegyric topos from a more optimistic past.

Marvell's admission that his lines of praise are "true" but "weakly said" suggests his continued allegiance to the early seventeenth-century cult of "strong lines," a frequent designation of the Donnean style.[96] He appropriately ends his poem with a quotation from Donne himself, for the final line echoes the refrain of Donne's *First Anniversarie*:

[95] Ben Jonson, "To ALPHONSO FERRABOSCO, on his Booke," ll. 1–4, 9–13, 15–18 in *Ben Jonson*, ed. C. H. Herford and Percy and Evelyn Simpson, 11 vols. (Oxford: Clarendon, 1925–1952), 8:82.
[96] Wilhelm Franke notes the allusion to "strong lines" in *Gattungskonstanten des englischen Vers-Epitaphs von Ben Jonson zu Alexander Pope* (Nuremberg: Carl, 1964), 125. On the cult of "strong lines," see George Williamson, "Strong Lines," in his *Seventeenth-Century Contexts* (Chicago: University of Chicago Press, 1960), 120–132.

Shee, shee is dead; shee's dead: when thou knowst this,
Thou knowst how poore a trifling thing man is.
....   how lame a cripple this world is.
....   how ugly'a monster this world is:
....   how wan a Ghost this our world is:
....   how drie a Cinder this world is.[97]

Restoration poets tended to follow Jonson precisely in the ways he differed from Donne, adopting his plain-style couplets and relative smooth-
ness of numbers (compared to Donne) while avoiding his compressed,
sometimes riddling, wit. Marvell recalls, by contrast, the double legacy
of these two early seventeenth-century masters when he moves from an
occupatio that imitates Jonson to an echo of one of Donne's most famous
passages. Marvell recalls Donne for the same reason he recalls Jonson,
in order to show poetry's supposed loss of power in a decadent age.
Donne asserts the cosmic importance of the death of his virgin, Elizabeth
Drury, by identifying her death with the death of the world.[98] He tries,
furthermore, to awaken his readers' "faint weake love of vertue and of
good" (l. 71) by recalling the supposed perfections of the deceased.[99] In
sharp contrast to Donne, Marvell does not claim that Jones's death has
changed the world, which was bad before and will continue to be so,
nor does he claim that he or his poem can in any way reform the living.

Marvell's use of the name-as-praise motif, which became rarer after
the Restoration, also self-consciously hearkens back to an earlier style.
There is a fundamental difference, however, between Marvell's use of
the motif and that of his predecessors. Earlier treatments of the name
sought to link the proper reader, who could appreciate its great meaning,
and the deceased. Marvell instead seeks to preserve a distance between
the reader (and writer) and the dead. He asserts not only that further
praise of the dead is superfluous for those in the know, as earlier poets
had done, but also that such praise would be an insult to the deceased,
who deserves to be free from the contaminating blandishments of the
living.

The decline of the name-as-praise motif in the late seventeenth century
reflected poets' impatience with a topos based on an outmoded stylistic
concern with the relationship between individual *verba* and *res*. It also

---

[97] John Donne, *The First Anniversarie: An Anatomy of the World*, ll. 183–184, 237–238,
325–326, 369–370, 427–428 in *The Epithalamions, Anniversaries, and Epicedes*, ed. W. Milgate
(Oxford: Clarendon, 1978), 27, 28, 31, 32, 34. George Williamson noted the echo in *The
Donne Tradition: A Study in English Poetry from Donne to the Death of Cowley* (1930; rpt., New
York: The Noonday Press, 1958), 153.

[98] Lewalski argues that Donne treats his subject as a "type" of the "regenerate soul and
restored image of God [in man]," and that her death is therefore appropriately treated
as the fall of the world in *Donne's Anniversaries* (see p. 244).

[99] Donne, *Epithalamions*, 24.

reflected suspicion of the humanist ideal of the self-made man that the motif so often expressed. The notion that a man could and should make his name meaningful no doubt disturbed Restoration writers looking back on its association with rebellious "upstarts" like Cromwell. An elegy on Cromwell had developed at excruciating length the normally brief name-as-praise motif:

> We'le wrong thee so no more, but drop a tear,
> And onely say, Here lieth *Oliver.*
> Tis *Oliver* lies here, and what's the rest,
> The *Spaniard, Scot,* and *Hollander* attest.
> Here lies Great *Oliver,* but all's not done,
> What Trophies lodge in that Trisyllabon?
> This word is bigge with *Caesars,* and indeed
> Contains more *Heroes* than the *Trojan* steed.
> How much of worth doth this small word contain?[100]

In his own elegy upon the Protector, Marvell had celebrated the supposed power of Cromwell's great name:

> Thee, many ages hence, in martial verse
> Shall th'English souldier, ere he charge, rehearse;
> Singing of thee, inflame themselves to fight,
> And with the name of Cromwell, armyes fright.
> As long as rivers to the seas shall runne,
>   . . . . .
> As long as future time succeeds the past,
> Always thy honour, praise and name, shall last.[101]

"Cromwell" was a name that could influence the world.[102] Times had changed, however, and in the Restoration epitaph Marvell can only praise the name of a private, all-too-uninfluential woman.

On the evidence of the epitaph, the virtuous dead no longer have

[100] Elegy by Sam Fuller in Cambridge University, *Musarum Cantabrigiensium luctus & gratulatio* (1658), H3r–v.

[101] Marvell, "A Poem upon the Death of O. C.," ll. 277–281, 285–286 in Marvell, *Poems,* 1:136.

[102] See also Marvell's 1651 epigram "In Legationem Domini Oliveri St. John ad Provincias Foederatas" (Marvell, *Poems,* 1:99), whose conceit is the great public meaning of the name of the Protectorate's negotiator with the Dutch, Oliver St. John (whose name combines the "olive" of peace and the warlike stance of Saint John of Patmos): "Even if you should be silent, your name is an embassy / And carries . . . *public words* [i.e. official weight]" ("Tu quoque si taceas tamen est Legatio Nomen / Et . . . publica verba refert," 13–14, emphasis mine). Marvell may also have written the epitaph upon Sir John Trott, d. 1658, which begins: "If the Just are praised when they are onely named how am I surprised with a Panegyricke whilst I am telling the reader that here lyes the body of John Trott. . . . " (Marvell, *Poems,* 1:339).

public force. Marvell's other poems from this period reveal a similar lack of faith in the ability of the dead to influence society. The epitaph upon Edmund Trott, whose death in 1667 at the age of twenty-three left his parents childless, praises this youth for uniquely avoiding the vices of the age: "He sailed / by the isle of Circe, and the Sirens' rocks, / And in this shipwreck of manners and of the age, / He alone lost nothing, but gained much."[103] As in the Jones epitaph, Marvell treats moral purity primarily in terms of sexual chastity: the young Trott avoids feminine tempters. By praising a male for a chastity normally celebrated in epitaphs upon women, Marvell suggests the importance of radical detachment from the world in "this shipwreck of manners and of the age." Such detachment has no perceptible effect, however, on the world left behind.

Written about the same time as the Trott epitaph, Marvell's major verse satire, *The Last Instructions to a Painter*, fully reveals the great resonance of virginal, unworldly innocence for Marvell.[104] The *Last Instructions*'s elegiac portrait of Archibald Douglas depicts a virginal youth whose relation to the world is strikingly close to that of Frances Jones. Dying in the hopelessly ill-conceived and mismanaged Second Dutch War, Douglas nevertheless retains his unworldly purity and thereby gains immortality:

> Not so brave *Douglas*; on whose lovely chin
> The early Down but newly did begin,
> And modest Beauty yet his Sex did Veil,
> While envious Virgins hope he is a Male.
> His yellow Locks curl back themselves to seek,
> Nor other Courtship knew but to his Cheek.
> · · · · ·
> Like a glad Lover, the fierce Flames he meets,
> And tries his first embraces in their Sheets.
> His shape exact, which the bright flames enfold,
> Like the Sun's Statue stands of burnish'd Gold.
> Round the transparent Fire about him glows,
> As the clear Amber on the Bee does close:
> And, as on Angels Heads their Glories shine,
> His burning Locks adorn his Face Divine.
> · · · · ·

---

[103] "Circaem Insulam, Scopulos Sirenum / Praeternavigavit, / Et in hoc naufragio morum & saeculi / Solus perdiderat nihil, auxit plurimum" (Marvell, *Poems*, 1:141). The Trott family were probably dissenters; see E. E. Duncan-Jones, "Marvell's Letter to Sir John Trott," *Notes and Queries*, n.s., 13 (1966):27. Their minority status gives added resonance to Marvell's description of Edmund Trott as a virtuous exception.

[104] Edmund Trott died on August 11, 1667, and internal evidence suggests that Marvell probably composed the *Last Instructions* between August 30, 1667 and November 29, 1667 (see note in Marvell, *Poems*, 1:346).

Fortunate Boy; if either Pencil's Fame,
Or if my Verse can propagate thy Name,
When *Oeta* and *Alcides* are forgot,
Our *English* youth shall sing the Valiant *Scot.*
　　　(ll. 649-654, 677-684, 693-696)[105]

Marvell invented the virginity of Douglas, who was in fact married.[106] Marvell uses this imagined virginity to suggest Douglas's solitary, unworldly form of heroism, perhaps the only kind of heroism still possible in a world of lust, ambition, and senseless war.[107] Like Jones, Douglas lives and dies outside the normal patterns of life. With his locks that "curl back themselves to seek" (l. 653) and become a halo at his death, Douglas attains a self-enclosed perfection that protects him from the degradations of the age. Like Jones, he escapes from "courtship" (l. 654) in all its senses, for Marvell presents the court not only as a center of sexual lust (ll. 50–64) but also as the cause of a war described as the rape of England (ll. 730–734). Drawing attention to the ornate, archaic rhetoric of the passage, George deF. Lord has called it "an elegy on ... old-fashioned and heroic virtues" that are out of touch with "the alien, cynical world of Charles II's court."[108] Marvell turns Douglas, like Jones, into a virginal anachronism.

The poet's promise to immortalize Douglas's name strikingly separates the poet's memorialization of the virtuous from the political order. Marvell echoes Virgil's promise to immortalize Nisus and Euryalus: "Happy pair! If aught my verse avail, no day shall ever blot you from the memory of time, so long as the house of Aeneas shall dwell on the Capitol's unshaken rock, and the Father of Rome hold unshaken sway."[109] While Virgil links his pair's heroic immortality to the endurance of the Roman state and the line of emperors, Marvell pointedly promises Douglas's immortality without mentioning the corrupt state. His promise that *"English* youth" will sing of Douglas also recalls but significantly differs from Marvell's claim in his elegy upon the Protector that soldiers would sing

---

[105] Marvell, *Poems*, 1:163–165.

[106] See editor's note in Marvell, *Poems*, 1:368.

[107] See also the discussions of Douglas's sexuality in Joseph Messina, "The Heroic Image in *The Last Instructions to a Painter*," in *Tercentenary Essays in Honor of Andrew Marvell*, ed. Kenneth Friedenreich (Hamden, Conn.: Archon Books, 1977), 297–310; and Jose, 116–117.

[108] George deF. Lord, "From Contemplation to Action: Marvell's Poetical Career," in *Andrew Marvell: A Collection of Critical Essays*, ed. George deF. Lord (Englewood Cliffs: Prentice-Hall, 1968), 71.

[109] "Fortunati ambo! si quid mea carmina possunt, / nulla dies umquam memori vos eximet aevo, / dum domus Aeneae Capitoli immobile saxum / accolet imperiumque pater Romanus habebit" (Virgil, *Aeneid* 9.446–449).

Cromwell's name. Marvell now praises not a victorious general but a defeated martyr, and he promises only that the English youth will sing of Douglas, not that Douglas's name will inspire soldiers to victory (as he once claimed that Cromwell's name would). Fame, rather than posthumous influence, is all that the poet dares promise, for Douglas as much as for Jones.

In the *Last Instructions*, Douglas the martyred virgin prepares the reader for the tableau of an innocent and forlorn virginal figure threatened by no less a figure than the monarch himself, lustful Charles II:

> There, as in the calm horrour all alone
> He [Charles II] wakes, and Muses of th'uneasy Throne:
> Raise up a sudden Shape with Virgins Face
> Though ill agree her Posture, Hour, or Place:
> Naked as born, and her round Arms behind,
> With her own Tresses, interwove and twin'd:
> . . . . .
> The Object strange in him no Terrour mov'd:
> He wonder'd first, then pity'd, then he lov'd:
> And with kind hand does the coy Vision press
> Whose Beauty greater seem'd by her distress;
> But soon shrunk back, chill'd with her touch so cold,
> And th'airy Picture vanisht from his hold
> In his deep thoughts the wonder did increase,
> And he Divin'd 'twas *England* or the *Peace*.
>
> (ll. 889–894, 899–906)

Instead of being aroused to save his country, the rakish Charles II attempts erotic conquest. The virgin who is "*England* or the *Peace*" can save herself only by flight. The poem does not wholly despair of political reform: it ends with an appeal to Charles II to dismiss his corrupt courtiers in favor of honest advisors (ll. 955–990).[110] The earlier portrait of Charles as debauchee does not, however, encourage optimism that the poet's plea will be heard. For Marvell at his most despairing, those who would escape the corruptions of the time can only vanish or die into their anachronistic, virginal self-perfection, like Trott, or Douglas, or Jones.

Though in his epitaph upon Frances Jones Marvell does not endow the deceased with cosmic significance, as Donne had hyperbolically done with Elizabeth Drury, readers of the epitaph could find commemorated the virtues of a vanished, "virginal" nation. In writing perhaps the last epitaph to incorporate early seventeenth-century motifs, Marvell nostalgically bids farewell to the poetic traditions that served an age when virtue was thought still to have public power.

---

[110] On the poem as advice to Charles II, see Wallace, 145–183.

Dryden considered the epigram and epitaph low genres unworthy of his genius. Throughout his poetic career he aspired to heroic verse and devoted himself to genres that could be related, at times with considerable strain, to epic. Sometimes he included epitaphic motifs within his major poems: *Absalom and Achitophel* (1681), for example, hearkens back to early seventeenth-century epitaphic poetics by introducing its panegyric of the loyal few, including the epitaphlike commemoration of Barzillai's son (ll. 831–859), with the claim that "Naming [them] is to praise" (l. 816).[111] Dryden was not, however, partial to the epitaph as an independent genre.[112] His most characteristic funerary poems are his long, high-style Pindaric odes in the manner of Cowley, such as "Threnodia Augustalis" (1685) and the Anne Killigrew ode (1686).[113] Nevertheless Dryden wrote seven epitaphs and translated one, and in two of his most interesting epitaphs, composed for relatives of his wife, he exploits the rhetoric of idealizing nostalgia to attack the times.

His epitaph upon John Paulet, the marquis of Winchester, commemorates one of Charles I's most loyal Catholic subjects. During the first Civil War Parliament laid siege to Winchester's garrisoned home, Basing House, whose windows were inscribed with the motto "Aymez Loyaulté." The house fell in 1645, Winchester was briefly imprisoned in the Tower, and his estate was sequestered. After the Restoration his lands were restored and he spent the remaining years of his life quietly practicing his religion in retirement upon his estate in Enfield until his death in 1675.[114] The prose inscription upon the plain black and white marble wall tablet in Englefield Parish Church dedicated to his memory notes that the monument was erected by Winchester's widow, a recusant rel-

[111] Dryden, *Poems*, 1:238–239.

[112] In "The Life of Plutarch" (1683), Dryden commends epigrams and the epitaphs not as independent literary genres but as minor "ornaments" in historical and biographical writing along with proverbs and apothegmes; see John Dryden, *Prose, 1668–1691: An Essay of Dramatick Poesie and Shorter Works*, ed. Samuel Holt Monk et al., The California Edition of the Works of John Dryden, vol. 17 (Berkeley: University of California Press, 1971), 248. "A Discourse Concerning the Original and Progress of Satire" (1693) condemns epigrammatic turns in "high" poetry by which poets descend "from *Homer* to the *Anthologia*, from *Virgil* to *Martial* and *Owen's* Epigrams, and from *Spencer* to *Flecknoe*; that is, from the top to the bottom of all Poetry" (Dryden, *Poems*, 2:609). Though Dryden himself could be accused of such shifts, his contemptuous reference to the *Greek Anthology* and Martial, the two most important classical models for epigrams and epitaphs, reveals his conscious disdain for these "low" genres.

[113] Dryden admired Cowley's Pindaric odes, and his own Pindaric funerary odes are clearly indebted to the earlier poet; see James D. Garrison, *Dryden and the Tradition of Panegyric* (Berkeley: University of California Press, 1975), 210–219.

[114] In addition to Kinsley's brief biographical note in Dryden, *Poems*, 4:2087–2088; see the *DNB* article on Winchester and J. C. H. Aveling, *The Handle and the Axe: The Catholic Recusants in England from Reformation to Emancipation* (London: Blond & Briggs, 1976), 164–165, 169, 173.

ative of Dryden's wife.[115] Dryden's verse epitaph upon Winchester celebrates the heroism of a bygone era:

> He who in impious times untainted stood,
> And midst rebellion durst be just and good;
> Whose arms asserted, and whose sufferings more
> Confirm'd the cause for which he fought before,
> Rests here, rewarded by an heav'nly prince,
> For what his earthly could not recompense.
> Pray, reader, that such times no more appear:
> Or, if they happen, learn true honor here.
>
> Ark of thy age's faith and loyalty,
> Which to preserve them, Heav'n confin'd in thee.
> Few subjects could a king like thine deserve;
> And fewer, such a king so well could serve.
> Blest king, blest subject whose exalted state
> By suff'rings rose, and gave the law to fate.
> Such souls are rare, but mighty patterns given
> To earth were meant for ornaments to heaven.[116]

With its periodic sentence of three couplets in praise of Winchester as the solitary good subject of Charles I, the grand style opening appropriately hearkens back to the rhetoric of Royalist Civil Wars and Interregnum poetry. Thus a panegyric addressing the Royalist soldier Sir Bevil Grenville, killed in battle in 1643, exclaims: "Thou that in those black times dard'st to be good, / When Treason was best virtue... / Dard'st love the King, when a whole Nation / Was growing one great Rebell; hast firm stood, / And gave the first great stop to th' growing flood."[117]

The first stanza's attitude toward the past is mixed. On the one hand the poet looks back on "impious times" (l. 1) from the safe vantage point of the present and bids the reader pray "that such times no more appear"

---

[115] The monument is described in Nikolaus Pevsner, *Berkshire*, rev. ed., The Buildings of England (Harmondsworth: Penguin, 1966), 137. Isabella Paulet, the marchioness dowager of Winchester, was the daughter of William Howard, viscount Stafford, a Catholic cousin of Elizabeth Dryden. James Anderson Winn discusses Dryden's relation to Viscount Stafford, whose execution during the Exclusion Crisis influenced Dryden's treatment of the "Popish Plot" and, perhaps, Dryden's final conversion to Catholicism, in *John Dryden and His World* (New Haven: Yale University Press, 1987), 336, 358, 361, 415 and passim. Winn does not, however, discuss either the marchioness dowager or the Winchester epitaph.

[116] Dryden, "Epitaph on the Monument of the Marquis of Winchester," in his *Poems*, 4:1800–1801.

[117] Included in Oxford University, *Verses on the Death of ... Sir Bevill Grenvill* (Oxford, 1643), 19. The epitaph upon Edward Penell, d. 1657, similarly praises him for having been "Good in bad times" (Ravenshaw, 112), while Brome's undated epitaph, "To the memory of ... I. Cordel *Kt.*," praises one "who durst be good when goodness was a crime" (Brome, 1:270).

(l. 7). On the other hand the poet bids that Winchester's "true honor" (l. 8) be learned and practiced should such a time of strife return, with the implication that such honor is relevant only in such a time. It is surely not an unmitigated gain that the present era of domestic peace has made Winchester's heroic loyalty irrelevant.

In the second stanza the living poet respectfully addresses, from the other side of a great divide, the hero of a bygone time: "Ark of *thy age's* faith and loyalty / Which to preserve them, Heaven confined in thee" (ll. 9–10; emphasis mine). The poem's final praise of both Winchester and the king he served—"Such souls are rare, but mighty patterns given / To earth" (ll. 15–16)—suggests that the two virtuous dead were didactic *exempla* for the living, but it is not clear how those living in Dryden's own unheroic times could or should imitate these heroes of suffering-unto-death. The final image of the dead as "ornaments of heaven" (l. 16) indeed stresses the distance between the blessed dead and the living. While early seventeenth-century poets sometimes invoked the astrological notion of "influence" in order to convey the continuing ethical influence of the heavenly dead upon the living, Dryden's dead, removed from earthly suffering to become heavenly "ornaments," have no clear link to the world that they have left behind.[118]

The epitaph indeed provides striking testimony to the continuing idealization of the heroes of the Civil Wars and the consequent belittling of the present. Though Winchester's life extended fifteen years after the Restoration, Dryden treats his life and death wholly in terms of his loyalty to Charles I. The years 1660 to 1675, which Winchester spent in retirement, are passed over in silence. Indeed Dryden does his best to make it sound as if Winchester did not outlive the period of civil conflict by closely linking the Royalist's life and death to the execution of Charles I. While the first stanza describes Winchester's suffering for his "earthly" (l. 6) ruler until "rewarded" (l. 5) by death and beatitude, the second stanza's parallel description of king and subject who "by suff'rings rose, and gave the law to fate" (l. 14)—that is, were victorious over the suffering and death ("fate" here means "death," *OED* 4b) inflicted upon them—makes it sound as if Winchester, like his king, was a casualty of the Great Rebellion who conquered death with Christian Stoic fortitude.[119]

[118] For the dead's heavenly influence upon the living, see Jonson's "To the memory of my beloved, The AUTHOR Mr. WILLIAM SHAKESPEARE: And what he hath left us," ll. 77–78 in Jonson, 8:392; and Carew's "To the Countesse of Anglesie, upon the immoderatly-by-her-lamented death of her Husband," ll. 81–82 in *The Poems of Thomas Carew*, ed. Rhodes Dunlap (Oxford: Clarendon, 1949), 71.

[119] The phrase "gave the law to fate" which I have glossed as "victorious over death," is admittedly difficult. I suspect it conflates famous phrases in praise of Cato Uticensis, the Stoic whose suicide was the example par excellence of a moral conquest over death. In an

The epitaph's distortion of the biography of the deceased would not have greatly shocked late seventeenth-century readers, who expected an idealizing emphasis on the activities of the dead during the Civil Wars. Thus an epitaph upon a Royalist soldier who died in 1691 compresses his long life after the Civil Wars to the single word "after": "after a faithfull discharge of his Duty to King Charles the First of blessed memory in his Wars during the wicked Rebellion he dyed on the 12. of Febr. 1691. aged 79. years."[120] Some epitaphs do, however, describe Royalists who suffered during the Civil Wars but then resumed the "arts of piece" at the glorious Restoration.[121] It is therefore rather surprising that Dryden, the poet laureate, chose to exploit the rhetoric of nostalgia rather than take the opportunity to praise the peace of Winchester's later days under the Restoration. I would suggest that Dryden's emphasis on Winchester's suffering loyalty to Charles I unto death is in fact a polemical defense of Winchester as a loyal English Catholic and an oblique but unmistakable criticism of such a man's continued suffering during the Restoration.

Dryden pointedly avoids explicit mention of Winchester's Catholicism. "Ark of thy age's faith and loyalty" may be read as a pleonastic doublet (cf. *OED* III. 10 "faith" as "faithfulness, fidelity, loyalty") that deliberately suggests that the all-important "faith" of Winchester was not his Catholicism but rather his loyalty to his king. The epitaph pointedly replaces what Protestants would consider popish superstition with eminently respectable patriotic sentiment: the poem asks not that the reader pray for the dead, as might a contemporaneous European Catholic epitaph, but instead requests that the reader "pray" (l. 7) that England never be

---

essay on Cato known to Dryden, Montaigne praises the Stoic hero and cites the major poetic panegyrics upon him. Horace describes "all the world subdued, except stern Cato's soul" ("cuncta terrarum subacta / praeter atrocem animum Catonis," *Ode* 2.1.23–24); Manilius praises the "unconquered, since death was conquered, Cato" ("Et invictum, devicta morte, Catonem," *Astronomica* 4.87, as cited in Montaigne); and Virgil describes Cato's "giving...laws" in Elysium ("dantem iura," *Aeneid* 8.670); see Michel de Montaigne, *Les Essais*, ed. Pierre Villey, rev. V.-L. Saulnier, 3rd ed., 2 vols. (1924; Paris: Presses Universitaires de Paris, 1978), 1:232. Dryden's "gave the law to fate" seems to combine Horace's and Manilius's depiction of the hero unconquered by death and the Virgilian law-giver. (Since the ancient commentators, readers have debated whether Virgil's line refers to Cato Uticensis or to his great grandfather, Cato the Censor. In the notes to his translation of *The Aeneid*, however, Dryden cites Montaigne's essay and argues that the passage refers to the younger Cato; see John Dryden, *The Works of Virgil in English: 1697*, ed. William Frost and Vinton A. Dearing, The California Edition of the Works of John Dryden, vols. 5–6 [Berkeley: University of California Press, 1987], 6:822–823.)

[120] Epitaph upon John Anguish, d. 1691, in John Le Neve, *Monumenta Anglicana: Being Inscriptions on the Monuments of several Eminent Persons . . . 1600–1715*, 5 vols. (London, 1718–1719), 3:131.

[121] I draw the phrase from the epitaph upon Peter Eliot, d. 1681, in Le Neve, 3:30–31. See also the epitaph upon John Sudbury, d.1684, in Le Neve, 3:64.

embroiled again in civil war.[122] The public memorial's simultaneous suppression of Winchester's religion and assertions of his quasi-religious faith toward Charles I clearly respond to the ubiquitous anti-Catholic sentiment of the 1670s.[123] Many English Protestants hated and feared Catholics as agents of foreign domination: a Catholic was regarded, to quote Edmund Waller in a 1675 House of Commons debate upon "popery," as "a person that has a Sovereign somewhere else than in England."[124] Dryden's epitaph combats such a response toward the Catholic Winchester by polemically implying that his fundamental faith was in fact patriotism-unto-death.

Winchester's final years were not happy ones for English Catholics.[125] The Restoration settlement reestablished the Church of England and revived the legal penalties inflicted on both Protestant nonconformists and Catholics. Catholics were not only barred from public office but also vulnerable—whenever the laws were actually enforced—to extensive fines and imprisonment. During Charles II's reign the court was heavily Catholic. Charles II himself, who officially converted to Catholicism on his deathbed, had evident Catholic sympathies, allied himself with the hated Catholic "tyrant" Louis XIV, pursued Catholic mistresses, and showed marked concern for the plight of English Catholics. Since he was dependent for his finances on a Parliament that viewed religious statues as Parliament's domain and linked "popery" to foreign domination, domestic tyranny, and clerical abuse of power, Charles did not, however, succeed in his various attempts to improve English Catholics' legal position. On March 15, 1672, with Parliament prorogued, he issued a Declaration of Indulgence suspending penal legislation against both nonconformists and Catholics and allowing the former public, the latter private, worship.[126] Though some members of Parliament were eager to extend toleration to the dissenters, many feared papist conspiracies

[122] Prayers for the dead were still very much an issue in this period. In his *Rehearsal Transpros'd*, for example, Marvell sharply criticizes the epitaph upon the minister Herbert Thorndike, d. 1672, which concludes: "Tu Lector requiem ei & beatam in Christo resurrectionem precare" ("You, o reader, pray that he receive rest and a blessed resurrection in Christ"). Thorndike was a maverick churchman who advocated following the practices of the early church, including prayers for the dead. Marvell cites his epitaph as one example of the general "slide on into Superstition" (see Marvell, *Rehearsal*, 100; 348, n. 24; and the *DNB* article upon Thorndike).

[123] On anti-Catholicism in the later seventeenth century, see John Miller, *Popery and Politics in England: 1660–1688* (Cambridge: Cambridge University Press, 1973); and Michael G. Finlayson, *Historians, Puritanism, and the English Revolution: The Religious Factor in English Politics before and after the Interregnum* (Toronto: University of Toronto Press, 1983), 119–158.

[124] Anchitell Grey, *Debates of the House of Commons from the Year 1667 to the Year 1694*, 10 vols. (London, 1763), 3:186.

[125] This paragraph relies primarily upon Miller, 102–153.

[126] The declaration is in Kenyon, *Stuart Constitution*, 382–383.

and viewed the declaration as a tyrannic attempt to encroach upon Parliament's domain.[127] In 1673, fears of Charles's Catholic brother and heir to the throne, the duke of York, greatly contributed to anti-Catholic sentiment. Parliament forced Charles to repeal his declaration and instituted the Test Act, which required all office holders to subscribe to a declaration against transubstantiation. The act forced York to resign from court office. The years 1673 to 1674 witnessed particularly virulent expressions of anti-Catholic feeling, and York's marriage to the Catholic Mary Beatrice of Modena in 1675 increased the anti-Catholic frenzy. In 1675, seeking to strengthen the court by appealing to the old Cavaliers hostile to both nonconformists and Catholics, Charles's new chief minister, Thomas Osborn, earl of Danby, had Catholics barred from the court, encouraged the passing of new anti-Catholic legislation, and prosecuted nonconformists and papists with new zeal. For reasons of state Charles supported Danby against the advice of his Catholic brother and abandoned toleration.

Dryden's epitaph implies a firm position in the Restoration debate concerning the treatment of Catholics, which was often justified on the basis not only of their perennial allegiances but also of their alleged role in the Civil Wars. In an early attempt to grant limited toleration to the Catholics, the declaration of December 26, 1662, Charles claimed that "our Roman Catholic subjects of this kingdom . . . deserved well from our royal father of blessed memory, and from us, and even from the Protestant religion itself, in adhering to us with their lives and fortunes for the maintenance of our Crown."[128] In a House of Commons debate concerning the constitutionality of Charles's 1672 Declaration of Indulgence, Sir Robert Carr argued for tolerance of Catholics on the grounds that "the Papists have fought for the King," while two other members of Parliament argued against tolerance by claiming that Charles I had complained that the papists had not done their duty at the battle of Edgehill.[129] A pro-Catholic satire of 1673, attacking the "Ungrateful wretches" who enacted the Test Act, asked rhetorically whether Catholic Royalists like Winchester deserved such treatment: "Did we contend for you with blood and treasure, / That you should plague and banish us at pleasure? / Did Worcester, Winchester, and Bellasis, / Bristol, Carnarvon, all engage for this?"[130]

---

[127] On Protestant, including nonconformist, suspicions of the declaration, see Miller, 117–119. In the *Rehearsal Transpros'd* Marvell walked a difficult tightrope, using the king's declaration to support his own argument against Parker for toleration of dissenters without endorsing its assertion of royal prerogative in religious matters (Wallace, 188–191).

[128] Kenyon, *Stuart Constitution*, 381.

[129] Grey, 2:32, 35.

[130] "The Banished Priests' Farewell to the House of Commons" (1673), ll. 37–42 in

The most emotionally charged aspect of the debate inevitably centered on the Catholics' relationship to Charles I's execution. While Charles I's support of the Arminians helped prompt Parliament to declare war in 1642 against "popish" tyranny, his execution in 1649 transformed him into a Protestant martyr whose execution was officially mourned each January 30 by the established Church. Throughout the century the regicide served as a polemical counter: all major political and religious groups denied that they were the regicides and ascribed to their opponents the blame for the greatest sin of English history.[131] The Protestant dissenters were the most obvious group to blame, and members of the established Church often did so. Nevertheless many Protestants, beginning with the Presbyterian William Prynne in the late 1640s and early 1650s and continuing among men of various shades of conformity and nonconformity up through the 1680s, argued that the regicide was the result of a popish plot to destroy Protestant England.[132] In 1672 a member claimed in the House of Commons that "there was great rejoicing at *Rome*, by the Cardinal Protector of the *English*, for the King's murder."[133] Implicitly responding to such contemporary aspersions upon English Catholics, Dryden not only praises Winchester for being a loyal subject but also closely links, indeed superimposes, Winchester's suffering-unto-death and the king's execution. Far from rejoicing in his king's death, Winchester, so Dryden's polemical rhetoric tries to suggest, in essence shared it.

Dryden had a long-standing commitment to toleration of Catholics, admiration for the Catholic York, and patrons among the Yorkist faction.[134] The epitaph implicitly endorses toleration for Catholics in gratitude for their loyalty, a commitment Charles II had himself earlier espoused but had now out of political prudence abandoned. The tablet is signed "John Dryden, Poet Laureate." In the late seventeenth century the names of poets began to appear upon their verse inscriptions. This trend reflected both the greater importance of the verbal element to the

George deF. Lord, ed., *Poems on Affairs of State*, vol. 1, *1660–1678* (New Haven: Yale University Press, 1963), 206.

[131] See, for example, J. P. Kenyon's discussion of the polemical treatment of the regicide in the 1690s, when supporters of the Glorious Revolution were at pains to distinguish their "legal" deposition of James II from the "illegal" trial of Charles I, in *Revolution Principles: The Politics of Party, 1689–1720* (Cambridge: Cambridge University Press, 1977), 61–82.

[132] Miller, 85–86; and Finlayson, 125–129.

[133] Grey, 2:76.

[134] Winn discusses Dryden's support of toleration and notes that Dryden's many Catholic in-laws and his wife's own possible Catholicism may have contributed to his position (pp. 119–124). He also notes that one of Dryden's patrons, Sir Thomas Clifford, a convert to Catholicism, resigned in 1673 from the office of lord treasurer along with York, while another, John Sheffield, the earl of Mulgrave, to whom Dryden dedicated *Aureng-Zebe* in 1676, was a York supporter (pp. 240–242, 252–254 and passim).

monument, particularly in the case of the plain inscriptional tablet, and the greater fame of poets in an age of increasing literacy and truly national poetry.[135] "John Dryden, Poet Laureate" adds undoubted prestige to the dignified but modest inscriptional tablet commemorating Winchester. In an epitaph idealizing a dead subject and his dead king, the signature evokes, furthermore, a living subject, Dryden, and the king whom he served, Charles II. By evoking the present king, however, Dryden might also be suggesting his critique of the present court policy. Though the claim that an "earthly king" could not "recompense" Winchester for his suffering refers primarily to the executed Charles I, Dryden also hints—he could do no more—that the present king has unfortunately failed fully to "recompense" loyal Catholic subjects. Dryden had Scriptural support for the notion that good men's true "recompense" is heavenly rather than earthly (cf. Hebrews 10:35 and 11:26), but the consolation of theology does not lessen Dryden's implicit criticism of the present order's all too earthly ingratitude.[136]

Neither the prose nor the verse inscription mentions the son and heir of the deceased, Charles Paulet, the sixth marquis of Winchester and first duke of Bolton. Early in the 1660s father and son quarrelled over financial matters,[137] and from the early years of the Restoration the son was outwardly Protestant enough to serve as a member of Parliament.[138] By 1675, the year his father died, Charles Paulet had indeed emerged not only as an apostate but also as a staunch member of the "country opposition" of Anthony Ashley Cooper, the earl of Shaftesbury, which feared the growing power of the court and its papist tendencies.[139] In

[135] Dryden's name is appended to the epitaph inscribed upon the Bath Abbey wall tablet commemorating Mary Frampton, d. 1698. "Edmund Waller, Esq." is appended to the epitaph inscribed upon the plain floor slab commemorating Edmund Dunch, d. 1686, in Stoke Newington Parish Church, and Waller's verse epitaph upon the wall tablet of John Howard, viscount Andover, d. 1663, in Ewelme Parish Church is introduced as a "funeral song by the renowned Edmund Waller, the British master-Virgil, our dearest friend" ("funebre carmen ab inclyto Edmundo Wallero archiMarone Brittano et nostri amicissimo"); see the transcription in F. N. Davis, ed., "Anthony à Wood's and Richard Rawlinson's Parochial Collections (Second Part)," *Oxfordshire Record Society* 4 (1922):139–140. Dryden's fame and laureate office and Waller's long-standing fame as a poet and his social standing as a courtier and member of Parliament explain the appearance of their names on these inscriptions.

[136] On Dryden's conception of gratitude as the all-important virtue of a healthy social and political order, see John M. Wallace, "John Dryden's Plays and the Conception of a Heroic Society," in *Culture and Politics from Puritanism to the Enlightenment*, ed. Perez Zagorin (Berkeley: University of California Press, 1980), 113–134.

[137] See the reference to the "unhappy difference" between father and son in *Calendar of State Papers, Domestic Series*, series 4, vol. 2, *1661–1662*, ed. Mary Anne Everett Green (London, 1861), 91.

[138] The law forbade Catholics to be members of Parliament, though several crypto- or quasi-Catholics managed to serve (Miller, 64–65).

[139] On Winchester's long association with the country opposition and his support of Shaftesbury's attempt to exclude York as a Catholic from the succession during the Ex-

1675 the new marquis proposed, with Shaftesbury's support, that all members of Parliament be required to swear that they would not be influenced in their votes by any thought of reward (from the court); in a pamphlet outlining the country opposition's case, Shaftesbury warmly praised the new marquis as "an expert Parliament Man" whose proposed oath was designed to prevent members of Parliament from being "too much for the King."[140] In the same period that Dryden commemorated the fifth Winchester for being a true Royalist, precisely because he was selflessly loyal to a king who could not reward him, Winchester's son sought to make sure that subjects were not too loyal to a king because of the rewards that he could in fact offer. Dryden may have written the epitaph after the appearance of Shaftesbury's pamphlet praising the sixth marquis for his attempt to limit the king's power. In any case the epitaph, while obliquely criticizing the failure of a king, idealizes a man supposedly loyal to a king unto death. Its silence concerning Winchester's heir hints at the truth, that Winchester was the last of his kind.

Dryden himself converted to Catholicism some time after York's succession as James II in 1685. James II's attempt to use the royal prerogatives to grant Catholics full toleration and right to office alienated the Protestant majority of England, who supported William of Orange's invasion of England in 1688 and William and Mary's accession to the throne in February 1689.[141] With the Glorious Revolution Dryden fell from court office and favor into the painful situation of a Catholic Jacobite. His epitaph upon Margaret Paston was probably composed shortly after the Revolution. Paston, the Catholic niece of Sir Henry Bedingfeld, the Catholic brother-in-law of Dryden's wife, died in August 1689 at the age of twenty-three.[142] The epitaph presents her as an ideal whose loss completes the depravity of the times:

> So fair, so young, so innocent, so sweet;
> So ripe a Judgement, and so rare a Wit,
> Require at least an Age, in One to meet.

---

clusion Crisis of 1678–1681, see J. R. Jones, *The First Whigs: The Politics of the Exclusion Crisis, 1678–1683* (London: Oxford University Press, 1961), 32.

[140] The proposed oath and Shaftesbury's praise of the sixth marquis may be found in Shaftesbury's anonymously published pamphlet, *A Letter from a Person of Quality, to his Friend in the Country* (London, 1675), 28–29. In the same pamphlet Shaftesbury voices his suspicions that despite Danby's official policy the court was in fact penalizing Protestant dissenters while only pretending to penalize Catholics (pp. 6–8).

[141] On James II's attempt to achieve full toleration for Catholics and its disastrous political consequences, see Miller, 196–263; and J. R. Jones, *The Revolution of 1688 in England* (London: Weidenfeld and Nicolson, 1972), 75–127.

[142] Concerning Margaret Paston, her family, and in-laws, see E. B. Burstall, "The Pastons and Their Manor of Binham," *Norfolk Archaeology* 30 (1952):112; and Rosamond Meredith, "The Eyres of Hassop, and Some of Their Connections, from the Test Act to Emancipation," *Recusant History* 9 (1967):13, 24–26.

> In her they met; but long they cou'd not stay,
> 'Twas Gold too fine to fix without Allay:
> Heav'ns Image was in her so well exprest,
> Her very Sight upbraided all the rest.
> Too justly ravish'd from an Age like this;
> Now *she* is gone, the World is of a Piece.[143]

The epitaph mixes sorrow for Paston's tragic early death and a bitterness with the age that must at least partially be explained by the state of England as Dryden viewed it. He praises with appropriate brevity a woman whose virtues "long could not stay" in what he now regards as an otherwise debased world.

The opening triplet uses the traditional panegyric topos of many-in-one, claiming that Paston united various virtues, including those qualities of mind normally treated in the late seventeenth century as antitheses: wit and judgment.[144] Dryden adds, however, an historical perspective to the usual praise of virtues unified: Paston's accomplishment required an "Age." Throughout his poetic career, Dryden's most distinctive panegyric strategy is to emphasize the historical nature of his subject's achievement. In panegyrics on artists from the period preceding the Paston epitaph, Dryden praises his subjects for uniting the separate virtues of predecessors: in 1687 he commends Henry Higden's blending of Horatian and Juvenalian style, and in 1688 he celebrates Milton's joining of Homer's "loftiness of thought" and Virgil's "majesty."[145] Such praise expresses Dryden's positive conception of his contemporaries—and, implicitly, himself—as heirs synthesizing the best features of the past.

Like many of Dryden's poems from the late 1680s and 1690s, however, this epitaph explicitly contrasts the exceptional individual to an otherwise debased age.[146] After the triplet, Dryden turns to Paston's death and the times. He emphasizes the contrast between Paston's individual achieve-

---

[143] Dryden, "Epitaph on Mrs. Margaret Paston of Barningham In Norfolk," in his *Poems*, 4:1801. The epitaph, which for some reason was not inscribed upon the tomb of the deceased, was first published in *Lintot's Miscellany* (1712).

[144] On the growing sense of opposition between wit and judgment in the mid and late seventeenth century, see George Williamson, *The Proper Wit of Poetry* (Chicago: University of Chicago Press, 1961), 18–21 and passim.

[145] Dryden, "To my Ingenious Friend, Mr. Henry Higden . . . ," and "[Lines on Milton]" in his *Poems*, 1:465–466, 2:540.

[146] Thus in 1694 Dryden praises the "promis'd hour" and "present Age" in which Congreve joins the "strength" of early seventeenth-century drama and the "beauties" of earlier Restoration dramatists while also attacking the age as one in which "Poetry is curs'd"; see "*To my Dear Friend Mr. Congreve, On his Comedy, call'd*, The Double-Dealer," in his *Poems*, 2:852–854. This emphasis already appears in the idealization of the deceased and the attack upon contemporary poetic profligacy in the fourth stanza of the Anne Killigrew ode (1686) as well as in the praise of James II and his newborn son and the attack upon the recalcitrant nation in "Britannia Rediviva" (1688) (especially ll. 61–70 and 277–297); see *Poems*, 1:461, 2:541–551. It is intensified, however, in the post-1688 poetry.

ment and the corrupt times by using the word "age" in two very different senses in this short poem. While Dryden claims that it takes "an Age" for such an ideal as Paston to appear, the poet who had once celebrated the Restoration as the "Happy Age" of Astraea's return now praises a woman whose brief perfection is rightly and necessarily removed from an "Age like this."[147]

It is striking but not ultimately surprising that Dryden, the virtual opposite of Marvell in politics, religion, and aesthetics, describes Paston's relation to her times in a way closely resembling that of Jones's relation to hers. Both poets idealize dead women in order to mourn the virtues supposedly destroyed by the course of history. In order to accentuate the contrast between a vanished ideal and the degraded present, Dryden ignores the fact that Paston had a surviving husband and daughter. Instead of praising a chaste wife and dutiful mother, as do so many epitaphic poets, Dryden transforms Paston into an ideal who, like Marvell's Jones, lived apart from the world and is saved by death from any connection to it. Like Marvell, Dryden recalls but significantly diverges from Donne's famous commemoration of a virgin, the *First Anniversarie*. While Dryden's praise of Paston as "gold" with mortal "allay" recalls Donne's praise of Drury's virtue entering the "allay" of sinful femininity (*First Anniversarie*, ll. 177–182),[148] the final line recalls the refrain of Donne's poem. Like Marvell, Dryden differs from Donne in neither claiming that the deceased caused the world's death nor seeking some way of improving the world. Paston's death returns the world to its bad state ("The world is of a piece"), and the poet can do nothing but commemorate a vanished perfection.

In the penultimate line, "Too justly ravish'd from an age like this," "ravish'd" primarily means "carried away...from earth" (*OED* 3), but in the context of a young woman's death, the commonplace of Death the amorous ravisher is also present.[149] By claiming that death's "ravishment" of Paston is just punishment upon the age, the epitaph obliquely suggests that Paston was saved from the age's potentially more ignominious violation. "Ravishment" had topical, political resonances in the late 1680s: just as Marvell described the invading Dutch of the Second Dutch War as rapists, so Jacobites like Dryden described William of Orange as the "ravisher" of England.[150] In *Don Sebastian* (1690), the

[147] See Dryden, "Astraea Redux," l. 320 in his *Poems*, 1:24.

[148] Donne, *Epithalamions*, 27.

[149] On this commonplace, see Theodore Spencer, *Death and Elizabethan Tragedy: A Study of Convention and Opinion in the Elizabethan Drama* (Cambridge: Harvard University Press, 1936), 71–77. Spencer cites with many parallels Romeo's speculation that "amorous" death has made Juliet "his paramour" in *Romeo and Juliet* V.iii.101–105.

[150] For examples of rape imagery applied to William III's conquest of England, see Howard Erskine-Hill, "Literature and the Jacobite Cause: Was There a Rhetoric of Jaco-

drama closest in date to the probable composition of the Paston epitaph, Dryden exploits the Jacobite resonances of "ravishment": shortly after the Muslim tyrant Muley-Moluch threatens Almeyda's "ravishment" (II.i.496–497), she tells her husband, the Christian prince Sebastian: "The Tyrant will not long be absent hence; / And soon I will be ravish'd from your arms" (II.i.557–558).[151] Muley-Moluch and Sebastian subsequently argue over Almeyda in terms of "usurpation" versus "lawful claim" (III.i.169–172), and the two men's struggle clearly parallels William III and James II's struggle over England.[152] Thus when Muley-Moluch threatens the "ravishment" of Almeyda and she fears to be "ravished from" Sebastian, a viewer or reader would naturally compare her situation to another female vulnerable to rape, England.[153] Death's "ravishment" of Paston both resembles and prevents her from suffering such a rape. The brute force of Dryden's own idealizing rhetoric makes Paston embody the ex-laureate's nostalgic view of the nation's lost virtue.

The intense polemicizing of the dead found in this and other late seventeenth-century epitaphs continues through the mid eighteenth century as partisan poets enlist the dead in the sociopolitical struggles of the living. The epitaph thereby loses credibility, however, and the greatest poet of the early and mid eighteenth century, Pope, treats the genre as the pernicious product and agent of a corrupt social order while seeking new ways for the poetic epitaph to both answer the needs of the living and be faithful to the dead.

---

bitism?" in *Ideology and Conspiracy: Aspects of Jacobitism, 1689–1759*, ed. Eveline Cruickshanks (Edinburgh: John Donald Publishers, 1982), 49; 61, n. 9.

[151] John Dryden, *Plays: Albion and Albanius, Don Sebastian, and Amphitryon*, ed. Earl Miner, George R. Guffey, and Franklin B. Zimmerman, The California Edition of the Works of Dryden, vol. 15 (Berkeley: University of California Press, 1976), 118, 120.

[152] Dryden, *Plays: Albion*, 132.

[153] David Bywaters convincingly argues for the Muley-Moloch / Sebastian and William III / James II parallels in "Dryden and the Revolution of 1688: Political Parallel in *Don Sebastian*," *JEGP* 85 (1986):346–365; see especially pp. 351–358. He further suggests that Dryden has the two men struggle over a woman instead of a throne in order to camouflage, and make possible the disclaiming of, his political intent. Though this is certainly true, Almeyda's womanhood here has its own political significance because of the Jacobite use of rape imagery.

PART 3

NEW SUBJECTS, NEW READERS:
THE EIGHTEENTH- AND EARLY
NINETEENTH-CENTURY EPITAPH

Chapter 8

"Your Distance Keep":
Pope's Epitaphs upon Himself

In *Spectator* 349 Joseph Addison argues that no man's life can be "pronounced vicious or virtuous" until completed by death. Men are more eager to praise the living than the dead, because the living can always change while the true characters of the dead have been fully revealed by their completed lives.[1] Like his contemporary Addison, Alexander Pope treats the completion of a man's life as the definitive disclosure of its meaning and value.[2] In the *Moral Essays*, for example, he posits the

[1] See *The Spectator*, ed. Donald F. Bond, 5 vols. (Oxford: Clarendon, 1965), 3:299. Bond's notes provide several classical and Renaissance sources for Addison's argument (3:299); for biblical and patristic parallels, see Erwin Panofsky, "Mors Vitae Testimonium. The Positive Aspect of Death in Renaissance and Baroque Iconography," in *Studien zur Toskanischen Kunst*, ed. Wolfgang Lotz and Lise Lotte Möller (Munich: Prestel-Verlag, 1964), 228–232.

[2] In this and the following chapter, I cite Pope's epitaphs and other brief poems from the Twickenham edition of Pope, vol. 6, *Minor Poems*, ed. Norman Ault and John Butt (New Haven: Yale University Press, 1954). All other citations of Pope's poetry are from the following volumes of the Twickenham edition, cited without page number: vol. 2, *The Rape of the Lock and Other Poems*, ed. Geoffrey Tillotson, 2d ed. (New Haven: Yale University Press, 1954); vol. 3, part i, *An Essay on Man*, ed. Maynard Mack (London: Methuen,1950); vol. 3, part ii, *Epistles to Several Persons*, ed. F. W. Bateson, 2d ed. (New Haven: Yale University Press, 1961); vol. 4, *Imitations of Horace with An Epistle to Dr. Arbuthnot and The Epilogue to the Satires*, ed. John Butt (New Haven: Yale University Press, 1961); and vol. 5, *The Dunciad*, ed. James Sutherland, 3d ed., revised (New Haven: Yale University Press, 1963). All citations of Pope's letters are from *The Correspondence of Alexander Pope*, ed. George Sherburn, 5 vols. (Oxford: Clarendon, 1956). Unless otherwise specified, all citations of Pope's prose are from *The Prose Works of Alexander Pope*, vol. 1, *1711–1720*, ed. Norman Ault (Oxford: Basil Blackwell, 1936); and *The Prose Works of Alexander Pope*, vol. 2, *The Major Works, 1725–1744*, ed. Rosemary Cowler (Oxford: Basil Blackwell, 1986).

Ruling Passion, which "sticks to our last sand" (*Epistle to Cobham*, l. 225), as the solution to the puzzles of human nature. He gives both the *Epistle to Cobham* and the *Epistle to Bathurst* strong closure by ending with depictions of various men's deaths as the definitive revelations of their true natures (*Cobham*, ll. 222–265, *Bathurst*, ll. 283–402).[3] Such death scenes have clear generic affinities to poetic epitaphs.[4] *The Dunciad's* magnificent conclusion attacks English (sub)culture by imagining the culture's end; in a letter Pope describes his satiric apocalypse as a "publick Epitaph or monumental Inscription, like that at Thermopylae, on a *whole people perish'd.*"[5]

Pope composed many actual epitaphs upon contemporaries in which he sought to define the significance of their completed lives. He also continually imagined his own death and the epitaph in which he could encapsulate for posterity the ultimate meaning of his own existence. Though in his earliest known poem he wished for no epitaph upon his grave, in letters throughout his life he discussed epitaphs that could be written about him; at the height of his poetic career he composed the prose inscription for his tomb; in his major poems he included epitaphic self-portraits; and early and late he wrote serio-comic poetic epitaphs upon himself. His epitaphic compositions assert his integrity unto death, putting forward the image of a completed, virtuous life against the forces of change and degradation.

Pope pits his epitaphic self-definitions against not only his own mutability but also others' attempts to define him. Both the idealization and

[3] Earl W. Wasserman noted that in *Bathurst* Pope puns on "end(s)" as temporal conclusion(s) and as goal(s) in order to suggest that men's deaths reveal their ultimate values; see *Pope's Epistle to Bathurst: A Critical Reading with an Edition of the Manuscripts* (Baltimore: Johns Hopkins University Press, 1960), 43–44. Kenneth Burke's discussion of how "the essence of a thing can be defined narratively in terms of its *fulfillment* or *fruition*" sheds light upon Pope's strategies; see his *A Rhetoric of Motives* (1950; rpt., Berkeley: University of California Press, 1969), 13–17.

[4] Both *Cobham* and *Bathurst* end with two dying men's self-characterizing last words— " 'Oh, save my Country, Heav'n!' shall be your last!" (*Cobham*, l. 265); "And sad Sir Balaam curses God and dies" (l. 402)—just as Pope's epitaph upon his exiled friend Francis Atterbury, written during the same period, concludes with Atterbury's dying cry: "—*Save my Country, Heav'n, /*—He said, and dy'd" ("EPITAPH. For Dr. FRANCIS ATTERBURY, Bishop of Rochester, Who died in Exile at Paris, in 1732," in *Minor Poems*, 344). *Bathurst* also refers to, and includes, epitaphs that reinforce the poem's absorption of epitaphic motifs: Dr. Arbuthnot's satiric epitaph upon Francis Chartres appears in a footnote to line twenty, while Pope's praise of the Man of Ross, buried without "monument, inscription, stone" (l. 283), compensates for the epitaph that the Man of Ross did not receive.

[5] See Pope, *Correspondence*, 3:143 (Pope to Gay, October 23, 1730). Noting that *The Dunciad*, like many eighteenth-century poems, ends with death, Margaret Doody argues that Pope and other eighteenth-century poets imagined their ultimate defeat by "death, and the end of utterance, which are one"; see *The Daring Muse: Augustan Poetry Reconsidered* (Cambridge: Cambridge University Press, 1985), 183–195 (quotation on p. 191). I argue, by contrast, that Pope seeks to *master* endings—of lives and poems—with definitive poetic statement.

the invective that had dominated the polemical epitaphs of the late seventeenth century continued in the heated political climate of the early and mid eighteenth century. Throughout his career Pope participated in literary skirmishes, and in the 1730s he became the most accomplished poet to oppose George II's court and the regime of Sir Robert Walpole.[6] He accordingly developed a keen sense of vulnerability to partisan attack and misrepresentation. In his epitaphs upon himself he tried to forestall both the slander of enemies and the degrading flattery of sycophants. In *The Dunciad*, Dulness bids her minions write foolish compositions that would deprive respectable authors of their identities, contaminating not only their books but even their graves: "Leave not a foot of verse, a foot of stone, / A Page, a Grave, that they can call their own" (4.127–128). Pope's epitaphs upon himself stem from an intense desire to prevent such a loss of posthumous identity, to ensure that he will have a grave that he can call his own by writing an epitaph that represents him as he wishes to be remembered. Pope tries to construct the definitive view of himself.[7]

Pope's epitaphic self-definitions seek not only to define a permanent self against flux and the misrepresentations of contemporaries and successors. They further attempt to distinguish him from his literary predecessors, the authors against whose work he defines what is truly his own.[8] Though he sometimes professes humility vis-à-vis the major poets of the past, Pope in fact attempts to outdo his predecessors, both English and classical. The *Epistle to Augustus*'s brief history of English poetry notes that Dryden, Pope's major predecessor, "wanted, or forgot, / The last and greatest Art, the Art to blot" (ll. 280–281); Pope will achieve what Dryden neglected. Conscious of his position at the end of the humanist, neoclassical tradition, Pope finds solace in closely associating

---

[6] On Pope's opposition to the Hanoverian-Walpole regime, see Maynard Mack, *The Garden and the City: Retirement and Politics in the Later Poetry of Pope, 1731–1743* (Toronto: University of Toronto Press, 1969); and the qualifications of Mack in Bertrand A. Goldgar, *Walpole and the Wits: The Relation of Politics to Literature, 1722–1742* (Lincoln: University of Nebraska Press, 1976).

[7] I am indebted to an unpublished essay by Anne Badger on Pope's desire to have the "last word" as a central motif in his poetry. See Pope's 1742 "EPIGRAM. On CIBBER's Declaration that he will have the Last Word with Mr. POPE": "Quoth Cibber to Pope, tho' in Verse you foreclose, / I'll have the last Word, for by G-d I'll write Prose. / Poor Colley, thy Reas'ning is none of the strongest, / For know, the last Word is the Word that lasts longest" (*Minor Poems*, 397). In his epitaphs upon himself, Pope tries to deliver the "last," in the sense of most enduring, word on himself.

[8] Compare Ronald Paulson's discussion of the role of the other in Pope's poetry in his "Satire, and Poetry, and Pope," in Leland Henry Carlson and Ronald Paulson, *English Satire*, Clark Library Seminar Papers (Los Angeles: University of California Press, 1972), 99–102. The revised and much expanded version of this essay in Paulson, *Breaking and Remaking: Aesthetic Practice in England, 1700–1822* (New Brunswick, N.J.: Rutgers University Press, 1989), 48–93, unfortunately arrived too late for me to take into consideration.

what is last with what is greatest. However constrained by his awareness
that other, possibly superior poetic values are no longer available, Pope's
early decision to excel as the poet of "correctness" makes his poetic
project the rectifying culmination of poetic tradition.[9] In his epitaphs
upon himself Pope imagines himself as a poet of retirement who unequivocally refused the blandishments of the world and the "great." By
distinguishing his uncompromising stance from the attitudes of Cowley
and Matthew Prior, the English poets whose epitaphs upon themselves
are closest to his own, and Horace and Virgil, the classical poets whom
he emulates throughout his career, Pope "corrects" the past and attempts
to immortalize himself as the definitive poet of retirement-unto-death.

In his earliest known work, the "Ode on Solitude," Pope wishes for a
life of country solitude and a death uncommemorated by elegy or epitaph. Here are the first and last stanzas of the poem's earliest version
of 1709:

> How happy he, who free from Care,
> The rage of courts, and noise of towns;
> Contented breathes his native air,
> In his own grounds.
>   . . . . . .
> Thus let me live, unheard, unknown,
> Thus unlamented let me dye;
> Steal from the world, and not a stone
> Tell where I lie.[10]

The poet's concluding wish moves smoothly from an "unheard, unknown" life to an "unlamented" death. A retired life and deathly oblivion
are parts of a continuous process of "steal[ing] from the world."
Throughout his life Pope described his retirement from the London
social world as a kind of "death."[11] The unmarked grave of this poem
is the ultimate extension of such a "death." To escape the world in both
life and death is to find contentment and freedom in a place that is
wholly one's own. Adapting a topos exploited in different ways by Herrick and Cowley and subsequently used by various late seventeenth- and

---

[9] On Pope's sense of himself as the culmination of poetic tradition, see also John Paul
Russo, *Alexander Pope: Tradition and Identity* (Cambridge: Harvard University Press, 1972),
224–225 and passim.

[10] Pope, *Minor Poems*, 3–4.

[11] In a 1710 letter Pope writes of being "buryd in solitude"; in 1716 he explains to
Thomas Parnell that it "would be like writing my own Epitaph" to tell "where I now repose
in Obscurity"; in a letter probably composed in 1718, he describes the "retreat" in which
he converses with the dead until he "return[s] to the living"; and in 1740 he writes of his
"Burial (at Twitnam)"; see *Correspondence*, 1:88, 1:348, 1:511, 4:227.

early eighteenth-century authors, Pope obliquely suggests that the grave is one's final, truest piece of private property: the poet who imagines the happy man dwelling undisturbed in his "own grounds," significantly changed in 1736 to the singular "own ground," wants to dwell equally undisturbed in the only ground that one can ultimately call one's own, the grave.[12] Living unknown and lying buried without an epitaph would ensure that the poet maintained his "own" place, not losing himself to that "fancy'd life in others breath, / A thing beyond us" (*An Essay on Man* 4.237–238), as Pope later described fame.[13]

Pope's wish to live upon his "own grounds" is a pathos-laden fantasy. Although he sometimes depicts himself in his poetry as a kind of landed country gentleman, Pope was legally excluded from such a life. Anti-papist statutes passed under William III in 1700 denied Catholics the right to purchase, transmit, or inherit land; though the statutes were not rigidly enforced, Pope and his family, who were Catholic, obeyed the law.[14] In a letter of 1717, Pope compared his condition as an English Catholic to that of a "slave" and lamented that he could not "call a foot of paternal Earth my owne."[15] Pope's legal status as a Catholic deepens the personal resonance of his concluding wish in "Ode on Solitude" for an anonymous grave as his ultimate place of retired freedom: the poet might well imagine an unmarked grave, outside the world and its oppressive laws, as the ground most truly his "own."

Pope's longing for an anonymous grave was clearly at odds, however, with his poetic ambition. He continued to polish the "Ode on Solitude," from its first, probably already revised, appearance in a letter to Henry Cromwell of 1709, to the final version in the *Works* of 1736. With each revision Pope continued to express both a longing for retreat unto death

[12] Dustin Griffin notes that the singular "own ground" may "hint at the place of eventual burial" in "Revisions in Pope's 'Ode on Solitude,'" *MLQ* 36 (1975):372. For late seventeenth- and early eighteenth-century expressions of the grave as one's ultimate piece of property, see, for example, John Oldham's imitation of Horace's *Ode* 2.14: "Nor [in death] wilt thou be allow'd of all thy Land, to have, / But the small pittance of a six-foot grave" ("Paraphrase Upon HORACE. BOOK II. ODE XIV," ll. 51–52 in *The Poems of John Oldham*, ed. Harold Brooks with Raman Selden [Oxford: Clarendon, 1987], 121); and John Dunton's 1700 discussion of the grave: "'Tis all we can call our own, for observe of a *Man new dead*; this was his Wife (says one)—that was his Land—This was his Brother—That was his building—This was his Garden—And thus they talk awhile of what WAS HIS—but if we go to the Church-yard, where his Body lies, 'tis said, this IS HIS GRAVE" (*The Art of Living Incognito* [London, 1700], 214–215).

[13] Compare Pope's early description of fame as "that second Life in others' Breath, / Th'Estate which Wits inherit after Death" (*The Temple of Fame*, ll. 505–506). In the "Ode on Solitude" the young poet wishes for an "Estate" he can call his own rather than one dependent upon "others' Breath."

[14] John M. Aden discusses the various early eighteenth-century laws against Catholics in *Pope's Once and Future Kings: Satire and Politics in the Early Career* (Knoxville: University of Tennessee Press, 1978), 3–20.

[15] Pope, *Correspondence*, 1:384–385.

and a commitment to a highly public career of poetic self-definition. Pope's poem, including its final desire for an unmarked grave, is heavily indebted to the translations, imitations, and original compositions in Cowley's *Essays*.[16] Pope not only imitates, however, but also attempts to outdo Cowley as the modern exemplar of the retirement ideal, writing a brief, graceful lyric that captures the retirement impulse more successfully than any single poem by Cowley himself. Pope's discussion of the poem in the 1709 letter to Cromwell reveals this emulative struggle. Pope offers the poem as proof of his early love of country life and, implicitly, as a sign of his poetic precocity: "I find by the Date [it] was written when I was not Twelve years old . . . you may perceive how long I have continued in my Passion for a rural life, & in the same Employments of it."[17] In subsequent publications of the poem he repeats the proud claim that he composed his first retirement poem when he was about twelve. Pope's assertion recalls Cowley's comments concerning his own first retirement poem in his final essay, "Of Myself": "That I was then of the same mind as I am now [concerning the delights of country retirement] . . . may appear by the latter end of an Ode, which I made when I was but thirteen years old, and which was then printed with many other Verses. The Beginning of it is Boyish, but of this part which I here set down (if a very little were corrected) I should hardly now be much ashamed."[18] Although both Pope and Cowley find in their first compositions proof of their consistency as men and poets, Pope implicitly points out that he was even more precocious than his predecessor. In both the letter and the subsequent revisions of the poem, furthermore, Pope finds nothing so "boyish" as to require wholesale omission but instead simply perfects the five stanzas he wrote as a child. Even while he explicitly wishes to maintain the self's isolated integrity by a retreat unto death, Pope publicly defines the self in its "distinction" (to use one of Pope's own terms) from a poetic predecessor.[19]

There is thus an unacknowledged tension in the "Ode on Solitude" between the poem as a wish for privacy and as an act of publicity. Pope's later epitaphs on himself stem from his realization that the ultimate retreat into what is one's "own" in fact depends on public assertions of the self in all of its uniqueness. While the ode posits an unmarked grave as a final place of retreat, Pope's epitaphs on himself publicly claim and

[16] For the major echoes of Cowley, see the notes in Pope, *Minor Poems*, 4–5; and Griffin, "Revisions," 371–374. Maynard Mack discusses the *beatus vir* tradition in Pope's poetry in *Garden and City*, 77–115; and Cowley's particular influence upon Pope in *Garden and City*, 113–115.

[17] Pope, *Correspondence*, 1:68.

[18] Abraham Cowley, *Essays, Plays, and Sundry Verses*, ed. A. R. Waller (Cambridge: Cambridge University Press, 1906), 456.

[19] See Pope, "On the Desire of Distinction" (1711) in *Prose Works*, 1:20–26.

defend such a private place and the self that it shelters. By shrewd marketing of his Homer translations (1715–1726), landless Pope became the first author to earn full financial independence.[20] By presenting his epitaphic self-portraits to the reading public, Pope similarly seeks to earn his ultimate "spiritual" independence from it. In *An Epistle to Dr. Arbuthnot* (1734–1735) he declares his wish to "live my own! and die so too!" (l. 261), and the poem reveals his public struggle to die in his own way. In a footnote to a line indignantly noting the abuse hurled at "His Father, Mother, Body, Soul, and Muse" (l. 381), he provides brief obituaries of his father and mother in which he counters the aspersions upon their ancestries. In the 1735 edition of the poem he adds to this footnote the Latin prose epitaph that he composed and had inscribed upon the family monument in Twickenham Church:

The following Inscription was placed by their Son on their Monument, in the Parish of Twickenham, in Middlesex.

D.O.M.

ALEXANDRO POPE, VIRO INNOCUO
PROBO, PIO, QUI VIXIT ANNOS LXXV, OB. MDCCXVII.
ET EDITHAE CONJUGI INCULPABILI, PIENTISSIMAE,
QUAE VIXIT ANNOS XCIII OB. MDCXXXIII.
PARENTIBUS BENEMERENTIBUS FILIUS FECIT, ET SIBI.[21]

The epitaph is neoclassical in style. Pope uses the formulae of ancient Roman inscriptions as adapted by Renaissance humanists by opening his epitaphic tribute to his parents with the abbreviated dedication "D. O. M." for "Deo Optimo Maximo"; continuing with the names of the deceased in the dative, their ages and dates of death, and a few well-chosen adjectives of praise; and concluding with the relative who erected the monument for the "well deserving" dead.[22] Pope's careful attention to the lineation of the epitaph makes his composition a *carmen lapidarium*, an inscriptional or pseudo-inscriptional form whose lineation underlines the meaning of the inscription rather than follows either the normal practices of prose or the requirements of meter. Used by the ancients

---

[20] On Pope's marketing of his Homer translations, see Maynard Mack, *Alexander Pope: A Life* (New Haven: Yale University Press, 1986), 266–268, 416–417.

[21] The epitaph was translated and published in the 1744 edition of Pope's *Last Will and Testament:* "To God the Creator and best of Beings, / To *Alexander Pope*, a Gentleman of Honesty, Probity and Piety, who Liv'd LXXV. Years, died M. DCC. XVII. / And to *Editha*, his Excellent and truely [*sic*] Pious Wife, who lived XCIII. Years, died M. DCC. XXXIII. / To his well-deserving Parents the Son erected this, and to himself" (Pope, *Prose Works*, 2:505).

[22] For discussion of the humanist conventions noted in Pope's epitaph, see Iiro Kajanto, "Origin and Characteristics of the Humanistic Epitaph," *Epigraphica: Rivista Italiana di Epigrafia* 40 (1978):20–30. On Pope's interest in classical and neoclassical inscriptions, see Morris R. Brownell, *Alexander Pope and the Arts of Georgian England* (Oxford: Clarendon, 1978), 335.

and popularized by Italian humanists for brief sepulchral inscriptions, the *carmen lapidarium* first became popular in England in the seventeenth century.[23] In England, however, the form was most often used for extended, florid praise, and beginning in the late seventeenth century lengthy *carmina lapidaria* became popular, like Pindaric funerary odes, for grand-style panegyric of the dead.[24] By returning to the form's original brevity, Pope's inscription pointedly rejects its association with extreme length and grandiloquence. Pope designed the simple funerary monument on which the epitaph is inscribed, a small, pedimented wall tablet free of the Baroque ornamentation common in contemporaneous monuments. Thus Pope provided an epitaph and monument whose chaste, neoclassical modesty befitted his unpretentious parents.

Pope is even more modest concerning himself than concerning his father and mother. Neoclassical inscriptions normally include the name of the erector of the monument.[25] The Twickenham tablet's omission of Pope's name dramatizes his humble attitude: the famous poet omits his own name in order to affirm that the commemoration of his parents' names is more important than his own, that his ultimate identity is no more and no less than that of the pious "filius" of the truly important "Alexand[er] Pope," not the son but the father. The concluding "et sibi" signals only in the most discreet manner possible that the inscription is in fact not only the epitaph of his parents, as his prefatory reference to "their Monument" would suggest, but also his own proleptic epitaph. Pope's omission of his own name in an epitaph upon himself thus displays even more pointedly his humble piety. This self-effacing tribute to sim-

---

[23] John Sparrow, *Visible Words: A Study of Inscriptions in and as Books and Works of Art* (Cambridge: Cambridge University Press, 1969), 101–135 and passim.

[24] For lengthy seventeenth-century *carmina lapidaria*, see, for example, Richard Crashaw's 54-line inscription upon William Herrys, d. 1631, in *The Complete Poetry of Richard Crashaw*, ed. George Walton Williams (New York: Norton, 1970), 572–575; Robert Waring's 136-line pseudo-inscriptional epitaph upon Jonson in *Jonsonus Virbius* (1638), reprinted in *Ben Jonson*, ed. C. H. Herford and Percy and Evelyn Simpson, 11 vols. (Oxford: Clarendon, 1925–1952), 11:476–479; and Francis Quarles's pseudo-inscriptional 253-line "Memorials upon the Death of Sir Robert Quarles, Knight," published in 1639, in Quarles, *Complete Works in Prose and Verse*, ed. Alexander B. Grosart, 3 vols. (London, 1880–1881), 3:27–31. The Restoration poet Thomas Flatman, who composed both Pindaric funerary odes and long *carmina lapidaria*, reveals the perceived connection between the two as alternative grand-style panegyrics when he explains that his lengthy panegyric upon Prince Rupert, d. 1682, appears "not in a Pindaric but a lapidary poem" ("Non carmine Pindarico ...sed Lapidario"); see *Minor Poets of the Caroline Period*, ed. George Saintsbury, 3 vols. (Oxford: Clarendon, 1905–1921), 3:388.

[25] John Le Neve's anthology provides numerous eighteenth-century examples of the "two-part" classical form revived by the Renaissance humanists; see the first volume of *Monumenta Anglicana: Being Inscriptions on the Monuments of several Eminent Persons ... 1600–1715*, 5 vols. (London, 1718–1719), passim. Possibly by Pope, the prose inscription that accompanies his verse epitaph upon John Knight follows this convention by naming Anna Craggs, Knight's widow, as the erector of the monument (*Minor Poems*, 364).

ple, unlearned parents in learned, polished Latin is, of course, a highly self-conscious, indeed ostentatious, gesture of modesty, and underlines Pope's will to be defined as a humble son despite the famous poet's evident claims to be something more. Pope did not in fact order the words "et sibi" to be inscribed upon the Twickenham monument until his final illness, when he directed in his will that his body be buried "near the monument of my dear parents at Twickenham, with the addition after the words *filius fecit*—of these only, *et sibi: Qui obiit anno 17—aetatis—*." As he approached death, Pope stressed his desire for a modest end: he told Joseph Spence that he wanted no other epitaph besides the additions to his parents' inscription and that he desired a funeral as "plain" as the epitaph.[26] By placing the "et sibi" in a footnote to *Arbuthnot* before its actual inscription, Pope proclaims to the public that no matter how they might define him, he will affirm unto death his humble role as a dutiful son.

The determination of the poet in *Arbuthnot* to die in his "own" way is a response to the various groups who desire to "kill" him by stifling his unique identity: *his* death, he proclaims, will be the occasion for self-definition rather than for others' control and manipulation. *Arbuthnot* presents both the poet's supposed friends and outright foes as "killers" who seek to reduce him to the passivity of the dead: "Or which must end me, a Fool's Wrath or Love? / A dire Dilemma! either way I'm sped, / If Foes, they write, if Friends, they read me dead" (ll. 30–32). This description of "murderers" combines comedy and brutal reality. Pope recalls the comic Horatian topos of mad poets' killing their unwilling, passive listeners with deafening, execrable verse (*Ars Poetica*, l. 475).[27] He also registers the harsh fact that attackers in verse had indeed alluded to killing him.[28] Pope connects these reading and writing murderers to the flatterers who also attempt to "kill" him by their ludicrous attempts to assimilate his flaws to those of ancient exempla:

[26] See Pope, "The Last Will and Testament," in *Prose Works*, 2:506; and Joseph Spence, *Observations, Anecdotes, and Characters of Books and Men*, ed. James M. Osborn, 2 vols. (Oxford: Clarendon, 1966), 1:259 (no. 624). For an interesting discussion of Pope's "art of dying," see Morris R. Brownell, " 'Like Socrates': Pope's Art of Dying," *SEL* 20 (1980):407–429. Brownell demonstrates that the dying Pope imitates Socrates confronting his end as described by Plato, Montaigne, and Addison. Pope's concern for a burial and epitaph that join him to his family distinguishes him, however, from the dying Socrates, who explicitly denies that his burial is of any importance (*Phaedo* 115c–e).

[27] See also the discussion of "aural oppression" in *Arbuthnot* in J. Paul Hunter, "Satiric Apology as Satiric Instance: Pope's *Arbuthnot*," *JEGP* 68 (1969): 634–637.

[28] In "VERSES Address'd to the IMITATOR of the FIRST SATIRE of the Second Book of Horace," Lady Mary Wortley Montagu and Lord Hervey allege that Pope is "unslain" only because he is too "mean" to be killed (ll. 66–72); they further claim that his supposedly "*deathless Satire*, and *immortal Song*" (l. 86) actually kills itself, for it but "stings and dies" (l. 88). See Montagu, *Essays and Poems, and Simplicity, A Comedy*, ed. Robert Halsband and Isobel Grundy (Oxford: Clarendon, 1977), 268–269.

> —One Flatt'rer's worse than all;
> Of all mad Creatures, if the Learn'd are right,
> It is the Slaver kills, and not the Bite.
>
> (ll. 104–106)
>
>   There are, who to my Person pay their court,
> I cough like *Horace*, and tho' lean, am short,
> *Ammon*'s great Son one shoulder had too high,
> Such *Ovid*'s nose, and 'Sir! you have an Eye—'
> Go on, obliging Creatures, make me see
> All that disgrac'd my Betters, met in me:
> Say for my comfort, languishing in bed,
> 'Just so immortal *Maro* held his head:'
> And when I die, be sure you let me know
> Great *Homer* dy'd three thousand years ago.
>
> (ll. 115–124)

The flatterers compare Pope to four poets whom he translated or imitated, Horace, Ovid, Virgil, and Homer, as well as to Alexander the Great, the poet's ancient namesake. The flatterers not only humiliate him by comparing him to ancient forbears on the basis of bodily defects: they also attempt to destroy his unique identity in their obsessive search for his resemblances to the dead. They do not realize that as an imitative poet, Pope defines himself by finding not only similarities but also vital differences between himself and models from the past. Their assertions of physical similarities between him and Alexander the Great and Ovid ignore, for example, the crucial ethical differences that are the poet's concern. Their periphrastic designation "*Ammon*'s great Son" reminds us that Alexander the Great, despite the superficial resemblance in name and bodily defect to Pope, exhibited a filial impiety by denying his mortal father that is the very opposite of Pope's professions of *pietas*. Their reference to "*Ovid's* Nose," punning on the cognomen that P. Ovidius Naso ("nose") received from his father, links long-nosed Pope to a poet with a ridiculous paternal legacy that once more contrasts with Pope's assertions of filial pride. Immediately after the comparisons of the flatterers, Pope imitates the Ovidian poetic autobiography given in *Tristia* 4.10.120–146 but suggests the fundamental difference between the ancient poet and himself: while Ovid rejected the advice of his father that he pursue a political career in order to become a poet, Pope did not disobey his father in becoming a writer (ll. 129–130). The flatterers simply will not see, however, the ways in which Pope differs from classical models. Only by interrupting their comparisons can he make them reveal, despite themselves and but for a moment, that he indeed has a living identity separate from the ancients: "Sir, you have an *Eye* [I]—" (l. 118).

Pope's final suggestion that the flatterers compare him in death to Homer literalizes their desire to "kill" him by identifying him with the dead. "Three thousand years ago" recalls the description of Juvenal's bad patron who writes poetry and only concedes that Homer was a greater poet "because of a thousand years" ("Propter mille annos").[29] Just as the foolish patron can admire Homer only because he is long dead, so the flatterers can admire Pope only by assimilating him to the ancient dead. There is a further irony in the flatterers' imagined comparison of Pope and Homer in death, for Homer was the most famous example of a poet honored in death instead of being nurtured in life. Celebrating his success with the reading public in the preface to his translation of *The Iliad*, Pope favorably contrasted his own success in life with the "pompous Honours" that Homer only "receiv'd after Death."[30] Pope's great achievement as the English Homer was not that he would die like Homer, as the flatterers in *Arbuthnot* suggest, but rather that his Homeric translations earned him a material success and consequent independence that penurious Homer had sadly lacked. Jonathan Swift drew the correct contrast when he wrote a few years before *Arbuthnot*, "By Homer dead [Pope] was taught to thrive, / Which Homer never could alive / And, sits aloft on Pindus' head, / Despising slaves that cringe for bread."[31] A few years after *Arbuthnot*, Pope echoed Swift when claiming that "(thanks to *Homer*) . . . I live and thrive, / Indebted to no Prince or Peer alive" (*Horatian Imitations: Epistle II.* 2, ll. 68–69). *Arbuthnot* suggests, however, that Pope's flatterers do not wish to let him thrive in all his vital freedom from both ancient poetic paradigms and the importunities of the world.

Against such murderous opponents, Pope retreats at the very beginning of the poem into a self-chosen, fictive death ("Shut, shut the door, good *John*! fatigu'd I said, / Tye up the knocker, say I'm sick, I'm dead," ll. 1–2), from which he then delivers his attack upon the world. The epitaph announces that he has planned for himself his ultimate place of retreat, but the epitaph has to be included in, and protected by, a poem that can act out the retreat and expel all those who attempt to deny the poet his self-fashioned identity.

Pope's attack on his various opponents distinguishes him, however, from familial as well as poetic tradition. Attacking others in order to

---

[29] Juvenal, *Satire* 7.39; noted in Howard Weinbrot, *Alexander Pope and the Traditions of Formal Verse Satire* (Princeton: Princeton University Press, 1982), 254–255.

[30] I cite the text in Alexander Pope, *The Iliad of Homer, Books I–IX*, ed. Maynard Mack et al., The Twickenham Edition of Pope, vol. 7 (New Haven: Yale University Press, 1967), 25.

[31] Jonathan Swift, "A Libel on the Reverend Dr. Delany and His Excellency John, Lord Carteret," ll. 85–88 in *The Complete Poems*, ed. Pat Rogers (Harmondsworth: Penguin, 1983), 406.

defend his parents' and his own reputations, he must reject one central value of his parents' retired life:

> ...[My] Father held it for a rule
> It was a Sin to call our Neighbour Fool,
> That harmless Mother thought no Wife a Whore,—
> Hear this! and spare his Family, *James More!*
> Unspotted Names!
>
> (ll. 382–386).

The juxtaposition of "James More! / Unspotted Names" reveals the ambiguities of Pope's filial role. James Moore is presented earlier in the poem as a son who, supposedly under the influence of Pope, disobeys his father by neglecting his legal career to take up writing: "*Arthur*, whose giddy Son neglects the Laws, / Imputes to me and my damn'd works the cause" (ll. 23–24). Either the father or son (or both) has in effect confused Pope with Ovid, the poet who did disobey his father in abandoning law for poetry. Like the flatterers, the slanderers thus ignore Pope's vital difference from ancient paradigms. In attacking Moore, Pope doubly asserts his non-Ovidian filial piety, not only defending his parents from a slanderer but also attacking one who embodies filial disobedience. Nevertheless, the attack on Moore also reveals why Pope cannot simply imitate his beloved parents: in order to protect his parents' names, he must abandon their innocence.[32] While Pope's father thought it a sin to call someone a fool (l. 383), Pope's *Dunciad* of 1728 committed precisely that sin in deriving the name "Moore" from the Greek *morus*, "foolish" (*The Dunciad Variorum*, 2.46, footnote).[33]

Pope thus defines himself against his innocent father just as he defines himself against his ancient models. His inability and unwillingness wholly to imitate his father indeed parallels his inability and unwillingness wholly to imitate the major ancient model for the apologia of *Arbuthnot*, Horace. Pope's defense of his humble but virtuous father resembles in general terms Horace's famous defense of his own humble but virtuous father in *Satire* 1.6.[34] To underscore the difference between himself and Horace, however, Pope contrasts his relationship to his father with the father-son relationship described by Horace in another poem, *Satire* 1.4. In that work Horace defends his own satiric practice by saying that he

---

[32] On the necessary distance between father and son in *Arbuthnot*, see also Ripley Hotch, "The Dilemma of an Obedient Son: Pope's *Epistle to Dr. Arbuthnot*," in *Recent Essays by Several Hands on Alexander Pope*, ed. Maynard Mack and James Winn (Hamden, Conn.: Archon Books, 1980), 428–443; and Weinbrot, *Pope and Satire*, 264–268.

[33] Pope also probably wrote an invective epitaph upon Moore making fun of his name; see *Minor Poems*, 326–327, 330.

[34] See Howard Erskine-Hill, *The Augustan Idea in English Literature* (London: Edward Arnold, 1983), 314.

is but following his father's practice of pointing out to him specific examples of follies to be avoided:

Tis a habit [speaking frankly] the best of fathers taught me *for, to enable me to stay clear of follies, he would brand them, one by one, by his examples [ut fugerem exemplis vitiorum quaeque notando]*. Whenever he would encourage me to live thriftily, frugally, and content with what he had saved for me, "Do you not see," he would say, "how badly fares young Albius, and how poor is Baius? A striking lesson not to waste one's patrimony!" When he would deter me from a vulgar amour, "Don't be like Scetanus".... "Your philosopher will give you theories for shunning or seeking this or that: enough for me, if I can *uphold the rule [morem servare]* our fathers have handed down."[35]

Horace presents himself as the heir of a moralizing tradition handed down to him by his proto-satiric father. Distancing himself from both his own father and the Horatian tradition, Pope reveals that he unfortunately cannot follow *his* father's "rule" (l. 382) of avoiding satiric attack. While Horace's father is for the Roman poet a simple model for imitation, both Pope's father and Horace's text serve the English poet as foils for his sometimes difficult but always necessary self-definition. Pope's exclamation at the end of the panegyric of his father, "Oh grant me thus to live! and thus to die!" testifies to his genuine filial piety. Nevertheless, like his wish for a country estate in "Ode on Solitude," Pope's desire to live and die like his father could not, as the poet knew, be fulfilled.[36] Pope's self-definition in the family epitaph seeks to lessen the unavoidable distance between father and son by exchanging the role of satirist for that of pious son. The family epitaph is, however, included in a footnote to verses that necessarily qualify and complicate this self-definition by revealing that Pope the satirist has a relation to his father that is neither Alexander the Great's, nor Ovid's, nor Arthur Moore's filial impiety nor Horace's straightforward filial imitation. Pope has no simple model, literary or historical, for his relation to his father. His sense of what it is to be a loyal son unto death is very much, perforce, his "own."

[35] "... insuevit pater optimus hoc me, / ut fugerem exemplis vitiorum quaeque notando. / cum me hortaretur, parce frugaliter atque / viverem uti contentus eo, quod mi ipse parasset: / 'nonne vides, Albi ut male vivat filius, utque / Baius inops? magnum documentum, ne patriam rem / perdere quis velit.' a turpi meretricis amore / cum deterreret: 'Scetani dissimilis sis.' /..../... 'sapiens, vitatu quidque petitu, / sit melius, causas reddet tibi: mi satis est, si / traditum ab antiquis morem servare'" (Horace, *Satire* 1.4.105–112, 115–117).

[36] Pope was always aware of the cost of poetry, how it could separate one from one's family and some of one's deepest personal values. In a letter of 1724 to Henry St. John, viscount Bolingbroke, Pope asked rhetorically, "To write well, lastingly well, Immortally well, must not one leave Father and Mother and cleave unto the Muse?" (*Correspondence*, 2:227).

By claiming in a footnote to *Arbuthnot* that he wishes to be buried in Twickenham Parish Church and to be remembered as a virtuous son, Pope hints to the reading public that he does not wish to be buried and commemorated in Westminster Abbey as a famous poet. Beginning in the Middle Ages, England's kings and many of the nobility had been buried in the Abbey, and since the early seventeenth century England's major poets had often been honored with Abbey burial and commemoration.[37] The Abbey, "where Kings and Poets lye" (as Pope notes in his imitation of Horace's *Epistle* 1.6, l. 51), consequently symbolized the supposed harmony between England's social and literary elite. Contemporaries might well have assumed that Pope, who was deeply involved in the commemoration of various poets in the Abbey, would himself wish to be buried there.[38] Pope's Catholicism would presumably not have precluded Abbey burial, since Pope's great Catholic predecessor Dryden had been buried in the Abbey when anti-Catholic sentiment was stronger than in Pope's own times. However, although Pope himself encouraged the erection of Abbey tombs in honor of Dryden and John Gay, *Arbuthnot* associates the Abbey with the social elite's mistreatment of these two poets (ll. 247–260). While the "great" give Dryden a magnificent funeral in the Abbey after having ignored the living poet (ll. 247–248), they refuse to finance Gay's Abbey burial and monument just as they neglected him when alive (ll. 256–258). Immediately after presenting Dryden and Gay as passive victims in death of aristocratic whim or disregard, Pope declares his resolve to be his own man, in death as in life: "Oh let me live my own! and die so too!" (l. 261). The Twickenham inscription indeed proves Pope's determination to die in his own way rather than to become a pawn of great men, honored or spurned in the Abbey.

Pope's "Epitaph. *For One who would not be buried in Westminster-Abbey*,"

[37] Chaucer and Spenser had both been buried in the Abbey not because they were great poets but because they died in Westminster. By the time a monument was erected to Spenser in the early seventeenth century, however, the Abbey was regarded as the proper place of burial for England's major poets. Thus Drayton in 1631 and Jonson in 1637 were buried in the Abbey in honor of their achievements as poets. See Arthur Penrhyn Stanley, *Historical Memorials of Westminster Abbey*, 3 vols. (New York: Anson D. F. Randolph, 1888), 2:106–115.

[38] On Pope's involvement in Poets' Corner, see Brownell, *Pope and the Arts*, 339–356. John Dart's "Westminster Abbey: A Poem" (1721), which Pope owned, concludes its panegyric survey of the poets buried in the Abbey by noting the inevitability of Congreve's and Pope's deaths with the clear implication that these two will take their rightful place amongst the great poets buried and commemorated in the Abbey. See Dart, "Westminster Abbey: A Poem" in *Westmonasterium, or The History and Antiquities of the Abbey Church of St. Peters Westminster*, 2 vols. (London, n.d.), 1:xliii. Maynard Mack lists Pope's copy of the poem in *Collected in Himself: Essays Critical, Biographical, and Bibliographical on Pope and Some of his Contemporaries* (Newark: University of Delaware Press, 1982), 405.

published in 1738, makes explicit the poet's rejection of the Abbey as the symbol of the alliance between poets and the "great":

> Heroes and Kings! your distance keep:
> In peace let one poor Poet sleep,
> Who never flatter'd Folks like you:
> Let Horace blush, and Virgil too.[39]

The epitaph's title is ambiguous: Pope suggests both that he would not be considered worthy of burial in the Abbey and, more importantly, that he would not choose to be buried there even if he were deemed acceptable. Though the epitaph might be read as an explanation of Pope's determination to be buried in Twickenham Parish Church, the poem does not specify where the poet desires to be buried but instead simply defines his burial place in opposition to the Abbey. In *Arbuthnot* Pope refuses to be flattered *to* death; in this epigram he proleptically refuses whatever chance he might have of being flattered *in* death by those whom he refused to flatter in life. He distinguishes himself, "one poor Poet," from the normal run of poets, who, he implies, flatter the great and are in turn "honored" in the Abbey with visits from, and burial near, those they flattered. Using brevity for a seemingly self-deflating, comic epitaph, Pope in fact proudly parades his own apparent lowliness, converting supposed concessions of weakness into assertions of strength. The title's announcement of the (self-)banishment of the poet from the Abbey gives way to the poet's grandiloquent banishment of "Heroes, and Kings" from his burial place. While the second line requests that the exalted of the realm not disturb the peace of "one poor Poet," the mock humility of the line is reversed by the third line's proud declaration that this supposedly humble poet never flattered such men.

Pope's contrast between "one poor Poet" and the kings of the Abbey exemplifies and promotes a crucial shift in cultural authority. The monarchy suffered considerable loss of power and prestige in the post-1688 period, with the abolishment of divine right succession and the establishment of an (increasingly) constitutional monarchy. During the same period men of letters like Addison and Pope rose in status as success and recognition in the literary marketplace made them increasingly independent of court and aristocratic patronage. The relative worth of monarchs and men of letters consequently became a resonant synecdoche for the continuing conflict between lineage and personal merit as determinants of social value. In a poem of the 1720s on Westminster Abbey, John Dart expresses joy that the dust of Addison is mingled with that of monarchs; he goes on, however, to assert that just as Virgil's

---

[39] Pope, *Minor Poems*, 376.

tomb has outlasted that of Augustus, so Addison's monument will last longer than any king's.[40] In his *Letters Concerning the English Nation* (1733), Voltaire notes the veneration Englishmen feel for their men of letters and contends that visitors to Westminster Abbey admire "not the mausoleums of the *English* Kings, but the Monuments... of those illustrious Men who contributed to its Glory."[41] Expressing his own particular contempt for monarchs during the reign of George II, Pope radicalizes the contrast between a writer of genius and mere royalty by rejecting any association with the Abbey and its regal monuments.

Pope's dismissive coupling of "heroes" with "kings" participates in yet another major cultural trend, the devaluation of traditional notions of heroism. The so-called "heroes" are those whose military valor gained them Abbey burial.[42] Since military leaders normally came from the aristocracy, such "heroes" conveniently embodied the aristocracy's original role and raison d'être as the warrior class. Although the cult of aristocratic, military valor by no means died in the early eighteenth century, it experienced great strain.[43] Memories of the Civil Wars encouraged, as we have seen, the idealization of martyrs rather than conquerors and thereby undermined the traditional image of the military hero. The partisan politics of the late seventeenth and early eighteenth centuries ensured that one party's glorious cause was the opposing party's ignominious and unprofitable slaughter, and that one party's patriotic hero was the opposing party's exemplum of destructiveness and lust for absolute power. The outpouring of panegyric and satiric epitaphs upon one figure, John Churchill, the duke of Marlborough, reveals just how divided were the attitudes of the nation toward its "heroes."[44] In recognition of his military services to the nation, Marlborough was buried in 1722 with splendid funerary pomp in the Henry VII chapel of the

[40] Dart, 1:xl.

[41] Voltaire, *Letters Concerning the English Nation* (London, 1733), 226.

[42] In 1722 Pope's Jacobite friend Francis Atterbury, then dean of the Abbey, wrote to Pope that he was building a Abbey monument for his wife and himself "as far from Kings and Kaisars, as the space will admit of" (Pope, *Correspondence*, 2:114). Pope's "heroes" are the equivalent of Atterbury's "kaisars."

[43] For various discussions of the decline of traditional notions of heroism from the late seventeenth through the eighteenth century, see the essays in Robert Folkenflik, ed., *The English Hero, 1660–1800* (Newark: University of Delaware Press, 1982).

[44] Numerous epitaphs upon Marlborough, both panegyric and satiric, are summarized and quoted in Robert D. Horn, ed., *Marlborough: A Survey* (New York: Garland, 1975), 480–511. Though it includes its Whig author's own panegyric epitaph upon Marlborough, Bernard Mandeville's *The Fable of the Bees: Part II* (1729) presents sharply contrasting assessments of Marlborough as examples of the difficulty of "unbiass'd" judgment; see *The Fable of the Bees, or, Private Vices, Publick Benefits*, ed. F. B. Kaye, 2 vols. (Oxford: Clarendon, 1924), 2:336–339. Voltaire notes that the "Spirit of Party" was so pronounced in England that he met people who claimed Marlborough was a coward (pp. 220–221).

Abbey.[45] Many Whig elegies and epitaphs affirmed his heroic status and celebrated his joining England's kings in death. Elkanah Settle, the official poet of the City of London and one of Pope's dunces, applauded Marlborough's burial near "Royal Dust," while another versifier praised Marlborough, "left among the Kings to sleep."[46] Tories who had opposed Marlborough's continental wars and been critical of his alleged cowardice and financial corruption ridiculed, by contrast, the deceased and his lavish Westminster Abbey funeral.[47] Pope's friend Francis Atterbury, who had to officiate at the funeral as dean of the Abbey, told a sympathetic Pope that he viewed the funeral as "the last Scene of Pompous Vanity."[48] Swift composed a satiric elegy that dispatched Marlborough as one of the "bubbles raised by breath of kings."[49] Using Marlborough as one of its satiric exemplum, Pope's An Essay on Man ridiculed military "heroes" for the violent propensities that cause them to make "an enemy of all mankind" (4.222).[50] A Whig epitaph upon Marlborough celebrated the hero's blending in death with England's poets as well as kings: "So! kings and bards their ashes round him blend, / Ambitious once the hero to befriend."[51] In his epitaph upon himself, by contrast, Pope the "poor Poet" refuses to be part of such a club. His dismissal of "heroes" so that he can lie in his grave in "peace" deflates traditional heroic ideals by wittily suggesting that Pope will not allow the bellicose, who have destroyed so many people's peace, to disturb the dead poet's.

The epitaph implicitly represents the poet himself as the true hero. In the final line Pope suggests that his independence makes him morally superior to the two ancient models, Horace and Virgil, who most shaped his literary career. The four-line poem thereby transforms Pope's designations of himself as the unnamed "one" of the title and the anonymous "one poor Poet" in the second line from gestures of modesty into proud assertions of his uniqueness against the duality, and perhaps duplicity, of his opening and closing binary opponents: "Heroes, and Kings" and "Horace...and Virgil." The poem indeed recalls the solitary, heroic

[45] For a discussion of the funeral and various contemporaneous comments upon it, see James Sutherland, Background for Queen Anne (London: Methuen, 1939), 204–224.

[46] Elkanah Settle, "THRENODIA BRITTANICA. A Funeral Oblation To THE MEMORY OF...MARLBOROUGH" (1723); and Arthur D'Anvers, "The FUNERAL, A Poem in Memory of...Marlborough" (1725); cited in Horn, 508, 517.

[47] See Sutherland, 206.

[48] Pope, Correspondence, 2:129.

[49] Swift, "A Satirical Elegy on the Death of a Late Famous General," in Swift, 242.

[50] Pope later expanded and made more explicit the attack upon Marlborough in an unpublished satiric portrait; see "[A Character]" in Pope, Minor Poems, 358–359.

[51] "EPITAPH on the Duke of Marlborough, translated," Gentleman's Magazine 23 (1753):484. This is a translation of a Latin epitaph, "Epitaphium in Ducem MARLBURIENSEM," published in Gentleman's Magazine 23 (1753): 437. The Latin epitaph was presumably written shortly after Marlborough's burial in the Abbey and certainly written before the removal of his body to Blenheim Palace in 1744.

figure in the *Epilogue to the Satires*, published in the same year, the "one" who is to be memorialized for his defiance of a social order wholly consumed by corruption: "All, all look up, with reverential Awe, / On Crimes that scape, or triumph o'er the Law: . . . / Yet may this Verse (if such a Verse remain) / Show there was one who held it in disdain" (*Dialogue* 1, ll. 167–168, 171–172).

Pope's critique of Horace and Virgil has topical relevance, for the supporters and opponents of the Hanoverian-Walpole regime used the ancient poets as polemical counters in their propaganda, with the pro-government party enlisting the "court poets" Horace and Virgil on their side and critics of the government attacking the ancient "court fawners."[52] Pope the (supposedly) poor but independent poet contrasts himself with the Roman poets who received gifts from the emperor Augustus (Horace, *Epistle* 2.1.245–247).[53] The poet who scorns burial among the heroes and kings he did not flatter pointedly defines himself against Horace, who, according to Suetonius, was buried beside his patron Maecenas, the aristocratic advisor of Augustus whom Horace praises at the opening of his *Odes* as "sprung from royal stock."[54]

Pope, however, does not wholly reject his ancient Roman models but instead uses them as foils for the purpose of self-affirmation. His assertion of superiority to Horace and Virgil is based on values ultimately derived from the ancient poets themselves.[55] Representing the humble poet of retirement as a heroic ideal, Pope is indebted to Horatian and Virgilian retirement poetry, particularly as mediated by Cowley's *Essays*. Indeed, Pope adopts the combination of epitaphic self-definition and simultaneous imitation and critique of Horatian-Virgilian poetry from Cowley's "Epitaphium Vivi Auctoris."[56] Pope follows Cowley in rejecting the great and asserting the moral superiority of the modern poet to his

[52] See Howard D. Weinbrot, *Augustus Caesar in "Augustan" England: The Decline of a Classical Norm* (Princeton: Princeton University Press, 1978), 120–149; and Erskine-Hill, 324–325.

[53] I am indebted to Howard Weinbrot for this suggestion.

[54] "Maecenas atavis edite regibus" (Horace, *Ode* 1.1.1). The concluding sentence of Suetonius's *Vita Horati* notes that Horace was buried "near the tomb of Maecenas" ("iuxta Maecenatis tumulum").

[55] The extent to which Pope in general accepts or rejects the persona and values of Horace has been extensively debated, but the most important proponents of what one may reductively call a "Horatian" and an "anti-Horatian" Pope, Howard Erskine-Hill and Howard Weinbrot, both explore, despite very different emphases, Pope's portrayal of both his similarities to and differences from Horace. Erskine-Hill argues that Pope's *Horatian Imitations*, like all great works of imitation, seek "points of significant difference as well as identification" with their models (p. 291), while Weinbrot concedes that Pope found in Horace a "sympathetic voice" and at least some "norms" that could serve as a standard (*Pope and Satire*, 333). I differ from both critics in emphasizing Pope's use of Horatian "norms" precisely in order to assert his own difference from, and superiority to, the ancient poet.

[56] The poem was reprinted in *Spectator* 551; see *The Spectator*, 4:475–476.

ancient models, Horace and Virgil. While Cowley treats retirement as a kind of death, Pope treats death, just as he did in "Ode on Solitude," as the ultimate form of retirement.[57] Pope's request that he be allowed to sleep in peace wittily combines two epitaphic motifs, the comic epitaphic wish that the passerby not awaken the deceased sleeping in his grave and the Catholic epitaphic prayer, *Requiescat in pace*.[58] Pope's request also adapts, however, a Horatian wish for the untroubled sleep of the humble, retired countryman. Cowley's various translations of Horace in the *Essays* reveal the connection between peaceful sleep and retirement:

> Sleep is a God too proud to wait in Palaces
> And yet so humble too as not to scorn
> The meanest Country Cottages....
>
> *(Ode 3. 1)*
>
> Is it not there [in retirement] that sleep (and only there)
> Nor noise without, nor cares within does fear?
>
> *(Epistle 1.10)*[59]

As a "poor Poet" who wishes for the sleep granted only to the humble in Roman poetry, Pope banishes those who would disturb such sleep. In

[57] In three of the letters in which Pope compares his retirement to death (see note 11), he imagines that an epitaph upon himself could or should be written: "I fear I must be forc'd... to write my own Epitaph"; "It would be like writing my own Epitaph to acquaint you... where I now repose"; "[Pope] is no longer a subject for any thing but an Epitaph" (*Correspondence* 1:87, 1:348, 4:227). "Heroes, and Kings" reverses the tenor-vehicle relationship between retirement and death found in both Cowley's epitaph upon himself and Pope's own musings upon the genre.

[58] As I discussed in Chapter 3, note 23, *Requiescat in pace* and *R.I.P* began to appear on English Catholic tombstones in the early eighteenth century. Pope's witty adaptation of the epitaphic formula plays on an ambiguity in its interpretation. Some eighteenth-century Catholic inscriptions make explicit that *Requiescat in pace* is a prayer for the repose of the soul. The conclusion of the inscription upon Lady Barbara Webb, d. 1740, for example, declares: "She made it her death bed request... that the repose of her soul may be remembered by all good Christians. This tomb was erected by her disconsolate husband. *Requiescat in pace*. Amen" (included in Frederick Teague Cansick, ed., *A Collection of Curious and Interesting Epitaphs... of Saint Pancras, Middlesex* [London, 1869], 2:38). The normal absence of explicit reference to the soul, however, licensed readers to interpret the phrase as a wish for the body's peaceful repose in the grave. While Pope here adapts the formula for a comic request, in "Elegy to the Memory of an Unfortunate Lady" (l. 69) he adapts it to give solemn religious significance to the body's rest in the grave. Later English Protestant poets also adapt the formula to express reverential concern for the repose of the body.

[59] Cowley, *Essays*, 435, 417. See also the evocation of untroubled sleep in Cowley's translation of Horace's *Epode* 2 (*Essays*, 413). Horatian poems not translated by Cowley similarly associate sleep and retirement: see *Odes* 2.16 and 3.4. Other retirement poems in Cowley's *Essays* also link the two. One such, after favorably contrasting the life of a simple countryman with that of any "king" or "hero," ends with the wish, "Let my Life sleep, and learn to love her End" (*Essays*, 420). In the retirement poem he wrote at thirteen, Cowley asks for "sleep, as undisturb'd as Death" (*Essays*, 457). Reversing the topos, Pope seeks a death as undisturbed as sleep.

so doing he demonstrates that he is true to the values Horace and Virgil only purported to uphold. The first line's sending the great away resembles epitaphs that send off those who would profane the dead: "Let no profane ignoble foot tread neere / This hallow'd peece of Earth" begins an early seventeenth-century epitaph.[60] The line also recalls, however, the opening of Horace's *Ode* 3.1, which banishes the "profanum vulgus" before launching into its celebration of country sleep. Cowley's rendering of Horace's line as "Hence, ye Profane; I hate ye all / Both the Great, Vulgar, and the small" transformed Horace's rejection of a low-class, uncultured "vulgus" into the poet's rejection of all those, high and low, who could not comprehend, and were in danger of disturbing, his retirement.[61] Pope goes beyond Cowley to complete the reversal of Horace's sense by sending off a "vulgus" now identified as the great "Folks" alone, the heroes and kings that the poet must banish to safeguard his peace and quiet.

Pope's critique of Horace and Virgil as flatterers is especially pointed because the two ancients, in their personae as humble, retired poets, delighted in the *recusatio*, purportedly declining to praise great men but in fact managing to praise in the very process of refusal. In *Ode* 2.12, for example, Horace claims that he could not adequately sing of "Caesar's battles and of kings, once threatening, led by the neck along the streets," even though this ode and much of his other poetry is filled with praise of Augustus's achievements.[62] Pope's claim that the Augustan poets should blush for flattering the great indeed turns a Horatian *recusatio* against Horace. In *Epistle* 2.1, addressed to Augustus, Horace declines to praise the Roman leader on the grounds that he would only embarrass the *princeps*, and contends that he would himself not want inept praise "lest I have to blush at the stupid gift."[63] Horace thereby manages indirectly to flatter Augustus's good taste. In his imitation of the epistle, Pope turns this *recusatio* into an authentic refusal to praise George II, and expands Horace's line to "Well may he blush, who gives it ["a vile Encomium"], or receives" (l. 414), thus transforming Horace's flattery into his own proud refusal to praise or be praised in a way that would cause himself to blush.[64] Pope thus makes the Roman fiction of the poet who avoids praising great men into a modern truth.

[60] Henry King, "An Epitaph on his most honour'd Freind [*sic*] Richard Earle of Dorset," ll. 1–2 in *The Poems of Henry King*, ed. Margaret Crum (Oxford: Clarendon, 1965), 67.

[61] Cowley, *Essays*, 434.

[62] "...proelia Caesaris, /...ductaque per vias / regum colla minacium" (*Ode* 2.12.10–12). For other Horatian *recusationes*, see Horace, *Odes* 1.6, 4.2 and *Satire* 4.1; and the discussion in R. G. M. Nisbet and Margaret Hubbard, *A Commentary on Horace: Odes*, 2 vols. (Oxford: Clarendon, 1970–1978), 1:81–83, 2:179–180.

[63] "...ne rubeam pingui donatus munere" (Horace, *Epistle* 2.1.267).

[64] On the difference between Horace's and Pope's line and its relevance to "Heroes, and Kings!" see also Weinbrot, *Augustus Caesar*, 211–212.

This epitaph clearly presents the two aspects of the self central to Pope's various epitaphic self-definitions: the satirist whose voice attacks and thus distances others and the "poor Poet," described in the third person, who sleeps protected by the attacking voice. Just as in *Arbuthnot* the poet must defend his own integrity unto death by expelling slanderers and flatterers from his retreat, so here the poet can only sleep peacefully by expelling his adversaries. In arguing that the peaceful sleep of death-as-retirement requires not Horatian-Virgilian deference to, but rather the banishment of, the great, Pope takes up a theme he explored some five years earlier in his imitation of Horace's *Satire* 2.1. The juxtaposition of two passages from the satire reveals the intimate connection between attack and sleep:

> Not write? But then I *think*,
> And for my Soul I cannot sleep a wink.
> I nod in Company, I wake at Night,
> Fools rush into my Head, and so I write.
> (ll. 11–14)

> Yes, while I live, no rich or noble knave
> Shall walk the World, in credit, to his grave.
> To VIRTUE ONLY and HER FRIENDS, A FRIEND,
> The World beside may murmur, or commend.
> Know, all the distant Din that World can keep
> Rolls o'er my *Grotto*, and but sooths my Sleep.
> (ll. 119–124)

In the original passage imitated in the first quotation above, Horace simply says that he writes because he cannot sleep ("verum nequeo dormire," l. 7), while Pope explains his own sleeplessness by suggesting that his interiority is threatened when "Fools rush into my Head." He writes in order to expel such fools. The second passage reveals that once he has attacked his adversaries, he can at last rest, for he draws an implicit connection, unparalleled in Horace, between his attack on "the rich and noble knave," who must be allowed no "credit" unto his "grave," and his own peaceful sleep in his Twickenham grotto, uncontaminated by the evil world that has been expelled. The juxtaposition of Pope's grotto and his opponent's grave clearly suggests that the poet's sleep of retirement is a beneficent form of "death" to the world and that the lapidary phrase "To VIRTUE ONLY and HER FRIENDS, A FRIEND," is a kind of epitaph upon the poet. One may compare Pope's description of his "Burial (at Twitnam)" from a letter of 1740 concerning his grotto.[65] But

---

[65] Pope, *Correspondence*, 4:227. Ann Badger's essay on Pope suggests the association of grotto and grave and the similarity of Pope's self-defining motto to an epitaph. The former association is not original to Pope. Both Charles Cotton and Pope's older contemporary Anne Finch, Lady Winchilsea, explicitly associate a "cave" of retirement and the grave:

as in the epitaph, so here Pope emphasizes that he cannot retire—into sleep, into death—except by violently forcing the "World" away.[66]

Pope's expulsion of the great in his epitaph distinguishes him not only from the classical retirement poets but also from his immediate predecessor in the epitaph upon oneself, Cowley. Despite Cowley's advocacy of retirement, the Restoration poet was buried with great ceremony in the Abbey.[67] The prefatory elegies in eighteenth century editions of Cowley's works present the poet's burial among kings as an appropriate honor: one anonymous elegist claims that "it was fit / Amongst our Kings to lay the King of Wit," while Denham hails Cowley's burial where "poets near our Princes sleep."[68] Cowley the anticourt poet of retirement was thus posthumously remade into a laureate poet exemplifying the harmony of the political and cultural orders.[69] In *Windsor-Forest* (1713), which wholeheartedly praised a Stuart monarch, Pope could proudly recall the "sad Pomp" (l. 274) of his fellow-poet Cowley's funeral. In the Hanoverian 1730s, however, Pope, contemptuous of all funerary associations of poets and kings, proleptically refuses Westminster Abbey as his own burial place and thereby spurns the absorption into the status quo that Cowley underwent in death.

"And Solitude in a dark Cave, / Where all things husht, and silent be, / Resembleth so the quiet Grave, / That there I would prepare to flee" (Cotton, "The World. Ode," ll. 51–54 in *Poems of Charles Cotton*, ed. John Buxton [London: Routledge, 1958], 243); "Had he [Crassus]... / Made that lonely wond'rous Cave / Both his Palace, and his Grave, / Peace and Rest he might have found, / (Peace and Rest are under Ground)" ("The Petition for an Absolute Retreat," ll. 229–233 in *The Poems of Anne Countess of Winchilsea*, ed. Myra Reynolds [Chicago: University of Chicago Press, 1903], 75). Pope's association of grotto and grave is further suggested by his (probably unconscious) echo in the couplet "Know, all the distant Din that World can keep / Rolls o'er my *Grotto*, and but sooths my Sleep" of Charles Cotton's Pindaric ode, "Death." Cotton proclaims that the noise of the world cannot disturb us when we sleep in our graves—"Nor all the rattle, that above they [the living] keep, / [Can] Break our repose, or rouse us from that everlasting sleep"—and dismisses anyone who desires to attack the dead—"all the clutter [i.e., "noisy turmoil or disturbance, hubbub," *OED* 4] he can keep / Will only serve to rock us whilst we soundly sleep" (*Poems of Charles Cotton: 1630–1687*, ed. John Beresford [London: Richard Cobden Sanderson, 1923], 222–223).

[66] Pope also connects attacking the world and peaceful sleep in *Arbuthnot*: "Out with it, *Dunciad*! let the secret pass, / That Secret to each Fool, that he's an Ass: / The truth once told, (and wherefore shou'd we lie?) / The Queen of *Midas* slept, and so may I" (ll. 79–82). While the "secret" that every fool is an "Ass" is based on Persius, *Satire* 1.9–12, 119–121, Pope's claim that he can sleep after telling this secret is his own. Though Pope does not develop the connection between peaceful sleep and retirement here, the passage reenforces *Arbuthnot's* dramatization of Pope's attacking the world in order to protect his retreat from it.

[67] See Stanley, *Historical Memorials*, 2:117–118.

[68] I cite *The Works of Mr. Abraham Cowley*, 2 vols. (London, 1710), 1:lxx, lxxvi.

[69] Also included in eighteenth-century editions of Cowley, Thomas Sprat's biography of his friend further associates the dead poet with the monarchy by recounting that Charles II "was pleas'd to bestow on him [Cowley] the best Epitaph, when ... his Majesty declar'd, *That Mr. Cowley had not left a better Man behind him in* England"; see *Works of Cowley*, xliii.

In his epitaph, Pope also echoes, but distances himself from, another well-known epitaph, a quatrain by the poet's older contemporary Matthew Prior:

> Nobles, and Heralds by Your leave,
> Here lyes what Once was MATTHEW PRIOR,
> The Son of Adam and of Eve,
> Can STUART, or NASSAW go higher.[70]

Pope's four-line, tetrameter epitaph has a formal similarity to Prior's composition. The two poems have similar openings ("Heroes, and Kings" recalling "Nobles, and Heralds") and similar proclamations of the poet's value against that of kings. Prior uses comic brevity to deflate supposed greatness and thereby advances his own claims as a son of Adam and Eve every bit as deserving of commemoration as pompous kings. His serio-comic epitaph was very popular throughout the eighteenth century for its jaunty deflation of kings and its assertion of a commoner's worth.[71] Despite his declaration that plain "MATTHEW PRIOR" was as good as "STUART, or NASSAW," Prior himself left five hundred pounds in his will for a grandiose monument in the Abbey with a long panegyric prose inscription declaring his great services to two monarchs, his rise to knighthood, and his literary achievements. Contemporaries criticized Prior for the vanity of erecting his own monument in the Abbey.[72] Pope himself spoke dismissively of Prior's monument and inscription.[73] Pope

[70] Matthew Prior, "Epitaph," in *The Literary Works of Matthew Prior*, ed. H. Bunker Wright and Monroe K. Spears, 2 vols. (Oxford: Clarendon, 1959), 1:195.

[71] Prior's epitaph was first published in 1721. Many different versions and answers were published in the years immediately following (see Wright's and Spear's commentary, 2:885), and its frequent reprinting suggests that it remained popular through the 1730s and 1740s: see, for example, [William Oldys, ed.], *A Collection of Epigrams*, 2d ed., 2 vols. (London, 1735–1737), 1:H1v; *Gentleman's Magazine* 15 (1745):217; and *London Magazine* 18 (1749):464.

[72] James Ralph criticizes Prior for "extending ... vanity beyond the grave"; see [Ralph], *A Critical Review of the Publick Buildings, Statues and Ornaments, In, and about London and Westminster* (London, 1734), 79. In his letter-writing manual, Samuel Richardson has a young lady claim that the monument "serves only to proclaim his [Prior's] vanity, being erected at his own desire and expence"; see *Familiar Letters on Important Occasions* (1741), ed. Brian W. Downs (London: George Routledge, 1928), 211. An early eighteenth-century epigram similarly attacks Prior's monument; see "On MATTHEW PRIOR," in *A New Select Collection of Epitaphs*, ed. T. Webb, 2 vols. (London, 1775), 1:137.

[73] In a 1728 letter to Lord Bathurst, Pope claims that he would rather spend money for an obelisk in Bathurst's garden than for a memorial like "Priors [*sic*] to Westminster" (*Correspondence* 2:525). Citing a remark Pope made to Spence (see Spence, no. 215, 1:93), Brownell plausibly suggests that Pope disapproved of the monument and epitaph because both the iconography and the inscription glorify Prior's writing of a history at the time of his death, a task for which Pope held Prior unfit (*Pope and Arts*, 344–345). I suspect, however, that like Ralph and Richardson, Pope was also more generally contemptuous of Prior's buying himself a monument in the Abbey.

was probably attacking the author of Prior's epitaph, Robert Freind, in an epigram written in 1736, only two years before the publication of Pope's epitaph on himself:

> Friend! for your Epitaphs I'm griev'd,
>   Where still so much is said,
> One half will never be believ'd,
>   The other never read.[74]

In his epitaph on himself, Pope follows Prior's verse epitaph in its brevity and debunking of greatness. At the same time, he implicitly criticizes Prior for wanting to be buried in Westminster Abbey with an absurd encomium. By echoing Prior but announcing his refusal of Abbey burial, Pope suggests that he will be serious, unlike Prior, in his rejection of the great. By differentiating his composition from both Cowley's and Prior's similar epitaphs, Pope attempts to compose the authentic and definitive version of the proud, independent epitaph upon oneself.

Pope's project of dying in his own way had no natural terminus short of his actual death. He composed yet another epitaph on himself, published anonymously in 1741:

> Under this Marble, or under this Sill,
> Or under this Turf, or e'en what they will;
> Whatever an Heir, or a Friend in his stead,
> Or any good Creature shall lay o'er my Head;
> Lies He who ne'er car'd, and still cares not a Pin,
> What they said, or may say of the Mortal within.
> But who living and dying, serene still and free,
> Trusts in God, that as well as he was, he shall be.[75]

There is a palpable letting go of the self here not present in the earlier epitaphs. While in earlier compositions Pope defined his ultimate self implicitly or explicitly against others' definitions and gave himself a final resting place of his own in opposition to others' attempts to "bury" him, here with comic exuberance Pope imagines himself "serene ... and free" despite his supposed uncertainty as to where and by whom he will be buried. He nevertheless still bases his epitaphic self-definition on the creation of a place of retreat free from the outside world: wherever and by whomever he is buried, Pope lays claim to a grave as an enclosure that will ensure, like his grotto, the separation of the outside world from

[74] Pope, "EPIGRAM. *On One who made long Epitaphs*," in *Minor Poems*, 363.
[75] Pope, "EPITAPH. *On Himself*," in *Minor Poems*, 386.

the "Mortal within." Though the poem ends with the poet's trust that he need not worry about self-definition because of an other, God, who will affirm rather than challenge the self, Pope must imagine his retreat from men in order to make contact with this protecting other.

The ultimate paradox of the poem, as David B. Morris points out, is that "Pope wishes to be remembered as not caring how he is remembered."[76] A related paradox is his need to define his serene indifference concerning men's opinions against other men's lack of such serenity. Johnson pointed out that the epitaph borrows its uncertainty as to where and by whom the deceased will be buried from Ludovico Ariosto's neo-Latin epitaph upon himself.[77] Ariosto's epitaph begins with his name ("Ludovico Ariosto's bones are buried [here]") and ends with the request that the epitaph be inscribed upon whatever monument is provided for the dead, so that the spirit of the deceased can find its "own ashes" at the Last Judgment.[78] The name that Ariosto can playfully imagine will help his soul at the end of time will in the meantime identify his monument for posterity. Though the wry acknowledgment of the uncertainty of things human gives a comic, self-deflating tone to the poem, the Italian poet expresses a desire for posthumous fame: if he should be buried, he wants people to know who he is. Pope's anonymous epitaph, with its final trust in God, defines itself against this pursuit of fame and consequent dependence upon men.

Pope's stance is more directly defined, however, against that of his major English predecessor in the serio-comic epitaph. The final couplet of assurance is written in a meter unusual in Pope's poetry, anapestic tetrameter.[79] Both this meter and the willful nonchalance of the poem recall another of Prior's epitaphs on himself, which concludes as follows:

> If his Bones lye in Earth, roll in Sea, fly in Air
>   To Fate We must yeild, and the things are the same,
> And if passing Thou giv'st Him a Smile, or a Tear
>   He cares not—Yet prythee be kind to his Fame.[80]

While Prior claims that it does not truly matter what happens to his corpse, the final couplet qualifies his nonchalance: he "cares not" whether

[76] David B. Morris provides a sensitive close reading of the poem but does not discuss its models in *Alexander Pope: The Genius of Sense* (Cambridge: Harvard University Press, 1984), 28–32.

[77] See Samuel Johnson, "Life of Pope," in *Lives of the English Poets*, ed. G. B. Hill, 3 vols. (Oxford: Clarendon, 1905), 3:272. (Johnson omits, however, the last five lines of the Ariosto epitaph.)

[78] "Ludovici Areosti humantur ossa" (Ludovico Ariosto, "For his own tomb," in *Renaissance Latin Verse: An Anthology*, ed. Alessandro Perosa and John Sparrow [Chapel Hill: University of North Carolina Press, 1979], 182–183).

[79] See Morris, 32.

[80] Matthew Prior, "For His own Epitaph," in Prior, 1:410.

men give him "a Smile, or a Tear" as they regard his (full or empty) monument because either gesture would be an appropriate sign of approbation for this serio-comic poet, but he does hope that people are "kind to his Fame." The poet's self-mocking tone, his humorous sense of his own vanity and frailty, attempts to charm the reader. Pope, who purportedly "cares not a pin" about what people say, rejects such a final plea for man's beneficence. Even while he declares that he looks to God instead of man for ultimate self-definition, Pope still feels the need to define himself against men who look to man for *their* self-definition. In a letter of 1710 the young Pope wonders whether "'tis a kind of Sacrilege ...to steal Epitaphs?"[81] Instead of stealing others' epitaphs, he continually rewrites them in order to affirm through emulative struggle what is, finally, his "own."

[81] Pope, *Correspondence*, 1:87.

Chapter 9

Grafting Fame:
Pope and the Dilemmas
of Epitaphic Praise

Commemorating the worthy is a central task of Pope's poetry, early and late. Pope, who in his epitaphs upon himself continually fights against slander and flattery, likewise struggles throughout his career to avoid these vices in his epitaphs upon others. In the dream vision of *The Temple of Fame* (1715) the young poet learns that he should save the virtuous from slander and oblivion in order to gain "honest Fame" (l. 524) for himself.[1] By writing benevolent epitaphs upon those who would otherwise be misjudged or forgotten, Pope extends the social and ideological range of the epitaph. He commemorates lowly but virtuous laborers, flawed women too harshly condemned by society, and poets who have not received the public recognition they deserve. Pope knows that the vulnerability of the dead to neglect or misinterpretation makes them propitious objects for his art and furthers his career as a poet of corrective, definitive statement. At the same time, he struggles with the ethical implications of his own poetic opportunism.

Although Pope composes some panegyric epitaphs upon the "great" indistinguishable from the "Sepulchral lyes" he attacks (*Dunciad Variorum* 1.41; 1742 *Dunciad* 1.43), his most innovative epitaphs upon members of the social elite attempt to counter imputations of flattery by expressing

[1] On Pope's self-appointed role as the bestower of fame, see Donald Fraser, "Pope and the Idea of Fame," in *Alexander Pope*, ed. Peter Dixon (Athens, Ohio: Ohio University Press, 1972), 286–310; Ronald Paulson, "Satire, Poetry, and Pope," in Leland Henry Carlson and Ronald Paulson, *English Satire*, Clark Library Seminar Papers (Los Angeles: University of California Press, 1972), especially pp. 68–74; and John Paul Russo, *Alexander Pope: Tradition and Identity* (Cambridge: Harvard University Press, 1972), 147–175.

his "sincere" grief for those whom he had intimately known and loved. Though his shifting of epitaphic rhetoric from impersonal panegyric to elegiac lament is a highly influential strategy, it provides no conclusive solution to the widespread suspicion of epitaphs upon the "great." While he tries to make his own reputation as a national poet and a moral arbiter serve as ethical proof of the virtues of the dead, his highly subjective rhetoric leaves him vulnerable to charges of both willful partiality and obtrusive self-display. The problematic moral status of Pope's epitaphs reveals a genre in crisis.

In some of his early compositions, Pope reveals a deep and shocking fantasy underlying his poetry of commemoration. He finds or creates social outcasts whose unconscious or conscious goal is to be saved from opprobrium by his commemorative art.

In the autumn of 1718, in the parish of Pope's friend Simon Viscount Harcourt, lightning struck and killed John Hewet and Sarah Drew, betrothed laborers working together in the fields. Pope, who happened to be staying with Harcourt, wrote three epitaphs on the lovers and corresponded with various friends concerning their deaths and his verses. The epitaphs and letters reveal his use of the dead to portray himself as a benevolent commemorative poet. Pope appears both as the Christian teacher, correcting uncharitable judgments upon the dead, and as the man of sensibility, sympathizing with true lovers, however lowly their condition.

On Pope's request, Lord Harcourt erected a monument to the two lovers, and an epitaph by Pope was accordingly inscribed upon a plain stone tablet on the outside wall of Stanton-Harcourt church:

> Think not by rigorous judgment seiz'd,
>   A pair so faithful could expire;
> Victims so pure Heav'n saw well pleas'd
>   And snatch'd them in Coelestial fire.
>
> Live well and fear no sudden fate;
>   When God calls Virtue to the grave,
> Alike tis Justice, soon or late,
>   Mercy alike to kill or save.
>
> Virtue unmov'd can hear the Call,
> And face the Flash that melts the Ball.[2]

Pope enclosed earlier versions of this epitaph in letters of September 1718 to his friends John Caryll and Francis Atterbury, explaining that

---

[2] Pope, "EPITAPH ON JOHN HEWET and SARAH DREW," in *Minor Poems*, 199.

he composed it in order to correct the Stanton-Harcourt parishioners' view of the lovers' deaths. Believing that the fatal lightning was God's punishment, the parishioners were angry that the local minister had allowed Hewet and Drew Christian burial. Such "superstitious" and "absurd" views stem, Pope explains in his letters, from an unchristian fear of "a gloomy, savage" God and from the uncharitable view that "misfortunes, when they happen to others, are a punishment of vice."[3] The epitaph instead asserts that the two lovers were rapt heavenward by "Coelestial fire." The description of the lovers as "faithful" suggests both their mutual fidelity and their faith in God; there is a sentimental hint that the lovers' devotion is in some sense analogous to, or even proof of, their religious devotion. Pope indeed discovers a heroic Christian Stoicism in such humble lovers. They become examples of a "Virtue unmov'd" that can respond to God's plan—whether it be death by lightning or the final conflagration of the Apocalypse—without fear.

By commemorating virtuous lovers who were both humble and misunderstood, Pope fulfills the task of the poet suggested by *The Temple of Fame*: he prevents slander from besmirching the innocent and ensures that the worthy, however humble in rank, are not lost in oblivion. Since early eighteenth-century laborers were normally buried in unmarked churchyard graves, the commemorative tablet emphatically singled out Hewet and Drew. Its placement on the outside wall of the church was particularly appropriate for a commemoration by the social elite of worthy members of the lower classes, since the outside wall marked a midpoint between the church's interior, with its grand monuments, and the churchyard, with its humble graves. The tablet communicates lessons from the elite to the humble, from the "inside" to the "outside." One may compare the epitaph of Humphrey How, a servant of the lord of Stoneleigh Manor, Warwickshire, who died in 1688. Inscribed upon the outer stones of Stoneleigh Parish Church, How's epitaph signals its own mediating function as a communication from the high to the low:

> Here lyes a Faithful Friend unto the Poore
> Who dealt Large Almes out of his Lord[shi]ps Store
> Weepe Not Poore People Tho' Ye Serva[n]t's Dead
> The Lord him selfe Will Give You Daily Bread.... [4]

The Hewet-Drew tablet, also erected by a local lord, is less explicitly but no less clearly a message from high to low. Invested with Lord Harcourt's

---

[3] Pope, *Correspondence*, 1: 497–500.

[4] Eighteenth-century masters (including Pope himself, as we shall see in chapter 11) continued to use the outside church wall as a site to commemorate servants appropriately located between high and low.

authority, Pope the didactic poet undertakes to correct the views of the humble parishioners by mixing authoritative assertion with strong commands ("Think not..."; "Live well and fear no sudden fate").

A Catholic reproving a misguided Protestant parish, Pope draws his authority from an ecumenical conception of Christianity. By sending versions of his epitaph to both Caryll, a devout and traditional Catholic, and Atterbury, the High Church bishop of Rochester and dean of Westminster Abbey, Pope self-consciously promotes such ecumenism.[5] Shortly before the Hewet-Drew affair, Atterbury, who had a lifelong antipathy to Catholicism, had suggested that Pope convert to the established church.[6] In his dignified refusal Pope declared his loyalty to the faith in which he was born, contending that all "honest and reasonable christians" were essentially of the same religion in their espousal of two central precepts, "to serve God and live in peace with...[one's] neighbour."[7] Pope's epitaph uses the two lovers to teach an unenlightened community precisely such ecumenical Christianity, for his lovers are faithful towards a merciful God and deserve charitable judgment from their former neighbors.

The suspicion of and discrimination against Catholics in eighteenth-century England, evident from the statutes concerning property noted in the preceding chapter, help explain Pope's eagerness to concentrate on shared fundamental beliefs. By giving Protestant dissenters full freedom of worship, the Toleration Act of 1689 had permanently weakened the established church's ability to control religious thought and its general hold over the beliefs of the nation.[8] With the general increase in religious tolerance and Catholics' evident lack of political power, acute fear and consequent persecution of Catholics declined considerably after 1689. Nevertheless, Catholics were still viewed with intense distrust by the Protestant majority, especially during peak periods of Jacobite activity, and were far less successful than Protestant dissenters in bypassing

[5] When Pope sent Atterbury the epitaph, he asked the latter's opinion of "the doctrine" as well as "the poetry" (Correspondence, 1:500).

[6] Atterbury was entering his career as the prime English Jacobite conspirator when he began his friendship with Pope. Atterbury's support of the Catholic Pretender and consequent exile in France never, however, diminished his antipathy to Catholicism or brought him closer to such Catholic gentlemen of Jacobite sympathies as Pope's friend Caryll, and he was undoubtedly deeply disappointed that he could not convert his talented young friend, Pope. See G. V. Bennett, The Tory Crisis in Church and State, 1688–1730: The Career of Francis Atterbury, Bishop of Rochester (Oxford: Clarendon, 1975), 28–29, 206–207, 296–298, 303–305.

[7] Pope, Correspondence, 1:454. Pope's compression of the Christian credo to these two precepts recalls Jesus's formulations in Mark 12:29–31, Matthew 22:37–40, and Luke 10:27.

[8] See Leonard J. Trinterud, "A. D. 1689: The End of the Clerical World," in Winthrop S. Hudson and Trinterud, Theology in Sixteenth- and Seventeenth-Century England (Los Angeles: University of California Press, 1971), 27–50.

the many laws discriminating against them.[9] In his epitaph Pope sought to foster Christian charity and tolerance, which was as necessary for him as for the reputations of the deceased.[10]

In a letter to Lady Mary Wortley Montagu composed a few days before those to Caryll and Atterbury, Pope reveals more than a Christian teacher's interest in the fate of the Stanton-Harcourt lovers. While to his male friends he emphasizes his moral reaction to the villagers' superstition, in his letter to Lady Mary he gives a disturbing erotic slant to his commemorative task. In addition to the epitaph we have just discussed, Pope sent Lady Mary the following composition upon the two lovers:

> When Eastern lovers feed the fun'ral fire,
> On the same Pile the faithful Fair expire;
> Here pitying Heav'n that virtue mutual found,
> And blasted both, that it might neither wound.
> Hearts so sincere, th'Almighty saw well-pleas'd,
> Sent his own Lightning, & the Victims seiz'd.[11]

Both epitaphs describe the lovers' deaths as the act of a God who, as in Genesis 1, looked upon his creation "well-pleas'd." There is a striking parallel between this God who "saw well-pleas'd" and Pope's self-portrait as the sensitive commemorator in his letter to Lady Mary. Describing the humble lovers' deaths as a pastoral "romance," he emphasizes his own pleasure with what he saw: "I have a mind to fill the rest of this paper with an accident that happen'd just under my eyes, and has made a great Impression upon me."[12] He concludes his description with this assessment: "Upon the whole, I can't think these people unhappy: The greatest happiness, next to living as they would have done, was to dye as they did. The greatest honour people of this low degree could have was to be remembered on a little monument."[13] The lovers' happiness

[9] On attitudes toward Catholics, see Roland N. Stromberg, *Religious Liberalism in Eighteenth-Century England* (Oxford: Oxford University Press, 1954), 5, 88–89.
[10] Despite his friendships with the traditional Catholic Caryll and the High Church Atterbury, Pope's ecumenical principles brought him near the eighteenth-century English religious mainstream. The benevolence of God and the duty to imitate Him through charitable action were fundamental principles of the Latitudinarian movement, which was very influential within the established church, and Pope's desire to reduce Christianity to a few essentials on which all Christians could agree was shared by prominent Low Church Protestants; see Norman Sykes, *Church and State in England in the XVIIIth Century* (1935; rpt., New York: Farrar, 1975), 257–268; and Norman Sykes, *From Sheldon to Secker: Aspects of English Church History, 1660–1768* (Cambridge: Cambridge University Press, 1959), 163–165, 176–177, 186–187.
[11] Pope, *Correspondence*, 1:495. (I have adopted "the" instead of "their" in line two from the first printed text of the poem, included in Pope, *Minor Poems*, 197–198).
[12] Pope, *Correspondence*, 1:494.
[13] Pope, *Correspondence*, 1:496.

is conferred both by divine providence and by the honor Pope vouchsafes them. When the epitaphs were published, Pope might well have added, the lovers' "little monument" would be known far and wide.[14] While God creates and beneficently destroys, Pope recreates and beneficently commemorates.

As commemorator, Pope self-consciously assumes his merciful, God-like role. To Teresa Blount he sent a bawdy couplet on the two lovers that replaces God's plan with an accident of nature: "Here lye two poor Lovers, who had the mishap / Tho very chaste people, to die of a Clap."[15] This epitaph uses comic anapests and the long-standing tradition of burlesque distichs upon the lowly to cut down to size a pair of lovers who were "poor" both in luck and social station. By contrast, in the two panegyric epitaphs Pope graciously treats the lovers as dignified poetic subjects and thereby raises them to immortality.

Pope suggests that Lady Mary could write a better epitaph, but her response could not have met his expectations. She denies that the two lovers were "either wiser or more virtuous than their neighbors" and asserts that had they survived "their lives would have passed in the common track with their fellow-parishioners."[16] Her counter-epitaph is in the comic style traditional for epitaphs upon the lower orders:

> Here lies John Hughes and Sarah Drew;
> Perhaps you'll say, What's that to you?
> Believe me, friend, much may be said
> On that poor couple that are dead.
> On Sunday next they should have married;
> But see how oddly things are carried!
> On Thursday last it rain'd and lighten'd,
> These tender lovers sadly frighten'd,
> Shelter'd beneath the cocking hay
> In hopes to pass the time away.
> But the BOLD THUNDER found them out
> (Commission'd for that end no doubt)
> And seizing on their trembling breath,
> Consign'd them to the shades of death.
> Who knows if 'twas not kindly done?
> For had they seen the next year's sun,

---

[14] Pope's claim that the two lovers were not "unhappy" in their deaths seems to recall Lord Bathurst's response in August, 1718 to Pope's description of the two lovers: "But why unhappy after all? ... their names would never have been recorded to posterity but for this accident, and therefore I may conclude them *fortunati ambo si quid carmina possunt*" (Pope, *Correspondence*, 1:488). Pope was undoubtedly flattered by Bathurst's comparing his epitaph to Virgil's commemoration of Nisus and Euryalus in *The Aeneid* 9.446–499.

[15] Pope, *Correspondence*, 1:349 (the letter is misdated by Sherburn; it should be dated 1718).

[16] Pope, *Correspondence*, 1:523.

A beaten wife and cuckold swain
Had jointly curs'd the marriage chain;
Now they are happy in their doom,
FOR POPE HAS WROTE UPON THEIR TOMB.[17]

The jaunty rhythm of these iambic tetrameters, reminiscent of Butler's *Hudibras* and Swift's aggressively "low" poetry, the colloquialisms, the awkward pleonasms, and the ironic, parenthetic assertion that the thunder was "no doubt" an act of special providence—all these features mock the idea of paying respect to such common lovers. The most untraditional aspect of the epitaph is its length, which serves to spoof all the more the claim that "much may be said" about such a trivial subject as the two lovers. The epitaph is devastating, but not simply because Lady Mary punctures the bubble of Pope's serious tone. Pope had done as much himself, after all, in the distich sent to Teresa Blount, which laughs at the expense of the two laborers. Lady Mary's epitaph deflates because its final couplet renders all too crudely explicit Pope's implication that the lovers found happy fates in being commemorated by him. "Happy in their doom," a ludicrous semi-oxymoron, combines with a final line in banner letters to ridicule Pope's smug assertions.

Herself unhappily married, Lady Mary projects her own sense of the inevitable disappointments of marriage onto the two lovers who escaped becoming quarreling spouses. Her comic epitaph nevertheless insists upon the social distance between herself and a pair of laborers.[18] At the close of her letter she rebuts any suggestion that she herself should relish to die like them: "I confess these sentiments are not altogether so heroic as yours; but I hope you will forgive them in favour of the last two lines. You see how much I esteem the honour you have done them; tho' I am not very impatient to have the same, and had rather continue to be your stupid, *living*, humble servant, than be *celebrated* by all the pens in Europe."[19] "I am not very impatient to have the same" implicitly construes Pope's epitaphs as oblique presentations of Lady Mary's and Pope's dying and being memorialized together, a Popean fantasy Lady Mary wholeheartedly rejects. She had good reason to find covert eroticism in the epitaph. Lady Mary was traveling with her husband in Asia Minor when

---

[17] Pope, *Correspondence*, 1:523.

[18] On Lady Mary's unhappy marriage, see Robert Halsband, *The Life of Lady Mary Wortley Montagu* (Oxford: Clarendon, 1956), 29–44 and passim. Lady Mary's 1724 poem, "Written ex tempore on the Death of Mrs[.] Bowes," seriously and grimly portrays death as an escape from the suffering of marriage; see Lady Mary Wortley Montagu, *Essays and Poems, and Simplicity, A Comedy*, ed. Robert Halsband and Isobel Grundy (Oxford: Clarendon, 1977), 233. Lady Mary could identify with Mrs. Bowes and bitterly congratulate her for escaping marriage's sorrows because the deceased was a member of Lady Mary's own social class.

[19] Pope, *Correspondence*, 1:523–524.

Pope sent her the poem. Pope's letter describes Lady Mary's "Oriental Self" and the "true nature & simplicity of manners" she has gained by "residence in the East" before presenting her with an epitaph comparing two English lovers to the extremes of "Eastern" amorous devotion unto death.[20] Pope's letter thus wistfully implies that the Stanton-Harcourt lovers' joint death and commemoration are the kind that he and she could have, if only she were willing. The letter and epitaph thus together assimilate the death of the two lovers to Pope's poetic obsession with self-commemoration.[21] In her reply, Lady Mary distances herself from Pope's fantasies by insisting upon the vast difference between herself and the "happy" lovers.

Since the beginning of their correspondence two years before the Hewet-Drew episode, Pope had attempted to draw Lady Mary into extravagant imaginings that involved their deaths and poetic commemoration together. Pope's epistolary fantasies provided him with a substitute for an actual love affair with Lady Mary, which he knew to be impossible. They countered his sense of vulnerability toward another living human being with a feeling of control over his own poetic fictions of death and immortality. Successive letters of 1716 describe Lady Mary's absence from England as a kind of death; treat her empty London home as "the Tomb of a Friend"; hope that Pope's correspondence will not be unanswered lest it "be like a Traffic with the Grave"; and pray to Lady Mary in Catholic fashion as a departed saint: "I cannot be satisfied with strowing flowers over you, & barely honoring you as a thing lost; but must consider you as a glorious, tho' remote Being, & be sending Addresses and prayers after you."[22] In one of these letters Pope also vows to pursue her but requests, should the attempt prove fatal, that she have the following epitaph placed over him: "Here stopt by hasty Death, Alexis lies, / Who crost half Europe, led by Wortley's eyes!"[23] Pope's epitaph upon himself imitates the one that the Roman love elegist Tibullus addressed to his mistress from a far-away island: "Here lies Tibullus devoured by savage death, / while he followed Messalla upon land and sea."[24] In the Tibullan elegy the epitaph is immediately followed by the poet's description of a lovers' Elysium of blissful sexuality, and the juxtaposition sug-

---

[20] Pope, *Correspondence*, 1:494.

[21] Pope earlier sent Martha Blount a letter similar to that he sent to Lady Mary (*Correspondence*, 1:481). In his letter to Blount, Pope more directly declares that he would be happy to die with a woman who loved him as Drew did Hewet (*Correspondence*, 1:481). Blount does not respond to this declaration, and I have concentrated on the correspondence with Lady Mary because it forms part of an extended and genuine exchange concerning Pope's fantasies of death and commemoration.

[22] Pope, *Correspondence*, 1:345, 354–355, 363, 367.

[23] Pope, *Correspondence*, 1:369.

[24] "HIC IACET IMMITI CONSUMPTUS MORTE TIBULLUS, / MESSALLAM TERRA DUM SEQUITURQUE MARI" (*Elegy* 1.3.55–56, translation mine).

gests that the afterlife will compensate him and his mistress for their earthly separation.[25] In his letter to Lady Mary, Pope immediately follows his epitaph with a description of their encounters in the afterlife; though he is less explicitly sexual, he hints at such bliss by means of the Tibullan epitaph. By joining Lady Mary's name to his own in the epitaph and then proceeding to describe their union after death, furthermore, Pope makes the epitaph not only his but also Lady Mary's. Thus he expresses a fantasy wish that he and Lady Mary may die into a lovers' Elysium and be immortalized together in a distich of his own composition.[26]

On occasion Lady Mary could accept Pope's role for her and describe her life in Asia Minor as a kind of death,[27] but her response to the Hewet-Drew epitaph renews earlier resistance to Pope's elaborate and oppressive fantasies.[28] In the "ODE for MUSICK. on St. CECILIA's Day" (1713), Pope implicitly identified with Orpheus, who, despite his eloquence, failed to regain the dead Eurydice and died while singing of his beloved (ll. 49–117).[29] Responding sometime after November 1716 to a report that Lady Mary was not returning to England, Pope laments with flirtatious hyperbole his Orphic inability to win Lady Mary back from the "death" of absence with his tender epistles: "Is Eurydice once more snatch'd to the Shades?"[30] In a letter of February 1717, Pope, who was concerned by Lady Mary's continued absence and reports of her illness, claims that she is "doubly dead" to him.[31] In reply Lady Mary assures him that she is not only a living being but also hopes to remain so. Describing how her boat almost overturned in the Hebrus, she offers a barbed comment similar to her response concerning the Hewet-Drew epitaphs:

[25] See Tibullus, *Elegy* 1.3.57–66.

[26] Pope continues with variations on the idea of a joint death in letters of 1717. In another letter in which he vows to follow Lady Mary, Pope compares himself to Leander, who died in pursuit of his beloved Hero, a revealing comparison since Hero herself subsequently died in sorrow (*Correspondence*, 1:406). In yet another he compares himself to a Provencal poet who pursued his beloved to Tripoli, died upon seeing her, and was rewarded when she "built him a Tomb of Porphyry, put his Epitaph upon it . . . and turnd Nun" (*Correspondence*, 1:440–441). Thus Lady Mary would reward him by commemorating him as her faithful lover and in turn "dying" to the world by becoming a nun.

[27] See Lady Mary's letter of June 17, 1717: "I had . . . [your letter] but yesterday, in which you suppose me to be dead and buried. I have already let you know that I am still alive; but to say truth, I look upon my present circumstances to be exactly the same with those of departed spirits" (Pope, *Correspondence*, 1:411–412).

[28] Patricia Meyer Spacks analyzes Lady Mary's attempt in her letters to escape Pope's amorous fantasies in "Imaginations Warm and Tender: Pope and Lady Mary," *South Atlantic Quarterly* 83 (1984): 207–215. Spacks does not discuss, however, the crucial role of imagined death and commemoration in the two writers' epistolary struggles and misunderstandings.

[29] Pope, *Minor Poems*, 32–34.

[30] Pope, *Correspondence*, 1:384.

[31] Pope, *Correspondence*, 1:389.

If I had much regard for the glories that one's name enjoys after death, I should certainly be sorry for having missed the romantic conclusion of swimming down the same river in which the musical head of *Orpheus* repeated verses, so many ages since:

> *Caput a cervice revulsum,*
> *Gurgite cum medio, portans Oeagrius Hebrus*
> *Volveret, Eurydicen vox ipsa, et frigida lingua*
> *Ah! miseram Eurydicen! anima fugiente vocabat*
> *Eurydicen toto referebant flumine ripae.*

Who knows but some of your bright wits, might have found it a subject affording many poetical turns ... I despair of ever having so many fine things said of me as so extraordinary a death would have given occasion for.[32]

Lady Mary rejects poetic immortality as an adequate compensation for death. She thereby rejects Pope's fantasies of her dying and thereby turning into the object of his Orphic song. Though the tone is ostensibly comic, there is an underlying pathos in her assertion of her (literally and figuratively) vital independence. Even as she imagines and rejects the role of commemorated poetic object, she figures herself as an Orpheus, a poet as well as poetic object. Lady Mary implicitly refuses to be a Eurydice, the wholly passive object of poetic desire that Pope addressed so often, in so many guises, in their correspondence.[33] Her proclamation of her identity as a living being, who would rather live than die in "romantic" fashion to be celebrated by a Pope, helps explain the aggressive tone of Lady Mary's epitaph and her comments upon the Hewet-Drew lovers. The two laborers had been absorbed into Pope's poetic schemes, but she would resist.

By the time she responded to the Hewet-Drew epitaph, Lady Mary would have known several poems in which Pope imagines the death of vulnerable women who in some sense need Pope's commemoration. Pope's epitaphs upon the humble lovers are the "real–life" equivalent

---

[32] Pope, *Correspondence*, 1:396–397. Lady Mary cites *Georgics* 4.523–527: "Even then, while Oeagrian Hebrus swept and rolled in midcurrent that head, plucked from its marble neck, the bare voice and death-cold tongue, with fleeting breath, called Eurydice—ah, hapless Eurydice! 'Eurydice' the banks re-echoed, all adown the stream."

[33] Since Pope's letter comparing Lady Mary to Eurydice cannot be precisely dated, it is probable but not certain that she had already received it when she alludes to the Orpheus tale. Pope's clear self-identification with Orpheus and his general attitude toward her are enough, in any case, to give pointed significance to her comparison of herself to Orpheus.

of such memorials as *Eloisa to Abelard* and the "Elegy to the Memory of an Unfortunate Lady," both published in 1717.[34]

Eloisa depicts a woman who longs to be commemorated by Pope.[35] Pope endows Eloisa with his own concerns, "the best of passions, Love and Fame" (l. 40), but he has Eloisa seek fame not within herself but from her male beloved. In John Hughes's translation of the Eloise-Abelard correspondence, which Pope used in composing his poem, Abelard desires burial near Eloisa so that "my tomb will by that means be more rich and more renowned."[36] Reversing the gender roles, Pope has Eloisa desire to be buried and commemorated with Abelard and thereby acquire the renown that will compensate for her suffering: "May one kind grave unite each hapless name, / And graft my love immortal on thy fame" (ll. 343–344). Eloisa's desire to gain fame from Abelard embodies Pope's own fantasy of a beloved who, like the Lady Mary he imagined, would find her ultimate fulfillment in the fame provided by and alongside Pope. The poem accordingly ends with a coda in which Eloisa envisages "some future Bard" (l. 359)—Pope himself—sympathetically commemorating the two lovers. Pope thereby imagines, in displaced form, his union in death with a beloved and represents himself as the commemorator of the vulnerable dead.

Eloisa appropriately ends Pope's first major collection, the *Works* of 1716. In its preface, Pope seeks the reader's benevolence by wondering whether or not the book will bring him fame or critical "death": "In this office of collecting my pieces, I am altogether uncertain, whether to look upon my self as a man building a monument, or burying the dead?"[37] In *Eloisa* he contrives to do both: he buries himself in his surrogates, Eloisa and Abelard, while building a monument to himself as the poet who commemorates them.

Pope's "Elegy to the Memory of an Unfortunate Lady" imagines a woman even more directly dependent upon the poet for her posthumous reputation. The poem defends the reputation of an imaginary woman whose love suicide made her an outcast from her family and society at large. The woman has been denied proper "rites" (ll. 48, 61–62), the "domestic tear" (l. 49), the mourning of friends (l. 55), and a funerary monument or epitaph. After attacking the "proud" who refused to for-

[34] In June, 1717, Pope sent Lady Mary the *Works* of 1717, which contained the last two mentioned poems.

[35] I have found suggestive the readings of *Eloisa* in Lawrence Lipking, *Abandoned Women and Poetic Tradition* (Chicago: University of Chicago Press, 1988), 144–152; and Ellen Pollak, *The Poetics of Sexual Myth: Gender and Ideology in the Verse of Swift and Pope* (Chicago: University of Chicago Press, 1985), 183–186.

[36] I cite the text in John Hughes, *Letters of Abelard and Heloise ... To which are added, poems ...* (Edinburgh, 1806), 105.

[37] Pope, "Preface to *The Works* (1717)," in *Prose Works*, 1:295.

give the lady because they had "ne'er learn'd to glow / For others' good, or melt at others' woe" (ll. 43, 45–46), the poet declares that the natural and divine orders respect the deceased in a way that society does not:

> What tho' no weeping Loves thy ashes grace,
> Nor polish'd marble emulate thy face?
> What tho' no sacred earth allow thee room,
> Nor hallow'd dirge be mutter'd o'er thy tomb?
> Yet shall thy grave with rising flow'rs be drest,
> And the green turf lie lightly on thy breast:
> There shall the morn her earliest tears bestow,
> There the first roses of the year shall blow;
> While Angels with their silver wings o'ershade
> The ground, now sacred by thy reliques made.
>   So peaceful rests, without a stone, a name,
> What once had beauty, titles, wealth, and fame.
>
> (ll. 59–70)

The cosmic order compensates for rejection by the human order. The natural "tears" of the morning dew and the supernatural tears of angels are a superior substitute for the mimic tears of stone cherubs, the "weeping Loves" so popular on eighteenth-century funerary monuments.[38] The cosmos and Pope are here, however, the same. Declaring that the unhallowed grave of a suicide is now a "sacred" place of "reliques," Pope blesses the deceased with his own poetic fiat. He asserts his power to realize his desires by transforming normally optative epitaphic formulae, the classical *sit tibi terra levis* and Catholic *Requiescat in pace*, into indicative assertions of fact—"the green turf [will] lie lightly on thy breast"; "So peaceful rests. . . ." The poem thus embodies his wildest fantasy of redressing the wrongs done to the dead: he does not confine himself to matters of earthly reputation but instead declares nature's and heaven's benign forgiveness of the woman's sin.

Pope never names the deceased, whose final repose indeed seems to depend upon the obliteration of her name: "So peaceful rests, without a stone, a name." The poem's title emphasizes the omission, since "to the memory of" normally and logically accompanies a name: one thinks of such famous panegyrics as Jonson's "To the Memory of . . . Mr. William Shakespeare" and Dryden's "To the Pious Memory of . . . Mrs. Anne Killigrew" as well as the many epitaphs that begin "Sacred to the Memory of," or "Memoriae Sacrum," followed by the name of the deceased. Pope defends the deceased from slander, but by making her an

---

[38] On the popularity of cherubs in eighteenth-century funerary monuments, see Brian Kemp, *English Church Monuments* (London: B. T. Batsford, 1980), 127–128.

anonymous, half-glimpsed figure, he suggests his own control over her posthumous significance.

The poem appropriately ends with a coda emphasizing the dependence of the deceased upon her poet for her continued existence in memory:

> Ev'n he, whose soul now melts in mournful lays,
> Shall shortly want the gen'rous tear he pays;
> Then from his closing eyes thy form shall part,
> And the last pang shall tear thee from his heart,
> Life's idle business at one gasp be o'er,
> The Muse forgot, and thou belov'd no more!
>
> (ll. 77–82)

This woman is the beloved of Petrarchan cliché, imprinted in the poet's heart. Because he has his love for the deceased all to himself, she will be "belov'd no more" once he has died. Since the deceased never comes fully into public view, Pope can expatiate upon himself as the "gen'rous" soul who corrects unto his death the insensitive responses of all others. Even more than the coda of *Eloisa*, this ending makes the death of an other the occasion for the poet's own flattering commemorative self-portrait.

Pope's drive to rescue the dead from oblivion or misunderstanding and to take credit for so doing is not limited to lower-class lovers and legendary or imaginary women in distress. His epitaphs on fellow poets also present vulnerable figures dependent on his memorializing art. Unlike laborers and women, however, whom Pope manipulates without moral reservation, Pope's fellow male poets provoke intense ethical qualms in their commemorator. To some degree Pope must deny the deceased what he insists upon for himself: self-definition in death. In different ways, however, he attempts to balance his urge to create the ultimate image of others with a counterimpulse to allow his fellow poets to define themselves for posterity.

In the three compositions on Dryden—the English poet who influenced him most—Pope tries to commemorate his great predecessor while also allowing him to memorialize himself. Though Dryden had been buried with great pomp in the Abbey upon his death in 1700, he did not at that time receive a tomb. Pope used an epitaph intended for the Westminster Abbey tomb of Nicholas Rowe, who died in 1718, to attack the nation that failed to give Dryden a proper monument:

> Thy reliques, *Rowe*, to this fair urn we trust,
> And sacred, place by *Dryden*'s awful dust:
> Beneath a rude and nameless stone he lies,
> To which thy tomb shall guide inquiring eyes.
> Peace to thy gentle shade, and endless Rest!
> Blest in thy genius, in thy love too blest!
> One grateful woman to thy fame supplies
> What a whole thankless land to his denies.[39]

Funerary poems on poets often treat the physical proximity of one poet's burial place to another's as a sign of poetic kinship.[40] Pope's epitaph, by contrast, does not explicitly link Rowe and nearby Dryden by pointing out, for example, that both men were poet laureates. Instead the poem starkly contrasts their fates and spends as much time lamenting the tombless Dryden as it does commemorating Rowe. Pope indeed implies the obvious but indecorous truth that Dryden, a far greater writer than Rowe, deserved national rather than merely "domestic" recognition in the Abbey. The poem thus suggests Pope's outrage: he must violate decorum in order to suggest the monstrous neglect of a "thankless land."[41]

Perhaps because Rowe's widow was displeased with Pope's emphasis, this epitaph was not inscribed on Rowe's monument.[42] Nevertheless the composition, first published in 1720, had its desired effect, as the poet proudly declared in a footnote when he republished it in 1726:

The Tomb of Mr. *Dryden* was erected soon after this upon this hint by the Duke of *Buckingham*; to which was originally intended this Epitaph...

> This *SHEFFIELD* rais'd. The sacred Dust below
> Was *DRYDEN* once: The rest who does not know?

[39] Pope, "Epitaph. Intended for Mr. Rowe. In *Westminster-Abbey*," in *Minor Poems*, 208.

[40] For English examples, see the epitaph upon Spenser beginning "Here near Chaucer Spenser is buried, closest to Chaucer in genius, as he is closest to him in burial" ("Hic prope Chaucerum situs est Spenserius illi / Proximus ingenio, proximus ut tumulo"), in William Camden, *Reges, Reginae, Nobiles...in ecclesia...Westmonasterii sepulti...*[London, 1600], *Reges*, I2v); William Basse's "Elegy on Shakespeare," reprinted in *Ben Jonson*, ed. C. H. Herford and Percy and Evelyn Simpson, 11 vols. (Oxford: Clarendon, 1925–1952), 11:145; and Sir John Denham's "On Mr Abraham Cowley, His Death and Burial amongst the Ancient Poets," in *The Poetical Works of Sir John Denham*, ed. Theodore Howard Banks, 2d ed. (1928; rpt., Hamden, Conn.: Archon Books, 1969), 149–152. The motif originates in Cardinal Bembo's early sixteenth-century epitaph on Jacopo Sannazaro, who was buried near his beloved Virgil; see *Renaissance Latin Verse: An Anthology*, ed. Alessandro Perosa and John Sparrow (Chapel Hill: University of North Carolina Press, 1979), 172.

[41] Johnson criticizes the indecorous emphasis upon Dryden in his essay upon Pope's epitaphs; see *Lives of the English Poets*, ed. G. B. Hill, 3 vols. (Oxford: Clarendon, 1905), 3:261.

[42] A revised, more decorous version of the epitaph was finally inscribed upon Rowe's tomb in 1743. It follows panegyric tradition by describing the dramatist lying near "his" Shakespeare, the dramatist whom Rowe edited and attempted to emulate; see Pope, *Minor Poems*, 400.

Which the author since chang'd into the plain Inscription now on the Tomb,
being only the name of that Great Man, in this manner

DRYDEN.

Natus Aug. 9. 1631
Mortuus Maii I. 1701
Johannes Sheffield, Dux Buckinghamiensis, fecit.[43]

The footnote allows Pope to take public credit for the poetic "hint" that
led to the erection of the monument and to demonstrate his eagerness
and skill in briefly but sufficiently eulogizing Dryden. The couplet that
Pope had composed for the inscription on Dryden revives the name-as-
praise motif popular in the sixteenth and early seventeenth centuries.[44]
The tomb's actual inscription literalizes the name-as-praise motif, however, by giving "only the name of that great Man." By rejecting the
distich he had composed for the monument, Pope effaces himself before
Dryden and suggests that his great predecessor immortalized himself.[45]
Because of his fame as a poet, many of Pope's sepulchral inscriptions
bear his own name, but Pope refrains from obtruding his own superfluous
poetic flourishes and his own name upon Dryden's monument.

The combined visual and verbal impact of the Dryden monument
nevertheless suggests Pope's identification with his great predecessor.
The Dryden memorial, a laurel-crowned bust of the poet in an architectural frame with Pope's brief inscription, is typical of the period in
proclaiming the poet's earthly fame. The early eighteenth century witnessed extensive innovation in funerary monuments. While the general
decline in radical Protestant fervor lessened suspicion of church monuments, monuments became all the more acceptable as they increasingly
concentrated solely on secular, earthly fame, substituting pagan motifs
for Christian imagery and avoiding figures in devotional poses that might
arouse the spectator's religious sensibilities.[46] The Dryden memorial is,

[43] Pope, *Minor Poems*, 209.

[44] Probably in 1729 Pope adapted the two-line epitaph upon Pico della Mirandola that
uses the name-as-praise motif for two satiric epitaphs (*Minor Poems*, 297–298). The Pico
epitaph is the most likely model for Pope's distich in praise of Dryden.

[45] Contemporaries interpreted the monument as implying that Dryden's name provided
the only possible and sufficient praise. John Dart exclaims that it would be "high Presumption to attempt thy [Dryden's] Praise, / A needless Task; for can that Creature be /
Who has not heard of Homer and of thee!" ("Westminster Abbey: A Poem" in *Westmonasterium, or The History and Antiquities of the Abbey Church of St. Peters Westminster*, 2 vols.
[London, n.d], 1:xli); compare "On Seeing Mr. DRYDEN's Bust, with nothing but his name,
in WESTMINSTER ABBEY," *Gentleman's Magazine* 22 (1752):234.

[46] On the secularization of funerary monuments in the eighteenth century, see Philippe
Ariès, *The Hour of Our Death*, trans. Helen Weaver (New York: Random, 1982), 263–265;
and Lawrence Stone, *The Family, Sex and Marriage in England, 1500–1800* (New York:
Harper, 1977), 226.

however, quite simple in comparison to the many grand monuments of the period and was accordingly praised by contemporaries for its plainness.[47] While seventeenth-century patrons relied mainly on expensive materials and sheer size to proclaim the social status of the dead, patrons in the eighteenth-century, anxious to demonstrate their learning and taste, increasingly sought elaborate designs revealing knowledge both of classical sculpture and continental baroque and rococo models. Sculptors rather than masons erected monuments, and eminent architects were often involved in their design.[48] Though the architect James Gibbs designed the Dryden monument, Pope, who had employed Gibbs at Twickenham and may have gained him the Dryden commission, insisted on the simple design: Atterbury writes of Pope's decision to have "Dryden's Name only below, and his Busto above."[49] Pope's "EPISTLE to Mr. JERVAS, With *Dryden's* Translation of *Fresnoy's Art* of *Painting*" (1716), a poem addressed to a painter and treating the sister-arts, suggests the significance of this design for Pope. The epistle is indebted to Dryden for both its occasion (Dryden's translation) and its generic model (Dryden's epistle on the sister-arts, "To Sir Godfrey Kneller"). Pope begins by explicitly comparing himself and Mr. Jervas to Dryden and Fresnoy (ll. 8–12) and ends by announcing the respective achievements of the visual and verbal artist, both pathetically limited by death: "Thou but preserv'st a Face and I a Name" (l. 78).[50] Dryden's monument preserves precisely such a name and face against death. While the sculptor's bust depicts Dryden in all of his irreducible otherness, the name allows Pope to affirm his own self-identification with Dryden as verbal artist, even as Pope excludes his own name from the monument.

Dryden's monument does include, however, another name, that of John Sheffield, the duke of Buckingham, who erected it. Pope viewed Sheffield as a living link between himself and Dryden. In *Absalom and Achitophel* Dryden praised Sheffield as a poet and a friend of poets (ll. 877–878); following Dryden, in *An Essay on Criticism* (ll. 723–724 and footnote) Pope praised Sheffield and cited Dryden's praise. Dryden had occasionally collaborated with Sheffield; Pope in turn edited Sheffield's verse for a posthumous edition. In *Arbuthnot*, some fifteen years after the erection of the monument, Pope listed Sheffield as one of those who

[47] On the Dryden monument, see Morris R. Brownell, *Alexander Pope and the Arts of Georgian England* (Oxford: Clarendon, 1978), 341–342; and Terry Friedman, *James Gibbs* (New Haven: Yale University Press, 1984), 99–100. The monument was subsequently much changed.

[48] On these general changes in funerary art during the eighteenth century, see Kemp, 121–122; and Margaret Whinney, *Sculpture in Britain: 1530 to 1830* (Baltimore: Penguin, 1964), 67–73.

[49] See Pope, *Correspondence*, 2:55. On Pope and Gibbs, see Brownell, *Pope and Arts*, 342.

[50] Pope, *Minor Poems*, 156–158.

"(great *Dryden*'s friends before) / With open arms receiv'd one Poet more" (ll. 141–142). Sheffield's name on the monument thus further associates self-effacing Pope and his great poetic predecessor.

Contemporaries were critical of the appearance of Sheffield's name on Dryden's monument. An epigram of 1733 declaimed: "Great *Peers*, 'tis known, can in Oblivion lie: / But no great *Poet* has the Pow'r to die. / At cheap Expence behold engrafted Fame; / . . . / S—d shall borrow *Life* / from *Dryden's Grave*."[51] In 1734, James Ralph criticized Sheffield for "complimenting" himself by inscribing his own name on Dryden's memorial and complained that by means of such inscriptions the erectors of monuments made the fame of the dead the "foundation" of their own.[52] Though he had omitted his own composition and name from the Dryden monument, Pope (so these attacks suggested) had encouraged another to use Dryden's fame in order to increase his own. The reactions to the Dryden monument may have made Pope all the more determined to reject burial and commemoration for himself in the Abbey. While in 1726 he thought it permissible to conjoin Dryden's name to Sheffield's, Pope sought to ensure that his epitaphic self-definition would be all his own by commemorating himself at his own expense far from Westminster Abbey.[53]

In the Dryden epitaph Pope obliquely but distinctly links himself to his great predecessor. In his epitaph upon Elijah Fenton, a minor poet who collaborated on his translations of Homer, Pope praises a humble figure with self-effacing generosity but takes credit for so doing. When William Broome, the third collaborator on the Homer translations, asked Pope to compose a memorial for Fenton in 1730, Pope replied, with an eye to posterity, as follows: "I shall with pleasure take upon me to draw

[51] "On the Old Bust, with a sour Air, on Mr. Dryden's Monument, in Westminster–Abbey," *Gentleman's Magazine* 3 (1733):95–96.

[52] [James Ralph], *A Critical Review of the Publick Buildings, Statues and Ornaments, In, and about London and Westminster* (London, 1734), 76–77, 92.

[53] In 1721 the London printer and alderman John Barber erected a monument to Samuel Butler in the Abbey with an inscription proudly identifying his role, and in 1737 the London architect William Benson erected a monument to Milton in the Abbey with a similar inscription. Though he never criticized Sheffield's inscription of his name upon the Dryden monument, in the 1740s Pope mocked Barber's and Benson's attempts to gain renown in this manner; see the 1742 *Dunciad* 3.325 and 4.109–112; and the epigram in Pope, *Minor Poems*, 395–397. In addition to his friendship with Sheffield, Pope's selective condemnation must partly be explained by his snobbish contempt for London citizens, a far more visceral reaction than his proud protestations of independence from the nobility. Compare this early eighteenth-century epigram's distinction between highborn Sheffield and "mean" Barber as erectors of monuments: "Respect to *Dryden* justly *Sheffield* paid; /. . . . / But whence is *Barber*? that a name so mean / Should, join'd with *Butler*, on a tomb be seen!" ("*On the Same Occasion*" ["*On Setting up Mr. Butler's Monument* in Westminster-Abbey"] in [William Oldys, ed.], *A Collection of Epigrams*, 2d ed., 2 vols. [London, 1735–1737], 1:R1v).

this Amiable, quiet, deserving, unpretending, Christian & Philosophical character, in His Epitaph. There, Truth may be spoken in a few words: as for Flourish, & Oratory, & Poetry, I leave them to Younger and more lively Writers, such as love Writing for writing-sake & would rather show their own Fine Parts, than Report the Valuable ones of any other man. So the Elegy I renounce."[54] Pope had much reason to protest that he would be a selfless reporter of Fenton's excellence. Broome had long felt that both he and Fenton had been exploited by Pope, and posterity has concurred in castigating Pope's shabby treatment of his collaborators. Pope's letter nevertheless expresses a genuine moral scruple, and his distinction between elegy and epitaph points up the ethical ambiguities in his manner of commemoration. Espousing the traditional but increasingly contested view that epitaphs should be short, Pope gives new ethical significance to the long-standing contrast between the epitaph's brief, impersonal praise and the elegy's extended, subjective grief by equating this contrast with the difference between the self-effacing communication of "Truth . . . in a few words" and poetic self-display. Since Pope himself indulged in elegiac self-display in such a poem as the "Elegy to . . . an Unfortunate Lady," his attack on "lively Writers" of elegies, whose liveliness is gained at the dead's expense, seems to be self-reproach as much as criticism of others. When he sent his epitaph upon Fenton to Broome, Pope modestly claimed, "It is not good in any sense but as it is true, and really therefore exemplary to others."[55] The poet who would later assert that he "stoop'd to Truth" in his poetry (*Arbuthnot*, l. 341) thus assured Broome that the brief, plain Fenton epitaph avoided both flattery of the dead and the opportunistic display of the poet.

Fenton was the tutor of Pope's friend William Trumbull, who erected a small marble wall tablet to his teacher in Easthamsted Parish Church. The tablet's only flourishes are the elegant cursive lettering of the inscription and a thin strip of plain marble at its base, a simple design that befits the humble man praised in Pope's epitaph:

> This modest Stone, what few vain Marbles can
> May truly say, here lies an honest Man.
> A Poet, blest beyond the Poet's fate,
> Whom Heav'n kept sacred from the Proud and Great.
> Foe to loud Praise, and Friend to learned Ease,
> Content with Science in the Vale of Peace,
> Calmly he look'd on either Life, and here
> Saw nothing to regret, or there to fear;

[54] Pope, *Correspondence*, 3:128–129.
[55] Pope, *Correspondence*, 3:156.

From Nature's temp'rate feast rose satisfy'd,
Thank'd Heav'n that he had liv'd, and that he dy'd.
                                        A. POPE[56]

Like the plainness of the tablet, the brevity of the epitaph decorously
conveys the modesty of the deceased. In addition, Pope's epitaph on
Fenton appropriately begins with an echo of Crashaw's epitaph upon
Mr. Ashton:

> The modest front of this small floore
> Beleeve mee, Reader can say more
> Than many a braver Marble can;
> *Here lyes a truly honest man.*[57]

Pope modifies Crashaw's opening in two significant ways. Avoiding Crashaw's unusual insertion of a self-referential "mee," Pope lets the "modest Stone" (l. 1) deliver the message, thus effacing himself. While making
the same distinction as Crashaw between modest and vain monuments,
Pope emphasizes the plain truth of what the monument can say rather
than how much it can say. The seventeenth-century proclamation of
epigrammatic sententiousness thus yields to Pope's concern for the supposed brief and simple truth.

Unlike the "honest" Protestant Ashton, "honest" (l. 2) Fenton is a *beatus
vir* in the Roman and neoclassical English retirement tradition. With the
decline of religious "enthusiasm" in the late seventeenth and eighteenth
centuries, the ideal of the honest man lost much of its heavily Protestant
resonance and became more and more associated with the retired country gentleman. Classical resonances and association with the plain yeoman made "honesty" the virtue of choice for the bluff, old-fashioned
country gentleman who rejected the strife of city and court. Cotton
praises the man "who from the busie World retires" and whose contentment stems from honesty: "A very little satisfies / An honest, and a
grateful heart."[58] The Restoration divine Robert South contrasts "the
honest country gentleman" who "sit[s] safe and warm in a moderate

---

[56] Pope, "EPITAPH. *On Mr.* ELIJAH FENTON...," in *Minor Poems*, 318. In this and
subsequent epitaphs I have added Pope's own name, which appears on the inscriptional
tablets, to the printed texts.

[57] Johnson, who pointed out this echo, treated it as a flaw that exemplified the unfortunate
ubiquity of literary copying and the difficulty of true originality; see Samuel Johnson,
"*Rambler* 143," in *The Rambler: Part 2*, ed. W. J. Bate and Albrecht B. Strauss, The Yale
Edition of the Works of Samuel Johnson, vol. 4 (New Haven: Yale University Press, 1969),
399–400; and Johnson, *Lives*, 3:267. I argue, by contrast, that Pope's borrowing constitutes
meaningful imitation.

[58] Charles Cotton, "Contentation. Directed to my Dear Father, and most Worthy Friend,
Mr. Isaac Walton," ll. 101, 89–90 in *Poems of Charles Cotton*, ed. John Buxton (London:
Routledge, 1958), 256.

fortune" with "the highest and richest grandees" who have "ill-got places to lose."[59] In one of his essays, "The dangers of an Honest Man in much Company," Cowley argues that the "honest man," the plain country gentleman, is incapable of the artifice of court or city.[60] He loosely imitates an epigram by Martial (*Epigram* 3. 38) that advises a newcomer to leave the capital quickly because an "Honest and Poor" man cannot survive there.[61] A 1735 epigram in Cowley's vein similarly advises the virtuous countryman "Honestus" to flee the town, because he cannot "pimp, nor cheat, nor swear, nor lye."[62]

Pope himself often associates honesty with the gentleman who plainly and candidly rejects the glittery, insubstantial values of the city and court.[63] Pope professes to write "free from all disguises" in corresponding with Yorkshire gentleman Hugh Bethel and "a few such plain honest men."[64] Pope, who sometimes obscured his own status as a professional writer and the tenant—not owner—of his Twickenham home by portraying himself as a retired country gentleman, similarly commemorates Fenton, who tutored and translated for a living, as an "honest" gentleman of retirement. Pope's flattering depiction of Fenton is faithful to Fenton's own self-idealization: Fenton translated several classical retirement poems and one of his original compositions, "An Epistle to Thomas Lambard, Esq.," adapts Horace's pretense that his epistles are not verse (*Epistle* 1.1.1–10) in order to celebrate in "honest prose" the tranquility of retired life.[65]

In praising Fenton's "learned Ease" (l. 5), the epitaph mixes truth and tact. Pope often complained of Fenton's inordinate laziness and in letters ascribed his death to "Indolencey and Inactivity."[66] In a conversation with Joseph Spence some ten weeks before Fenton's death, Pope deliv-

---

[59] Robert South is cited for a different point in Peter Dixon, *The World of Pope's Satires: An Introduction to the Epistles and Imitations of Horace* (London: Methuen, 1968), 186.

[60] Abraham Cowley, *Essays, Plays, and Sundry Verses,* ed. A. R. Waller (Cambridge: Cambridge University Press, 1906), 443–448. Rachel Trickett discusses Cowley's use of "honest" in *The Honest Muse: A Study in Augustan Verse* (Oxford: Clarendon, 1967), 11.

[61] Cowley, *Essays,* 445.

[62] "*Advice to* HONESTUS," in [Oldys], *Collection,* 1:P3v.

[63] Compare the discussions of Pope's vision of the "honest man" in Dixon, 131–133; and Trickett, 220–222. Pope's epitaphs upon Lord John Caryll and Sir William Trumbull, Sr., proclaim the unusual worth of the dead by using a phrase that would seem almost an oxymoron to the poet and his contemporaries: "An honest Courtier" (*Minor Poems,* 81 and 169). A 1731 essay, "Of Honesty," for example, contrasts the plain virtue of honesty with the courtly show of honor: "*Honesty* is discover'd in a regular course of laudable Actions; *Honour* is wholly external . . . a perpetual *Courtier*" (*Gentleman's Magazine* 1 [1731]:384–385).

[64] Pope, *Correspondence,* 3:519. I quote an undated fragment.

[65] See Elijah Fenton, "An Epistle to Thomas Lambard, Esq.," "Claudian's Old Man of Verona," and "Martial, Lib. X. Epigr. XLVII," in *The Works of the English Poets from Chaucer to Cowper,* ed. Alexander Chalmers, 21 vols. (London, 1810), 10:415–418, 422. Fenton's claim to write "honest prose" is on p. 415.

[66] I cite a 1730 letter from Pope to John Gay in Pope, *Correspondence,* 3:121; see also Pope, *Correspondence,* 2:45, 2:125.

ered a judgment more balanced than that in the panegyric epitaph: "Fenton is a right honest man. He is fat and indolent; a very good scholar: sits within and does nothing but read or compose."[67] The epitaph dignifies such laziness by treating the deceased as the embodiment of a wholly admirable Epicureanism. Since Epicurus led a life of retired contemplation and advocated "tranquility of mind and indolence of body,"[68] Pope could with little strain make Fenton into a modern exemplar of the Epicurean life. Pope's Fenton, who wisely treats life as a "feast" (l. 9) to be enjoyed and then left without fear or fuss, recalls the Epicurean sage against whom Lucretius and Horace measure the mass of men. Lucretius imagines Nature asking man: "Why not, like a banqueter fed full of life, withdraw with contentment and rest in peace, you fool?"[69] Echoing Lucretius, Horace ends *Satire* 1.1 by lamenting that "seldom can we find one who says he has had a happy life, and who, when his time is sped, will quit life in contentment, like a guest who has had his fill."[70]

Eighteenth-century Englishmen often identified Epicureanism with sinful indulgence. A satiric epitaph, "On the Death of an Epicure," projects the baneful consequences of the Epicurean view of life as a feast: "At length, my friends, the *feast* of life is o'er: / I've eat sufficient—and I'll drink no more: / My night is come; I've spent a jovial day; / 'Tis time to part; but oh!—what is to pay?"[71] Pope's claim that the deceased enjoyed "Nature's temp'rate feast" (l. 9) defends Fenton's Epicureanism by implicitly distinguishing between a natural, moderate pursuit of pleasure and unnatural luxury. The contrast was traditional in seventeenth- and eighteenth-century defenses of the ancient philosophical school. Invoking Epicurus's authority for his own retired way of life, for example, Cowley praises the ancient sage for enjoying nature's "cheap and virtuous" delights and avoiding gluttony.[72] A work attributed to Saint-Évremond, the most well-known of the modern Epicureans, imagines Epicurus reproaching the gluttonous banqueter Nero for not taking pleasure in the food and drink that "the Simplicity of Nature" provides.[73]

Christians also often attacked Epicureanism for its supposed atheism,

[67] Spence, 1:213 (no. 501).

[68] I cite the description of Epicurus in Sir William Temple's "Upon the Gardens of Epicurus; or, Of Gardening, in the Year 1685," in *Five Miscellaneous Essays by Sir William Temple*, ed. Samuel Holt Monk (Ann Arbor: University of Michigan Press, 1963), 10.

[69] "Cur non ut plenus vitae conviva recedis, / Aequo animoque capis securam, stulte, quietam?" (Lucretius, *De Rerum Nature* 3.938–939).

[70] "... raro, qui se vixisse beatum / dicat et exacto contentus tempore vita / cedat uti conviva satur, reperire queamus" (Horace, *Satire* 1.1.117–119).

[71] "On the Death of an Epicure" in [Richard Graves, ed.], *The Festoon, A Select Collection of Epigrams*, 4th ed. (London, 1767), 212.

[72] Cowley, "The Garden," in his *Essays*, 424–425.

[73] "Reflections upon the Doctrine of Epicurus," in *The Works of Monsieur de St. Evremond*, trans. Mr. Des Maizeaux, 3 vols. (London, 1728), 3:291.

but Pope Christianizes Fenton's pursuit of pleasure. His claim that "Heav'n kept" Fenton "sacred from the Proud and Great" (l. 4) suggests the beneficent guidance of a Christian God in Fenton's pursuit of Epicurean retirement. Pope's assertion that Fenton "thank'd Heav'n" (l. 10) after he rose from his "feast" casts Fenton as a Christian Epicurean in the tradition of Erasmus. In his colloquy "The Epicurean" ("Epicureus"), Erasmus argues, in the words of an early eighteenth-century translator, that "*Christians truly pious are true* Epicureans."[74] In the same colloquy the gluttons' feasts are contrasted with the truly Epicurean meal of the "godly Man" who humbly receives his modest repast from a "kind Father." The religious man concludes his meal just as Fenton concludes his "temp'rate feast" of life: "*having return'd Thanks* [to God], at last he rises from the Table, not stuffed, but recreated; not loaded, but refreshed in Mind, as well as Body."[75]

Fenton looks backward upon life without "regret" and forward to the afterlife without "fear" (l. 8) in a cast of mind that further recalls Erasmus. "The Epicurean" argues that the good man alone can attain "the Remembrance of a Life innocently pass'd, and the Hope of a better to come."[76] Erasmus is Christianizing a classical formulation. In another colloquy that treats a modest meal as a synecdoche of the Christian life, "The Religious Feast" ("Convivium Religiosum"), the banqueters applaud Cato the Elder's declaration in Cicero's *De senectute* (22.83) that he has neither regrets concerning his life nor fears concerning his death.[77] The symposiasts nevertheless criticize Cato's Stoic equanimity because it involves no trust in God. They prefer the dying Socrates's more diffident expression of "hope, that God, of his Goodness, would accept him for the Honesty of his Intentions."[78] Like Cato neither regretting the past nor fearing the future, but like Socrates displaying humble piety, Fenton perfectly fulfills the Erasmian ideal.[79]

[74] N. Bailey, trans., *All the Familiar Colloquies of Desiderius Erasmus* . . . , 2d ed. (London, 1733), 553.

[75] Bailey, 564 (italics mine). The Latin reads: " . . . et gratiarum actio succedens; postremo surgit a mensa non distentus, sed recreatus, non onustus, sed refectus, et refectus mente pariter et corpore"; see Desiderius Erasmus, *Colloquia*, ed. L.-E. Halkin, F. Bierlaire, and R. Hoven, Opera Omnia Desiderii Erasmi Roterodami, vol. 3 (Amsterdam: North-Holland Publishing Company, 1972), 731. Pope owned Jean Le Clerc's eleven-volume edition of Erasmus's *Opera Omnia* (1703–1706); see Maynard Mack, *Collected in Himself: Essays Critical, Biographical, and Bibliographical on Pope and Some of his Contemporaries* (Newark: University of Delaware Press, 1982), 308, 320. I cite Bailey's accurate and felicitous eighteenth-century English translation in the text for convenience.

[76] Bailey, 559–560 (" . . . vitae innocenter actae recordatio ac spes vitae melioris"; Erasmus, *Colloquia*, 727).

[77] Bailey, 117; Erasmus, *Colloquia*, 253.

[78] Bailey, 118–119 ("Est tamen mihi bona spes, quod ille conatus nostros sit boni consulturus"; Erasmus, *Colloquia*, 254).

[79] Other writers who influenced Pope adopted the Erasmian definition of the good life

Pope considered himself an Erasmian Catholic. He admired Erasmus's humanist synthesis of Christian piety and classical learning as well as his attempt to moderate between Catholic and Protestant extremists. The poet defined his own ecumenism as an *imitatio Erasmi*.[80] In a 1729 letter to Swift, Pope declared, "Yet am I of the Religion of Erasmus, a Catholick; so I live; so I shall die; and hope one day to meet you, Bishop Atterbury, poor Craggs, Dr. Garth, Dean Berkley, and Mr. Hutchenson, in that place, To which God of his infinite mercy bring us, and every body!"[81] In his imitation of Horace's *Satire* 2.1, published in 1733, he compares himself to Erasmus: "Papist or Protestant, or both between, / Like good *Erasmus* in an honest Mean / In Moderation placing all my Glory" (ll. 65–67). Pope's association of "honest" virtue and Erasmian religious moderation is characteristic.[82]

The Erasmian resonances of the Fenton epitaph compel reconsideration of the opening echo of Crashaw. In 1710 Pope selected the epitaph upon Ashton as one of Crashaw's best compositions.[83] Focusing on style, Pope praises the poems that Crashaw composed in a "natural, middleway."[84] Pope's approval of stylistic moderation suggests, however, his approval of other kinds of moderation. While probably knowing little of the precise historical context of the Ashton epitaph, Pope would have seen in the poem a religious via media rare in English poetry. As an Erasmian, ecumenical Catholic who adhered to the "honest Mean," Pope was undoubtedly drawn to an epitaph by a soon-to-be-Catholic poet in praise of a Protestant "honest man" who avoided religious controversy and attacks upon Rome. Pope's Fenton shares with Crashaw's Ashton more than an epithet: both men avoid the "loudness" of vainglory and strife, seek peace, and experience appropriately quiet deaths. Unlike Crashaw's poem, Pope's does not explicitly treat religious divisions, but

---

and death. Montaigne, who was profoundly indebted to Erasmus, claims in his *Essays*, "I neither complain of the past, nor do I fear the future"; see Michel de Montaigne, "Of Repentance," in *Essays*, trans. Charles Cotton, 3 vols. (London, 1685–1693), 3:46. In *Spectator* 349, Addison follows Erasmus in praising the calm of Socrates's death stemming from the Greek philosopher's "Consciousness of a well-spent Life, and the Prospect of a happy Eternity" (*The Spectator*, ed. Donald F. Bond, 5 vols. [Oxford: Clarendon, 1965], 3:300).

[80] On Erasmus as a religious model for Pope, see Chester Chapin, "Alexander Pope, Erasmian Catholic," *Eighteenth-Century Studies* 6 (1973):411–430.

[81] Pope, *Correspondence*, 3:81.

[82] Thus in a letter of 1714 to Caryll he contrasted moderate members of religious and political factions with the extremists on both sides: "while the most honest and moral of each [religious and political] party think me no ill man, I can easily support it, tho' the most violent and mad of all parties rose up to throw dirt at me" (*Correspondence*, 1:238–239). See also his self-definition as "a Christian and honest man" who avoids extremism in another 1714 letter to Caryll (*Correspondence*, 1:220); and the 1717 response to Atterbury's attempt to convert him, previously cited, in which Pope claims that all "honest" Christians share fundamental beliefs (*Correspondence*, 1:455).

[83] Pope, *Correspondence*, 1:111.

[84] Pope, *Correspondence*, 1:110.

such silence itself supports the poet's own form of Christian irenicism: the Protestant Fenton led an "honest" life, and that is enough for the Catholic Pope and, so he hopes, for his charitable readers.

By linking the religious irenicism of the Ashton epitaph to the retirement ideal, however, the Fenton epitaph differs from Crashaw's work in pointedly rejecting the political status quo. While Crashaw's opening lines are followed by a proclamation of Ashton's allegiances to the Caroline religious and political establishment ("His Conscience was a thing / That troubled neither Church nor King"), Pope's opening couplet is followed by the claim that Fenton was protected from "the Proud and Great." By modifying Crashaw, Pope underscores his anticourt ideal: only among such retired men as Fenton, not among the social elite of the Hanoverian-Walpole regime, can true peace be found.

The epitaph is thus very generous in presenting Fenton, whom Pope in fact considered a good but flawed man, as the embodiment of the poet's central ideals. Pope is nevertheless patronizing towards Fenton. Like most of the poet's sepulchral inscriptions, the epitaph upon Fenton acknowledges the fame of its self-effacing author by bearing his name at its close. Also like most of Pope's epitaphs, the Fenton epitaph was not only published in various editions of Pope's poems but also quickly appeared in several London journals.[85] Pope knows that it is he who preserves Fenton's unassuming merit, which would otherwise go unrecognized. No more is said of Fenton as a poet than that "Heav'n blest" him "beyond the Poet's fate" (l. 3) by keeping him away from the high and mighty. Pope thus hints that Fenton did not have the talent to sustain public exposure. Providence protected Fenton from the challenges faced by Pope himself, who "live[s] among the Great" but remains, by virtue of his integrity, "No Pimp of Pleasure, and no Spy of State" (*Imitations of Horace: Satire* II.1, l. 134). While he portrays himself as necessarily marshaling all his poetic power in order to assert his own virtue against those who would corrupt him, Pope commemorates Fenton as a man of minor poetic gifts to whom Heaven grants an uncorrupted life.

Fenton is the earliest of the major portraits of the plain "honest" man as "other" in Pope's oeuvre. Such figures are morally superior to, but also simpler than, Pope, who must save them from oblivion or slander, thus affirming his own commitment to "honesty" while transcending that virtue as courageous poet. Pope's portrait of Fenton notably resembles the portrait of Alexander Pope, Sr., in *Arbuthnot*. Like Fenton, Pope's father lived a life of retirement, was "by Nature honest" (l. 400), and avoided "Civil and Religious Rage" (l. 394). His father's peacefulness

---

[85] See note in Pope, *Minor Poems*, 319.

does not save him from others' attacks, and Pope must ward off slander by doing public battle with his father's enemies. Pope similarly saves Fenton from oblivion.[86]

In commemorating his fellow poet and friend John Gay, who died in 1732, Pope simultaneously allows Gay to define himself for posterity and redefines the deceased by posthumously enlisting him with Pope as an embattled opponent of the powers that be. The prominent sculptor Rysbrack designed Gay's Abbey monument, which was finally erected in 1737.[87] Masks and musical instruments representing the various arts at which Gay excelled crown a pyramidal backdrop. A mourning putto at the pyramid's base holds a portrait medallion of Gay. Gay's own two-line epitaph upon himself appears on the pedestal of the medallion, with Pope's verse epitaph below, on the monument's base, and, lower still, a panegyric prose inscription.[88] The pyramid and the medallion portrait, derived from classical medals, are two of the most common eighteenth-century pagan symbols of immortality.[89] While these, along with the symbols of the various arts, proclaim Gay's fame as an artist, the two verse compositions by Pope and Gay provide contrasting comments upon the life and career of the deceased.

Pope had been asked by Gay to arrange that the latter poet's distich upon himself be placed on his grave. In October 1727, Gay was seriously ill and greatly depressed by the fact that his court ambitions had resulted in nothing more than an offer of the menial position of gentleman-usher to the two-year old Princess Louisa. In a letter to Pope he exclaimed, "O that I had never known what a Court was!" Near the end of the letter, Gay requested that Pope make sure that Gay's monument be inscribed with the epitaph, "Life is a Jest, and all Things show it; / I thought so once, but now I know it," and "what more" Pope should "think proper."[90] Pope seems to have responded to this letter with a

[86] Even Pope's famous praise of the "honest man" in the *Essay on Man*—"A Wit's a feather, and a Chief a rod; / An honest Man's the noblest work of God" (4. 247–248)—is not free of condescension. William Empson comments aptly: "Pope...retains a certain patronage towards the most ideal man he can conceive, perhaps even compared to the chiefs and wits in Pope's own set; but it is from this that he gets the dignity of his assertion; only God could afford to take such a tone, so a sentence that takes it to point out God's noblest work is sure to be well-informed" (*The Structure of Complex Words* [London: Chatto & Windus, 1977], 196).

[87] On the erection of the Gay monument, see *Gentleman's Magazine* 7 (1737):313.

[88] For a description of the monument, see M. I. Webb, *Michael Rysbrack: Sculptor* (London: Country Life Limited, 1954), 87. The text of all the inscriptions may be found in *Gentleman's Magazine* 7 (1737):313.

[89] See Kemp, 169; and Katharine A. Esdaile, "Sculpture," in *Johnson's England: An Account of the Life & Manners of His Age*, ed. A. S. Turberville, 2 vols. (Oxford: Clarendon, 1933), 2:76.

[90] *The Letters of John Gay*, ed. C. F. Burgess (Oxford: Clarendon, 1966), 66–67. I here

comic epitaph of his own commemorating "honest Jack" and his "death" to the court.[91] He later saw to it, however, that Gay's epitaph upon himself was inscribed upon the monument followed by Pope's own composition. Pope's epitaph defends Gay's composition from misinterpretation:

> Of Manners gentle, of Affections mild;
> In Wit, a Man; Simplicity, a Child;
> With native Humour temp'ring virtuous Rage,
> Form'd to delight at once and lash the age;
> Above Temptation, in a low Estate,
> And uncorrupted, ev'n among the Great;
> A safe Companion, and an easy Friend,
> Unblam'd thro' Life, lamented in thy End.
> These are Thy Honours! not that here thy Bust
> Is mix't with Heroes, or with Kings thy dust;
> But that the Worthy and the Good shall say,
> Striking their pensive bosomes—*Here* lies GAY.
>
> A. POPE[92]

"In Wit, a Man; Simplicity, a Child" (l. 2) seeks to quell harsh reactions to Gay's epitaph upon himself. Gay's composition is, Pope suggests, a piece of childlike "simplicity" to be indulged rather than a mature expression of godless cynicism to be decried.[93] Pope concedes the foibles of his friend in order to shield him from more severe criticism.[94]

Pope not only defends but also corrects Gay's epitaph: the distich is a rueful *jeu d'esprit* stemming from disappointment with the court, and Pope counters Gay's disappointment with an affirmation of the immortal "honours" (l. 9) that will distinguish Gay's moral superiority from the courtly corruptions of "heroes" and "kings" (l. 10). The two verse epitaphs thus place in dialogue the two men whose names appear together

---

adopt Burgess's dating of the letter (65–66, n. 2) rather than the later 1729 date adopted by Sherburn in Pope, *Correspondence*, 3:19, n. 3.

[91] See Pope, *Minor Poems*, 295.

[92] Pope, "EPITAPH. On Mr. GAY. In *Westminster-Abbey*, 1732," in *Minor Poems*, 349–350.

[93] Pope's description echoes Dryden's praise of Anne Killigrew: "Her Wit was more than Man, her Innocence a Child!" ("To the Pious Memory of . . . Mrs. Anne Killigrew," l. 70 in *The Poems of John Dryden*, ed. James Kinsley, 4 vols. [Oxford: Clarendon, 1958], 1:461). "Simplicity" is, however, far more equivocal than Dryden's "innocence." In a letter to Pope, Swift, indeed, criticized Pope's use of the word because the "vulgar" might not be able to distinguish "simplicity" from "folly" (Pope, *Correspondence* 3:361).

[94] Despite Pope's efforts, Gay's epitaph upon himself provoked much criticism because its denial of life's seriousness seemed blasphemous. See, for example, Samuel Johnson's 1738 criticism of the epitaph reprinted in *Samuel Johnson*, ed. Donald Greene, The Oxford Authors (Oxford: Oxford University Press, 1984), 51–53; Samuel Richardson, *Familiar Letters on Important Occasions* (1741), ed. Brian W. Downs (London: Routledge, 1928), 211; and Myles Cooper, "Epitaph," in his *Poems on Several Occasions* (Oxford, 1761), 23.

on the monument. This dialogue is similar to those of Pope's contemporaneous Horatian imitations, in which Pope addresses a "friend" whose weak or compromising attitude serves as a foil to Pope's own heroic, independent stance.

Pope's composition modifies a traditional epitaphic structure: a list of attributes that grammatically depend upon a "Here lies X" clause that is withheld, for maximum closure, until the end of the poem.[95] Pope's epitaph initially frustrates but ultimately fulfills the reader's expectations. After eight lines of adjectives and epithets that would normally lead directly into the statement *"Here* lies GAY" (l. 12), upon which all would syntactically and emotionally turn, Pope adds three and a half lines that change the sense of the closing statement. In so doing Pope makes the first eight lines an ungrammatical fragment, as Samuel Johnson objected,[96] but the anacoluthon emphasizes, however awkwardly, Pope's determination to redefine what *"Here* lies GAY" means. By contrasting Gay's physical burial among the "great" with Gay's spiritual dwelling in the "bosoms" of the "Worthy and the Good" (l. 11), Pope supplies the expected closing formula only when the "here" has been defined in opposition to the actual tomb in Westminster Abbey. Adding topical political resonance to the traditional conceit that the living are the true monument of the deceased, Pope removes Gay from the contamination of the Abbey just as he removes himself from the potential of such contamination in his epitaph upon himself.[97]

Johnson's further complaint that "the Worthy" and "the Good" are redundant specifications reveals that Pope is not in fact very interested in defining the virtuous comrades of Gay: their identity is less important than their function as the opponents of the social establishment.[98] A complimentary epigram of 1733, "To Mr. Pope, on his Epitaph on Gay," by John Boyle, the fifth earl of Cork and Orrery, indeed imagines Pope alone defending Gay against the court:

> Entomb'd with kings though Gay's cold ashes lie,
> A nobler monument thy strains supply.
> Thy matchless muse, still faithful to thy friend,
> By courts unaw'd, his virtues dares commend.

[95] For examples of this epitaphic form, see Sidney Godolphin's and James Clayton's epitaphs upon Jonson in *Jonsonus Virbius* (1638), in Jonson, 11:450–451; the epitaph by Lucius Cary, viscount Falkland, upon the countess of Huntingdon, d. 1633, in Thomas Joseph Pettigrew, *Chronicles of the Tombs* (London, 1857), 339; and Sidney Godolphin's epitaph upon Lady Rich, first published in 1658 and reprinted in [Oldys], 2:B6r.

[96] Johnson, *Lives*, 3:269.

[97] Maynard Mack plausibly suggests that Pope may have composed "Heroes, and Kings!" shortly after the erection of the Gay monument in *Alexander Pope: A Life* (New Haven: Yale University Press, 1986), 733.

[98] Johnson, *Lives*, 3:269.

> Lamented Gay! forget thy treatment past,
> Look down, and see thy merit crown'd at last.
> A destiny more glorious who can hope?
> In life belov'd, in death bemoan'd by Pope.[99]

Orrery follows Pope's lead in addressing Gay and answering his disappointments in life with an assertion of his posthumous honors. Orrery, however, reduces Pope's original contrast between the Abbey's heroes and kings and "the Worthy and the Good" to a contrast between the court and Pope, the heroic poet who glorifies by commemorating his friend. Written during the same period as the Gay epitaph and possibly influenced by the Orrery epigram, Pope's *Epistle to Arbuthnot* does much the same. It contrasts the "great" who neglected Gay and two solitary figures, the poet Pope and Gay's patron, the duke of Queensberry:

> Blest be the *Great*! For those they take away,
> And those they left me—For they left me GAY,
> Left me to see neglected Genius bloom,
> Neglected die! and tell it on his Tomb;
> Of all thy blameless Life the sole Return
> My Verse, and QUEENSB'RY weeping o'er thy Urn!
>   (ll. 255–260)

Pope's epitaph upon Gay has been absorbed into Pope's portrait of himself in the act of saving the worthy from neglect. Pope now uses the deceased to indulge the self-display he had so self-consciously renounced a few years earlier in his letter to Broome.

Pope's epitaphs upon aristocrats and major public figures also reveal the poet's struggles against the corruption of funerary verse. In humanist fashion Pope attacked those prouder of their lineage than their personal achievements (*Essay on Man* 4.205–216) and inveighed against the "Sepulchral Lyes" written by Grub-Street hacks for their patrons (*Dunciad Variorum* 1.41; 1742 *Dunciad* 1.43). He therefore rightly worried that he would be charged with flattery in his own epitaphs upon the "great."[100] When members of the social elite sought epitaphs from him for their relatives or loved ones, Pope occasionally complied and composed flattering epitaphs such as those he himself condemns. In the *Epilogue to the Satires, Dialogue II* Pope complains, "Each Mother asks it ["random

---

[99] [John Boyle, Lord Orrery], "To Mr. Pope, on the Same [i.e., his epitaph on Gay]," in *Gentleman's Magazine* 3 (1733):319. In May, 1733 Swift sent the poem to Pope and Pope acknowledged in reply his pleasure at being praised by a man of "virtue" (*Correspondence*, 5:13 and 3:372).

[100] See also Pope's description of epitaphs as "Flatteries and False History" in a 1736 letter to Richard Allen (*Correspondence*, 4:13).

Praise"] for her Booby Son, / Each Widow asks it for the Best of Men, / For him she weeps, and him she weds agen. / Praise cannot stoop, like Satire, to the Ground" (ll. 107–110). The Twickenham editor, John Butt, suggests that these lines refer to the requests of the duchess of Buckingham for an epitaph upon her son and of Anna Knight, née Craggs, for an epitaph upon her second (but not last) husband. Since Pope complied with both requests and composed epitaphs upon "a Mother's justest Pride" ("EPITAPH. *On* EDMUND *Duke of* BUCKINGHAM...," l. 3) and a beloved "fond Husband" ("EPITAPH. On *JOHN KNIGHT*," l. 4), there is self-criticism in his declaration that such praise is unthinkable.[101]

In his most innovative compositions upon the "great," however, Pope tries to avoid the charge of flattery by introducing a new way of declaring the worth of the dead. Financially independent and proud by temperament, Pope declines to have aristocratic patrons but claims a chosen few as his "friends."[102] In some epitaphs on members of the social elite, he justifies his commemorative role by asserting his deep personal feelings for the deceased, replacing the impersonal, panegyric "maker" that dominates the genre before him with the sincere, lamenting friend.[103] Pope thereby influentially suggests that the best demonstration of the value of the dead, however socially exalted, is the grief of those who knew them well. He also raises anew, however, the problematic ethical status of his own self-display in commemorating others.

In his epitaphs upon Simon Harcourt the Younger, written between 1722 and 1724 and inscribed upon a wall tablet in Stanton-Harcourt Church, and upon Robert and Mary Digby, written sometime between 1727 and 1730 and inscribed upon a wall tablet in Sherbourne Abbey, Pope mingles his personal sorrow with that of the fathers who erected the monuments. While the first stanza of the Harcourt epitaph is a traditional, impersonal panegyric, the second stanza introduces Pope himself:

> To this sad Shrine, who'er thou art, draw near,
> Here lies the Friend most lov'd, the Son most dear:
> Who ne'er knew Joy, but Friendship might divide,
> Or gave his Father grief, but when he dy'd.

---

[101] Pope, *Minor Poems*, 362, 364.

[102] On "friendship" as opposed to patronage in Pope's work, see Dixon, 108–121. On Pope's cult of friendship, see also Dustin H. Griffin, *Alexander Pope: The Poet in the Poems* (Princeton: Princeton University Press, 1978), 100–126.

[103] On "sincerity" in Pope's poetry, see also Leon Guilhamet, *The Sincere Ideal: Studies on Sincerity in Eighteenth-Century English Literature* (Montreal: McGill-Queen's University Press, 1974), 136–151; and Trickett, 222–223.

> How vain is Reason, Eloquence how weak,
> If *Pope* must tell what HARCOURT cannot speak?
> Oh let thy once-lov'd Friend inscribe thy Stone,
> And with a Father's Sorrows mix his own![104]

The fiction of the poem is that its poet composes the epitaph only because the father, struck dumb by grief, cannot. By asking the deceased to allow him as a "once-lov'd Friend" to inscribe the epitaph, Pope suggests that he would not be worthy of writing the poem merely as a commissioned poet; he also reveals, by his humble address to his deceased friend, precisely why he feels he is worthy. Simon Harcourt, Sr., rightly called this epitaph upon his son "a perpetual monument of your [i.e. Pope's] friendship": the epitaph displays the bond between Pope and the deceased rather than concentrating solely upon the virtues of the latter.[105]

While the first two verse paragraphs of the Digby epitaph consist of frigid exclamations that attempt to evoke the triumphant entrance of the dead into eternity, the brief, closing verse paragraph movingly renders the grief of both father and poet:

> Yet take these tears, Mortality's relief,
> And till we share your joys, forgive our grief;
> These little rites, a Stone, a Verse, receive,
> 'Tis all a Father, all a Friend can give!
> A. POPE[106]

Father and friend are presented together in the very process of offering all that they can give to the deceased—their tears, the memorial tablet, the epitaph itself—with full awareness of how little their "rites" can do either for themselves or the dead. The appeal to "Mortality's Relief" suggests that only the mourners' grief and need to console themselves validates the inscription.[107]

The Harcourt and Digby compositions may be termed elegiac epitaphs. By conjuring up at the end of the poems an imagined moment

---

[104] Pope, "EPITAPH. *On the Honble.* SIMON HARCOURT, *Only Son of the Lord Chancellor* HARCOURT. . . . ," in *Minor Poems*, 242.

[105] Pope, *Correspondence*, 2:147.

[106] Pope, "EPITAPH. *On the Monument of the Honble.* ROBERT DIGBY . . . *erected by . . . the Lord* DIGBY . . . ," ll. 17–20 in *Minor Poems*, 314.

[107] The Digby epitaph's final couplet recalls Pope's 1709 translation of the Sarpedon episode from *Iliad* 16, where Zeus exclaims upon the death of his son: "His Friends a Tomb and Pyramid shall rear; / These unavailing Rites he may receive, / These, after Death, are All a God can give!" (ll. 333–335). While Homer's Zeus says only that a mound and commemorative pillar are "the due [*to . . . geras*] of the dead" (*Iliad* 16.675), Pope adds that these are "unavailing" but all that friends and a god can provide. Thus while Homer states the objective privileges of heroes slain in battle, Pope emphasizes the mourners' subjective feelings, which lead to "rites" that can do nothing but attest to love for the dead.

at which the mourning poet actually inscribes the monument or begs the inscription's acceptance by the deceased, Pope prevents the reader from separating the epitaph as a public memorial from its origins in the poet's own personal mourning process.[108] Unlike the traditional elegy-epitaph combination, which moves from the grief expressed in the temporal rites of mourning to the praise rendered in an enduring monumental inscription, these elegiac epitaphs end by dramatizing rather than suppressing or transcending the poet's time-bound, personal grief.

Pope tries to avoid confining the deceased to a private world of grieving family and friends, however, by implicitly or explicitly positing his friendship with the dead as an ideal against which the general corruption of England can be judged. His elegiac inscriptions bear his name. Both the Harcourt and Digby wall tablets are relatively modest memorials, and like Dryden's name on the wall tablet in memory of the marquis of Winchester, the well-known name of Pope adds great prestige to these otherwise undistinguished monuments. Pope clearly expects his readers, furthermore, to consider his announcement of personal sorrow as a public act of discrimination between those who are worthy of his grief and those who are not. Pope's epitaph upon Secretary of State James Craggs, published and placed on Craggs's monument in Westminster Abbey in 1727, further reveals the public status of Pope's friendships:

> Statesman, yet Friend to Truth! of Soul sincere,
> In Action faithful, and in Honour clear!
> Who broke no promise, serv'd no private end,
> Who gain'd no Title, and who lost no Friend,
> Ennobl'd by Himself, by All approv'd,
> Prais'd, wept, and honour'd, by the Muse he lov'd.
>   A. POPE[109]

Pope asserts the sincerity of his praise by introducing himself at the end as a "Muse" lamenting the loss of a friend.[110] While the concluding line

---

[108] Such "elegiac epitaphs" are examples of what Alastair Fowler terms "modal transformation." On the distinction between a "genre," which has an external form and can be named nominatively, and a "mode," a vaguer, adjectival concept, see his *Kinds of Literature: An Introduction to the Theory of Genres and Modes* (Cambridge: Harvard University Press, 1982), 106–111. Although Fowler concentrates on a later period, his discussion of "elegiac modulations" in the nineteenth century sheds light upon Pope's practice (206–212).

[109] Pope, "EPITAPH on JAMES CRAGGS, Esq.; In *Westminster-Abbey*," in *Minor Poems*, 281–282.

[110] The epitaph repeats, with only the last line modified to acknowledge Craggs's death, Pope's praise of Craggs in "To Mr. ADDISON, Occasioned by his Dialogues on MEDALS," ll. 70–72 (*Minor Poems*, 204). The self-quotation evinces the cult of friendship, for in the early poem Pope imagined a commemorative medal being cast of the still-living Craggs: "Then shall thy CRAGS (and let me call him mine) / On the cast ore, another Pollio, shine" (ll. 63–64). Virgil not only praises Pollio as a consul and patron (*Eclogue* 4.1–14) but also

personalizes the preceding brief, impersonal praise, the panegyric itself
suggests the public significance of Pope's personal friendship with
Craggs. Craggs was an exceptional public figure, the poet claims, precisely because he escaped the corruptions of office to be a true friend.
He was, first of all, a "Friend to Truth." The couplet "Who broke no
promise, serv'd no private end, / Who gain'd no Title, and who lost no
Friend" further suggests that his personal attachments had public significance, for friendship is a true public virtue opposed to the all too
common pursuit of "private end[s]" by public officials.[111] Once more
the two names upon the epitaph, Craggs and Pope, are designed to
link, in a fashion simultaneously intimate and public, the living and
the dead.

Pope's protestations of friendship and sorrow in his elegiac epitaphs
do not provide a viable solution, however, to the problem of praise in
a period when the social elite and public officials were increasingly dis-
credited. Pope's elegiac epitaphs indeed raise anew the issue of whether
the famous poet who displays his grief overshadows the deceased as the
true subject of interest. Though admired by Pope, Craggs was notorious
for his involvement in the South-Sea Bubble scandal, and the Craggs
epitaph could easily be read as evidence of Pope's partiality toward one
who simply happened to be his friend rather than as a fitting tribute to
a man of public virtue. In a left-handed compliment to Pope, Aaron
Hill "redeems" the epitaph on Craggs by celebrating the poet's glorious
transformation of base material into art:

> How *lost* this *pomp of verse*! how *vain* the *hope*,
> That thought can dwell on *Craigs* [*sic*], in view of *Pope*!
> When, upon *Rubicon*'s fam'd bank is shown
> *Caesar*'s press'd foot, on the remember'd stone;
> No traveller once asks the *quarry*'s name,
> Whence the coarse *grit*, by chance distinguish'd came;

---

describes him as one who loves the pastoral Muse and whom the pastoral poet loves in
return (*Eclogue* 3.84, 88). Craggs, the new Pollio, will likewise be a friend to the new Virgil,
Pope.

[111] Pope's celebration of true friendship as the basis of public virtue is an idealizing
counter-response to the practical need for "friends" (i.e., clients and allies) in eighteenth-
century politics; see Randolph Trumbach, *The Rise of the Egalitarian Family: Aristocratic
Kinship and Domestic Relations in Eighteenth-Century England* (New York: Academic Press,
1978), 61–68. For Pope, true friends promoted the virtuous society, while false friends
preserved the Walpolean status quo. The "Temple of Friendship" of Pope's friend Lord
Cobham at Stowe suggests the political resonances of ideal friendship: it had emblems of
"Friendship . . . [and] . . . Justice, and Liberty" as well as busts of leading Whig patriots
opposed to Walpole. See the description in George Bickham, *The Beauties of Stow* (1750),
intro. George B. Clarke, Augustan Reprint Society nos. 185–186 (Los Angeles: University
of California Press, 1977), 53–54.

But thinks, with *rev'rence,* here *great Julius* trod,
And *hails* the footstep of a *Roman God!*[112]

For Hill one name upon the monument outshines the other, and Pope's commemoration of a beloved friend becomes simply another monument to Pope's own glory. It is hard to know whether the dull but prickly Hill, who both admired and envied Pope, fully intended this compliment to be as doubled-edged as it is. Whatever his conscious intentions, by praising Pope's poetic skill but denying the worthiness of Craggs, Hill undercuts Pope as a credible arbiter of enduring worth and reduces Pope's lament for the dead to another of the poet's self-displays.[113]

Hill's reaction to the Craggs epitaph parallels eighteenth-century reactions to the Craggs funerary monument. The rise in status of funerary art in the eighteenth century was sometimes obtained at the expense of the supposedly great men who were commemorated. Spectators increasingly viewed funerary monuments as expressions of the artistry of their makers rather than as memorials of the dead, concentrating upon the display of skill rather than the alleged probity of the highborn or wealthy men who were commemorated. While Pope himself was concerned that the statue of Craggs accurately capture the likeness of his departed friend,[114] others were far more interested in Gibbs's novel and arresting design of the statue, which adapted a classical pose in order to depict the deceased standing cross-legged and leaning upon the urn ostensibly containing his own ashes (Figure 5). When he comments on the Craggs monument, James Ralph, for example, says nothing of the deceased but praises the pose as "pathetique and judicious."[115] The Craggs statue was often imitated, so that the monument was quickly admired as a powerful artistic innovation, rather than condemned as a monument to a corrupt secretary of state.[116] Gibbs's artistry, like that of Pope, overshadowed the deceased. Aesthetic appreciation was born of disbelief.

Over the course of the eighteenth century critics increasingly com-

[112] Aaron Hill, "*An* Epigram, *occasion'd by some Verses, on a Monument, in* Westminster Abbey," in *Works of the late Aaron Hill, Esq.,* 4 vols. (London, 1754), 3:31. These lines were reportedly attached to the monument itself; see John Hackett, *Select and Remarkable Epitaphs on Illustrious and Other Persons . . . ,* 2 vols. (London, 1757), 1:149.

[113] The passage is cited as extravagant praise in Dorothy Brewster, *Aaron Hill: Poet, Dramatist, Projector* (New York: Columbia University Press, 1913), 207. Brewster's careful chronological treatment of Hill's and Pope's several quarrels and reconciliations (pp. 201–238) underestimates, however, the uncontrollable ambivalence Hill felt towards his great contemporary and Pope's wary contempt for an admirer-critic who continually demanded Pope's attention.

[114] On the poet's concern, see Pope, *Correspondence,* 2:242–243.

[115] [Ralph], 73.

[116] On the influence of the Craggs monument throughout the later eighteenth century, see Kemp, 133; and Whinney, 80–81. The most famous eighteenth-century imitation was Peter Scheemakers's monument for Shakespeare, erected in February 1741 in the Abbey.

Figure 5. Monument of James Craggs, d. 1727, in Westminster Abbey. By permission of the dean of Westminster Abbey.

mented upon the gap between the artistic genius of commemorative artists and the insignificance of the "great" men they commemorated. Oliver Goldsmith's description in 1761 of Louis François Roubiliac's Westminster Abbey monuments resembles Hill's comments on Pope's commemoration of Craggs: "There [in Westminster Abbey] I found several new monuments erected to the memory of several great men; the names of the great men I absolutely forget, but well I remember that Roubillac was the statuary who carved them ... Alas, alas, cried I, such monuments as these confer honour, not upon the great men but upon little Roubillac."[117] Both verbal and visual artists, meanwhile, tried with new urgency to convince their audiences of the enduring significance of the commemorated dead. Many epitaphic poets after Pope followed him in composing elegiac epitaphs that expressed their grief for (real or supposed) friends as demonstrations of the value of the deceased. Lacking Pope's intense conviction of the public significance of his own feelings, however, poets were starkly confronted with the task of reestablishing a connection between their private responses to the dead, however sincere, and the public realm of their readers. Epitaphic poets therefore began to implore the reader to play a role in rediscovering the social significance of the dead. Funerary sculptors similarly began challenging the spectator to share in reimagining the dead. Both epitaphs and monuments increasingly implied that only through an act of sympathetic imagination on the part of the living reader or viewer could the dead, however exalted, become once more a vital part of the ongoing social order.

[117] Oliver Goldsmith, *The Citizen of the World* ("Letter CIX") in *The Collected Works of Oliver Goldsmith*, ed. Arthur Friedman, 5 vols. (Oxford: Clarendon, 1966), 2:424. Compare the more tactful but similar comment of a critic in the *Spectator* of 1753 concerning Roubiliac's monument to the duchess of Montagu: "These monuments shall be wept over when the Duke and Duchess shall be forgotten, if it is in the power of time to obliterate the memory of his Grace's charities and her beauty" (cited in Esdaile, "Sculpture," in Turberville, 2:83).

Chapter 10

"Kindred Spirits": The Proper Reader in the Mid-Eighteenth- to Early Nineteenth-Century Epitaph

The eighteenth-century cult of sentiment encouraged a new treatment of the dead. The mid eighteenth century witnessed the rise of what Ariès calls "the death of the other," an intensified focus on mourners' memory of, and enduring grief for, irreplaceable loved ones who have died.[1] Personal lament rather than impersonal, edifying panegyric began to dominate the poetic epitaph.

Lawrence Stone argues that this new emphasis on mourners' feelings reflects the growth of a more affectionate relationship between family members.[2] Yet although such affection certainly became more widespread as a cultural ideal in the eighteenth century, Stone, as his critics have noted, ignores evidence from earlier periods of intense familial feeling to support his argument for a dramatic change in familial relations.[3] At least insofar as it manifests itself in epitaphic rhetoric, the new emphasis reveals not so much the increase of feeling within the family

---

[1] See Philippe Ariès, *The Hour of Our Death*, trans. Helen Weaver (New York: Random, 1982), 407–556; and Michel Vovelle, *La mort et l'Occident de 1300 à nos jours* (Paris: Gallimard, 1983), 443–446. On the sentimental novel's emphasis on mourning, see R. F. Brissenden, *Virtue in Distress: Studies in the Novel of Sentiment from Richardson to Sade* (London: Macmillan, 1974), 6 and passim.

[2] Lawrence Stone, *The Family, Sex, and Marriage, 1500–1800* (New York: Harper, 1977), 246–253. His argument concerning the change in family sentiments is on p. 247. Compare Ariès, 471–473.

[3] See, for example, Ralph A. Houlbrooke, *The English Family, 1450–1700* (London: Longman, 1984), 14–16, 202–227; and Keith Wrightson, *English Society: 1580–1680* (New Brunswick: Rutgers University Press, 1982), 89–118.

as a new relationship between feelings for intimates, both inside and outside the family, and the public domain. With continuing disagreement over "objective" social criteria for assessing the worth of the dead, intimate grief increasingly seemed the most, and perhaps the only, authentic testimony to the enduring value of the deceased. Expressions of deep personal sorrow thus came to fill the vacuum in authoritative public utterance.

The new epitaphic style appealed to men and women of diverse beliefs. As the virulence of religious conflict declined over the course of the eighteenth century, men of various religious and nonreligious persuasions— conformists and nonconformists, evangelicals and latitudinarians, Methodists and freethinkers—adopted a common rhetoric of feeling. With the established church's decrease in power and authority, furthermore, even conforming poets sought new ways, not envisaged in Anglican doctrine, for the living to express their continuing personal attachment to, and desire for intimate communion with, the beloved dead.[4]

With economic expansion, increased urbanization, and the growth of the middle classes, more and more literate people of diverse backgrounds composed and read epitaphs.[5] Epitaphs were often published several times in the numerous magazines of the period and in the many epitaph anthologies, more common now than at any earlier time.[6] Unlike seventeenth- and early eighteenth-century collections, which often included untranslated Latin inscriptions, these later collections presented translations of Latin inscriptions or English compositions alone and thereby appealed to a wider audience. By expressing what were conceived to be

---

[4] English epitaphs support Ariès's claim that whereas eighteenth- and nineteenth-century Catholics increasingly viewed purgatory as "an opportunity to prolong beyond death the solicitude and affections of earthly life," Protestants of the same period, torn between their religious traditions denying contact with the dead and the need to display their continuing feelings for their deceased loved ones, "discovered" various new forms of communication across the barrier of death (pp. 454–468).

[5] Statistics on literacy are notoriously unreliable, but recent studies suggest a dramatic rise from the post–Civil Wars period through the 1750s; though stagnant from the second half of the eighteenth through the early nineteenth century, literacy remained higher throughout this period than at any time before 1740. See David Cressy, *Literacy and the Social Order: Reading and Writing in Tudor and Stuart England* (Cambridge: Cambridge University Press, 1980), 177; and R. S. Schofield, "Dimension of Illiteracy, 1750–1850," *Explorations in Economic History* 10 (1972/1973):445. Stagnation in minimal literacy for the whole population seems to have coincided in the late eighteenth century, moreover, with the growth in reading and writing among the middle classes. Paul Kaufman notes that there was a rapid increase in circulating libraries in the 1750s and that the number rose steadily throughout the second half of the century, which suggests a growing number of readers among the predominantly middle-class patrons of such enterprises; see "The Community Library: A Chapter in English Social History," *Transactions of the American Philosophical Association*, n. s., 57 (1967): part 7.

[6] The epitaph anthologies of John Hackett, W. Toldervy, T. Webb, George Wright, John Bowden, and Thomas Caldwell, among others, all came out between 1750 and 1815.

"natural" human feelings rather than the values of a particular class, the new epitaphic style largely "transcended" the social divisions among readers and writers of epitaphs.

While the influence of classical models declined, certain widely published English authors had far greater impact than ever before. Pope was especially influential. Though his epitaphs upon himself, with their emulation of the classics and their topical assertions of his independence-unto-death from the Hanoverian-Walpole regime, were little imitated, his innovative elegiac epitaphs became extremely popular models.

Epitaphs of the mid eighteenth and early nineteenth century often copy or adapt the endings of the Harcourt and the Digby epitaphs, which memorably express the sorrow of the poet as "friend" of the deceased. Since the word "friend" could in this period refer to a relative, some epitaphs closely echo Pope's lines in order to present mourning relatives addressing the dead.[7] Other compositions, by contrast, imitate Pope less directly but follow his practice of blending the mourning of the actual relatives who erected the monument with that of the poet-friend who composed the elegiac inscription, as in the following couplet: "The friend and heir here join their duty: One / Erects the busto, one inscribes the stone."[8] Other epitaphs make explicit Pope's implicit contrast between the sincere tribute of the poet-friend and the mere flattery of a hired hand, as in these two examples:

[7] For close echoes of the closing lines of the Harcourt or Digby epitaphs (or both), see, for example, "An EPITAPH made by Mr. PITT, and inscribed on a stone, that covers his Father, Mother, and Brother," Gentleman's Magazine 16 (1746):37; the epitaph upon Sarah Newman in T. Webb, ed., A New Select Collection of Epitaphs, 2 vols. (London, 1775), 1:247; "An EPITAPH, supposed to be written by WEEPING ORPHANS over the Grave of their dear PARENTS, in a Church-yard in Kent" in George Wright, Pleasing Melancholy (London, 1793), 55; "Inscription on a SINGLE LADY'S Monument, in a Church, in Somersetshire..." in Wright, Pleasing Melancholy, 144; the epitaph upon Joseph and Sarah Hinds, d. 1801, in Francis Haslewood, The Parish of Benenden, Kent: Its Monuments, Vicars, and Persons of Note (Ipswich, 1889), 48; the epitaph upon Anne Jane Williams, d. 1801, in Bath Abbey; the epitaph upon Lucy Hippsley in Thomas Caldwell, ed., A Collection of Epitaphs and Inscriptions, Ancient and Modern (London, 1802), 172–173; Hannah More, "On the Reverend Mr. Hunter," in The Poems of Hannah More (London, 1816), 310; the epitaph upon Susannah Hadden in William Graham, ed., A Collection of Epitaphs and Monumental Inscriptions, Ancient and Modern (Carlisle, 1821), 123; and the epitaph upon James Sanler, d. 1823, in Haslewood, 82–83.

[8] Sir C[harles] H[anbury] W[illiams], "An Epitaph on... Thomas Winnington, Esq.," London Magazine 19 (1750):566. For other examples of the poet placing himself in the poem as a mourning "friend," see "Epitaph on the Rev. Mr A—— Rector of B—— ...," Gentleman's Magazine 17 (1747):96; epitaph upon Richard Children, d. 1753, in John Thorpe, Registrum Roffense: or, A Collection of Antient Records... of the Diocese and Cathedral Church of Rochester (London, 1769), 856; "An Epitaph in Wisbich church-yard," Scots Magazine 26 (1764):200; G. Colman, "Epitaph on Mr. Powell's Monument at Bristol," Scots Magazine 33 (1771):548; and the epitaph upon Charles Jenner, d. 1774, in Caldwell, 271–272.

No venal muse this faithful picture draws,
Blest saint! desert like yours extorts applause.
Oh! let a weeping friend discharge his due,
His debt to worth, to excellence, and you!

A Son this [monument] rais'd, by holy Duty fir'd,
This sung a Friend, by friendly Zeal inspir'd;
No venal Falsehood stain'd the filial Tear,
Unbought, unask'd, the friendly Praise sincere.[9]

By their very protestations, such epitaphs suggest that poets continued to be rewarded for their panegyrics upon the social elite. What had changed was not the actual relations between patrons and poets but rather the poets' manner of conceiving and justifying their commemorative function. Assuming the role of the impersonal, public trumpeter of fame, earlier epitaphic poets defended themselves against charges of flattery by appealing to the didactic efficacy of idealized moral exempla. Epitaphic poets from the mid eighteenth century onward, by contrast, authenticated their compositions and testified to the value of the dead by either assuming the voice of the mourning relatives or presenting themselves as grieving friends of the deceased.

Poets also often called upon those readers who knew and loved the deceased to show proper responsive feeling. Pope's epitaph upon Gay was a crucial model. Poets imitated Pope's final couplet—". . . the Worthy and the Good shall say, / Striking their pensive bosoms—*Here* lies GAY"— in order to imagine or demand that friends of the deceased pronounce the epitaph's final line:

When ask'd to whom these lovely truths belong,
Thy friends shall answer, weeping, "Here lies STRONG."

. . . o'er his grave each worthy friend replies
Clasping their friendly hands, "HERE DUGGAN LIES."

. . . pensive think of your departed friend,
Repeat the tale convey'd in simple strain,
And sighing say—here lies poor honest HAYNE.[10]

---

[9] Nathaniel Cotton, "*On a* LADY, *who had laboured under a Cancer,*" in his posthumous *Various Pieces in Verse and Prose,* 2 vols. (London, 1791), 1:55; and William Hamilton, "Epitaph on Sir James Sooty," d. 1730, in *The Poems and Songs of William Hamilton of Bangour,* ed. James Patterson (Edinburgh, 1850), 32–33. See also the epitaph upon Mary Basnet, d. 1756, in Graham, 89–90; and the "*Inscription on a* LADY's *Monument, in Bath Cathedral,*" in Wright, *Pleasing Melancholy,* 122–123.

[10] I cite Nathaniel Cotton, "*An* EPITAPH *upon Mr. Thomas Strong . . .*," d. 1736, in Cotton, 1:82, an early example; the epitaph upon Mr. Duggan, d. 1779, in *A Collection of Epitaphs and Monumental Inscriptions,* 2 vols. (London, 1806), 1:29; and the epitaph upon John Hayne, d. 1797, in Thomas F. Ravenshaw, ed., *Antiente Epitaphes (from* A.D. *1250 to* A.D. *1800)* (London, 1878), 175.

Such epitaphs suggest that only friends can meaningfully enunciate the most traditional of epitaphic statements, "Here lies X." A formula traditionally associated with epitaphic impersonality must be reauthorized and revitalized by the grief of intimates.

While ignoring Pope's own distinction in the Gay epitaph between worldly rank and moral worth, between heroes and kings and the "Worthy and the Good," imitations of Pope's composition betray the sense of a fundamental division between a small group of intimates, who can truly mourn the deceased, and all other members of society, who cannot. They thereby indirectly suggest the crucial problem of the mid-eighteenth- to early nineteenth-century epitaph. If only those closely tied to the deceased by blood or affection can truly feel the pathos and significance of his or her loss, the public role of the deceased and of the epitaph as a genre is unclear. How can a mere passerby who reads an epitaph truly view the deceased as a friend? The problem was all the more pressing because the growth of a more heterogeneous reading public made the responses of readers increasingly unpredictable. During the same period that some epitaphs explicitly address the intimates of the deceased, others grapple with the problematic relationship between the deceased and the general reading public by addressing the reader as "stranger." "Stranger" is a common form of address in classical epitaphs (Greek *xenos*; Latin *hospes*), where it is simply a variant on the various terms for "traveler" or "passerby." Sixteenth- and seventeenth-century English and neo-Latin epitaphs occasionally address the "stranger" in the manner of classical epitaphs. The term becomes widespread in the English epitaph, however, only in the mid eighteenth century, when it emerges in an emotionally charged, dialectical relationship to "friend."[11] Epitaphs often implicitly or explicitly implore a "stranger" of highly developed sensibility to mourn for the deceased with something close to the feelings of a "friend," as in this early nineteenth-century composition:

> Stranger!
> If virtue o'er thy bosom bear control,
> If thine the generous, thine the exalted soul,
> Stranger! approach. This consecrated earth

---

[11] For classical examples of addresses to the "stranger" (*xenos* or *hospes*), see Richmond Lattimore, *Themes in Greek and Latin Epitaphs* (Urbana: University of Illinois Press, 1962), 230–234. The *xenos* or *hospes* of ancient epitaphs did not have the emotionally charged meaning of "stranger" as opposed to "friend" because both the Greek and Latin terms could mean "friend" as well as "stranger"; for a discussion of the antithetical meanings of the classical words and the light they shed on ancient conceptions of friendship, see Émile Benveniste, *Le vocabulaire des institutions indo-européennes*, 2 vols. (Paris: Les Éditions de Minuit, 1969), 1:87–101, 360–361.

Demands thy tribute to departed worth.
Beneath this tomb, her spirit sleeps,
Here friendship sighs, here fond affection weeps.... [12]

Requesting that the stranger display sorrow for the deceased akin to that of intimates, the epitaph suggests that the unknown reader can respond properly only if he or she has certain qualities. This poem reveals the most striking rhetorical innovation of mid-eighteenth- through early nineteenth-century epitaphs: their calls for, and expressions of deep uncertainty concerning, the benevolence of strangers.

Thomas Gray's *Elegy Written in a Country Church Yard*, first published in 1751, is both exemplary and extremely influential in its dramatization of the uncertainty surrounding the response of the epitaphic reader. Gray meditates in solitary darkness upon the poor buried in the church-yard and upon his own obscure life.[13] While the next chapter will discuss the significance of the new attention that Gray and his contemporaries pay to the poor buried in churchyards, here I wish to emphasize Gray's sense of the vulnerability of the churchyard dead and their monuments to contempt or neglect. Gray notes how "frail" the memorials are that protect the buried poor "from insult" and beg "the passing tribute of a sigh" (ll. 77–80).[14] Though the poet may himself respond sympathetically to the epitaphs of "the unlettered muse" (l. 81), there is no guarantee

---

[12] Epitaph upon Elizabeth Soane, d. 1815 (Graham, 88, punctuation modified). For other examples of such pathetic appeals to strangers not discussed elsewhere in my text, see "Epitaph," *Scots Magazine* 24 (1762):544; Hannah More's undated epitaphs upon C. Dicey and Reverend Mr. Love in More, 311, 313; and Anna Seward's epitaph, composed in 1792, upon David Garrick in *The Poetical Works of Anna Seward*, ed. Walter Scott, 3 vols. (Edinburgh, 1810), 2:186.

[13] I have found the following works concerning Gray's *Elegy* helpful: F. W. Bateson, "Gray's 'Elegy' Reconsidered," in his *English Poetry: A Critical Introduction*, rev. ed. (London: Longmans, 1966), 127–135; Charles J. Rzepka, *The Self as Mind: Vision and Identity in Wordsworth, Coleridge, and Keats* (Cambridge: Harvard University Press, 1986), 2–9; Peter M. Sacks, *The English Elegy: Studies in the Genre from Spenser to Yeats* (Baltimore: Johns Hopkins University Press, 1985), 133–137; John Sitter, *Literary Loneliness in Mid-Eighteenth-Century England* (Ithaca: Cornell University Press, 1982), 97–100; Howard D. Weinbrot, "Gray's *Elegy*: A Poem of Moral Choice and Resolution," *SEL* 18 (1978):537–551; George T. Wright, "Stillness and the Argument of Gray's *Elegy*," *MP* 74 (1977):381–389; the essays by Frank Brady, Bertrand H. Bronson, and Ian Jack in *From Sensibility to Romanticism: Essays Presented to Frederick A. Pottle*, ed. Frederick W. Hilles and Harold Bloom (London: Oxford University Press, 1965), 139–190; and the essays in Herbert W. Starr, ed., *Twentieth-Century Interpretations of Gray's Elegy: A Collection of Critical Essays* (Englewood Cliffs, N.J.: Prentice-Hall, 1968).

[14] I use the text of the *Elegy* in *The Poems of Thomas Gray, William Collins, and Oliver Goldsmith*, ed. Roger Lonsdale (London: Longmans, 1969), 117–140. All quotations and translations of Gray's poems are from this edition, hereafter cited as Gray.

that others will. The poet who goes on to imagine his own death as "A youth to fortune and to fame unknown" (l. 118) knows that he, too, is not assured that his gravestone will be read with proper sympathy. Imagining the *possible* appearance of a "kindred spirit" (l. 96) who will *possibly* learn of his fate from a local rustic and be guided to read his epitaph, Gray suggests that one's memory after death depends upon chance encounters:

> *If chance,* by lonely Contemplation led,
> Some kindred spirit shall inquire thy fate,
>
> *Haply* some hoary-headed swain *may* say....
>   (ll. 95–97, emphasis mine)

His hope for a "kindred spirit" reminds one of Eloisa's hope that sympathetic lovers will visit her tomb in Pope's *Eloisa to Abelard*:

> *If ever chance* two wandring lovers brings
> To *Paraclete*'s white walls, and silver springs,
> O'er the pale marble shall they join their heads,
> And drink the falling tears each other sheds,
> Then sadly say, with mutual pity mov'd,
> Oh may we never love as these have lov'd!
>   . . . . . .
>   ...*if* some relenting eye
> Glance on the stone where our cold reliques lie,
> Devotion's self shall steal a thought from heav'n,
> One human tear shall drop, and be forgiv'n.
>   (ll. 347–352, 355–358, emphasis mine)[15]

Pope heaps up the pathos of mere possibility with "if" clauses that describe the responding lovers and the relenting eye.[16] The ending of the poem, however, suggests the central difference between Pope's poetics of death and that of Gray. The final image in Pope's poem is of Eloisa's wish for what she has, in fact, already received, not a reader of her epitaph but the writer of her tale:

[15] Alexander Pope, *The Rape of the Lock and Other Poems,* ed. Geoffrey Tillotson, The Twickenham Edition of Pope, vol. 2, 2d ed. (New Haven: Yale University Press, 1954), 348.

[16] The pathetic uncertainty concerning the appearance of sympathetic mourners is Pope's addition to the tradition of Ovidian female love complaint: such uncertainty does not appear in the various passages in Ovid's *Heroides* in which abandoned women conclude their laments by imagining their monuments and epitaphs, passages from which Pope drew his major inspiration for the ending of *Eloisa.*

And sure if fate some future Bard shall join
In sad similitude of griefs to mine,
. . . . .
Such if there be, who loves so long, so well;
Let him our sad, our tender story tell;
The well-sung woes will sooth my pensive ghost;
He best can paint 'em, who shall feel 'em most.
(ll. 359–360, 363–366)

In this self-referential coda, Pope not only praises his artful song of woe but also moves away from uncertainty concerning others' reactions in order to focus instead upon his usual subject, his own sensitive response. He appears in his poem as an active writer who has done his all to honor Eloisa's memory and to commemorate himself as a suffering lover. Gray, by contrast, finally appears in his own poem not as an active writer but as the passive, vulnerable object of a hypothetical reader's gaze.

Gray's work is an elegy in the common eighteenth-century sense of a reflective poem, usually about love or death, that is in some way indebted to the Latin love elegy.[17] It is also an elegy in the more specific sense of a poem mourning someone's death—in this case, the speaker's own.[18] Gray emphasizes his own passivity in death by transforming a traditional generic combination that partakes of both senses. The poem imagines the country "swain" (l. 97) recounting the poet's melancholic behavior, sudden disappearance, and funeral, and then inviting the "kindred spirit" to read the poet's tombstone (ll. 97–116). By turning to his own funeral and epitaph, Gray recalls the generic combination of Herrick's "The cruell Maid," in which a speaker foresees his own burial and provides the inscription he wishes engraved upon his tomb. Pseudo-Tibullus's *Elegy* 3.2 introduced this generic combination to Roman elegy, and James Hammond's *Love Elegies* (1742), which established the elegiac associations of the quatrain form used by Gray, contains a poem closely following pseudo-Tibullus.[19] More than any other poet who uses this generic combination, Gray surrenders control over his own posthumous self-image. In the compositions of pseudo-Tibullus, Hammond, and even of modest Herrick, the poet who dictates his epitaph counters his

[17] On the eighteenth-century sense of elegy, see Ian Jack, "Gray's *Elegy* Reconsidered," in *From Sensibility to Romanticism*, 152–155.

[18] See also Sacks, 133.

[19] See James Hammond, "*Elegy* IX: He has lost Delia" in *The Works of the English Poets from Chaucer to Cowper*, ed. Alexander Chalmers, 21 vols. (London, 1810), 11:143. Jack suggests Gray's knowledge of Hammond's poetry in "Gray's *Elegy* Reconsidered," in *From Sensibility to Romanticism*, 155. Lonsdale reviews the general evidence of Hammond's influence and cites *Elegy* IX as a parallel to Gray's concluding epitaph (Gray, 108–109, 138–139).

powerlessness in life with an act of self-definition. Gray's *Elegy*, by contrast, eliminates the poet's active dictation of his epitaph in order to
imagine, instead, the epitaph's possibly being read with sympathy.
(Within the fiction of the poem, it is not even clear who composed the
final inscription.) In all other examples of the generic combination, the
speaker is an unhappy lover. Gray transforms the conventional love
theme to underscore his dependence on others for his posthumous identity. The "swain" who postulates that the poet was in life "forlorn, / Or
crazed with care, or crossed in hopeless love" (ll. 107–108) clearly does
not comprehend the poet's more general sorrow for mortal human
beings.[20] By presenting a rustic who does not understand him, Gray
underscores his need for a sensitive reader, whose posthumous appearance alone can save him from being misunderstood.[21]

The epitaph itself emphasizes the dependence of the deceased upon
the reader's response:

> *Here rests his head upon the lap of earth*
> *A youth to fortune and to fame unknown.*
> *Fair Science frowned not on his humble birth,*
> *And Melancholy marked him for her own.*
>
> *Large was his bounty and his soul sincere,*
> *Heaven did a recompense as largely send:*
> *He gave to Misery all he had, a tear,*
> *He gained from Heaven ('twas all he wished) a friend.*
>
> *No farther seek his merits to disclose,*
> *Or draw his frailties from their dread abode,*
> *(There they alike in trembling hope repose)*
> *The bosom of his Father and his God.*
>
> (ll. 117–128)

Framed by an evocation of the earth as the mother upon whom the
deceased lays his head and a description of the "bosom of his Father"
in which the soul of the deceased can "repose," the epitaph depicts death
as an escape from the burdens of adult life. Gray's posthumous peace
seems somehow dependent, however, upon the reader. While "He gave
to Misery all he had, a tear" looks back to the poet's sorrowful tribute
to the rural dead, the description of the single friend that he had in life

---

[20] Ironically, some of Gray's contemporaneous readers considered the poet of the *Elegy*
a traditional unhappy lover: Phillip Doddridge's epitaph "*On a* YOUNG MAN *who died for
Love; after the Manner of* GRAY" (Wright, *Pleasing Melancholy*, 62), for example, is a pastiche
of Gray's epitaph whose title makes explicit what its writer thought implicit in (or at least
consistent with) Gray's poem.

[21] On the "swain" and the "kindred spirit" as "contrasting kinds of audiences," see also
Rzepka, 7.

hints at the friendly reader he hopes to have in death. Though the poet longs for someone to "inquire his fate," he also hopes that this sympathetic inquirer will not attempt to discover more of his virtues or faults than he sees fit to tell. The reticent epitaph clearly demands a reader whose combination of sympathy and tact can save the deceased from both neglect and intrusion.

By his very admission of unspecified "frailties," Gray increases his dependence on the sympathetic forbearance of the reader. The poet's acknowledgment of flaws and his implicit plea for sympathy is both innovative and influential. Any reference at all to character flaws in the deceased is very rare in nonsatiric epitaphs before Gray. In the seventeenth century, Jonson's epitaph upon Elizabeth, L. H. is unique in this regard. In the early eighteenth century, Pope felt compelled to concede the childlike foibles of his friend Gay in order to protect him from harsher criticism, but otherwise Pope commemorates only legendary or fictional female figures, like Eloisa and the "unfortunate lady," as flawed heroines who nevertheless deserve forgiveness and sympathetic remembrance. Gray and later eighteenth-century poets, some directly indebted to him, are the first to portray their contemporaries and themselves as frail human beings who can only hope for the sympathy and forgiveness of the reader. In the late 1750s, for example, William Beattie concludes his epitaph upon himself by noting his failings and by making explicit the call for sympathetic response that Gray keeps beautifully oblique:

> Forget my frailties;—thou art also frail:
>   Forgive my failings;—thou thyself mayst fall:
> Nor read unmov'd my artless, tender tale,
>   I was a friend, O man, to thee, to all.[22]

Beattie tries to capture the sympathy of his unknown readers by insisting that he was a friend to all of humanity whose flaws were those to which all human beings are sadly prone. Less confident than earlier poets in their readers' reverence for the dead, Gray and his successors try to arouse their readers' pity. Epitaphic poets tend not to present the de-

---

[22] [William Beattie], "An EPITAPH. Designed for its author," *Scots Magazine* 19 (1757):238. For other late eighteenth-century evocations of the frailties of the deceased, see, for example, the epitaphs upon Richard Savage, d. 1743, in John Hackett, *Select and Remarkable Epitaphs on Illustrious and Other Persons . . .* , 2 vols. (London, 1757), 1:260; Mrs. Rocky Squire, d. 1760, in *A Collection*, 2:182; William King, d. 1763, in *Gentleman's Magazine* 34 (1764):139; Laurence Sterne, d. 1768, in Webb, *New Select Collection*, 1:130; George Campion, d. 1774, in *The Nottinghamshire and Derbyshire Notes and Queries* 2 (1894):125; and the epitaph closely modelled upon Gray's at the conclusion of "The FUNERAL. An ELEGY," *Scots Magazine* 28 (1766):317.

ceased as powerful moral examples; instead, they beg the sensitive passerby to show his or her benevolence toward the all too vulnerable dead.

Like many inscriptions, Gray's epitaph piously declares the Christian hope of the deceased in the Resurrection.[23] The description of such hope as "trembling" is, however, unusual. It is true that Christians work out their salvation in "fear and trembling," and that the mixture of hope and fear is a common response of the living, and even more of the dying, as they confront their God. Epitaphs, however, normally speak of the dead's confidently lying "in hope(s)" of the "joyful Resurrection," for the decorum of Christian panegyric demands that the inscription record the untroubled hope of one whose time to work out his or her salvation is, after all, past.[24] The image of the deceased in the "bosom" of God suggests in Calvinist fashion that the afterlife is a period of waiting for full bliss or damnation, and "trembling" increases the reader's sense of the dead's vulnerability in this interim state. The epitaph thus hints at an analogy between God and the reader, both of whom are implicitly implored to be beneficent—one by judging with mercy and the other by mercifully respecting the deceased.

In an early version of the end of the *Elegy* preserved in manuscript, Gray described himself, rather than the "kindred spirit," as being "By Night & lonely Contemplation led / To linger in the gloomy Walks of Fate." Instead of ending with the reading of his tombstone, the poet concluded with advice to himself:

> No more with Reason & thyself at strife;
> Give anxious Cares & endless Wishes room
> But thro' the cool sequester'd Vale of Life
> Pursue the silent Tenour of thy Doom.[25]

In the early 1740s Gray decided, not without regret, to live on his limited inheritance in the relatively modest, retired manner of a fellow at Cambridge rather than to pursue a lucrative legal career.[26] The stanza ex-

---

[23] On the piety of the final stanza, see Weinbrot, "Gray's Elegy," 548–549.

[24] Lonsdale cites as possible sources for Gray's line several combinations of fear or trembling and hope, all of which describe the living or dying, not the dead (Gray, 140). For some early eighteenth-century examples of epitaphs that use the formulaic "in hope(s) or "in spe(m)" to describe the dead who confidently await the Resurrection, see John Le Neve, ed., *Monumenta Anglicana: Being Inscriptions on the Monuments of several Eminent Persons ... 1600–1715*, 5 vols. (London, 1718–1719), 1:22, 28, 45–46, 99, 186, 213, 276; 5:195, 238–239, 241, 249, 253–254.

[25] Gray, 131.

[26] By his death in 1741 Gray's father, a scrivener, had dissipated the family fortune. Gray consequently received a far smaller inheritance than he had hoped; see R. W. Ketton-Cremer, *Thomas Gray: A Biography* (Cambridge: Cambridge University Press, 1955), 66–68.

presses Gray's wish to accept fully his (comparatively) modest station, which he figures hyperbolically as a life and death of silence and obscurity. In the final version of the poem, Gray transforms his desire not to be at "strife" with himself and his "silent...Doom" into the wish for someone to read about the completed life of a "youth unknown" with sympathetic understanding. The "kindred spirit" who would save the retired poet from total oblivion is both a stranger and a friend in the classical sense of an alter ego or other self. He is both the projection and imagined cure of an unhappy, divided self that seeks both to escape, and to receive recognition from, the world.

The "kindred spirit" is not Gray's earliest version of a friend who would save him from oblivion. The poet's turn to an unknown figure for validation is a compensatory response to tragedy within his intimate circle. In his 1742 translation of Propertius's *Elegy* 2.1, Gray celebrated his posthumous survival in the memory of his closest friend, Richard West; in the *Elegy*, composed some years after the death of West, Gray could only anxiously hope to be remembered by an unknown reader. While reflecting Gray's specific loss of a friend upon whose memory he could rely, the movement from the Propertius translation to the *Elegy* also reveals in diachronic form the combination of trust in intimates and anxious uncertainty concerning the reading public that pervades the funerary poetry of the period.

In Propertius's *Elegy* 2.1, the Roman poet rejects public, political poetry in favor of private elegies celebrating his love. He concludes, however, by reconnecting himself to the public realm by imagining his own death and suggesting that his great patron, Maecenas, might pronounce the true epitaph upon the poet who died for love: "Therefore when at last the Fates demand my life, and I shall be no than a brief name on a little stone of marble, then... *if perchance* [*si...forte*] thy journeying lead thee near my tomb, stay awhile thy chariot with carven yoke, and weeping pay this tribute to the silent dust: 'An unrelenting maid wrought this poor mortal's death'" (emphasis mine).[27] While Propertius imagines Augustus's right-hand man publicly validating the poet's private experience, he also emphasizes, out of deference to his high-ranking patron, that such validation would come only if the busy Maecenas should happen to come upon the poet's humble tomb. Gray's translation, sent in a letter of April 1742 to his friend West, wholly eliminates the uncertainty of "if perchance" ("si...forte"):

[27] "Quandocumque igitur vitam mea fata reposcent, / et breve in exiguo marmore nomen ero, /..... / si te forte meo ducet via proxima busto, / esseda caelatis siste Britanna iugis, / taliaque illacrimans mutae iace verba favillae: / 'Huic misero fatum dura puella fuit' " (Propertius, *Elegy* 2.1.71–72, 75–78).

When that my fates that breath they gave shall claim,
When the short marble but preserves a name,
A little verse, my all that shall remain,
Thy passing courser's slackened speed retain
   . . . . .
Then to my quiet urn awhile draw near,
And say, while o'er the place you drop a tear,
Love and the fair were of his life the pride;
He lived while she was kind, and, when she frowned, he died.[28]

Gray and West frequently sent one another translations from the classics, and their versions of Roman poems are simultaneously literary exercises and displaced but still deeply felt explorations of their personal relationship.[29] In July 1737 West, sick and "melancholy," sent Gray a translation of pseudo-Tibullus's *Elegy* 3.5. In the Latin elegy the poet fears his approaching death and hopes that his friends will remember him after death: "May ye live happy and with thoughts of me" the poet exclaims.[30] Making the voice of the Roman poet his own but increasing the sense of the poet's isolation, West adds to the Latin poem that he will die "unknown" without even "nature" noticing his death. Only some friends will cherish his memory, a small group who are all the more important because of the general oblivion.[31] In his letter of April 1742, Gray reciprocates such a poetic gesture. He translates another Roman elegist's imagining of his own death, and by implicitly identifying Maecenas with West, asks his friend to remember Gray's own "quiet urn."[32] In his translation of pseudo-Tibullus, West had made more pri-

---

[28] Gray, "[Translation from Propertius, *Elegies* II.i]," ll. 99–102, 105–108 in Gray, 47.

[29] Ian Jack treats Gray's and West's versions of Roman poetry as personal exchanges whose basis in classical poems provides a balancing "element of formality and convention" ("Gray's *Elegy* Reconsidered," in *From Sensibility to Romanticism*, 150–151). This characterization is somewhat misleading, for the poems are, with significant exceptions, quite faithful translations of their Roman models rather than free imitations: they do not modernize the details or, most importantly, change the names of the Roman speaker and addressee. Jack is nevertheless correct that the poems are, in an important sense, personal communications: ancient poets allow the friends to express through authoritative voices their own sentiments to and for one another.

[30] "Vivite felices, memores et vivite nostri" (pseudo-Tibullus, *Elegy* 3.5.31).

[31] *The Correspondence of Thomas Gray*, ed. Paget Toynbee and Leonard Whibley, 3 vols. (Oxford: Clarendon, 1935), 1:63–64.

[32] In a letter of December 1736, West sent Gray a translation of an elegy of Tibullus, now lost, saying that his "low spirits and constant ill health" led him to "elegies of woe" (*Correspondence of Gray*, 58). Besides pseudo-Tibullus's *Elegy* 3.5, the most sorrowful Tibullan elegy is *Elegy* 1.3, in which Tibullus complains of being sick in a foreign land, imagines his death, and hopes that a stone with the epitaph he has composed will be placed over his body (ll. 1–56). If this was indeed the poem that West translated, Gray would have further motivation to reciprocate his friend's translations of appeals for posthumous commemoration with a similar translation of his own.

vate the relationship between the poet and his friends. Insofar as Gray identifies Maecenas with West, he similarly privatizes his poem by transforming Propertius's address to a major public figure into a personal epistle to his intimate friend. Thus, like many compositions of the period, Gray's translation imagines a friend speaking—and thus authenticating—a final epitaphic message. This explains the change, whether consciously made or not, from Propertius's "si . . . forte" to Gray's indicative: Gray is confident that his closest friend will speak the appropriate commemorative words. The very year in which Gray translated Propertius, however, West died. Their private realm of friendship having became a world of solitude, Gray lost his assurance of a friend's loving memory.

Gray's well-known sonnet lamenting West's death ends with the despairing poet addressing, vainly, one who cannot hear him: "I fruitless mourn to him that cannot hear, / And weep the more because I weep in vain."[33] Gray also wrote a Latin elegy upon his friend. While the first book of De Principiis Cogitandi opens with an address to the living West, the fragmentary second book laments West's death. In the Latin poem, Gray not only addresses the deceased but also implores a response from him: "But, if, released from cares as you are, but not beyond mortal concerns, you look back with pity on once-familiar toils and are free to perceive our trivial anxieties; if, by chance [si forte] you look down from your lofty seat on the storm of human passion, the fears, the fierce promptings of desire, the joys and sorrows and the tumult of rage so huge in our tiny hearts, the furious surges of the breast; then look back on [i.e., look down upon] these tears."[34] Despite the view of the established church that the dead have no consciousness of the living, Gray longs for the sympathetic attention of his deceased friend. He reintroduces precisely what was omitted from the Propertius translation: the "si forte" of now truly pathos-laden conditionality. It is this phrase that also reappears in the Elegy, completed in 1750 but still in some sense reflecting Gray's loss of West.[35] While the Latin poem for West expresses

---

[33] Gray, "Sonnet [on the Death of Mr. Richard West]," ll. 13–14 in Gray, 68.

[34] " . . . atque oh si secura, nec ultra / Mortalis, notos olim miserata labores / Respectes, tenuesque vacet cognoscere curas; / Humanam si forte alta de sede procellam / Contemplere, metus stimulosque cupidinis acres, / Gaudiaque et gemitus, parvoque in corde tumultum / Irarum ingentem, et saevos sub pectore fluctus: / Respice, et has lacrimas . . . " (De Principiis Cogitandi: Liber Secundus, ll. 20–27 in Gray, 328, 332, emphasis in translation mine).

[35] The Elegy was sent to Horace Walpole in 1750 but its dates of origin are less certain. In a scrupulous account of the evidence, Lonsdale argues that the poem was probably begun in 1745–1746, rather than shortly after West's death in 1742, as Gray's friend William Mason suggested (see Gray, 103–110). The Elegy is nevertheless partly a response, distanced both by time and by the imaginative workings of the poet, to a death that so affected him. Sacks rightly notes that Gray's "residual grief for Richard West" is an important context for the Elegy (p. 133).

uncertainty as to whether a deceased friend will remember the living, mourning poet, the English elegy expresses uncertainty whether there will be a living friend to remember the dead poet. Both reveal Gray's lack of assurance, after West's death, in the death-transcending response of a friend. The unknown reader who would respond as a "kindred spirit" is Gray's imagined substitute for the now-dead West, and the "If chance" (l. 91) of the *Elegy* echoes the original uncertainty of Propertius concerning Maecenas, an uncertainty that Gray happily eliminated from his Propertian translation when he was confident of his friend's answering love.

Gray did have an important friend at the time he composed the *Elegy*, Horace Walpole, the son of the former prime minister, but Gray's ambivalence toward Walpole encouraged all the more his turn to an unknown reader for sympathetic understanding. Gray had loved Walpole since their school days at Eton, but in 1741 the two quarreled while on their continental tour. After they were uneasily reconciled in 1745, Walpole slowly replaced the deceased West as the reader of Gray's poems, and it was to him that Gray first sent his *Elegy* in 1750.[36] Difference in rank greatly complicated the two men's relations. After their reconciliation, Gray viewed the prime minister's son, ambivalently, as a tie to the world of the rich and powerful that he had forsworn.[37] The "kindred spirit" is an imagined substitute not only for the absent West but also for the present yet elusive Walpole, whose Maecenas-like greatness made it uncertain whether he could truly be the the alter ego whom Gray craved.

Gray was highly ambivalent about the publication of his poem. Walpole, not Gray, circulated the *Elegy* and finally arranged for the work's publication when unauthorized publication was imminent.[38] Gray's hope for a "kindred spirit" nevertheless suggests that he needed as well as feared the responses of unknown readers to the epitaph that portrayed his retired life. The *Elegy* indeed provides a powerful metaphor for Gray's authorial relationship to the public. Like Herrick's epitaphs upon himself, which represent a vulnerable self to the world in a time of sociopolitical crisis, Gray's representation of himself as dead and dependent for his posthumous reputation on a sympathetic reader reveals his sense of the author as a vulnerable figure who confronts, at a distance, a public of strangers upon whose goodwill he must rely.

[36] On Gray's love for Walpole, see Bruce Redford, *The Converse of the Pen: Acts of Intimacy in the Eighteenth-Century Familiar Letter* (Chicago: University of Chicago Press, 1986), 100–107; on their subsequent relationship and its relevance to Gray's poetry, see Roger Lonsdale, "The Poetry of Thomas Gray: Versions of the Self," *Proceedings of the British Academy* 59 (1973):114, 118–119.

[37] On Gray's ambivalence toward Walpole, see also Lonsdale, 118.

[38] On the publication of the *Elegy*, see Lonsdale's discussion in Gray, 110–111.

In a poem about the dead, Gray's highly unusual term for his desired reader, "kindred spirit,"[39] suggests not only a person who shares the sympathies of the deceased, but also one who is all spirit, one who has in some way transcended earthly existence and can therefore respond with the greatest sensitivity to the dead. The poet Anna Seward clearly registered the strange evocativeness of the term. In an epitaph upon a woman who died in 1781, Seward addresses the reader thus:

> O, gentle Stranger! may one generous tear
> Drop, as thou bendest o'er this hallow'd earth!

> Are truth, and science, love, and pity thine,
> With liberal charity and faith sincere?
> Then rest thy wandering step beneath this shrine,
> And greet a kindred Spirit hovering near![40]

Here the "kindred Spirit" is the spirit of the deceased hovering near the tombstone. Seward's use of Gray's term to refer to the deceased rather than the living reader suggests the interchangeability of the living and the dead as imagined by both Gray and Seward. Seward invites only a certain kind of "stranger" to "greet" the deceased—a virtuous Christian whose spiritual values ensure sympathy with the dead. She hints that the "kindred Spirit" will truly appear only if the proper reader of faith and charity is present. Like other compositions of the period, Seward's epitaph imagines the living and the dead somehow communicating across the barrier of death. Such communication depends, however, upon the presence of a deeply sensitive reader, and Seward's question, like Gray's "If chance," emphasizes that one cannot be sure that such a reader will appear.[41]

Gray's "If chance" clause and Seward's question are both restrained versions of an epitaphic formula that emerges in the mid eighteenth century concerning the ideal reader. The following two passages are representative:

> Oh! if from early youth one friend you've lov'd,
> Whom warm affection chose, and taste approv'd;

---

[39] Lonsdale, who finds numerous verbal echoes in Gray's *Elegy*, finds no parallels for "kindred spirit."

[40] Seward, "On Lady Miller," in Seward, 2:183.

[41] Compare Robert Southey's 1796 inscription for the cenotaph of Rousseau at Ermenonville: "Stranger!.../ Here, if thy breast be full, / If in thine eye the tear devout shall gush, / His SPIRIT shall behold thee, to thine home / From hence returning, purified of heart" (Southey, *The Minor Poems*, 3 vols. [London, 1815], 2:115). The lines seem to suggest that Rousseau's "SPIRIT" will "behold" the stranger if, and only if, that stranger has the requisite sensibility to mourn the deceased.

If you have known what anguish rends the heart,
When such, so known, so lov'd, for ever part;
Approach!—For you the mourner rears this stone,
To sooth your sorrows, and record his own.

Reader, if youth should sparkle in thine eye,
    If on thy cheek the flower of beauty flows;
Here shed the tear, and heave the pensive sigh,
    Where beauty, youth, and innocence repose.
Doth wit adorn thy mind? doth science pour
    Its ripen'd bounties on thy vernal year?
Behold where death has cropp'd the plenteous store,
    And heave the sigh, and shed the pensive tear.[42]

A long clause or series of clauses characterizing the ideal reader of the epitaph, either interrogatives or conditionals beginning with "if": this rhetorical formula first emerges in epitaphs of the 1740s and is ubiquitous from about 1750 through the first two decades of the nineteenth century.[43] Like the copious praise of the deceased's place in history that was popular in late seventeenth- and early eighteenth-century epitaphs, the extended characterization of the ideal reader lengthens the epitaph and further separates it from its epigrammatic roots. Though some elements of the rhetorical formula may be found in earlier epitaphs, the long description of the ideal reader and the emphasis upon the uncertainty of his or her appearance is novel. Two Theocritean epitaphs ask

[42] More, "Inscription on a Cenotaph in a Garden...," in More, 312; and the epitaph upon Miss Thicknesse (no date) in Wright, *Pleasing Melancholy*, 181–182.

[43] For some mid-eighteenth- to early nineteenth-century epitaphs, not cited elsewhere in my discussion, which have at least three lines demanding, either with a question or an "if" clause, whether the reader has the requisite qualities, see: Richard Rolt's epitaph upon Samuel Burt, d. 1751, in W. Toldervy, ed., *Select Epitaphs*, 2 vols. (London, 1755), 2:188–189; William Mason, "EPITAPH on Mrs. MASON...," *Gentleman's Magazine* 18 (1778):598; "On a Lady" in Webb, *New Select Collection*, 1:126–127; "An EPITAPH" in [Robert Dodsley, ed.], *A Collection of Poems*, 6 vols. (London, 1766), 5:92–93; epitaph upon George Campion, d. 1774, in *Nottinghamshire and Derbyshire Notes and Queries* 2 (1894):125; epitaph upon Mr. Worth, d. 1779, in Caldwell, 51; epitaph upon Robert Lowth, d. 1787, in *A Collection*, 1:140; epitaph upon Miss Croft, d. 1789, in Nathaniel Frobisher (publisher), *Frobisher's New Select Collection of Epitaphs: Humorous, Whimsical, Moral and Satyrical* (London, c. 1790s), 201; "On a benevolent YOUNG LADY, aged Twenty-three" in Wright, *Pleasing Melancholy*, 104; epitaph upon John Danby, d. 1798, in Graham, 98; epitaph upon Sarah Fletcher, d. 1799, in *The Oxford Book of Death*, ed. D. J. Enright (Oxford and New York: Oxford University Press, 1983), 326; Anna Seward's epitaph upon Rev. William Bagshot Stevens, d. 1800, in Seward, 2:194; "Designed for a Stone in the Church Yard of Haddington...," in *A Select Collection of Epitaphs and Monumental Inscriptions, with Anecdotes* (Ipswich, 1806), 62; epitaph upon Thomas Wakefield, d. 1806, in Richmond Parish Church; epitaph upon Mrs. Mary Franklin, d. 1811, in Graham, 102; More, "Reverend Mr. Penrose," in More, 307, and the undated epitaph upon a "young man" in Silvester Tissington, ed., *A Collection of Epitaphs and Monumental Inscriptions...* (London, 1857), 165–166. Several of Southey's (pseudo-inscriptional) "Inscriptions" of the 1790s use the conventional "if" clauses: see Southey, 2:109, 115–116, 121, 122, 127–128.

readers, if they are virtuous, to show reverence for the deceased (*Greek Anthology* 7.658, 13.3), but Greek compositions do not normally express, even so briefly, concern about their readers.[44] A few Latin sepulchral inscriptions briefly single out those who, if they have the requisite humanity or have had a similar experience of loss, can mourn the deceased properly, but the brevity of these rare passages suggests little genuine anxiety concerning readers.[45] Early seventeenth-century English epitaphs sometimes devote a line or couplet to castigating a reader who, if he is as "hard" as the tombstone, will not mourn or appreciate the deceased. The hyperbole of such attacks suggests little uncertainty concerning the assumed reader.[46] Like the occasional classical inscription, some late seventeenth- and early eighteenth-century English epitaphs use a brief "if" clause to describe the virtuous reader they wish to address.[47] The restraint of the gesture still suggests little worry, however, about obtaining this reader.

With its long, hypothetical descriptions of the reader, the epitaph from the mid eighteenth through the early nineteenth century reveals, by contrast, a radical shift in the relationship between the living and the dead and the epitaph and its readers. The clause or clauses can postulate either a reader who could sympathize with the mourner that composed the inscription, or one who could truly grieve for the deceased. The precise qualities that the reader must have varies. In all cases, however, epitaphs that use the new formula focus less on what they teach the reader than on what the reader must already be, know, and feel in order to commune as a friend with the mourner or the deceased. By suggesting

---

[44] It is suggestive that the two Theocritean epitaphs were probably first translated into English in the late eighteenth century; see Francis Fawkes, *The Idylliums of Theocritus* (London, 1767), 276–277, 280.

[45] Thomas Warton's *Inscriptionum Romanarum Metricarum Delectus* (London, 1758), a collection of Roman inscriptions, includes a rare classical example of an "if" clause that evokes a properly humane reader: "Stay, traveler, and if you have any humanity, weep, / While you see my melancholy bones gathered together [here]" ("Hospes sta, et lacruma [*sic*], si quicquam humanitus [*sic*] in te est, / Ossua dum cernis consita maesta mihi"; ("Lesbiae ossa hic sita sunt" in *The Poetical Works of the Late Thomas Warton*, ed. Richard Mant, 2 vols. [Oxford, 1802], 2:351). The inscription clearly appealed to later eighteenth-century taste. For another Roman example, discovered in the nineteenth century, see Franciscus Buecheler, ed., *Anthologia Latina, Pars Posterior: Carmina Latina Epigraphica* (Leipzig: Teubner, 1895–1897), 2:456 (no. 988).

[46] See, for example, the epitaphs upon Cecilia Bulstrode in *The Complete Works of Ben Jonson*, ed. C. H. Herford and Percy and Evelyn Simpson, 11 vols. (Oxford: Clarendon, 1925–1952), 8:371–372; Salomon Hext, d. 1606, in Le Neve, 4:13; Sir John Newdigate, Knight, d. 1610, in Harefield Parish Church; and Lucy Bromfield, d. 1618, in Ravenshaw, 62. Donne's brief evocation of the good reader in his epitaph upon Elizabeth Drury is a rare early seventeenth-century example of an "if" clause describing the desired reader.

[47] See, for example, the epitaphs upon Marmaduke Carvox, d. 1665, and Thomas Rokeby, d. 1699, in Le Neve, 2:109–110, 204–205.

the possibility that the reader will not have the requisite qualities, such epitaphs express a new kind of pathos. In addition to the sorrow of death and mourning, these epitaphs evoke, and seek to overcome, the additional pathos of the dead's possible neglect by the living or of mourners' possible emotional isolation in a society that ignores their loss.

The new epitaphic style both reflects and reflects upon the changing nature of the reading public. Noting the growing "call for fellow-feeling" in poetry of the later eighteenth century, Eric Rothstein suggests that poets simplified the responses they demanded in order to address a larger and less learned readership.[48] While epitaphs reveal this striving for simple emotional responses, their avowed uncertainty concerning readers' reactions—despite such simplification—is equally striking and registers their anxiety concerning their increasingly diverse audience.[49] Increased emphasis on the necessity of sincere feeling coupled with the intensified awareness of a heterogeneous public explain the epitaph's obsessive calls for proper readers: poets addressed themselves to a feeling few.[50] Even when men and women composed inscriptions for their relatives or loved ones with no thought of publication, they imitated the many published epitaphs centering on the reader and adopted the period style's formula as the "natural" way of expressing their feelings toward the dead.

Epitaphic calls for an ideal reader parallel contemporary funerary monuments that challenge the spectator to feel the proper emotions. In the 1760s and 1770s, compositions become popular in which a group of mourners with diverse reactions surrounds an urn. The lack of any actual representation of the deceased, whose dust is hidden in the urn, reveals the necessary role of subjective feeling in evoking the dead and thus challenges the spectator to manifest the appropriate response.[51] A

---

[48] Eric Rothstein, *Restoration and Eighteenth-Century Poetry, 1660–1780* (Boston: Routledge, 1981), 119–120.

[49] For recent discussions of the ways in which an enlarged readership affected eighteenth-century literary production, see Alvin Kernan, *Samuel Johnson and the Impact of Print* (Princeton: Princeton University Press, 1987), 62–70 and passim; and, with particular reference to the rise of the novel, J. Paul Hunter, " 'The Young, the Ignorant, and the Idle': Some Notes on Readers and the Beginnings of the English Novel," in *Anticipations of the Enlightenment in England, France, and Germany*, ed. Alan Charles Kors and Paul J. Korshin (Philadelphia: University of Pennsylvania Press, 1987), 259–282.

[50] For discussions of the ways in which eighteenth-century texts thematize the problematic relationship between authors and readers, see Bertrand H. Bronson, "Strange Relations: The Author and His Audience," in his *Facets of the Enlightenment: Studies in English Literature and Its Contexts* (Berkeley: University of California Press, 1968), 298–325; Sitter, passim; and, with reference to the novel, J. Paul Hunter, "Novels and 'the Novel': The Poetics of Embarrassment," *MP* 85 (1988):480–498, which discusses novelists' self-conscious engagement with a readership diverse in its social, educational, political, and religious background.

[51] Ronald Paulson argues that in the period 1760–1770 painting and sculpture, including funerary monuments, concentrated on "the pathetic response (among other responses) to

funerary form ubiquitous from the 1780s to the middle of the nineteenth century consists of a woman mourning over an urn. Though she sometimes represents an actual widow or other female relative of the deceased, the woman also personifies grief, the emotion the spectator should feel confronting the urn whose intense inner significance only the sensitive can appreciate.[52]

The new monumental style challenged the spectator to display proper sensitivity toward the dead during the very period when the public to whom funerary monuments appealed was becoming larger and more socially diverse. Beginning in the late eighteenth century, more and more middle-class patrons acquired monuments. While costly and elaborate allegorical monuments declined, smaller and simpler monuments sharply rose in popularity. By depicting grief in an emotionally direct, easily comprehensible fashion, the woman mourning over an urn appealed to the taste and pocketbooks of numerous patrons. The motif was extensively reproduced in monuments of every scale.[53] The gender-specific depiction of grief as a mourning woman underscores, however, the problematic relationship between the dead and the public. Increasingly in the eighteenth and nineteenth centuries, upper- and middle-class women were confined to the family and home and consequently participated only in the domestic aspects of mourning. While they were discouraged from attending funerals because they were deemed too sensitive to bear the public ritual, they were expected to remain in secluded mourning for long periods.[54] The woman mourning over an urn thus suggests that the truest mourning is deeply private. Publicizing deeply personal sorrow, the mourning woman challenges the sensitive spectator somehow to enter into the intimacy of private grief. Whether such a feeling spectator will be forthcoming is as uncertain as the appearance of the "kindred spirit" in Gray's *Elegy*.

---

a center of emptiness and/or transcendence"; see his "The Aesthetics of Mourning," in *Studies in Eighteenth-Century British Art and Aesthetics*, ed. Ralph Cohen (Berkeley: University of California Press, 1985), 148–181; the quotation summarizing his argument is on p. 166. (I unfortunately saw too late to take into account the expanded version of this essay in Ronald Paulson, *Breaking and Remaking: Aesthetic Practice in England, 1700–1822* [New Brunswick, N.J.: Rutgers University Press, 1989], 203–245.) See also the discussion of mourning figures in late eighteenth-century monuments in David Irwin, "Sentiment and Antiquity: European Tombs, 1750–1830," in *Mirrors of Mortality: Studies in the Social History of Death*, ed. Joachim Whalley (New York: St. Martin's, 1981), 136–137, 148–150.

[52] On the rise of this form, see Nicholas Penny, *Church Monuments in Romantic England* (New Haven: Yale University Press, 1977), 67–70; and Margaret Whinney, *Sculpture in Britain: 1530 to 1830* (Baltimore: Penguin, 1964), 155–156. Penny notes that one often cannot identify the grieving woman as a relative of the deceased.

[53] See Whinney, 155–156.

[54] See Leonore Davidoff and Catherine Hall, *Family Fortunes: Men and Women of the English Middle Class, 1780–1850* (Chicago: University of Chicago Press, 1987), 408–410.

Samuel Johnson was deeply interested in the epitaph: he wrote critical essays on the genre in general, on Gay's epitaph upon himself, and on Pope's epitaphs; in *The Lives of the English Poets* he criticized the pompous epitaphs upon poets and inserted several passages that are, in effect, his own prose epitaphs upon men whom he admired; he composed or coauthored numerous Latin prose epitaphs in honor of family, friends, acquaintances, and famous men; and he produced a small number of English poetic epitaphs that are the finest of the late eighteenth century. Critics have discussed Johnson's treatment of the epitaph either in isolation or in relation to a broad, long-standing humanist tradition.[55] Johnson's epitaphic poetics is very much a product of his particular times, however, for he self-consciously both adapts and resists features of the prevailing epitaphic style.

In "An Essay on Epitaphs" (1740) Johnson propounds a view of the genre that his own compositions seldom support. He argues: "The principal intention of epitaphs is to perpetuate the examples of virtue, that the tomb of a good man may supply the want of his presence, and veneration for his memory produce the same effect as the observation of his life. Those epitaphs are, therefore, the most perfect which set virtue in the strongest light, and are best adapted to exalt the reader's ideas, and rouse his emulation."[56] Johnson's earliest poetic epitaph, published in the *Gentleman's Magazine* in 1747, is unique among his compositions in seeking to follow such a traditional humanist theory of didactic exempla. The poem is based on Dr. Freind's Latin inscription commemorating Sir Thomas Hanmer, Speaker of the House of Commons. Though he follows the basic contours of the original inscription, however, Johnson replaces Freind's lengthy introductory account of Hanmer's distinguished lineage, which commemorates but does not instruct, with an opening address to the reader that emphasizes the virtues to be learned from the deceased:

> Thou, who survey'st these walls with curious eye,
> Pause at this tomb where Hanmer's ashes lie;

---

[55] Paul Fussell, *The Rhetorical World of Augustan Humanism: Ethics and Imagery from Swift to Burke* (Oxford: Clarendon, 1965), 289–293, 297–299; and Rachel Trickett, *The Honest Muse: A Study in Augustan Verse* (Oxford: Clarendon, 1967), 251–256 provide useful brief discussions of Johnson's theory and practice of the epitaph (and elegy) in terms of the neoclassical tradition. For "internal" readings, see Dustin Griffin, "Johnson's Funeral Writings," *ELH* 41 (1974):192–211; and David F. Venturo, "The Poetics of Samuel Johnson's Epitaphs and Elegies and 'On the Death of Dr. Robert Levet,'" *SP* 85 (1988):73–91. I am most indebted to Griffin, who rightly emphasizes the tensions in Johnson's theory and practice, and I most sharply disagree with Venturo, who ignores such tensions.

[56] Samuel Johnson, "An Essay on Epitaphs" (1740) in *Samuel Johnson*, ed. Donald Greene (Oxford: Oxford University Press, 1984), 97. Compare the very similar argument in Johnson's 1738 essay on Gay's epitaph in *Samuel Johnson*, 52.

His various worth, through varied life attend,
And learn his virtues, while thou mourn'st his end.[57]

The poem assumes that any "curious" reader can learn from, as well as mourn the loss of, a virtuous public figure. This early epitaph, however, is the only one in which Johnson simply and explicitly addresses the general reader in order to teach him the exemplary lesson of a good life.

One of Johnson's essays, *Rambler* 78 (1751), suggests the difficulties the writer perceived in the epitaphic project of commemorating virtuous, exemplary persons. The essay presupposes an eighteenth-century urban environment in which men and women constantly confront the deaths of strangers, such as the London in which Johnson and most of his readers lived.[58] The essay notes that people normally view a funeral as "a common spectacle in which we have no concern," instead of as a "summons" to us all.[59] Johnson emphasizes the weak sense of community in such a world by exploiting the various meanings of one of his favorite words, "common": a funeral is perceived as a "common" or "ordinary" event without "common" or "general" significance. After claiming that many people unfortunately look upon others "only as inhabitants of the common earth,"[60] Johnson discusses the indifference with which people generally greet the deaths of public figures:

Events...excite little sensibility, unless they affect us more nearly than as sharers in the common interest of mankind...little concern is caused by the eternal departure even of those who have passed their lives with publick honours. ...It is not possible to be regarded with tenderness except by a few. That merit which gives greatness and renown...is placed at a distance from common spectators....The wit, the hero, the philosopher, whom their tempers or their fortunes have hindered from intimate relations, die without any other effect than that of adding a new topic to the conversation of the day....because none had

[57] Samuel Johnson, *Poems*, ed. E. L. McAdam, Jr., The Yale Edition of the Works of Samuel Johnson, vol. 6 (New Haven: Yale University Press, 1964), 80–82. For the text of Dr. Freind's Latin inscription, see *Gentleman's Magazine* 17 (1747):239.

[58] The mortality rate in eighteenth-century London, which was substantially higher than that in the rest of England, was particularly high in the early to mid eighteenth century; see E. A. Wrigley, "A Simple Model of London's Importance in Changing English Society and Economy 1600–1750," *Past and Present* 37 (1967):46–49. Johnson himself linked high mortality rates to the impersonality of a city of strangers: James Boswell records Johnson's claim that numerous poor people died of hunger in London because the city was "so large" that people were "not known"; see *Boswell's Life of Johnson*, ed. G. B. Hill, rev. L. F. Powell, 6 vols. (Oxford: Clarendon: 1934–1950), 3:401.

[59] Samuel Johnson, "*Rambler* 78," in *The Rambler: Part 2*, ed. W. J. Bate and Albrecht B. Strauss, The Yale Edition of the Works of Samuel Johnson, vol. 4 (New Haven: Yale University Press, 1969), 47, 49.

[60] Johnson, "*Rambler* 78," in *The Rambler: Part 2*, 48.

any particular interest in their lives, or was united to them by a reciprocation of benefits and endearments.

Thus it often happens, that those who in their lives were applauded and admired, are laid at last in the ground without the common honour of a stone; because by those excellencies with which many were delighted, none had been obliged, and, though they had many to celebrate, they had none to love them.[61]

Johnson's continuing play with the different senses of "common" reveals the primacy of private relations in ordinary life. Since human beings generally do not have strong feelings for "the common interest," "common spectators" are not much affected by the deaths of important public figures. While the living commemorate those they personally knew and loved, therefore, great public men often do not receive even the "common honour" of a memorial stone. One can infer that those among the dead who do receive a gravestone and inscription because of the "particular interest" of their surviving relatives and friends will not necessarily elicit, in consequence, the "common interest" of society as a whole. In a world of private attachments, a public monument has little credibility as an assertion of a dead person's enduring social value, and the epitaph as a public, didactic genre faces the difficult task of promoting the virtues of the deceased among strangers who have little sense of their connection to the dead.

In his finest poetic epitaph, that upon William Hogarth, composed in 1771, Johnson reveals his doubts concerning a deceased public figure's exemplary power and the epitaph's effectiveness as a didactic genre:

> The hand of art here torpid lies
>   That traced th'essential form of grace,
> Here death has clos'd the curious eyes
>   That saw the manners in the face.
>
> If genius warm thee, reader, stay,
>   If merit touch thee, shed a tear,
> Be vice and dulness far away
>   Great Hogarth's honour'd dust is here.[62]

While the first stanza fulfills the traditional panegyric function of an epitaph, it does not seek, as Johnson's essay on epitaphs advises, to "supply the want" of the deceased by encouraging imitation of a moral example. In both his essay on epitaphs and his essay upon Pope's sepulchral inscriptions, first published in 1757 and republished as an appendix to the Life of Pope, Johnson criticizes what he perceives to be a

---

[61] Johnson, "Rambler 78," in The Rambler: Part 2, 48–49.
[62] Johnson, Poems, 268.

common fault in epitaphs, the lack of "particular and appropriate praise."[63] Johnson composed the Hogarth poem after receiving an epitaph upon the painter by David Garrick. Johnson considered Garrick's composition inadequate because it failed to provide a "discriminative character" that distinguished the deceased from other men of "intellectual eminence."[64] Johnson's first stanza provides such an individualizing portrait, but in so doing emphasizes the distance rather than the potential connection between the deceased and the epitaph's readers. The second and fourth lines provide a highly compressed account of Hogarth's particular achievements as the inventor of the Line of Beauty and the painter of expressive physiognomies. By starkly depicting the dead man in his grave, the first and third lines underscore the irreplaceable individuality of Hogarth. Hogarth's unique accomplishments seem all too inseparable from his motionless hand and closed eyes for there to be any possibility of imitating the deceased.

An emphasis on particularity of praise is typical of the period. One may compare the remark of Johnson's friend Edmund Burke, who in 1775 explained to the widow of William Dowdeswell that in his epitaph upon her late husband he had attempted to "characterize him in *particulars*, as I knew, felt, loved, and honourd him" rather than bestowing "general [praise] . . . as well fitted for one great publick man as another."[65] Burke's desire to portray the unique personality of his deceased friend suggests that he conceives of the genre primarily as a personal expression of friends' and relatives' attachment to the dead. He does not explicitly address the problem of connecting the deceased in all of his uniqueness to the living "stranger" who reads the epitaph. It is this problem with which Johnson proceeds to grapple in the second stanza of the Hogarth epitaph. An exclusive focus on "particulars," Johnson suggests, is not sufficient.

The epitaph's second stanza does not provide the reader with a model for imitation, but it does try to link the living and the dead by appealing to a reader who can appreciate the general virtues of "genius" and "merit" embodied in the painter's particular accomplishments. While Hogarth's unique hand is forever "torpid," the sensitive reader will feel

[63] Samuel Johnson, "Life of Pope," in *Lives of the English Poets*, ed. G. B. Hill, 3 vols. (Oxford: Clarendon, 1905), 3:263; and Johnson, *Samuel Johnson*, 100.

[64] See Johnson's letter to Garrick of December 12, 1771, in *The Letters of Samuel Johnson*, ed. R. W. Chapman, 3 vols. (Oxford: Clarendon, 1952), 1:273.

[65] *The Correspondence of Edmund Burke*, ed. Thomas W. Copeland et al., 10 vols. (Cambridge: Cambridge University Press; Chicago: University of Chicago Press, 1958–1978), 3:241. For similar comments by Burke on the necessity of "particularity" in epitaphs, see *Correspondence of Burke*, 7:38 and 9:360. For an early nineteenth-century critique of general praise in epitaphs, see Robert Bland, *Translations Chiefly from the Greek Anthology*, intro. Donald H. Reiman (1806; rpt., New York: Garland Publishing, 1978), vii–viii.

the posthumous "touch" of the painter's "merit." Though as a theorist of the epitaph Johnson emphasized the necessity of particularity as a counterweight to the common flaw of empty generality, elsewhere in his criticism he argued for generality as a counterweight to excessive particularity. Above all he praised the writer who judiciously related the two. In literary treatments of humanity, such a combination both reflects and reinforces our sense of individual human beings' shared qualities and concerns.[66] *Rambler* 60 (1750) argues that effective biographies reveal the good and evil "common to human kind" in the lives of "particular persons."[67] Johnson's "Preface to Shakespeare" (1765) extolls the playwright's consummate ability to depict "discriminated" and "distinct" characters who are nevertheless all "the genuine progeny of common humanity."[68] The Hogarth epitaph's movement from the painter's particular achievements to his general virtues attempts to establish his membership in the ongoing human community. The epitaph stresses, however, that Hogarth's connection to the living depends upon the reader, who must recognize and respect the painter's general virtues. By using the typical "if" clauses of the period, Johnson emphasizes that Hogarth may not find the reader that he deserves. The poet further underscores Hogarth's vulnerability by expelling "vice and dulness" from the gravesite, thus suggesting the dead's possible contamination by all who are inimical to his spirit.

Johnson was very concerned with the proper placement of the name of the deceased in epitaphs,[69] and he here uses the common device of placing the name of the deceased at the end as a resounding conclusion. While "Great Hogarth's honour'd dust is here" returns to the individual buried in his grave, the identifying name seems to gather into itself all the preceding praise. Nevertheless "Great Hogarth's honour'd dust" is

---

[66] On Johnson's conception of particularity and generality, see Lionel Basney, " 'Lucidus Ordo': Johnson and Generality," *ECS* 5 (1971):39–57; Jean Hagstrum, *Samuel Johnson's Literary Criticism* (1952; rpt., Chicago: University of Chicago Press, 1967), 83–89; and Howard D. Weinbrot, "The Reader, the General, and the Particular: Johnson and Imlac in Chapter Ten of *Rasselas*," *ECS* 5 (71):80–96. These works focus on the aesthetic, epistemological, and metaphysical implications of Johnson's treatment of the general and the particular. Though he oversimplifies Johnson's position by treating only Imlac's discussion of the poet in *Rasselas*, John Barrell rightly calls attention to the sociopolitical implications of Johnson's concerns in *The Political Theory of Painting from Reynolds to Hazlitt: "The Body of the Public"* (New Haven: Yale University Press, 1986), 90–93.

[67] Samuel Johnson, "*Rambler* 60," in *The Rambler: Part 1*, ed. W. J. Bate and Albrecht B. Strauss, The Yale Edition of the Works of Samuel Johnson, vol. 3 (New Haven: Yale University Press, 1969), 319–320.

[68] Samuel Johnson, *Johnson on Shakespeare*, ed. Arthur Sherbo with intro. Bertrand H. Bronson, 2 vols., The Yale Edition of the Works of Samuel Johnson, vols. 7–8 (New Haven: Yale University Press, 1968), 1: 62, 64.

[69] Johnson heaped scorn on epitaphs that omitted the name of the deceased and singled out for praise an epitaph by Pope that "inserted [the name] with a particular felicity" ("Essay," in *Samuel Johnson*, 277; and *Lives*, 3:259).

not confident panegyric. Coming after the conditional clauses and banishment of vice in the preceding lines, the word "honour'd" hovers between the indicative and the hortatory. The final line suggests both that Hogarth's dust *is* honored and that it will be if, and only if, the reader has proper respect for the painter's virtues.

While Johnson adopts the period style's call for a proper reader, his epitaph's use of "if" clauses is far briefer and more emotionally restrained than those of most compositions of the period. Unlike many of his contemporaries, Johnson does not portray his ideal reader and the deceased as interchangeable "kindred spirits" who in some sense mingle across the barrier of death. One may contrast the Hogarth epitaph in this respect with contemporaneous epitaphs that use the same device of a series of "if" clauses followed by the final identification of the dead. Johnson certainly knew, for example, the 1751 epitaph upon his old friend and mentor, Gilbert Walmesley. The first stanza of the Walmesley epitaph moves from six prolix lines of "if" clauses describing the proper reader's many virtues to a concluding couplet naming the deceased. Unlike Johnson's conclusion, the final couplet asserts what one might call a sentimental appropriation of the dead. The couplet bids the properly responsive reader, "With sympathetic love these relics see! / But think not Walmesley dead—he lives in thee."[70] The second stanza of Richard Graves's epitaph upon William Shenstone, published the same month that Johnson composed his composition, similarly moves from six slack lines of "if" clauses characterizing the ideal reader to a final couplet asking that reader to recognize his close tie to the deceased, who is at last identified: "Ah! smite thy breast, and drop a tear, / For, know, thy Shenstone's dust lies here!"[71] "*Thy* Shenstone" suggests that the deceased in some sense belongs to, and lives in, the reader who can appreciate him. The Hogarth epitaph, by contrast, avoids such identifications, allowing no easy blurring of the distinction between the living reader and the deceased. Johnson no more can envisage the appropriation of the dead by the living through fellow-feeling than he can proclaim the exemplary influence of the dead upon the living. Instead

---

[70] *London Magazine* 20 (1751):424. The epitaph was reprinted in several late eighteenth-century anthologies; see, for example, Toldervy, 2:209; and Webb, *New Select Collection*, 1:108. Much later Johnson himself commemorated Walmesley, with far greater sense of irreparable loss, in the "Life of Edmund Smith" (*Lives*, 2:20–21). On Walmesley's formative influence upon Johnson, see Walter Jackson Bate, *Samuel Johnson* (New York: Harcourt, 1975), 71–86.

[71] [Richard Graves,] "*On an* URN *(now erecting) to the Memory of* WILLIAM SHENSTONE, *Esq. in Hales Owen Church-yard, Shropshire,*" *Gentleman's Magazine* 41 (1771): 564. For other epitaphs with "if" clauses that lead up to the proper name, see "*An* EPITAPH *on the Rev. Mr.* T. BEAUMONT," *Gentleman's Magazine* 14 (1744):672 (an early example); and the first stanza of the epitaph upon Samuel Richardson, d. 1761, in Webb, *New Select Collection*, 1:128.

he can only hope that the reader will appreciate "genius" and "merit" and consequently respect Hogarth's "dust" in all its distinctive and vulnerable otherness.

Johnson banishes "vice and dulness" from Hogarth's grave lest they in some sense harm the artist's "dust." The protection of the painter's remains is a resonant figure for the protection of his posthumous reputation. The epitaph suggests a fundamental connection between the bodies and the reputations of the dead: both are defenseless against the malice or neglect of the living.

Johnson's concern for the body of the deceased here is at odds with his critical pronouncements. In "An Essay on Epitaphs," he decries such pagan expressions as the wish that "the earth might be light upon" the dead because "all regard for the senseless remains of a dead man [is] impertinent and superstitious."[72] Bishop Sprat's epitaph upon Cowley, which requests that the remains of the deceased may "lie undisturbed," is similarly "too ludicrous for reverence or grief," because "the repose of the body" is not important for a Christian.[73] Johnson's funerary writings often, however, express precisely such "superstitious" concern for the dead's physical remains. Even while condemning regard for the bodies of the deceased, Johnson's essay on epitaphs commends medieval Catholic epitaphs that request prayers for the dead because such requests "flowed naturally from the religion then believed, and awakened in the reader sentiments of benevolence for the deceased."[74] Whatever the effect of prayer on the souls of the dead, requests for prayers evinced and inspired proper feelings toward the deceased. In his own epitaphs, Johnson was unwilling to depart from mainstream Protestantism so far as to request prayers, but his "superstitious" expressions of concern for the frail physical remains of the dead similarly display, and attempt to arouse in the sensitive reader, feelings of benevolence toward the deceased.[75] Lawrence Stone argues that a general obsession with the physical remains of the dead among the English upper and middle classes in the eighteenth century reveals a decline in religious faith regarding

[72] Johnson, "Essay," in *Samuel Johnson*, 98.
[73] Johnson, "Essay," in *Samuel Johnson*, 99. Compare his castigation of the line "Peace to thy [gentle] shade" in Pope's epitaph upon Rowe in *Lives*, 3:261.
[74] Johnson, "Essay," in *Samuel Johnson*, 100.
[75] In his private devotions Johnson displays his benevolence toward the dead by actually praying for their souls, though he uses a qualifying "so far as it may be lawful" lest he should be deviating not only from the custom of the English church but also from the divine will. On these prayers, whose "papist" character shocked some of Johnson's Protestant contemporaries when published after his death, see Maurice J. Quinlan, *Samuel Johnson: A Layman's Religion* (Madison: University of Wisconsin Press, 1964), 17, 20, 171–172. In a public genre like the epitaph Johnson was unwilling to be so heterodox.

the immortal soul.[76] The example of Johnson suggests, however, that the concern with the mortal bodies of the deceased may betoken not a decrease in faith regarding the *heavenly* afterlife but an increase in anxiety regarding the *earthly* kindness and respect vouchsafed the dead by the living.[77]

In his epitaph upon the musician Charles Claudius Phillips, composed and published the same year as his essay on epitaphs, Johnson expresses tender concern for the bodily repose of the deceased:

> Phillips! whose touch harmonious could remove
> The pangs of guilty pow'r, and hapless love,
> Rest here, distrest by poverty no more,
> Find here that calm thou gav'st so oft before;
> Sleep undisturb'd within this peaceful shrine,
> Till angels wake thee with a note like thine.[78]

Though the poem didactically suggests the ultimate heavenly reward of those who suffer on earth, Johnson reveals more sense of the frailty of the deceased than of his potential power as an exemplum. While he describes the ability of the living Phillips to sway others with his music, Johnson imagines no such power over others for the dead Phillips. The poet instead displays a protective tenderness toward the deceased by wishing that he lie in peace until the Last Judgment. Focusing on what Johnson the critic dismisses as the mere "senseless remains," the penultimate three lines emphasize, like some of Herrick's epitaphs, the vulnerability of the sleeping body. By thrice repeating the wish that the deceased rest undisturbed in his grave until the Resurrection,[79] the lines act as a kind of incantatory charm, protecting the deceased from the disturbances of the living.[80]

---

[76] Stone, *Family*, 248–249.

[77] Griffin ("Funeral Writings": 197–199) discusses Johnson's contradictory attitudes toward the body in his theory and practice of the epitaph and elegy in terms of the tension between Christian joy and natural sorrow for the dead. I think that Johnson's feelings for the bodily remains of the dead involve not only grief but also a profound desire to show, and awaken in his readers, benevolence toward the dead.

[78] Johnson, *Poems*, 68–69.

[79] Johnson's composition is a revision of an epitaph upon Phillips by Richard Wilkes. Johnson expands from one to three lines the original epitaph's wish that the deceased "Rest here in peace, till angels bid thee rise" (Johnson, *Poems*, 68). The Wilkes epitaph's echo of the Catholic *Requiescat in pace* adds religious solemnity to the request for the body's repose; the emphatic repetition of Johnson's three lines does the same.

[80] The Phillips epitaph's movement from a repeated wish for the body's peaceful repose to a final evocation of the Resurrection recalls Crashaw's "An Epitaph Upon Husband and Wife, which died, and were buried together," a poem that Johnson admired. Johnson used the second half of the poem for his entry on "peace" in the *Dictionary*: "Peace, good reader, do not weep; / Peace, the lovers are asleep; / . . . / Let them sleep, let them sleep on, / 'Till this stormy night be gone; / And th'eternal morrow dawn, / Then the curtains will be

One of his greatest occasional poems, the prologue to Hugh Kelly's *A Word to the Wise* (1777), most clearly reveals Johnson's desire to stimulate the public's benevolence toward the vulnerable dead. The prologue defends a play that was a total failure when first performed but was revived after the author's death in a benefit performance for his family. Johnson reminds his audience of the author's helpless state:

> This night presents a play, which publick rage,
> Or right, or wrong, once hooted from the stage;
> From zeal or malice now no more we dread,
> For English vengeance *wars not with the dead.*
> A generous foe regards, with pitying eye,
> The man whom fate has laid, where all must lye.
> To wit, reviving from its author's dust,
> Be kind, ye judges, or at least be just:
> Let no resentful petulance invade
> Th'oblivious grave's inviolable shade.
> Let one great payment every claim appease,
> And him who cannot hurt, allow to please.[81]

Echoing Agamemnon's decision to allow the Trojans to bury their dead in Pope's translation of *The Iliad*, "I war not with the Dead" (7.485), Johnson evokes a battlefield, in which the bodies of the dead are at their most defenseless, in order to arouse his audience's sympathies for the deceased.[82] Just as the phrase "honour'd dust" in the Hogarth epitaph is both a claim and a hope, so the Kelly poem mingles the indicative, telling the audience of its English generosity towards the dead, and the hortatory, bidding the audience show a kindness toward the deceased to which it might not be disposed. By requesting that the living "allow to please" one who "cannot hurt," Johnson again reveals his sense, so evident in the Hogarth epitaph, that the influence of the vulnerable dead depends wholly on the receptivity of the living.[83]

---

drawn, / And they waken with that light, / Whose day shall never sleep in night" (cited in Johnson, *Poems*, 388–389). Thomas Percy attributed to Johnson a Latin translation of the last eight lines of the poem, presumably composed while he was working on his dictionary (see text and note in Johnson, *Poems*, 388–389). Like some of Herrick's epitaphs, Crashaw's composition is among the few serious seventeenth-century epitaphs to request that the reader not awaken the deceased. Johnson's singling out of this seventeenth-century epitaph further reveals his concern with protecting the dead from disturbance.

[81] Johnson, "Prologue to *A Word to the Wise*," ll. 1–12 in *Poems*, 290–291.

[82] See note in Johnson, *Poems*, 290; and Alexander Pope, *The Iliad of Homer, Books I–IX*, ed. Maynard Mack et al., The Twickenham Edition of Pope, vol. 7 (New Haven: Yale University Press, 1967), 388.

[83] Johnson's actions as well as his verse reveal his sense of the protective kindness that the living owed the vulnerable dead and of the frequent failures on the part of the living to show such kindness. Near the end of his life, Johnson arranged for tombstones to "protect" the remains of his wife and his parents, who had all died decades before; see

In the Hogarth and Kelly poems, Johnson self-consciously addressed a socially diverse public whose responses could not be predicted. In his numerous Latin epitaphs, by contrast, Johnson sought from the outset to limit his readership to the few who could truly appreciate the deceased. While his contemporaries increasingly composed their epitaphs in the native tongue, Johnson preferred Latin to English for sepulchral inscriptions because Latin was "ancient and permanent."[84] Such linguistic permanence was for him inseparable from Latin's restriction to a cultural elite. In 1773 he argued against the wish of Lord Kames that an English inscription be placed on the monument Kames had erected along the Glasgow road in honor of Tobias Smollett. According to Boswell, Johnson claimed that "all to whom Dr. Smollet's [sic] merit could be an object of respect and imitation, would understand it as well in Latin; and that surely it was not meant for the Highland drovers, or other such people, who pass and repass that way."[85] The phrase "such people, who pass and repass" literalizes the notion of the mobile vulgus, the mob whose fickle immersion in passing things makes them unable to appreciate "permanent" merit.[86] The Latin prose epitaph Johnson composed upon Smollett emphasizes its selectivity of address: "You who come here, o traveler, either gifted of mind, or polished by learning, pause for a brief moment in honor of the memory of Tobias Smollett, M. D."[87]

Johnson's Greek verse epitaph upon Oliver Goldsmith, who died in 1774, similarly forbids the foolish "stranger" to disturb the dust of the deceased while inviting the learned few to reveal themselves by mourning for Goldsmith: "Behold the tomb of Goldsmith, but do not, stranger, tread upon this solemn dust with foolish feet. You [plural] who care for nature, the beauty of rhythm, and past deeds, bewail the poet, the his-

---

the letters of 1784 to Thomas Bagshaw and to Richard Greene in Johnson, *Letters*, 3:181, 251–252. Johnson clearly believed that he had failed to show proper care for the dead by not having erected the gravestones earlier; his request that the stone be laid on his parents' grave with "all possible haste" while he was "yet alive" suggests that he feared divine punishment should he die before the stone was set in place (Johnson, *Letters*, 3:252). Johnson felt that as a son and husband he had failed to show proper benevolence toward the dead. What, he might well have asked, could be expected of strangers?

[84] Though Boswell reports a preference for Latin only with regard to inscriptions upon the learned, Johnson's many Latin prose inscriptions, including those on his parents, his wife, and Mr. Thrale, suggest a more general preference; see *Boswell's Life*, 3:84–85.

[85] *Boswell's Life*, 5:366.

[86] Compare Johnson's assocation of the instability of English with the "casual and mutable" diction of the "laborious and mercantile part of the people" in "A Preface to *A Dictionary of the English Language*" (1755) in Samuel Johnson, *Selected Poetry and Prose*, ed. Frank Brady and W. K. Wimsatt (Berkeley: University of California Press, 1977), 293.

[87] "Quisquis ades, viator, / Vel mente felix, vel studiis cultus, / Immorare paululum memoriae / TOBIAE SMOLLETT, M. D." (included in *Boswell, Life*, 5:367).

torian, and the natural philosopher."[88] As in the Hogarth and Kelly poems, Johnson associates the posthumous reputation of the deceased with his physical remains, for both are vulnerable and in need of the proper response. Here he professes no uncertainty, however, that he addresses at least some readers who can appreciate Goldsmith the polymath's several virtues. Johnson's assurance stems at least partially from the very language that he employs: while purporting to send off the foolish "stranger," Johnson's learned Greek epitaph, even more than his Latin inscriptions, actually eliminates from the start all but those with the learning necessary to appreciate the deceased.[89]

In order to protect the dead from the ignorant mob, Johnson's Greek and Latin epitaphs exclude the larger public that Johnson confronted in his greatest works. Johnson also uses translations of Greek and Latin epitaphs, however, as vehicles for dramatizing his own difficult relationship as a writer to the general reading public. Like Gray, Johnson sees a resonant analogy between the relationship of the dead to the living and the relationship of an author to his readership. In the opening *Rambler* essays, Johnson discusses the difficult task he is undertaking as a periodical essayist, noting how hard it is to gain the respectful attention of the public, "a multitude fluctuating in pleasures, or immersed in business."[90] In the final essay of *The Rambler*, he translated for his epigraph an epitaph upon Heraclitus from the *Greek Anthology* (7.128) that scorns to address such a "multitude":

> Be gone, ye blockheads, Heraclitus cries,
> And leave my labours to the learn'd and wise:
> By wit, by knowledge, studious to be read,
> I scorn the multitude, alive and dead.[91]

As an epigraph to Johnson's concluding *Rambler*, the Heraclitus epitaph is both apposite and deliberately misleading. When Johnson thinks of any ending he thinks about ultimate ends, and Heraclitus's epitaphic

[88] "Ton taphon eisoraas ton Olibarioio, koniên / Aphrasi mê semnên, Xeine, podessi patei. / Hoisi memêle phusis, metrôn kharis, erga palaiôn, / Klaiete poiêtên, historikon, phusikon" (Johnson, *Poems*, 281, my translation).

[89] Contrast William Seward's 1798 English translation of the Goldsmith epitaph, which, because it addresses a large English readership, appropriately (even if unconsciously) reintroduces the conventional uncertainty concerning the sensitivity of its readers: "Whoe'er thou art, with reverence tread / Where Goldsmith's letter'd dust is laid. / *If nature and the historic page, / If the sweet muse thy care engage,* / Lament him dead, whose powerful mind / Their various energies combin'd" (Johnson, *Poems*, 281, emphasis mine).

[90] Johnson, "*Rambler 2*," in *The Rambler: Part 1*, 13–14.

[91] Samuel Johnson, "*Rambler 208*," in *The Rambler: Part 3*, ed. W. J. Bate and Albrecht B. Strauss, The Yale Edition of the Works of Samuel Johnson, vol. 5 (New Haven: Yale University Press, 1969), 315. Johnson particularly liked this epitaph: in the 1780s, he translated it once more, into Latin (Johnson, *Poems*, 317).

proclamation of his posthumous relationship to the world introduces the essayist's discussion of his own achievement as a periodical writer *sub specie aeternitatis*. Johnson explains what he has sought to accomplish as an essayist and finally prays for a "last reward" from heaven for his labors.[92] The Heraclitus epitaph expresses an attitude toward the world, however, with which Johnson sympathizes but in the course of the essay rejects. Johnson claims that he avoided courting a popular audience at the expense of his own integrity and that the number of his "friends" among the public was never great.[93] He does not, however, follow the Greek epitaph in proudly rejecting the "multitude." Indeed the final essay explains why at the end of his "life" as the writer of the *Rambler* Johnson actually deserves—like Hogarth, Goldsmith, and Kelly—"kindness" in the "final sentence of mankind" for his efforts on mankind's behalf.[94]

Johnson's hope for kindness as the bond between readers and writers is not one–sided. Johnson provides one of his most suggestive formulations of the relationship between a writer and his public in yet another first-person epitaph. He concludes a *Rambler* essay on his favorite theme, the difficulty and necessity of self-knowledge, by quoting and discussing the Italian neo-Latin poet Giovanni Pontano's epitaph upon himself:

> Death, says Seneca, falls heavy upon him who is too much known to others, and too little to himself; and Pontanus, a man celebrated among the early restorers of literature, thought the study of our own hearts of so much importance, that he has recommended it from his tomb.... "I am Pontanus, beloved by the powers of literature, admired by men of worth, and dignified by the monarchs of the world. Thou knowest now who I am, or more properly who I was. For thee, stranger, I who am in darkness cannot know thee, but I intreat thee to know thyself."
>
> I hope every reader of this paper will consider himself as engaged to the observation of a precept, which the wisdom and virtue of all ages have concurred to enforce, a precept dictated by philosophers, inculcated by poets, and ratified by saints.[95]

The Pontano epitaph is on one level a memento mori, for Pontano asks his reader to know himself, which is primarily to know that he or she is mortal. Unlike most memento mori warnings, however, Pontano's poem emphasizes the epistemological distance between the dead and the living rather than their ultimate ontological identity. Pontano's inability from his home of "darkness" to know the "stranger" at his tomb provides a

[92] Johnson, "*Rambler* 208," in *The Rambler: Part 3*, 320.
[93] Johnson, "*Rambler* 208," in *The Rambler: Part 3*, 316.
[94] Johnson, "*Rambler* 208," in *The Rambler: Part 3*, 318.
[95] Johnson, "*Rambler* 28," in *The Rambler: Part 1*, 157.

resonant metaphor for the inability of the writer Johnson to know the readers that he addresses. The most benevolent act a writer can perform is to encourage each and every unknown reader to learn to know him or herself. Johnson presents the ideal relationship between writers and readers as a mutual charity based on the severe limits to which either party can know or help the other across the divide of "death."

Johnson accepted the limitations of the epitaph's powers as one aspect of the limits of social and literary interactions in a world of "strangers." The declining faith in the epitaph's public, didactic efficacy and the overriding emphasis on the personal feelings of intimates also lead in the mid eighteenth century, however, to the development with which I will conclude, a new kind of anti-epitaph. Writers reject epitaphs not only for the traditional reason that they are mere vanities in the face of death and judgment, but also because they now appear to be useless barriers to the spontaneous feelings of the true mourners. Since only those who knew the deceased intimately can fully appreciate what has been lost, a public inscription addressed to general readers is not only superfluous but perhaps even a betrayal of the dead. A desire for intimate, unmediated communion between the living and the dead, without any written obstruction, thus emerges.

In the extremely popular evangelical meditation on death, *Meditations among the Tombs* (1745–1746), a possible influence upon Gray's *Elegy*, James Hervey reads and moralizes on the sepulchral inscriptions in a country church. The direction of Hervey's moralizing is decisively new. An early eighteenth-century meditation, such as Isaac Watts's "The Church-Yard," clearly states its moral: "Go to the Church-yard then, O sinful and thoughtless Mortal, go learn from every Tomb-stone and every rising Hillock, that *The Wages of Sin is Death.*"[96] Watts focuses wholly on the inevitability of death and the consequent necessity of repentance. Hervey, on the other hand, focuses less on inevitable death than on the suffering of those who have been bereaved: he meditates on inscriptions not merely as memento moris but also as springboards for imagining mourning scenes, such as the parents at the funeral of their child or the family surrounding a father's death-bed.[97] Personal responses, his own and those he imagines, replace the actual inscriptions, which are not quoted but simply paraphrased and woven into Hervey's meditation. Toward the end of the work, Hervey declares that he does not even want a monument or inscription for himself. He would rather have his

[96] Isaac Watts, *Reliquiae Juveniles: Miscellaneous Thoughts in Prose and Verse* (1734; rpt., Gainesville, Fla.: Scholars' Facsimiles and Reprints, 1968), 108.

[97] See James Hervey, *The Whole Works of the Late James Hervey*, 6 vols. (London, 1819), 1:58–59, 72–73.

name written in the book of life than in "solid rock"—a traditional assertion of Christian priorities—but he would also prefer to an inscription the responses of those who pass by his unmarked grave and, without the promptings of a material memorial, spontaneously eulogize the deceased:

Let me leave a memorial in the breasts of my fellow-creatures. Let surviving friends bear witness that I have not lived to myself alone, nor been altogether unserviceable in my generation. O! let an uninterrupted series of beneficent offices be the inscription, and the best interests of my acquaintance the plate that exhibits it.... Let the poor, as they pass by my grave, point out the little spot, and thankfully acknowledge, "There lies the man, whose unwearied kindness was the constant relief of my various distresses...." Let a person, once ignorant and ungodly, life up his eyes to heaven, and say within himself, "Here are the last remnants of that sincere friend, who watched for my soul.... Methinks his discourses, seasoned with religion, and blessed by grace, are still warm in my heart; and I trust, will be more and more operative, till we meet each other in the house not made with hands, eternal in the heavens."[98]

By ruling out an epitaph upon himself in favor of the responses of the local community, Hervey takes to the extreme the emphasis upon friends' vocalization of the "true" epitaph found in Pope's epitaph upon Gay and its later eighteenth-century imitations. Hervey does not even consider the potential usefulness of an inscription depicting a moral exemplum for strangers. Though the *Meditations* is itself written for a general audience, Hervey's imagination is sparked by the edifying power he has (or imagines he has) in the smaller community of those who know and hear him as their parish priest and their personal friend. His rejection of an epitaph suggests uncertainty concerning his whole project of reaching and teaching unknown readers.

The substitution of intimates' memories for a public inscription is equally striking in another very popular didactic work, the children's story *Goody Two-Shoes* (1766), which tells of a poor orphan who rises through virtue and industry to become a rich and benevolent pillar of her community. When the heroine Mrs. Margery Two-Shoes dies, she is commemorated in the parish churchyard by "a Monument... without Inscription... over which the Poor as they pass weep continually, so that the Stone is ever bathed in Tears."[99] Without being cheapened by unnecessary panegyric, Goody's monument becomes a unifying focus of the local community, linking the living poor to their deceased benefactress. The book ends with an "extempore" poem delivered by a "young Gentleman" inspired by Goody and her modest monument. While giving

[98] Hervey, 1:89–90.
[99] *Goody Two-Shoes*, intro. Charles Welsh (1766; rpt., London, 1881), 140.

the book the strong closure often provided by an epitaph, these verses differ from an actual epitaph in that they purportedly are a spontaneous, oral ejaculation rather than a premeditated, inscribed panegyric.[100] Goody's lack of a public inscription means that within the fiction of the tale only a small community of intimates can be moved and inspired by her example. Thus the didactic purpose of a highly successful publishing venture like *Goody-Two Shoes* has no place in the story's celebration of a local community's feelings: the tale ignores its own telling.

Sentimental novels portraying avowedly private response are sometimes more self-conscious about such tensions. Henry Mackenzie's *The Man of Feeling* (1771) uses the topos of the discovered manuscript and several narrative frames in order to emphasize that the story of the radically private Harley, the man of retiring sensibility, comes to the public only by chance. The book is framed by the protagonist Harley's lack of an epitaph. As a character explains in an early scene, Harley would not dare prepare himself an epitaph because " [bashfulness] often goes with a man to his grave; nay, he dares not even pen a *hic jacet* to speak out for him after his death."[101] In the final paragraph of the book the narrator responds to Harley's grave:

He had hinted that he should like to be buried in a certain spot near the grave of his mother. This is a weakness; but it is universally incident to humanity; 'tis at least a memorial for those who survive: for some indeed a slender memorial will serve; and the soft affections, when they are busy that way, will build their structures, were it but on the paring of a nail. . . .

  I sometimes visit his grave; I sit in the hollow of the tree. 'Tis worth a thousand homilies! every nobler feeling rises within me! every beat of my heart awakens a virtue!—but 'twill make you hate the world—No: there is such an air of gentleness around, that I can hate nothing; but, as to the world—I pity the men of it.[102]

Mackenzie takes the emphasis on subjective response found in Gray's *Elegy* to its limit. Gray sees and responds to the "frail memorial[s]" that unknown rustics have erected for themselves as minimal assertions of enduring social identity and then hopes for the response of a "kindred spirit" to his own churchyard monument and inscription. The narrator here responds, by contrast, to a "slender memorial" whose objective status outside of his own consciousness is uncertain. It is unclear—and irrelevant—whether Harley has been given a monument or simply a covering of earth, but it is clear that no epitaph is here allowed to delimit

---

[100] *Goody*, 140.
[101] Henry Mackenzie, *The Man of Feeling* (1771; rpt., New York: Garland, 1974), 2.
[102] Mackenzie, 267–268.

the free play of the narrator's sentiment. Harley does not "speak out" from the grave, but this allows the narrator to feel ever so much more about him. The reader and the public world are, meanwhile, separated by many layers of mediating frame from this picture of unmediated communion.

A final example reveals how the suspicion of the epitaph as a public message appears even in works devoted to the very task of publishing epitaphs. An anonymous collection of epitaphs published in 1806 has as its frontispiece a picture of mourners standing around a churchyard gravestone (Figure 6). The frontispiece blends two famous works, one visual and one verbal, concerning reactions to an inscription. Three figures surround the stone: an old man in black, standing before the stone in profile on the left, leaning on a cane with his chin on his hand in a traditional gesture of melancholy; a young lady dressed in mourning in three-quarter view on the right, leaning sorrowfully on the gravestone from behind and pointing down toward, but not looking at, the inscription whose meaning she so well knows; and a second young lady in white, her back to the spectator, kneeling in front of the stone and reading the inscription. The various poses of the figures—leaning, pointing, kneeling, reading—are rearranged versions of the poses in Poussin's masterpiece *The Arcadian Shepherds*, in which three shepherds and a shepherdess around a tomb slowly come to understand, with elegiac pensiveness, its inscription, "Et in Arcadia Ego," which was interpreted by Poussin and his eighteenth-century admirers to mean "I [a fellow shepherd] too once lived in Arcadia" (Figure 7). The painting was very popular in the eighteenth century for its rendering of elegiac response, and the frontispiece stiffly adapts Poussin's evocative pastoral to dignify a contemporary, "realistic" scene of the sadness called forth by a modest gravestone and epitaph.[103]

In the mid and late eighteenth century, members of the upper classes began commemorating the dead on their private estates, burying the deceased in family mausolea rather than in local parish churches and erecting cenotaphs and memorial urns in gardens influenced by Poussin.[104] The more humble mourners of the frontispiece of this anonymous

[103] On Poussin's painting in eighteenth-century England, see Erwin Panofsky, "*Et in Arcadia Ego*: Poussin and the Elegiac Tradition," in his *Meaning in the Visual Arts* (Garden City, N.Y.: Doubleday, 1955), 295–320; the opening pages discuss a 1769 painting by Sir Joshua Reynolds based upon Poussin's work (pp. 295–296).

[104] On the rise of the mausoleum, see Penny, 44–64. Richard A. Etlin, *The Architecture of Death: The Transformation of the Cemetery in Eighteenth-Century Paris* (Cambridge: MIT Press, 1984), 179–184, traces the incorporation of Poussin's painting and its inscription, both as motif and general inspiration, in eighteenth-century English gardens, which included urns with pathetic inscriptions commemorating beloved relatives and friends.

Figure 6. Frontispiece of *A Select Collection of Epitaphs and Monumental Inscriptions,* *with Anecdotes* (Ipswich, 1806).

Figure 7. Nicolas Poussin, *The Arcadian Shepherds* (*Les Bergers D'Arcadie*), Louvre Museum. Courtesy of Giraudon/Art Resource.

collection create their own personal space of mourning within a public churchyard. The two mourning figures flanking the tomb are clearly the relatives of the deceased, and together they simultaneously draw us toward and keep us away from the inscription, for while the index finger of the woman on the right gestures us forward, the cane of the man on the left obstructs our view. The kneeling woman who reads the inscription, dressed in the white of innocence rather than the black of mourning, is presumably the beloved of the deceased.[105] She also partially covers the inscription, but we can make out, though an "S" is covered and an "H" only half visible, "HERE RESTS / A YOUTH," a fragment of Gray's epitaph upon himself ("Here rests his head upon the lap of earth / A youth to fortune and to fame unknown").[106] By presenting an obstructed, partial view of a drastically reduced version of Gray's already self-consciously reticent epitaph, the frontispiece suggests how difficult it is for us as would-be "kindred spirits" to know or feel the brief inscription's full meaning, which can ultimately be understood only by the true mourners who knew the deceased.[107]

Recalling the woman mourning over an urn common in contemporary funerary monuments, the kneeling woman also represents both grief as such, her face turned away from the viewer because the deepest grief is unrepresentable,[108] and the viewer-reader, insofar as he or she is properly responsive. Just as our reading of the inscription seems to be both invited and prevented, so we seem both included in and excluded from the grief of the kneeling woman. As the introduction to a collection of inscriptions, the frontispiece asks us simultaneously to read with sym-

[105] Compare the depiction of the beloved dressed in white grieving over the tomb of the unhappy lover in the frontispiece to the 1801 English translation of Goethe's sentimental novel *Die Leiden des Jungen Werthers* (1796), reprinted in Brissenden, facing p. 264.

[106] Gray's *Elegy* explains the presence of the beloved in the frontispiece: she mourns a young man who loved her too dearly, the speaker of the *Elegy* whom some readers assumed was an unhappy lover (see note 20).

[107] In his study of the relationship between poetry and painting in Augustan literature, Jean H. Hagstrum argues plausibly that the first illustrator of the *Elegy*, the poet's friend Richard Bentley, linked Gray's epitaph to Poussin's painting by borrowing from Poussin's kneeling shepherd the action of his "swain," who, with no basis in Gray's text, traces out the letters of the inscription for the "kindred spirit." Hagstrum also argues, less convincingly, for Poussin's direct influence upon Gray. See *The Sister Arts: The Tradition of Literary Pictorialism and English Poetry from Dryden to Gray* (Chicago: University of Chicago Press, 1958), 295–299. Perhaps inspired by the Bentley illustration, the engraver of the frontispiece for the 1806 anthology makes the merging of Gray and Poussin even clearer.

[108] On the impossibility of directly representing the profoundest grief, see Hervey's description of a skillful painter "who, having placed around a beautiful expiring virgin, her friends in all the agonies of grief, represented the unequalled anguish of the father with far greater liveliness and strength, or rather with an expressible emphasis, by drawing a veil over his face" (1:70). Hervey has adapted the famous story of the painter Timanthes of Cythnos's placing a veil over the face of Agamemnon in order to suggest the Greek general's profound anguish at the sacrifice of Iphigenia (see Cicero, *Orator* 21.74).

pathetic feeling and to recognize our inevitable distance as readers from the deepest, truest, and ultimately private grief: it thus combines the epitaph's call for the proper reader's sympathy and the related distrust of public communications traced in this chapter.

Chapter 11

Praising Honest Creatures: Paternalist Commemoration from the Mid Eighteenth to the Early Nineteenth Century

With the gradual deterioration of the paternalist social hierarchy and the growth of capitalist relations beginning around the middle of the eighteenth century, the upper and middle classes began to view the lower orders as a distant, independent, and sometimes dangerously discontented "other."[1] The social elite increasingly treated the humble churchyard graves and inscriptions of their social inferiors as alien but important forms of cultural production. In various ways members of the privileged classes sought to bridge the sociocultural gap that they perceived in funerary practices: they chose burial in the churchyard rather than the church interior to assert their sympathetic connection to the poor; they admired and collected the epitaphs of the humble; and they sought to "improve" the lower orders' literary efforts by providing them with "correct" epitaphic models.

While Pope displayed his unique sensibility by commemorating persons society would otherwise have misinterpreted or forgotten, from the mid eighteenth century onward numerous members of the elite displayed their benevolence by memorializing humble creatures whom society would otherwise have wholly ignored. It became fashionable for

[1] On the widening social and cultural gap between the upper and middle ranks and the poor around the middle of the eighteenth century, see Ralph Malcolmson, *Popular Recreations in English Society, 1700–1850* (Cambridge: Cambridge University Press, 1973), 89–171; Ralph Malcolmson, *Life and Labour in England, 1700–1780* (New York: St. Martin's, 1981), 146–153; and E. P. Thompson, "Patrician Society, Plebeian Culture," *Journal of Social History* 7 (1974):382–405.

the privileged to compose epitaphs upon their laborers, domestic servants, and pets. Paternalist epitaphs upon the lower classes, or upon pets that could represent the lower classes, nostalgically reaffirmed the affective bond between the ostensibly benign elite and the supposedly contented lower orders. Such epitaphs suggested that the lowly at their most vulnerable—in death—could depend upon their social superiors for rescue from oblivion.

The cult of feeling manifested itself in very different ways in epitaphs upon the "great" and in epitaphs upon the lowly. While the former increasingly consisted of personal laments for irreplaceable individuals and extended pleas for the sympathetic response of strangers, the latter redeployed brief, impersonal panegyric rhetoric in order to commemorate the simple, generic virtues of the lowly. The humble thus became vehicles for affirming supposedly common, uncontested social values. Because of their crucial ideological function, epitaphs upon the lowly were widely published and quickly became highly conventional. While their formulaic quality seemed to demonstrate the social elite's conceptual mastery over potential challenges to its cultural hegemony, it also contributed to poets' growing sense of the epitaph as a hollow, subliterary genre.

Gray's *Elegy* is an early and influential example of the new concern for the laboring poor, a hitherto neglected group of the dead. The poem contrasts the church monuments of the elite and the humble churchyard tombstones of the poor: on the one hand, the church's "storied urn[s]" and "animated bust[s]" (l. 41) and, on the other, the "frail memorial[s]" (l. 78) placed among the "rugged elms" and "yew-tree's shade" (l. 13) and decked with "shapeless sculpture" (l. 79) and inscriptions by the "unlettered muse" (l. 81).[2] Pope's "Elegy to the Memory of an Unfortunate Lady" may have suggested Gray's contrast between two kinds of commemoration, one associated with elite art and the other with "humble" nature. Both Pope's and Gray's poems explore society's differential treatment of the dead, and both embrace the cause of the outcast— Pope's condemned suicide, Gray's disdained poor—to attack the "proud" ("Elegy to the Memory," l. 43, *Elegy*, l. 37).[3] While Pope affirms the dignity of a unique, fictional character, however, Gray affirms the moral worth of an entire social group.

Gray distinguishes between great and poor not only in terms of art

[2] I cite the text of Gray's *Elegy* in *The Poems of Thomas Gray, William Collins, and Oliver Goldsmith*, ed. Roger Lonsdale (London: Longmans, 1969), 117–140.

[3] F. W. Bateson suggests that Pope's "Elegy" was the major model for Gray's *Elegy* as an attack on the "proud" in "Gray's 'Elegy' Reconsidered," in his *English Poetry: A Critical Introduction*, rev. ed. (London: Longmans, 1966), 131–132.

and nature but also in terms of silence and sound.[4] The contrast is here paradoxical. The commemorative art of the elite, for all its noisy claims, cannot overcome the silence of death:

> Can storied urns or animated bust
> Back to its mansion call the fleeting breath?
> Can Honour's voice provoke the silent dust,
> Or Flattery soothe the dull cold ear of Death?
>
> (ll. 41–44)

By contrast, the churchyard monuments of the poor, who in life "kept the noiseless tenor of their way" (l. 76), make the poet hear the cries of the dead for recognition:

> Yet even these bones from insult to protect,
> Some frail memorial still erected nigh,
> With uncouth rhymes and shapeless sculpture decked,
> Implores the passing tribute of a sigh.
>
> Their name, their years, spelt by the unlettered muse,
> The place of fame and elegy supply:
> And many a holy text around she strews,
> That teach the rustic moralist to die.
>
> For who to dumb Forgetfulness a prey,
> This pleasing anxious being e'er resigned,
> Left the warm precincts of the cheerful day,
> Nor cast one longing lingering look behind?
>
> On some fond breast the parting soul relies,
> Some pious drops the closing eye requires;
> Ev'n from the tomb the voice of nature cries,
> Ev'n in our ashes live their wonted fires.
>
> (ll. 77–92)

Gray hears the humble churchyard monuments "implore" the sympathetic stranger's attention. He suggests that the desire for remembrance shared by rich and poor is best expressed by the latter because their artless monuments in the natural landscape most authentically articulate, for those willing to listen, the "voice of nature" in all its humble neediness. By being so near the silence of death, the poor's obscure lives of "noiseless tenor" reveal what the social elite attempt to forget, the closeness of all mortals to death. By their evident vulnerability to contempt or neglect,

---

[4] For other discussions of sound and silence in the Elegy, see Bateson, 133; Peter M. Sacks, *The English Elegy: Studies in the Genre from Spenser to Yeats* (Baltimore: Johns Hopkins University Press, 1985), 134–136; and George T. Wright, "Stillness and the Argument of Gray's *Elegy*," *MP* 74 (1977):381–389.

the poor's "frail memorial[s]" similarly lay bare what the social elite's grand monuments attempt to hide, the weakness of all mortal attempts to escape oblivion. Those who are most silent in life are thus the most expressive in death.

Gray's meditation upon the universal desire for posthumous recognition may be contrasted with such a classical treatment of the same subject as Cicero's in the *Tusculan Disputations*:

The begetting of children, the prolongation of a name . . . the very burial monuments, the epitaphs—what meaning have they except that we are thinking of the future as well as the present? . . . somehow it comes about that there is in men's minds a sort of deeply rooted presentiment of future ages, and this feeling is strongest and most evident in men of the greatest genius and the loftiest spirit. . . . So far, I am speaking of statesmen, but what of poets? Have they no wish to become famous after death? . . . But if universal agreement is the voice of nature [*Quod si omnium consensus naturae vox est*], and all throughout the world agree that there is something appertaining to those who have passed away from life, we too are bound to hold the same opinion; and if we think that spirits of outstanding ability or moral worth have the clearest insight into the meaning of nature [*vim naturae*], because they are blest with the highest nature [*natura optima*], then, inasmuch as all the best characters do most service for posterity, the probability is that there is something of which they will have sensation after death.[5]

Cicero argues that the "voice of nature" (*naturae vox*) or "universal agreement" pronounces the human spirit immortal. Like Gray, Cicero treats monuments and epitaphs as signs of the universal human desire for remembrance, a desire that seems to presuppose human immortality and the consequent ability to enjoy posthumous fame. Following Plato's *Symposium* (208c–209e), however, Cicero discerns a hierarchy in the human striving for remembrance: though all human beings desire to be remembered, only men of the "highest nature," such as the great statesmen and poets, actively seek fame in the noblest ways and thereby best reveal the human desire for remembrance.[6] While Gray's *Elegy* recalls

---

[5] "Quid procreatio liberorum, quid propagatio nominis . . . quid ipsa sepulcrorum monumenta, elogia significant nisi nos futura etiam cogitare? . . . sed nescio quo modo inhaeret in mentibus quasi saeclorum quoddam augurium futurorum, idque in maximis ingeniis altissimisque animis et exsistit maxime et apparet facillime. . . . Loquor de principibus: quid poëtae? nonne post mortem nobilitari volunt? . . . Quod si omnium consensus naturae vox est omnesque, qui ubique sunt, consentiunt esse aliquid quod ad eos pertineat, qui vita cesserint, nobis quoque idem existimandum est et si, quorum aut ingenio aut virtute animus excellit, eos arbitramur, quia natura optima sint, cernere naturae vim maxime, veri simile est, cum optimus quisque maxime posteritati serviat, esse aliquid, cuius is post mortem sensum sit habiturus" (Cicero, *Tusculan Disputations* 1.14.31–1.15.35).

[6] For several other Ciceronian passages arguing that great men's desire for posthumous fame is proof of man's immortality, see *De senectute* 23.82 and the list of parallels in J. G. F. Powell, ed., *Cato Maior: De senectute* (Cambridge: Cambridge University Press, 1988), 261.

the classical notion of the universal need to be remembered, the poet pointedly relocates the *naturae vox*. Instead of among men of the "highest nature," he hears the "voice of nature" most clearly among the lowly who cry out from their churchyard graves.[7]

Gray makes clear his revision of classical conceptions of immortality by suggesting a connection between the buried villagers and great men of the sort singled out by Cicero, those who consciously pursue immortality because they possess the "highest nature." Between his attack on proud church monuments and his sympathetic response to humble churchyard gravestones, he reflects on the unrealized potential for fame of those buried in the churchyard:

> Perhaps in this neglected spot is laid
> Some heart once pregnant with celestial fire;
> Hands that the rod of empire might have swayed,
> Or waked to ecstasy the living lyre.
>   .   .   .   .   .
> Some village-Hampden that with dauntless breast
> The little tyrant of his fields withstood;
> Some mute inglorious Milton here may rest,
> Some Cromwell guiltless of his country's blood.
>   (ll. 45–48, 57–60)

By suggesting that the villagers may have had the heroic capacities and genius of great statesmen and poets, the kind of men Cicero commended, Gray defends the worth of those whose social position denied them both the glory and the guilt of public achievement. Gray's ensuing meditation upon the "voice of nature" and "wonted fires" (l. 92) of the dead further suggests that the poor achieve in death what they could not in life: those who in life had only potential "voice" ("Some mute inglorious Milton") and "celestial fire" attain in death a voice and fire deserving the sympathetic attention of the living.[8]

Like Pope's benevolent commemorations of the vulnerable dead, Gray's elegiac focus on the churchyard inhabitants contributes to the poet's memorializing portrait of himself as a man whose sentiments transcend the unfeeling norms of polite society. By imagining his own burial

---

[7] Gray certainly knew the *Tusculan Disputations*: he paraphrases a passage from the work (5.3) in a January 1747 letter to Walpole; see *The Correspondence of Thomas Gray*, ed. Paget Toynbee and Leonard Whibley, 3 vols. (Oxford: Clarendon, 1935), 1:262–263.

[8] In the earlier version of the poem preserved in the Eton manuscript, "Hampden" was "Cato," "Milton" was "Tully," and "Cromwell" was "Caesar" (see Gray, 127–128, notes 57, 59, and 60). Gray wished to give the poem a greater English flavor, but the earlier version's Roman references, including the reference to Cicero, make clear that Gray invokes classical values in order to reject classical elitism.

and monument in the churchyard, Gray links himself in death to the poor whose worth he defends against the "proud." It is true that unlike the poor, he is commemorated not by name and the formulaic pieties of an "unlettered muse" but instead by an anonymous poetic epitaph that reveals his unique sensibility far better than could any name or formula. Nevertheless his churchyard epitaph, like theirs, authentically expresses the vulnerability of mortal men through its self-conscious humility: the epitaph that declares the "frailties" of an "unknown youth" who humbly "lies upon the lap of earth" awaiting the sympathetic response of the "kindred spirit" is the poet's self-chosen analogue to the rustics' "frail" churchyard monuments and inscriptions.

By treating the buried poor as the truest representatives of all the vulnerable dead, Gray makes explicit the association often implicit among his contemporaries of the poor with the dead as groups all too frequently neglected by society. Such an association is evident in the work of the influential moral philosopher and economist Adam Smith. In both *The Theory of Moral Sentiments* (1759), one of the most popular expositions of "sentimental" morality, and his classic treatise on economics, *An Inquiry into the Nature and Causes of the Wealth of Nations* (1776), Smith argues that a free market economy, which relies on humanity's "natural selfishness and rapacity" rather than on its "benevolence," produces extreme economic inequality but increases the wealth of all.[9] *The Theory of Moral Sentiments* qualifies the approval of "commercial society," however, by suggesting that such a society depends upon a disregard for the poor that renders their lot akin to death.[10]

Smith's ethical treatise argues that "sympathy" or "fellow feeling" depends on imagining oneself in the situation of those with whom one sympathizes.[11] Because human beings find it far easier to sympathize with others' joys than with others' sorrows,[12] they sympathize more readily with the rich and powerful than with the poor and powerless.

[9] See Adam Smith, *The Theory of Moral Sentiments*, ed. D. D. Raphael and A. L. Macfie, corr. ed. (Oxford: Clarendon, 1979), 184–185; and Adam Smith, *An Inquiry into the Nature and Causes of the Wealth of Nations*, ed. R. H. Campbell and A. S. Skinner; textual ed. W. B. Todd, 2 vols. (Oxford: Clarendon, 1976), 1:26–27. On the popularity and influence of Smith's ethical treatise, see Brissenden, 36–37.

[10] My discussion of Smith's ambivalent attitude toward "commercial society" is indebted to Istvan Hont and Michael Ignatieff, "Needs and Justice in the 'Wealth of Nations': An Introductory Essay," in their anthology *Wealth and Virtue: The Shaping of Political Economy in the Scottish Enlightenment* (Cambridge: Cambridge University Press, 1983), 1–44. On Smith's concern for the conditions of the poor, see also Gertrude Himmelfarb, *The Idea of Poverty: England in the Early Industrial Age* (New York: Vintage, 1983), 42–63.

[11] Smith, *Theory*, 9.

[12] See Smith, *Theory*, 47. On Smith's concern with the limits of human sympathy, see also David Marshall, *The Figure of Theater: Shaftesbury, Defoe, Adam Smith, and George Eliot* (New York: Columbia University Press, 1986), 167–192.

People scramble for wealth and station in order to be "taken notice of with sympathy."[13] Though moralists rightly urge the fortunate to show "fellow feeling" for the poor,[14] the poor are normally despised or "overlooked."[15]

The dead are also vulnerable to disregard. Though the opening chapter of the moral treatise argues that human beings "sympathize even with the dead," such sympathy largely depends, paradoxically, upon the living's neglect of the deceased:

It is miserable, we think, to be deprived of the light of the sun; to be shut out from life and conversation; to be laid in the cold grave . . . to be no more thought of in this world, but to be obliterated, in a little time, from the affections, and almost from the memory, of . . . dearest friends and relations. Surely, we imagine, we can never feel too much for those who have suffered so dreadful a calamity. The tribute of our fellow-feeling seems doubly due to them now, when they are in danger of being forgot by every body; and, by the vain honours which we pay to their memory, we endeavour, for our own misery, artificially to keep alive our melancholy remembrance of their misfortune.[16]

The notion that "dearest friends and relations" soon grow emotionally distant from the dead exemplifies in extreme form the eighteenth-century social elite's sense of the living's disregard for the deceased. While many of his contemporaries suggest that only intimates truly care about the dead, who are forgotten by society as a whole, Smith suggests that not even intimates care deeply about the deceased. Since Smith later defines "affection" as "habitual sympathy,"[17] his assertion that the living "sympathize" with the dead because they pity them for being "obliterated . . . from the affections" of intimates means that such sympathy is only a second-order, compensatory response to the lack of "habitual sympathy." By means of "vain honours" such as monuments and epitaphs, the living "artificially" remember the "misfortune" of those whom they are naturally inclined to forget because of their "dull sensibility to the afflictions of others."[18]

Smith's descriptions of the neglected poor recall his opening description of the dead: the poor are deprived of the "daylight of honour and approbation," just as the dead are "deprived of the light of the sun"; the poor man is "out of the sight of mankind" and "in the midst of a crowd is in the same obscurity as if shut up in his own hovel," just as

---

[13] Smith, *Theory*, 50.
[14] Smith, *Theory*, 225–226.
[15] Smith, *Theory*, 50–51.
[16] Smith, *Theory*, 12–13.
[17] Smith, *Theory*, 220.
[18] Smith uses this phrase later in the work when arguing that "our sorrow at a funeral generally amounts to no more than an affected gravity" (*Theory*, 47).

the dead are "shut out from life and conversation . . . in the cold grave."[19] Smith's other writings similarly describe the poor's lot as akin to death: his 1763 lectures on jurisprudence note that the poor man is "buried in obscurity" and "thrust down into the lowest part of the earth";[20] in one of its bleaker moments, *The Wealth of Nations* describes the urban poor "sunk in obscurity and darkness."[21] Smith's ethical treatise notes, however, that the upper classes regard the poor's condition as even "worse than death,"[22] and their state is indeed worse in Smith's view, for the poor generally evoke no second-order sympathetic response from their fellow men. To sympathize with the deceased poor would therefore be, in Smith's scheme, to sympathize with those who are doubly forgotten in the general pursuit and admiration of wealth and power. With the widening gap between rich and poor beginning in the mid eighteenth century, however, members of the social elite increasingly reassert their bond with the poor by displaying precisely such sympathy.

Over the course of the later eighteenth and early nineteenth centuries, for example, the upper and middle classes increasingly chose churchyard burial, like Gray in the *Elegy*, as a sentimental assertion of their ultimate kinship to the churchyard poor. This new trend represented a major shift in conceptions of churchyard burial. During the sixteenth and early seventeenth centuries, fears of mixing worship of the living God with worship of the dead resulted in a minority of the Protestant elite, especially those of the Puritan faction, chosing churchyard burial despite the prestige of church burial and commemoration.[23] In the late seventeenth century the percentage of the social elite buried in the churchyard rose considerably.[24] Though the crowding of churches with bodies and monuments was partially responsible for the increasing use of the

---

[19] Smith, *Theory*, 51.

[20] Adam Smith, *Lectures on Jurisprudence*, ed. R. L. Meek, D. D. Raphael, and P. G. Stein (Oxford: Oxford University Press, 1978), 341.

[21] Smith, *Wealth*, 2:795.

[22] Smith, *Theory*, 50.

[23] Philippe Ariès notes without adequately explaining the churchyard burials of members of the elite in England in *The Hour of Our Death*, trans. Helen Weaver (New York: Random, 1982), 90–92. For examples of Puritan ministers who chose churchyard burial in the late sixteenth and early seventeenth centuries, see Patrick Collinson, *The Elizabethan Puritan Movement* (Berkeley: University of California Press, 1967), 370–371; and R. C. Richardson, *Puritanism in North-West England: A Regional Study of the Diocese of Chester to 1642* (Manchester: Manchester University Press; Totowa, N.J.: Rowman & Littlefield, 1972), 30.

[24] See Ariès, 338–339; and Clare Gittings, *Death, Burial and the Individual in Early Modern England* (London: Croom Helm, 1984), 139–141 and 145–146. John Le Neve's anthology of epitaphs upon the elite, *Monumenta Anglicana: Being Inscriptions on the Monuments of several Eminent Persons . . . 1600–1715*, 5 vols. (London, 1718–1719), reveals a rise in the percentage of churchyard inscriptions beginning in the second half of the seventeenth century: there are 10 churchyard inscriptions out of total of 454, around 2 percent, for the years 1600–1649; 20 such inscriptions out of 818, almost 2.5 percent, for the years

churchyard, more men and women than ever before chose to be buried in the churchyard out of religious conviction that the dead should be separated from the living. Sir Matthew Hale, who died in 1676, expressed the views of many of his contemporaries when he claimed that "churches were for the living . . . Churchyards for the dead."[25] In addition to increasing the popularity of the plain wall tablet, the iconoclasm of the Civil Wars dissuaded some of the social elite from continuing burial practices that were at best divisive and at worst temptations to idolatry.

The religious scruples of the elite did not prevent them, however, from asserting social distinctions in death. Some families distinguished between the churchyard as the appropriate burial place and the church as the site of monuments expressing enduring social status: a family who in the 1690s buried a gentlewoman in the churchyard "by her own appointment" also erected a cenotaph to her memory in the church, thus affirming her status and their own.[26] In the late seventeenth century those who chose churchyard burial also began erecting substantial churchyard monuments, in imitation of the church monuments they had forsaken.[27]

Gray's contrast between church and churchyard in terms of social class and the distinction between art and nature both exemplifies and influences the new eighteenth-century sense of the distinction between indoor and outdoor commemoration. Increasingly, the upper and middle ranks chose simpler, outdoor memorials not out of specifically religious scruples but out of a desire to assert in death their links to "simple" nature and to the socially humble, who were deemed closest to nature. Both the private gardens of the social elite and the public churchyards reveal this new cult of natural simplicity. William Shenstone's garden at Leasowes, for example, had urns dedicated to friends absent or dead with inscriptions that honored the person's simplicity and love of nature.[28]

1650–1679; 30 out of 515, almost 6 percent, for the years 1680–1699; and 31 out of 347, almost 9 percent, for the years 1700–1715.

[25] Quoted in Samuel Clarke, *The Lives of Sundry Eminent Persons in this Later Age* (London, 1683), 130. In 1692, an Oxfordshire gentleman, Griffith Higgs, "meekly" chose to be buried outside near the church door because he "fear'd" church burial; see F. N. Davis, ed., "Anthony à Wood's and Richard Rawlinson's Parochial Collections (Third Part)," *Oxfordshire Record Society* 11 (1929):275–276. Protestants of all religious persuasions increasingly rejected church burial: Gittings cites the similar sentiments of the Low Church bishop Hall and the High Church, non-juror archbishop Sancroft (p. 141).

[26] See the epitaph of Bridget Wilford, d. 1692, in Le Neve, 3:137.

[27] Thomas Parnell's "A Night-Piece on Death," published posthumously in 1722, describes the proudly ascending churchyard monuments that "Adorn the rich, or Praise the great" (l. 44); see *The New Oxford Book of Eighteenth Century Verse*, ed. Roger Lonsdale (Oxford: Oxford University Press, 1984), 117.

[28] See *The Poetical Works of William Shenstone*, ed. Rev. George Gilfillan (1854; rpt., New York: Greenwood Press, 1968), 274, 278–281; and the discussion of Shenstone's inscrip-

Shenstone chose to be buried and commemorated in the local churchyard, and his 1771 epitaph by Richard Graves, cited earlier for its address
to the reader, contrasted his "simple urn" with the "monumental bust,
/ Or sumptuous tomb" typical of the "great."[29] Some echoed Gray's *Elegy*
to suggest the significance of churchyard burial: an epitaph upon a
middle-class woman who died in 1779 praises the "frail memorial" of
the deceased, placed amid the "rude branches" and "green sod" of the
churchyard, as superior to "all the monuments of proudest art"; in a
1791 composition entitled "Epitaph on and by Himself in a Country
Church-yard," a poet imagines his "poor clay" buried in lowly "sod"
rather than in a church's "proud tomb"; in an early nineteenth-century
churchyard epitaph, a grieving sister contrasts the "simple stone" that
she erected to her brother, an army officer, with the "storied urn" and
"monumental bust" (cf. *Elegy*, l. 41) of the proud.[30]
    Some members of the eighteenth-century social elite made explicit
their wish to be buried in the churchyard in order to assert, in death,
their link to the poor. In 1740, for example, Lady Beatrice Webb chose,
as her epitaph states, churchyard burial "in compassion for the poor."[31]
Goody Two-Shoes (1766) provides a fictional analogue for such a choice.
In an early episode of the book, a local gentlewoman's elaborate church
burial is described as an unwholesome "display [of] the Pride of the
Living, or the Vanity of the Dead."[32] Goody's monument stands at the
end of the story in pointed contrast to such aristocratic pride, since the
prosperous, benevolent heroine is commemorated in the churchyard
where she was buried so that the poor can continue to "encounter" in
their own milieu their middle-class friend.

    During the late eighteenth century members of the social elite also
began to take note of, and to provide models for, churchyard epitaphs
upon the lower classes. Magazines printed correspondents' transcriptions
and praise of humble churchyard inscriptions. Gray responded sympathetically to epitaphs that "teach the rustic moralist to die," and others

---

tions in Richard A. Etlin, *The Architecture of Death: The Transformation of the Cemetery in
Eighteenth-Century Paris* (Cambridge: MIT Press, 1984), 176–184.
    [29] See [Richard Graves], "*On an* URN *(now erecting) to the Memory of* WILLIAM
SHENSTONE, *Esq. in Hales Owen Church-yard, Shropshire,*" *Gentleman's Magazine* 41 (1771):
564.
    [30] Epitaph upon Mrs. Ann Cooper, d. 1779, in Frederick Teague Cansick, ed., *A Col-
lection of Curious and Interesting Epitaphs . . . of Saint Pancras, Middlesex*, 2 vols. (London, 1869),
1:59; *Gentleman's Magazine* 61 (1791):1047; and epitaph upon Archibald Septimus Hedge,
d. 1805, in William Graham, ed., *A Collection of Epitaphs and Monumental Inscriptions, Ancient
and Modern* (Carlisle, 1821), 177.
    [31] Cansick, 1:38.
    [32] *Goody Two-Shoes*, intro. Charles Welsh (1766; rpt., London, 1881), 47.

began to appreciate the piety of humble churchyard inscriptions.[33] While over the course of the seventeenth century medieval memento mori formulae virtually disappeared from epitaphs upon the social elite, they continued to be inscribed upon modest churchyard gravestones; in 1793 George Wright praised an anonymous churchyard inscription that used such a formula as the most "suitable" epitaph for "rich or poor."[34] The educated classes not only appreciated, however, but also sought to control the epitaphic compositions of the lower orders. The Methodist *Arminian Magazine*, which had a wide circulation among the middle and lower classes, often included model epitaphs and campaigned against both morally improper and grammatically incorrect inscriptions. In one issue readers were warned not to leave the composition of epitaphs "to illiterate Relations, Parish-Clerks, or Stone-Masons, to the great scandal of the Nation in general, and of Religion in particular."[35] John Bowden's *The Epitaph Writer* (1791) was one of several anthologies designed specifically for "the Use of those Artists who write or engrave Epitaphs for the middle and lower Ranks of People." It contains brief, pious compositions deemed suitable for the most modest kinds of memorials, plain tombstones and wooden markers.[36]

Those who associated churchyard commemoration with the poor and provided models for their epitaphs often ignored the fact that the vast majority of the poor neither sought nor received memorials, however humble. The majority of churchyard memorials during the eighteenth and nineteenth centuries were not for laboring poor but for the more prosperous yeomen farmers, craftsmen, and tradesmen, whose brief gravestone inscriptions expressed Christian pieties or proclaimed the enduring value of their simple but dignified way of life.[37] By contrast,

[33] See, for example, the comments of an anonymous "tourist" upon his collection of churchyard epitaphs by "village poets" in *Kentish Register* 2 (1794):355–356; and the praise of a military private's churchyard epitaph, cited in support of Gray's claim that humble epitaphs "teach the rustic moralist to die," in *Monthly Magazine and British Register* 1 (1796):98–99.
[34] George Wright, *Pleasing Melancholy* (London, 1793), 97. For a critique of such interest in humble churchyard pieties, see Charles Lamb's attack upon the "Such as I am, such you shall be" formula as one of "those impertinent and misbecoming familiarities, inscribed upon your ordinary tombstones," in his essay "New Year's Eve" (1821) in *Elia and the Last Essays of Elia*, ed. Jonathan Bate (Oxford: Oxford University Press, 1987), 35.
[35] *Arminian Magazine* 7 (1784):564. On the circulation of the *Arminian Magazine*, see Louis Billington, "The Religious Periodical and Newspaper Press, 1770–1870," in *The Press in English Society from the Seventeenth to the Nineteenth Centuries*, ed. Michael Harris and Alan Lee (Rutherford, N.J.: Fairleigh Dickinson University Press; London: Associated University Press, 1986), 115–116.
[36] John Bowden, *The Epitaph-Writer* (1791), i. The early nineteenth-century *Epitaphs for Country Church Yards* (London, n.d.) is another anthology of brief, pious churchyard inscriptions intended for the humble. Both Wright's *Pleasing Melancholy* of 1793 and the anonymous *Collection* of 1806 also contain numerous inscriptions of this kind.
[37] For discussion and examples of such epitaphs, see Frederick Burgess, *English Church-*

while many of the laboring poor wished for a "decent" funeral, far fewer felt the need for a material monument celebrating their way of life. In the eighteenth and early nineteenth centuries many laborers joined groups known as "friendly societies," one of whose chief tasks was to provide funerals for their members. There were also burial societies devoted exclusively to this task.[38] To the consternation of some upper-class reformers, such societies often provided very elaborate funeral ceremonies. If members had received less extravagant funerals, they could certainly have purchased modest monuments with brief inscriptions.[39] The members of such groups desired, however, to reaffirm the community of relatives, friends, and neighbors in the face of death, and this intense focus on the local community did not encourage the erection of monuments with epitaphs addressed to the unknown passerby. Illiteracy, which remained high among the poor, especially in the countryside, further discouraged interest in epitaphs.[40] A monument with an inscription clearly meant far less to an illiterate laborer and to his or her surviving family and friends than the show of communal respect at a funeral.

Ironically, however, during the same period in which authors such as Hervey and Mackenzie imagined the rejection of public epitaphs, focusing instead on the memories of a smaller community of "friends," other authors projected their concern with public commemoration onto the laboring poor. Assuming that all men desired public memorials, with self-conscious generosity they began publishing brief panegyric epitaphs upon the poor, for whom they also erected humble churchyard me-

---

yard Memorials (London: Lutterworth Press, 1963), 114, 229–241; Kenneth Lindley, *Of Graves and Epitaphs* (London: Hutchinson, 1965), 113–128; and Kenneth Lindley, *Graves and Graveyards* (London: Routledge, 1972), 50–59.

[38] On "friendly" and burial societies, see Gittings, 60–65; M. Dorothy George, *London Life in the Eighteenth Century* (1925; rpt., New York: Harper, 1964), 302–303, 399–400, n. 94; and Margaret D. Fuller, *West Country Friendly Societies* (Lingfield, Surrey: Oakwood Press for University of Reading, 1964), 83–87. Peter Linebaugh discusses the intense concern with "decent" burial—which normally meant, at a minimum, a Christian burial rite, a shroud, and a coffin—among condemned criminals and the sympathetic working-class crowds at Tyburn in "The Tyburn Riot against the Surgeons," in *Albion's Fatal Tree: Crime and Society in Eighteenth-Century England*, ed. Douglas Hay et al. (London: Penguin, 1975), 65–118.

[39] In the early nineteenth century, funerals financed by burial societies were reported to cost as much as ten to fifteen pounds (George, 303); in the same period one could obtain a modest tombstone for a few pounds (Burgess, 271–281).

[40] During the 1750s 63 to 64 percent of the women and about 40 percent of men were unable to sign their names; see R. S. Schofield, "Dimension of Illiteracy, 1750–1850," *Explorations in Economic History* 10 (1972/1973):445. Gray's *Elegy* itself acknowledges the widespread illiteracy of the rural poor by including the illiterate "swain" who beckons the "kindred spirit" to peruse Gray's gravestone epitaph because the stranger can read (l. 115). Gray's sympathetic response to the churchyard epitaphs does not bridge the gap between himself and such a "swain."

morials. Such epitaphs clearly responded to increasing social unrest. The living conditions of much of the laboring poor deteriorated around the middle of the eighteenth century. Laborers lost their land to enclosures, were deprived of various customary rights, and experienced a decline in real wages. They expressed their discontent in rioting, particularly during the many harvest crises. The French Revolution further alarmed the English upper and middle classes, who feared that the laboring poor's discontent might lead to revolution at home. The social elite reacted to the suffering and discontent of the poor both with humanitarian attempts to improve their condition and with efforts to instill in them the "industry" and self-discipline that would supposedly alleviate their plight.[41] While earlier in the century Pope displayed his benevolence by commemorating laborers who had been dramatically singled out in death by lightning, from the mid eighteenth century onward members of the elite commemorated laborers—some of them real, some imaginary— simply for being hardworking and contented. Such epitaphs offered models for imitation to those among the poor who were literate and reassuringly proved to the commemorators, if not to the poor themselves, the enduring bond of sentiment between high and low.

Some epitaphs upon contented laborers describe the peaceful "verdant" setting of their humble churchyard graves in order to suggest that the lot of the laborer, in death as in life, is part of the natural and beneficent order of things.[42] Others extend the social range of the "honest" ideal in order to praise the "honest" labor of the hardworking poor. The opening and close of a brief epitaph upon "a Poor Labouring Man" is typical: "Honest, industrious, without guile or art, / His task performing with a cheerful heart... / So pass'd his days; and, having done his best, / This honest, faithful poor man sunk to rest."[43] One glimpses the harsher attitudes that underlie and necessitate such sentimentalization of "honest" labor in J. Arbuthnot's claim in 1773 that the enclosure of

[41] On changing socioeconomic conditions and rural laborers' riots, see E. J. Hobsbawm and George Rudé, *Captain Swing* (New York: Random, 1968); on the attitude of the social elite to the conditions of the poor, see Daniel A. Baugh, "Poverty, Protestantism, and Political Economy: English Attitudes toward the Poor," in *England's Rise to Greatness, 1660–1763*, ed. Stephen B. Baxter, Clarke Library Professorship Publications, no. 7 (Berkeley: University of California Press, 1983), 63–108 (especially pp. 84–93); and Himmelfarb, 23–146.

[42] See, for example, "In a Country Churchyard," in W. Toldervy, ed., *Select Epitaphs*, 2 vols. (London, 1755), 2:211; "*On a Poor but truly Worthy* MAN, *aged Forty-three*," in Wright, *Pleasing Melancholy*, 136–137; and "*On a poor Labouring* MAN, *in a Church-yard, in Lincolnshire*," in Wright, *Pleasing Melancholy*, 172–173.

[43] A *Collection*, 1:179. For other epitaphs upon "honest" laborers not discussed in my text, see "An Epitaph on a poor honest Man," *London Magazine* 12 (1743):514; "*On a poor Industrious* HUSBANDMAN, *in Yorkshire*," in Wright, *Pleasing Melancholy*, 126; "On a truly pious woman...," in Wright, *Pleasing Melancholy*, 196; and the untitled quatrain upon a "poor... honest man," in Graham, 132.

common lands was socially beneficial because common lands encouraged the poor's "idleness" and independence, whereas enclosure drove the poor to "honest industry" in the service of others, and in the argument of a "Kentish freeholder" in 1776 that the lower orders' response to "hard times" could only be "honest labour" and "patient resignation."[44]

It was not unusual for rural clergymen to compose epitaphs upon the "honest" members of their flock. Edward Young, for example, composed several epitaphs upon lowly parishioners, including a simple churchyard inscription of 1749 upon an "honest man" who had been "Industrious in low estate."[45] In 1810 the Somerset rector John Skinner erected a churchyard tombstone to a day laborer with the following didactic inscription: "Here lieth James Britten / who was what every true Briton should be, / An honest, Good Man, / he died December 17, 1810. Aged 70. / Reader Mayest thou both live and die as he did."[46] Skinner's diary suggests the motives behind such commemoration: he considered Britten a hardworking, contented, church-attending man, the very opposite of so many of Skinner's unruly parishioners.[47] The epitaph provided a moral example to those humble members of the parish who could read simple English prose. Whatever the epitaph's efficacy as lesson, furthermore, Skinner could feel that as both a benevolent gentleman and a parish minister he had shown commendable respect for a virtuous man of low degree.[48]

Johnson's "An Essay on Epitaphs" (1740) is an early example of the interest in commemoration of the socially humble. Like many of his contemporaries and successors, Johnson believed that virtuous men of low estate deserved epitaphic commemoration and that such commemoration could help preserve the social order by inculcating virtuous obedience. His models for epitaphs upon the lowly are unusual, however, in not sentimentalizing the lot of the poor.

[44] J. Arbuthnot, *An Inquiry into the Connection between the Present Price of Provisions and the Size of Farms* (1773), 128, cited in K. D. M. Snell, *Annals of the Labouring Poor: Social Change and Agrarian England, 1660–1900* (Cambridge: Cambridge University Press, 1985), 173; and *Gentleman's Magazine* 36 (1766):524.

[45] Edward Young, "Epitaph at Welwyn, Hertfordshire," in his *Poetical Works*, intro. Rev. J. Mitford, 2 vols. (London: 1896), 2:193–194. Young also wrote epitaphs upon a servant, a cook, and a thresher; see Harold Forster, *Edward Young: The Poet of the Night Thoughts, 1683–1765* (Alburgh Harleston, Norfolk: Erskine Press, 1986), 263.

[46] John Skinner, *Journal of a Somerset Rector, 1803–1834*, ed. Howard and Peter Coombs (Oxford: Oxford University Press, 1984), 59.

[47] Skinner, 58.

[48] One may contrast the plain, didactic English inscription upon Britten with the Latin inscription Skinner wrote two years later upon his wife, in which he bids "farewell" ("Vale") to his "dearest" ("charissima"); see Skinner, 72–73. While the Britten epitaph attempts to instruct the many, the epitaph upon Skiner's wife expresses personal feelings accessible only to the more educated few.

Johnson criticizes both the generic hierarchy in literature and the harsh excesses of the prevailing social hierarchy that have encouraged, so he suggests, the neglect of both the epitaph as a genre and the many who deserve epitaphic commemoration. He opens his essay by arguing that the focus of contemporary criticism on such topics as Homer rather than on epitaphs is strange, because "to afford a subject for heroic poems is the privilege of very few, but every man may expect to be recorded in an epitaph."[49] Because of an anachronistic generic hierarchy in which epic poetry is deemed highest despite its irrelevance to ordinary peoples' lives, criticism has unjustly ignored the epitaph. Both criticism and literary practice should concern themselves with "every man," their proper subject and audience, rather than with the exceptional few. Though throughout his career Johnson in fact reacts ambivalently to the large reading public of his time, in this essay he considers the epitaph a crucial genre precisely because it has the potential both to depict and teach the "bulk of mankind."[50]

As he certainly knows, Johnson's claim that all "may be expected" to receive epitaphic commemoration is false as an empirical observation of eighteenth-century social realities. Rather than discuss the actual restriction of epitaphs to the privileged few, however, Johnson implies that every good man or woman, regardless of rank, is morally entitled to an epitaph. He claims that all societies have been led by "Nature and reason" to commemorate good actions and that all literate societies therefore commemorated their "heroes and wise men" with panegyric inscriptions.[51] He suggests that the category of "heroes and wise men" has traditionally been too restrictive, however, by concluding the essay with a discussion of two Greek epitaphic distichs upon Stoic slaves, Epictetus and the otherwise unknown Zosima. For the benefit of his diverse readership he provides Latin and the following English translations of the two epitaphs, which can, he claims, "animate multitudes":

> Zosima, who, in her life, could only have her body enslaved,
>   now finds her body, likewise, set at liberty.
>
> Epictetus, who lies here, was a slave and a cripple, poor as
>   the beggar in the proverb, and the favourite of heaven.[52]

Since Johnson calls Zosima a heroine and Epictetus was a famous philosopher, these final epitaphs break down the distinction between the

---

[49] Samuel Johnson, "An Essay on Epitaphs," in *Samuel Johnson*, ed. Donald Greene (Oxford: Oxford University Press, 1984), 96.

[50] Johnson, *Samuel Johnson*, 101.

[51] Johnson, *Samuel Johnson*, 96.

[52] Johnson, *Samuel Johnson*, 101. In his old age Johnson again translated both these epitaphs into Latin; see Johnson, *Poems*, 320–321.

"bulk of mankind" and "heroes and wise men."[53] If people looked carefully enough, so these epitaphs suggest, they could find heroic and wise individuals even among the very lowest ranks. By concluding his essay with two epitaphic distichs and his commentary upon them, Johnson ends with a reminder of the powerful sententiousness of a genre apparently so slight that it can be exemplified by two distichs. His literary revaluation of the brief but weighty genre parallels the two epitaphs' ethical revaluations of high and low in their praise of heroic and wise slaves.

As a conservative moralist, Johnson argues that ethical reformation rather than socioeconomic transformation is the key to improving the lives of the poor. The two Greek epitaphs contain lessons for both the privileged and the "bulk of mankind": they teach the former to ignore "a man's outward circumstances in making an estimate of . . . [a person's] real value"; they teach the latter "that virtue is impracticable in no condition," since even these slaves were able to resist "the temptations of poverty and slavery."[54] Johnson further distinguishes his "heroes and wise men" from those of tradition by suggesting their different approaches to the problem of freedom: "He that has delivered his country from oppression, or freed the world from ignorance and error, can excite the emulation of a very small number; but he that has repelled the temptations of poverty, and disdained to free himself from distress at the expense of his virtue, may animate multitudes, by his example."[55] The most important lesson the "multitudes" can learn is not how to "free" themselves from their conditions but how *not* to free themselves "at the expense of . . . virtue." Those who remain virtuous will thereby gain the inner freedom of the Stoic. While accepting the outward slavery of her body in life, Zosima retained the inner freedom of her virtuous soul and thereby obtained full freedom when she left her body at death.[56] Hers is the combination of virtue and true freedom to which the "bulk of mankind" should aspire.

Johnson associates the epitaphic distichs' brief but weighty lessons concerning humble virtue and true freedom with the *sermo humilis* of

[53] Johnson, *Samuel Johnson*, 101.
[54] Johnson, *Samuel Johnson*, 102.
[55] Johnson, *Samuel Johnson*, 101.
[56] On the freedom of the Stoic slave's soul, compare Seneca: "Only the body [of the slave] is at the mercy and disposition of a master; but the mind is its own master." ("Corpora obnoxia sunt et adscripta dominis; mens quidem sui iuris"; *De beneficiis*, 3.20.1). Donald Greene discusses several passages in which Johnson, as a Christian intensely aware of human beings' frailties and need of God's grace, attacks the Stoics' proud claims to freedom from human miseries; see "Johnson, Stoicism, and the Good Life," in *The Unknown Samuel Johnson*, ed. John J. Burke, Jr., and Donald Kay (Madison: University of Wisconsin Press, 1983), 17–38. Johnson was nevertheless attracted to the Stoic ideal; for a balanced discussion, see Carey McIntosh, "Johnson's Debate with Stoicism," *ELH* 33 (1966):327–336.

Scripture. He glosses the Zosima epitaph by noting that the deceased is now where "the poor cease from their labours, and the weary be at rest."[57] He underscores that men can expect full freedom only at death by conflating two New Testament promises of rest to the godly (Matthew 11:28; Revelations 14:13) and a passage from Job that envisions death as the only escape from earthly labor, oppression, and servitude: "There the wicked cease from troubling; and there the weary be at rest. There the prisoners rest together; they hear not the voice of the oppressor. The small and great are there; and the servant is free from his master" (Job 3:17–19).

By choosing as models applicable to "the bulk of mankind" two epitaphs upon virtuous slaves, Johnson hints that the mass of mankind must bear burdens similar to those of slaves. In *Rambler* 12 Johnson pointedly gives the name Zosima to a poor gentlewoman who seeks employment as a servant and discovers how harshly the upper- and middle-ranks treat those below them.[58] The modern "slave" presumably requires the same heroic virtues as his or her ancient forbears in order to gain his or her inner freedom in life and complete freedom—after death.

Though Johnson was not alone in seeing a similarity between the conditions of servants and that of slaves,[59] most eighteenth-century masters would undoubtedly have been shocked at the explicit comparison of the two. Indeed benevolent epitaphs upon servants, which greatly idealized the master-servant relationship, became very common beginning in the mid eighteenth century.[60] The changing relationship between masters and servants exemplified the general decline of paternalism.

[57] Johnson, *Samuel Johnson*, 101.

[58] See Samuel Johnson, "*Rambler* 12," in *The Rambler: Part 1*, ed. W. J. Bate and Albrecht B. Strauss, The Yale Edition of the Works of Samuel Johnson, vol. 3 (New Haven: Yale University Press, 1969), 62–68; and Edward A. Bloom, "Symbolic Names in Johnson's Periodical Essays," *MLQ* 13 (1952):346.

[59] Philip Thicknesse's *Memoirs* (1788), for example, compares the lot of London maidservants to that of slaves; see E. S. Turner, *What the Butler Saw: Two Hundred and Fifty Years of the Servant Problem* (New York: St. Martin's, 1962), 95.

[60] One can obtain a rough idea of the dramatic increase in epitaphs upon servants around 1750 from two nineteenth-century anthologies of such epitaphs, [J. W. Streeten, ed.], *Epitaphia, or a Collection of Memorials, Inscribed to the Memory of Good and Faithful Servants* (London, 1826); and Arthur J. Munby, ed., *Faithful Servants: Being Epitaphs and Obituaries* (London, 1891). These anthologies together contain 5 epitaphs from the seventeenth century, 19 from 1700 to 1750, 105 from 1751 to 1800, and 220 from 1801 to 1826, the time of the first anthology's publication. Because memorials to servants were normally inscribed upon churchyard monuments of inexpensive stone or wood, they quickly became illegible or disappeared; these collections thus obviously underrepresent the earlier periods. Nevertheless, if epitaphs upon servants had been plentiful and of interest to the social elite before the 1750s, more of them would have been transcribed and eventually published in the numerous epigram and epitaph anthologies; as later notes will attest, I have found few other epitaphs elsewhere upon servants before the 1750s.

Over the course of the eighteenth century the burgeoning of the middle classes caused increased demand for domestics, which led to the rise of a seller's market and, in consequence, increased mobility and freedom for servants.[61] During the same period the aristocracy gradually reduced their claims to control the personal lives of their domestics.[62] Servants' growing independence led to frequent complaints concerning the self-ishness and pride of servants who were not loyal to their masters.[63] Such developments also turned truly devoted servants into cultural ideals tinged with nostalgia for older, more stable days. Because a servant was a member of his master's household, a kind master's epitaph upon a servant devoted unto death provided the most compelling literary rep-resentation of a paternalist order that was being increasingly under-mined by social change.[64]

Before the mid eighteenth century there are few English epitaphs on servants. An early seventeenth-century example suggests the rarity of such epitaphs by praising the unusually benevolent master who saves his faithful servant from oblivion: "O read these Lines again! you'll seldom find / A Servant faithful and a Master kind" reads the memorial tablet in Westminster Abbey in memory of a servant who died in 1621.[65] Though he had classical models in Martial's various epitaphs upon slaves, Herrick is unusual for his time in writing an epitaph upon his maidservant:

[61] See J. Jean Hecht, *The Domestic Servant Class in Eighteenth-Century England* (London: Routledge, 1956), 1–34.

[62] See Randolph Trumbach, *The Rise of the Egalitarian Family: Aristocratic Kinship and Domestic Relations in Eighteenth-Century England* (New York: Academic Press, 1978), 141–150.

[63] On the rarity of long-term service and the consequent complaints of masters, see Hecht, 81–82. Complaining of servants' mobility in the 1750s, John Shebbeare notes that "servants have very little attachment to those they serve ... self is the sole motive" (Batista Angeloni [pseudo], *Letters on the English Nation*, 2d ed., 2 vols. [London, 1756], 2:39). Making the same complaint in the 1770s, Jonas Hanway laments that "pride ... is often the cause of servants changing *places*.... [and] renders domestics more inconstant than other people" (*Virtue in Humble Life*, 2 vols. [London, 1777], 1:103).

[64] Throughout the early modern period the term "servant" was indeed used of all laborers who lived with, and thus were considered to some extent part of the family of, their master. It thus included not only domestic servants but also farm laborers who boarded with their masters. The majority of epitaphs, however, commemorate domestic servants.

[65] Epitaph upon Gabriel Lawrence, d. 1621, in John Hackett, *Select and Remark-able Epitaphs on Illustrious and Other Persons . . .*, 2 vols. (London, 1757), 1:229. For other seventeenth-century epitaphs upon servants, in addition to those cited in *Epitaphia* and Munby, see the epitaphs upon John Richards, d. 1612, in Thomas F. Ravenshaw, ed., *Antiente Epitaphes (from A.D. 1250 to A.D. 1800)* (London, 1878), 53; George Pickering, d. 1645, in Davis, "Parochial Collections," 278; and Humphrey How, d. 1688, on the outside wall of Stoneleigh Parish Church.

> In this little Urne is laid
> *Prewdence Baldwin* (once my maid)
> From whose happy spark here let
> Spring the purple Violet.
>   ("*Upon* Prew *his Maid*," H-782)[66]

Herrick provides a decorously "little" memorial for a lowly creature who, as the parenthetic "once my maid" suggests, gained commemoration because of her humble connection to the poet. Though he does not claim any greatness for his former servant, Herrick reveals his sense of his maid's humble but genuine value by requesting that "the purple Violet" spring from her "happy," that is, "blessed" (*OED* 2b), remains. Because in ancient cult the living showed their piety towards the dead by strewing graves with violets,[67] the growing of violets at the graves of the deceased was a traditional symbol of nature's own modest beneficence toward the worthy dead. In a fifteenth-century neo-Latin epitaph, Antonio Beccadelli prays that a woman's grave "may exhale violets"; in *Hamlet*, Laertes bids "violets spring" from Ophelia's "fair and unpolluted flesh."[68] While Herrick similarly requests that nature show respect for his former servant, his use of the generic singular, "the purple Violet," in place of the usual plural form, "violets," suggests that even a single exemplary flower would be enough for his humble maid.

Even so modest a composition is an idiosyncratic response to unsettling times. The epitaph is a literary fantasy, since Prudence outlived Herrick.[69] The fantasy here is as serious as in Herrick's many epitaphs upon himself, however, for it allows the poet once more to imagine a small but sufficient realm of retreat. In "His Grange, or private wealth," Baldwin appears as a central comfort in Herrick's little home: "I have / A maid (my *Prew*) by good luck sent, / To save / That little, Fates me gave or lent" (H-724). Since the poet claims to "have" his maid, she seems

---

[66] I cite the text in *The Complete Poetry of Robert Herrick*, ed. J. Max Patrick (Garden City, N.Y.: Doubleday, 1963). I use Patrick's numbering of Herrick's poems throughout my discussion.

[67] For the Roman custom of strewing violets, see Ovid, *Fasti* 2.539; and J. M. C. Toynbee, *Death and Burial in the Roman World* (Ithaca: Cornell University Press, 1971), 62. Christians of late antiquity adopted the pagan rite: see Prudentius, *Liber Cathemerinon* 10: "Hymnus Circa Exequias Defuncti," ll. 169–170. In one epitaph Herrick revives ancient practice by having an infant request that his or her grave be strewn with "Violets" ("An Epitaph upon a child" H-125, l. 6).

[68] "[Oro tuum] violas spiret...sepulcrum" (Antonio Beccadelli, "Optat pro Nichina defuncta," l. 1, in *Renaissance Latin Verse: An Anthology*, ed. Alessandro Perosa and John Sparrow [Chapel Hill: University of North Carolina Press, 1979], 19); and William Shakespeare, *Hamlet*, ed. Harold Jenkins, The Arden Shakespeare (London: Methuen, 1982), 389 (V.i.233–234). For an ancient example of the topos, see Persius, *Satire* 1.39–40.

[69] Prudence Baldwin died and was buried at Dean Prior in 1678; see Patrick's note to "*Upon* Prudence Baldwin *her sicknesse*" (H-302).

herself to be part of Herrick's "little" but precious "private wealth." By immortalizing Baldwin in a modest epitaph that resembles so many of those upon himself, Herrick preserves in imagination a small but blessed world of master and servant, possessor and possessed, that escapes the social disorder at large.

Through the early eighteenth century the practice of commemorating servants remained uncommon. Pope was unusual in composing a short epitaph in honor of his nurse, Mary Beach, who died in 1725. Inscribed on a modest but elegantly rusticated memorial tablet on the outer wall of Twickenham Parish Church, the brief *carmen lapidarium* reads as follows:

TO THE MEMORY OF
MARY BEACH
WHO DIED NOV 5. 1725 AGED 78
ALEX. POPE, WHOM SHE NURSED IN
HIS INFANCY AND CONSTANTLY AT-
TENDED FOR THIRTY EIGHT YEARS
IN
GRATITUDE TO A FAITHFUL OLD SERVANT,
ERECTED THIS STONE.

Praising his nurse wholly in terms of her "faithful" service, Pope maintains the social distance between the servant and himself. He displays his concern for hierarchy by placing this English epitaph to a servant on the outside wall of the church whose inside walls bore the Latin epitaphs upon his parents and himself. Singling out his nurse as he had singled out John Hewet and Sarah Drew, Pope separates her not only from the mass of unmarked churchyard graves but also from the church monuments of her social betters. It is thus not surprising that the most likely models for Pope's simple inscription are Roman masters' plain, brief *carmina lapidaria* honoring their "most faithful" slaves and freedmen.[70]

Despite his clear assertions of the social hierarchy, however, Pope made himself vulnerable to ridicule simply by commemorating a servant—especially a female servant!—in the 1720s. An anonymous pamphlet of 1729 seized upon the Beach memorial as evidence of Pope's sexual relations with his nurse, which presumably alone could explain his concern for so lowly a creature's memory. The pamphlet mocked Pope in biblical style: "And Pope knew his nurse, and she conceived and

[70] For Roman inscriptions dedicated to "most faithful" ("fidelissim[o/ae]") slaves and freedmen, see Jan[us] Gruter[us] et al., *Inscriptiones Antiquae Totius Orbis Romani* . . . , 2 vols. in 4 parts (Amsterdam, 1707), vol. 2, part 1: DCCCCXXXVII, DCCCCXLIII, DCCCCLIIII, DCCCCLVII.

bare a child.... And it came to pass that the nurse died, being full of years, and was buried in the cave of Twickenham, called Kneller's Cave [i.e., Twickenham Parish church]; and a stone was set upon the cave's mouth [i.e., the tablet] and Pope and all the ancient men and ancient women of Twickenham mourned forty days for the nurse: and then the mourning of Pope the son of the hatter was ended."[71] Pope's mourning and monument for his nurse are treated as ludicrous devotion that could only stem from the vulgar love affair of "the son of a hatter."[72]

From the mid eighteenth century onward, by contrast, epitaphs upon servants become increasingly common and uncontroversial attempts to imagine and inculcate social harmony. They often evoke the biblical parable of the "good and faithful servant" who increases the talents given him by his master (Matthew 25:14–30) in order to emphasize that the "good and faithful" servant has inherited heaven by assiduously performing his or her lowly service in the lot assigned by God.[73] Epitaphs idealize "honest" servants, as in this late eighteenth-century poem:

> Tho o'er his humble Grave no costly Bust,
> Or Sculptured Marble points to titled dust:
> An honest Man the noblest work of GOD,
> Has left his cares, beneath this Verdant Sod.[74]

This epitaph's contrast between the "humble Grave" and "Verdant Sod," on the one hand, and the "costly Bust" and "sculptured Marble," on the

[71] I cite the text in *Horace Walpole's Correspondence*, ed. W. S. Lewis et al., 42 vols. (New Haven: Yale University Press, 1937–1983), 18:35–36. The editor notes that the pamphlet was reprinted in 1742 (p. 34).

[72] For a similar sociosexual smear on Pope, see Lady Mary Wortley Montagu's reference to his kissing his "antient Nurse" in "P[ope] to Bolingbroke," l. 83 in Montagu, *Essays and Poems, and Simplicity, A Comedy*, ed. Robert Halsband and Isobel Grundy (Oxford: Clarendon, 1977), 283.

[73] For panegyrics upon servants that echo the parable of the talents, see the epitaphs upon John Warner, d. 1738 (Mundy, 9); Thomas Cooke, d. 1739 (in Silvester Tissington, ed., *A Collection of Epitaphs and Monumental Inscriptions...* [London, 1857], 215); Ursula Swinbourn, d. 1781 (Tissington, 217–218); Samuel Cane, d. 1782 (*Epitaphia*, 45); Nestor, d. 1787 (Mundy, 133); Thomas Stockford, d. 1790 (*Epitaphia*, 64); George Purkis, d. 1808 (*Epitaphia*, 153); Ann Poole, d. 1810 (Munby, 192); Janet Peterkin, d. 1816 (*Epitaphia*, 224); and Thomas Reece, d. 1821 (*Epitaphia*, 277).

[74] Epitaph upon Thomas Ballinger, d. 1789 (*Epitaphia*, 60). *Epitaphia* and Mundby's anthology together contain three epitaphs upon "honest" servants who died between 1700 and 1750 and sixty-eight who died between 1751 and 1826 (*Epitaphia*, 21–291; Munby, 6–288). For other such epitaphs, see those upon Thomas Cooke, d. 1739 (Tissington, 215); Thomas Fanton, who died in the late 1740s or early 1750s (Lindley, *Of Graves*, 116); Samuel Burt, d. 1751 (Toldervy, 2:188–189); John James Cooke, d. 1760 (Ravenshaw, 163); Susanna Prince, d. 1774 (cited in Turner, 207); John Bayley, d. 1792 (Tissington, 214); Elizabeth Harrison, d. 1797 (Tissington, 220–221); Elizabeth William and Mary Waters, d. 1815 and 1816 (included in William Pulleyn, ed., *Church-yard Gleanings and Epigrammatic Scraps...* [London, 1830?], 68); William Brassington, d. 1817 (Lindley, *Of Graves*, 115); and John Owen, d. 1821 (Tissington, 214–215).

other, exploits the conventional opposition between "humble" nature and "proud" art in order to affirm the natural and beneficent basis of the virtuous servant's low social status in life and death. The poem also implicitly contrasts its own brief but sufficient praise of the humble deceased with the florid panegyrics upon the "great." Applying Pope's pithy declaration "An honest Man's the noblest work of God" (*Essay on Man*, 4.248) far beyond the social range envisaged by Pope, the epitaph asserts that the "honest" servant has lived the ethically "noblest" life.[75] Though the word "cares" acknowledges the harshness of the servant's condition, the brief panegyric dignifies the servant's humble acceptance of his earthly lot by suggesting that he has received his posthumous reward, an escape from his worldly troubles and the enduring regard of his master and other benevolent social superiors.

From the mid eighteenth century onward epitaphs also increasingly commemorate servants as "friends" of their masters. The epitaph upon the Duke of Newcastle's chief domestic servant, who died in 1751, for example, proclaimed, "Fidelity made him rather esteemed as a Friend, / Than a Servant," while an epitaph of 1797 praised a servant who was "in all things faithful, everywhere a friend."[76] Since friendship was traditionally conceived as the intimate relationship between equals, panegyrics upon faithful servants-as-friends added egalitarian resonances to traditional hierarchical notions. Masters' desire to combine the hierarchical concept of service with the egalitarian ideal of friendship not only reveals their increasing "benevolence." It also reveals their attempts to defend, by modifying almost to the point of incoherence, a vulnerable paternalist ideology.

Two examples suggest that before the mid eighteenth century such rhetoric was considered too demeaning even by those who erected monuments to their servants. In a letter of 1725 written upon the loss of Mary Beach, Pope discussed emotions "good-natur'd minds" (like his own) felt towards "this Sort of Friend."[77] Nevertheless the poet whose sepulchral compositions proclaim him the "friend" of men of substance like Simon Harcourt the Younger, the two Digby children, and James Craggs was apparently unwilling to declare himself the "friend" of his

[75] For similar applications of Pope's line to servants, see the epitaphs upon Matthew Rogers, d. 1816, and Stephen King, d. 1819, in *Epitaphia*, 222, 252.

[76] Epitaphs upon Samuel Burt, d. 1751 (Toldervy, 2:188–189); and Elizabeth Harrison, d. 1797 (Tissington, 220–221). For other panegyrics upon servants-as-friends, see the epitaphs upon Phebe Ambler, d. 1756 (*Epitaphia*, 18); Samuel Tomes, d. 1761 (*Epitaphia*, 16); Samuel Cane, d. 1782 (*Epitaphia*, 45); William Chapman, d. 1793 (*Epitaphia*, 75); Thomas Cranston, d. 1798 (*Epitaphia*, 91); James Wells, d. 1799 (Munby, 9); Elizabeth Glover, d. 1805 (Munby, 138); Mary Poole, d. 1811 (*Epitaphia*, 183); and Elizabeth Pezzey, d. 1825 (Munby, 315).

[77] *The Correspondence of Alexander Pope*, ed. George Sherburn, 5 vols. (Oxford: Clarendon, 1956), 2:337.

nurse in the public inscription to her memory. Jonathan Swift, who like his fellow poet and close friend Pope was an early composer of an epitaph upon a faithful servant, self-consciously refrained from commemorating a beloved servant as a "friend." The brief inscription in Saint Patrick's Cathedral upon a servant who died in March 1721 explains that the servant's "grateful Master caused this monument to be erected in Memory of his Discretion, Fidelity and Diligence in that Humble Station."[78] In his 1754 memoir upon Swift, Patrick Delany claimed that one of Swift's acquaintances, a man of more "vanity than wisdom," had convinced the dean to substitute "grateful master" for Swift's original formulation, "grateful Friend, and master." Arguing that the original formulation better expressed Swift's own view that "an affectionate, and faithful servant, should always be considered in the character of an *humble friend*," Delany did not explain why Swift agreed to the change.[79] Presumably, Swift realized that he would be lowering himself too much in the eyes of his contemporaries to acknowledge that his servant was indeed a friend. In the 1720s commemorating a servant as a friend was still very rare; by the more troubled times of the mid eighteenth century, such rhetoric had become a far less exceptional and exceptionable way of reaffirming the emotional bond between high and low.

In oblique but striking fashion, epitaphs upon dogs also idealize the master-servant relationship in a period of increased social tension. In the mid and late eighteenth century, epitaphic commemoration of lowly creatures widened to include domestic animals. Keith Thomas argues that growing concern for the welfare of animals in the late eighteenth century paralleled the spread of humane feeling toward previously despised human beings.[80] The epitaph upon a man who died in 1787 explicitly connects his benevolence toward animals with his fellow-feeling for other, presumably less fortunate, people: "The most prominent and remarkable features in his Character were his real and invincible attachment to dogs and cats, and his unbounded benevolence towards them, as well as towards his fellow creatures."[81] It is not surprising, therefore, that the elite's epitaphs upon "honest" and "faithful" dogs, the pet most often treated as part of the family, should resemble the upper classes' epitaphs upon servants, the only group among lowly human laborers to be welcomed into the families of the elite.

---

[78] Jonathan Swift, *The Correspondence of Jonathan Swift*, ed. Harold Williams, 5 vols. (Oxford: Clarendon: 1963–1965), 2:422–423, n. 5.

[79] See Patrick Delany, *Observations upon Lord Orrery's Remarks on the Life and Writings of Dr. Jonathan Swift* (London, 1754), 195–196; and Swift, *Correspondence*, 2:423, n. 5.

[80] K. V. Thomas, *Man and the Natural World: A History of the Modern Sensibility* (New York: Pantheon, 1983), 184.

[81] Epitaph upon Philip Shall Cross, d. 1787 (Tissington, 179).

Epitaphs upon dogs displayed the commemorators' status: only men of substance had the leisure time and sensibility to commemorate their pets. Erecting elegant monuments to their dogs on their estates, gentlemen could simultaneously display their wealth and their sensitive, if often self-consciously and comically exaggerated, appreciation of lowly creatures.[82] Far from being the mere *vers de société* of a self-assured elite, however, epitaphs upon dogs provided a wholly imaginary but emotionally compelling solution to a crucial problem in social relationships. While employing a rhetoric similar to that of epitaphs upon servants, epitaphs upon dogs attempted to ground the master-servant relationship even more thoroughly in "nature." The "honest" dog's wholly "natural" feelings of "fidelity" and "friendship" toward his master or mistress exemplified an ideal against which relations between human servants and their masters—and, more generally, between the lower orders and their social superiors—could be judged.[83]

The dog epitaphs that became popular in the mid eighteenth century had few antecedents in classical or earlier English tradition.[84] One lovely but uninfluential epitaph from the *Greek Anthology* commemorated a faithful dog (*Epigram* 7.211).[85] One Martial epitaph praised a dog "faithful to its master" ("domino fidissima "), but the Roman poet singled out this dog only because of its "noble" ("nobilis") death at the hands of a boar (*Epigram* 11.69).

It is no accident that the two major English poets who anticipate the later eighteenth-century benevolent epitaph upon servants, Herrick and Pope, also anticipate the period's sentimental epitaphs upon dogs. Herrick's "*Upon his Spaniell* Tracie" (H-967) is as unusual for its time as his epitaph upon his maid:

[82] For a thorough but noninterpretive survey of funerary monuments commemorating dogs from the early eighteenth to the early nineteenth century, see N. B. Penny, "Dead Dogs and Englishmen," *The Connoisseur* 192 (1976):298–303.

[83] Though neither treats the relationship between dogs and servants central to my analysis here, I owe a general debt to William Empson, *The Structure of Complex Words* (London: Chatto & Windus, 1977), 158–174; and Ronald Paulson, *Popular and Polite Art in the Age of Hogarth and Fielding* (Notre Dame: University of Notre Dame Press, 1979), 49–63, both of which brilliantly analyze the centrality and multivalency of the dog in eighteenth-century English culture. My discussion of the social function of epitaphs upon dogs challenges Paulson's claim, however, that the sentimental treatment of the dog "faithful unto death" was "totally apolitical" (*Popular and Polite Art*, 53, 62).

[84] The evidence here runs directly against A. Lytton Sells's thesis that animal poetry from the Renaissance to the Romantics, including epitaphs upon pets, is heavily dependent upon classical models rather than an expression of contemporaneous social and cultural attitudes; see his *Animal Poetry in French and English Literature and the Greek Tradition* (Bloomington: Indiana University Press, 1955).

[85] It is indicative of the epitaph's lack of influence that James Hutton's two-volume study of translations of the *Greek Anthology* in Italy, France, and the Low Countries to 1800 lists no translations of the poem.

Now thou art dead, no eye shall ever see,
For shape and service, *Spaniell* like to thee.
This shall my love do, give thy sad death one
Tear, that deserves of me a million.

In "His Grange, or private wealth," Tracie appears, alongside Prew, as one of Herrick's comforts in his little "home" of retreat—"[In addition] To these / A *Trasy* I do keep, whereby / I please / The more my rurall privacie" (H-724)—and the epitaph makes clear that Tracie was yet another faithful servant, beloved by his master for his "shape and *service*."

Pope was a great lover of dogs, whose unquestioning acceptance of him seems to have provided some solace for the rejections he suffered at the hands of other human beings.[86] One of Pope's earliest verses commemorated a faithful, loving dog.[87] In 1709 Pope sent Henry Cromwell an epitaphlike imitation of Homer's description of the death of Ulysses's old, devoted dog Argus in book 17 of *The Odyssey*:

When wise *Ulysses*, from his native coast
Long kept by wars, and long by tempests tost,
Arriv'd at last, poor, old, disguis'd, alone,
To all his friends, and ev'n his Queen, unknown,
Chang'd as he was, with age, and toils, and cares,
Furrow'd his rev'rend face, and white his hairs,
In his own Palace forc'd to ask his bread,
Scorn'd by those slaves his former bounty fed
Forgot of all his own domestic crew;
The faithful Dog alone his rightful Master knew!
Unfed, unhous'd, neglected, on the clay,
Like an old servant now cashier'd, he lay;
Touch'd with resentment of ungrateful Man,
And longing to behold his ancient Lord again.
Him when he saw—he rose, and crawl'd to meet,
('Twas all he cou'd) and fawn'd, and lick'd his feet,
Seiz'd with dumb joy—then falling by his side,
Own'd his returning Lord, look'd up, and dy'd![88]

Pope found it less threatening to combine the hierarchical notion of service with the egalitarian resonances of friendship when commemorating a dog than when commemorating a human servant. The relationship between Ulysses, the "master" (l. 10), and Argus, his "faithful

---

[86] See Norman Ault, "Pope and his Dogs" in his *New Light on Pope* (London: Methuen, 1949), 337–350.

[87] Probably Pope's last piece of verse also commemorated a dog, the distich upon Bounce; see Alexander Pope, *Minor Poems*, ed. Norman Ault and John Butt, The Twickenham Edition of Pope, vol. 6 (New Haven: Yale University Press, 1954), 405.

[88] Pope, "ARGUS," in *Minor Poems*, 51–52.

Dog" (l. 10), clearly combines the master-servant relationship with the intimacy of friendship. The dog that is compared to "an old servant" (l. 12) is in fact Ulysses's truest servant, devoted unto death. Since both master and servant are, however, aged and outcast—a parallel Pope underscores by devoting nine lines to each—the two also have a deep bond of fellow-feeling. In the course of his letter to Cromwell, Pope suggests that a good dog is indeed both a friend who resembles a servant and a servant who resembles a friend. He playfully argues that if "the chief point of Friendship" is "to comply with [a] Friend's Motions & Inclinations," his own dog is a true friend, and he concludes his letter with a salutation that jocularly suggests the analogy between a faithful dog and a devoted servant: "Of all Dogs, you shall find none more faithfull than Dear Sir, Your most Affectionate humble Servant, A: Pope."[89] Though a conventional epistolary formula, Pope's self-designation as "Your most Affectionate humble Servant" suggests the mixture of emotional bonding (friendship) and subservience (service) that the good dog represents.[90]

A verbal echo reveals how closely Pope associated the commemoration of humble, loyal dogs and that of lowly, faithful human beings. In his letter of 1725 to the earl of Oxford lamenting the death of his nurse, Pope quotes a verse from a 1706 ode by Prior: "—and by his side / A Good man's greatest loss, a faithful Servant, dy'd!"[91] Both the rhyme and context recall the final couplet of Pope's poem upon Argus: "—then falling by his side, / Own'd his returning Lord, look'd up, and dy'd!" In the *Odyssey* Argus does not die at his master's side (17.324–327), and Pope probably followed Prior rather than Homer when composing the final couplet of his Homeric imitation in 1709. In reapplying these lines to a human servant in 1725, Pope betrays the similarity of his attitude toward servants and dogs and the great mobility, from human to animal and back, of benevolent sentiment.

While Pope's need for and appreciation of a dog's unquestioning love had strong personal roots, the epitaphs upon dogs from the mid eighteenth through the early nineteenth century display an entire social elite's need to imagine the spontaneous affection and utter devotion not always

[89] Pope, *Correspondence*, 1:75.

[90] Sherburn notes that "Dear Sir" and "Servant" were not in the original letter but were inserted by Pope in all his printed texts; see Pope, *Correspondence*, 1:75. I think Pope added them because they deepened the wit of his comparing himself to a dog.

[91] Pope, *Correspondence*, 2:336–337. Sherburn does not provide the source, which is "An Ode, Humbly Inscrib'd to the Queen. On the Glorious Success of Her Majesty's Arms, 1706," ll. 159–160; see *The Literary Works of Matthew Prior*, ed. H. Bunker Wright and Monroe K. Spears, 2 vols. (Oxford: Clarendon, 1959), 1:238. The lines, which concern the death of Marlborough's subordinate, Colonel Bringfield, were well known because the newspapers made much of Bringfield's death (see note in Prior, 2:897). Quoting from memory, Pope slightly modifies Prior's lines.

forthcoming from socially inferior human beings. With varying combinations of humor and sentimentality, epitaphs often commemorate a
dog who died in the course of "honest" service to its friend and master.
Published in the early 1780s, Richard Graves's epitaph on a "favourite
dog," for example, praises the deceased for being "[t]rue to his master,
generous, brave; / His friend, companion; not his slave"; a 1793 epitaph
commemorates a canine "friend" of "service just"; while a 1795 epitaph
memorializes an "honest" and "faithful" dog who was also a "friend."[92]

Epitaphs occasionally reveal with astonishing directness just how much
masters wished their servants would resemble their faithful, friendly
dogs. Just as Pope commemorated his nurse on the outside wall of the
church in which his family was commemorated, so the gentleman William
Ashby, whose ancestors were commemorated by various monuments in
Harefield Parish Church, erected a tablet on the outside wall of the same
church to commemorate his "faithfull Servant" and gamekeeper Robert
Mossendew, who died in 1744. After devoting more lines to a pointer
who had accompanied Mossendew than to the deceased himself, the
brief verse epitaph concludes by praising Mossendew for imitating the
dog's humble thankfulness toward his master: "[The dog Tray's] gratitude inflam'd his mind. / This servant in an honest way / In all his actions
copy'd Tray."[93]

Just as Pope mourns his nurse by echoing his own epitaphic poem
upon a dog, so a late eighteenth-century minister composes memorial
verses upon his faithful servant that echo a mid-eighteenth-century epitaph upon a dog. A comic epitaph of 1747 commemorates a canine
servant-friend whose virtues put man to shame:

> Here lies a pattern for the human race,
> A dog that did his work and knew his place:
> A trusty servant, to his master dear;
> A safe companion and a friend sincere.
> In spight of bribes and threats severely just;

---

[92] Richard Graves, "Epitaph on a Favourite Dog" in his *Euphrosyne: or, Amusements on
the Road of Life*, 2 vols. (London, 1776–1780), 2:145–146; "A TALE," *Kentish Register* 1
(1793):70; and "EPITAPH *on a favourite Dog . . .*," *Kentish Register* 3 (1795):228. One may
instructively contrast the later eighteenth- and early nineteenth-century treatment of the
dog as "servant-friend" with contemporary attitudes. Anthropologists argue that in contemporary English and American culture dogs are considered friends of the family and
analogous, in terms of taboo status, to kin; see Edmund Leach, "Anthropological Aspects
of Language: Animal Categories and Verbal Abuse," in *New Directions in the Study of
Language*, ed. Eric H. Lenneberg (Cambridge: MIT Press, 1964), 23–63; and Marshall
Sahlins, *Culture and Practical Reason* (Chicago: University of Chicago Press, 1976), 171–
175. The dog as kin-friend reveals the values of the contemporary egalitarian, nuclear
family, just as the dog as servant-friend reveals the older values of the paternalist, extended
family that included, though in an increasingly uneasy fashion, servants.
[93] The tablet is photographed and cited in Penny, "Dogs," 299.

He sought no pension, and he broke no trust.
The midnight thief and strolling gypsie found
That faithful *Sancho* watch'd the mansion round:
        . . . . .
Truth warm'd his breast, and love without disguise,
His heart was grateful, and his actions wise.
In him, through life, all social virtues shone;
Blush, foolish man, by brutes to be outdone!
—May no rude hands disturb his peaceful grave,
Who us'd as nature taught, what nature gave;
For nature's gifts to use in nature's way,
Is all the duty beast or man can pay.
("EPITAPH *on an old favourite* DOG," ll. 1–8, 19–26)[94]

Praising humble Sancho at humorously inordinate length, the epitaph
playfully dignifies the humble dog's fidelity and friendship with panegyric rhetoric reminiscent of Pope. The lighthearted epitaph expresses
a serious conservative social message, however, in its attack on the corruption of "foolish man," who has lost all commitment to the ideal of
friendly service that the dog, however comically, embodied. It is therefore shocking but not surprising that a late eighteenth-century minister
chose to adapt this epitaph for the wholly serious commemoration of
his "Friend and Servant" Samuel Cane. Omitting the lines applicable
only to a dog, the Cane epitaph repeats lines 1–6 and lines 19–24, only
changing "A dog that did his work and knew his place" to "A Man who
did his work, and knew his place" and "Blush, foolish man, by beasts to
be outdone!" to a concluding "O blush ye great by CANE to be undone."[95]
The minister, who had this epitaph upon his servant inscribed on a
modest wooden churchyard monument, undoubtedly felt himself sin-
cerely generous in commemorating a lowly servant whom he deigned
to call his "friend." He presumably saw nothing wrong with borrowing
his benevolent praise of a fellow human being from a comic panegyric
upon a dog: one good servant was much like another, whether dog or
man.[96]

When the 1747 epitaph praises a dog-servant as one who possessed
all "social virtues" but "us'd as nature taught, what nature gave," it makes
explicit what many epitaphs upon dogs imply: dogs "follow nature" and
thereby reveal the deficiencies of socially corrupted man. Some early
and mid-eighteenth-century satiric epitaphs hold up the dog as the nat-

[94] *Gentleman's Magazine* 17 (1747):145.
[95] Epitaph on Samuel Cane, d. 1782, servant of the Reverend W. Price (*Epitaphia*, 45).
[96] I suspect that the minister was inspired to echo the epitaph upon a dog because of a (half-conscious?) pun on "Cane" and "canine," a pun that further suggests the conde-scension in his benevolent praise of his servant.

ural ideal betraying man's falsities.[97] In his garden at Stowe, Pope's friend
Lord Cobham placed a satiric inscription, possibly written by Pope, commemorating "Signor Fido," a dog who gained "an honest Livelihood"
and "follow[ed] Nature."[98] Other mid- and late eighteenth-century epitaphs were more sentimental than satiric in their praise of dogs who
"naturally" fulfilled the ideal of faithful service. Thus Pope's friend John
Boyle, Lord Orrery, composed a panegyric epitaph upon his dog Hector
describing the deceased as a "friend" who was "By nature faithful, vig-
ilant and true."[99] Such praise could presumably not be bestowed upon
many human servants, who all too often forgot their "natural" servitude.

Following in the footsteps of several eighteenth-century aristocrats,
Lord Byron erected a large and elegant tomb on the grounds of his
ancestral estate to his dog Boatswain, who died in 1808.[100] Byron's conspicuous extravagance displayed both his status and his sentiment. The
verse inscription, published in 1809, combines sentimental praise of
Boatswain's exemplary, "natural" life with satire upon the corrupt social
life of human beings. While presenting its commemoration of a "poor
dog" as if it were a radical rejection of social norms, Byron's poem, like
so many earlier epitaphs upon dogs, in fact defends the traditional social
hierarchy by imagining its supposedly "natural" basis.

The twenty-six line epitaph is quite long for a sentimental panegyric
upon a humble dog, and its very length underscores Byron's ostensible
contempt for mere human conceptions of social decorum. The epitaph
begins with a contrast between the commemoration given a "proud son
of man" and the oblivion normally vouchsafed a "poor dog" of "honest
heart," a contrast that recalls—and significantly extends—Shirley's early
seventeenth-century contrast between the monument erected to a worthless gentleman and the oblivion normally bestowed upon an "honest
parson":

> When some proud son of man returns to earth,
> Unknown to glory, but upheld by birth,
> The sculptor's art exhausts the pomp of woe,
> And storied urns record who rests below;
> When all is done, upon the tomb is seen,
> Not what he was, but what he should have been:
> But the poor dog, in life the firmest friend,

[97] On eighteenth-century satiric uses of dogs, see also Paulson, *Popular and Polite Art*,
51–53.

[98] The inscription is included in Bickham, 45–46.

[99] Included in [Richard Graves, ed.], *The Festoon: A Select Collection of Epigrams* (London,
1767), 138. The epitaph was composed sometime between 1737, when Orrery mentions
the living Hector in a letter to Swift (Swift, *Correspondence* 5:25), and Orrery's death in
1762.

[100] See Penny, "Dead Dogs," 301–302.

> The first to welcome, foremost to defend,
> Whose honest heart is still his master's own,
> Who labours, fights, lives, breathes for him alone;
> Unhonoured falls, unnoticed all his worth. . . .
>
> (ll. 1–11)[101]

Ignoring the conventionality of commemorating a beloved pet, the poet suggests that he alone appreciates the dog whom he saves from otherwise certain oblivion, memorializing him as a devoted friend of his master. After condemning human beings for believing that heaven is open only to them and not to virtuous animals like Boatswain (ll. 12–14), the poem continues with an attack on brutish man's corrupt social relations:

> Oh man! thou feeble tenant of an hour,
> Debased by slavery, or corrupt by power,
> Who knows thee well must quit thee with disgust,
> Degraded mass of animated dust!
> Thy love is lust, thy friendship all a cheat,
> Thy smiles hypocrisy, thy words deceit!
> By nature vile, ennobled but by name,
> Each kindred brute might bid thee blush for shame.
>
> (ll. 15–22)

Byron's assault upon his "corrupt" fellow men might to some extent reveal his disgust as a reformist, Foxite Whig with the sociopolitical "corruption" of late Hanoverian England, which was a constant target of the Foxite Whigs.[102] His hyperbolic attack primarily expresses, however, an extreme, misanthropic repulsion from the falsity of all social relations. The revealing oddness of the poem lies in its implicit contention that the dog who "labours, fights, lives, breathes for . . . [its master] alone" is not "debased by slavery" and that the master who accepts such a relationship is not "corrupt by power." In commemorating his humble pet, Byron simultaneously launches a radical attack upon the corruption of social life and indulges in a highly conventional fantasy of a "natural," beneficent social hierarchy.

---

[101] George Gordon, Lord Byron, "Inscription on the Monument of a Newfoundland Dog," in *The Complete Poetical Works of Lord Byron*, ed. Jerome J. McGann, 5 vols. to date (Oxford: Clarendon, 1980–), 1:224–225.

[102] On Byron's allegiance to the reformist Whig faction of Charles James Fox, see Malcolm Kelsall, *Byron's Politics* (Brighton: Harvester Press; Totowa, N.J.: Barnes, 1987); and Carl Woodring, *Politics in English Romantic Poetry* (Cambridge: Harvard University Press, 1970), 148–229. J. G. A. Pocock notes the Foxite Whigs' attacks upon "corruption" and places such attacks within the tradition of eighteenth-century oppositional political rhetoric in "The Varieties of Whiggism from Exclusion to Reform: A History of Ideology and Discourse," in his *Virtue, Commerce, and History: Essays on Political Thought and History* (Cambridge: Cambridge University Press, 1985), 284–286.

By exploiting one of the social elite's favorite epithets for an obedient and contented member of the lower orders, Byron's praise of his dog's "*honest* heart" underscores the conventional cast of a poem that presents itself as radical critique. In a letter written shortly after Boatswain's death, Byron suggests the similarity of his feelings toward his dog and toward his human servants. "Boatswain is dead!" he exclaimed, "I have lost everything except Old Murray," referring to an elderly family servant. In letters from the same period he describes Murray with the same epithet he used of Boatswain: Murray is a "poor honest fellow!" and an "honest & faithful" servant.[103] Byron's epitaph upon an "honest" creature firmly upholds the paternalist hierarchy of master and servant, human as well as canine.

Despite the formulaic quality of his praise of Boatswain, the poet melodramatically concludes the epitaph by claiming that no reader of the epitaph can truly appreciate the loss he has suffered:

> Ye! who perchance behold this simple urn,
> Pass on—it honours none you wish to mourn:
> To mark a Friend's remains these stones arise,
> I never knew but one, and here he lies.
>
> (ll. 23–26)

Like Pope in his elegiac epitaphs, Byron ends his panegyric by declaring his own personal grief for a friend. While Pope sought to give public meaning to his friendship, however, Byron contends that his friendship with Boatswain runs wholly counter to the degraded norms of human society. Inverting the pleas common in epitaphs of the period for the passerby to reveal himself a "kindred spirit," Byron tells the unfeeling traveler to pass on. By moving from an extended third-person panegyric upon his dog to a defiantly solitary, first-person assertion of his unique bond to the deceased, however, Byron does not transcend the literary and cultural conventions and preoccupations of the social elite. He simply moves from the fashionable commemoration of an "honest" creature to an extreme version of, and response to, the equally fashionable doubt whether the epitaphic "stranger" could truly be a feeling "friend."

Byron's description of the elaborate monument to his dog as a "simple urn" underscores the aristocratic hauteur in the poet's rejection of human fellowship. In his 1811 will, Byron declared his wish to be buried "without any ceremony or burial-service whatever, or any inscription,

---

[103] For these various remarks concerning Murray, see George Gordon, Lord Byron, *Byron's Letters and Journals*, ed. Leslie A. Marchand, 12 vols. (Cambridge: Harvard University Press, 1973–1983), 1:176, 1:181, and 3:106.

save his name and age" in the vault below the Boatswain monument.[104] Byron's plan to be buried not among his aristocratic ancestors in the local parish church, Newstead Abbey, but instead with his devoted dog in unconsecrated ground upon the family property expressed on one level his defiance of social and religious norms. Yet his wish for burial on his estate was an extreme version of the privatization of mourning common among the upper classes of his time, just as his eccentric plan to be reunited with his faithful dog in death was based on an ideological conception of the "natural" hierarchy that was very popular among, and comforting to, the social elite.

Only when the social construction of reality is not taken for granted do men feel the need to (re)construct and assert, over and over again, the social order's "natural" foundations. In the epitaphs upon laborers, servants, and dogs examined in this chapter, for the first time in English literature the social elite deign to commemorate in great numbers and in serious—or in the case of many epitaphs upon dogs, semiserious— fashion the very lowest members of the social hierarchy. The highly formulaic panegyric motifs of such epitaphs simultaneously idealize and conventionalize a potentially dangerous, potentially incomprehensible "other." After offering the "virtuous servant" as a model for the laboring poor, a magazine moralist of 1795 went on to attack the "common peo- ple" of revolutionary France, who, lacking proper guidance, had become "the very worst of animals."[105] Fearing the ever-present danger of wild men and beasts, epitaphs praise, and thereby sought to perpetuate, the tamest of creatures, servants canine and human. Though they continue to be written throughout the nineteenth century, such panegyrics as- sociate the epitaph as a genre with literary commonplaces and social conservatism and thereby contribute to the developments I shall discuss in the next and final chapter, poets' increasing rejection of the epitaph and its demise as a vital literary genre.

[104] See the copy of the will in Byron, *Letters and Journals*, 1:71–72. Byron relinquished this plan only when he sold his estate.
[105] See "The Moralist (III)," *The Kentish Register* 1 (1793):83, 86.

Chapter 12

Wordsworth and the End
of the Epitaphic Tradition

The epitaph is central to William Wordsworth's poetry and poetics.[1] Many of his poems are inspired by epitaphs or use epitaphic motifs, and his treatment of the genre in his *Essays upon Epitaphs* is one of his major works of poetic theory. Nevertheless, Wordsworth composed few actual poetic epitaphs, and they are not among his major works. Critics have explored the way in which the poet's use of the epitaph informed his highly influential transformations of nature poetry, lyric, and autobiographical epic.[2] My focus is different: I will here briefly analyze Words-

[1] I cite Wordsworth's poetry from *The Poetical Works of William Wordsworth*, ed. Ernest de Selincourt and Helen Darbishire, 5 vols. (Oxford: Clarendon, 1940–1949), hereafter cited as *PW*. I have used both the text and critical apparatus of Selincourt and Darbishire in order to cite, unless otherwise noted, the earliest printed version of all poems. All citations of Wordsworth's prose works and letters come respectively from *The Prose Works of William Wordsworth*, ed. W. J. B. Owen and Jane Worthington Smyser, 3 vols. (Oxford: Clarendon, 1974); and *The Letters of William and Dorothy Wordsworth*, ed. Ernest de Selincourt, 2d ed., rev. Chester L. Shaver, Mary Moorman, and Alan G. Hill, 7 vols. (Oxford: Clarendon, 1967–1988).

[2] On Wordsworth's use of the epitaph, see Ernest Bernhardt-Kabisch, "Wordsworth: The Monumental Poet," *Philological Quarterly* 44 (1965):503–518; Paul de Man, "Autobiography as De-facement," in his *The Rhetoric of Romanticism* (New York: Columbia University Press, 1984), 67–81; D. D. Devlin, *Wordsworth and the Poetry of Epitaphs* (Totowa, N.J.: Barnes, 1981); Angus Easson, *The Lapidary Wordsworth: Epitaphs and Inscriptions* (Winchester: King Alfred's College, 1981); Frances Ferguson, *Wordsworth: Language as Counter-Spirit* (New Haven: Yale University Press, 1977), 155–172 and passim; Paul H. Fry, "The Absent Dead: Wordsworth, Byron, and the Epitaph," *Studies in Romanticism* 17 (1978):413–433; Geoffrey Hartman, "Wordsworth, Inscriptions, and Romantic Nature Poetry," in his *Beyond Formalism* (New Haven: Yale University Press, 1970), 206–230; Geoffrey Hartman, *Wordsworth's Poetry: 1787–1814* (1964; rpt., Cambridge: Harvard University Press, 1971),

worth's epitaphic poetry to exemplify the process by which the poetic epitaph ceased to be a vital literary genre in the early nineteenth century. Some critics have explained Wordsworth's neglect of the epitaph itself in favor of a more general "epitaphic mode" as a matter of his individual poetic impulses.[3] His epitaphic poetry is, however, the culmination of the developments analyzed in the two preceding chapters, the social elite's new interest in churchyard inscriptions upon the humble and its new anxiety concerning the response of the "stranger" to the poetic epitaph.[4]

Profoundly affected by the early loss of his parents and by his brother's death in 1805 and the deaths of two of his children in 1812, Wordsworth sought to treat death not simply as a personal tragedy but also as a sociocultural problem. More self-consciously than any of his epitaphic predecessors, Wordsworth explored the relationship between changing social relations among the living and changing attitudes toward the dead. He believed that the humble members of traditional, rural communities felt a closeness to the dead that softened the blow of mortality. Because of their weak sense of community and their contempt for the past, he felt, the educated and urbanized classes of an increasingly industrial England had lost such intimacy across the barrier of death. Implicitly in his epitaphic poetry, and explicitly in his *Essays upon Epitaphs*, Wordsworth treats the best epitaphs as the written embodiment of what he calls "a community of the living and the dead," a community increasingly eroded and forgotten.[5] Like Gray's *Elegy*, the *Essays* celebrate brief,

---

3–30 and passim; J. Douglas Kneale, *Monumental Writing: Aspects of Rhetoric in Wordsworth's Poetry* (Lincoln: University of Nebraska Press, 1988), 72–100, 129–147, 179–185, and passim; and J. Hillis Miller, *The Linguistic Moment: From Wordsworth to Stevens* (Princeton: Princeton University Press, 1985), 59–113.

[3] I borrow the term "epitaphic mode" from Ferguson, 155.

[4] Geoffrey Hartman's "Wordsworth, Inscriptions, and Romantic Nature Poetry," which discusses Wordsworth's debt to, and transformation of, the late eighteenth-century convergence of the epitaph and nature inscription, is the major exception to the critical tendency to ignore the sources of Wordsworth's epitaphic poetics. Yet although he notes the association of nature and the "common man" in late eighteenth-century and Wordsworthian epitaphic poetry (pp. 210–211), Hartman is interested in Wordsworth and his predecessors' vision of nature rather than their conception of society, and in the epitaph as a source for nature poetry rather than as an aspect of the social construction of the dead. He therefore does not focus on the developments that are my concern. Alan Bewel argues that Wordsworth's poetry provides a "history of death," that is, a history of changing relationships between the living and the dead, in *Wordsworth and the Enlightenment: Nature, Man, and Society in the Experimental Poetry* (New Haven: Yale University Press, 1989), 197–234. Though he treats neither the English literary and cultural context of Wordsworth's poetics of death nor the generic issue I address here, his sense of Wordsworth's epitaphic poetics as deeply historical parallels my own.

[5] Wordsworth, *Prose Works*, 2:56. The Burkean ring of this formulation reveals the general influence of Burke's conservatism upon Wordsworth's thought concerning the relationship of the living and the dead. In his *Reflections on the Revolution in France* (1790), Burke argued against supporters of the radical political and social changes taking place

humble country churchyard epitaphs as the best examples of the genre. Wordsworth defends the often formulaic quality of such epitaphs, with their conventional praise of humble virtues and simple expressions of Christian piety, by arguing that epitaphs should remind us of our "common nature" as mortals.[6] Commonplaces uphold community.

Not part of a traditional rural community himself, Wordsworth in his writing responds to, but generally does not compose, "lowly" epitaphs. Fearing that the educated, urban reader of his day cannot appreciate the "common" messages of humble epitaphs, he composes elegiac meditations that seek to reveal, expand upon, and answer the feelings underlying simple inscriptions. He thereby tries to recapture, for both himself and his readers, the traditional bond between the living and the dead. Wordsworth in effect treats the epitaph as a para-literary stimulus to his personal response, which becomes the decisive poetic act.

Poets after Wordsworth largely ignored his championing of country churchyard epitaphs as nostalgic conservatism. While continuing to mistrust their readership, instead of embracing forms with the potential to speak to all through literary and cultural commonplaces, poets increasingly proclaimed their individual visions.[7] By the early decades of the nineteenth century, while bereaved survivors continued to compose verse inscriptions and anthologies of formulaic epitaphs continued to be published, those who stood as poets in their own and others' regard largely avoided the epitaph as a "subliterary" form.[8] Poetic expressions of personal feeling or visionary insight concerning the dead continued

in revolutionary France that society was "a partnership not only between those who are living, but between those who are living, those who are dead, and those who are to be born"; see *The Works of the Right Honorable Edmund Burke*, rev. ed., 12 vols. (Boston: Little, 1865–1867), 3:359. James K. Chandler's *Wordsworth's Second Nature: A Study of the Poetry and Politics* (Chicago: University of Chicago Press, 1984) argues for the centrality of Burke's anti-Enlightenment traditionalism to Wordsworth's poetics from the early poetry onward. Though I emphasize the specific generic traditions that shape Wordsworth's epitaphic poetics, these traditions and Burke's social vision have a common origin in the cult of sentiment, which Burke politicizes in a conservative direction in response to the French Revolution; see, for example, his defense of "inbred sentiments" and "untaught feelings" in the *Reflections* (Burke, 3:345–346). It is therefore not surprising that Wordsworth could express a Burke-influenced conception of the "community of the living and the dead" in an epitaphic poetics based on late eighteenth-century sentimental motifs.

[6] See Wordsworth, *Prose Works*, 2:59, 65.

[7] On the increasingly difficult relations between the poet and the reading public in the early nineteenth century, see Marilyn Butler, *Romantics, Rebels and Reactionaries: English Literature and Its Background, 1760–1830* (Oxford: Oxford University Press, 1981), 178–187; and Raymond Williams, *Culture and Society, 1780–1950* (New York: Harper, 1958), 30–48.

[8] In a survey of English Romantic poetic epitaphs, Ernest Bernhardt-Kabisch notes that poets virtually abandoned the genre around 1810 but provides no explanation for this poetic shift; see "The Epitaph and the Romantic Poets: A Survey," *HLQ* 30 (1967):144.

to thrive in the elegy, but the poetic epitaph's attempt to define the enduring social significance of the dead was itself effectively dead.

Though *Lyrical Ballads* contains several poems with epitaphic motifs, "A Poet's Epitaph," written during Wordsworth's stay in Goslar, Germany in 1798–1799 and published in the second edition of *Lyrical Ballads* in 1801, is the only poem that he calls an epitaph. Its peculiarities as an epitaph reveal the poet's intense concern with the responses of readers. Purporting to be a gravestone inscription upon an unnamed rural poet, the epitaph neglects to describe the deceased in order to concentrate wholly on the reactions of readers, good and bad. Wordsworth writes what is really a meta-epitaph that dramatizes the confrontation between the expectations of his imagined readers and the traditional values that he believes are embodied in the genre at its best.

Nine stanzas address various fictional readers and, with one exception, expel them from the grave as persons who cannot and will not appreciate the dead. This address to inadequate readers, far longer than in any earlier epitaph, suggests by its very length the rarity of "proper" readers:

> Art thou a Statesman in the van
> Of public business trained and bred?
> —First learn to love one living man;
> *Then* may'st thou think upon the dead.
>
> A Lawyer art thou?—draw not nigh!
> Go, carry to some other place
> The hardness of thy coward eye,
> The falsehood of thy sallow face.
>
> Art thou a Man of purple cheer?
> A rosy Man, right plump to see?
> Approach; yet, Doctor, not too near,
> This grave no cushion is for thee.
>
> Art thou a man of gallant pride,
> A Soldier and no man of chaff?
> Welcome!—but lay thy sword aside,
> And lean upon a peasant's staff.
>
> Physician art thou?—one, all eyes,
> Philosopher!—a fingering slave,
> One that would peep and botanize
> Upon his mothers' grave?
>
> Wrapt closely in thy sensual fleece,
> O turn aside,—and take, I pray,
> That he below may rest in peace,
> Thy pinpoint of a soul, away!

> A Moralist perchance appears;
> Led, Heaven knows how! to this poor sod:
> And he has neither eyes nor ears;
> Himself his world, and his own God;
>
> One to whose smooth-rubbed soul can cling
> Nor form, nor feeling, great or small;
> A reasoning, self-sufficing thing,
> An intellectual All-in-all!
>
> Shut close the door; press down the latch;
> Sleep in thy intellectual crust;
> Nor lose ten-tickings of thy watch
> Near this unprofitable dust.
>
> (ll. 1–36)[9]

Except for the soldier, who can take up a "peasant's staff" (l. 16) and thereby return to the intimacy with the dead still supposedly strong in traditional rural communities, all the imagined readers are men of learned professions who are unable or unwilling to appreciate the deceased. Like the "Heroes, and Kings" addressed in Pope's epitaph upon himself, such readers could only destroy the "peace" (l. 23) of the buried poet. Despite its obvious satiric exaggerations, the poem suggests the genuine difficulties Wordsworth imagined when contemplating readers.[10] The succession of figures resembles the various readers whom Wordsworth lists in the 1802 version of the "Preface to *Lyrical Ballads*" where he argues that the poet must please "a human Being possessed of that information which may be expected from him, not as a lawyer, a physician, a mariner, an astronomer, or a natural philosopher, but as a Man."[11] Responding to the specialization and professionalization inherent in a complex modern society, Wordsworth imagines the poet as a person who can still address and recall the common concerns of human beings. "A Poet's Epitaph" suggests, however, that the educated classes, in their pursuit of specialized interests, have forgotten one of the fundamental items of common "information" to be expected of them as humans—reverence for the dead.[12] Even those whose occupations

[9] Wordsworth, *PW*, 4:65–66.

[10] On Wordsworth's difficult relationship to his readers, see also the succinct discussion in David Simpson, *Wordsworth's Historical Imagination: The Poetry of Displacement* (New York: Methuen, 1987), 104–107.

[11] Wordsworth, *Prose Works*, 1:139.

[12] Stephen Maxfield Parrish notes the influence upon "A Poet's Epitaph" of two compositions by Robert Burns, "A Bard's Epitaph" and the epitaph at the conclusion of "Elegy on Capt. M—H—," in *The Art of the Lyrical Ballads* (Cambridge: Harvard University Press, 1973), 176; see *The Poems and Songs of Robert Burns*, ed. James Kinsley, 3 vols. (Oxford: Clarendon, 1968), 1:247, 441–442. Like Wordsworth's epitaph, both poems by Burns apply the questions or "if"-clauses normally used to describe the ideal reader to a succession of readers. There is a crucial difference, however, between Burns's two poems and Words-

should involve special concern for people's common bonds—the politician, the minister, and the moral philosopher—feel no love for others and are therefore incapable of being moved by the deceased.

Wordsworth devotes the most lines to the last negative figure, the "moralist" (l. 25), a broad caricature of all the Enlightenment moral philosophers who, rejecting traditional sentiments, specialize in applying their individual "naked reason" to the understanding of man and society. Both a symptom and a proponent of a divided and divisive society, the philosopher who should discern the moral relations between human beings is an ethical solipsist, "self-sufficing" and "All-in-All" (l. 32). He is concerned only with the "tickings of . . . [his] watch" (l. 35), the rational calculation of time, rather than with the "unprofitable dust" (l. 36) of the dead.

Wordsworth's last six stanzas, by contrast, call upon an ideal addressee:

> But who is He, with modest looks,
> And clad in homely russet brown?
> He murmurs near the running brooks
> A music sweeter than their own.
>
> He is retired as noontide dew,
> Or fountain in a noon-day grove;
> And you must love him, ere to you
> He will seem worthy of your love.
>
> The outward shows of sky and earth,
> Of hill and valley, he has viewed;
> And impulses of deeper birth
> Have come to him in solitude.
>
> In common things that round us lie
> Some random truths he can impart,—
> The harvest of a quiet eye
> That broods and sleeps on his own heart.
>
> But he is weak; both Man and Boy,
> Hath been an idler in the land;
> Contented if he might enjoy
> The things which others understand.
>
> —Come hither in thy hour of strength;
> Come, weak as is a breaking wave!
> Here stretch thy body at full length;
> Or build thy house upon this grave.
>   (ll. 37–60)[13]

---

worth's composition: while all but one of Burns's projected readers are sympathetic, Wordsworth concentrates on insensitive readers.

[13] Wordsworth, *PW*, 4:66–67.

The poem tells us nothing concerning the deceased except that he was a poet who now lies in a grave of "poor sod" (l. 26). Instead the poem describes a rustic figure who will feel a connection to the deceased because, one must infer, he is the dead man's living embodiment. The first stanza bids the politician, "First learn to love one living man; / Then may'st thou think upon the dead" (ll. 3–4). The rustic becomes the living man whom the actual readers of the poem must learn to love: "And you must love him, ere to you / He will seem worthy of your love" (ll. 43–44). The readers of the epitaph must love the rustic, without demanding reasons, before they can perceive the rustic's worth; they must love the deceased even more unconditionally, for he will only "seem worthy of . . . love" as a result of the love that readers have first learned to feel for his living double. The poem's failure to perform the normal function of an epitaph, to name the deceased and to characterize his or her achievement, underscores how much sense of their human bonds readers need to *bring to* an epitaph in order to appreciate the dead.

By not spelling out the rustic's own respect for the dead, Wordsworth hints that the rustic does not in fact separate the dead from the living. The rustic finds significance in "common things" (l. 49), things that are both ordinary and (potentially) shared by all. His appreciation of the common things "that round us lie" (l. 49) spontaneously includes the deceased members of the human community who indeed round us lie, though readers may forget them and therefore not find them in Wordsworth's line. The final stanza appropriately requests that the rustic not mourn for, but rather display his continuing connection to, the deceased. He is told either to rest upon the grave in a deathlike posture ("Here stretch thy body at full length," l. 59) or to build a home that acknowledges by propinquity his bond to the deceased dwelling below ("Or build thy house upon this grave," l. 60). The rustic will thereby become like a "breaking wave" (l. 58), losing his individual identity in the continuity of the living and the dead, the present and the past, just as a wave breaks to join the sea of which it is part. The author's commands to the rustic are the opposite of those to the moralist, who is to sleep alone in the "house" of his individual ego: "Shut close the door; press down the latch; / Sleep in thy intellectual crust" (ll. 33–34). The solitary will embody an intimacy between the living and the dead unimaginable to those addressed at the opening of the poem.

"A Poet's Epitaph" suggests, however, its author's own distance from those who embody the poem's ideals. Gray imagines a "mute inglorious Milton" possibly buried among the churchyard poor; Wordsworth similarly imagines the "retired" (l. 41) rustic and presumably the humble deceased as those he elsewhere calls "silent" poets, men who have the wise passivity of poets but neither the occasion nor the need to publicize their wisdom.[14] He thereby splits the role of poet into the pair of retired, unknown country poets on the one hand, and the actual author of the epitaph, on the other. While the former embody the traditional relationship between the living and the dead, the latter presents to (and defends from) the reading public a way of life and death that he admires but of which he is not himself a part. The very length of Wordsworth's epitaph, which is far too long to be an actual inscription on a humble gravestone, underscores the distance between its author and the ideal he describes.

Wordsworth's request that the rustic sleep or build his house upon the grave is one version of a motif that runs throughout his poetry. The poet often treats the proximity of homes and graves in rural communities as the spatial correlative of a traditional intimacy between the living and the dead. In "We are Seven," written six months to a year before "A Poet's Epitaph," the child who continues to count dead siblings as part of the "seven" family children is incomprehensible to her adult, educated interlocutor. Since the child lives in a "church-yard cottage" (l. 23) only "twelve steps or more" (l. 39) from her siblings' graves, her viewpoint expresses in extreme form the wisdom of a traditional community as expressed in its topography.[15] The lack of resolution to the conversation suggests that the author himself can admire but cannot fully adopt the perspective of the child or her community.

Wordsworth himself was indeed unable to bear the extreme closeness to the dead that he perceived in traditional communities. After losing two of his children in 1812, he left his Grasmere home because it was too near the churchyard where his children were buried. In 1813 he wrote to Lord Lonsdale: "The House which I have for some time occupied is the Parsonage of Grasmere. It stands close by the Churchyard; and I have found it absolutely necessary that we should quit a Place, which, by recalling to our minds at every moment the losses we have sustained in the course of the last year, would grievously retard our progress towards that tranquility of mind which it is our duty to aim at."[16] Wordsworth's need to distance himself from the dead prompted him to idealize all the more the spatial and

---

[14] See Wordsworth's description of his brother John, who "didst...become / A *silent* Poet; from the solitude / Of the vast sea didst bring a watchful heart / Still couchant, an inevitable ear / And an eye practised like a blind man's touch" ("When, to the attractions of the busy world," ll. 79–83 in *PW*, 2:122); and of the Wanderer in *The Excursion*, one of those "poets" who "live out their time, / Husbanding that which they possess within, / And go to the grave, unthought of" (*The Excursion* 1:77–91, in *PW*, 5:10–11).

[15] Wordsworth, *PW*, 1:237.

[16] Wordsworth, *Letters*, 3:66 (January 8, 1813). Compare Wordsworth's letter of January 13, 1813 to Samuel Rogers explaining the necessity of his leaving "a Residence which forces upon us at every moment so many memorials of the happy but short lives of our departed Innocents" (*Letters*, 3:69).

emotional closeness of the living and the dead among simple countryfolk. In the churchyard section of *The Excursion*, much of it written not long after Wordsworth left Grasmere, the pastor emphasizes such closeness by turning his attention back and forth between the graves of the dead and the nearby cottages of their relatives. Thus he begins and ends one tale by shifting from a woman's grave to the home in which her enduring spirit dwells among the surviving family: "Here rests a Mother. But from her I turn / And from her grave.—Behold......./ the Cottage where she dwelt"; "Thrice happy, then, the Mother may be deemed, / The Wife, from whose consolatory grave / I turned, that ye in mind might witness where, / And how, her Spirit yet survives on earth!"[7] In most of his epitaphic poetry Wordsworth tries to recapture such intimacy, for himself and for his readers, by encouraging the "stranger" to respond properly to a humble epitaph or grave.

"Matthew," which appeared in the *Lyrical Ballads* of 1800, responds to a inscription that provides the bare name of a dead man. Wordsworth presents his poem as a supplement to a tablet in memory of the teachers of a country school:

In the School of——is a tablet, on which are inscribed, in gilt letters, the Names of the several persons who have been Schoolmasters there since the foundation of the School, with the time at which they entered upon and quitted their office. Opposite to one of those Names the Author wrote the following lines.

> If Nature, for a favorite child,
> In thee hath tempered so her clay,
> That every hour thy heart runs wild,
> Yet never once doth go astray,
>
> Read o'er these lines; and then review
> This tablet, that thus humbly rears
> In such diversity of hue
> Its history of two hundred years.
>
> —When through this little wreck of fame,
> Cipher and syllable! thine eye
>
> Has travelled down to Matthew's name,
> Pause with no common sympathy.

[7] Wordsworth, *The Excursion* 6:1115–1119 and 6:1188–1191, in *PW*, 5:223, 227. These passages were probably composed between 1813 and 1814; see Mark L. Reed, *Wordsworth: The Chronology of the Middle Years, 1800–1815* (Cambridge: Harvard University Press, 1975), 24. Compare Wordsworth's remark in *Essays upon Epitaphs* that it was unfortunate when shifts of population caused the the inhabitants of a parish to have "small knowledge" of the dead buried in their churchyard (*Prose Works*, 2:66); and his 1820 sonnet, "A Parsonage in Oxfordshire," which celebrates the beneficent lack of demarcation between the "unhallowed" property of the living and the churchyard where "kindred, friends, / And neighbours rest together" (ll. 1, 5–6, *PW*, 3:41). See also Paul H. Fry's discussion of metonymy as the trope linking the living and the dead in the churchyard books of *The Excursion* (pp. 418–421).

And, if a sleeping tear should wake,
Then be it neither checked nor stayed:
For Matthew a request I make
Which for himself he had not made.

Poor Matthew, all his frolics o'er,
Is silent as a standing pool;
Far from the chimney's merry roar,
And murmur of the village school.

The sighs which Matthew heaved were sighs
Of one tired out with fun and madness;
The tears which came to Matthew's eyes
Were tears of light, the oil of gladness.

Yet, sometimes, when the secret cup
Of still and serious thought went round,
It seemed as if he drank it up—
He felt with spirit so profound.

—Thou soul of God's best earthly mould!
Thou happy Soul! and can it be
That these two words of glittering gold
Are all that must remain of thee?[18]

The poet offers his composition as a link in an emotional chain, calling for the reader's response to the poet's response to the name upon an inscription. Wordsworth does not in fact provide the full name of the deceased purportedly inscribed upon the tablet but only his own sorrowful reaction to "these two words of glittering gold" (l. 31). By making his published poem an emotional response to a half-present name from an absent memorial of an unnamed school, Wordsworth suggests the distance between his published poem and its reader, on the one hand, and the deceased and his community, on the other. As in "A Poet's Epitaph," he thereby underscores how much the reader must bring to the poem in order to establish a connection to the deceased.

The first four stanzas use the ubiquitous "if" clause to describe the qualities the reader must have in order to appreciate the dead. The opening hyperbolic clause claims that only a reader who feels the impulses of nature "every hour" while "never once" falling into vice (ll. 3–4)—a person whose natural joy resembles that of the deceased as the poem will portray him—is worthy to read the inscription. By professing uncertainty whether "a sleeping tear" will "wake" (l. 13) even in such a

<hr>

[18] Wordsworth, *PW*, 4:68–69. The poem's 1800 title was "Lines written on a tablet in a School." I use the later, better-known title "Matthew" for convenience.

reader, a second "if" clause emphasizes that the poet cannot be sure whether even an ideal reader will bring the dormant feelings necessary for the inscription to arouse his or her grief.

In trying to awaken the sympathies of unknown readers, the poet reveals his own distance from Matthew's humble sense of the individual's place within an ongoing local community. Wordsworth contrasts his own singling out of Matthew and the modest demands of the deceased: "For Matthew a request I make / Which for himself he had not made" (ll. 15–16). Matthew himself would presumably have been satisfied with the small part in the communal memory ensured by his unadorned name upon the "little wreck of fame" (l. 9) that "humbly" (l. 6) memorializes generations of country schoolmasters. He presumably would not have asked for more than "common sympathy" (l. 12), which the poet considers insufficient. More explicitly than "A Poet's Epitaph," then, "Matthew" acknowledges its author's simultaneous respect for, and remoteness from, a "common" way of life and death.

The penultimate three stanzas further suggest the sociocultural gap between the poet and the deceased. Describing Matthew in both his joyful and pensive moods, Wordsworth idealizes the humble sanctity of the deceased, who is both "lower" and "higher" than the poet and his educated readers. Matthew's pleasures are described with the obtrusively "low" word "fun" (l. 22), which Johnson's *Dictionary* describes as "a low cant word" (*OED* 2, note) and which Wordsworth elsewhere uses to describe the mirth of a simple rural festival and of a carefree tinker.[19] The poet finds in Matthew's simple joys a sacred dignity, however, for his "oil of gladness" (l. 24) recalls Christ, anointed by God the Father with "the oil of gladness" (Hebrews 1:9). The description of the deceased in his moments of deep thought suggests that the silence of death fulfills an aspect of his unworldly nature. While the fifth stanza describes the now dead Matthew as "silent as a standing pool" (l. 21), the seventh evokes his once silent inner spiritual life: "Yet, sometimes, when the secret cup / Of still and serious thought went round, / It seemed as if he drank it up, / He felt with spirit so profound" (ll. 25–28). By its minimalism, the original memorial list respects the silence of humble Matthew's inner life, which eludes representation; the poet's words, by contrast, attempt simultaneously to honor and to break this silence with their own evocation of the deceased.[20]

[19] See Wordsworth, "The Waggoner," 2:94 (*PW*, 2:190); and "The Tinker," l. 47 (*PW*, 4:367).
[20] See Ferguson, 87. Ferguson's excellent analysis of the poem as a "war of words" between Wordsworth's writing and the original inscription (pp. 84–88) does not treat the specifically social dimension of the distance between Matthew and his community and the commemorative poet.

The final stanza's elegiac address both laments and seeks to overcome the poet's distance from the deceased. "Thou soul of God's best earthly mould / Thou happy Soul" (ll. 29–30) asserts that the soul of the deceased is now in heaven ("happy" here means "blessed, beatified," *OED* 2b). The heavenly state of the deceased is not consolation enough for the living poet, however, who laments the separation of the soul from the beloved "earthly mould" of which it was once a part. By the very anguish with which it is posed, the final elegiac question—"can it be / That these two words of glittering gold / Are all that must remain of thee?" (ll. 30–32)—suggests that the "two words" of the reticent inscription would be all that remained of modest Matthew but for the poet's—and, he hopes, the reader's—intense reaction to those minimal words. By its very inadequacy for the poet, the original inscription provokes his feelings of loss and stimulates his compensatory elegiac lament. While excessive from the point of view of Matthew himself, such an elegiac response helps rebind the poet—and, the poet hopes, the responsive reader—to the dead.

Like "Matthew," Wordsworth's *Essays upon Epitaphs*, written and partially published in 1810, center on the reader's response. The three essays try to reform the educated reader so that he or she can read lowly epitaphs with the requisite sympathy. Like Johnson in his essay on epitaphs, Wordsworth praises epitaphs that briefly present the moral achievement and eternal reward of "Men in a lowly Condition"; like Gray in his *Elegy*, Wordsworth focuses in particular upon the brief, pious country churchyard epitaphs of the (more prosperous) "Peasants and rural Artizans."[21] Wordsworth cites with approval such a short, Bible-inspired epitaph as the following quatrain upon a child who died at three months: "What Christ said once he said to all: / Come unto me, ye Children small; / None shall do you any wrong, / For to my kingdom you belong."[22] Like the Gospel message on which this epitaph is based, such churchyard epitaphs address "all." In the first essay, Wordsworth praises churchyard inscriptions for their humble accessibility:

An epitaph is not a proud writing shut up for the studious; it is exposed to all—to the wise and the most ignorant; it is condescending, perspicuous, and lovingly

[21] Wordsworth, *Prose Works*, 2:64. According to his nephew Christopher Wordsworth, the poet did not know of Johnson's essay when he wrote his own but "afterwards spoke of it with much commendation"; see Christopher Wordsworth, *Memoirs of William Wordsworth*, 2 vols. (London, 1851), 1:434.

[22] Wordsworth, *Prose Works*, 2:92. Wordsworth quotes and echoes Gray's *Elegy* several times in the *Essays*: he uses the "frail memorial" stanzas of the *Elegy* (ll. 77–80) as an epigraph; discusses churchyard epitaphs as evidence of the "piety of the rude Forefathers of the hamlet" (cf. *Elegy*, l. 16); and describes the churchyard gravestone that bears only the name of the deceased as a "frail memorial" (*Prose Works*, 2:63, 2:69, 2:93).

solicits regard; its story and admonitions are brief, that the thoughtless, the busy, and indolent, may not be deterred, nor the impatient tired: the stooping old man cons the engraven record like a second horn-book;—the child is proud that he can read it;—and the stranger is introduced through its mediation to the company of a friend: it is concerning all, and for all:—in the churchyard it is open to the day; the sun looks down upon the stone, and the rains of heaven beat against it.[23]

Wordsworth's image of the epitaph as "exposed to all" introduces an ideal "community of the living and the dead." The "stooping old man" and the child not only embody the extremes of the community's living generations but also reveal the efficacy of the epitaph among the socially humble: the child's and old man's pride in reading simple churchyard texts allows Wordsworth to suggest the beneficent role of the epitaph in a community in which literacy is minimal.

Wordsworth imagines the churchyard epitaph's not only reinforcing a traditional community's sense of its own past, however, but also achieving what the social elite considered the genre's central goal: the conversion of the outsider, the epitaphic "stranger," into a "friend." Yet precisely because of their simplicity, churchyard epitaphs are likely to be neglected or despised by the sophisticated readers whom Wordsworth addresses. The second essay consequently opens with the image of a "stranger" who responds inappropriately to the epitaphs in a country churchyard and proceeds to demand that its reader develop the "habits of reflection" and the "correspondent" feelings necessary to appreciate humble churchyard inscriptions.[24]

Wordsworth demands of his readers no less than an intellectual and moral transformation. His calls for the educated reader to learn how to appreciate simple, pious churchyard epitaphs resemble Protestant calls for the Christian's reformation so that he or she can grasp the *sermo humilis* of the Gospel.[25] The properly reformed reader will be able to

[23] Wordsworth, *Prose Works*, 2:59.

[24] Wordsworth, *Prose Works*, 2:63, 2:70.

[25] Compare, for example, Milton's proclamation concerning the transformation necessary for readers to comprehend the simple message of Scripture: "If we will but purge with sovrain eyesalve that intellectual ray which God hath planted in us, then we would beleeve the Scriptures protesting their own plainnes, and perspicuity, calling to them to be instructed, not only the *wise*, and *learned*, but the *simple*, the *poor*, the *babes*" (*The Complete Prose Works of John Milton, vol. 1: 1624–1642*, ed. Don M. Wolfe [New Haven: Yale University Press, 1953], 566). M. H. Abrams discusses the centrality of the *sermo humilis* in Wordsworth's poetry as a whole in his *Natural Supernaturalism: Tradition and Revolution in Romantic Literature* (New York: Norton, 1971), 390–399. His argument that Wordsworth uses the *sermo humilis* for an "egalitarian revolution" against "class consciousness and social prejudices" ignores, however, the way in which Wordsworth simultaneously asserts the spiritual nobility of the humble and defends a traditional social hierarchy. Abrams cites a passage from the "Essay, Supplementary to the Preface" (1815) in which Wordsworth points out the necessity of the poet's "making him [the reader] ashamed of vanity that

find much significance in a seemingly slight message. In one passage Wordsworth describes his own exemplary reaction to the briefest of churchyard inscriptions:

In an obscure corner of a Country Church-yard I once espied, half-overgrown with Hemlock and Nettles, a very small Stone laid upon the ground, bearing nothing more than the name of the Deceased with the date of birth and death, importing that it was an Infant which had been born one day and died the following. I know not how far the Reader may be in sympathy with me, but more awful thoughts of rights conferred, of hopes awakened, of remembrances stealing away or vanishing were imparted to my mind by that Inscription there before my eyes than by any other that it has ever been my lot to meet with upon a Tomb-stone.[26]

This elegiac meditation enacts the reversals inherent in the concept of the *sermo humilis*: Wordsworth finds the greatest expressivity in a "half-overgrown . . . very small" gravestone and its minimal epitaph. His re-action exemplifies Adam Smith's claim that men "sympathize" with the dead because the latter are so vulnerable to being forgotten: Wordsworth is moved by an inscription that conveys the inevitability of "remem-brances stealing away and vanishing." He has no assurance, however, that his reader will share his sympathetic response to the frail inscription. The remark with which he introduces his reflections—"I know not how far the Reader may be in sympathy with me"—implicitly challenges his readers: Wordsworth does not know the feelings of his reader, but he does know that only the reader in sympathy with him can truly appreciate his reaction and the epitaph to which he responds.

Wordsworth's emphasis on the all-important role of the reader's feel-ings dignifies the plainest prose epitaph or the most formulaic inscription as the stimulus for meditations upon life and death. The poet suggests that because of the reality to which it refers, the simplest epitaph can be the most profound, the least self-consciously literary the most af-fecting. Wordsworth's emphasis upon the proper feelings of the living for the dead indeed leads him to commend not only the simplest in-scriptions but also the complete absence of epitaphs. Like eighteenth-century writers of "anti-epitaphs" such as James Hervey, who wished to be remembered in his humble parishioners' spontaneous effusions at his

---

renders him insensible of the appropriate excellence *which civil arrangements, less unjust than might appear, and Nature illimitable in her bounty,* have conferred on men who may stand below him in the scale of society" (*Prose Works,* 3:80, italics mine). By omitting the words in italics, Abrams highlights Wordsworth's respect for the moral worth of the lower orders while suppressing the complementary affirmation of the social hierarchy (Abrams, 397). Like Johnson's praise of the epitaphs upon Epictetus and Zosima, Wordsworth's praise of lowly epitaphs has a fundamentally conservative thrust.

[26] Wordsworth, *Prose Works,* 2:93.

grave rather than to be commemorated by a written tablet addressed to strangers, Wordsworth sometimes suggests that a community's unwritten memories of its dead are far superior to written memorials.[27] Unlike those of his contemporaries who assumed a universal desire for monumental and epitaphic commemoration, Wordsworth exalts simple countryfolk who do not need tombstones and epitaphs because they consider the dead a vital part of the ongoing local community. "The Brothers" (1800) and *The Excursion* (1814) depict "strangers" from outside the community, figures for both Wordsworth and his readers, learning or failing to learn how to respond correctly to unmarked graves. In "The Brothers," Leonard, who has gone off to sea in search of his fortune and thereby become a "stranger" (l. 37) to his village, suggests to the local minister that the churchyard's lack of monuments and epitaphs shows the living to be "heedless of the past" (l. 168). Teaching Leonard what he has apparently forgotten, the minister replies: "We have no need of names and epitaphs; / We talk about the dead by our firesides. . . . / The thought of death sits easy on the man / Who has been born and dies among the mountains" (ll. 178–179, 182–183).[28] *The Excursion* describes the response of various outsiders to the pastor's "oral record" concerning the unmemorialized but unforgotten dead of a community. The "I" of the poem comes to realize that the "Dalesmen trust / The lingering gleam of their departed lives / To oral record, and the silent heart; / Depositories faithful and more kind / Than fondest epitaph" (6:610–614).[29] The epitaph seems doomed in Wordsworth's hand either to minimum gestures or to complete absence, both of which can stimulate the poet's and—so Wordsworth hopes—his reader's reflections.

Wordsworth's poetry in the "epitaphic mode" after *The Excursion* reveals his continuing emphasis upon response. Though worried by the "extreme length" of the first version of his memorial poem upon Charles Lamb, originally intended for the latter's monument, Wordsworth lengthened rather than shortened the composition and converted the epitaph into "a Meditation supposed to be uttered by his [Lamb's] Graveside."[30] Published in 1837, the final version of the poem runs to 131

[27] On Wordsworth's general committment to oral tradition as part of his "traditionalism," see also Chandler, 120–183 and passim.

[28] Wordsworth, *PW*, 2:6. Though Wordsworth treats the pastor with considerable irony, his 1800 note to "The Brothers" corroborates the pastor's view: "There is not anything more worthy of remark in the manners of the inhabitants of these mountains, than the tranquility, I might say indifference, with which they think and talk upon the subject of death. Some of the country churchyards, as here described, do not contain a single tombstone, and most of them have a very small number" (*PW*, 2:467–468).

[29] Wordsworth, *PW*, 5:205.

[30] See his letters of November 20, 1835, to Edward Moxon and of November 25, 1835, to H. C. Robinson in *Letters*, 6:114, 122.

lines. Wordsworth begins with the third-person panegyric verses originally intended as the epitaph (ll. 1–38), proceeds to explain that his
"reflecting mind and sorrowing heart" (l. 39) failed to compose a suitable
inscription (ll. 39–49), and then provides his elegiac address to the deceased (ll. 50–130).[31] Treating his inability to write a brief, impersonal
epitaph as an expression of his profound grief, Wordsworth makes his
response to the impersonal epitaph that he could not write the occasion
of his personal elegy.[32]

Wordsworth did sometimes try, however, to compose brief epitaphs
that expressed the simple piety he perceived in the humblest examples
of the genre. Both the successes and failures of two late poems demonstrate the difficulties he encountered in such attempts. In a sonnet
published in 1829, "A Gravestone upon the Floor in the Cloisters of
Worcester Cathedral," he responds to a brief epitaph with his own brief
epitaphic counterstatement:

> "*MISERRIMUS!*" and neither name nor date,
> Prayer, text, or symbol, graven upon the stone;
> Naught but that word assigned to the unknown,
> That solitary word—to separate
> From all, and cast a cloud around the fate
> Of him who lies beneath. Most wretched one,
> *Who* chose his epitaph?—Himself alone
> Could thus have dared the grave to agitate,
> And claim, among the dead, this awful crown;
> Nor doubt that He marked also for his own
> Close to these cloistral steps a burial-place,
> That every foot might fall with heavier tread,
> Trampling upon his vileness. Stranger, pass
> Softly!—To save the contrite, Jesus bled.[33]

As is characteristic of much of Wordsworth's later work, this poem enun-
ciates traditional Christian values, but its interest lies not in its own
message but in its obtrusive attempt to subdue the message of the epitaph
to which it responds. Rejecting the strong emphasis on particularity of
praise common in late eighteenth- and early nineteenth-century discussions of the epitaph, Wordsworth recommends in the *Essays* that epitaphs
subordinate "what was peculiar to the individual . . . to a sense of what
he had in common with the species" in order more forcefully to bind

[31] Wordsworth, "Written after the Death of Charles Lamb," *PW*, 4:272–276.
[32] Compare Wordsworth's 1830 "Elegiac Musings . . . " upon Sir George Beaumont (*PW*,
4:270–272), which responds to the very brief inscription that Beaumont modestly requested
for his tomb with a sixty-four line elegy in which the poet addresses the deceased, copiously,
because "genuine grief" cannot find "relief" in "*silent* admiration" (l. 44–45).
[33] Wordsworth, *PW*, 3:48. See also the analysis of the poem in Easson, 18–19.

the living and the dead.[34] This sonnet goes beyond Wordsworth the critic's concept of subordination; the poet here tries to reaffirm commonality by completely eliminating the peculiarity of the individual. The epitaph "Miserrimus!" ("Most wretched!") is shocking to Wordsworth because of the dead man's claims to spiritual uniqueness as he abases himself before God and his fellow mortals. After registering his shock, however, the poet vigorously reabsorbs the deceased into the "community of the living and the dead." He first interprets the deceased as a recognizable Wordsworthian figure, the solitary proud of his isolation, the extreme version of the "stranger" alienated from traditional communal life.[35] He then places him in the universalizing perspective of Christ's mercy. The dead man wished for the "heavier tread" of the passerby, but Wordsworth wishes that the "Stranger, pass / Softly!" While the deceased desired to be remembered by the reader as a solitary sinner, Wordsworth reminds his reader that "to save the contrite, Jesus bled." The solitude of private despair gives way to Christian fellowship. The "stranger" who heeds the poet's Christian lesson will respect the deceased as a fellow member of the community promised eternal life.[36]

The final lines provide an epitaphic response to "Miserrimus!" The concluding address to the "stranger" only makes sense if either the entire sonnet or the final lines are imagined as inscribed or left upon the gravestone. The sonnet, which began as the poet's personal meditation on a willfully private epitaph, ends with a public counterstatement. "To save the contrite, Jesus bled" is indeed the kind of brief, pious formula that appears on churchyard gravestones and that Wordsworth commends in the Essays. The poem "normalizes" the epitaph to which it responds in order to proclaim in simple, devout language the shared condition of men, living and dead. The disturbing yields to the commonplace. The concluding "epitaph" inadvertently suggests, however, the problem that arises when Wordsworth himself tries to compose, rather than respond to, the kind of epitaph he recommends as a critic. Only the intensity of Wordsworth's initial, personal response saves his sonnet from banality; his attempt at actual epitaphic counterstatement is a poetic dead end.

[34] Wordsworth, *Prose Works*, 2:89.

[35] One may compare him to the figure commemorated in "Lines Left upon a . . . Yew-Tree" (*PW*, 1:92–94) and to the Solitary of *The Excursion*.

[36] Despite his attachment to the established church, the late Wordsworth's conception of the relationship between the living and the dead was in one respect unorthodox. In 1835 he defended prayers for the dead as natural expressions of grief that led to "the barriers between the two worlds [of life and death] dissolving before the power of love and faith" (Wordsworth's note to "Stanzas Suggested in a Steamboat off Saint Bees' Heads, on the Coast of Cumberland," ll. 73ff., in *PW*, 4:403). Wordsworth tempered church dogma in order to strengthen the living Christian's link to the dead.

A brief poem composed one year later reveals, however, Wordsworth's occasional ability to recapture the brief, generalizing spirit of the simple epitaph upon a humble creature without falling into cliché. He sent an inscription written in 1830 to his friend John Kenyon:

[Enclosed is]...a serious Stanza or two, intended for an Inscription in ... a field adjoining our Garden which I purchased two or three years ago. ...in that field we have lived no small part of the long bright days of the summer gone by; and in a hazel nook of this favourite piece of ground is a Stone, for which I wrote one day the following serious Inscription, you will forgive its Egotism.

> In these fair Vales, hath many a tree
> At Wordsworth's suit been spared,
> And from the builder's hand this Stone,
> For some rude beauty of its own,
> Was rescued by the Bard;
> Long may it rest in peace! and here
> Perchance the tender-hearted
> Will heave a gentle sigh for him
> As One of the departed.[37]

Throughout his career Wordsworth composed poems purporting to be inscriptions upon some natural feature of a landscape; many of these are epitaphic in mood, associating a natural scene with the dead who once dwelt in it.[38] "In these fair Vales..." is in a sense an epitaph commemorating both a humble stone and Wordsworth himself. The poet asks that the stone be allowed to "rest in peace" as if it were a dead creature. Foreseeing the time when he will himself have "departed," he also imagines a reader who might remember him. The movement from "Long may it rest in peace!" to "heave a gentle sigh for him / As One of the departed" blurs the distinction between stone and poet, both of whom deserve commemorative solicitude.[39]

Wordsworth's epigrammatic inscription resembles paternalist epitaphs upon the humble, but it avoids their formulaic quality by displacing onto a "rude" stone the attention normally given humble persons and pets and thus reveals just how far down the ladder of creation one can and should extend commemoration. The inscription also differs from such epitaphs by its author's unblinkered awareness of the self-interest in-

---

[37] Wordsworth, *Letters*, 5:426.
[38] See Hartman, "Wordsworth, Inscriptions, and Romantic Nature Poetry," in *Beyond Formalism*, 206–230.
[39] On the blurring of the stone and the poet, see Miller, 112–113.

herent in all commemoration of the lowly. By preventing the builder from dislodging the stone from its natural setting, the poet thereby saves it as a "living" stone, to use a favorite Wordsworthian locution.[40] Nevertheless, he himself not only treats the stone as dead by inscribing it with its own "epitaph" but also uses it to express his concern for his own mortality and posthumous remembrance. In the letter to Kenyon, Wordsworth appropriately admits his poetic "egotism." Wordsworth's epigrammatic poem in effect distills the movement in Gray's *Elegy* from the poet's compassionate meditation upon the "frail memorials" of the lowly to his hope for a "kindred spirit" who may by "chance" respond sympathetically to the poet's own humble gravestone. Wordsworth the sensitive poet commemorates a mere stone and then imagines a "tender-hearted" passerby "perchance" remembering the poet who himself remembered the lowliest thing of nature.

As the letter to Kenyon explains, however, the inscription commemorates not any simple stone but one upon Wordsworth's property. The inscription thereby both links the poet to, and distinguishes him from, his rustic neighbors. Throughout his career Wordsworth praised the intense attachment of yeoman farmers to their small properties, treating the yeomanry as the humble analogue to the landed aristocracy devoted to their ancestral estates.[41] Two passages, one composed some thirty years before the inscription and another some fifteen years after it, help clarify the poet's relationship to the yeomen that he idealized. In an 1801 letter to Charles James Fox, Wordsworth lamented the impact of industrialization and urbanization upon the farmers who labored upon "little properties" that "have descended to them from their ancestors." He argued that such men's "little tract of land serves as a kind of permanent rallying point for their domestic feelings, as a tablet upon which they are written which makes them objects of memory in a thousand instances when they would otherwise be forgotten."[42] The yeomen inscribe their "domestic feelings" upon their small piece of property so that it binds them to their ancestors. Wordsworth drew Fox's particular attention to "The Brothers" and "Michael" as expressions of his social views, and there is a close connection between the poet's assertion that

[40] For Wordsworthian expressions suggesting the vitality of untouched stone, see the references to a "living" or "live" rock or stone in "To Joanna," l. 83 (*PW*, 2:114); "Effusion in the Pleasure-Ground...," l. 50 (*PW*, 3:103); "In a Garden of the Same," l. 10 (*PW*, 4:196); *The Excursion* 6:1145 (*PW*, 5:225); and a poem close in date to "In these fair vales...," "Composed when a Probability Existed of our Being Obliged to Quit Rydal Mount...," l. 66 (*PW*, 4:383).

[41] On Wordsworth's idealization of yeomen as property owners, see also Simpson, 81–96, who notes that far fewer Lake District yeomen probably owned their land than Wordsworth suggests (87–88).

[42] Wordsworth, *Letters*, 1:314–315.

the rustics treat their ancestral property as a figurative memorial tablet and the claim in "The Brothers" that the local countrymen do not erect memorial gravestones because the dead are so much a part of their collective memory.

Forty years later Wordsworth was still defending the beleaguered yeomen and their love of modest ancestral grounds. In 1844 he composed a sonnet attacking plans for the Kendal and Windermere railway that would have displaced Lake District farmers from their "paternal fields." In a note to the poem, Wordsworth told the following anecdote as an example of the "attachment which many of the yeomanry feel to their small inheritances": "Near the house of one of of them stands a magnificent tree, which a neighbour of the owner advised him to fell for profit's sake. 'Fell it!' exclaimed the yeoman, 'I had rather fall on my knees and worship it.' It happens, I believe, that the intended railway would pass through this little property."[43] The farmer presumably treasures his "magnificent tree" as a visible proof of the longevity of his property and the familial continuity that it embodies.

In the inscription Wordsworth expresses feelings for a humble stone on his property both similar to and significantly different from those of the yeoman for his tree. The inscription was composed some five years after Wordsworth had acquired the field in which the stone was found. He bought the field in 1825 because it was adjacent to the house he rented, Rydal Mount. His relationship with his landlady being difficult, Wordsworth planned to escape eviction by threatening to build a grand house in the field should he be asked to leave his residence.[44] The stratagem having proved unnecessary, the poem obliquely celebrates Wordsworth's escape from eviction and his consequent transformation of the field from a potential building site to a place of pleasurable contemplation of nature. The poet who rented his home and singled out a stone in a field that he bought as a scheme had neither the traditional attachment to his property nor the close relation to the dead that he perceived in humble rustics. By literally writing his feelings upon a natural object and awaiting the response of the "tender-hearted," Wordsworth indeed revealed his distance from those whose property he had described many years before as a tablet upon which "domestic feelings" were spontaneously and figuratively written. Unlike those who could dispense with epitaphs because of their close ties to the dead, Wordsworth inscribed a humble stone in a high-culture attempt to forge a link between the living "stranger" and the dead poet analogous to the intimacy between the living and the dead into which the yeomen were born.

[43] Wordsworth, "On the Projected Kendal and Windermere Railway," *PW*, 3:61–62.
[44] On Wordsworth's buying of the field in 1825, see Stephen Gill, *William Wordsworth, A Life* (Oxford: Clarendon, 1989), 359.

In his peculiar inscription "In these fair Vales..." Wordsworth avoided the clichés of so many epitaphs upon lowly creatures by self-consciously going outside the mainstream of the epitaphic tradition. Like "A Poet's Epitaph," a poem too long to be a humble gravestone epitaph that neglects the usual task of characterizing the deceased, or "Matthew," which uses an epitaphic inscription only as its initial stimulus, this epigrammatic inscription reveals that Wordsworth's "epitaphic mode" is most poetically fruitful when the poet self-consciously transcends the confines of the epitaph as a genre.

Wordsworth's epitaphic poetry simultaneously combats and confirms the demise of the epitaph as a vital literary form. Both the emphasis on the reader's elegiac response as the locus of significance and the highly formulaic quality of epitaphs themselves turned poets away from the genre. Later poets admired Wordsworth not as the defender of a traditional "community of the living and the dead" but as the individual, lyric interpreter of the relationship between the living and the dead, the past and the present. In his sonnet "To Wordsworth," Percy Bysshe Shelley laments what he considers Wordsworth's political apostasy as the "death" of a poet who had formerly stood like a "lone star" and "wept to know / That things depart."[45] In his "Memorial Verses: April, 1850," Matthew Arnold mourns Wordsworth's death as the return to the grave of an "Orpheus" who had single-handedly revived "spirits that had long been dead."[46] While elegiac expressions of personal feeling or visionary insight concerning the dead have continued to be major features of lyric poetry, since the early nineteenth century the poetic epitaph's attempt to identify the enduring social significance of the dead has come to seem increasingly futile.[47]

The poetic epitaph's demise as a vital literary genre coincides not only with the rise to dominance of the personal elegy as the poetic expression of feelings for the dead but also with the emergence of the obituary as the major para-literary expression of the dead's public significance. While the poetic epitaph's long-standing conventions become increas-

[45] Percy Bysshe Shelley, "To Wordsworth," ll. 2, 7 in *The Complete Poetical Works*, ed. Neville Rogers, 2 vols. (Oxford: Clarendon, 1975), 1:10.

[46] Matthew Arnold, "Memorial Verses: April, 1850," ll. 38, 55 in *The Poems of Matthew Arnold*, ed. Kenneth Allot (New York: Barnes, 1965), 228–229.

[47] On the importance of elegy and its influence on various genres in the nineteenth century, see Alastair Fowler, *Kinds of Literature: An Introduction to the Theory of Genres and Modes* (Cambridge: Harvard University Press, 1982), 206–212. While often rejecting elegiac conventions, twentieth-century elegists continue to assume that poetry has a central role to play in mourning personal loss; on their rejection of conventions, see Peter M. Sacks, *The English Elegy: Studies in the Genre from Spenser to Yeats* (Baltimore: Johns Hopkins University Press, 1985), 299–328.

ingly problematic as a result of vast social change and the transformation of the reading public, the obituary emerges as a modern form responsive to a large, socially diverse audience eager for information about their society. The differences between the two genres suggest a fundamental shift in the social construction of the dead: while the poetic epitaph attempts to assert the enduring public significance of the deceased in memorable verse as part of a (real or imagined) material monument, the obituary normally reports in unadorned prose an event—a death— as one item in society's ever-changing news.

The obituary column arises in the eighteenth-century English news-paper and magazine as a list of recent deaths of "notable" persons. Newspapers and magazines strove simply for timeliness and accuracy.[48] Over the course of the late eighteenth and early nineteenth centuries, however, obituary columns began including longer biographical sketches of the deceased.[49] The obituary thus posed a challenge to poetic rep-resentations of the dead. In the "Preface to *Lyrical Ballads*," Wordsworth associates his poetry with rural permanence as opposed to modern urban ephemerality: he defends "low and rustic life" as his subject matter and source of diction on the grounds that rustics' occupations are "durable" and their speech (relatively) "permanent," and he laments the "rapid communication of intelligence" that "gratifies" and corrupts the literary taste of "men in cities."[50] Criticizing Wordsworth for the "minute matters of fact" in his descriptions of rustics, Samuel Taylor Coleridge compares his former collaborator's style at its worst to that of an "obituary of a magazine" in commemoration of "some obscure ornament of society lately deceased."[51] Although he denigrates Wordsworth and rejects his championing of humble rural life as the locus of permanence, Coleridge posits an opposition similar to Wordsworth's between literature and tran-sient news. He uses the obituary, which fails to raise the dead to lasting significance, as a synecdoche for the ephemerality of modern journalistic

[48] On the obituary in the early newspaper, see Michael Harris, *London Newspapers in the Age of Walpole: A Study of the Origins of the Modern English Press* (Rutherford, N.J.: Fairleigh Dickinson University Press; London: Associated University Presses, 1987), 157–158, 168–169.

[49] Changing nomenclature in the *Gentleman's Magazine* reflects the gradual enlargement of the obituary column: the simple list titled "Deaths" becomes "Obituaries of considerable Persons" in 1780 (*Gentleman's Magazine* 50 [1780]: 494–496) and "Obituaries of considerable Persons; with Biographical notices" from 1781 onward (*Gentleman's Magazine* 51 [1781]:194–196).

[50] Wordsworth, *Prose Works*, 1:124, 128.

[51] Samuel Taylor Coleridge, *Biographia Literaria*, ed. James Engell and W. Jackson Bate, The Collected Works of Samuel Taylor Coleridge, vol. 7 (Princeton: Princeton University Press, 1983), 2:134 (2 vols. in 1).

"subliterature" and of literature that does not attain its goal of permanence.

In his obituary upon John Cavanagh, a hands-five player, William Hazlitt, the greatest Romantic journalist, launches a rejoinder to the critics of the obituary. Hazlitt composed his obituary "between jest and earnest," as he noted when he republished the piece (which first appeared in *The Examiner* in 1819), as the conclusion of his 1821 essay "The Indian Jugglers."[52] With serio-comic gusto, Hazlitt etches a lasting portrait of a man who was immersed wholly in the "presentness" of urban life, one for whom "the noisy shout of the ring happily stood . . . instead of the unheard of voice of posterity."[53] In the process Hazlitt raises the obituary itself to enduring "literary" status.

Hazlitt ends his obituary by alluding to an epitaph upon the deceased: "We have paid this willing tribute to his memory. Let no rude hand deface it, / And his forlorn '*Hic Jacet*.' "[54] The final line is humorous, for Hazlitt knows that his obituary has ensured Cavanagh's memory better than any gravestone inscription.[55] Indeed, Hazlitt pits his obituary against Wordsworthian epitaphic poetry. The essay's closing couplet is based on the conclusion of "Ellen Irwin, or the Braes of Kirtle," a Wordsworth ballad that ends with a churchyard inscription: "Now ye, who willingly have heard / The tale I have been telling, / May in Kirkconnel churchyard view / The grave of lovely Ellen: / By Ellen's side the Bruce is laid; / And, for the stone upon his head, / May no rude hand deface it, / And its forlorn *hic jacet*!" (ll. 49–56).[56] Wordsworth's invitation to those who have "heard" his tale to "see" the churchyard graves of his subjects exploits folk ballad convention in order to substitute for the distant, textual relation between the poet and his readers an imagined community of oral tales, local inscriptions, and intimacy across the barrier of death. Hazlitt's obituary upon Cavanagh, as a self-consciously modern composition addressed to a large readership interested in the changing urban scene, implicitly rejects Wordsworth's nostalgic evocation of a rural "community of the living and the dead."[57] Although

---

[52] I cite the text in William Hazlitt, *The Complete Works*, ed. P. P. Howe, 21 vols. (London: Dent, 1931–1934), 8:86. David Bromwich discusses the Cavanagh obituary in *Hazlitt: The Mind of a Critic* (New York: Oxford University Press, 1983), 354–355.

[53] Hazlitt, 8:89.

[54] Hazlitt, 8:89.

[55] See Bromwich, 354.

[56] Wordsworth, *PW* 3:72.

[57] Hazlitt's rejection of Wordsworth's vision also emerges in his praise of Cavanagh for not having been "lumbering like Mr. Wordsworth's epic poetry" (Hazlitt, 8:89). In his review of Wordsworth's "epic," *The Excursion*, some five years earlier, Hazlitt delivered a balanced judgment concerning the poet's obsessive focus on the "common and the permanent" (Hazlitt, 19:11) but vigorously attacked those portrayed in *The Excursion* as the

Hazlitt's carefully crafted obituary is the exception that proves the rule concerning the obituary as a para-literary form, its implicit farewell to a "forlorn"—and irrelevant—"Hic Jacet'" provides a fitting valediction to a poetic genre that had largely lost its cultural significance.

---

embodiment of the "common and the permanent," the "common country people," for their "stagnant" and petty lives (Hazlitt, 19:21–24).

Epilogue

The Victorian period witnessed an intense revival of public ceremonial for the dead. The upper and middle classes paid for elaborate funerals, made a cult of visiting the tombs of the dead, and had cliché-studded verses inscribed upon their monuments.[1] Poets nevertheless largely continued to avoid the epitaph as a "subliterary" form.

Various interrelated trends over the last hundred years have encouraged the "occultation" of death and the dead in England and the other Western nations. The vast increase in life expectancy that began in the late nineteenth century has resulted in people generally dying in old age, when they are relatively disengaged from economic and cultural production and their deaths less likely to cause a profound reaction in the society at large.[2] The increase in geographical mobility, the rise of the impersonal modern hospital, and the frequent transfer of responsibility for the dying and dead from local communities to the state have

[1] On Victorian funerary culture, see James Stevens Curl, *The Victorian Celebration of Death* (Newton Abbot: David and Charles, 1972); and John Morley, *Death, Heaven, and the Victorians* (London: Studio Vista, 1971).

[2] On the dramatic and steady improvements in life expectancy that began in the late nineteenth century, see E. A. Wrigley, *Continuity, Chance, and Change: The Character of the Industrial Revolution in England* (Cambridge: Cambridge University Press, 1988), 89, n. 31, which cites the data provided in Samuel H. Preston, Nathan Keyfitz, and Robert Schoen, *Causes of Death: Life Tables for National Populations* (New York: Harcourt, 1972), 236–263. For a speculative discussion of the way in which increased life expectancy, and the consequent association of death with the elderly, decreases the social importance of the dead, see Robert Blauner, "Death and Social Structure," *Psychiatry* 29 (1966):378–394.

all contributed to a decrease in the living's contact with death and the dead.[3] Today, ever fewer people are buried and ever fewer graves are visited. Tombstone inscriptions normally consist of the barest prose identifications of the dead for the benefit of immediate relatives.[4] The contemporary "invisible death," as Ariès calls it, has reinforced the marginality of the poetic epitaph.[5]

The exceptions to the overall obsolescence of the English poetic epitaph in this century are revealing. Comic and satiric epitaphs, which do not advance serious claims for the enduring social role of the deceased, have continued as a staple of light verse. Epitaphs that define a fictional character's view of life and death, such as Thomas Hardy's various epitaphs upon anonymous cynics and pessimists, are a twentieth-century transformation of comic epitaphs upon generic character types. Like comic epitaphs, such compositions assert no faith in the dead's public significance.[6]

National calamities such as wars tend to revive a sense of the public importance of the dead.[7] Poetic epitaphs upon soldiers and other victims of war are, not surprisingly, the most common twentieth-century form of the serious epitaph. Such poetic epitaphs reveal, however, the problematic status of the genre in this century. The most famous and characteristic English poetic epitaphs from World War I, for example, commemorate symbolic characters, as in Kipling's "Epitaphs on the War, 1914–1918," or groups, as in A. E. Housman's "Epitaph on an Army of Mercenaries" and "Here dead lie we because we did not choose...."[8] In their generic quality, such epitaphs resemble the Westminster Abbey memorial inscription commemorating the "unknown warrior," which was the annual focus of national mourning on Armistice Day during the interwar years. The unprecedented notion of commemorating an "un-

[3] On the decrease in the living's contact with the dead in modern Western societies, see Jack Goody, "Death and the Interpretation of Culture," in *Death in America*, ed. David E. Stannard (Philadelphia: University of Pennsylvania Press, 1975), 6–7.

[4] Jean Didier-Urbain discusses the "mutism" and "immense silence" of contemporary Western epitaphs in *La société de conservation: Étude sémiologique des cimitières d'Occident* (Paris: Payot, 1978), 438–450.

[5] On the contemporary "invisible death," see Philippe Ariès, *The Hour of Our Death*, trans. Helen Weaver (New York: Random, 1982), 559–601; and Geoffrey Gorer, *Death, Grief and Mourning in Contemporary Britain* (Garden City, N.Y.: Doubleday, 1965).

[6] See Thomas Hardy, "Epitaph," "Cynic's Epitaph," "Epitaph on a Pessimist," and "A Placid Man's Epitaph," in *The Complete Poems of Thomas Hardy*, ed. James Gibson (London: Macmillan, 1976), 695, 795, 803, 901.

[7] See Goody, 7.

[8] See *A Choice of Kipling's Verse*, ed. T. S. Eliot (London: Faber, 1941), 161–168; and *The Complete Poems of A. E. Housman*, intro. Basil Davenport, Centennial Edition (New York: Henry Holt, 1959), 144, 197. For epitaphs of the same two types inspired by World War II, see Roy Fuller, "Epitaph on a Bombing Victim," "Epitaphs for Soldiers," and "Epitaph" in his *Collected Poems, 1936–1961* (London: Andre Deutsch, 1962), 42, 90, 104.

known warrior" was a response both to the mass casualties of World War
I, many of whom could not be identified, and to the mass public of post–
World War I Britain, the multitudes of bereaved survivors who sought
public recognition of their personal losses. Representing all soldiers by
virtue of being no soldier in particular, the unknown warrior provided
a public object for individuals' otherwise private grief.[9] Like this anonymous soldier, the subjects of twentieth-century poetic epitaphs of war
are publicly significant precisely because they have no individual identity.
Such compositions are thus the dialectical complements of ordinary
tombstone inscriptions, which memorialize individuals but do not demand public attention.

Except for comic, clearly fictive, or war-related compositions, twentieth-century poetic epitaphs normally exploit the genre's very anachronism in order to imagine an escape from modernity. Attracted by the
genre's distance from contemporary society, poets generally repudiate
the epitaph's traditional assertions of the continuity between the living
and the dead as a sentimental or pious fraud. One of the most famous
twentieth-century poetic epitaphs, William Butler Yeats's epitaph upon
himself at the conclusion of his last poem, "Under Ben Bulben," is exemplary in its simultaneously anachronistic and iconoclastic exploitation
of the genre. The preceding passages signal that the epitaph is part of
a rejection of the present in favor of a heroic past: in the penultimate
section of the poem, Yeats bids the Irish poet do what Yeats himself has
done, "Scorn the sort now growing up" (l. 71) and "sing" of "heroic
centuries" (ll. 79–81); in the final section immediately preceding the
epitaph Yeats describes his burial place, Drumcliff churchyard, as the
embodiment of antiquity, where an ancestor of his was rector "Long
years ago" and an "ancient cross" still stands (ll. 87–90).[10] The final
epitaph addresses a reader remote from Yeats's contemporaries:

> Cast a cold eye
> On life, on death.
> Horseman, pass by!
> (ll. 93–95)

[9] On the memorial ceremonies for the "unknown warrior" as an "opportunity for making
private and individual sorrow for a time public and corporate," see David Cannadine,
"Death and Grief in Modern Britain," in *Mirrors of Mortality: Studies in the Social History of
Death*, ed. Joachim Whalley (New York: St. Martin's, 1981), 226. Noting that monuments
to an unknown soldier have been erected by many twentieth-century nations, Benedict
Anderson discusses the figure as a potent symbol of the modern nation, which Anderson
describes as an "imagined community" of persons who "will never know most of their
fellow members"; see *Imagined Communities: Reflections on the Origin and Spread of Nationalism*
(London: Verso, 1983), 14–20. The "unknown soldier" is the appropriately abstract public
representation of a mass society of strangers.
[10] William Butler Yeats, "Under Ben Bulben," in *The Collected Poems of William Butler
Yeats* (New York: Macmillan, 1933), 341–344.

The "horseman" whom the epitaph singles out recalls both the aristocracy of a heroic past, the "hard-riding country gentlemen" (l. 76) mentioned in the penultimate stanza as fit subjects for song, and the
supernatural "horsemen" of the poem's opening (ll. 5–11), who in Yeats's
poetic mythology embody the spirit of ancient nobility. Valuing the poetic epitaph precisely because it is a genre out of fashion, Yeats avoids
all "sentimental" requests that he be remembered by actual, living readers. The poet consequently breaks with the epitaphic tradition as well
as with modern realities: Yeats pointedly replaces the pedestrian *viator*
of tradition, who is too much an Everyman, with his imaginary proud
rider; instead of commanding the reader to stop and mourn a man who
has gone where all mortals must go, as might a traditional epitaphic poet,
he commands the equestrian to "pass by" with heroic disdain for the
merely mortal.[11] Yeats introduces his epitaph by claiming that it avoids
"conventional phrase" (l. 90), and his highly original composition rejects
the goal of so many epitaphs from Jonson to Wordsworth, that of linking
the living reader to the deceased.

The poetic epitaph's attempt to define the social significance of the
dead appears equally anachronistic in present-day North America. Contemporary gravestone inscriptions in the United States normally provide
only the name and dates of the deceased or add to these a brief, formulaic
expression of sentiment; they make no appeal to those beyond the intimates of the deceased.[12] The contemporary American obituary reveals
the lack of a compelling public rhetoric concerning the dead. Newspaper
and television obituaries provide timely but ephemeral accounts of the
lives of famous people. Newspaper obituaries on "ordinary" people normally provide only formulaic lists of facts concerning the dead, their
surviving relatives, and funeral arrangements. While gravestone inscriptions offer no public message concerning the dead, the average newspaper obituary delivers a public message that is largely, to quote one
sociologist, "person-empty."[13]

[11] On these inversions of epitaphic conventions, see also Hugh Kenner, "The Sacred
Book of the Arts," in *Yeats: A Collection of Critical Essays*, ed. John Unterecker (Englewood
Cliffs: Prentice-Hall, 1963), 20–21.

[12] In his study of the "dying of death" in nineteenth- and early twentieth-century America, James J. Farrel notes that the movement against inscriptions expressing ideas and
feelings about death or the dead in favor of inscriptions with only names and dates began
around the turn of the century; see *Inventing the American Way of Death, 1830–1920* (Philadelphia: Temple University Press, 1980), 126–127. On the poetic inscription's disappearance in twentieth-century America, see also Thomas C. Mann and Janet Greene, *Over
Their Dead Bodies: Yankee Epitaphs and History* (Brattleboro, Vt.: The Stephen Greene Press,
1962), 78–79; and for mordant commentary on the sentimental formulae that have replaced poetry on contemporary American gravestones, see Jessica Mitford, *The American
Way of Death* (New York: Simon, 1963), 188–189.

[13] On the development of the American obituary into a "person-empty" summary of
"recorded, publicly accessible, traceable facts, events, and experiences," see Gary L. Long,

The most widely visited public memorial of recent times, the Vietnam Veterans Memorial erected in Washington, D.C., in 1982, reflects not only Americans' complex attitudes toward the Vietnam War but also the contemporary cultural establishment's suspicion of public pronouncements concerning the dead. Claiming that death is a "personal and private matter," Maya Lin, the designer of the memorial, stated that it was meant to foster "personal reflection and private reckoning."[14] Selected by a group of eminent architects and sculptors, the design recalls contemporary gravestones in its minimalist identification of the deceased. A list of names inscribed upon a V-shaped black marble slab set into the earth and devoid of figurative representation, the memorial eschews the proud verticality and pomp of monumental assertions of immortality and avoids the potential hollowness of a straightforward message concerning the Americans who died in the Vietnam War. While the inscription on the tomb of the American unknown soldier, erected after World War I in imitation of its British counterpart, commemorates a soldier whose lack of identity enabled him to represent a collective glory—"Here rests in honored glory an American soldier known but to God"—the Vietnam War Memorial records individual names but leaves open their ultimate collective significance. Thus it allows its viewers their intensely personal responses. Some have seen the list of names as a powerful indictment of war, others as a patriotic commemoration of forgotten heroes.[15] Still others have noted that each viewer must endow the list with significance: as one essayist puts it, the list provides only the "pure data" and thus acknowledges that the individual viewer's "interpretation of the data, not someone else's, is what matters."[16] Discussions and photographs of the memorial in the media often focus on individual reactions.[17] Just as Wordsworth's own elegiac response—and, so he hopes, his reader's— gives significance to "two words" inscribed upon a commemorative tablet in "Matthew," so personal responses give meaning to this spare cenotaphic message.

"Organizations and Identity: Obituaries 1856–1972," *Social Forces* 65 (1987):964–1001. I cite pp. 987 and 993.

[14] Cited in Charles L. Griswold, "The Vietnam Veterans Memorial and the Washington Mall: Philosophical Thoughts on Political Iconography," *Critical Inquiry* 12 (1986):718.

[15] See Elizabeth Hess, "A Tale of Two Memorials," *Art in America* 71 (1983):126.

[16] "Notes and Comment," *The New Yorker*, 18 March 1985:35. Frederick Hart, the designer of a figurative sculpture later added at a distance to the original memorial, criticizes the original precisely for its openness to interpretation: "People say you bring what you want to...[the] memorial. But I call that brown bag esthetics. I mean you better bring something, because there ain't nothing being served" (cited in Hess, p. 124).

[17] Lin has noted that the mirroring surface of the black marble forces one to see oneself reflected in the names (Hess, p. 123). Others have adopted the trope of reflection to capture the crucial role of individual responses to the memorial; see, for example, the photographs of visitors' reactions in "Reflections on 'The Wall,'" *Smithsonian Magazine* 17 (1987):149.

A poetic epitaph of the early 1950s exemplifies the obsolescence of the genre in contemporary America. W. S. Merwin's "Epitaph" rejects public rhetoric concerning the dead by refusing even to identify the deceased:

> Death is not information.
> Stone that I am,
> He came into my quiet
> And I shall be still for him.[18]

This epitaph is on one level a modernist poet's elegant literary exercise, a *reductio ad silentium* of a traditionally brief genre. "Death is not information" launches a serious attack, however, on the dehumanizing modern discourses exemplified by the contemporary "objective" obituary, all the related discourses—of the mass media, of bureaucratic organizations, of the sciences and social sciences—that try to reduce every human experience, including death, to manageable "information."[19] Merwin's minimalist epitaph suggests that when public discourse can encompass no more than "information," the poetic epitaph's traditional role of commemorating the deceased is not an expression but rather a betrayal of individual values.

Though Merwin rejects the traditional function of the poetic epitaph, he revives conventions of the genre precisely in order to defend the dead against the stultifying norms of contemporary public discourse. Like the concluding couplet of Herrick's "To the Passenger," "He that wants a buriall roome / *For a Stone, ha's Heaven his Tombe*," Merwin's opening line, "Death is not information," exploits the gnomic, epigrammatic aspect of the traditional epitaph in order to reject with curt authority the traditional premises of the genre. Transforming the ancient and Renaissance epitaphic topos of the speaking stone in order to have the stone announce its paradoxical preservation of "quiet"—the diminished, modern substitute for the spiritual rest (*re-quies*) once wished upon the dead (*Requiescat in pace*)—the poem seems to invoke the anachronistic

---

[18] W. S. Merwin, "Epitaph," in his *The First Four Books of Poems* (New York: Atheneum, 1975), 35. Reprinted by permission of Georges Borchardt Inc. and the author. Copyright © 1952, 1975.

[19] When Merwin's poem first appeared in 1952, the attempt to reduce human experience to controllable "information" was particularly evident in the growing popularity of "information theory." First developed in communication engineering, "information theory" was quickly applied in the early 1950s to such diverse humanistic fields as sociology, psychology, linguistics, and journalism; see Randall L. Dahling, "Shannon's Information Theory: The Spread of an Idea," in Institute for Communication Research, Stanford University, *Studies of Innovation and of Communication to the Public* (Palo Alto: Stanford University Press, 1962), 117–139.

motif of the speaking stone as a synecdoche for the poetic tradition itself
in all its salutary distance from modernity's "information explosion."

Both Yeats's and Merwin's poetic epitaphs simultaneously revive and
bury the tradition studied in this book. They suggest that the poetic
epitaph now is a genre not only about, but of, the past.

Index

Library of Congress Cataloging-in-Publication Data

Scodel, Joshua, 1958–
    The English poetic epitaph : commemoration and conflict from
Jonson to Wordsworth / Joshua Scodel.
        p.   cm.
    Includes index.
    ISBN 0-8014-2482-8 (alk. paper)
    1. English poetry—History and criticism.   2. Epitaphs—Great
Britain—History and criticism.   3. Funeral rites and ceremonies in
literature.   4. Literature and society—Great Britain.   5. Praise in
literature.   6. Death in literature.   I. Title.
PR508.E55S36 1991
821'.0409354—dc20   90-55714